The Oxford Dictionary of

Proverbs

Edited by

JENNIFER SPEAKE

Previously co-edited with

JOHN SIMPSON

OXFORD
UNIVERSITY PRESS

OXFORD
UNIVERSITY PRESS

Great Clarendon Street, Oxford OX2 6DP

Oxford University Press is a department of the University of Oxford. It furthers the University's objective of excellence in research, scholarship, and education by publishing worldwide in

Oxford New York

Auckland Bangkok Buenos Aires Cape Town Chennai Dar es Salaam Delhi Hong Kong Istanbul Karachi Kolkata Kuala Lumpur Madrid Melbourne Mexico City Mumbai Nairobi São Paolo Shanghai Singapore Taipei Tokyo Toronto

Oxford is a registered trade mark of Oxford University Press in the UK and in certain other countries

Published in the United States by Oxford University Press Inc., New York

First published as *The Concise Oxford Dictionary of Proverbs*, edited by John Simpson, 1982
Second edition, edited by John Simpson and Jennifer Speake, 1992
Third edition, edited by John Simpson and Jennifer Speake, 1998
Fourth edition, edited by Jennifer Speake, 2003
Reissued in paperback, 2004

British Library Cataloguing in Publication Data

Data available

Library of Congress Cataloging in Publication Data

Data available

ISBN 0-19-860894-2

2

Typeset by Kolam Information Services Pvt. Ltd, Pondicherry, India
Printed in Great Britain by Clays Ltd., St Ives plc

Editor's Preface

This new *Oxford Dictionary of Proverbs* represents the latest stage in Oxford University Press's coverage of proverbs and reflects the changes that have taken place in the two decades since the *Concise Oxford Dictionary of Proverbs* first appeared. The *Concise* itself grew out of the monumental *Oxford Dictionary of English Proverbs*, first published in 1935 and substantially revised by F. P. Wilson in 1970. A massive work of historical scholarship, the *Oxford Dictionary of English Proverbs* cast its net over the corpus of English literature and brought together a rich haul of metaphor, idiom, and proverb from all stages of the language. From the outset, however, the *Concise* was intended to fulfil a different need from the larger volume, in its focus on contemporary usage and on what the late twentieth-century English-speaker regarded as a proverb—as John Simpson explains in his Introduction. It is this conception that underlies the present dictionary.

Research for the *Oxford Dictionary of Proverbs* has shown that the proverb in Britain and North America is as vital and varied as ever, and the resources of the Internet, tapped for the first time for this book, will clearly play an increasing role in future. Over forty additional current proverbs have been included. Some of these are apparently recent coinages; others have venerable roots but have been revived in the later years of the twentieth century.

For this dictionary some citations of older proverbs in the third edition of the *Concise* have been deleted, but material showing different forms of the proverb has been retained. Some proverbs settle quickly to a standard form; others seem to be more susceptible of variation, and by citing variants it is possible to trace their evolution. The notes on the individual proverbs draw attention to such points of interest.

Proverb usage once again shows itself an index of linguistic and social change. Whereas many older proverbs use 'man' for the human subject, modern users often attempt to avoid such non-inclusive language, preferring 'someone' or 'a person'. While examples of up-to-date usage have been found for nearly four hundred of the proverbs in this book, it seems clear that other proverbs are starting to undergo obsolescence by reason of social change. Expressions of the received wisdom of a patriarchal agrarian society that organized itself according to the rhythms of the seasons and the Church's calendar become antiquarian oddities in a modern environment. Thus *a woman, a dog, and a walnut tree, the more you beat them the better they be* offends a slew of twenty-first-century sensibilities, while *Candlemas day, put beans in the clay* has little to say to an urban secular society.

On the other hand, recent pithy expressions of universal predicaments (*when all you have is a hammer, everything looks like a nail*) or truths (*justice delayed is justice denied*) demonstrate a good proverb's ability to circulate, thrive, and evolve in a variety of contexts. Cartoonists and humorists can assume the easy familiarity of their audience with proverbs, as is shown by recent examples of *the opera isn't over till the fat lady sings* and *two heads are better than one*. Although proverbs may be used as resounding clichés, very frequently they are used in contexts that show the user's often playful awareness of their resonance.

For this dictionary, as for the *Concise Oxford Dictionary of Proverbs*, I am greatly indebted to the work of Mr William F. Deeck, doyen of proverb-spotters, for his invaluable contributions; the work would be much poorer without his numerous trans-Atlantic contributions. I would also like to thank the late Kenneth Scholes for drawing my attention to the painted proverbs at Ascott House and all other readers who have contributed proverb citations.

Jennifer Speake
Oxford
September 2002

Contents

Introduction

The *Concise Oxford Dictionary of Proverbs* provides a general history of proverbs in common use in Britain in the last two hundred years. Some of the proverbs have been in use throughout the English-speaking world for many years; others (especially Scottish proverbs) have spread from regional use to attain general currency in the nineteenth and twentieth centuries. Proverbs which originated in the United States and in other countries outside the British Isles, such as *If you don't like the heat, get out of the kitchen* or *The apple never falls far from the tree*, are included if they are now current in Britain, or if they are particularly prevalent in their region of origin.

A proverb is a traditional saying which offers advice or presents a moral in a short and pithy manner. Paradoxically, many phrases which are called 'proverbial' are not proverbs as we now understand the term. We might for instance refer to 'the proverbial fly on the wall' or say that something is 'as dead as the proverbial dodo', although neither of these phrases alludes to a proverb. The confusion dates from before the eighteenth century, when the term 'proverb' also covered metaphorical phrases, similes, and descriptive epithets, and was used far more loosely than it is today. Nowadays we would normally expect a proverb to be cast in the form of a sentence.

Proverbs fall readily into three main categories. Those of the first type take the form of abstract statements expressing general truths, such as *Absence makes the heart grow fonder* and *Nature abhors a vacuum*. Proverbs of the second type, which include many of the more colourful examples, use specific observations from everyday experience to make a point which is general; for instance, *You can take a horse to water, but you can't make him drink* and *Don't put all your eggs in one basket*. The third type of proverb comprises sayings from particular areas of traditional wisdom and folklore. In this category are found, for example, the health proverbs *After dinner rest a while, after supper walk a mile* and *Feed a cold and starve a fever*. These are frequently classical maxims rendered into the vernacular. In addition, there are traditional country proverbs which relate to husbandry, the seasons, and the weather, such as *Red sky at night, shepherd's delight; red sky in the morning, shepherd's warning* and *When the wind is in the east, 'tis neither good for man nor beast*.

Several of the more common metaphorical phrases are included in the dictionary if they are also encountered in the form of a proverb. The phrases *to cut off your nose to spite your face* and *to throw the baby out with the bathwater*, for example, would not ordinarily qualify for inclusion, but have been admitted because they are often found in proverb form—*Don't cut off your nose to spite your face* and *Don't throw the baby out with the bathwater*. Other metaphorical phrases (*to win one's spurs*, *to throw in the towel*, etc.), similes (*as red as a rose*, *as dull as ditchwater*), and aphoristic quotations (*Power grows out of the barrel of a gun*) are not included. Nevertheless, proverbs which originated in English as quotations, such as *Hope springs eternal* or *Fools rush in where angels fear to tread*, are included when the origins of the quotations are no longer popularly remembered.

It is sometimes said that the proverb is going out of fashion, or that it has degenerated into the cliché. Such views overlook the fact that while the role of the proverb in English literature has changed, its popular currency has remained constant. In medieval times, and even as late as the seventeenth century, proverbs often had the status of universal truths and were used to confirm or refute an argument. Lengthy lists of proverbs were compiled to assist the scholar in debate; and many sayings from Latin, Greek, and the continental languages were drafted into English for this purpose. By the eighteenth century, however, the popularity of the proverb had declined in the work of educated writers, who began to ridicule it as a vehicle for trite, conventional wisdom. In Richardson's *Clarissa Harlowe* (1748), the hero, Robert Lovelace, is congratulated on his approaching marriage and advised to mend his foolish ways. His uncle writes: 'It is a long lane that has no turning.—Do not despise me for my proverbs.' Swift, in the introduction to his *Polite Conversation* (1738), remarks: 'The Reader must learn by all means to distinguish between Proverbs, and those polite Speeches which beautify Conversation:..As to the former, I utterly reject them out of all ingenious Discourse.' It is easy to see how proverbs came into disrepute. Seemingly contradictory proverbs can be paired—*Too many cooks spoil the broth* with *Many hands make light work*; *Absence makes the heart grow fonder* with its opposite *Out of sight, out of mind*. Proverbs could thus become an easy butt for satire in learned circles, and are still sometimes frowned upon by the polished stylist. The proverb has none the less retained its popularity as a homely commentary on life and as a reminder that the wisdom of our ancestors may still be useful to us today. This shift is reflected in the quotations which accompany the entries in the dictionary: recent quotations are often taken from the works of minor writers, or from newspapers and magazines, while earlier quotations are more frequently from the works of major writers.

It is a reflection of the proverb's vitality that new ones are continually being created as older ones fall into disuse. Surprisingly, *A trouble shared is a trouble halved* is not recorded before the twentieth century, and *A change is as good as a rest* apparently dates only from the last decade of the nineteenth; the popular saying *A watched pot never boils* first occurs as late as 1848. The computer world has recently given us a potential classic, *Garbage in, garbage out*, and economics has supplied us with *There's no such thing as a free lunch*. Proverbs continue—as the early collectors never tired of stating—to provide the sauce to relish the meat of ordinary speech.

*

Proverb dictionaries differ in their manner of ordering material. There are a number of choices open to the compiler. One method favoured in early dictionaries was a straight alphabetical sequence, starting with all proverbs beginning with the word *a*, such as *A bird in the hand is worth two in the bush* and *A stern chase is a long chase*, and continuing in this rigid style until *z*. The problems caused by this system are manifold, the most apparent being the grouping of large numbers of unrelated proverbs under a few words such as *a*, *every*, *one*, and *the*, forcing the user to engage on a long search for the proverb of his choice. Another option is thematic presentation, whereby proverbs relating to cats, dogs, the Devil, Pride, etc., are each placed together. Despite the many advantages of this method, confusion can occur when there is no clear subject, as when a proverb falls under two or more thematic headings.

The manner of arrangement chosen here is that favoured by most major proverb collections of recent years, such as M. P. Tilley's *Dictionary of the Proverbs in England in the Sixteenth and Seventeenth Centuries* (1950) and B. J. Whiting's *Early American Proverbs and Proverbial Phrases* (1977). This method combines the advantages of alphabetical and thematic presentation by listing proverbs by the *first significant word*; thus *All cats are grey in the dark* may be found at *cats*, *You cannot put an old head on young shoulders* at *old*, while *Every picture tells a story* occurs at *picture*. Furthermore, a generous selection of cross-references is given in the text to assist the reader in cases of difficulty. The first of the three examples above, for example, is cross-referenced at *grey* and *dark*, the second at *head*, *young*, and *shoulder*, and the third at *every*, *tell*, and *story*. Variant forms are always noted at the main form when they are important enough to merit inclusion.

Illustrative quotations of proverbs are a major feature of the dictionary, as in *ODEP*. Accordingly, the earliest known example of each proverb's occurrence in literature is always given as the first quotation. Many of the proverbs were probably in common oral use before being recorded in print, but this dictionary clearly must rely upon the evidence of the printed word. When a proverb is known to have existed in another language before its emergence in English, this is indicated in the headnote preceding the quotations. For instance, although *There's many a slip 'twixt cup and lip* is first recorded in English in 1539, its parent form is found in both Greek and Latin, and this information is provided before the sixteenth-century English citation. Similarly, *Nothing succeeds like success*, first noted in English in 1867, was current in French some decades earlier. It is interesting to note that a high proportion of traditional 'English' proverbs are of foreign origin. Like many of the words in our language, proverbs frequently passed into English from Latin or Greek, through the learned disciplines of medicine or the law, or from a knowledge of the classical authors; or they came into English from French in the years following the Conquest. A number of modern proverbs, such as *The opera isn't over till the fat lady sings* or *The family that prays together stays together*, originated in the United States. Predictably, one classic proverb of English origin is the old saying *It never rains but it pours*.

Each entry is provided with several illustrative quotations which show the contexts in which the proverb has been used, up to the present day. The standard form of a proverb often changes during its development: the first recorded use of the current form is always cited. Short headnotes are added when there is some obscurity in the meaning or use of a proverb which is not resolved in the quotations, or when there is some point of grammatical or syntactical interest which deserves mention. Thus, the legal implications of *Possession is nine points of the law* and *Every dog is allowed one bite* are explained, as are the historical origins of *Caesar's wife must be above suspicion* and *One might as well be hanged for a sheep as a lamb*. The original meanings of words such as *handsome* in *Handsome is as handsome does* are also discussed when necessary.

Much of the work involved in the compilation of the dictionary has concerned the verification of quotations. In the past, quotations have often been carried forward from one proverb dictionary to another without being checked; this is especially true of the older quotations. All quotations have been rechecked for this dictionary, and are quoted from the first edition of the relevant work, unless otherwise stated in the citation or in the Bibliography. Many quotations in other collections were found to have been wrongly dated, principally because they were taken from later (often bowdlerized Victorian) editions of the work in question, and frequently the true first edition contains a less-familiar version of the proverb, or no proverb at all.

Self-evident short titles are occasionally used in citations, but whenever possible the title and author of each work are given in full. Titles have been modernized, quotations (with the exceptions of the Bible and Shakespeare) have not. Quotations are cited by reference to chapter; other styles are consistently employed when a work is not subdivided thus. Full references are given for the Bible, Shakespeare, and several other major writers; plays are cited by act and scene (failing scene, then page). Biblical quotations are cited from the Authorized Version of 1611 unless otherwise stated: similar quotations may often be found in earlier translations, sermons, and homilies, but the modern form of a proverb usually reflects this translation. Contractions, which occur frequently in medieval sources, have been silently expanded.

John Simpson
Oxford
March 1982

Abbreviations used in the dictionary

a	*ante* (before)
Apr.	April
Aug.	August
AV	Authorized Version (of the Bible), 1611
BCP	Book of Common Prayer
c	*circa* (about)
cent.	century
cf.	*confer* (compare)
COD	Concise Oxford Dictionary
Dec.	December
Dict.	dictionary (of)
Du.	Dutch
ed.	edition
EETS	Early English Text Society
esp.	especially
et al.	*et alii* (and others)
Feb.	February
Fr.	French
Ger.	German
Gr.	Greek
Hist.	history (of), historical
Ibid.	*ibidem* (in the same place)
Ital.	Italian
Jan.	January
L.	Latin
Mag.	Magazine
Mar.	March
mod.	modern
MS(S)	manuscript(s)
Nov.	November
NY	New York
Oct.	October
ODEP	Oxford Dictionary of English Proverbs
OED	Oxford English Dictionary
Pt.	part
quot.	quotation
rev.	revised
Sept.	September
Ser.	series
St.	Saint
STS	Scottish Text Society
tr.	translation (of)
US	United States (of America)
vol.	volume

A *see* who SAYS A must say B.

abhors *see* NATURE abhors a vacuum.

a-borrowing *see* he that GOES a-borrowing, goes a-sorrowing.

abroad *see* GO abroad and you'll hear news of home.

ABSENCE makes the heart grow fonder

Cf. PROPERTIUS *Elegies* II. xxxiii[b]. I. 43 *semper in absentes felicior aestus amantes*, passion [is] always warmer towards absent lovers.

□ *c* **1850** in T. H. Bayly *Isle of Beauty* (rev. ed.) iii. Absence makes the heart grow fonder. **1923** *Observer* 11 Feb. 9 These saws are constantly cutting one another's throats. How can you reconcile the statement that 'Absence makes the heart grow fonder' with 'Out of sight, out of mind'? **1992** A. LAMBERT *Rather English Marriage* (1993) xi. 178 Absence may have made his heart grow fonder, but it hasn't done wonders for mine. **2002** *Spectator* 9 Feb. 63 In this way you can keep her at bay indefinitely, or at least until such time as her absence has made your heart grow fonder. ■ **absence; love**

He who is ABSENT is always in the wrong

Cf. Fr. *les absents ont toujours tort*; *c* **1440** J. LYDGATE *Fall of Princes* (EETS) III. l. 3927 For princis ofte .. Wil cachche a qu[a]rel .. Ageyn folk absent.

□ **1640** G. HERBERT *Outlandish Proverbs* no. 318 The absent partie is still faultie. **1710** S. PALMER *Proverbs* xxi. The absent party is always to blame. **1736** B. FRANKLIN *Poor Richard's Almanack* (July) The absent are never without fault, nor the present without excuse. **1912** 'SAKI' *Unbearable Bassington* iv. The absent may be always wrong, but they are seldom in a position to be inconsiderate. **1981** A. PRICE *Soldier no More* 57 I will quote first that fine old French saying—which covers any claim Charlie may or may not have on that cake—'he who is absent is always in the wrong.' ■ **absence; error**

absolute *see* POWER corrupts.

abundance *see* out of the FULLNESS of the heart the mouth speaks.

ACCIDENTS will happen (in the best-regulated families)

□ **1763** G. COLMAN *Deuce is in Him* I. 22 Accidents, accidents will happen—No less than seven brought into our infirmary yesterday. **1819** 'P. ATALL' *Hermit in America* i. Accidents will happen in the best regulated families. **1850** DICKENS *David Copperfield* xxviii. 'Copperfield,' said Mr. Micawber, 'accidents will occur in the best-regulated families; and in families not regulated by .. the influence of Woman, in the lofty character of Wife, they must be expected with confidence, and must be borne with philosophy.' **1939** W. S. MAUGHAM *Christmas Holiday* x. Accidents will happen in the best regulated families, and .. if you find you've got anything the matter with you, .. go and see a doctor right away. **2002** *Country Life* 14 Feb. 51 No-one should underestimate the pain and suffering caused. However, the CPS [Crown Prosecution Service] has to recognise that, even in this determinedly scapegoat society, accidents do happen. ■ **misfortune**

There is no ACCOUNTING for tastes

It is impossible to explain why different people like different things (especially things that do not appeal to the speaker). Also now in the form *there is no accounting for taste.* The saying is a version of the Latin tag *de gustibus non est disputandum,* there is no disputing about tastes. Cf. **1599** J. MINSHEU *Dialogues in Spanish* 6 Against ones liking there is no disputing.

□ **1794** A. RADCLIFFE *Mysteries of Udolpho* I. xi. I have often thought the people he disapproved were much more agreeable than those he admired;—but there is no accounting for tastes. **1889** GISSING *Nether World* II. viii. There is no accounting for tastes. Sidney..not once..congratulated himself on his good fortune. **1985** R. REEVES *Doubting Thomas* iv. 'You're usually in here with a little guy, wears a rug. Looks like he gets his suits from Sears. Paisley ties. ..There's no accounting for taste.' ■ **idiosyncrasy; taste**

accumulate *see* if you don't SPECULATE, you can't accumulate.

accuse *see* he who EXCUSES, accuses himself.

accuser *see* a GUILTY conscience needs no accuser.

acorn *see* GREAT oaks from little acorns grow.

ACTIONS speak louder than words

First recorded in its current form in the United States.

□ **1628** J. PYM *Speech* 4 Apr. in Hansard *Parliamentary Hist. England* (1807) II. 274 'A word spoken in season is like an Apple of Gold set in Pictures of Silver,' and actions are more precious than words. **1736** *Melancholy State of Province* in A. M. Davis *Colonial Currency* (1911) III. 137 Actions speak louder than Words, and are more to be regarded. **1856** A. LINCOLN *Works* (1953) II. 352 'Actions speak louder than words' is the maxim; and, if true, the South now distinctly says to the North, 'Give us the *measures,* and you take the *men.*' **1939** M. STUART *Dead Men sing no Songs* xii. Deeds speak louder than words. First she tells you the most damning things she can.., and then she begs you to believe he's innocent in spite of them? **2001** *Washington Times* 1 Aug. A13 Democrats market themselves as the party of the common man, but actions (and inactions) speak louder than words. ■ **words and deeds**

When ADAM delved and Eve span, who was then the gentleman?

The rhyme is particularly associated with the itinerant preacher John Ball, a leader of the 1381 'Peasants' Revolt', who used it to incite the people against their feudal lords.

□ *c* **1340** R. ROLLE in G. G. Perry *Religious Pieces* (EETS) 88 When Adam dalfe [dug] and Eue spane..Whare was than the pride of man? **1381** in Brown & Robbins *Index Middle English Verse* (1943) 628 Whan adam delffid and eve span, Who was than a gentilman? **1562** J. PILKINGTON *Aggeus & Abdias* I. ii. When Adam dalve, and Eve span, Who was than a gentle man? Up start the carle, and gathered good, And thereof came the gentle blood. **1979** C. E. SCHORSKE *Fin-de-Siècle Vienna* vi. When Adam delved and Eve span Who was then the gentleman? The question had ironic relevance for the *arrivé.* ■ **equality; gentry**

As good be an ADDLED egg as an idle bird

□ **1578** LYLY *Euphues* I. 325 If I had not bene gathered from the tree in the budde, I should beeing blowne haue proued a blast, and as good it is to bee an addle egge as an idle bird. **1732** T. FULLER *Gnomologia* no. 681 As good be an addled Egg, as an idle Bird. **1974** D. CARTER *Ghost Writer* iii. The chickens are feeling the heat, poor creatures. I'm afraid I gave them a bit of a ticking off. As good be an addled egg, I told them, as an idle bird. ■ **action and inaction; idleness**

ADVENTURES are to the adventurous

□ **1844** DISRAELI *Coningsby* III. 1. 244 'I fear that the age of adventures is past.'..'Adventures are to the adventurous,' said the stranger. **1952** 'T. HINDE' *Mr Nicholas* iv. He told himself that adventure was to the adventurous. ..If he could not make the effort for the small he would miss the big adventure. ■ **boldness; opportunity, taken; risk**

ADVERSITY makes strange bedfellows

While the underlying idea remains the same, there has always been some variation in the first word of the proverb: see also POLITICS *makes strange bedfellows.*

□ **1611** SHAKESPEARE *Tempest* II. ii. 37 My best way is to creep under his gaberdine; there is no other shelter hereabout. Misery acquaints a man with strange bedfellows. **1837** DICKENS *Pickwick Papers* xli. (*heading*) Illustrative..of the old proverb, that adversity brings a man acquainted with strange bedfellows. **1927** *Times* 27 Aug. 12 The..alliance of 1923–5 was an illustration of the adage that adversity makes strange bedfellows. **1982** *Times* 15 Mar. 9 (*heading*) Poverty makes strange bedfellows. ■ **adversity; misfortune**

afraid *see* he who RIDES a tiger is afraid to dismount.

Africa *see* there is always something NEW out of Africa.

AFTER a storm comes a calm

Cf. *a* **1250** *Ancrene Riwle* (1962) 191 Iblescet ibeo thu laverd the makest stille efter storm [blessed are you, Lord, who makes a calm after the storm]; **1377** LANGLAND *Piers Plowman* B. XVIII. 409 After sharpe shoures..moste shene [bright] is the sonne.

□ **1576** C. HOLYBAND *French Littleton* E1^{v} After a storme commeth a calme. **1655** T. FULLER *Church Hist. Britain* IX. viii. After a storm comes a calm. Wearied with a former blustering they began now to repose themselves in a sad silence. **1979** 'J. LE CARRÉ' *Smiley's People* i. For the next two weeks nothing happened. ..After the storm had come the calm. ■ **peace; trouble**

AFTER dinner rest a while, after supper walk a mile

The sense turns on the fact that dinner is a heavy meal, while supper is a light one. The precept was current in medieval Latin: *post prandium stabis, post coenam ambulabis*, after luncheon you will stand still, after supper you will walk about.

□ **1582** G. WHETSTONE *Heptameron of Civil Discourses* E3 After dynner, talke a while, After supper, walke a mile. **1584** T. COGAN *Haven of Health* ccxi. That olde English saying: After dinner sit a whyle, and after supper walke a myle. **1979** *Daily Telegraph* 24 Dec. 3 'The physiological reaction to a heavy indigestible meal.. seems to be to sleep it off.' What it all seems to boil down to is the old adage: After dinner rest a while, after supper walk a mile. ■ **health**

AFTER the feast comes the reckoning

Mainly in late 20th-cent. North American use.

□ **1620** F. QUARLES *Feast for Wormes* VI. vi. But Young-man, know, there is a Day of doome, The Feast is good, untill the reck'ning come. **1996** *Random House Dict. Popular Proverbs & Sayings* 3 After the feast comes the reckoning. **1999** *Time* 29 July (electronic ed., *heading*) After the Monica feast comes the reckoning. ■ **action and consequence**

after *see also* it is easy to be WISE after the event.

Agamemnon *see* BRAVE men lived before Agamemnon.

age *see* the age of MIRACLES is past; if YOUTH knew, if age could.

agree *see* BIRDS in their little nests agree; TWO of a trade never agree.

alive *see* if you want to LIVE and thrive, let the spider run alive.

ALL good things must come to an end

The addition of 'good' is a recent development. The earlier forms may be compared with EVERYTHING *has an end.*

□ *c* **1440** *Partonope of Blois* (EETS) l. 11144 Ye wote [know] wele of all thing moste be an ende. **1562** G. LEGH *Accidence of Armoury* 182 All worldly thinges haue an ende (excepte the housholde wordes, betwene man and wife). **1738** SWIFT *Polite Conversation* i. 85 All Things have an End, and a Pudden [a kind of sausage] has two. **1857** H. H. RILEY *Puddleford Papers* xxiii. All things must have an end, and the grand caravan, in time, came to its end. **1924** 'D. VANE' *Scar* xxv. All good things come to an end. The feast was over. **2002** *Washington Times* 17 Mar. C12 For more than a decade, Roy Kramer reigned as the most powerful figure in college athletics—not just in the Southeastern Conference but arguably the entire nation. But all good things must come to an end, and that end is now. ■ **finality; good things**

It takes ALL sorts to make a world

□ **1620** T. SHELTON tr. *Cervantes' Don Quixote* II. vi. In the world there must bee of all sorts. **1767** S. JOHNSON *Letter* 17 Nov. (1952) I. 194 Some Lady surely might be found.. in whose fidelity you might repose. The World, says Locke, has people of all sorts. **1844** D. W. JERROLD *Story of Feather* xxviii. Click can't get off this time?.. Well, it takes all sorts to make a world. **1975** J. I. M. STEWART *Young Pattullo* iii. 'My father's a banker during the week and a country gent at week-ends. Takes all sorts, you know.' 'Takes all sorts?' 'To make a world.' **1993** BILL RICHARDSON *Bachelor Brothers' Bed & Breakfast* (1997) 74 There is no nightlife. ..I suppose that what we have here is the working out of the adage that it takes all kinds to make a world. ■ **idiosyncrasy; tolerance; variety**

ALL things are possible with God

With allusion to MATTHEW xix. 26 (AV).. with God all things are possible; cf. HOMER *Odyssey* x. 306 *θεοὶ δέ τε πάντα δύνανται*, with the gods all things can be done.

□ **1694** P. A. MOTTEUX tr. *Rabelais' Pantagruel* V. xliii. Drink.. and you shall find its taste and flavor to be exactly that on which you shall have pitched. Then never presume to say that anything is impossible to God. **1712** C. MATHER *Letter* 22 Nov. (1971) 117 However, take it again; all things are possible with God. **1826** L. BEECHER *Letter* 11 June in *Autobiography* (1865) II. viii. Sometimes it seems as if persons had too much.. intellect to be converted easily. But all things are possible with God. **1965** M. SPARK *Mandelbaum Gate* vi. It would be interesting, for a change, to prepare and be ready for possibilities of, I don't know what, since all things are possible with God and nothing is inevitable. **1971** 'S. CHANCE' *Septimus and*

Danedyke Mystery (1973) iii. 31 'All things are possible—but some are not very likely. As the Apostle should have said, but didn't.' ■ **possibility and impossibility**

ALL things come to those who wait

Cf. Fr. *tout vient à celui qui sait attendre*, all comes to him who knows how to wait.

□ **1530** A. BARCLAY *Eclogues* (EETS) II. 843 Somewhat shall come who can his time abide. **1642** G. TORRIANO *Select Italian Proverbs* 26 He who can wait, hath what he desireth. **1847** DISRAELI *Tancred* II. IV. viii. I have got it at last, everything comes if a man will only wait. **1872** V. FANE *Tout vient à qui sait Attendre* in *From Dawn to Noon* II. 85 Ah! 'All things come to those who wait.'.. They *come*, but often come *too late*. **1980** M. SELLERS *Leonardo & Others* viii. Everything comes to those who wait. The theory fitted well into my lazy way of thinking. **2002** *Times 2* 14 Feb. 7 Until last week I considered the proverb 'All things come to those who wait' to be up there with 'Every cloud has a silver lining' on the list of fatuous remarks to make when your best friend has failed a vital job interview, been dumped by the love of his life, dropped his dentures down a drain or been trapped for hours on the Tube. ■ **patience and impatience**

all *see also* all's for the BEST in the best of all possible worlds; all CATS are grey in the dark; DEATH pays all debts; why should the DEVIL have all the best tunes?; don't put all your EGGS in one basket; all's FAIR in love and war; all is FISH that comes to the net; all that GLITTERS is not gold; all is GRIST that comes to the mill; when all you have is a HAMMER, everything looks like a nail; HEAR all, see all, say nowt; to KNOW all is to forgive all; there is MEASURE in all things; MODERATION in all things; ONE size does not fit all; to the PURE all things are pure; a RISING tide lifts all boats; all ROADS lead to Rome; the THIRD time pays for all; all's WELL that ends well; you can't WIN them all; all WORK and no play makes Jack a dull boy.

alone *see* he TRAVELS fastest who travels alone.

alter *see* CIRCUMSTANCES alter cases.

always *see* he who is ABSENT is always in the wrong; there is always a FIRST time; ONCE a —, always a —; there is always ROOM at the top; the UNEXPECTED always happens.

Good AMERICANS when they die go to Paris

The person alluded to in quot. 1858 was Thomas Gold Appleton (1812–84). Quot. 2002 alters the sense from the implied equivalence of Paris with Heaven.

□ **1858** O. W. HOLMES *Autocrat of Breakfast-Table* vi. To these must certainly be added that other saying of one of the wittiest of men: 'Good Americans, when they die, go to Paris.' **1894** O. WILDE *Woman of no Importance* I. l. 16 They say.. that when good Americans die they go to Paris. **1932** T. SMITH *Topper takes Trip* xxi. We are those good Americans who come to Paris when they die. **2002** *Times Literary Supplement* 22 Mar. 23 'Like any other city.. Big, noisy, crowded.' You don't have to believe that Paris is worth a Mass or the place where good Americans go to die to disagree. ■ **death**; **just deserts**

and *see* if IFS and ands were pots and pans, there'd be no work for tinkers' hands.

angel *see* FOOLS rush in where angels fear to tread.

anger *see* never let the SUN go down on your anger.

angry *see* a HUNGRY man is an angry man.

ANOTHER day, another dollar

Quot. 1897 links the form *more days, more dollars* to sailors being paid by the day: the longer the voyage the greater the financial reward. Later uses suggest that *another day, another dollar* occurs as world-weary comment on routine toil to earn a living. It has also generated a quantity of by-forms.

□ **1897** J. CONRAD *Nigger of 'Narcissus'* (1955) v. 114. The common saying, 'More days, more dollars,' did not give the usual comfort because the stores were running short. **1957** D. ERSKINE & P. DENNIS *Pink Hotel* (1958) 8 ''Nother sleepless night,' Mr. Baldwin said. 'Heard the clock strike four again.' 'That's a shame, Mr. Baldwin,' Mary said. She yawned and stretched, knowing that her landlord was about to say Another Day, Another Dollar. **1992** J. E. DOMINGUEZ & V. ROBIN *Your Money or Your Life* v. 157 For those opting for Financial Independence it reinforces the awareness that work is no longer about 'another day, another dollar.' **1993** *Time International* 18 Jan. 4 Another day, another deadline. And another backdown by Saddam Hussein, for what seems like the zillionth time. **2002** *Times 2* 10 Jan. 7 And I haven't even mentioned . . Bobby Fischer, stripped of his title by Fide in 1975 (another decade, another squabble), but never defeated, and still only 58. ■ **action and consequence; work**

answer *see* ASK a silly question and you get a silly answer; a CIVIL question deserves a civil answer; a SOFT answer turneth away wrath.

anvil *see* the CHURCH is an anvil which has worn out many hammers.

ANY port in a storm

□ **1749** J. CLELAND *Memoirs of Woman of Pleasure* II. 133 It was going by the right door, and knocking desperately at the wrong one. . . I told him of it: 'Pooh,' says he 'my dear, any port in a storm.' **1821** SCOTT *Pirate* I. iv. As the Scotsman's howf [refuge] lies right under your lee, why, take any port in a storm. **1965** J. PORTER *Dover Three* ii. It was not quite the sort of company with which Dover would mix from choice but, as the jolly sailors say, any port in a storm. **1983** M. BOND *Monsieur Pamplemousse* iv. On the principle of any port in a storm he made a dive for the nearest cubicle. ■ **necessity; trouble**

If ANYTHING can go wrong, it will

Commonly known as *Murphy's Law*, the saying has numerous variations. It is said to have been invented by George Nichols in 1949. Nichols was then a project manager working in California for the American firm of Northrop, and developed the maxim from a remark made by a colleague, Captain E. Murphy, of the Wright Field Aircraft Laboratory. The contexts of the early quotations appear to support this explanation: **1955** *Aviation Mechanics Bulletin* May–June 11 Murphy's Law: If an aircraft part can be installed incorrectly, someone will install it that way.

□ **1956** *Scientific American* Apr. 166 Dr. Schaefer's observation confirms this department's sad experience that editors as well as laboratory workers are subject to Murphy's Laws, to wit: 1. If something can go wrong it will, [etc.]. **1958** *Product Engineering* 21 Apr. 32 If anything can go wrong with an experiment—it will. **1974** *New York Times Magazine* 8 Sept. 33 'If anything can go wrong, it will,' says Murphy's law. In this computer age, the 'law' has been helped along by clever con men. **1980** A. E. FISHER *Midnight Men* vii. Of course, the up train was delayed. There was some vast universal principle. If anything can go wrong it will. **2000** *Washington Post* 28 Dec. E1 Tune out the pundits. . . I subscribe to a corollary of Murphy's Law ('Anything that can go wrong, will'), which is Pundit's Law: Anything experts predict will happen, will not. ■ **error**

An APE's an ape, a varlet's a varlet, though they be clad in silk or scarlet

A varlet was formerly a menial servant, but the word also took on the sense of 'scoundrel' or 'rogue'. Scarlet was the colour of the official or ceremonial dress of various dignitaries, including judges. Cf. LUCIAN *Adversus Indoctum* 4 *πίθηκος ὁ πίθηκος.. κἂν χρυσέα ἔχῃ σύμβολα*, an ape is an ape.. even if it has gold insignia; ERASMUS *Adages* I. vii. *simia simia est, etiamsi aurea gestet insignia.*

□ **1539** R. TAVERNER tr. *Erasmus' Adages* 21 An ape is an ape although she weare badges of golde. **1659** J. HOWELL *Proverbs* (English) I An Ape's an Ape, A Varlett's a Varlett, Though they be cladd in silk, or scarlett. **1732** T. FULLER *Gnomologia* no. 6391 An Ape's an Ape: a Varlet's a Varlet, Tho' they be clad in Silk or Scarlet. **1967** D. MORRIS *Naked Ape* i. The naked ape is in danger of.. forgetting that beneath the surface gloss he is still very much a primate. ('An ape's an ape, a varlet's a varlet, though they be clad in silk or scarlet.') Even a space ape must urinate. ■ **appearance, deceptive; nature and nurture**

ape *see also* the HIGHER the monkey climbs the more he shows his tail.

appear *see* TALK of the Devil, and he is bound to appear.

APPEARANCES are deceptive

A common US form is *appearances are deceiving.*

□ **1666** G. TORRIANO *Italian Proverbs* 12 Appearance oft deceives. **1784** in *Collections of Massachusetts Hist. Society* (1877) III. 186 The appearances in those mountainous regions are extremely deceptive. **1846** H. MELVILLE *Typee* xxiv. Appearances.. are deceptive. Little men are sometimes very potent, and rags sometimes cover very extensive pretensions. **1927** E. F. BENSON *Lucia in London* v. Mr. Merriall.. watched the three figures at Georgie's door. 'Appearances are deceptive,' he said. 'But isn't that Olga Shuttleworth and Princess Isabel?' **2002** A. VANNEMAN *Sherlock Holmes and Giant Rat of Sumatra* xviii. 128 'Why, Mr. Holmes, you are the most wide-awake man here.' 'Appearances are deceiving,' returned Holmes. ■ **appearance, deceptive; deception**

APPETITE comes with eating

Desire or facility increases as an activity proceeds. Cf. **1534** RABELAIS *Gargantua* I. v. *l'appétit vient en mangeant*, appetite comes with eating; **1600–1** SHAKESPEARE *Hamlet* I. ii. 143 Why, she would hang on him As if increase of appetite had grown By what it fed on.

□ **1653** URQUHART & MOTTEUX tr. *Rabelais' Gargantua* I. v. Appetite comes with eating. *a* **1721** M. PRIOR *Dialogues of Dead* (1907) 227 But as we say in France, the Appetite comes in Eating; so in Writing You stil found more to write. **1906** W. MAXWELL *From Yalu to Port Arthur* i. Appetite comes with eating. Having absorbed Port Arthur and begun on Manchuria, Russia saw no reason why she should not have Korea also. **1943** S. CLOETE *Congo Song* xxiv. The appetite came with eating. The more he had of her, the more he wanted. ■ **wanting and having**

appetite *see also* HUNGER is the best sauce.

An APPLE a day keeps the doctor away

□ **1866** *Notes & Queries* 3rd Ser. IX. 153 A Pembrokeshire Proverb.—'Eat an apple on going to bed, And you'll keep the doctor from earning his bread.' **1913** E. M. WRIGHT *Rustic Speech* xiv. Ait a happle avore gwain to bed, An' you'll make the doctor beg his bread (Dev.); or as the more popular version runs: An apple a day keeps the doctor away. **2001** *Times* 12 Dec. 2 Have you resolved to be a well person?.. Do you eat an apple a day to keep the doctor away? ■ **doctors; health**

The APPLE never falls far from the tree

Apparently of Eastern origin, it is frequently used to assert the continuity of family characteristics. Quot. 1839 implies return to one's original home. Cf. 16th-cent. Ger. *der Apfel fellt nicht gerne weit vom Baume*, the apple does not usually fall far from the tree.

□ **1839** EMERSON *Letter* 22 Dec. (1939) II. 243 As men say the apple never falls far from the stem, I shall hope that another year will draw your eyes and steps to this old dear odious haunt of the race. **1939** H. W. THOMPSON *Body, Boots & Britches* xix. As a.. farmer remarked, 'If you breed a pa'tridge, you'll git a pa'tridge.' Another way of setting that truth forth is,.. 'An apple never falls far from the tree.' **1981** *Women's Journal* Apr. 179 He's a fool, Muffie, as his father was. The apple never falls far from the tree. **2001** *Washington Post* 28 June C10 The social worker had summed up the child's future: 'Don't expect to do miracles. An apple can't fall too far from the tree.' ■ **family; nature and nurture; origins**

apple *see also* the ROTTEN apple injures its neighbours; SMALL choice in rotten apples; STOLEN fruit is sweet.

An APPLE-PIE without some cheese is like a kiss without a squeeze

□ **1929** C. BROOKS *Seven Hells* v. 63 Let me advise you to take a bit of cheese with it. They have a good proverb, these folks: 'Apple pie without the cheese, is like the kiss without a squeeze.' **1989** *Courier-Journal* (Louisville, KY) 2 July 4M There was an old English rhyme popular about 1750 that went: An apple-pie without some cheese Is like a kiss without a squeeze. **2002** *Spectator* 21 Sept. 61 'Apple cake without cheese,' they used to say in Yorkshire, 'is like a kiss without a squeeze.' ■ **food and drink**

APRIL showers bring forth May flowers

□ *c* **1560** in T. Wright *Songs & Ballads* (1860) 213 Aprell sylver showers so sweet Can make May flowers to sprynge. **1670** J. RAY *English Proverbs* 41 April showers bring forth May flowers. **1846** M. A. DENHAM *Proverbs relating to Seasons, &c.* 36 March winds and April showers bring forth May flowers. **1921** *Sphere* 14 May 152 If there was anybody left to believe in the saying that 'April showers bring forth May flowers' their simple faith must have been rudely shattered by May's behaviour this year. **2001** *Washington Post* 1 July F1 If April showers bring May flowers, what do June brides bring? ■ **weather lore**

architect *see* EVERY man is the architect of his own fortune.

arm *see* KINGS have long arms; STRETCH your arm no further than your sleeve will reach; YORKSHIRE born and Yorkshire bred, strong in the arm and weak in the head.

An ARMY marches on its stomach

The proverb has been attributed to both Napoleon and Frederick the Great; this figurative use of (*on one's*) *stomach* is unusual in English.

□ **1904** *Windsor Magazine* Jan. 268 'An army marches on its stomach.' '*C'est la soupe qui fait le soldat.*' These Napoleonic aphorisms.. have been increasingly appreciated by our War Office. **1977** J. B. HILTON *Dead-Nettle* x. 'They say an army marches on its stomach,' Gilbert Slack began to say. 'You mean that Frank was a cook?' **1992** W. DONALDSON *Root into Europe* ii.16 'Didn't see service as such. Supply and demand myself. Pay and personnel. Laundry and so forth. An army marches on its stomach.' **2002** *Washington Times* 30 Jan. E4 (*Hazel comic strip*) 'An army marches on its stomach.' 'And retreats on its . . ' ■ **food and drink; soldiers**

around *see* what GOES around comes around.

arrive *see* it is BETTER to travel hopefully than to arrive.

ART is long and life is short

Hippocrates (*Aphorisms* I. I. *ὁ βίος βραχύς, ἡ δὲ τέχνη μακρή*, life is short, but art is long) compared the difficulties encountered in learning the art of medicine or healing with the shortness of human life. Hippocrates' saying was alluded to by Seneca in his dialogue 'On the Brevity of Life' (*De brevitate vitae* I: *vitam brevem esse, longam artem*) and from this version the usual Latin form of the tag is derived: *ars longa, vita brevis*, art is long, life is short. *Art* is now commonly understood in the proverb in a less specific sense. In quot. 1958, it refers to (the durability of) a work of art.

□ *c* **1380** CHAUCER *Parliament of Fowls* l. 1 The lyf so short, the craft so long to lerne. **1558** W. BULLEIN *Government of Health* 5ᵛ And although oure life be shorte, yet the arte of phisicke is long. **1581** G. PETTIE tr. *S. Guazzo's Civil Conversation* I. 16 An art is long and life is short. **1710** S. PALMER *Proverbs* 380 Art is Long, Life Short. Our Philosophical Meditations on Time are very Obscure and Confus'd. **1869** M. ARNOLD *Culture & Anarchy* vi. If . . we take some other criterion of man's well-being than the cities he has built . . our Liberal friends . . take us up very sharply. 'Art is long', says the *Times*, 'and life is short.' **1958** L. DURRELL *Balthazar* IV. xiii. The shapely hand on his shoulder still wore the great ring taken from the tomb of a Byzantine youth. Life is short, art long. **1987** 'C. AIRD' *Dead Liberty* viii. 'The art is long,' Sloan heard himself saying aloud. . . 'And life is short. I know that.' Dr. Bressingham completed the quotation brusquely. ■ **life; mortality**

ash *see* when the OAK is before the ash, then you will only get a splash; beware of an OAK it draws the stroke.

ASK a silly question and you get a silly answer

With allusion to PROVERBS xxvi. 5 (AV) Answer a fool according to his folly, lest he be wise in his own conceit.

□ *c* **1300** *South-English Legendary* (EETS) 494 Ffor-sothe thou axest as a fol, and swich ansuere me schul the yive. **1484** CAXTON *Aesop* (1967) V. xiii. 158 And thus they wente withoute ony sentence For to a folysshe demaunde behoueth a folysshe ansuere. **1551** R. ROBYNSON tr. *T. More's Utopia* I E4 For Salomon the wise sayeth: Answer a foole according to his folishnes, like as I do now. *c* **1600** *Tarlton's Jests* (1638) E2ᵛ The fellow seeing a foolish question had a foolish answere, laid his legges on his neck, and got him gone. **1721** J. KELLY *Scottish Proverbs* 35 A thraward [perverse] Question should a thraward Answer. **1934** C. RYLAND *Murder on Cliff* vi. If you ask me damned silly questions, I'm going to give you damned silly answers. **1969** 'A. GILBERT' *Missing from her Home* v. No, don't bother to answer that. Ask a silly question and you get a silly answer. **1985** M. WESLEY *Harnessing Peacocks* (1990) v. 46 'Are you happy at school?' Ask a silly question. 'It's all right.' 'What sort of answer is that?' she cried in distress. ■ **action and consequence; stupidity**

ASK no questions and hear no lies

□ **1773** GOLDSMITH *She stoops to Conquer* III. 51 Ask me no questions and I'll tell you no fibs. **1818** SCOTT *Heart of Midlothian* I. ix. If ye'll ask nae questions, I'll tell ye nae lees. **1900** H. LAWSON *Over Sliprails* 135 'Where did you buy the steer, father?' she asked. 'Ask no questions and hear no lies.' **1906** R. KIPLING *Puck of Pook's Hill* 252 Them that asks no questions isn't told a lie—Watch the wall, my darling, while the Gentlemen go by! **1997** R. BOWEN *Evans Above* vi. 65 Charlie put his finger to his nose. 'Them that asks no questions, don't get told no lies, that's what my old mother used to say,' he said. ■ **curiosity; lying**

ask *see also* if you WANT something done, ask a busy person.

a-sorrowing *see* he that GOES a-borrowing, goes a-sorrowing.

ATTACK is the best form of defence

The idea of the pre-emptive strike expressed in a form approaching this appears to be American in origin; cf. **1775** W. H. DRAYTON in R. W. Gibbes *Documentary Hist. American Revolution* (1855) I. 174 It is a maxim, that it is better to attack than to receive one; **1799** G. WASHINGTON *Writings* (1940) XXXVII. 250 Make them believe, that offensive operations, often times, is the surest, if not the only.. means of defence. Recent usage shows a clear British–US divergence, however, with *the best* DEFENSE *is a good offense* as the US form.

□ **1930** C. F. GREGG *Murder on Bus* xxxvii. Inspector Higgins fired his revolver at the sound, deeming attack the better part of defence, whilst someone from the other side of the room had a similar notion. **1965** N. S. GRAY *Apple-Stone* xi. 'Attack', she said, 'is the best means of defence.' She sounded so smug that I told her the thought was not original. **1980** F. OLBRICH *Desouza in Stardust* iv. Attack is the best form of defence, they say, and when politicians lose their principles they play a dirty game. **2002** *Times* 19 June 24 Clearly, the big banks have stuck to their policy of attack being the best form of defence on this issue [of price controls]. ■ **boldness; warfare**

away *see* when the CAT's away, the mice will play.

B *see* who SAYS A must say B.

babe *see* out of the MOUTHS of babes—.

baby *see* don't THROW the baby out with the bathwater.

back *see* GOD makes the back to the burden; what is GOT over the Devil's back is spent under his belly; it is the LAST straw that breaks the camel's back; you SCRATCH my back, I'll scratch yours.

A BAD excuse is better than none

□ **1551** T. WILSON *Rule of Reason* S6 This is as thei saie in English, better a badde excuse, then none at all. **1579** S. GOSSON *School of Abuse* 24 A bad excuse is better, they say, then none at all. **1821** W. WIRT *Letter* 29 Aug. in J. P. Kennedy *Memoirs* (1849) II. vii. The old fellow's look had a glimpse of passing cunning as much as to say, 'A bad excuse is better than none.' **1981** P. VAN GREENAWAY *'Cassandra' Bill* xiii. What excuse is better than none? ■ **excuses**

BAD money drives out good

Commonly known as Gresham's Law, after Sir Thomas Gresham (*c* 1519–79), founder of the Royal Exchange. Gresham saw the economic need to restore the purity of the coinage, though there is no evidence that he actually used this expression. Quot. 1902 states that the principle, not the proverb, is mentioned in Gresham's letter to the Queen. (**1858** H. D. MACLEOD *Elements of Political Economy* 477 He [Gresham] was the first to perceive that a bad and debased currency is the cause of the disappearance of the good money.)

□ **1902** *New English Dictionary* VI. 116 *Gresham's law*, the principle, involved in Sir Thomas Gresham's letter to Q. Elizabeth in 1558, that 'bad money drives out good'. **1933** A. HUXLEY *Letter* 18 Nov. (1969) 438 Gresham's Law holds good in every field..and bad politics tends to drive out good politics just as bad money drives out good money. **1982** R. NISBET *Prejudices* 178 Genuine scholars receive grants too, but this misses the crucial point, which is that bad money drives out good, and that only a few years of such handouts to putterers will be enough to convince the American people that Everyman is a humanist. **2002** *Times 2* 12 June 5 In potatoes as in currency, Gresham's law applies: bad drives out good. The new new, in potatoes, is old. ■ **money**

BAD news travels fast

Cf. **1539** R. TAVERNER tr. *Erasmus' Adages* II. A4 Sad and heuy tydynges be easly blowen abroade be they neuer so vaine and false and they be also sone beleued. In quots. 1592 and 1694 *news* is construed as a plural noun, as was usual at this period.

□ **1592** KYD *Spanish Tragedy* I. B2^{V} Euill newes flie faster still than good. **1694** *Terence's Comedies made English* 46 Bad News always fly faster than good. **1792** T. HOLCROFT *Road to Ruin* II. i. All these bills..brought..this morning. Ill news travels fast. **1935** W. IRWIN *Julius Caesar Murder Case* xxv. 'Where'd you get it [a knife]?' 'On the Plains of Philippi.' 'Bad news travels fast,' said Hercules. **1991**

L. SANDERS *McNally's Secret* (1992) iv. 38 'I've already had a dozen phony sympathy calls—including one from a cousin in Sarasota. Bad news certainly travels fast.' **2002** *Times* 1 Feb. 22 Media processes are not forensic but sensational. Their light shines uncertainly. It often distorts and can be unfair. 'Ill news hath wings.' ■ **misfortune; news**

A BAD penny always turns up

The proverb, also used allusively in simile and metaphor (see quot. 1766), refers to the predictable, and usually unwelcome, return of a disreputable or prodigal person after some absence.

□ **1766** A. ADAMS in L. H. Butterfield et al. *Adams Family Correspondence* (1963) I. 55 Like a bad penny it returnd, to me again. **1824** SCOTT *Redgauntlet* II. ii. Bring back Darsie? little doubt of that—the bad shilling is sure enough to come back again. **1884** R. H. THORPE *Fenton Family* iii. Just like as not he'll be coming back one of these days, when he's least wanted. A bad penny is sure to return. **1922** JOYCE *Ulysses* 149 Who's dead, when and what did he die of? Turn up like a bad penny. **1941** A. UPDEGRAFF *Hills look Down* vi. 'I miss Bart.' 'Oh, a bad penny always turns up again.' **1979** G. MITCHELL *Mudflats of Dead* iii. 'Stop worrying. The bad pennies always turn up.' 'Oh, Adrian, I don't think she's a bad penny, not really.' ■ **wrong-doers**

BAD things come in threes

Bad things may be specified as *accidents*, *deaths*, or other mishaps; cf. MISFORTUNES *never come singly*. This is a well-attested folk superstition on both sides of the Atlantic: **1891** *Notes & Queries* 7th Ser. XII. 489 One of my servants having accidentally broken a glass shade, asked for two other articles of little value, a wine bottle and jam crock, that she might break them, and so prevent the two other accidents. ..which would otherwise follow. Cf. THIRD *time lucky*.

□ **1997** D. HANSEN *Sole Survivor* xvi. 82 He was a superstitious man and believed that bad joss always struck in threes. **2002** *Times* 20 Mar. 22 They say bad things come in threes. I don't know who the they are that say this, mind, or how they found out that that was how bad things came,..but..last weekend, they were spot on. ■ **misfortune; superstition**

There is no such thing as BAD weather, only the wrong clothes

□ **1980** *Washington Post* 15 Feb. D1 'There's no such thing as bad weather, only bad clothes,' said Peterson. 'You want to wear the least you can, and still not get frostbitten.' [illegible] *Daily Telegraph* 23 Sept. 13 As someone once said, there is no such [illegible] only the wrong clothes. **1994** *St. Louis Post-Dispatch* 7 Aug. 1T [illegible] may encounter, Muckley says, 'There is no such thing as [illegible] clothes.' ■ **weather**

A BAD workman blames his tools

Cf. late 13th-cent. Fr. *mauvés ovriers ne trovera ja bon hostill*, a bad workman will never find a good tool.

□ **1611** R. COTGRAVE *Dict. French & English* s.v. Outil, A bungler cannot find (or fit himselfe with) good tooles. **1640** G. HERBERT *Outlandish Proverbs* no. 67 Never had ill workeman good tooles. **1859** S. SMILES *Self-Help* iv. It is proverbial that the bad workman never yet had a good tool. **1940** J. G. COZZENS *Ask Me Tomorrow* vii. I've read somewhere that a poor workman quarrels with his tools. **1979** A. FOX *Threat Signal Red* xv. Damn! Dropped the screwdriver. ..Bad workmen blame their tools. **2001** *Washington Times* 19 Aug. B8 'Virtuous War' starts off with a bad idea, proceeds to a pair of disasters, then gets worse. As for the fundamental reason for its failure—for now let's just say, it's a poor workman who blames his lousy tools. ■ **efficiency and inefficiency; work**

bad *see also* give a DOG a bad name and hang him; FIRE is a good servant but a bad master; a GOOD horse cannot be of a bad colour; HARD cases make bad law; HOPE is a good breakfast but a bad supper; NOTHING so bad but it might have been worse; THREE removals are as bad as a fire.

bag *see* EMPTY sacks will never stand upright; there's many a GOOD cock come out of a tattered bag.

bairn *see* FOOLS and bairns should never see half-done work; the SHOEMAKER's son always goes barefoot.

As you BAKE, so shall you brew

As you begin, so shall you proceed. Complementary to *as you* BREW, *so shall you bake*.

□ *c* **1577** *Misogonus* III. i. As thou bakst, so shat brewe. **1775** D. GARRICK *May-Day* ii. To keep..My bones whole and tight, To speak, nor look, would I dare; As they bake they shall brew. **1909** W. DE MORGAN *It never can happen Again* I. v. Each one [i.e. young person]..was..the centre of an incubation of memories that were to last a lifetime. 'As they bake, so they will brew,' philosophized Mr. Challis to himself. ■ **action and consequence**

bake *see also* as you BREW, so shall you bake.

bandit *see* the more LAWS, the more thieves and bandits.

bare *see* there goes more to MARRIAGE than four bare legs in a bed.

barefoot *see* the SHOEMAKER's son always goes barefoot.

bargain *see* it takes TWO to make a bargain.

bark *see* DOGS bark, but the caravan goes on; why KEEP a dog and bark yourself?

A BARKING dog never bites

Cf. Q. CURTIUS *De Rebus Gestis Alexandri Magni* VII. iv. 13 *canem timidum vehementius latrere quam mordere*, a timid cur barks more furiously than he bites [said there to be a Bactrian saying]; 13th-cent. Fr. *chascuns chiens qui abaie ne mort pas*, the dog that barks does not bite.

□ *c* **1550** *Thersytes* E1 Great barking dogges, do not most byte And oft it is sene that the best men in the hoost Be not suche, that vse to bragge moste. **1595** *Locrine* (1908) IV. i. Soft words good sir. ..A barking dog doth sildome strangers bite. **1629** *Book of Merry Riddles* 22 A barking dog seldome bites. **1837** F. CHAMIER *Arethusa* III. x. Our dogs which bark, Abdallah, seldom bite. **1980** *Daily Telegraph* 1 May 18 A canvassing candidate came to a house where there was an Alsatian who barked ferociously. His agent said: 'Just go in. Don't you know the proverb "A barking dog never bites"?' 'Yes,' said the candidate, 'I know the proverb, you know the proverb, but does the dog know the proverb?' ■ **words and deeds**

BARNABY bright, Barnaby bright, the longest day and the shortest night

St. Barnabas' Day, 11 June, was reckoned the longest day of the year under the

Old Style calendar. Cf. **1595** SPENSER *Epithalamion* l. 266 This day the sunne is in his chiefest hight, With Barnaby the bright.

□ **1659** J. HOWELL *Proverbs* (English) 20 Barnaby bright, the longest day and shortest night. **1858** *Notes & Queries* 2nd Ser. VI. 522 In some parts of the country the children call the lady-bird Barnaby Bright, and address it thus:—'Barnaby Bright, Barnaby Bright, The longest day and the shortest night.' **1906** E. HOLDEN *Country Diary of Edwardian Lady* (1977) 72 Barnaby bright All day and no night. **1978** R. WHITLOCK *Calendar of Country Customs* vii. Barnaby bright, Barnaby bright, The longest day and the shortest night, is a reminder that, before the change in the calendar in 1752, 11 June *was* the longest day of the year. ■ **calendar lore**

basket *see* don't put all your EGGS in one basket.

bathwater *see* don't THROW the baby out with the bathwater.

battalion *see* PROVIDENCE is always on the side of the big battalions.

battle *see* the RACE is not to the swift, nor the battle to the strong.

BE what you would seem to be

Cf. AESCHYLUS *Seven against Thebes* l. 592 *οὐ γὰρ δοκεῖν ἄριστος ἀλλ᾽ εἶναι θέλει*, for he wishes not to appear but to be the best; SALLUST *Catilina* liv. *Esse, quam videri, bonus malebat*, he [*sc.* Cato] preferred to be good, rather than to seem good.

□ *c* **1377** LANGLAND *Piers Plowman* B. x. 253 Suche as thow semest in syghte, be in assay [trial] y-founde. **1640** G. HERBERT *Outlandish Proverbs* no. 724 Be what thou wouldst seeme to be. **1721** J. KELLY *Scottish Proverbs* 68 Be what you seem, and seem what you are. The best way! for Hypocrisy is soon discovered. **1865** 'L. CARROLL' *Alice's Adventures in Wonderland* ix. It's a vegetable. It doesn't look like one, but it is. . . the moral of that is—'Be what you would seem to be.' **1980** G. SIMS in H. Watson *Winter Crimes 12* 158 The Benningworth family motto *Esse quam videri*, 'To be rather than to seem to be'. ■ **appearance**

bean *see* CANDLEMAS day, put beans in the clay, put candles and candlesticks away.

BEAR and forbear

Cf. EPICTETUS *Fragments* x. *ἀνέχου καὶ ἀπέχου*, be patient and endure; ERASMUS *Adages* II. vii. 13 *sustine et abstine*.

□ **1573** T. TUSSER *Husbandry* (rev. ed.) II. 12ᵛ Both beare and forbeare, now and then as ye may, then wench God a mercy [reward you], thy husband will say. **1688** BUNYAN *Discourse of Building, &c. House of God* 53 To bear and forbear here, will tend to rest. **1871** S. SMILES *Character* xi. The golden rule of married life is, 'Bear and forbear'. **1940** H. W. THOMPSON *Body, Boots & Britches* xix. You must take two bears two live with you—Bear and Forbear. ■ **patience and impatience**; **tolerance**

bear (noun) *see* don't SELL the skin till you have caught the bear.

beard *see* it is MERRY in hall when beards wag all.

beast *see* when the WIND is in the east, 'tis neither good for man nor beast.

If you can't BEAT them, join them

Lick is more usual in the US.

□ **1941** Q. REYNOLDS *Wounded don't Cry* i. There is an old political adage which says 'If you can't lick 'em, jine 'em'. **1953** P. GALLICO *Foolish Immortals* xvii. It was vital to him to get the reins back into his own hands again. He remembered an old adage: 'If you can't lick 'em, join 'em.' **1979** D. LESSING *Shikasta* 266 I said, Running things, what's the point? He said, If you can't beat them, join them! **1996** *Washington Times* 2 July B8 Having taken it on the chin so convincingly, brokers have decided that, if you can't beat 'em, join 'em. **2002** *Washington Times* 26 Feb. A20 In fact, he began an attempt to win over the Catholic party to his side; the Teutonic version of 'can't lick 'em, join 'em.' ■ **enemies; self-preservation**

beat *see also* one ENGLISHMAN can beat three Frenchmen; it is easy to find a STICK to beat a dog; a WOMAN, a dog, and a walnut tree, the more you beat them the better they be.

beautiful *see* SMALL is beautiful.

BEAUTY draws with a single hair

□ **1591** J. FLORIO *Second Fruits* 183 Ten teemes of oxen draw much lesse, Than doth one haire of Helens tresse. **1640** G. HERBERT *Outlandish Proverbs* no. 685 Beauty drawes more then oxen. **1666** G. TORRIANO *Piazza Universale* 199 One hair of a woman draws more than a hundred yoke of oxen. **1712** POPE *Rape of Lock* II. 28 And beauty draws us with a single hair. **1941** 'M. COLES' *They tell no Tales* xxii. Beauty draws me with a single hair if it's blonde enough. **1945** R. L. HINE *Confessions* (ed. 2) 91 The old adage.. that 'beauty draws more than oxen.' ■ **beauty**

BEAUTY is in the eye of the beholder

Beauty is not judged objectively, but according to the beholder's estimation. The idea is a very old one: THEOCRITUS *Idyll* vi. 18 *ἦ γὰρ ἔρωτι πολλάκις.. τὰ μὴ καλὰ καλὰ πέφανται*, for in the eyes of love that which is not beautiful often seems beautiful. Cf. **1742** HUME *Essays Moral & Political* II. 151 Beauty, properly speaking, lyes.. in the Sentiment or Taste of the Reader.

□ **1769** F. BROOKE *Hist. Emily Montague* IV. 205 You should remember, my dear, that beauty is in the lover's eye. **1788** R. CUMBERLAND in *Observer* IV. cxviii. Beauty, gentlemen, is in the eye, I aver it to be in the eye of the beholder and not in the object itself. **1878** M. W. HUNGERFORD *Molly Bawn* I. xii. 'I have heard she is beautiful—is she?' 'Beauty is in the eye of the beholder,' quotes Marcia. **2001** *Spectator* 8 Dec. 58 This at once confirmed the conclusion that I had just reached after studying the photographs of the child Wladyslaw..: beauty is not merely in the eye but also in the imagination of the beholder. ■ **beauty; love; taste**

BEAUTY is only skin-deep

Physical beauty is no guarantee of good character, temperament, etc. Cf. *a* **1613** T. OVERBURY *Wife* (1614) B8v All the carnall beautie of my wife, Is but skinne-deep.

□ **1616** J. DAVIES *Select Second Husband* B3 Beauty's but skin-deepe. **1829** COBBETT *Advice to Young Men* III. cxxix. The less favoured part of the sex say, that 'beauty is but skin deep'.. but it is very agreeable though, for all that. **1882** E. M. INGRAHAM *Bond & Free* xiii. Mother used to say that beauty was only skin deep, but I never before realized that bones could be so fearfully repulsive. **1978** A. PRICE *'44 Vintage* xix. Beauty is only skin-deep, but it's only the skin you see. ■ **beauty**

bed *see* EARLY to bed and early to rise, makes a man healthy, wealthy, and wise; as you MAKE your bed, so you must lie upon it; there goes more to MARRIAGE than four bare legs in a bed.

bedfellow *see* ADVERSITY makes strange bedfellows; POLITICS makes strange bedfellows.

beer *see* he that DRINKS beer, thinks beer; LIFE isn't all beer and skittles; TURKEY, heresy, hops, and beer came into England all in one year.

Where BEES are, there is honey

Cf. L. *ubi mel, ibi apes*, where there is honey, there are bees.

□ **1616** T. DRAXE *Adages* 77 Where Bees are, there is honie. **1670** J. RAY *English Proverbs* 60 Where Bees are, there is honey. Where there are industrious persons, there is wealth, for the hand of the diligent maketh rich. **1748** M. FREEMAN *Word in Season* 6 Take away the *Bees*, and.. you shall have no *Honey* in the Hive,.. but there always *will be Honey where there are Bees*. **1931** P. A. TAYLOR *Cape Cod Mystery* ix. It'd look.. like they was something afoot, bein' as how there's bees where's honey. ■ **associates; diligence**

beforehand *see* PAY beforehand was never well served.

beget *see* LENGTH begets loathing; LOVE begets love.

Set a BEGGAR on horseback, and he'll ride to the Devil

A proverb (now frequently used elliptically) with many variations, meaning that one unaccustomed to power or luxury will abuse it or be corrupted by it.

□ **1576** G. PETTIE *Petit Palace* 76 Set a Beggar on horsebacke, and he wyl neuer alight. **1592** NASHE *Pierce Penniless* I. 174 These whelpes.. drawne vp to the heauen of honor from the dunghill of abiect fortune, haue long been on horseback to come riding to your Diuelship. **1616** T. ADAMS *Sacrifice of Thankfulness* 6 He that serues the Flesh serues his fellow: And a Beggar mounted on the backe of Honour, rides post to the Diuell. **1669** W. WINSTANLEY *New Help to Discourse* 151 Set a Beggar on Horse-back, and he will ride to the Devil. **1855** GASKELL *North & South* I. x. You know the proverb.. 'Set a beggar on horseback, and he'll ride to the devil,'—well, some of these early manufacturers did ride to the devil in a magnificent style. **1923** C. WELLS *Affair at Flower Acres* ii. I should think your early days of forced economy would have taught you not to be quite so extravagant. But there's an old proverb—'Set a beggar on horse-back—' and so forth, that jolly well fits you. **1961** W. H. LEWIS *Scandalous Regent* x. He had a good deal of the vulgarity and insolence of the beggar on horseback. ■ **good fortune; pride**

beggar *see also* SUE a beggar and catch a louse; if WISHES were horses, beggars would ride.

BEGGARS can't be choosers

The substitution of *can't* for *must not* is a recent development. Cf. mid 15th-cent. Fr. *qui emprunncte ne peult choisir*, he who borrows cannot choose.

□ **1546** J. HEYWOOD *Dialogue of Proverbs* I. x. D1 Folke say alwaie, beggers shulde be no choosers. **1728** VANBRUGH *Journey to London* III. i. My Lords, says I, Beggars must not be Chusers; but some Place about a thousand a Year.. might do pretty weel. **1888** N. J. CLODFELTER *Snatched from Poor House* iv. Crawl out o' that bed! I'spose you do feel a little bad, but 'beggars can't be choosers!' **1939** J. SHEARING *Blanche Fury* 72 'I suppose.. you would marry any man with a good character and a fine estate.'.. 'Beggars can't be choosers, you mean!' **2000** J. ALTMAN *Gathering of Spies* ix. 150 It would ruin the dress, no doubt about that. But beggars couldn't be choosers. She drew a breath and then jumped, tucking and rolling as she came out of the train. ■ **necessity; poverty**

begin *see* CHARITY begins at home; LIFE begins at forty; the LONGEST journey begins with a single step; when THINGS are at the worst they begin to mend; *also* BEGUN.

beginning *see* a GOOD beginning makes a good ending.

begun *see* the SOONER begun, the sooner done; WELL begun is half done.

beholder *see* BEAUTY is in the eye of the beholder.

BELIEVE nothing of what you hear, and only half of what you see

Cf. *a* **1300** *Proverbs of Alfred* (1907) 35 Gin thu neuere leuen alle monnis spechen, Ne alle the thinge that thu herest singen; **1770** C. CARROLL *Letter* 4 Sept. in *Maryland Hist. Mag.* (1918) XIII. 58 You must not take Everything to be true that is told to you.

□ **1845** E. A. POE in *Graham's Mag.* Nov. 194 You are young yet.. but the time will arrive when you will learn to judge for yourself. ..Believe nothing you hear, and only one half that you see. **1933** 'R. ESSEX' *Slade of Yard* xix. It's a good plan to believe half you see and nothing you hear. **1979** D. KYLE *Green River High* ii. I listened with the old magician's warning lively in my mind; believe nothing of what you hear—and only half of what you see! **2002** *Washington Times* 16 Aug. A19 The Democratic candidates are lined up, and they are making hot and heavy pitches for our votes. But, as the old saying goes, believe half of what you see and none of what you hear. ■ **rumour; trust and scepticism**

believing *see* SEEING is believing.

A BELLOWING cow soon forgets her calf

An excessive show of grief (at a bereavement) quickly passes. Cf. **1553** T. WILSON *Art of Rhetoric* 42 The Cowe lackyng her Caulfe, leaueth Loweyng within three or foure daies at the farthest.

□ **1895** S. O. ADDY *Household Tales* 142 In the East Riding they say, 'A bletherin' coo soon forgets her calf,' meaning that excessive grief does not last long. **1928** *London Mercury* Feb. 439 Common proverb in the West Country is 'A belving cow soon forgets her calf'. **1945** F. THOMPSON *Lark Rise* xxxiv. When a woman, newly widowed, had tried to throw herself into her husband's grave at his funeral.. some one.. said drily.. 'Ah, you wait. The bellowing cow's always the first to forget its calf.' ■ **forgetfulness; words and deeds**

belly *see* what is GOT over the Devil's back is spent under his belly.

bent *see* as the TWIG is bent, so is the tree inclined.

All's for the BEST in the best of all possible worlds

This saying translates Voltaire's *Tout est pour le mieux dans le meilleur des mondes possibles*, the observation which the philosophical optimist Dr Pangloss in *Candide* (1759) persists in making, despite overwhelming evidence to the contrary.

□ **1911** G. B. SHAW *Shewing-up of Blanco Posnet* 299 The administrative departments were consuming miles of red tape in the correctest forms of activity, and everything was for the best in the best of all possible worlds. **1943** A. CHRISTIE *Moving Finger* xv. I agreed with happy Miss Emily that everything was for the best in the best of possible worlds. **1961** WODEHOUSE *Ice in Bedroom* ii. Fate had handed him the most stupendous bit of goose [luck] and.. all was for the best in this best of all possible worlds. ■ **content and discontent; optimism**

The BEST is the enemy of the good

Also *the* GOOD *is the enemy of the best*. Cf. **1770** VOLTAIRE *Questions sur L'Encyclopédie* II. 250 *c'est bien ici qu'on peut dire Il meglio e l'inimico del bene*, and **1772**——*La Béguele* in *Œuvres Complètes* (1877) X. 50 *le mieux est l'ennemi du bien*.

□ **1861** R. C. TRENCH *Commentary on Epistles to Seven Churches in Asia* p. v. 'The best is oftentimes the enemy of the good'; and . . many a good book has remained unwritten . . because there floated before the mind's eye . . the ideal of a better or a best. **1925** *Times* 1 Dec. 16 This is not the first time in the history of the world when the best has been the enemy of the good; . . one single step on . . solid ground may be more profitable than a more ambitious flight. **1960** D. JONES *Letter* 1 June in R. Hague *Dai Greatcoat* (1980) III. 182 Tom told me a very good Spanish proverb: 'The best is the enemy of the good.' **1981** *Times* 2 Mar. 13 To maintain that all that a school provides must be provided free makes the best the enemy of the good. ■ **good things**

The BEST-laid schemes of mice and men gang aft agley

Often used allusively in shortened form (see quot. 1911). *Gang aft agley* means 'often go awry'.

□ **1786** BURNS *Poems* 140 The best laid schemes o' Mice an' Men, Gang aft agley. **1911** D. H. LAWRENCE *Letter* 21 Sept. (1979) I. 305 I am sorry the bookbinding has gone pop. But there 'The best laid schemes' etc. etc. **1996** H. P. JEFFERS *Reader's Guide to Murder* xxvii. 179 But, like the man said, 'The best laid plans of mice and men often go awry.' ■ **intentions; wanting and having**

The BEST of friends must part

Cf. *c* **1385** CHAUCER *Troilus & Criseyde* v. 343 Alwey frendes may nat ben yfeere [may not be together].

□ **1611** G. CHAPMAN *May-Day* IV. 70 Friends must part, we came not all together, and we must not goe all together. **1685** J. DUNTON in *Publications of Prince Society* (1867) 10 But the dearest friends must part. **1784** J. F. D. SMYTH *Tour in USA* I. xxxvii. Sooner or later, all, even the dearest of friends, must part. **1821** SCOTT *Kenilworth* I. xi. 'You are going to leave me, then?' . . 'The best of friends must part, Flibbertigibbet.' **1979** W. GOLDING *Darkness Visible* ii. 'Aren't there going to be any more lessons?' . . 'The best of friends must part.' ■ **absence; friends**

The BEST of men are but men at best

The General Lambert referred to in quot. 1680 was the Parliamentarian commander John Lambert (1619–83), who played an important role in Cromwell's military victories over the Royalists in the English Civil War.

□ **1680** J. AUBREY *Letter* 15 June in *Brief Lives* (1898) I. 12 I remember one sayeing of generall Lambert's, that 'the best of men are but men at best'. **1885** T. HARLEY *Moon Lore* 191 We can but repeat to ourselves the saying, 'The best of men are but men at best'. ■ **human nature; virtue**

The BEST things come in small packages

Parcels sometimes replaces *packages*. Cf. 13th-cent. Fr. *menue[s] parceles ensemble sunt beles*, small packages considered together are beautiful; **1659** J. HOWELL *Proverbs* (French) 10 The best ointments are put in little boxes.

□ **1877** B. FARJEON *Letter* 22 Jan. in E. Farjeon *Nursery in Nineties* (1935) v. As the best things are (said to be) wrapped in small parcels (proverb), I select the smallest sheet of paper I can find . . to make you acquainted with the . . state of affairs. **1979** R. THOMAS *Eighth Dwarf* xviii. 'The little gentleman.' . . 'The best things sometimes come in small packages,' Jackson said, wincing at his own banality. **2002** *Country Life* 15 Aug. 61 Back at the lodge, the scales turn at 18 pounds, four ounces—my personal best, and an *über*-trout by any standards. .. Sometimes good things come in big packages. ■ **great and small**

The BEST things in life are free

□ **1927** B. G. DE SILVA et al. *Best Things in Life are Free* (*song*) 3 The moon belongs to ev'ryone, The best things in life are free, The stars belong to ev'ryone, They gleam there for you and me. **1955** W. GADDIS *Recognitions* II. ii. Someone once told them the best things in life are free, and so they've got in the habit of not paying. **2002** *Washington Post* 12 Jan. C12 The best things in life are free—friendships and sunshine still cost nothing—but some of the worst things are also free. ■ **good things; money**

It is BEST to be on the safe side

□ **1668** DRYDEN & NEWCASTLE *Sir Martin Mar-all* V. i. I'm resolv'd to be on the sure side. **1811** J. AUSTEN *Sense & Sensibility* III. iv. Determining to be on the safe side, he made his apology in form as soon as he could say any thing. **1847** MARRYAT *Children of New Forest* I. xi. Be on the safe side, and do not trust him too far. **1935** L. I. WILDER *Little House on Prairie* iii. Best to be on the safe side, it saves trouble in the end. **1981** *Economist* 28 Nov. 100 The Rowland–Molina hypothesis about the damaging effects of CFCs has not been disproved, so it is best to be on the safe side. ■ **prudence; security**

best *see also* ACCIDENTS will happen (in the best-regulated families); ATTACK is the best form of defence; the best DEFENSE is a good offense; why should the DEVIL have all the best tunes?; the best DOCTORS are Dr Diet, Dr Quiet, and Dr Merryman; EAST, west, home's best; EXPERIENCE is the best teacher; FIRST thoughts are best; the GOOD is the enemy of the best; HONESTY is the best policy; HOPE for the best and prepare for the worst; HUNGER is the best sauce; he LAUGHS best who laughs last; LAUGHTER is the best medicine; it is best to be OFF with the old love before you are on with the new; an old POACHER makes the best gamekeeper; SECOND thoughts are best; SILENCE is a woman's best garment.

BETTER a dinner of herbs than a stalled ox where hate is

Herbs here is used in the archaic sense of 'plants of which the leaves are used as food', and a *stalled ox* is one that is fattened in a stall for slaughter. With allusion to PROVERBS xv. 17 (Geneva (1560) translation, which is closely followed by AV) Better is a dinner of green herbs where love is, than a stalled ox and hatred therewith.

□ **1817** S. SMITH *Letter* 13 Mar. in S. Holland *Memoir* (1855) II. 138 When you think of that amorous and herbivorous parish of Covent Garden, and compare it with my agricultural benefice, you will say, 'Better is the dinner of herbs where love is, than the stalled ox,' etc. etc. **1914** 'SAKI' *Beasts & Super-Beasts* 227 The ox had finished the vase-flowers . . and appeared to be thinking of leaving its rather restricted quarters. . . I forget how the proverb runs. . . Something about 'better a dinner of herbs than a stalled ox where hate is'. **1979** J. DRUMMOND *I saw Him Die* viii. Lunch was a silent affair. . . I said, ' "Better a dinner of herbs than a stalled ox where hate is." ' ■ **content and discontent; food and drink; malice**

BETTER a good cow than a cow of a good kind

A good character is better than a distinguished family.

□ **1922** J. BUCHAN *Huntingtower* x. I'm no weel acquaint wi' his forbears, but I'm weel eneuch acquaint wi' Sir Erchie, and 'better a guid coo than a coo o' a guid kind', as my mither used to say. ■ **family; human nature**

BETTER are small fish than an empty dish

□ **1678** J. RAY *English Proverbs* 204 Better are small fish then an empty dish. **1862** A. HISLOP *Proverbs of Scotland* 171 Sma' fish are better than nane. **1874** painted on cornice at Ascott House, Wing, Bucks., UK. Better are small fish than an empty dish. **1971** J. GLUSKI *Proverbs* 133 Better are small fish than an empty dish. **2000** *Pravda* (English version, online ed.) 17 Oct. Why should the great ones of this world settle such particular questions? However, the answer is simple: better a small fish than an empty dish. ■ **content and discontent**

BETTER be an old man's darling, than a young man's slave

□ **1546** J. HEYWOOD *Dialogue of Proverbs* II. vii. 13[V] Many yeres sens, my mother seyd to me, Hyr elders wold saie, it ys better to be An olde mans derlyng, then a yong mans werlyng [object of scorn]. **1721** J. KELLY *Scottish Proverbs* 74 Better an old Man's Darling, than a young Man's Wonderling, say the Scots, Warling, say the English. **1859** J. R. PLANCHÉ *Love & Fortune* 8 Let defeated rivals snarling, Talk of one foot in the grave. Better be an old man's darling, Than become a young man's slave. **1980** J. MARCUS *Marsh Blood* ix. Find yourself an older man. Much better to be an old man's darling, than a young man's slave. **1992** 'C. AIRD' 'Man Who Rowed for Shore' in *Injury Time* (1995) 14 [S]he had been brought up by her mother on the well-attested aphorism that it was better to be an old man's darling than a young's [*sic*] man's slave.. ■ **love; wives and husbands**

BETTER be envied than pitied

Cf. PINDAR *Pythian Odes* I. 163 *κρέσσων γὰρ οἰκτιρμοῦ φθόνος*, envy is stronger than pity; HERODOTUS *Hist.* iii. 52 *φθονέεσθαι κρέσσον ἐστὶ ἢ οἰκτείρεσθαι*, it is better to be envied than to be pitied; mid 15th-cent. Fr. *trop plus vaut estre envié que plaint*, it is much better to be envied than pitied; ERASMUS *Adages* IV. iv. 87 *praestat invidiosum esse quam miserabilem.*

□ **1546** J. HEYWOOD *Dialogue of Proverbs* I. xi. D2[V] Sonne, better be envied then pitied, folke sey. *a* **1631** DONNE *Poems* (1633) 94 Men say, and truly, that they better be Which be envyed then pittied. **1902** G. W. E. RUSSELL *Onlooker's Note-Book* xxxiii. Her friend responded sympathetically, 'My dear, I'd much rather be envied than pitied.' ■ **malice; pity**

BETTER be out of the world than out of the fashion

□ **1639** J. CLARKE *Parœmiologia Anglo-Latina* 171 As good out of th' world as out o' th' fashion. **1738** SWIFT *Polite Conversation* ii. 117 'Why, Tom, you are high in the Mode.'..'It is better to be out of the World, than out of the Fashion.' **1903** E. F. MAITLAND *From Window in Chelsea* IV. Women seem seldom hindered by lack of money when it is a case of follow-my-leader. 'Better be out of the world than out of the fashion.' **1935** J. MAXTON *If I were Dictator* i. Dictatorships are fashionable just now. There was an old-time song which said 'If you are out of the fashion you had better leave the world.' ■ **novelty**

BETTER be safe than sorry

Now very often in the form *better safe than sorry.*

□ **1837** S. LOVER *Rory O'More* II. xxi. 'Jist countin' them,—is there any harm in that?' said the tinker: 'it's betther be sure than sorry'. **1933** *Radio Times* 14 Apr. 125 Cheap distempers very soon crack or fade. Better be safe than sorry. Ask for

Hall's. **1972** J. WILSON *Hide & Seek* vii. It's not that I want to shut you in .. but—well, it's better to be safe than sorry. **2002** *Washington Post* 12 Jan. C10 (*Garfield comic strip*) 'You're breaking up with me? But we've never dated. You don't want to take any chances?' 'Better safe than sorry.' ■ **prudence; security**

BETTER late than never

Cf. DIONYSIUS OF HALICARNASSUS *Roman Antiquities* ix. 9 *κρεῖττον γάρ ἐστιν ὀψὲ ἄρξασθαι τὰ δέοντα πράττειν ἢ μηδέποτε*, it is better to start doing what one has to late than not at all; LIVY *Hist.* IV. ii. *potius sero quam nunquam.*

c **1330** in C. Keller *Die Mittelenglische Gregoriuslegende* (1941) 146 A. Better is lat than neuer blinne [cease] Our soules to maken fre. *c* **1450** LYDGATE *Assembly of Gods* (EETS) l. 1204 Vyce to forsake ys bettyr late then neuer. **1546** J. HEYWOOD *Dialogue of Proverbs* I. x. C4 Things done, can not be vndoone, .. But better late then neuer to repent this. **1708** S. OCKLEY *Conquest of Syria* I. 276 Whilst he was murdering the unhappy Aleppians, Caled (better late than never) came to their Relief. **1954** A. HUXLEY *Letter* 16 Sept. (1969) 711 I am sorry your holiday will have to be postponed so long; but better late than never. **2002** *Washington Post* 17 Feb. SC4 (*Sally Forth comic strip*) 'Consider these a "late Valentine's Day" bouquet.' 'It was three days ago.' 'I know, but better late than never, I always say.' 'Better never late, I always say.' ■ **lateness**

BETTER one house spoiled than two

Said of two foolish or wicked people joined in marriage and troubling only themselves. *Spoiled* (or *spilled* [destroyed]) is sometimes contrasted with *filled* (see quots. 1670 and 1805).

□ **1586** T. B. tr. *de la Primaudaye's French Academy* xlvi. The wicked and reprobate, of whom that common proverbe is spoken, that it is better one house be troubled with them than twaine. **1587** R. GREENE *Penelope's Web* V. 162 The old prouerb is fulfild, better one house troubled than two. **1670** J. RAY *English Proverbs* 51 Better one house fill'd then two spill'd. This we use when we hear of a bad Jack who hath married as bad a Jyll. **1805** W. BENTLEY *Diary* 28 May (1911) III. 161 One of the company discovering a disposition to speak much of his own wife .. the Gen. observed .. One house filled was better than two spoiled. **1924** *Folk-Lore* XXXV. 358 Better one house spoilt than two (said when a witless a man marries a foolish woman). ■ **marriage**

The BETTER the day, the better the deed

Frequently used to justify working on a Sunday or religious festival. Cf. early 14th-cent. Fr. *a bon jour bone euvre*, for a good day, a good deed.

□ **1607** MIDDLETON *Michaelmas Term* III. i. Why, do you work a' Sundays, tailor? The better day the better deed, we think. **1721** J. KELLY *Scottish Proverbs* 328 The better Day, the better Deed. I never heard this used but when People say that they did such an ill thing on Sunday. **1896** J. C. HUTCHESON *Crown & Anchor* xiii. The better the day, the better the deed .. It was only the Pharisees who objected to any necessary work being done on the Sabbath. **1995** D. WILLIAMS *Death of Prodigal* 'And he was coming back here with us after, for Sunday lunch. I've just cleaned the car in his honour, too.The better the day, the better the deed, like.' ■ **action and inaction**

BETTER the devil you know than the devil you don't know

Cf. **1539** R. TAVERNER tr. *Erasmus' Adages* 48 *Nota res mala, optima.* An euyl thynge knowen is best. It is good kepyng of a shrew [a scolding or ill-tempered woman] that a man knoweth; **1576** G. PETTIE *Petit Palace* 84 You had rather keepe those whom you know, though with some faultes, then take those whom you knowe not, perchaunce with moe faultes; **1586** D. ROWLAND tr. *Lazarillo de Tormes* H6[v] The olde prouerbe: Better is the euill knowne, than the good which is yet to knowe.

□ **1857** TROLLOPE *Barchester Towers* II. vii. 'Better the d—you know than the d—you don't know,' is an old saying.. but the bishop had not yet realised the truth of it. **1937** W. H. SAUMAREZ SMITH *Letter* 16 May in *Young Man's Country* (1977) ii. Habit has practically made me resigned to Madaripur—'Better the devil you know than the devil you don't.' **1987** S. STEWART *Lifting the Latch* 166 I knowed he'd never change, it 'ud always be 'Don't-be-so-daft' and no appreciation; but better the Black 'un thee knows than the devil thee don't. **2002** *Spectator* 23 Feb. 34 Probably the Tories are still seen as unelectable, so better the devil you know. ■ **familiarity**

It is BETTER to be born lucky than rich

□ **1639** J. CLARKE *Parœmiologia Anglo-Latina* 49 Better to have good fortune then be a rich mans child. **1784** *New Foundling Hospital for Wit* (new ed.) IV. 128 Estate and honours!—mere caprich! Better be fortunate than rich: Since oft me find..Is verify'd what proverbs prate. **1846** M. A. DENHAM *Denham Tracts* (1892) I. 224 Better to be born lucky than rich. **1926** D. H. LAWRENCE in *Harper's Bazaar* July 97 'Then what *is* luck, mother?' 'It's what causes you to have money. If you are lucky you have money. That's why it's better to be born lucky than rich. If you're rich you may lose your money. But if you're lucky, you will always get more money.' **1980** T. MORGAN *Somerset Maugham* xv. This was Maugham at his most lighthearted, exposing the fallacy of the moralist position. 'I'm glad to be able to tell you that it has a moral,' he said, 'and that is: it's better to be born lucky than to be born rich.' ■ **luck; riches**

It is BETTER to give than to receive

The AV form is also used (see quot. 2001): ACTS xx. 35 It is more blessed to give, than to receive.

□ *c* **1390** GOWER *Confessio Amantis* v. 7725 Betre is to yive than to take. *c* **1527** T. BERTHELET tr. *Erasmus' Sayings of Wise Men* B2 It is better to gyue than to take, for he that takethe a gyfte of another is bonde to quyte [repay] it, so that his lyberte is gone. **1710** S. PALMER *Proverbs* 351 'Tis better to Give than to Receive, but yet 'tis Madness to give so much Charity to Others, as to become the Subject of it our Selves. **1980** *Times* (Christmas Supplement) 15 Nov. p. i. There is no harm in reminding your relatives and friends that it is better to give than to receive. **2001** *Washington Times* 2 July B9 (*Herb & Jamaal comic strip*) 'Herb, you know the old saying: "It is more blessed to give than to receive."' 'What, presents?' 'No, advice.' ■ **giving and receiving**

BETTER to have loved and lost, than never to have loved at all

□ **1700** CONGREVE *Way of World* II. i. Say what you will, 'tis better to be left, than never to have lov'd. **1812** G. CRABBE *Tales* xiv. Better to love amiss than nothing to have lov'd. **1850** TENNYSON *In Memoriam* xxvii. 44 'Tis better to have loved and lost Than never to have loved at all. **1953** B. PYM *Jane & Prudence* i. One wondered if it was really better to have loved and lost than never to have loved at all, when poor Prudence seemed to have lost so many times. **2002** *Times 2* 15 Oct. 9 That cliché, it is better to have loved and lost than never to have loved at all, applies to me. ■ **love, blighted**

BETTER to light one candle than to curse the darkness

The motto of the American Christopher Society (founded 1945), said by the society to derive from 'an ancient Chinese proverb'.

□ **1962** Adlai Stevenson in *New York Times* 8 Nov. 34 She [Eleanor Roosevelt] would rather light a candle than curse the darkness, and her glow has warmed the world. **2000** *Straits Times* (online ed.) 26 Aug. He is certainly one who believes it is better to light a candle than to curse the darkness. **2002** *Spectator* 12 Jan. 26 A fortnight ago, protesters.. wound their way on a candlelit walk through deep snow from the forest up into the citadel. 'There is an English saying,' one of them.. told me. 'It is better to light a candle than to curse the darkness.' ■ **action and inaction**

BETTER to live one day as a tiger than a thousand years as a sheep

Recorded as the view of Tipu Sahib *c* 1750–99, sultan of Mysore in India; see quot. 1800.

□ **1800** A. BEATSON *View of Origin and Conduct of War with Tippoo Sultaun* x. 153 'In this world I would rather live two days like a tiger, than two hundred years like a sheep.' **1997** *Daily Telegraph* (online ed.) 8 Mar. The title of Anne Haverty's novel [*One Day as a Tiger*] derives from an old Tibetan proverb: 'It is better to have lived one day as a tiger than a thousand years as a sheep.' ■ **action and inaction; boldness**

BETTER to marry than to burn

With allusion to I CORINTHIANS vii. 8–9 (AV) I say therefore to the unmarried and widows, It is good for them if they abide even as I. But if they cannot contain, let them marry: for it is better to marry than to burn.

□ **1911** G. B. SHAW *Getting Married* 116 St Paul's reluctant sanction of marriage; .. his contemptuous 'better to marry than to burn' is only out of date in respect of his belief that the end of the world was at hand and that there was therefore no longer any population question. **1973** J. PORTER *Murder with Dover* 58 'You didn't approve?' Miss Marsh pursed her lips. 'We are told it is better to marry than to burn,' she said. 'And he could have done worse, I suppose.' **2000** *Washington Times* 15 Nov. E12 (*Herb & Jamaal comic strip*) [T]hey say, .. 'It is better to marry than to burn'.. But I'll tell ya, among the things they say, what I'm most curious about is.. who are '*they*'? ■ **marriage**

It is BETTER to travel hopefully than to arrive

□ **1881** R. L. STEVENSON *Virginibus Puerisque* IV. 190 To travel hopefully is a better thing than to arrive, and the true success is to labour. **1918** D. H. LAWRENCE in *English Review* Jan. 29 Love is strictly a travelling. 'It is better to travel than to arrive,' somebody has said. **1959** 'J. DUNCAN' *My Friend Muriel* II. 83 Remember, .. it is better to travel hopefully than to arrive. The satisfaction lies mainly in the travelling. **2002** *Rough News* Spring 2 (*comic strip*) 'They say it's better to travel than to arrive.' '"They" have obviously never been on this bus!' ■ **expectation; optimism; travel**

BETTER to wear out than to rust out

It is better to remain active than to succumb to idleness: used particularly with reference to elderly people. Frequently attributed in its current form to Bishop Richard Cumberland (d. 1718). Cf. **1557** R. EDGEWORTH *Sermons* A1^{V} Better it is to shine with laboure, then to rouste for idlenes; **1598** SHAKESPEARE *Henry IV*,

Pt. 2 I. ii. 206 I were better to be eaten to death with a rust than to be scoured to nothing with perpetual motion.

□ **1820** in Southey *Life of Wesley* II. xxv. I had rather wear out than rust out. **1834** M. EDGEWORTH *Helen* II. xiii. Helen.. trembled for her health.. but she repeated her favourite maxim—'Better to wear out, than to rust out.' **1947** S. BELLOW *Victim* xvii. It was better to wear out than to rust out, as was often quoted. He was a hard worker himself. **1972** *Times* 24 May 16 'A man will rust out sooner'n he'll wear out' is one of his oft-repeated maxims. ■ **action and inaction; old age**

BETTER wed over the mixen than over the moor

It is better to marry a neighbour than a stranger. For *mixen*, see quot. 1661.

□ *a* **1628** in M. L. Anderson *Proverbs in Scots* (1957) no. 320 Better to wow [woo] over middin, nor [than] over mure. *a* **1661** T. FULLER *Worthies* (Cheshire) 174 Better Wed over the Mixon [midden] then over the Moor.. that is, hard by or at home, Mixon being that heap of Compost which lyeth in the yards of good husbands. **1818** SCOTT *Heart of Midlothian* III. vi. He might hae dune waur [worse] than married me. .. Better wed over the mixen as over the moor, as they say in Yorkshire. **1874** T. HARDY *Far from Madding Crowd* I. xxii. 'That means matrimony.' .. 'Well, better wed over the mixen than over the moor,' said Laban Tall. ■ **familiarity; marriage**

better *see also* DISCRETION is the better part of valour; the GREY mare is the better horse; a LIVE dog is better than a dead lion.

BETWEEN two stools one falls to the ground

Inability to choose between, or accommodate oneself to, alternative viewpoints or courses of action is likely to end in disaster. Now more common in the metaphorical phrase *to fall between two stools*. Cf. medieval L. *labitur enitens sellis herere duabus*, he falls trying to sit on two seats; also current in early 16th-cent. German (woodcut in Thomas Murner's *Schelmenzunft*, 1516).

□ *c* **1390** GOWER *Confessio Amantis* IV. 626 Thou farst [farest] as he betwen tuo stoles That wolde sitte and goth to grounde. *c* **1530** R. HILL *Commonplace Book* (EETS) 129 Betwen two stolis, the ars goth to grwnd. **1841** DICKENS *Old Curiosity Shop* I. xxxiii. She was.. still in daily occupation of her old stool opposite to that of her brother Sampson. And equally certain it is, by the way, that between these two stools a great many people had come to the ground. **1907** W. DE MORGAN *Alice-for-Short* xvi. Your mother wants to put it off on me. .. But I won't be let into saying anything. .. Charles saw that between the two stools the young couple wouldn't fall to the ground, but would go to the altar. **1979** A. CHISHOLM *Nancy Cunard* xxi. Politically, Nancy had fallen between stools. ■ **decision and indecision**

beware *see* let the BUYER beware; beware of an OAK it draws the stroke.

bicycle *see* a WOMAN without a man is like a fish without a bicycle.

Never BID the Devil good morrow until you meet him

□ **1873** J. MORRIS *Wanderings of Vagabond* ii. 19 The firm of Giles & Morris never looked ahead to meet trouble, but were firm believers in an old Irish adage, which affirms that, 'It's time enough to bid the devil good morning when you meet him.' **1905** A. CARNEGIE *James Watt* iv. 77 Roebuck, on the contrary, continued hopeful and energetic, and often rallied his pessimistic partner on his propensity to look upon the dark side. He was one of those who adhered to the axiom, 'Never bid the devil good-morning till you meet him.' **1923** *Seanad Eireann* 14 June (electronic ed.) MR. LINEHAN: Have you any indication as to whether the National Health Insurance Bill will be certified as a Money Bill? It looks very like the Unemployment Insurance Bill. AN CATHAOIRLEACH: It may be, but never bid the devil good morrow until you meet him. MR. LINEHAN: It may be too late then. **1929** F. D. GRIERSON *Green Diamond Mystery* vi. 66 By the time they reached Calais Kit had wisely resolved, in the classic phrase, not to bid the Devil good-morrow till he met him; in other words, to wait until he saw June, and then be guided by her reception of him. **1998** *Beloit Daily News* 19 Mar. (electronic ed.) Over the weekend, Ryan responded to hypothetical questions about having Fitzgerald on the ticket by saying 'We should never bid the devil good morning until we meet him.' ■ **good and evil**

BIG fish eat little fish

□ *a* **1200** *Old English Homilies* (EETS) 2nd Ser. 179 The more [bigger] fishes in the se eten the lasse [smaller]. *c* **1300** in J. Small *English Metrical Homilies* (1862) 136 Al this werld es bot a se,..And gret fisches etes the smale. For riche men of this werd [world] etes, That pouer [the poor] wit thair travail getes. **1608** SHAKESPEARE *Pericles* II. i. 27 Master, I marvel how the fishes live in the sea.—Why, as men do a-land—the great ones eat up the little ones. **1979** *New Society* 6 Dec. 557 The state today..seems like nothing so much [as] a huge aquarium. ..Big fish eat little fish, and the great fish eat the big. ■ **great and small**

BIG fleas have little fleas upon their backs to bite them, and little fleas have lesser fleas, and so *ad infinitum*

□ **1733** SWIFT *Poems* II. 651 The Vermin only teaze and pinch Their Foes superior by an Inch. So Nat'ralists observe, a Flea Hath smaller Fleas that on him prey, And these have smaller Fleas to bite 'em, And so proceed *ad infinitum*. **1872** A. DE MORGAN *Budget of Paradoxes* 377 Great fleas have little fleas upon their backs to bite 'em, And little fleas have lesser fleas, and so *ad infinitum*. And the great fleas themselves, in turn, have greater fleas to go on; While these again have greater still, and greater still, and so on. **1979** R. BARNARD *Posthumous Papers* ii. There will be a long article in the *Sunday Chronicle*..and I'm afraid the *Sunday Grub* has got onto the story as well. Big fleas and little fleas, you know—. **2001** *Times* 22 Dec. 19 They [CERN scientists] would identify another lacuna in our knowledge which would require even bigger and better facilities to decide whether it could or could not be explained. 'Great fleas have little fleas upon their backs to bite 'em, and little fleas have lesser fleas and so ad infinitum.' ■ **associates**; **great and small**

big *see also* PROVIDENCE is always on the side of the big battalions.

The BIGGER they are, the harder they fall

Commonly attributed to the boxer Robert Fitzsimmons, prior to a fight *c* 1900 (see quot. 1902). (*Come* is sometimes used instead of *are*; see quot. 1971.) A similar form is however found in earlier related proverbs, such as: **1493** H. PARKER *Dives & Pauper* R7^{v} It is more synne in the man For the higher degre [position] the harder is the fal; **1670** J. RAY *English Proverbs* 102 The higher standing the lower fall. The idea can be traced back at least as far as the 4th-cent. AD Latin poet Claudian (*In Rufinum* I. 22 *Tolluntur in altum Ut lapsu graviore ruant*, men are raised on high in order that they may fall more heavily).

□ **1902** *National Police Gazette* 27 Sept. 6 'If I can get close enough,' he [Fitzsimmons] once said, 'I'll guarantee to stop almost anybody. The bigger the man, the heavier the fall.' **1927** 'C. BOYER' *Mosaic Earring* i. 'I haven't seen..even an imitation of the blossom I would have to find before I surrender my sweet freedom.' 'The bigger they are, the harder they fall.' **1971** J. CLIFF (*song-title*) The bigger they come the harder they fall. **1981** H. & B. BRETT *Promises to Keep* ix. 'I thought a big, beautiful place like this would be an exception to the general decline.' 'Sometimes,' Mrs. Benjamin said sagely, 'the bigger they are, the harder they fall.' **2002** *New Scientist* 30 Mar. 14 (*headline*) The bigger you are, the harder you fall. ■ **great and small; misfortune**

bill *see* DEATH pays all debts.

billet *see* every BULLET has its billet.

bind *see* SAFE bind, safe find.

binding *see* you can't tell a BOOK by its cover.

A BIRD in the hand is worth two in the bush

It is better to accept or be content with what one has than to try to get more and risk losing everything. Cf. 13th-cent. L. *plus valet in manibus avis unica quam dupla silvis*, one bird in the hands is worth more than two in the woods. Parodied by the American actress Mae West (1892–1980) in the 1934 movie *Belle of the Nineties*: 'A man in the house is worth two in the street.'

□ *c* **1450** J. CAPGRAVE *Life of St. Katharine* (EETS) II. iii. It is more sekyr [certain] a byrd in your fest, Than to haue three in the sky a-boue. *c* **1470** *Harley MS 3362* f.4 Betyr ys a byrd in the hond than tweye in the wode. **1581** N. WOODES *Conflict of Conscience* IV. i. You haue spoken reasonably, but yet as they say, One Birde in the hande, is worth two in the bush. **1678** BUNYAN *Pilgrim's Progress* I. 42 That Proverb, A Bird in the hand is worth two in the Bush, is of more Authority with them, then are all.. testimonies of the good of the world to come. **1973** G. GREENE *Honorary Consul* II. iii. We have an expression in English—A bird in the hand is worth two in the bush. I don't know anything about that 'afterwards'. I only know I would like to live another ten years. **2002** *Oxford Times* 18 Jan. 15 The firm could realise a very good price now. .. The situation may not be as good as this in three or four years. A bird in the hand is worth two in the bush. ■ **prudence; risk**

A BIRD never flew on one wing

Mainly Scottish and Irish. Now frequently used to justify a further gift, esp. another drink.

□ **1721** J. KELLY *Scottish Proverbs* 308 The Bird must flighter [flutter] that flies with one Wing. Spoken by them who have Interest only in one side of the House. **1824** S. FERRIER *Inheritance* III. xxxii. 'The bird maun flichter that flees wi' ae wing'—but ye's haud up your head yet in spite o' them a'. **1914** K. F. PURDON *Folk of Furry Farm* ii. He held out a shilling to Hughie. 'A bird never yet flew upon the one wing, Mr. Heffernan!' said Hughie, that was looking to get another shilling. **1925** S. O'CASEY *Juno & Paycock* III. 89 Fourpence, given to make up the price of a pint, on th' principle that no bird ever flew on wan wing. **1980** J. O'FAOLAIN *No Country for Young Men* iii. I'll just have another quick one. A bird never flew on wan wing. ■ **food and drink**

bird *see also* as good be an ADDLED egg as an idle bird; you cannot CATCH old birds with chaff; the EARLY bird catches the worm; FINE feathers make fine birds; it's an ILL bird that fouls its own nest; in vain the NET is spread in the sight of the bird.

There are no BIRDS in last year's nest

Circumstances have altered.

□ **1620** T. SHELTON tr. *Cervantes' Don Quixote* II. lxxiv. I pray you go not on so fast, since that in the nests of the last yeere, there are no birds of this yeere. Whilom [formerly] I was a foole, but now I am wise. **1732** T. FULLER *Gnomologia* no. 4863 There are no Birds this Year, in last year's Nest. **1845** LONGFELLOW *Poems* 62 All things are new..even the nest beneath the eaves;—There are no birds in last year's nest. **1946** H. MCELROY *Unkindly Cup* I. ii. 23 'I am not as bad, or as unfeeling as I sound. It was my memory that was groaning—not the other part of my anatomy.' '"There are no birds in last year's nests",' Bland quoted sententiously. ■ **change; circumstances**

BIRDS in their little nests agree

A nursery proverb, also used as a direction, which states that young children should not argue among themselves.

□ **1715** I. WATTS *Divine Songs* 25 Birds in their little Nests agree; And 'tis a shameful Sight, When Children of one Family Fall out, and chide, and fight. **1868** L. M. ALCOTT *Little Women* i. 'Birds in their little nests agree,' sang Beth, the peacemaker. **1961** J. STEINBECK *Winter of our Discontent* I. i. 'Birds in their little nests agree,' he said. 'So why can't we?..You kids can't get along even on a pretty morning.' **1980** A. T. ELLIS *Birds of Air* (1983) 52 Her mother used to say to her and Mary: 'Birds in their little nests agree.' ■ **harmony and disharmony**

BIRDS of a feather flock together

People of the same (usually, unscrupulous) character associate with one another, as do birds of the same species. Cf. APOCRYPHA *Ecclesiasticus* xxvii. 9 (AV) The birds will resort unto their like, so will truth return unto them that practise in her.

□ **1545** W. TURNER *Rescuing of Romish Fox* B8 Byrdes of on kynde and color flok and flye allwayes together. **1599** J. MINSHEU *Spanish Grammar* 83 Birdes of a feather will flocke together. **1660** W. SECKER *Nonsuch Professor* 81 Our English Proverb..That birds of a feather will flock together. To be too intimate with sinners, is to intimate that you are sinners. **1828** BULWER-LYTTON *Pelham* III. xv. It is literally true in the systematised roguery of London, that 'birds of a feather flock together.' **2001** *Washington Times* 15 July D7 Birds of a feather flock together, so the second thing you should do is find another friend who's less troubled than the first. ■ **associates; human nature; similarity and dissimilarity**

Little BIRDS that can sing and won't sing must be made to sing

□ **1678** J. RAY *English Proverbs* (ed. 2) 343 The bird that can sing and will not sing must be made to sing. **1846** DICKENS *Cricket on Hearth* ii. 'The bird that can sing and won't sing, must be made to sing, they say,' grumbled Tackleton. 'What about the owl that can't sing, and oughtn't to sing, and will sing?' **1888** A. QUILLER-COUCH *Troy Town* i. 'A little music might perhaps leave a pleasant taste.'..'Come, Sophy! Remember the proverb about little birds that can sing and won't sing?' **1904** G. K. CHESTERTON *Napoleon of Notting Hill* II. i. When the disdainful oligarchs declined to join in the songs of the men of the Broadway.., the great Republican leader, with his rough humour, said the words which are written in gold upon his monument, 'Little birds that can sing and won't sing, must be made to sing.' **1952** J. KNOX *Little Benders* 18 Heaven wasn't so far away when you could do your own singing about it. Mama believed that and many a time she said, 'A body who *can* sing and *won't* sing ought to be *made* to sing.' ■ **obstinacy; speech and silence**

bite *see* (noun) a BLEATING sheep loses a bite; every DOG is allowed one bite; (verb) a BARKING dog never bites; BIG fleas have little fleas upon their backs to bite them; DEAD men don't bite.

bitten *see* ONCE bitten, twice shy.

black *see* the DEVIL is not so black as he is painted; FEBRUARY fill dyke, be it black or be it white; TWO blacks don't make a white.

blame *see* a BAD workman blames his tools; COMMON fame is seldom to blame.

A BLEATING sheep loses a bite

Opportunities are missed through too much chatter.

□ **1599** J. MINSHEU *Dialogues in Spanish* 20 That sheepe that bleateth looseth a bit [mouthful]. **1659** G. TORRIANO *English & Italian Dict.* 37 A bleating sheep loseth her pasture. **1861** T. HUGHES *Tom Brown at Oxford* II. vii. He said something about a bleating sheep losing a bite; but I should think this young man is not much of a talker. **1978** R. V. JONES *Most Secret War* xlv. I thought of reminding him [Churchill] of an adage that I had learnt from my grandfather: 'Every time a sheep bleats it loses a nibble.' ■ **opportunity, missed; speech and silence**

BLESSED is he who expects nothing, for he shall never be disappointed

□ **1727** POPE *Letter* 6 Oct. (1956) II. 453 I have..repeated to you, a ninth Beatitude..'Blessed is he who expect nothing, for he shall never be disappointed.' **1739** B. FRANKLIN *Poor Richard's Almanack* (May) Blessed is he that expects nothing, for he shall never be disappointed. **1931** A. R. & R. K. WEEKES *Emerald Necklace* xix. 'When I get back..I shall expect to find *all* our luggage in the hall.' 'Blessed is he that expecteth nothing,' said Louis, 'for he shall not be disappointed.' **1997** *Washington Times* 28 Feb. C16 My dear grandmother..gave me a plaque many years ago that contains a motto to live by: 'Blessed are those who expect nothing, for they will not be disappointed.' ■ **blessings; disappointment**

blessed *see also* it is BETTER to give than to receive; blessed are the DEAD that the rain rains on.

BLESSINGS brighten as they take their flight

Cf. **1732** T. FULLER *Gnomologia* no. 989 Blessings are not valued, till they are gone.

□ **1742** YOUNG *Night Thoughts* II. 37 How blessings brighten as they take their flight. **1873** 'S. COOLIDGE' *What Katy Did* xi. Blessings brighten as they take their flight. Katy began to appreciate for the first time how much she had learned to rely on her aunt. **1929** G. M. WHITE *Square Mark* i. It has been said that one never knows one's blessings until one has lost them. ■ **blessings; gains and losses**

There's none so BLIND as those who will not see

Parallel to *there's none so* DEAF *as those who will not hear*. In both proverbs, *will not* has the force of 'does not wish to' or 'refuses to'.

□ **1546** J. HEYWOOD *Dialogue of Proverbs* II. ix. K4 Who is so deafe, or so blynde, as is hee, That wilfully will nother here nor see. **1551** CRANMER *Answer to Gardiner* 58 There is no manne so..blynd as he that will not see, nor so dull as he that wyll not vnderstande. **1659** P. HEYLYN *Examen Historicum* 145 Which makes me wonder..that having access to those Records..he should declare himself unable to decide the doubt. ..But none so blind as he that will not see. **1738** SWIFT *Polite Conversation* iii. 191 You know, there's none so blind as they that won't see. **1852** E. FITZGERALD *Polonius* 58 'None so blind as those that won't see.'..A single effort of the will was sufficient to exclude from his view whatever he judged hostile to his immediate purpose. **2000** P. LOVESEY *Reaper* xv. 185 Owen shook his head and picked up his drink. 'There's none so blind as those that will not see.' ■ **ignorance; obstinacy**

When the BLIND lead the blind, both shall fall into the ditch

Now more common in the metaphorical phrase, *the blind leading the blind*. With allusion to MATTHEW xv. 14 (AV) Let them alone: they be blind leaders of the blind. And if the blind lead the blind, both shall fall into the ditch.

□ *c* **897** ALFRED *Gregory's Pastoral Care* (EETS) i. Gif se blinda thone blindan læt, he feallath begen [both] on ænne pytt. *c* **1300** *Body & Soul* (1889) 49 Ac hwanne the blinde lat the blinde, In dike he fallen bothe two. **1583** B. MELBANCKE *Philotimus* 165 In the ditch falls the blind that is led by the blind. **1836** CARLYLE *Sartor Resartus* II. iii. It is written, When the blind lead the blind, both shall fall into the ditch. .. May it not sometimes be safer, if both leader and led simply—sit still? **1908** H. M. SYLVESTER *Olde Pemaquid* 12 If the blind lead the blind, the ditch is but a little way on. **1947** L. P. HARTLEY *Eustace & Hilda* xvi. To get Hilda out of the house was a step forward, even in a Bath chair .. even if they could see nothing b
the blind leading the blind. ■ **ignorance; rulers and ruled**

A BLIND man's wife needs no paint

□ **1659** J. HOWELL *Proverbs* (Spanish) 4 The blind mans wife needs no painting. **1736** B. FRANKLIN *Poor Richard's Almanack* (June) God helps them that help themselves. Why does the blind man's wife paint her self? **1892** C. M. YONGE *Old Woman's Outlook in Hampshire Village* 166 His [the schoolmaster's] copies too were remarkable. One was 'A blind man's wife needs no paint.' 'Proverbs, sir, Proverbs,' he answered, when asked where it came from. ■ **appearance; wives and husbands**

blind *see also* in the COUNTRY of the blind, the one-eyed man is king; a DEAF husband and a blind wife are always a happy couple; LOVE is blind; a NOD'S as good as a wink to a blind horse; NOTHING so bold as a blind mare.

bliss *see* where IGNORANCE is bliss, 'tis folly to be wise.

You cannot get BLOOD from a stone

Frequently used, as a resigned admission, to mean that it is hopeless to try extorting money, etc., from those who have none. Other unyielding or unlikely substances are sometimes substituted for *stone*; the *turnip* version is frequent in North America.

□ *c* **1435** J. LYDGATE *Minor Poems* (EETS) 666 Harde to likke hony out of a marbil stoon, For ther is nouthir licour nor moisture. **1666** G. TORRIANO *Italian Proverbs* 161 There's no getting of bloud out of that wall. **1836** MARRYAT *Japhet* iv. There's no getting blood out of a turnip. **1850** DICKENS *David Copperfield* xi. Blood cannot be obtained from a stone, neither can anything on account be obtained .. from Mr. Micawber. **1925** J. S. FLETCHER *False Scent* ix. 'You'll never get it. .. ' 'He'll have to pay me when he loses!' 'You can't get blood out of a stone.' **2001** K. HALL PAGE *Body in Moonlight* vii. 120 ' "You can't get blood from a stone," Nick was saying. They were both really ripping. You could tell.' **2002** *London Review of Books* 3 Jan. 5 In Dr Eckener's time you couldn't get blood from a turnip, and you couldn't get helium from any place but the United States of America. ■ **meanness; possibility and impossibility**

BLOOD is thicker than water

Predominantly used to mean that a family connection will outweigh other relationships. Cf. 12th-cent. Ger. *ouch hoer ich sagen, daz sippebluot von wassere niht verdirbet*, also I hear it said that kin-blood is not spoiled by water; **1412** LYDGATE *Troy Book* (EETS) III. 2071 For naturely blod will ay of kynde Draw vn-to blod, wher he may it fynde.

□ **1813** J. RAY *English Proverbs* (ed. 5) 281 Blood's thicker than water. **1815** SCOTT *Guy Mannering* II. xvii. Weel—blood's thicker than water—she's welcome to the cheeses. **1914** WODEHOUSE *Man upstairs & Other Stories* 115 But though blood, as he was wont to remark while negotiating his periodical loans, is thicker than water, a brother-in-law's affection has its limits. **2000** G. FARRELLY *Duped by Derivatives* i. 1 They say blood is thicker than water. That was all Theresa Clancy could think about that Wednesday morning when she opened the office door. ■ **family**

The BLOOD of the martyrs is the seed of the Church

The Church has thrived on persecution. Cf. TERTULLIAN *Apologeticus* l. *semen est sanguis Christianorum*, the blood of Christians is seed.

□ **1560** J. PILKINGTON *Aggeus the Prophet* U4V Cipriane wrytes that the bloud of Martirs is the seede of the Church. **1655** T. FULLER *Church Hist. Britain* I. iv. Of all Shires in England, Stafford-shire was.. the largest sown with the Seed of the Church, I mean, the bloud of primitive Martyrs. **1889** J. LUBBOCK *Pleasures of Life* II. xi. The Inquisition has even from its own point of view proved generally a failure. The blood of the martyrs is the seed of the Church. **1979** *Church Times* 15 June 10 It is not merely that 'the blood of the martyrs is the seed of the Church'; it is that a little persecution is good for you. ■ **adversity; Christianity**

BLOOD will have blood

Violence begets violence. Cf. GENESIS ix. 6 (AV) Who so sheddeth man's blood, by man shall his blood be shed.

□ *a* **1449** J. LYDGATE *Minor Poems* (EETS) 512 Blood will have wreche [vengeance], that wrongfully is spent. **1559** *Mirror for Magistrates* (1938) 99 Blood wyll haue blood, eyther fyrst or last. **1605–6** SHAKESPEARE *Macbeth* III. iv. 122 It will have blood; they say blood will have blood. **1805** SOUTHEY *Madoc* I. vii. Blood will have blood, revenge beget revenge. **1974** A. FOREST *Cricket Term* i. 'Blood will have blood,' quoted Lawrie smugly. ■ **revenge; violence**

BLOOD will tell

Family characteristics or heredity cannot be concealed.

□ **1850** G. H. BOKER *World a Mask* IV. in S. Bradley *Glaucus* (1940) 38 He looked like the tiger in the Zoological, when I punch him with my stick. ..Game to the backbone—blood will tell. **1914** WODEHOUSE *Man upstairs & Other Stories* 253 Blood will tell. Once a Pittsburgh millionaire, always a Pittsburgh millionaire. **2002** *Oldie* June 63 By the end, she herself has turned out to be the cousin of 'darling Clare', and the daughter of long-lost Sir David Beaumont,.. which is a bit of a cheat really because blood will out, won't it, and it's not surprising that Daisy is such a marvel. ■ **family**

bloom *see* when the FURZE is in bloom, my love's in tune; when the GORSE is out of bloom, kissing's out of fashion.

blow *see* it's an ILL wind that blows nobody any good; NORTH wind doth blow, we shall have snow; SEPTEMBER blow soft, till the fruit's in the loft; STRAWS tell which way the wind blows.

BLUE are the hills that are far away

A northern proverb comparable to DISTANCE *lends enchantment to the view*. *Green* is sometimes found instead of *blue*. Cf. *the* GRASS *is always greener on the other side of the fence*.

□ **1887** T. H. HALL CAINE *Deemster* I. v. 'What's it sayin',' they would mutter, 'a green hill when far away from me; bare, bare, when it is near.' **1902** J. BUCHAN *Watcher by Threshold* IV. 236 'Blue are the hills that are far away' is an owercome [common expression] in the countryside. **1914** *Spectator* 6 June 955 It is the habit of the Celt to create fanciful golden ages in the past—'Blue are the faraway hills,' runs the Gaelic proverb. **1949** J. L. MORRISSEY *Necktie for Norman* iii. 21 It was so much like the attitude of the habitual stay-at-home. They say that 'distant hills are always the greenest.' ■ **absence; content and discontent**

blush *see* TRUTH makes the Devil blush.

boat *see* a RISING tide lifts all boats.

body *see* CORPORATIONS have neither bodies to be punished nor souls to be damned.

boil *see* a WATCHED pot never boils.

bold *see* NOTHING so bold as a blind mare.

bolted *see* it is too late to shut the STABLE-door after the horse has bolted.

bond *see* an ENGLISHMAN'S word is his bond.

bone *see* what's BRED in the bone will come out in the flesh; you BUY land you buy stones; a DOG that will fetch a bone will carry a bone; HARD words break no bones; the NEARER the bone, the sweeter the meat; STICKS and stones may break my bones, but words will never hurt me; while TWO dogs are fighting for a bone, a third runs away with it.

You can't tell a BOOK by its cover

□ **1929** *American Speech* IV. 465 You can't judge a book by its binding. **1946** ROLFE & FULLER *Glass Room* i. 'Forgive me, sir,' he said. 'I had you all wrong. You can never tell a book by its cover.' **1954** R. HAYDN *Journal of Edwin Carp* 131 This is a nice respectable street, wouldn't you say, sir?.. Unfortunately, sir, you can't tell a book by its cover. **1969** S. MAY et al. *You can't judge Book by its Cover (song)* 1 I can't let you know you're getting to me.. 'cause you can't judge a book by its cover. My pappa used to say, look, child, look beyond a tender smile. **1984** D. CANNELL *Thin Woman* xii. Appreciate your allowing me to participate, but you should be less trusting, Ellie—can't always judge a book by its cover. **2001** *Bookseller* 9 Nov. 28 Don't judge a book by its cover, read it for yourself at BookBrowse.com. ■ **appearance, deceptive**

book *see also* a GREAT book is a great evil.

If you're BORN to be hanged then you'll never be drowned

Commonly used to qualify another's apparent good luck. Cf. mid 14th-cent. Fr. *noyer ne peut, cil qui doit pendre*, he cannot drown who must hang; *c* **1503** A. BARCLAY tr. *Gringore's Castle of Labour* (1506) A8 He that is drowned may no man hange.

□ **1593** J. ELIOT *Ortho-Epia Gallica* 127 He thats borne to be hangd shall neuer be drownde. **1723** DEFOE *Colonel Jack* (ed. 2) 126 He had a Proverb in his Favour, and he got out of the Water..not being born to be drown'd, as I shall observe afterwards in its place. **1956** H. LEWIS *Witch & Priest* v. There is another picture, and underneath it says..*If you're born to be hanged, then you'll never be drowned.* **1986** M. SLUNG *More Momilies* 16 If you're born to hang, you won't drown. ■ **fate and fatalism; luck**

born *see also* it is BETTER to be born lucky than rich; because a MAN is born in a stable that does not make him a horse; YORKSHIRE born and Yorkshire bred, strong in the arm and weak in the head.

borrow *see* the EARLY man never borrows from the late man.

Neither a BORROWER nor a lender be

□ **1601** SHAKESPEARE *Hamlet* I. iii. 73 Neither a borrower nor a lender be; For loan oft loses both itself and friend. **1985** R. CURTIS & B. ELTON *Blackadder II* in R. Curtis et al. *Black-Adder* (1998) 192 Take heed the moral of this tale, Be not a borrower or lender, And if your finances do fail, Make sure your banker's not a bender. **2002** *Times 2* 11 Mar. 7 The moral architecture of my childhood was supported by a series of massive, neo-Victorian precepts, among which 'neither a borrower nor a lender be' occupied a particularly imposing position. ■ **borrowing and lending**

borrowing *see* he that GOES a-borrowing, goes a-sorrowing.

bottle *see* you can't put NEW wine in old bottles.

bottom *see* TRUTH lies at the bottom of a well; every TUB must stand on its own bottom.

bought *see* GOLD may be bought too dear.

bowls *see* those who PLAY at bowls must look out for rubbers.

You can take the BOY out of the country but you can't take the country out of the boy

Originally North American, it has generated a large variety of humorous by-forms.

□ **1938** 'B. BAER' in Baer & Major *Hollywood* (*caption to caricature of James Stewart*) You can take a boy out of the country but you can't take the country out of a boy. **1950** F. BUNCE *So Young a Body* vii. 'You can take the girl out of the country, but you can't take the country out of the girl,' Remington interjected casually. 'Ginnie's from a crossroads in Vermont, and she's still a small-town kid at heart.' **1978** W. B. MURPHY *Leonardo's Law* x. 'He was just something I picked up off the counter.' She smiled. I guess you can take the girl out of the chorus line but you can't take the chorus line out of the girl. **1987** *Washington Post* 27 Apr. C2 Back in the good old days, when eager young rubes were descending upon the great metropolises in search of fame and fortune, it used to be said that you can take the boy out of the country but you can't take the country out of the boy. **1997** *Times* 19 Sept. 33 And, while you can take Björk out of Iceland, it seems you cannot take Iceland out of Björk's music. **2001** *National Review* 20 Aug. 56 My own visceral responses to the case are distinctly Southern, which is about as far removed from the civilized response as you can get. You can take the girl out of the South but you can't take the South out of the girl, e.g., 'Why doesn't her father kill him?' ■ **nature and nurture; origins**

Never send a BOY to do a man's job

□ **1931** G. FOWLER *Great Mouthpiece* xii. Mr. Alfred J. Talley..took command of the..prosecution. He was an able man. ..'It's about *time* they gave me a run for the money,' Fallon said. 'The People shouldn't send boys on men's errands.' **1941** 'T. CHANSLOR' *Our Second Murder* xxviii. Never send a boy to do a man's work. **1967** E. MCGIRR *Hearse with Horses* vi. He blushed. Piron thought that he shouldn't have sent a boy to do a man's job. **1987** *Washington Post* 21 Jan. D10 Research proves that in more than 99 percent of these cases, the defender who has overruffed endears himself by uttering the old cliche, 'Never send a boy to do a man's job.' ■ **efficiency and inefficiency; work**

Two BOYS are half a boy, and three boys are no boy at all

The more boys that help, the less work they do.

□ *c* **1930** F. THOMPSON *Country Calendar* 114 Their parents do not encourage the joining of forces. ..We have a proverb here: 'Two boys are half a boy, and three boys are no boy at all.' **1971** *New York Times* 31 Jan. IV. 12 Rural New England of the mid-nineteenth century, not commonly sophisticated in mathematics but witty enough about man's condition, used to [say].. 'One boy helping, a pretty good boy; two boys, half a boy; three boys, no boy.' **2002** *Times: Weekend* 6 Apr. 9 I..have been warned by my neighbours not to let him have any friends round. Because the more boys there are, the less work will get done. Apparently there is a country proverb that goes: 'One boy is a boy. Two boys are half a boy. And three boys are no boys at all.' ■ **assistance; efficiency and inefficiency; work**

BOYS will be boys

Occasionally *girls will be girls*.

□ **1601** A. DENT *Plain Man's Pathway* 64 Youth will be youthfull, when you haue saide all that you can. **1826** T. H. LISTER *Granby* II. vii. Girls will be girls. They like admiration. **1848** THACKERAY *Vanity Fair* xiii. As for the pink bonnets..why boys will be boys. **1964** WODEHOUSE *Frozen Assets* iii. I tried to tell him that boys will be boys and you're only young once. **2000** W. NORTHCUTT *Darwin Awards* iv. 108 Firecrackers are illegal in Indonesia. However, they can be purchased on the black market during celebrations such as Eid Al-Fitr..And boys will be boys, the world over. ■ **human nature**

brae (slope, hill-side): *see* put a STOUT heart to a stey brae.

BRAG is a good dog, but Holdfast is better

Tenacity and quietness of manner are preferable to ostentation. Cf. **1580** A. MUNDAY *Zelauto* 146 Brag is a good Dogge, whyle he will holde out: but at last he may chaunce to meete with his matche; **1599** SHAKESPEARE *Henry V* II. iii. 52 And Holdfast is the only dog, my duck.

□ **1709** O. DYKES *English Proverbs* 123 Brag is a good Dog, but Hold-fast is a Better. ..Nothing edifies less in an ingenuous Conversation, than Boasting and Rattle. **1752** S. JOHNSON *Rambler* 4 Feb. VIII. 92 When I envied the finery of any of my neighbours, [my mother] told me, that 'brag was a good dog, but holdfast was a better'. **1889** *Pictorial Proverbs for Little People* 11 Brag's a good dog, but Holdfast is better. **1937** R. W. WINSTON *It's Far Cry* xxi. In golf, as in life..the exceptional has no staying qualities. To quote a Southern [US] saying, 'Brag is a good dog, but Holdfast is better'. **1952** J. F. DOBIE *Some Part of Myself* vii. I remember my mother's repeating once after he left an old proverb: 'Brag's a good dog, but Hold Fast is a better.' ■ **boasting; words and deeds**

brain *see* an IDLE brain is the Devil's workshop.

brass *see* where there's MUCK there's brass.

None but the BRAVE deserve the fair

The pair referred to in Dryden's poem (*Alexander's Feast*) are Alexander the Great and the Athenian courtesan Thaïs.

□ **1697** DRYDEN *Poems* (1958) III. 148 Happy, happy, happy Pair!.. None but the Brave deserves the Fair. **1829** P. EGAN *Boxiana* 2nd Ser. II. 354 The tender sex.. feeling the good old notion that 'none but the brave deserve the fair', were sadly out of temper. **1873** TROLLOPE *Phineas Redux* II. xiii. All the proverbs were on his side. 'None but the brave deserve the fair,' said his cousin. **1978** F. WELDON *Praxis* xii. She frequented the cafe where the Rugger set hung out, and on a Saturday, after closing hours, could be seen making for the downs, laughing heartily and noisily in the company of one or other of the brave, who clearly deserved the fair. ■ **courage; just deserts**

BRAVE men lived before Agamemnon

The exploits of Agamemnon, king of Mycenae, in the Trojan War were celebrated by Homer and by the tragic poets of ancient Greece. The point, made first by Horace, was that heroes need writers to commemorate them if they are to achieve eternal fame: HORACE *Odes* IV. ix. 25 *vixere fortes ante Agamemnona multi*, many brave men lived before Agamemnon.

□ **1616** JONSON *Forest* VIII. 114 There were braue men, before Aiax or Idomen, or all the store That Homer brought to Troy. **1819** BYRON *Don Juan* I. v. Brave men were living before Agamemnon And since, exceeding valorous and sage. **1980** *Times* 23 June 16 Brave men lived before Agamemnon, lots of them. But on all of them.. eternal night lies heavy, because they have left no records behind them. ■ **courage; fame and obscurity**

brave *see also* (adjective used as noun) FORTUNE favours the brave; (verb) ROBIN Hood could brave all weathers but a thaw wind.

The BREAD never falls but on its buttered side

A formulation of Murphy's Law; cf. *if* ANYTHING *can go wrong, it will.*

□ **1867** A. D. RICHARDSON *Beyond Mississippi* iii. *His* bread never fell on the buttered side. **1891** J. L. KIPLING *Beast & Man* x. We express the completeness of ill-luck by saying, 'The bread never falls but on its buttered side.' **1980** *Guardian* 3 Dec. 12 Murphy's (or Sod's) Law. .. Murphy's many relatives always quote it as 'Buttered bread falls buttered side down—and if it's a sandwich it falls open.' ■ **luck; misfortune**

bread *see also* HALF a loaf is better than no bread; MAN cannot live by bread alone.

break *see* (noun) never give a SUCKER an even break; (verb) HARD words break no bones; if it were not for HOPE, the heart would break; it is the LAST straw that breaks the camel's back; OBEY orders, if you break owners; STICKS and stones may break my bones, but words will never hurt me; also BREAKING, BROKEN.

breakfast *see* HOPE is a good breakfast but a bad supper; SING before breakfast, cry before night.

breaking *see* IGNORANCE of the law is no excuse for breaking it; you cannot make an OMELETTE without breaking eggs.

What's BRED in the bone will come out in the flesh

Lifelong habits or inherited characteristics cannot be concealed (cf. BLOOD *will tell*). The form and emphasis of the proverb have been altered in recent years by the omission of a negative. Cf. medieval L. *osse radicatum raro de carne recedit*, that which is rooted in the bone rarely comes out from the flesh.

□ *c* **1470** MALORY *Morte d'Arthur* (1947) I. 550 Sir Launcelot smyled and seyde, Harde hit ys to take oute off the fleysshe that ys bredde in the bone. **1546** J. HEYWOOD *Dialogue of Proverbs* II. viii. K2 This prouerbe prophecied many yeres agone, It will not out of the fleshe, thats bred in the bone. **1603** J. FLORIO tr. *Montaigne's Essays* III. xiii. They are effects of custome and vse: and what is bred in the bone will never out of the flesh. **1832** J. P. KENNEDY *Swallow Barn* III. v. What is bred in the bone—you know the proverb. *a* **1957** L. I. WILDER *First Four Years* (1971) iv. We'll always be farmers, for what is bred in the bone *will* come out in the flesh. **1981** B. HEALEY *Last Ferry* iv. There's bad blood there. . . What's bred in the bone comes out in the flesh. ■ **family; habit; human nature**

bred *see also* YORKSHIRE born and Yorkshire bred, strong in the arm and weak in the head.

breed *see* FAMILIARITY breeds contempt; LIKE breeds like.

BREVITY is the soul of wit

In quot. 1600–1 *soul of wit* should be understood as 'essence of wisdom'; *wit* is now commonly understood in its modern sense, the '(power of giving sudden intellectual pleasure by) the unexpected, quick, and humorous combining or contrasting of ideas or expressions' (COD).

□ **1600–1** SHAKESPEARE *Hamlet* II. ii. 90 Since brevity is the soul of wit. . I will be brief. **1833** M. SCOTT *Tom Cringle's Log* II. v. Brevity is the soul of wit,—ahem. **1946** D. WELCH *Maiden Voyage* x. I will not repeat myself, since brevity is the soul of wit. **1996** *Washington Post* 8 Sept. C5 Clinton is Southern and given to garrulousness while brevity, as they say, is the soul of wit. ■ **brevity and long-windedness**

As you BREW, so shall you bake

Cf. *As you* BAKE, *so shall you brew*. Medieval usage makes the connection between brewing and drinking rather than between brewing and baking, as in the following: **1264** in C. Brown *English Lyrics of XIIIth Century* (1932) 131 Let him habbe ase he brew, bale [misery] to dryng [drink] *a* **1325** *Cursor Mundi* (EETS) l. 2848 Nathing of that land [is not submerged], Suilk [such] als thai brued now ha thai dronken. *c* **1450** *Towneley Play of Second Shepherd* (EETS) l. 501 Bot we must drynk as we brew And that is bot reson.

□ *c* **1570** T. INGELEND *Disobedient Child* D8v As he had brewed, that so shulde bake. **1766** COLMAN & GARRICK *Clandestine Marriage* I. 3 As you sow, you must reap—as you brew, so you must bake. **1922** S. J. WEYMAN *Ovington's Bank* xxiii. No, you may go, my lad. As you ha' brewed you may bake. ■ **action and consequence**

brew *see also* as you BAKE, so shall you brew.

You cannot make BRICKS without straw

Nothing can be made or performed without the necessary materials. Frequently used as a metaphorical phrase, *to make bricks without straw*. A (misapplied) allusion to EXODUS v. 7 (AV) Ye shall no more give the people straw to make brick, as heretofore: let them go and gather straw for themselves. Cf. **1624** BURTON *Anatomy of Melancholy* (ed. 2) I. ii. (Hard taske-masters as they [patrons] are) they take away their straw, & compell them to make their number of bricke.

□ **1658** T. HYDE *Letter* in *Verney Memoirs* (1904) II. xxxviii. I have made the enclosed. It is an hard task to make bricks without straw, but I have raked together some rubbish. **1737** in *Publications of Prince Society* (1911) III. 170 Let Men be never so willing and industrious, they can't make Brick without Straw. **1909** A. BENNETT *Literary Taste* iv. You can only acquire really useful general ideas by first acquiring particular ideas. ..You cannot make bricks without straw. **1995** A. G. TAYLOR *Simeon's Bride* xxxi. 208 'What would you have us do, sir?' Jack asked. 'We can't make bricks without straw.' ■ **possibility and impossibility; work**

Happy is the BRIDE that the sun shines on

An equivalent superstition is *blessed are the* DEAD *that the rain rains on.*

□ **1648** HERRICK *Hesperides* 129 Blest is the Bride, on whom the Sun doth shine. And thousands gladly wish You multiply, as doth a fish. **1787** F. GROSE *Provincial Glossary* (Superstitions) 61 It is reckoned a good omen, or a sign of future happiness, if the sun shines on a couple coming out of the church after having been married. ..Happy is the bride that the sun shines on. **1926** 'P. WENTWORTH' *Black Cabinet* xxxvi. 'Happy's the bride that the sun shines on,' is how the proverb goes. But where there's real true love..there's always sunshine in a manner of speaking. **1984** C. A. O'MARIE *Novena for Murder* 181 And the weather is cooperating! 'Blessed the bride that the sun shines on!' ■ **blessings; weddings**

Always a BRIDESMAID, never a bride

□ **1882** E. M. INGRAHAM *Bond & Free* i. Always a maiden [bridal attendant], never a wife. **1903** V. S. LEAN *Collectanea* II. 81 Three times bridesmaid, never a bride. **1917** LEIGH, COLLINS, & MORRIS *'Why am I always the Bridesmaid?' (song)* Why am I always the bridesmaid, Never the blushing bride? **1951** WODEHOUSE *Old Reliable* xi. Then they'd leave me..and go off and buy candy and orchids for the other girls. ..Often a bridesmaid but never a bride. ■ **weddings**

It is good to make a BRIDGE of gold to a flying enemy

The rationale is 'an enemy closely pursued may become desperate. ..By all means, then, let the vanquished have a free course' (T. Fielding *Proverbs of all Nations* (1824) 14). The idea is attributed to Aristides (480 BC), who warned Themistocles not to destroy the bridge of boats which Xerxes had built across the Hellespont in order to invade Greece (PLUTARCH *Themistocles* xvi). Cf. ERASMUS *Apophthegms* viii. *Hostibus fugientibus pontem argenteum exstruendum esse*, for a fleeing enemy one should construct a bridge of silver.

□ **1576** W. LAMBARDE *Perambulation of Kent* 323 It was well sayde of one..If thine enemie will flye, make him a bridge of Golde. **1642** T. FULLER *Holy State* IV. xvii. He [the good general] makes his flying enemy a bridge of gold, and disarms them of their best weapon, which is necessity to fight whether they will or no. **1889** R. L. STEVENSON *Master of Ballantrae* iv. You may have heard a military proverb: that it is a good thing to make a bridge of gold to a flying enemy. I trust you will take my meaning. ■ **enemies; warfare**

bridge *see also* don't CROSS the bridge till you come to it; everyone SPEAKS well of the bridge which carries him over.

brighten *see* BLESSINGS brighten as they take their flight.

bring *see* NIGHT brings counsel; the WORTH of a thing is what it will bring.

If it ain't BROKE, don't fix it

Principally known in North America; the British equivalent is LET *well alone*.

□ **1977** *Nation's Business* May 27 Bert Lance [President Carter's Director of the Office of Management and Budget] believes he can save Uncle Sam billions if he can get the government to adopt a single motto: 'If it ain't broke, don't fix it.' **1984** R. WILDER *You All Spoken Here* 25 If it ain't broke, don't fix it: Don't mess with a clock that runs on time. **1988** *Washington Post* 5 Dec. C11 The sleep pattern you have worked out is normal for you, and since you have been fairly successful in planning your life around it, why change? 'If it ain't broke, don't fix it.' **2001** *Times Literary Supplement* 30 Nov. 14 A healthy libertarianism rubs shoulders with the 'if it ain't broke, don't fix it' style of conservatism. ■ **busybodies; content and discontent**

broken *see* PROMISES, like pie-crust, are made to be broken; RULES are made to be broken.

broom *see* NEW brooms sweep clean; SWEEP the house with broom in May, you sweep the head of the house away.

broth *see* TOO many cooks spoil the broth.

build *see* FOOLS build houses and wise men live in them; where GOD builds a church, the Devil will build a chapel; it is easier to PULL down than to build up.

built *see* ROME was not built in a day.

Every BULLET has its billet

Fate determines who shall be killed; quot. 1922 implies more generally that fate plays a part in all human affairs.

□ **1575** G. GASCOIGNE *Fruits of War* I. 155 Suffiseth this to proove my theame withall, That every bullet hath a lighting place. **1765** WESLEY *Journal* 6 June (1912) V. 130 He never received one wound. So true is the odd saying of King William [III], that 'every bullet has its billet'. **1922** JOYCE *Ulysses* 366 The ball rolled down to her as if it understood. Every bullet has its billet. **1932** R. C. WOODTHORPE *Public School Murder* XI. iv. 237 It is said that every bullet finds its billet. I am afraid this is yet another instance of a shaft at random sent finding a mark the archer never meant. ■ **death; fate and fatalism**

A BULLY is always a coward

1817 M. EDGEWORTH *Ormond* in *Harrington & Ormond* III. xxiv. Mrs. M'Crule, who like all other bullies was a coward, lowered her voice. **1826** LAMB *Elia* in *New Monthly Magazine* XVI. 25 A Bully is always a coward. .. Confront one of the silent heroes with the swaggerer of real life, and his confidence in the theory quickly vanishes. **1853** T. C. HALIBURTON *Wise Saws* iv. I never saw a man furnished with so much pleasure in my life. A brave man is sometimes a desperado. A bully is always a coward. **1981** *Times* 9 May 2 The old adage holds good: all bullies are cowards, and most cowards are bullies. ■ **cowardice**

bung-hole *see* SPARE at the spigot, and let out at the bung-hole.

burden *see* GOD makes the back to the burden.

burn (verb) *see* BETTER to marry than to burn.

burned *see* ONCE bitten, twice shy.

A BURNT child dreads the fire

□ *c* **1250** *Proverbs of Hending* in *Anglia* (1881) IV. 199 Brend child fuir fordredeth [is in dread of]. *c* **1400** *Romaunt of Rose* l. 1820 'For evermore gladly,' as I rede, 'Brent child of fier hath mych drede.' **1580** LYLY *Euphues & his England* II. 92 A burnt childe dreadeth the fire. .. Thou mayst happely forsweare thy selfe, but thou shalt neuer delude me. **1777** P. THICKNESSE *Journey* I. xviii. He then observed, that a burnt child dreads the fire; .. that a Jew had lately passed thro' France, who had put off false Bank notes, and that I might .. have taken some. **1889** *Pictorial Proverbs for Little People* 5 She will not touch a match or a lighted candle .. which proves that the proverb is true which says: a burnt child dreads the fire. **1948** WODEHOUSE *Uncle Dynamite* II. vii. The burnt child fears the fire, and bitter experience had taught Pongo Twistleton to view with concern the presence in his midst of Ickenham's fifth earl. **1984** *Newsweek* 5 Nov. 98 The burned child fears the fire and when dawn breaks next Tuesday voters may pull the covers over their ringing heads and refuse to get out of bed. ■ **experience**

burnt *see also* if you PLAY with fire you get burnt.

bury *see* let the DEAD bury the dead.

bush *see* a BIRD in the hand is worth two in the bush; GOOD wine needs no bush.

The BUSIEST men have the most leisure

Complementary to IDLE *people have the least leisure* and the rationale behind *if you* WANT *something done, ask a busy person*. Cf. **1866** S. SMILES *Self-Help* (new ed.) i. Those who have most to do .. will find the most time.

□ **1884** J. PAYN *Canon's Ward* II. xxxiv. It is my experience that the men who are really busiest have the most leisure for everything. **1911** *Times Literary Supplement* 6 Oct. 365 The busiest men have always the most leisure; and while discharging the multifarious duties of a parish priest and a guardian he found time for travelling.

BUSINESS before pleasure

The two nouns are frequently contrasted in other, non-proverbial, expressions. Cf. *c* **1640** *Grobiana's Nuptials* (*MS Bodley 30*) 15 Well to the businesse.—On; businesse is senior to complement; **1767** T. HUTCHINSON *Diary & Letters* (1883) I. v. Pleasure should always give way to business.

□ **1837** C. G. F. GORE *Stokeshill Place* III. vi. 'Business before pleasure' is a golden rule which most of us regard as iron. **1943** S. STERLING *Down among Dead Men* v. This is business, Sarge. You know what business comes before. **1986** J. HESS *Strangled Prose* vi. Douglas drifted past with the department chairman, engrossed in conversation. He gave me a quick nod, but steered his captive toward a sofa. Business before pleasure. **1997** R. BOWEN *Evans Above* xxii. 232 'I think I should buy you a drink first.' .. 'Business before pleasure, major,' Evan said. ■ **business; work**

business *see also* EVERYBODY's business is nobody's business; PUNCTUALITY is the soul of business.

busy *see* if you WANT something done, ask a busy person.

butter *see* (noun) there are more WAYS of killing a dog than choking it with butter; (verb) FINE words butter no parsnips.

buttered *see* the BREAD never falls but on its buttered side.

BUY in the cheapest market and sell in the dearest

□ **1595** T. LODGE *Fig for Momus* H2 Buy cheape, sell deare. **1862** RUSKIN *Unto this Last* II. 60 Buy in the cheapest market?—yes; but what made your market cheap?..Sell in the dearest?..But what made your market dear? **1880** J. A. FROUDE *Bunyan* vii. 'To buy in the cheapest market and sell in the dearest' was Mr. Badman's common rule in business. ..In Bunyan's opinion it was knavery in disguise. ■ **buying and selling**

You BUY land, you buy stones; you buy meat, you buy bones

Cf. **1595** *Pedler's Prophesy* B4V You shall be sure to haue good Ale, for that haue no bones.

□ **1670** J. RAY *English Proverbs* 211 He that buys land buys many stones; He that buys flesh buys many bones; He that buys eggs buys many shells, But he that buys good ale buys nothing else. **1721** J. KELLY *Scottish Proverbs* 172 He that buys Land, buys Stones; He that buys Beef, buys Bones; He that buys Nuts, buys shells; He that buys good Ale, buys nought else. **1970** *Countryman* Autumn 172 Welsh butcher to customer complaining of bony meat: 'Well, missus, you buy land, you buy stones; buy meat, you buy bones.' ■ **buying and selling; property**

buy *see also* why buy a cow when milk is so cheap?; MONEY can't buy happiness; one WHITE foot, buy him.

Let the BUYER beware

A warning that the buyer must satisfy himself of the nature and value of a purchase before proceeding with the transaction. The Latin tag *caveat emptor* is also frequently found: *caveat emptor, quia ignorare non debuit quod jus alienum emit*, let the purchaser beware, for he ought not to be ignorant of the nature of the property which he is buying from another party. See also the next proverb.

□ **1523** J. FITZHERBERT *Husbandry* 36 And [if] he [a horse] be tame and haue ben rydden vpon than caveat emptor be ware thou byer. **1592** NASHE *Pierce Penniless* I. 155 Sed caueat emptor, Let the interpreter beware. **1607** E. SHARPHAM *Fleire* II. C4 They are no prouerb breakers: beware the buyer say they. **1927** *Times* 29 Sept. 10 We dislike very much, whether it is put in Latin or in English, the phrase 'Let the buyer beware!' **1974** D. FRANCIS *Knock Down* xi. '*Caveat emptor*,' I said. 'What does that mean?' 'Buyer beware.' 'I know one buyer who'll beware for the rest of his life.' **2001** *Washington Times* 24 Sept. A11 It's caveat emptor as charities and others appeal for relief donations in the wake of the Sept. 11 terrorist attacks. Only this time 'let the buyer beware' should probably read 'let the donor beware.' ■ **buying and selling; caution**

The BUYER has need of a hundred eyes, the seller of but one

Cf. It. *chi compra ha bisogna di cent' occhi; chi vende n'ha assai di uno*, he who buys needs a hundred eyes; he who sells but one.

□ **1640** G. HERBERT *Outlandish Proverbs* no. 390 The buyer needes a hundred eyes, the seller not one. **1745** B. FRANKLIN *Poor Richard's Almanack* (July) He who buys had need have 100 Eyes, but one's enough for him that sells the Stuff. **1800** M. EDGEWORTH *Parent's Assistant* (ed. 3) III. 86 He taught him..to get..from customers by taking advantage of their ignorance. ..He often repeated..'The buyer has need of a hundred eyes, the seller of but one.' **1928** *Illustrated Sporting & Dramatic News* 7 Jan. 27 (*caption*) The buyer has need of a hundred eyes. The seller of but one. ■ **buying and selling; caution**

CAESAR's wife must be above suspicion

Julius Caesar replied thus (according to Plutarch) when asked why he had divorced his wife Pompeia. He considered his honour and position compromised, since she was indirectly associated with Publius Clodius' trial for sacrilege. Cf. **1580** LYLY *Euphues & his England* II. 101 Al women shal be as Caesar would haue his wife, not onelye free from sinne, but from suspition.

□ **1779** A. ADAMS *Letter* 4 Jan. in L. H. Butterfield et al. *Adams Family Correspondence* (1973) III. 148 It is a very great misfortune that persons imployed in the most important Departments should.. have seperate interests from the publick whom they profess to serve. Caesars wife ought not to be suspected. **1847** J. C. & A. W. HARE *Guesses at Truth* (ed. 3) 1st Ser. 263 Caesar's wife ought to be above suspicion. ..Caesar himself ought to be so too. **1965** O. MILLS *Dusty Death* xxi. Policemen.. are like. ..candidates for the Church of England ministry. ..and Caesar's wife. ..Not only they, but all their relations, must be above suspicion. **1990** *Washington Times* 9 July D2 He [i.e. Governor D. Wilder] ought to bear in mind the maxim of one of Caligula's more lucid predecessors: Caesar's wife must be above suspicion. And so should Caesar. ■ **associates; conduct**

cake *see* you cannot HAVE your cake and eat it.

calf *see* a BELLOWING COW soon forgets her calf.

call *see* call no man HAPPY till he dies; he who PAYS the piper calls the tune.

called *see* MANY are called but few are chosen.

calm *see* AFTER a storm comes a calm.

camel *see* it is the LAST straw that breaks the camel's back.

He who CAN, does; he who cannot, teaches

There are many (frequently humorous) variations on this proverb.

□ **1903** G. B. SHAW *Maxims for Revolutionists* in *Man & Superman* 230 He who can, does. He who cannot, teaches. **1979** *Daily Telegraph* 6 Aug. 8 A version of an old adage came to me—those who can, do, those who can't, attend conferences. **1981** P. SOMERVILLE-LARGE *Living Dog* i. He who can, does sang the train wheels, he who cannot, teaches. **1999** 'H. CRANE' *Miss Seeton's Finest Hour* iii. 19 'A teacher of art,' she corrected him politely with a sigh. 'Those who can,' she explained as he seemed about to protest her modesty, 'do—as Mr. Shaw has so pithily expressed it. Those who cannot.. ' She sighed. 'Teach,' she concluded sadly. **2002** *Washington Times* 11 July D8 (*Herb & Jamaal comic strip*) 'Rev. Croom, as a man of the cloth, do you consider yourself an example of perfection?' 'No. ..I may wear this collar, but I struggle with being a human as much as the next guy. I guess that's what's meant when they say.. 'He who can, does; he who cannot, *preaches*.' ■ **efficiency and inefficiency; work**

candle *see* BETTER to light one candle..; CANDLEMAS day, put beans in the clay, put candles and candlesticks away.

candlelight *see* never CHOOSE your women or your linen by candlelight.

If CANDLEMAS day be sunny and bright, winter will have another flight; if Candlemas day be cloudy with rain, winter is gone, and won't come again

In the Church calendar, the feast of the Purification of the Virgin Mary and the Presentation of Christ in the Temple falls on 2 February, which is known as Candlemas Day because candles are blessed at church services on that festival. In North America, 2 February is popularly known as Groundhog Day; the very similar weather prediction associated with it arises through the notion that if the groundhog emerges from its burrow on that day into bright sunlight and is frightened by its own shadow it will go back for a further six weeks' hibernation. The superstition was known from at least as early as the early sixteenth century: cf. **1523** SKELTON *Works* I. 418 Men were wonte for to discerne By candlemas day what wedder shulde holde. Quot. 1584's version of the rhyme is close to the Latin lines in quot. 1678.

□ **1584** R. SCOT *Discovery of Witchcraft* XI. XV. If Maries purifieng daie, Be cleare and bright with sunnie raie, The frost and cold shalbe much more, After the feast than was before. **1678** J. RAY *English Proverbs* (ed. 2) 51 If Candlemas day be fair and bright Winter will have another flight: If on Candlemas day it be showre and rain, Winter is gone and will not come again. This is a translation.. of that old Latin Distich; *Si Sol splendescat Maria purificante, Major erit glacies post festum quam fuit ante.* **1980** *Times* 2 Feb. 11 Today is Candlemas Day. So let us see if the old legend holds good again as it did last year. 'If Candlemas day be sunny and bright, winter will have another flight; if Candlemas day be cloudy with rain; winter is gone and won't come again.' ■ **weather lore**

CANDLEMAS day, put beans in the clay; put candles and candlesticks away

For *Candlemas Day* see preceding proverb. The two halves of the proverb appear to have come together comparatively recently, with the instruction about sowing beans possibly being displaced from St Valentine's day (14 Feb.) in response to the shift from the Old Style to the New Style calendar; cf. the rhyme attested from *c* 1640 *On Saint Valentine's Day cast beans in clay But on Saint Chad* (2 Mar.) *sow good or bad* (John Smyth, *Berkeley MSS* 33. no. 89).

□ **1678** J. RAY *English Proverbs* (ed. 2) 344 On Candlemas day throw candle and candlestick away. **1876** T. F. THISELTON-DYER *British Popular Customs* 55 From Candlemas the use of tapers at vespers and litanies, which had continued through the whole year, ceased until the ensuing All Hallow Mass.. On Candlemas Day, throw candle and candlestick away. **1948** F. THOMPSON *Still glides Stream* ii. Broad beans were planted.. on Candlemas Day. *Candlemas Day, stick beans in the clay, Throw candle and candlestick right away*, they would quote. **1974** K. BRIGGS *Folklore of Cotswolds* ii. Candlemas Day was the time.. when lights were extinguished. ..An old rhyme said: Candlemas Day, put beans in the clay: Put candles and candlesticks away. ■ **calendar lore; garden lore**

If the CAP fits, wear it

Used with reference to the suitability of names or descriptions as demonstrated by the behaviour of the person concerned. Cf. *if the* SHOE *fits, wear it*. The cap in question was originally a dunce's cap, as is shown by the following: **1600** N. BRETON *Pasquil's Fools-Cap* A3 Where you finde a head fit for this Cappe, either bestowe it vpon him in charity, or send him where he may haue them for his money.

□ **1732** T. FULLER *Gnomologia* no. 2670 If any Fool finds the Cap fit him, let him wear it. **1750** RICHARDSON *Clarissa* (ed. 3) VII. ii. If indeed thou findest . . that the cap fits thy own head, why then . . clap it on. **1854** DICKENS *Hard Times* II. vii. 'Mercenary. . . Who is not mercenary?' . . 'You know whether the cap fits you. . . If it does, you can wear it.' **1985** 'J. GASH' *Pearlhanger* xi. Little crooks get chased. Big crooks . . get knighted and freedom. I don't mean bankers and insurance syndicates, incidentally, though if the cap fits . . ■ **conduct**; **reputation**

capacity *see* GENIUS is an infinite capacity for taking pains.

caravan *see* DOGS bark, but the caravan goes on.

Where the CARCASE is, there shall the eagles be gathered together

With allusion to MATTHEW xxiv. 28 (AV) Wheresoever the carcase is, there will the Eagles be gathered together. Modern translations read 'vultures' for 'eagles'.

□ *c* **1566** W. P. tr. *Curio's Pasquin in Trance* 33 Where the caraine [carrion] is, thither do the Eagles resort. **1734** B. FRANKLIN *Poor Richard's Almanack* (Jan.) Where carcasses are, eagles will gather, And where good laws are, much people flock thither. **1929** C. BUSH *Perfect Murder Case* x. On the way he explained his appearance at the inquest on the twin lines of busman's holiday and that where the carcass is there will the vultures be gathered together. **1979** 'S. WOODS' *Proceed to Judgement* 190 [He] was surprised to find Sir Nicholas and Vera, as well as Roger and Meg, having tea with Jenny. 'Where the carcase is, there shall the eagles be gathered together,' he commented, not very politely. ■ **associates**

card *see* LUCKY at cards, unlucky in love.

CARE killed the cat

Cf. CURIOSITY *killed the cat*. There is some shift in meaning between *care* = worry, grief and *care* = carefulness, caution, and in quot. 1962 the meaning is 'care lavished on the cat', rather than care exercised by it.

□ **1598–9** SHAKESPEARE *Much Ado about Nothing* V. i. 133 Though care kill'd a cat, thou hast mettle enough in thee to kill care. **1726** SWIFT *Poems* II. 761 Then, who says care will kill a cat? Rebecca shews they're out in that. **1890** 'R. BOLDREWOOD' *Miner's Right* II. xxiii. He was always ready to enjoy himself. . . 'Care killed a cat.' **1949** S. SMITH *Holiday* xii. We must be careful of that. Care killed the cat, said Caz. **1962** A. CHRISTIE *Mirror Crack'd* xxii. Care killed the cat, they say. . . You don't want kindness rubbed into your skin, . . do you? **1979** F. SELWYN *Sergeant Verity & Blood Royal* xx. 'Pretty sure, Mr. Crowe? I was bloody near ten feet short of it, that's all!' . . 'Come on now, Verity. Care might kill a cat! Look to the future!' ■ **stress**

Don't CARE was made to care

Quot. 1959 gives the version of the traditional children's rhyme found at Hackney, London.

□ **1959** I. & P. OPIE *Lore and Language of Schoolchildren* iii. 50 To 'don't-cares' the traditional saying is: Don't care was *made* to care, Don't care was hung, Don't care was put in a pot And boiled till he was done. **1992** D. LESSING *African Laughter* 223 Look at the maize. How do we know what bugs the Portuguese brought in with maize? We don't know! We don't care! Well, don't care was made to care . . you ought to be able to stick a finger easily into real soil. **2001** *Spectator* 19 May 13 And as the crime spawned by permissiveness reaches even into the most secluded cul-de-sac, they will find that an egalitarian government is neutral between victim and offender, so that while they cannot defend themselves, there is nobody out there to protect them. Don't care will be made to care then. ■ **trouble**

care *see also* CHILDREN are certain cares, but uncertain comforts; take care of the PENCE and the pounds will take care of themselves.

careful *see* if you can't be GOOD, be careful.

A CARPENTER is known by his chips

□ *a* **1533** LD. BERNERS *Hist. Arthur* (1582) 162[b] I know well my lorde Arthur hath been here. . . He is a good carpenter, for he hath made here a faire sight of chips. **1546** J. HEYWOOD *Dialogue of Proverbs* I. vii. 14 Muste she not (quoth he) be welcome to vs all, Amonge vs all, lettyng suche a farewell fall? But such carpenters, such chips. Quoth she folke tell. **1738** SWIFT *Polite Conversation* ii. 153 'You have eaten nothing.' . . 'See all the Bones on my Plate: They say, a carpenter's known by his Chips.' **1962** *Washington Daily News* 24 July 14 In the idiom of the Middle West, you can tell a wood chopper by his chips. President Kennedy's economic report . . was based on the scientific estimates of his Council of Economic Advisers. ■ **appearance; human nature**

carry *see* a DOG that will fetch a bone will carry a bone; everyone SPEAKS well of the bridge which carries him over.

cart *see* don't PUT the cart before the horse.

case *see* CIRCUMSTANCES alter cases; HARD cases make bad law; no one should be JUDGE in his own cause.

Ne'er CAST a clout till May be out

A warning not to leave off old or warm clothes until the end of May. The proverb does not refer to May blossom, as is sometimes assumed.

□ **1706** J. STEVENS *Spanish & English Dict.* s.v. Mayo, *Hasta passado Mayo no te quites el sayo*, Do not leave off your Coat till May be past. **1732** T. FULLER *Gnomologia* no. 6193 Leave not off a Clout [item of clothing], Till May be out. **1832** A. HENDERSON *Scottish Proverbs* 154 Cast ne'er a clout till May be out. **1948** R. GRAVES *White Goddess* x. In ancient Greece, as in Britain, this [May] was the month in which people went about in old clothes—a custom referred to in the proverb 'Ne'er cast a clout ere May be out,' meaning 'do not put on new clothes until the unlucky month is over.' **1970** N. STREATFEILD *Thursday's Child* xxv. I still wear four petticoats . . Ne'er cast a clout till May be out. **1996** C. DUNN *Murder on Flying Scotsman* i. 7 Brought up on 'Ne'er cast a clout till May be out' (May month or may blossom? she had always wondered), Daisy was wearing her green tweed winter coat. ■ **calendar lore; dress**

cast *see also* COMING events cast their shadows before; OLD sins cast long shadows; do not throw PEARLS to swine.

castle *see* an ENGLISHMAN's house is his castle.

casualty *see* TRUTH is the first casualty of war.

A CAT in gloves catches no mice

Restraint and caution (or 'pussyfooting') achieve nothing. Cf. 14th-cent. Fr. *chat engaunté ne surrizera ja bien*, a gloved cat will never mouse well.

□ **1573** J. SANFORDE *Garden of Pleasure* 105 A gloued catte can catche no myse. **1592** G. DELAMOTHE *French Alphabet* II. 1 A mufled Cat is no good mouse hunter. **1758** B. FRANKLIN *Poor Richard's Almanack* (Preface) Handle your Tools without Mittens; remember that the Cat in Gloves catches no Mice. **1857** DICKENS *Little Dorrit* II. xiv. Mrs. General, if I may reverse the common proverb .. is a cat in gloves who *will* catch mice. That woman .. will be our mother-in-law. **1922** E. PHILLPOTTS *Red Redmaynes* ix. As we say in Italy, 'if you put a cat into gloves, she will not catch mice.' You have been in gloves ever since you knew Madonna was a widow. **1979** *Country Life* 21 June 2047 There is hardly one [cat] but flings back the lie in the face of the old saying that a cat in gloves catches no mice. Why dirty your paws when your servants will do it for you? ■ **efficiency and inefficiency**

A CAT may look at a king

□ **1546** J. HEYWOOD *Dialogue of Proverbs* II. v. H3 What, a cat maie looke on a king, ye know. **1590** R. GREENE *Never too Late* VIII. 181 A Cat may look at a King, and a swaynes eye hath as high a reach as a Lords looke. **1721** N. BAILEY *English Dictionary* s.v. Cat, A Cat may look upon a King. This is a saucy Proverb, generally made use of by pragmatical Persons. **1935** I. COMPTON-BURNETT *House & its Head* xi. There is no harm in that, dear. A cat may look at a king; and it is only in that spirit that my poor brother looks at Alison. **2001** *Times* 23 Nov. 20 Our trivia quiz shows are intended to show that taxi drivers are as clever as philosophers and poets. A cat may look at a king. ■ **equality; society**

When the CAT's away, the mice will play

Cf. early 14th-cent. Fr. *ou chat na rat regne*, where there is no cat the rat is king; *c* **1470** *Harley MS 3362* in *Retrospective Review* (1854) May 309 The mows lordchypythe [rules] ther a cat ys nawt; **1599** SHAKESPEARE *Henry V* I. ii. 172 To her unguarded nest the weasel Scot Comes sneaking, and so sucks her princely eggs, Playing the mouse in absence of the cat.

□ **1607** T. HEYWOOD *Woman killed with Kindness* II. 135 Mum; there's an old prouerbe, when the cats away, the mouse may play. **1670** J. RAY *English Proverbs* 68 When the cat is away, the mice play. **1876** I. BANKS *Manchester Man* III. xiv. Mrs. Ashton, saying 'that when the cat's away the mice will play', had decided on remaining at home. **1925** S. O'CASEY *Juno & Paycock* I. 13 It's a good job she has to be so often away, for when the cat's away, the mice can play! **2001** R. HILL *Dialogues of Dead* xxx. 258 'When I'm having the time of my life, you'd not deprive me of the pleasure of thinking about all those poor sods back here working their fingers to the bone.' 'You don't really believe that, do you? When the cat's away ..' ■ **discipline; opportunity, taken**

The CAT, the rat, and Lovell the dog, rule all England under the hog

The allusion is explained in quot. 1586.

□ **1516** R. FABYAN *New Chronicles of England & France* VIII. 219v The Catte the Ratte And Louell our dogge Rulyth all Englande under a hogge. The whiche was ment that Catisby Ratclyffe And the Lord Louell Ruled the lande under the kynge. **1586** R. HOLINSHED *Chronicles* III. 746 [Richard III executed] a poore gentleman called Collingborne [in 1484], for making a small rime of three of his .. councellors, .. lord Louell, sir Richard Ratcliffe .. and sir William Catesbie. .. The Cat, the Rat, and Louell our dog, Rule all England vnder an hog. Meaning by the hog, the .. wild boare, which was the Kings cognisance [coat of arms]. **1816** SCOTT *Antiquary* ii. 'His name .. was Lovel.' 'What! the cat, the rat, and Lovel our dog? Was he descended from King Richard's favourite?' **1973** A. CHRISTIE *Postern of Fate* I. ii.

The cat, the rat and Lovell, the dog, Rule all England under the hog. ..The hog was Richard the Third. ■ **rulers and ruled**

The CAT would eat fish, but would not wet her feet

Cf. medieval L. *catus amat piscem, sed non vult tingere plantas*, the cat loves a fish, but does not wish to wet its feet.

□ *c* **1225** in *Englische Studien* (1902) XXXI. 7 Cat lufat visch, ac he nele his feth wete. *c* **1380** CHAUCER *House of Fame* III. 1783 For ye be lyke the sweynte [tired] cat That wolde have fissh; but wostow [do you know] what? He wolde nothing wete his clowes. *c* **1549** J. HEYWOOD *Dialogue of Proverbs* I. xi. B8^{V} But you lust not to do, that longeth therto. The cat would eate fyshe, and wold not wet her feete. **1605–6** SHAKESPEARE *Macbeth* I. vii. 44 Letting 'I dare not' wait upon 'I would', Like the poor cat i' th' adage. **1732** T. FULLER *Gnomologia* no. 6130 Fain would the Cat Fish eat, but she's loth her Feet to wet. **1928** *Sphere* 7 Jan. 36 'The cat would fain eat fish, but would not wet his feet.'..In modern days one might paraphrase it into 'bad sailors would fain enjoy the sun, but would not cross the channel'. ■ **decision and indecision; wanting and having**

cat *see also* CARE killed the cat; CURIOSITY killed the cat; KEEP no more cats than will catch mice; WANTON kittens make sober cats; there is more than one WAY to skin a cat; there are more WAYS of killing a cat than choking it with cream; also CATS.

You cannot CATCH old birds with chaff

The wise and experienced are not easily fooled.

□ **1481** CAXTON *Reynard the Fox* (1880) xl. Wenest [do you think] thou thus to deceyue. ..I am no byrde to be locked ne take by chaf. I know wel ynowh good corn. *c* **1590** *Timon* (1842) IV. ii. Tis well.—An olde birde is not caught with chaffe. **1670** J. RAY *English Proverbs* 126 You can't catch old birds with chaff. **1853** THACKERAY *Newcomes* II. xv. They ogled him as they sang..with which chaff our noble bird was by no means to be caught. **1961** 'L. BRUCE' *Die All, Die Merrily* (1986) xx. 188 'But why, headmaster? On what do you base that?' 'Aha,' said Mr. Gorringer, 'old birds are not to be caught with chaff. I sensed it as soon as you failed to name him among your "possibles."' ■ **experience; wisdom**

catch *see also* a CAT in gloves catches no mice; a DROWNING man will clutch at a straw; EAGLES don't catch flies; the EARLY bird catches the worm; FIRST catch your hare; HONEY catches more flies than vinegar; KEEP no more cats than will catch mice; if you RUN after two hares you will catch neither; a SHUT mouth catches no flies; if the SKY falls we shall catch larks; SUE a beggar and catch a louse; set a THIEF to catch a thief; *see also* caught.

CATCHING's before hanging

□ **1818** A. N. ROYALL *Letters from Alabama* (1830) xxxvi. Yes, says Marchant, but catching's before hanging—the villain's cleared out. **1876** W. G. NASH *New England Life* vii. Catchin' before spankin' is the rule. **1961** E. SEEMAN *In Arms of Mountain* 60 Ketchin' comes before hangin', I always say. ■ **action and consequence**

All CATS are grey in the dark

The proverb, which turns on the concept that the night obscures all distinguishing features, is used in a variety of contexts.

□ *c* **1549** J. HEYWOOD *Dialogue of Proverbs* I. v. A6^{V} When all candels be out, all cats be grey. All thyngs are then of one colour. **1596** T. LODGE *Margarite of America* H2^{V}

All cattes are grey in the darke..and therefore (good madam) you doe well to preferre the eie. **1745** B. FRANKLIN *Letter* 25 June in *Papers* (1961) III. 31 And as in the dark all Cats are grey, the Pleasure of corporal Enjoyment with an old Woman is at least equal, and frequently superior. **1886** H. JAMES *Princess Casamassima* I. xiv. 'If she isn't, what becomes of your explanation?'..'Oh, it doesn't matter; at night all cats are grey.' **1990** R. RICHARDSON *Dying of Light* xi. 130 He braked as a cat scuttled in front of him. ..'Was that black?' 'All cats are grey in the dark,' Tess quoted. 'But it could have been. That's lucky.' ■ **similarity and dissimilarity**

cattle *see* HURRY no man's cattle.

caught *see* don't SELL the skin till you have caught the bear.

cause *see* no one should be JUDGE in his own cause.

cease *see* WONDERS will never cease.

certain *see* CHILDREN are certain cares, but uncertain comforts; NOTHING is certain but death and taxes; NOTHING is certain but the unforeseen.

chaff *see* you cannot CATCH old birds with chaff; a KING's chaff is worth more than other men's corn.

A CHAIN is no stronger than its weakest link

□ **1856** C. KINGSLEY *Letter* 1 Dec. (1877) II. 499 The devil is very busy, and no one knows better than he, that 'nothing is stronger than its weakest part'. **1868** L. STEPHEN in *Çornhill Mag.* XVII. 295 A chain is no stronger than its weakest link; but if you show how admirably the last few are united..half the world will forget to test the security of the..parts which are kept out of sight. **1986** L. J. PETER *Peter Pyramid* ii. A chain is only as strong as its weakest link; and the longer the chain, the more weak links. ■ **strength and weakness**

Don't CHANGE horses in mid-stream

The proverb is also used in the phrase *to change horses in mid-stream.*

□ **1864** A. LINCOLN *Collected Works* (1953) VII. 384 I am reminded..of a story of an old Dutch farmer, who remarked to a companion once that 'it was best not to swap horses when crossing streams'. **1929** R. GRAVES *Good-bye to All That* xxiii. 'If ours is the true religion why do you not become a Catholic?'..'Reverend father, we have a proverb in England never to swap horses while crossing a stream'. **1967** RIDOUT & WITTING *English Proverbs Explained* 41 Don't change horses in mid-stream. ..If we think it necessary to make changes, we must choose the right moment to make them. **1979** D. MAY *Revenger's Comedy* ix. Changing horses, love? I should look before you leap. ■ **decision and indecision**

A CHANGE is as good as a rest

□ **1890** A. CONAN DOYLE in *Lippincott's Monthly Mag.* Feb. x. 198 Well, I gave my mind a thorough rest by plunging into a chemical analysis. One of our greatest statesmen has said that a change of work is the best rest. So it is. **1895** J. THOMAS *Randigal Rhymes* 59 Change of work is as good as touchpipe [a short interval of rest]. **1903** V. S. LEAN *Collectanea* III. 439 Change of work is rest. (Manx.) **1951** M. COLES *Now or Never* ii. On the principle that a change of work is a rest, we redecorated the bathroom. ..We came to the conclusion that the saying is a fallacy. **1967** O. MILLS *Death enters Lists* viii. There would be no fish-bits for Whiskers..but she could buy him some fish-pieces; and a change was as good as a rest, she remembered. **1984** D. CANNELL *Thin Woman* xiii. Me old grandpa used to say 'a change is as good as a rest', and at my time of life variety don't often come aknocking. **1994** S. SHAW

Villain of Earth (1995) iv. 33 'No disrespect to John Quennell, but my career's not really advancing as it ought to, and perhaps our relationship's a little on the stale side. A change is as good as a rest, as they say.' ■ **change; recreation**

CHANGE the name and not the letter, change for the worse and not the better

Explained in William Henderson's *Notes on the Folk Lore of the Northern Counties of England and the Borders* (1866): 'It is unlucky for a woman to marry a man whose surname begins with the same letter as her own' (p. 26).

□ **1853** *Notes & Queries* 1st ser. VIII. 150 Is the following distich known in any part of England? 'To change the name but not the letter, Is to marry for worse, and not for better.' I met with it in an American book, but it was probably an importation. **1936** T. C. H. JACOBS *Appointment with Hangman* ii. 18 'Change the name and not the letter, change for the worse and not the better. She ought to be warned about that.' **1950** woman from Forfar, Angus, quoted in I. OPIE & M. TATEM *Oxford Dictionary of Superstitions* (1996) 238 A change of name and not of letter Is a change for the worse and not the better. ■ **marriage; superstition**

change *see also* (verb) the LEOPARD does not change his spots; TIMES change and we with time.

chapel *see* where GOD builds a church, the Devil will build a chapel.

CHARITY begins at home

□ *c* **1383** in Wyclif *English Works* (EETS) 78 Charite schuld bigyne at hem-self. *a* **1625** BEAUMONT & FLETCHER *Wit without Money* v. ii. Charity and beating begins at home. **1659** T. FULLER *Appeal of Injured Innocence* I. 25 Charity begins, but doth not end, at home. .. My Church-History .. began with our own Domestick affairs. .. I intended .. to have proceeded to forrain Churches. **1748** SMOLLETT *Roderick Random* I. vi. The world would do nothing for her if she should come to want—charity begins at home. **1910** 'SAKI' *Reginald in Russia* 2 With her, as with a great many of her sex, charity began at homeliness and did not generally progress much farther. **1985** C. MACLEOD *Plain Old Man* xiv. 'You know Aunt Emma never gives anybody a complimentary ticket. If she did, .. there'd be no money raised for charity.' 'I thought charity began at home.' **1996** *Washington Post* 30 July C16 True, charity begins at home, but it shouldn't end there. ■ **charity; home**

CHARITY covers a multitude of sins

Cf. ERASMUS *Responsio ad Albertum Pium* (1529) 35v *quid est charitas? Est pallium monachi. Qui sic? Quia operit multitudinem peccatorum*, What is Charity? A monk's cloak. Why? Because it covers a multitude of sins. With allusion to I PETER iv. 8 (AV) For charity shall cover the multitude of sins.

□ *a* **1633** G. HERBERT *Priest to Temple* (1652) xii. Many and wonderfull things are spoken of thee. .. To Charity is given the covering of sins. **1794** J. Q. ADAMS *Letter* 26 May in *Writings* (1913) I. 191 *Faction* covers at least as great a multitude of sins as *charity*. **1836** E. HOWARD *Rattlin the Reefer* I. xxx. The blue coat, like charity, covereth a multitude of sins. **1908** 'O. HENRY' *Gentle Grafter* 47 According to the old proverb, 'Charity covers a multitude of skins'. **1982** G. HAMMOND *Game* xvi. Charity, after all, can cover up a multitude of sins. ■ **charity; forgiveness**

chase *see* a STERN chase is a long chase.

It is as CHEAP sitting as standing

Commonly applied literally.

□ **1666** G. TORRIANO *Italian Proverbs* 277 The English say, It is as cheap sitting as standing, my Masters. **1858** SURTEES *Ask Mamma* xlix. Let's get chairs, and be snug; it's as cheap sitting as standing. **1932** 'J. J. CONNINGTON' *Sweepstake Murders* ix. He returned to Tommie Redhill's car. 'Jump in, Inspector,' Tommie suggested, opening the door at his side. 'It's as cheap sitting as standing.' **1946** 'R. T. CAMPBELL' *Bodies in Bookshop* xix. The old man.. grunted angrily and lowered himself into a chair. I had already taken a seat. It was as cheap to sit as to stand. ■ **idleness**

cheap *see also* why buy a cow when milk is so cheap; TALK is cheap.

cheapest *see* BUY in the cheapest market and sell in the dearest.

CHEATS never prosper

Also *cheaters*, esp. in US. Cf. *a* **1612** J. HARINGTON *Epigrams* (1618) IV. 5 Treason doth neuer prosper, what's the reason? For if it prosper, none dare call it Treason.

□ **1805** R. PARKINSON *Tour in America* II. xxix. It is a common saying in England, that 'Cheating never thrives': but, in America, with honest trading you cannot succeed. **1903** V. S. LEAN *Collectanea* II. 38 'Cheating never prospers.' A proverb frequently thrown at each other by young people when playing cards. **1935** R. CROMPTON *William—the Detective* vi. They avenged themselves upon the newcomer.. by shouting the time-honoured taunt 'Cheats never prosper.' **1971** R. L. FISH *Green Hell Treasure* ii. 'So you figured.. that someone in the classroom had been helping him with his homework, and that was cheating. Which you frown on.' 'With reason,' Da Silva said virtuously. 'Cheaters never prosper.' **2001** *Washington Times* 30 Aug. B8 Cheaters never prosper. They only receive the keys to the city from Mayor Rudolph Giuliani. ■ **wrong-doers**

cheeping *see* MAY chickens come cheeping.

cheese *see* an APPLE-PIE without some cheese is like a kiss without a squeeze.

A CHERRY year, a merry year; a plum year, a dumb year

□ **1678** J. RAY *English Proverbs* (ed. 2) 52 A cherry year a merry year: A plum year a dumb year. This is a puerile and senceless rythme.. as far as I can see. **1869** R. INWARDS *Weather Lore* 14 The progress of the seasons may be watched by observing the punctuality of the vegetable world. .. A cherry year, a merry year. A plum year, a dumb year. **1979** V. CANNING *Satan Sampler* ix. Warboys was studying an arrangement of cherry blossom. .. The blossom was good this year. A cherry year, a merry year. ■ **garden lore**

chicken *see* don't COUNT your chickens before they are hatched; CURSES, like chickens, come home to roost; MAY chickens come cheeping.

Monday's CHILD is fair of face

Each line of the verse (quot. 1838) may be used separately. Examples relating to different days of the week are illustrated here for convenience. In quot. 1838 'Christmas' is an unusual variant, 'Sabbath' being far more common.

□ **1838** A. E. BRAY *Traditions of Devon* II. 287 Monday's child is fair of face, Tuesday's child is full of grace, Wednesday's child is full of woe, Thursday's child has far to go, Friday's child is loving and giving, Saturday's child works hard for its living, And a child that's born on the Christmas day Is fair and wise and good and gay. **1915** J. BUCHAN *Salute to Adventurers* i. I was a Thursday's bairn, and so, according to the old rhyme,'had far to go'. **1935** D. JONES *Journal* 12 Nov. in R. Hague *Dai Greatcoat* (1980) II. 81 Which day's child is 'loving and giving' in the rhyme?.. Is it

Wednesday's? **1957** V. BRITTAIN *Testament of Experience* I. ii. From the outset Shirley sustained the nursery adage which commends 'Sunday's child', for she put on weight steadily and was the easiest of infants to rear. **1980** A. WILSON *Setting World on Fire* II. iii. She showed her contrition by stroking his hair. 'Saturday's child works hard for his living,' she murmured. **1997** *Washington Post* 18 Dec. C27 Monday's child is fair of face. | Tuesday's child is full of grace. | Wednesday's child is full of woe. | Thursday's child has far to go. | Friday's child is loving and giving. | Saturday's child works hard for a living. | And the child born on the Sabbath day | Is bonny and blithe, and good and gay. ■ **children**

The CHILD is the father of the man

An assertion of the unity of character from youth to manhood. Cf. **1671** MILTON *Paradise Regained* IV. 220 The childhood shews the man, As morning shews the day.

□ **1807** WORDSWORTH *Poems* (1952) I. 226 My heart leaps up when I behold A rainbow in the sky: So was it when my life began.. The Child is father of the Man. **1871** S. SMILES *Character* ii. The influences which contribute to form the character of the child.. endure through life. .. 'The child is father of the man.' **1907** E. GOSSE *Father & Son* xii. We are the victims of hallowed proverbs, and one of the most classic of these tells us that 'the child is the father of the man'. **2002** *Washington Post* 31 May C7 'The child is father of the man' is an idea that's been around for a while, but Gail Tsukiyama takes this notion and tweaks it, ever so gently. ■ **children; human nature**

child *see also* a BURNT child dreads the fire; PRAISE the child, and you make love to the mother; SPARE the rod and spoil the child; it is a WISE child that knows its own father.

CHILDREN and fools tell the truth

Cf. late 14th-cent. Fr. *pour savoir vrai de chose toute, yvre, enffant, sot et femme escoute,* to know the truth about everything, listen to drunkards, children, idiots, and women; *c* **1425** in *Anglia* (1885) VIII. 154 Atte laste treuthe was tryed oute of a childe and dronken man.

□ **1537** in *Letters & Papers of Reign of Henry VIII* (1929) Addenda I. I. 437 It is 'an old saying that a child, a fool and a drunken man will ever show.. the truth'. **1591** LYLY *Endymion* IV. ii. Children must not see Endimion, because children and fooles speake true. **1652** J. TATHAM *Scots Figgaries* III. 23 I am a fool 'tis confest, but children and fooles tell truth sometimes; you know. **1805** SCOTT *Letter* Jan. (1932) I. 233 It is a proverb, that children and fools talk truth and I am mistaken if even the same valuable quality may not sometimes be extracted out of the tales made to entertain both. **1921** *Evening Standard* 21 Oct. 9 Solicitor.. 'Are you telling the truth in this case?' Witness.—Only children and fools tell the truth. **1972** 'D. SHANNON' *Murder with Love* ii. All he said was that children and fools speak the truth. ■ **children; fools; truth**

CHILDREN are certain cares, but uncertain comforts

The sense is reversed in the last quotation.

□ **1639** J. CLARKE *Parœmiologia Anglo-Latina* 240 Children are uncertaine comforts, but certaine cares. **1641** R. BRATHWAIT *English Gentleman* (ed. 3) 27 Children reflect constant cares, but uncertaine comforts. **1732** T. FULLER *Gnomologia* no. 1095 Children are certain Cares, but uncertain comforts. **1885** E. J. HARDY *How to be Happy though Married* xvi. Children are *not* 'certain sorrows and uncertain pleasures' when properly managed. **1915** J. WEBSTER *Dear Enemy* 203 My new little family has driven everything out of my mind. Bairns are certain joy, but nae sma' care. ■ **children and parents**

CHILDREN should be seen and not heard

Originally applied specifically to (young) women.

□ *c* **1400** J. MIRK *Festial* (EETS) I. 230 Hyt ys an old Englysch sawe [saying]: 'A mayde schuld be seen, but not herd.' **1560** T. BECON *Works* I. Bbb2 This also must honest maids provide, that they be not full of tongue. . . A maid should be seen, and not heard. **1773** R. GRAVES *Spiritual Quixote* I. III. xviii. It is a vulgar maxim, 'that a pretty woman should rather be seen than heard'. **1820** J. Q. ADAMS *Memoirs* (1875) V. xii. My dear mother's constant lesson in childhood, that children in company should be seen and not heard. **1959** M. BRADBURY *Eating People is Wrong* ii. 'You think that children should be seen and not heard then?' asked the novelist. **2002** *Times 2* 2 May 8 But although mothers may not want to draw attention to themselves, . . there is never any guarantee that their baby . . has yet learnt the old maxim that children should be seen and not heard. ■ **children; manners**

children *see also* the DEVIL's children have the Devil's luck; FOOLS and bairns should never see half-done work; HEAVEN protects children, sailors, and drunken men.

chip *see* a CARPENTER is known by his chips.

choice *see* you PAYS your money and you takes your choice; SMALL choice in rotten apples.

choke *see* it is idle to SWALLOW the cow and choke on the tail.

choking *see* there are more WAYS of killing a cat than choking it with cream; there are more WAYS of killing a dog than choking it with butter.

Never CHOOSE your women or your linen by candlelight

□ **1573** J. SANFORDE *Garden of Pleasure* 51 Choose not a woman, nor linnen clothe by the candle. **1678** J. RAY *English Proverbs* (ed. 2) 64 Neither women nor linnen by candle-light. **1737** B. FRANKLIN *Poor Richard's Almanack* (May) Fine linnen, girls and gold so bright. Chuse not to take by candlelight. **1980** *Woman's Journal* Dec. 105 'Never choose your women or your linen by candlelight,' they used to say: a testimony to the soft, flattering glow that candles always give. ■ **appearance, deceptive; women**

choose *see also* of two EVILS choose the less.

chooser *see* BEGGARS can't be choosers.

chosen *see* MANY are called but few are chosen.

Christmas *see* the DEVIL makes his Christmas pies of lawyers' tongues and clerks' fingers; a DOG is for life, not just for Christmas; a GREEN Yule makes a fat churchyard.

The CHURCH is an anvil which has worn out many hammers

The saying originated in the reply of the Calvinist theologian Theodore Beza (1519–1605) to the King of Navarre after the massacre of the Huguenots at Vassy in March 1562. The king had attempted to excuse the massacre on the grounds of the Protestants' having provoked the Duke of Guise and his followers by throwing stones at them.

□ **1853** G. DE FELICE *Hist. Protestants of France* I. II. v. 156 (tr. Beza to King of Navarre, 1562) It is the peculiarity of the Church of God..to endure blows, not to give them; but yet you will be pleased to remember, that it is an anvil on which many a hammer has been broken. **1908** A. MACLAREN *Acts of Apostles* I. 136 The Church is an anvil which has worn out many hammers and the story of the first collision is, in essentials, the story of all. **1920** J. BUCHAN *Path of King* vii. 'From this day I am an exile from France so long as it pleases God to make His Church an anvil for the blows of His enemies.'..'God's church is now an anvil, but remember..it is an anvil which has worn out many hammers.' ■ **Christianity**

church *see also* the BLOOD of the martyrs is the seed of the Church; where GOD builds a church, the Devil will build a chapel; he is a GOOD dog who goes to church; the NEARER the church, the farther from God.

churchyard *see* a GREEN Yule makes a fat churchyard.

CIRCUMSTANCES alter cases

□ **1678** T. RYMER *Tragedies of Lost Age* 177 There may be circumstances that alter the case, as when there is a sufficient ground of partiality. **1776** W. HEATH *Memoirs* (1798) 92 Our General reflected for a moment, that as circumstances alter cases, Gen. Washington..might possibly wish for some aid. **1895** J. PAYN *In Market Overt* xxxix. Circumstances alter cases even with the best of us, as was shown in a day or two in the conduct of the Lord Bishop. **1938** A. CHRISTIE *Appointment with Death* xiii. It is undoubtedly true that circumstances alter cases. I do feel..that in the present circumstances decisions may have to be reconsidered. **1998** 'C. AIRD' *Stiff News* (2000) v. 56 'I didn't say anything before,' the Matron murmured awkwardly, 'because I couldn't imagine that it could be important.' 'Circumstances alter cases,' said Crosby prosaically. ■ **circumstances**

circus *see* if you can't RIDE two horses at once, you shouldn't be in the circus.

cite *see* the DEVIL can quote Scripture for his own ends.

city *see* if every man would SWEEP his own doorstep the city would soon be clean.

A CIVIL question deserves a civil answer

□ **1853** T. C. HALIBURTON *Sam Slick's Wise Saws* II. ii. Give a civil answer to a civil question. **1858** S. A. HAMMETT *Piney Woods Tavern* xxvii. The Squire there asked me a civil question, and that desarves a civil answer,—at least that's manners where I come from. **1935** E. GREENWOOD *Pins & Needles* xi. 'Thank you for those few words,' Aunt said effusively. 'I've got what I wanted—a civil answer to a civil question.'

CIVILITY costs nothing

Politeness now often replaces *civility*. Cf. late 15th-cent. Fr. *de bouche honnesteté.. petit couste et vault plenté*, courteous words..cost little and are worth much.

□ **1706** J. STEVENS *Spanish & English Dict.* s.v. Cortesía, Mouth civility is worth much and costs little. **1765** LADY M. W. MONTAGU *Letter* 30 May (1967) III. 107 Remember Civility costs nothing, and buys every thing. **1765** H. TIMBERLAKE *Memoirs* 73 Politeness..costs but little. **1873** W. ALLINGHAM *Rambles* xiv. Civility costs nothing, it is said—Nothing, that is, to him that shows it; but it often costs the world very dear. **1980** E. HARRIS *Medium for Murder* x. 'It made me hopping mad to hear you kow-towing to him.'..'Politeness costs nothing,' said Brooker. **1992** C. GRAHAM *Death in Disguise* v. 95 There was no call, Jill's boss had agreed whilst comforting his employee with an iced Malibu, to take that tone. Politeness cost nothing. ■ **manners; politeness**

clay *see* CANDLEMAS day, put beans in the clay, put candles and candlesticks away.

clean *see* a clean CONSCIENCE is a good pillow; NEW brooms sweep clean; if every man would SWEEP his own doorstep the city would soon be clean.

CLEANLINESS is next to godliness

Next in this proverb means 'immediately following', as in serial order. Cf. **1605** BACON *Advancement of Learning* II. 44 Cleannesse of bodie was euer esteemed to proceed from a due reuerence to God.

□ *a* **1791** WESLEY *Works* (1872) VII. 16 Slovenliness is no part of religion. .. 'Cleanliness is indeed next to godliness.' **1876** F. G. BURNABY *Ride to Khiva* X. 'Cleanliness is next to Godliness.' The latter quality, as displayed in a Russian devotee, is more allied with dirt than anything else. **1979** C. EGLETON *Backfire* i. The hospital staff had a thing about personal cleanliness, next to godliness, you might say. **2002** *Washington Post* 14 Aug. C2 But a $6,000 shower curtain? Even if cleanliness is next to godliness, isn't that kinda steep? ■ **cleanliness**

CLERGYMEN's sons always turn out badly

□ **1885** E. J. HARDY *How to be Happy though Married* xix. The Proverb says that 'Clergymen's sons always turn out badly'.. because the children are surfeited with severe religion, *not* with the true religion of Christ. **1922** W. R. INGE *Outspoken Essays* 2nd Ser. vii. An Eton boy.. when asked why the sons of Eli turned out badly, replied 'The sons of clergymen always turn out badly'. **1982** B. PYM *Unsuitable Attachment* iii. Yes, sons of the clergy often go to the bad, and daughters, too. ■ **children and parents**

clerk *see* the DEVIL makes his Christmas pies of lawyers' tongues and clerks' fingers.

client *see* a man who is his own LAWYER has a fool for his client.

climb *see* he that would EAT the fruit must climb the tree; the HIGHER the monkey climbs the more he shows his tail.

Hasty CLIMBERS have sudden falls

□ *a* **1439** J. LYDGATE *Fall of Princes* (EETS) III. 953 The wheel of Fortune tourneth as a ball; Sodeyn clymbyng axeth a sodeyn fall. *c* **1511** S. HAWES *Comfort of Lovers* (1975) A4 Clymbe not to fast, lest sodenlye ye slyde. **1592** R. GREENE *Repentance* in *Works* XII. 158 For a yong man led on by selfe will. .. Hee forseath not that such as clime hastely fall sodainely. **1605** *Capt. Thomas Stukeley* D1 But there are many daungers by the way, and hastie climers quicklie catch a fall. **1616** N. BRETON *Crossing of Proverbs* II. A4 Hasty climbers haue sodaine falls. .. Not if they sit fast. **1869** C. H. SPURGEON *John Ploughman's Talk* xix. Hints as to thriving. .. Hasty climbers have sudden falls. **1987** *Daily Telegraph* 27 Apr. 12 The ambition to send spaceships to the red planet reminds me of the old saying: 'Hasty climbers quickly catch a fall.' ■ **ambition**

From CLOGS to clogs is only three generations

Said to be a Lancashire proverb. Similar to *from* SHIRTSLEEVES *to shirtsleeves in three generations*. The clog, a shoe with a thick wooden sole, was commonly used by factory and other manual workers in the north of England. Cf. **1700** DRYDEN

Wife of Bath in *Fables Ancient & Modern* 493 Seldom three descents continue good. **1721** J. KELLY *Scottish Proverbs* 312 The Father buys, the Son biggs [builds], The Grandchild sells, and his Son thiggs [begs].

□ **1871** *Notes & Queries* 4th Ser. VII. 472 'From clogs to clogs is only three generations.' A Lancashire proverb, implying that, however rich a poor man may eventually become, his great-grandson will certainly fall back to poverty and 'clogs'. **1938** R. G. COLLINGWOOD *Principles of Art* v. But the poor, who are always the last guardians of a tradition, knew that the curse of God rested on idleness, and spoke of three generations from clogs to clogs. **1993** 'C. AIRD' *Going Concern* (1994) vii. 51 Claude Miller, Chairman and Managing Director of Chernwoods' Dyestuffs, was a living exemplification of the old saw about it being 'only three generations from clogs to clogs.' His father hadn't been the man his father was and, worse still, Claude Miller wasn't even the man his father had been. ■ **family; proverty**

close *see* when ONE door shuts, another opens.

cloth *see* CUT your coat according to your cloth.

CLOTHES make the man

Cf. Gk. εἵματα ἀνήρ, the man is his clothing; ERASMUS *Adages 'Divitiae' vestis virum facit.*

□ *a* **1400** *Prov. Wisdom* l. 59 in *Archiv* (1893) XC. 245 Euer maner and clothyng makyth man. *c* **1445** *Peter Idley's Instructions to his Son* (1935) I. 82 Ffor clothyng oft maketh man. **1591** J. FLORIO *Second Fruits* 115 Though manners makes, yet apparell shapes. **1617** R. GREENE *Alcida* B3 The Hood makes not the Monke, nor the apparrell the man. **1836** CARLYLE *Sartor* I. v. Clothes gave us individuality, distinctions, social polity. Clothes have made men of us. **1933** J. HILTON *Lost Horizon* 3 Still, it *did* happen—and it goes some way to show that clothes make the man, doesn't it? **2001** *Washington Post* 17 Dec. C12 Gem of the day (credit Mark Twain): Clothes make the man. Naked people have little or no influence on society. ■ **appearance, significant; dress**

clothes *see* there is no such thing as BAD weather, only the wrong clothes.

Every CLOUD has a silver lining

A poetic sentiment that even the gloomiest outlook contains some hopeful or consoling aspect. Cf. **1634** MILTON *Comus* I. 93 Was I deceiv'd, or did a sable cloud Turn forth her silver lining on the night?

□ **1863** D. R. LOCKE *Struggles of P. V. Nasby* (1872) xxiii. Ther is a silver linin to evry cloud. **1869** P. T. BARNUM *Struggles & Triumphs* 406 'Every cloud', says the proverb, 'has a silver lining.' **1991** T. MO *Redundancy of Courage* xxii. 283 This misfortune of hers had done wonders for our up and down relationship—all clouds have a silver lining, don't they say. **2002** *Spectator* 13 Apr. 74 Still, every cloud has a silver lining, and he was quiet for the rest of the meal, which is something of a delightful first. ■ **optimism**

clout *see* ne'er CAST a clout till May be out.

clutch *see* a DROWNING man will clutch at a straw.

coat *see* CUT your coat according to your cloth.

Let the COBBLER stick to his last

Attributed to the Greek painter Apelles (4th cent. BC): see quot. 1721. The 'shoemaker' variant is a long-standing one in British proverb lore, but is now mainly North American. A *last* is a wooden or metal model on which a shoemaker fashions shoes or boots. Cf. PLINY *Natural History* XXXV. 85 *ne supra crepidam sutor iudicaret*, the cobbler should not judge beyond his shoe; ERASMUS *Adages* I. vi. 16 *ne sutor ultra crepidam*.

□ **1539** R. TAVERNER tr. *Erasmus' Adages* 17 Let not the shoemaker go beyond hys shoe. **1616** J. WITHALS *Dict.* (rev. ed.) 567 Cobler keepe your last. **1639** J. CLARKE *Parœmiologia Anglo-Latina* 21 Cobler keepe to your last. **1721** J. KELLY *Scottish Proverbs* 242 Let not the Cobler go beyond his last. ..Taken from the famous Story of Apelles, who could not bear that the Cobler should correct any part of his Picture beyond the Slipper. **1868** W. CLIFT *Tim Bunker Papers* lix. I understood the use of a plow.. better than the use of a pen.. remembering the old saw 'Let the cobbler stick to his last.' **1930** C. F. GREGG *Murder on Bus* xxx. Yet even then, Mapell had been mixed up with a gang of blackmailers. The shoemaker sticks to his last! **1984** A. MACLEAN *San Andreas* viii. Point taken, Mr. McKinnon. You see before you a rueful cobbler who will stick to his last from now on. ■ **work**

The COBBLER to his last and the gunner to his linstock

A fanciful variant of the preceding proverb. A *linstock* is a staff with a forked head to hold a lighted match.

□ **1748** SMOLLETT *Roderick Random* II. xlii. I meddle with no body's affairs but my own; The gunner to his linstock, and the steersman to the helm, as the saying is. **1893** H. MAXWELL *Life of W. H. Smith* II. v. He.. never showed any disposition to trespass on the province of science or literature. ..There is sound sense in the adage, 'The cobbler to his last and the gunner to his linstock.' ■ **work**

cobbler *see also* the SHOEMAKER's son always goes barefoot.

Every COCK will crow upon his own dunghill

Everyone is confident or at ease when on home ground. Cf. SENECA *Apocolocyntosis* vii. *gallum in suo sterquilinio plurimum posse*, the cock is most powerful on his own dunghill; the work is a satire on Claudius' deification at death, and Seneca is punning on Claudius' provincial origin and interests, as *gallus* means both a cock and a Gaul.

□ *a* **1250** *Ancrene Wisse* (1952) 62 Coc is kene [bold] on his owune mixerne [midden]. **1387** J. TREVISA tr. *Higden's Polychronicon* (1879) VIII. 5 As Seneca seith, a cok is most myghty on his dongehille. **1546** J. HEYWOOD *Dialogue of Proverbs* I. xi. D2 He was at home there, he myght speake his will. Euery cocke is proude on his owne dunghill. **1771** SMOLLETT *Humphry Clinker* II. 178 Insolence.. akin to the arrogance of the village cock, who never crows but upon his own dunghill. **1935** D. L. SAYERS *Gaudy Night* xix. 'I believe you're showing off.'.. 'Every cock will crow upon his own dunghill.' **1980** M. GILBERT *Death of Favourite Girl* vii. Mariner seemed to be easy enough. A cock on his own dunghill. ■ **home**

cock *see also* there's many a GOOD cock come out of a tattered bag; the ROBIN and the wren are God's cock and hen.

COLD hands, warm heart

□ **1903** V. S. LEAN *Collectanea* III. 380 A cold hand and a warm heart. **1910** W. G. COLLINGWOOD *Dutch Agnes* 206 I did take her hand. .. Cold hand, warm heart! **1927** J. M. BARRIE *Shall We join Ladies in Plays* (1928) 840 I knew you would be on my side. .. Cold hand—warm heart. That is the saying, isn't it? **1962** E. LININGTON *Knave of Hearts* xv. A hot, humid night, but her hands cold. Cold hands, warm heart. **1985** D. & S. ROSEN *Death & Blintzes* xxvi. 'Belle, your hands are cold,' he said.

'Cold hands, that's funny?' 'You know the old saying, "cold hands, warm heart".' ■ **love**

cold *see also* (noun) as the DAY lengthens, so the cold strengthens; FEED a cold and starve a fever; (adjective) REVENGE is a dish that can be eaten cold.

colour *see* a GOOD horse cannot be of a bad colour.

come *see* ALL things come to those who wait; the BIGGER they are, the harder they fall; don't CROSS the bridge till you come to it; EASY come, easy go; never do EVIL that good may come of it; FIRST come, first served; what GOES around comes around; all is GRIST that comes to the mill; LIGHT come, light go; come LIVE with me and you'll know me; MARCH comes in like a lion, and goes out like a lamb; if the MOUNTAIN will not come to Mahomet, Mahomet must go to the mountain; when POVERTY comes in at the door, love flies out of the window; QUICKLY come, quickly go; when THIEVES fall out, honest men come by their own; TOMORROW never comes.

comfort *see* CHILDREN are certain cares, but uncertain comforts.

COMING events cast their shadows before

□ **1803** T. CAMPBELL *Poetical Works* (1907) 159 'Tis the sunset of life gives me mystical love, And coming events cast their shadows before. **1857** TROLLOPE *Barchester Towers* II. v. The coming event of Mr. Quiverful's transference to Barchester produced a delicious shadow in the shape of a new outfit for Mrs. Quiverful. **1979** D. LESSING *Shikasta* 231 'Coming events cast their shadows before.' This Shikastan [Earthly] observation was of particular appropriateness during an epoch when the tempo of events was so speeded up. ■ **future**

command *see* he that cannot OBEY cannot command.

COMMON fame is seldom to blame

Cf. **1597** H. LOK *Sundry Christian Passions* 149 Though prouerbe truely say, by fames affect, Gods iudgement lightly doth a truth detect.

□ **1639** J. CLARKE *Parœmiologia Anglo-Latina* 227 Common fame's seldome to blame. **1721** J. KELLY *Scottish Proverbs* 80 *Common Fame sindle* [seldom] *to blame*. A man will seldom be under an universal ill Report, unless he has given some occasion for it. **1853** R. C. TRENCH *Lessons in Proverbs* 13 Common fame is seldom to blame. **1936** R. A. J. WALLING *Corpse in Crimson Slippers* i. But though, as the proverb says, common fame is seldom to blame, don't believe everything you hear about me. ■ **public opinion**

communication *see* EVIL communications corrupt good manners.

A man is known by the COMPANY he keeps

Originally used as a moral maxim or exhortation in the context of (preparation for) marriage.

□ **1541** M. COVERDALE tr. *H. Bullinger's Christian State of Matrimony* F6 So maye much be spyed also, by the company and pastyme that a body vseth. For a man is for the moost parte condicioned euen lyke vnto them that he kepeth company wythe all. **1591** H. SMITH *Preparative to Marriage* 42 If a man can be known by nothing els, then he maye bee known by his companions. **1672** W. WYCHERLEY *Love in Wood* I. i. There is a Proverb, Mrs. Joyner, You may know him by his Company. **1912** 'SAKI' *Chronicles of Clovis* 286 (*heading*) A man is known by the company he keeps. **1976** L. ALTHER *Kinflicks* ii. People knew a man by the company he kept, but they generally knew a woman by the man who kept her. **2002** *Washington Times* 5 Feb. A19 Planned Parenthood denies that [Margaret] Sanger was a racist or an eugenicist, but there's truth to the adage that we are known by the company we keep. ■ **associates**

The COMPANY makes the feast

□ **1653** I. WALTON *Compleat Angler* iii. Take this for a rule, you may pick out such times and such companies, that you may make yourselves merrier, .. for 'tis the company and not the charge [expense] that makes the feast. **1911** F. W. HACKWOOD *Good Cheer* xxxii. Epicurus maintained that you should rather have regard to the company with whom you eat .. than to what you eat. .. This has been crystallised into the terse English proverb, 'The company makes the feast.' **1981** 'J. STURROCK' *Suicide most Foul* vi. It is the company which makes the occasion, not the surroundings. ■ **friends; hospitality**

company *see also* MISERY loves company; TWO is company, but three is none.

COMPARISONS are odious

Cf. early 14th-cent. Fr. *comparaisons sont hay̆neuses*, comparisons are hateful.

□ *c* **1440** J. LYDGATE *Minor Poems* (EETS) 561 Odious of old been all comparisouns. **1456** *Gilbert of Hay's Prose MS* (STS) 282 I will nocht here mak questioun .. quhy [why] that alwayis comparisoun is odious. *c* **1573** G. HARVEY *Letter-Book* (1884) 7 But thai wil sai, Comparisons ar odius: in deed, as it fals out, thai ar too odious. **1724** SWIFT *Drapier's Letters* X. 82 A Judge .. checked the Prisoner .. taxing him with 'reflecting on the court by such a Comparison, because Comparisons were odious'. **1939** G. MITCHELL *Printer's Error* ii. 'I will study the psychology of pigs instead of that of .. refugees.' 'Comparisons are odious,' observed Carey. **2001** P. J. O'ROURKE *CEO of Sofa* v. 82 And poets? Comparisons being odious, only a comparison will do to illustrate the odium of modern poesy. ■ **similarity and dissimilarity**

He that COMPLIES against his will is of his own opinion still

□ **1678** S. BUTLER *Hudibras* III. iii. He that complies against his Will, Is of his own Opinion still; Which he may adhere to, yet disown, For Reasons to himself best known. **1965** M. SPARK *Mandelbaum Gate* v. No one should submit their mind to another mind: He that complies against his will Is of his own opinion still—that's *my* motto. I won't be brainwashed. **1985** G. V. HIGGINS *Penance for Jerry Kennedy* xiii. But Ed Maguire did what he did against his own convictions. And what they say is true .. 'A man convinced against his will is of the same opinion still.' ■ **free will and compulsion**

CONFESS and be hanged

□ **1589** 'MISOPHONUS' *De Caede Gallorum Regis* A2^{V} Confesse and be hangede man In English some saie. **1604** SHAKESPEARE *Othello* IV. i. 37 Handkerchief—confessions—handkerchief! To confess, and be hanged for his labour. **1672** MARVELL *Rehearsal Transprosed* 74 After so ample a Confession as he hath made, must he now be hang'd too to make good the Proverb? **1821** SCOTT *Pirate* III. xii. At the gallows! .. Confess and be hanged is a most reverend proverb. **1951** M. C. BARNES *With all my Heart* vii. 'People who commit high treason get hanged.' .. 'Very well, confess and be hanged!' ■ **confession**

confessed *see* a FAULT confessed is half redressed.

CONFESSION is good for the soul

□ *c* **1641** in E. Beveridge *D. Fergusson's Scottish Proverbs* (1924) no. 159 Ane open confessione is good for the soul. **1721** J. KELLY *Scottish Proverbs* 270 Open Confession is good for the Soul. Spoken ironically, to them that boast of their ill Deeds. **1881** J. PAYN *Grape from Thorn* III. xxxix. Confession may be good for the soul; but it is doubtful whether the avowal of incapacity to the parties desirous of securing our services is quite judicious. **1942** R. A. J. WALLING *Corpse with Eerie Eye* v. That's open confession, but I don't know that it does my soul any good. **1983** R. HILL *Deadheads* IV. iv. Confession may be good for the soul but it's pretty lousy for marriages. **2002** *Washington Times* 1 Sept. D7 Confession may be good for the soul but not if it's being broadcast. ■ **confession**

A clean CONSCIENCE is a good pillow

There are a number of traditional ways of expressing the notion that a clear conscience enables its possessor to sleep soundly, even, as a well-attested variant claims, through a thunderstorm—as in *c* **1605** SHAKESPEARE *Macbeth* IV. i. 85 I may tell pale-hearted fear it lies, And sleep in spite of thunder. Cf. Ger. *Gut Gewissen ist ein sanftes Ruhekissen*; Fr. *Une conscience pure est un bon oreiller.*

□ **1721** J. KELLY *Scottish Proverbs* 14 A safe Conscience makes a sound Sleep. **1747** B. FRANKLIN *Poor Richard's Almanack* (July) A quiet conscience sleeps in thunder. **1902** F. E. HULME *Proverb Lore* 216 A good conscience makes an easy couch. **1929** 'P. OLDFELD' *Alchemy Murder* ii. 18 [The bed] was hard and cold, and he found poor comfort in a copybook maxim which came back vaguely to him—something about a good conscience providing the softest pillow for a weary head. **1992** MIEDER *Dict. American Proverbs* 112 A clean conscience is a good pillow. ■ **conscience**

CONSCIENCE makes cowards of us all

Quot. 1912 is a humorous perversion of the proverb. Cf. **1594** SHAKESPEARE *Richard III* I. iv. 133 Where's thy conscience now?—I'll not meddle with it—it makes a man a coward.

□ **1600–1** SHAKESPEARE *Hamlet* III. i. 83 Conscience does make cowards of us all. **1697** VANBRUGH *Provoked Wife* v. 75 It mayn't be amiss to deferr the Marriage till you are sure they [mortgages] are paid off. ..Guilty Consciences make Men Cowards. **1912** 'SAKI' *Chronicles of Clovis* 134 The English have a proverb, 'Conscience makes cowboys of us all.' **1941** H. G. WELLS *You can't be too Careful* viii. 'Why doesn't he face it out?'.. 'Conscience makes cowards of us all, Whittaker.' **1976** J. S. SCOTT *Poor Old Lady's Dead* iv. There was something funny here. Bloody funny. So the inspector, who lived, like any other policeman, with the sure knowledge that conscience doth make cowards of us all, began to lean. ■ **conscience; cowardice**

conscience *see also* a GUILTY conscience needs no accuser.

consent *see* SILENCE means consent.

CONSTANT dropping wears away a stone

Primarily used to mean that persistence will achieve a difficult or unlikely objective (but see also quots. 1874 and 1912). *Continual* frequently occurs instead of *constant* in the US. Cf. CHOERILUS OF SAMOS *Fragments* x. (Kinkel) *πέτρην κοιλαίνει ῥανὶς ὕδατος ἐνδελεχείῃ*, with persistence a drop of water hollows out the stone; TIBULLUS *Elegies* I. iv. 18 *longa dies molli saxa peredit aqua*, length of time eats away stones with soft water.

□ *a* **1250** *Ancrene Wisse* (1962) 114 Lutle dropen thurleth (pierce) the flint the (that) ofte falleth theron. *c* **1477** CAXTON *Jason* (EETS) 26 The stone is myned and holowed by contynuell droppyng of water. **1591** SHAKESPEARE *Henry VI, Pt. 3* III. ii. 50 He plies her hard; and much rain wears the marble. **1793** T. COKE *Extracts from Journals* III. ii. The Negroes of Barbadoes.. are much less prepared for the reception of genuine religion. But constant dropping, 'tis said, will wear out a stone. **1841** DICKENS *Old Curiosity Shop* I. vii. As to Nell, constant dropping will wear away a stone, you know you may trust me as far as she is concerned. **1874** G. J. WHYTE-MELVILLE *Uncle John* I. vi. Constant dropping wears away a stone; constant flirtation saps the character. **1912** D. H. LAWRENCE *Letter* 19 Dec. (1962) I. 169 She says a woman can only have one husband. .. Constant dropping will wear away a stone, as my mother used to say. **1963** E. S. GARDNER *Case of Mischievous Doll* vii. The constant dripping water.. can wear away the toughest stone. ■ **persistence**

contempt *see* FAMILIARITY breeds contempt.

continual *see* CONSTANT dropping wears away a stone.

contrary *see* DREAMS go by contraries.

cook *see* GOD sends meat, but the Devil sends cooks; TOO many cooks spoil the broth.

corn *see* a KING's chaff is worth more than other men's corn.

CORPORATIONS have neither bodies to be punished nor souls to be damned

A large organization, unlike a private individual, can act unjustly or highhandedly without fear of being brought to account.

□ **1658** E. BULSTRODE *Reports* II. 233 The opinion of Manwood, chief Baron [*c* 1580], was this, as touching Corporations, that they were invisible, immortall, and that they had no soule; and therefore no Subpœna lieth against them, because they have no Conscience nor soule. *c* **1820** J. POYNDER *Literary Extracts* (1844) I. 268 Lord Chancellor Thurlow said [*c* 1775] that the corporations have neither bodies to be punished nor souls to be damned. *a* **1845** S. SMITH in S. Holland *Memoir* (1855) I. xi. Why, you never expected justice from a company, did you? They have neither a soul to lose, nor a body to kick. **1932** ERNST & LINDEY *Hold your Tongue* xii. A corporation is just like any natural person, except that it has no pants to kick or soul to damn, and, by God, it ought to have both. ■ **business**; **conscience**

corrupt *see* EVIL communications corrupt good manners; POWER corrupts.

cost *see* CIVILITY costs nothing.

cough *see* LOVE and a cough cannot be hid.

COUNCILS of war never fight

People discussing matters in a group never reach the decision to fight, which an individual would make.

□ **1863** H. W. HALLECK *Telegram* 13 July (1877) III. 148 Act upon your own judgment and make your Generals execute your orders. Call no counsel [*sic*] of war. It is proverbial that counsels of war never fight. **1891** A. FORBES *Barracks, Bivouacs & Battles* 191 Solomon's adage that in the multitude of counsellors there is wisdom does not apply to war. 'Councils of war never fight' has passed into a proverb. ■ **action and inaction**; **decision and indecision**; **warfare**

counsel *see* a FOOL may give a wise man counsel; NIGHT brings counsel.

Don't COUNT your chickens before they are hatched

An instruction not to make, or act upon, an assumption (usually favourable) which might turn out to be wrong. The metaphorical phrase *to count one's chickens* is also used.

□ *c* **1570** T. HOWELL *New Sonnets* C2 Counte not thy Chickens that vnhatched be. **1579** S. GOSSON *Ephemerides of Phialo* 19 I woulde not haue him to counte his Chickens so soone before they be hatcht, nor tryumphe so long before the victorie. **1664** S. BUTLER *Hudibras* II. iii. To swallow Gudgeons ere th'are catch'd, And count their Chickens ere th'are hatch'd. **1829** SCOTT *Journal* 20 May (1946) 69 I see a fund.. capable of extinguishing the debt.. in ten years or earlier. ..But we must not reckon our chickens before they are hatchd. **1906** in Lady D. Nevill *Reminiscences* xxii. A victory may be snatched, But never count your little chicks, Before they're safely hatched. **1935** 'R. HULL' *Keep it Quiet* xxiv. To Cardonnel, he wrote his congratulations, adding that as to convicting the thief, he feared that they were far from proof, and ought not to count their chickens. **1964** RIDOUT & WITTING *English Proverbs Explained* 42 Mr. Smith hoped to be made manager before the end of the year. ..'Don't count your chickens before they are hatched,' warned his wife. **2002** *New Scientist* 5 Jan. 17 Ultimately it's a question of how much oil is down there, and how quickly it can be extracted. No one really knows, but the geological evidence suggests that the US might be counting its chickens before they're hatched. ■ **optimism**

In the COUNTRY of the blind, the one-eyed man is king

'A little wit, among foolish people, will pass a man for a great genius' (T. Fielding *Proverbs of all Nations* (1824) 23); also used of ability as well as wit. Cf. ERASMUS *Adages* III. iv. *in regione caecorum rex est luscus*, in the kingdom of the blind the one-eyed man is king.

□ **1522** J. SKELTON *Works* (1843) II. 43 An one eyed man is Well syghted when He is amonge blynde men. **1640** G. HERBERT *Outlandish Proverbs* no. 469 In the kingdome of blind men the one ey'd is king. **1830** J. L. BURCKHARDT *Arabic Proverbs* 34 The one-eyed person is a beauty in the country of the blind. **1904** H. G. WELLS in *Strand* Apr. 405 Through his thoughts ran this old proverb.. 'In the Country of the Blind, the One-Eyed Man is king.' **1937** W. H. SAUMAREZ SMITH *Letter* 7 Mar. in *Young Man's Country* (1977) ii. You exaggerate the alleged compliment paid to me by the Bengal Govt. in wanting to retain my services. 'In the country of the blind the one-eyed man is king.' **2002** B. MONAHAN *Sceptred Isle Club* i. 9 His success with crime-solving suggested an extraordinary intelligence, but he could never know from his limited vantage point in provincial Brunswick whether he was merely the one-eyed man in the land of the blind and the Jekyl Island Club solution a fluke. ■ **ignorance; rulers and ruled**

Happy is the COUNTRY which has no history

Carlyle (see quot. 1864) attributed this observation to the French political philosopher Montesquieu (1689–1755). Cf. **1740** B. FRANKLIN *Poor Richard's Almanack* (Feb.) Happy that Nation,—fortunate that age, whose history is not diverting.

□ **1807** T. JEFFERSON *Letter* 29 Mar. in *Writings* (1904) XI. 182 Blest is that nation whose silent course of happiness furnishes nothing for history to say. **1860** G. ELIOT *Mill on Floss* VI. iii. The happiest women, like the happiest nations, have no history. **1864** CARLYLE *Frederick the Great* IV. XVI. i. Happy the people whose annals are blank in history. **1957** V. BRITTAIN *Testament of Experience* I. iv. Quoting the familiar dictum: 'Happy is the country which has no history,' I remarked that I belonged, like Edward VIII, to a generation which was still on the early side of middle age but had already seen almost more history than any generation could bear. **1981** *Nature* 23 Apr. 698 An old proverb.. tells us that 'happy is the nation that has no history.'.. DNA.. is the unhappiest of molecules, for it is the subject of innumerable biographies. ■ **blessings; past**

country *see also* you can take the BOY out of the country but you can't take the country out of the boy; GOD made the country, and man made the town; OTHER times, other manners; a PROPHET is not without honour save in his own country.

couple *see* a DEAF husband and a blind wife are always a happy couple.

The COURSE of true love never did run smooth

□ **1595** SHAKESPEARE *Midsummer Night's Dream* I. i. 134 For aught that I could ever read.. The course of true love never did run smooth. **1836** M. SCOTT *Cruise of Midge* I. xi. 'The course of true love never did run smooth.' And the loves of Saunders Skelp and Jessy Miller were no exception to the rule. **1980** *Tablet* 26 Jan. 89 The course of true love could never run smooth with Sybylla's temperament. ■ **love, blighted**

course *see also* HORSES for courses.

court *see* HOME is home, as the Devil said when he found himself in the Court of Session.

cover *see* (noun) you can't tell a BOOK by its cover; (verb) CHARITY covers a multitude of sins.

coverlet *see* everyone STRETCHES his legs according to the length of his coverlet.

Why buy a COW when milk is so cheap?

An argument for choosing the least troublesome alternative; frequently used as an argument against marriage. One of the few proverbs in the form of a rhetorical question; cf. *why* KEEP *a dog, and bark yourself?*

□ **1659** J. HOWELL *Proverbs* p. ii. It is better to buy a quart of Milk by the penny then keep a Cow. **1680** BUNYAN *Mr. Badman* 293 Who would keep a Cow of their own, that can have a quart of milk for a penny? Meaning, Who would be at the charge to have a Wife, that can have a Whore when he listeth (wishes)? **1895** S. BUTLER *Note-Books* (1926) xvii. It was cheaper to buy the milk than to keep a cow. **1942** S. ACRE *Yellow Overcoat* v. 'He ain't marryin'.. any more!.. 'Why buy a cow when milk is so cheap, eh?' **1984** W. TEVIS *Color of Money* vi. 'I don't have a wife.' 'That's the best way. Why buy a cow when you can get milk free?' **2000** E. GUNN *Five Card Stud* iii. 36 She said she thought people who wanted to live together 'ought to get married and be done with it.' 'I don't want to be done with it,' Trudy said. 'I want it to go on and on.' 'Fat chance of that. Men don't buy the cow if they can get the milk for—' ■ **marriage**

cow *see also* a BELLOWING cow soon forgets her calf; BETTER a good cow than a cow of a good kind; it is idle to SWALLOW the cow and choke on the tail; THREE things are not to be trusted.

coward *see* a BULLY is always a coward; CONSCIENCE makes cowards of us all.

COWARDS die many times before their death

The popular form is a misquotation of Shakespeare (see quot. 1599) Cf. **1596** DRAYTON *Mortimeriados* S1 Every houre he dyes, which ever feares.

□ **1599** SHAKESPEARE *Julius Caesar* II. ii. 32 Cowards die many times before their deaths: The valiant never taste of death but once. **1800** M. EDGEWORTH *Castle Rackrent* p. xliv. In Ireland, not only cowards, but the brave 'die many times before their death.' **1927** *Sphere* 3 Dec. 414 It is true that cowards die many times before their death, and Noel Coward will come back again and again, and.. win his niche among the great dramatists. ■ **cowardice**

The COWL does not make the monk

Appearance is no reliable guide to a person's true character. Cf. medieval L. *cucullus non facit monachum*, the cowl does not make the monk; *a* **1250** *Ancrene Wisse* (1962) 10 Her in is religiun, nawt i the wide hod ne i the blake cape.

□ **1387** T. USK *Testament of Love* in Chaucer *Complete Works* (1897) II. xi. For habit maketh no monk; ne weringe of gilte spurres maketh no knight. **1588** R. GREENE *Pandosto* IV. 289 Trueth quoth Fawnia, but all that weare Cooles [cowls] are not Monkes. **1613** SHAKESPEARE *Henry VIII* III. i. 23 They should be good men, their affairs as righteous; But all hoods make not monks. **1820** SCOTT *Abbot* II. xi. 'Call me not doctor.. since I have laid aside my furred gown and bonnet.'.. 'O, sir.. the cowl makes not the monk.' **1891** G. B. SHAW *Music in London* (1932) I. 217 Such impostures are sure of support from the sort of people.. who think that it is the cowl that makes the monk. ■ **appearance, deceptive**

cradle *see* the HAND that rocks the cradle rules the world.

A CREAKING door hangs longest

Usually said consolingly about, by, or to the infirm, though sometimes implying that a weak or faulty thing continues to be a nuisance the longest. *Gate* sometimes replaces *door*.

□ **1776** T. COGAN *John Buncle, Junior* I. vi. They say a creaking gate goes the longest upon its hinges; that's my comfort. **1888** F. HUME *Madame Midas* II. ii. It is said that 'creaking doors hang the longest'. Mrs. Pulchop.. was an excellent illustration of the truth of this saying. **1944** A. CHRISTIE *Towards Zero* 62 But it seems I am one of these creaking gates—these perpetual invalids who never die. **1970** L. DEIGHTON *Bomber* vi. The Flight Engineer said, 'A creaking door hangs longest.' Digby christened her [an aeroplane] 'Creaking Door'. **1985** J. MORTIMER *Paradise Postponed* viii. I'll probably last like this another thirty years. I'll be a creaking gate.. and they goes on swinging forever. ■ **mortality; old age**

cream *see* there are more WAYS of killing a cat than choking it with cream.

Give CREDIT where credit is due

The older form with *honour* (principally in the sense 'obeisance, homage') is now rare. Cf. ROMANS xiii. 7 (Reims) Render therefore to all men their due:.. to whom honour, honour.

□ **1777** S. ADAMS *Letter* 29 Oct. in *Collections of Massachusetts Hist. Society* (1917) LXXII. 375 May Honor be given to whom Honor may be due. **1834** M. FLOY *Diary* 17 Jan. (1941) 50 Loudon must be a man of taste.. and disposed to give all credit where any credit is due. **1894** *Girl's Own Paper* 6 Jan. 228 The justice and magnanimity which would show 'honour to whom honour is due'.. is not always found equal to the occasion when it involves the granting of a degree. **1968** M. WOODHOUSE *Rock Baby* xxii. You aren't half as daft as I thought. .. Credit where credit's due. **1976**

T. SHARPE *Wilt* viii. 'Some maniac. ..' 'Come now, give credit where credit is due,' interrupted Dr. Board. **2002** *Washington Post* 1 Jan. C14 Express your gratitude. Give credit when it's due—and even when it isn't. ■ **fair dealing; just deserts**

CRIME doesn't pay

A US slogan particularly associated with the radio crime series *The Shadow*, in which it was spoken by The Shadow at the end of each broadcast (see quot. 1937), and with the cartoon detective Dick Tracy (see quot. 1954).

□ **1892** *Catholic World* Dec. 364 Until our laws are so made and executed as to prove that crime doesn't pay.. then only will religion and common-sense.. work out the great plan of creation. **1905** *Harper's Weekly* 18 Feb. 231/2 If only Christopher had stuck to Sherlock Holmes it would have been impressed upon him that crime doesn't pay, and that the cleverest criminal gets caught. **1937** E. H. BIERSTADT *Shadow: Death House Rescue* 26 Sept. (*script of radio broadcast*) 18 The weed of crime bears bitter fruit. ..Crime does not pay. ..The Shadow knows. ..(Laugh). **1954** S. BECKER *Comic Art in America* 5 Dick Tracy is the daddy of all cops-and-robbers strips, and Chester Gould.. has been announcing to the world since 1931 that crime does not pay. **1959** *Times Literary Supplement* 12 June 356 War, like crime, may not pay, but that does not make the problem of preventing it any easier. **2001** *Country Life* 20/27 Dec 85 We hear of..David Steele's meanness (he was known as 'Crime' because he never bought a drink - 'Crime doesn't pay'). ■ **action and consequence**

crime *see also* POVERTY is not a crime.

crop *see* good SEED makes a good crop.

Don't CROSS the bridge till you come to it

Do not concern yourself with difficulties until they arise. Now also common as the metaphorical phrase *to cross one's bridges when one comes to them*.

□ **1850** LONGFELLOW *Journal* 29 Apr. in *Life* (1886) II. 165 Remember the proverb, 'Do not cross the bridge till you come to it.' **1895** S. O. ADDY *Household Tales* xiv. One who anticipates difficulty is told not to cross the bridge till he gets to it. **1927** 'J. TAINE' *Quayle's Invention* xv. Why cross our bridges before we come to them? **1967** T. STOPPARD *Rosencrantz & Guildenstern are Dead* II. 43 We cross our bridges when we come to them and burn our bridges behind us, with nothing to show for our progress except a memory of the smell of smoke, and a presumption that once our eyes watered. ■ **trouble**

cross (noun) *see* NO cross, no crown.

CROSSES are ladders that lead to heaven

There are two strands to the proverb, punning on two meanings of *cross*: in one, *cross* signifies the crucifix; in the other, it means 'trouble, misfortune'.

□ **1616** T. DRAXE *Adages* 36 The Crosse is the ladder of heauen. **1670** J. RAY *English Proverbs* 6 Crosses are ladders that do lead to heaven. **1859** S. SMILES *Self-Help* xi. If there be real worth in the character.. it will give forth its finest fragrance when pressed. 'Crosses' says the old proverb, 'are ladders that lead to heaven.' **1975** J. O'FAOLAIN *Women in Wall* iv. The cross, they say, is the ladder to heaven and so I have sent your lordship.. two. ■ **misfortune**

crow *see* (noun) on the FIRST of March, the crows begin to search; HAWKS will not pick out hawks' eyes; ONE for the mouse, one for the crow; (verb) every COCK will crow upon his own dunghill; *also* CROWING.

crowd *see* TWO is company, but three is none.

crowing *see* a WHISTLING woman and a crowing hen are neither fit for God nor men.

crown *see* (verb) the END crowns the work; (noun) NO cross, no crown.

Don't CRY before you're hurt

Cf. early 14th-cent. Fr. *follie fait plorer deuant que on soit batu.*

□ **1548** *Reliquiæ Antiquæ* (1843) II. 16 Ye may the better understand that I cry not before I am pricked. **1678** J. RAY *English Proverbs* (ed. 2) 237 You cry before you're hurt. **1721** J. KELLY *Scottish Proverbs* 204 It is time enough to cry, Oh, when you are hurt. Spoken to dissuade People from groundless Fears. **1930** N. B. MAVITY *Other Bullet* xxviii. Don't cry out before you're hurt. **1981** J. WRIGHT *Devil's Parole* xvi. You mean.. that one shouldn't cry before one is hurt. ■ **cowardice; expectation**

cry *see also* MUCH cry and little wool; SING before breakfast, cry before night.

It is no use CRYING over spilt milk

It is pointless to repine when it is too late to remedy the misfortune.

□ **1659** J. HOWELL *Proverbs* (British) 40 No weeping for shed milk. **1738** SWIFT *Polite Conversation* i. 27 'I would cry my Eyes out.'.. ''Tis a Folly to cry for spilt Milk.' **1884** J. PAYN *Canon's Ward* I. xv. There would be a row.. but he would say, like a wise man, 'There's no use in crying over spilt milk.' **1936** M. DE LA ROCHE *Whiteoak Harvest* xxv. It's no use crying over spilt milk. The money's gone.. and that's that. **1995** R. ORMEROD *And Hope to Die* ix. 115 I said this dismissively. No good crying over spilt milk. ■ **misfortune; past**

cup *see* FULL cup, steady hand; the LAST drop makes the cup run over; there's MANY a slip between cup and lip.

He that will to CUPAR maun to Cupar

Cupar is a town in Fife, Scotland.

□ **1721** J. KELLY *Scottish Proverbs* 141 He that will to Cowper [Cupar], will to Cowper. A Reflection upon obstinate Persons, that will not be reclaim'd. **1817** SCOTT *Rob Roy* III. i. The Hecate.. ejaculated, 'A wilfu' man will hae his way—them that will to Cupar maun [must] to Cupar!' **1893** R. L. STEVENSON *Catriona* xiii. He stood part of a second.., hesitating. 'He that will to Cupar, maun to Cupar,' said he, and.. was hauled into the skiff. **1958** J. CANNAN *And be Villain* v. 'I shall take the first plane to Paris.'.. 'Well, he who will to Cupar maun to Cupar, but I think it's very silly of you.' ■ **obstinacy**

cure *see* NO cure, no pay; PREVENTION is better than cure.

What can't be CURED must be endured

Cf. **1377** LANGLAND *Piers Plowman* B. x. 439 When *must* comes forward, there is nothing for it but to *suffer*; *c* **1408** LYDGATE *Reason & Sensuality* (EETS) l. 4757 For thyng that may nat be eschiwed But of force mot be sywed [followed].

□ **1579** SPENSER *Shepherd's Calendar* (Sept.) 88 And cleanly couer, that cannot be cured. Such il, as is forced, mought nedes be endured. **1763** C. CHURCHILL *Prophecy of Famine* 18 Patience is sorrow's salve; what can't be cur'd, so Donald right areeds [counsels], must be endur'd. **1870** C. KINGSLEY *Madam How* i. That stupid resignation which some folks preach.. is merely saying—what can't be cured, must be endured. **1936** W. HOLTBY *South Riding* VI. i. We all have our bad turns. What can't be cured must be endured, you know. **1997** *Washington Post* 18 Dec. C1 'What cannot be cured must be endured,' the chained man says, trying to smile. But it comes out as a grimace. ■ **patience and impatience**

CURIOSITY killed the cat

□ **1921** E. O' NEILL *Diff'rent* II. 252 'What'd you ask 'em, for instance?' .. 'Curiosity killed a cat! Ask me no questions and I'll tell you no lies.' **1973** A. CHRISTIE *Postern of Fate* I. iv. 'A curiosity death,' said Tommy. 'Curiosity killed the cat.' **1984** J. R. RIGGS *Last Laugh* iii. 'I'm curious, that's all.' 'Curiosity killed old tom.' **2002** *Times 2* 17 May 9 'Well, you've probably heard the saying, "curiosity killed the cat". Well that's what I'm doing here.' For one horrible minute, I thought that he was about to .. reveal that he was Ben Vol-au-Vent from Curiosity Killed the Cat, killing a cat. ■ **curiosity**

curried (combed): *see* a SHORT horse is soon curried.

curse (verb) *see* BETTER to light one candle than to curse the darkness.

CURSES, like chickens, come home to roost

Also without specific reference to *curses*, as in quot. 2001.

□ *c* **1390** CHAUCER *Parson's Tale* l. 620 And ofte tyme swich cursynge wrongfully retorneth agayn to hym that curseth, as a bryd that retorneth agayn to his owene nest. **1592** *Arden of Feversham* G4 For curses are like arrowes shot upright, Which falling down light on the suters [shooter's] head. **1810** SOUTHEY *Kehama* (*title-page*) Curses are like young chicken; they always come home to roost. **1880** S. SMILES *Duty* iv. Their injustice will return upon them. Curses, like chickens, come home to roost. **1932** S. GIBBONS *Cold Comfort Farm* vii. Curses, like rookses, flies home to nest in bosomses and barnses. **1986** *Washington Post* 10 July A23 The proverb teaches us that 'curses, like chickens, come home to roost.' The Supreme Court taught that lesson one more time last week in an opinion that combined bad law with rough justice. **2001** *Spectator* 8 Dec. 71 The Brits used diplomatic language which is as useless as the Draft Dodger's oath in a court of law. As they say down on the farm, the chickens have come home to roost. ■ **malice; retribution**

The CUSTOMER is always right

□ **1917** B. PAIN *Confessions of Alphonse* iii. The great success of a restaurant is built up on this principle—*le patron n'a jamais tort*—the customer is always in the right! **1928** C. SANDBURG *Good Morning, America* 17 Behold the proverbs of a nation. .. Let one hand wash the other. The customer is always right. **1941** D. LODGE *Death & Taxes* ii. 'I'm drunk.' .. 'You shouldn't do it, George.' 'Business,' he said solemnly. 'The customer is always right.' **1980** *Times* 30 Sept. 9 That the customer is always right is a theory attributed to John Wanamaker, the American retail prince who founded the stores which bear his name. **2001** *Washington Times* 3 Sept. A12 The old man wasn't much on theory, but he understood value received, good will, repeat business, that the customer is always right and above all the importance of a trusted brand. ■ **buying and selling**

Don't CUT off your nose to spite your face

A warning against spiteful revenge which results in one's own hurt or loss. The metaphorical phrase *to cut off one's nose to spite one's face* is very frequently found. Cf. medieval L. *male ulciscitur dedecus sibi illatum, qui amputat nasum suum*, he who cuts off his nose takes poor revenge for a shame inflicted on him; mid 14th-cent. Fr. *qui cope son nès, sa face est despechie*, the man who cuts off his nose spites his face.

□ *c* **1560** *Deceit of Women* I1 He that byteth hys nose of, shameth hys face. **1788** F. GROSE *Dict. Vulgar Tongue* (ed. 2) U3v He cut off his nose to be revenged of his face, said of one who, to be revenged of his neighbour, has materially injured himself. **1889** R. L. STEVENSON *Master of Ballantrae* x. He was in that humour when a man—in the words of the old adage—will cut off his nose to spite his face. **1964** RIDOUT & WITTING *English Proverbs Explained* 43 Don't cut off your nose to spite your face. **1980** A. CRAIG *Pint of Murder* vi. So the next thing anybody knew she'd run off an' married that no-good Bob Bascom an' if that ain't cuttin' off your nose to spite your face, I'd like to know what is. ■ **malice; revenge**

CUT your coat according to your cloth

Actions should suit circumstances or resources. Also common as the metaphorical phrase *to cut one's coat according to one's cloth.*

□ **1546** J. HEYWOOD *Dialogue of Proverbs* I. viii. C1 I shall Cut my cote after my cloth. **1580** LYLY *Euphues & his England* II. 188 Be neither prodigall to spende all, nor couetous to keepe all, cut thy coat according to thy cloth. **1778** G. WASHINGTON *Writings* (1936) XIII. 79 General McIntoch.. must.. yield to necessity; that is, to use a vulgar phraze, 'shape his Coat according to his Cloth'. **1951** 'P. WENTWORTH' *Miss Silver comes to Stay* xxxvii. 'You must cut your coat according to your cloth.'.. 'My trouble is that I do like the most expensive cloth.' **1974** T. SHARPE *Porterhouse Blue* iii. I'm afraid the.. exigencies of our financial position do impose certain restraints. ..A case of cutting our coats to suit our cloth. ■ **circumstances; poverty; thrift**

cut *see also* (participial adjective) a SLICE off a cut loaf isn't missed; (verb) DIAMOND cuts diamond.

daisy *see* it is not SPRING until you can plant your foot upon twelve daisies.

damned *see* CORPORATIONS have neither bodies to be punished nor souls to be damned.

They that DANCE must pay the fiddler

Cf. *he who* PAYS *the piper calls the tune*, where the emphasis is reversed. *To pay the piper* (*fiddler*, etc.) means 'to bear the cost (of an enterprise)'. The proverb is now predominantly found in US use.

□ **1638** J. TAYLOR *Taylor's Feast* in *Works* (1876) 94 One of the Fidlers said, Gentlemen, I pray you to remember the Musicke [musicians], you have given us nothing yet. ..Alwayes those that dance must pay the Musicke. **1837** A. LINCOLN *Speech* 11 Jan. in *Works* (1953) I. 64 I am decidedly opposed to the people's money being used to pay the fiddler. It is an old maxim and a very sound one, that he that dances should always pay the fiddler. *a* **1957** L. I. WILDER *First Four Years* (1971) i. Laura was going to have a baby. ..She remembered a saying of her mother's: 'They that dance must pay the fiddler.' ■ **action and consequence**

dance *see also* he that LIVES in hope dances to an ill tune.

danger *see* the post of HONOUR is the post of danger; OUT of debt, out of danger.

dangerous *see* DELAYS are dangerous; a LITTLE knowledge is a dangerous thing.

dark *see* all CATS are grey in the dark.

The DARKEST hour is just before the dawn

□ **1650** T. FULLER *Pisgah Sight* II. xi. It is always darkest just before the Day dawneth. **1760** in J. Wesley *Journal* (1913) IV. 498 It is usually darkest before day break. You shall shortly find pardon. **1897** 1897 J. MCCARTHY *Hist. our Own Times* V. iii. Ayoob Khan now laid siege to Candahar. ..As so often happens in the story of England's struggles in India, the darkest hour proved to be that just before the dawn. **2002** *Washington Times* 4 Feb. B5 It is always darkest before the dawn, the old saying goes, and often a declarer reaches a dark point during the early play that precedes his ultimate step toward victory. ■ **hope and despair**

darkness *see* BETTER to light one candle than to curse the darkness.

darling *see* BETTER be an old man's darling, than a young man's slave.

daughter *see* like FATHER, like son; like MOTHER, like daughter; my SON is my son till he gets him a wife, but my daughter's my daughter all the days of her life.

dawn *see* the DARKEST hour is just before the dawn.

As the DAY lengthens, so the cold strengthens

□ **1631** E. PELLHAM *God's Power* 27 The New Year now begun, as the Days began to lengthen, so the Cold began to strengthen. **1639** J. CLARKE *Parœmiologia Anglo-Latina* 18 As the day lengthens so the cold strengthens. **1721** J. KELLY *Scottish*

Proverbs 52 As the Day lengthens the Cold strengthens. It is often found that February and March are much more cold and piercing than December or January. **1899** A. WEST *Recollections* II. xxi. The weather at this time was bearing out the old adage and the cold strengthened as the days lengthened. **1978** R. WHITLOCK *Calendar of Country Customs* iii. As the day lengthens, So the cold strengthens, is still a well-known country proverb, applicable to January and early February. ■ **weather lore**

Be the DAY weary or be the day long, at last it ringeth to evensong

□ **1509** S. HAWES *Pastime of Pleasure* xlii. R8^{v} For thoughe the day, be neuer so longe, At last the belles ryngeth to euensonge. **1612** T. ADAMS *Gallant's Burden* 20 If you could indent with the Sunne to stand still.. yet it shall sette: Be the day never so long, at length comes evensong. **1732** T. FULLER *Gnomologia* no. 6132 Be the day never so long, At length cometh Even-song. **1935** 'J. J. CONNINGTON' *In whose Dim Shadow* xv. ' "Be the day weary or be the day long, At last it ringeth to evensong",' quoted the Chief Constable. **1969** N. HALE *Life in Studio* 120 Be the day short or be the day long, At length it cometh to evensong. ■ **perseverance**

day *see also* ANOTHER day, another dollar; an APPLE a day keeps the doctor away; BARNABY bright, Barnaby bright, the longest day and the shortest night; the BETTER the day, the better the deed; BETTER to live one day as a tiger..; every DOG has his day; FAIR and softly goes far in a day; FISH and guests smell after three days; OTHER times, other manners; ROME was not built in a day; my SON is my son till he gets him a wife, but my daughter's my daughter all the days of her life; SUFFICIENT unto the day is the evil thereof; TOMORROW is another day.

Let the DEAD bury the dead

With allusion to MATTHEW viii. 22 (AV) Jesus said unto him, Follow me; and let the dead bury their dead.

□ **1815** L. DOW *Hist. Cosmopolite* (1859) 340 A religious bigot made a motion to mob me; but none would second it. A worldling replied to him, 'Let the dead bury their dead.' **1931** J. S. HUXLEY *What dare I Think?* vi. Let, then, the dead bury the dead. The task for us is to rejuvenate ourselves and our subject. **1997** *Spectator* 8 Nov. 28 There is something repellent, as well as profoundly unhistorical, about judging the past by the standards or prejudices of another age. Let the dead bury the dead. ■ **death**

DEAD men don't bite

The words put by Plutarch into the mouth of Theodotus, a teacher of rhetoric, advising the Egyptians to murder Pompey when he came seeking refuge in Egypt after his defeat at Pharsalia in 48 BC: PLUTARCH *Pompeius* lxxvii. νεκρὸς οὐ δάκνει, a dead man does not bite. Cf. ERASMUS *Adages* III. vi. *mortui non mordent*, the dead do not bite.

□ *a* **1547** E. HALL *Chronicle* (1548) Hen. VI 92^{v} A prouerbe.. saith, a dead man doth no harme: Sir John Mortimer.. was attainted [convicted] of treason and put to execucion. **1655** T. FULLER *Church Hist. Britain* IX. iv. The dead did not bite; and, being dispatch'd out of the way, are forgotten. **1883** R. L. STEVENSON *Treasure Island* xi. 'What are we to do with 'em anyway?.. Cut 'em down like that much pork?'.. 'Dead men don't bite,' says he. **1902** A. LANG *Hist. Scotland* II. xii. The story that Gray 'whispered in Elizabeth's ear, The dead don't bite', is found in Camden. **1957** L. REVELL *See Rome & Die* xvi. A dead man cannot bite, as it says somewhere in Plutarch. Pompey's murderers, I think. Anyhow, that was the way their minds worked then. ■ **revenge**

DEAD men tell no tales

Cf. **1560** T. BECON *Works* II. 97 He that hath his body loden with meat and drinke is no more mete to prai vnto god then a dead man is to tel a tale.

□ **1664** J. WILSON *Andronicus Comnenius* I. iv. 'Twere best To knock 'um i' th' head. .. The dead can tell no tales. **1702** G. FARQUHAR *Inconstant* v. 76 Ay, ay, Dead Men tell no Tales. **1850** C. KINGSLEY *Alton Locke* I. iv. Where are the stories of those who have .. ended in desperation? .. Dead men tell no tales. **2001** S. KENDRICK *Night Watch* iv. 159 Dead men tell no tales. But their bodies sometimes do. ■ **revenge; speech and silence**

Blessed are the DEAD that the rain rains on

A similar belief is *happy is the* BRIDE *that the sun shines on.*

□ **1607** *Puritan* I. i. If, Blessed bee the coarse [corpse] the raine raynes vpon, he had it, powring downe. **1787** F. GROSE *Provincial Glossary* (Superstitions) 61 It is .. esteemed a good sign if it rains whilst a corpse is burying: .. Happy is the corpse that the rain rains on. **1925** F. S. FITZGERALD *Great Gatsby* 210 I could only remember, without resentment, that Daisy hadn't sent a message or a flower. Dimly I heard someone murmur, 'Blessed are the dead that the rain falls on.' ■ **blessings; death**

dead *see also* the only GOOD Indian is a dead Indian; it's ILL waiting for dead men's shoes; a LIVE dog is better than a dead lion; never SPEAK ill of the dead; STONE-dead hath no fellow; THREE may keep a secret, if two of them are dead.

deadly *see* the FEMALE of the species is more deadly than the male.

There's none so DEAF as those who will not hear

Similar to *there's none so* BLIND *as those who will not see.* Cf. mid 14th-cent. Fr. *il n'est si mavais sours que chuis ch'oër ne voeilt*, there is no person so deaf as the one who does not wish to hear.

□ **1546** J. HEYWOOD *Dialogue of Proverbs* II. ix. K4 Who is so deafe, or so blynde, as is hee, That wilfully will nother here nor see? *c* **1570** T. INGELEND *Disobedient Child* C2^{V} I perceyve by thys geare, That none is so deaf, as who wyll not heare. **1766** in B. Franklin *Papers* (1969) XIII. 18 I have not interfered in this Trial one word, only in my Applications to you and Mr. Foxcraft, both of which turn a deaf Ear: for none so deaf as those who will not hear. **1993** F. SECOMBE 'Hello, Vicar!' in *Chronicles of a Vicar* (1999) i. 8 'Don't worry, Vicar. Of course you've got to be up at the parish church more than here. He ought to know that but there you are, there's none so deaf as him who won't listen.' ■ **obstinacy**

A DEAF husband and a blind wife are always a happy couple

□ **1578** J. FLORIO *First Fruits* 26 There neuer shal be chiding in that house, where the man is blynd, and the wife deafe. **1637** T. HEYWOOD *Pleasant Dialogues* VI. 334 Then marriage may be said to be past in all quietnesse, When the wife is blind, and the husband deafe. **1940** H. W. THOMPSON *Body, Boots & Britches* xix. When the wooing is o'er and the maid wed .. the neighbours will observe .. 'A deaf husband and a blind wife are always a happy couple.' **1988** *Washington Times* 8 July E2 Nothing brings out advice mongers like a summer wedding. .. 'A deaf husband and a blind wife are always a happy couple.' ■ **harmony and disharmony; marriage**

dear *see* EXPERIENCE keeps a dear school; GOLD may be bought too dear.

dear-bought *see* FAR-FETCHED and dear-bought is good for ladies.

dearest *see* BUY in the cheapest market and sell in the dearest.

DEATH is the great leveller

Cf. CLAUDIAN *De Raptu Proserpinae* II. 302 *omnia mors aequat*, death levels all things.

□ **1732** T. FULLER *Gnomologia* no. 1250 Death is the grand leveller. **1755** E. YOUNG *Centaur* ii. Is diversion grown a leveller, like death? **1961** M. DICKENS *Heart of London* I. 101 'All this is going to be a great leveller.'.. 'It is death which is the great leveller.' **1973** 'C. AIRD' *His Burial Too* vi. Dr. Dabbe took a last look. ..'A classic case, you might say, Sloan, of Death, the Great Leveller.' ■ **death**

DEATH pays all debts

Cf. **1597–8** SHAKESPEARE *Henry IV, Pt. 1* III. ii. 157 The end of life cancels all bands [bonds].

□ **1611** SHAKESPEARE *Tempest* III. ii. 126 He that dies pays all debts. **1827** SCOTT *Two Drovers* in *Chronicles of Canongate* I. xiv. 'It must be sorely answered.'.. 'Never you mind that—Death pays all debts; it will pay that too.' **1979** K. BONFIGLIONI *After You* xvi. I have no particular objection to death as such; it pays all bills. **1991** G. KEILLOR *WLT: Radio Romance* xli. I am not responsible anymore. Death pays all debts. Fix the damn furnace yourself. ■ **death**

death *see also* COWARDS die many times before their death; NOTHING is certain but death and taxes; there is a REMEDY for everything except death.

debt *see* DEATH pays all debts; OUT of debt, out of danger; SPEAK not of my debts unless you mean to pay them.

deceive *see* FOOL me once, shame on you..

deceptive *see* APPEARANCES are deceptive.

deed *see* the BETTER the day, the better the deed; no GOOD deed goes unpunished.

deep *see* STILL waters run deep.

defence *see* ATTACK is the best form of defence.

The best DEFENSE is a good offense

The usual US version of ATTACK *is the best form of defence*. Also as *a good offense is the best defense*.

□ **1989** *Washington Times* 13 Sept. C9 The reigning corporate strategy these days is that the best defense is a good offense. **1992** MIEDER *Dict. of American Proverbs* 436 A good offense is the best defense. **2002** *Washington Times* 6 Apr. B2 There is a saying, 'The best defense is a good offense.' Your sister-in-law's behavior was an example of that. ■ **boldness; warfare**

deferred *see* HOPE deferred makes the heart sick.

defiled *see* he that TOUCHES pitch shall be defiled.

delayed *see* JUSTICE delayed is justice denied.

DELAYS are dangerous

Cf. *c* **1300** *Havelok* (1915) l. 1352 Dwelling haueth ofte scathe [harm] wrouht.

□ **1578** LYLY *Euphues* I. 212 Delayes breed daungers, nothing so perillous as procrastination. **1655** J. SHIRLEY *Gentlemen of Venice* v. 62 Shall we go presently [immediately], delaies are dangerous. **1824** J. FAIRFIELD *Letters* (1922) p. xxxi. I have always found on all subjects that 'delays are dangerous'. . . It is expedient that we marry young. **1930** B. FLYNN *Murder en Route* xxxiii. What a pity Master Hector left it too late. . . Delays are proverbially dangerous. ■ **action and inaction; procrastination**

delved *see* when ADAM delved and Eve span, who was then the gentleman?

denied *see* JUSTICE delayed is justice denied.

Derbyshire *see* YORKSHIRE born and Yorkshire bred, strong in the arm and weak in the head.

deserve *see* none but the BRAVE deserve the fair; a CIVIL question deserves a civil answer; one GOOD turn deserves another.

DESPERATE diseases must have desperate remedies

The proverb is found in many variant forms. Cf. L. *extremis malis extrema remedia*, extreme remedies for extreme ills.

□ **1539** R. TAVERNER tr. *Erasmus' Adages* 4 A stronge disease requyreth a stronge medicine. **1600–1** SHAKESPEARE *Hamlet* IV. iii. 9 Diseases desperate grown By desperate appliance are reliev'd, Or not at all. **1639** J. CLARKE *Parœmiologia Anglo-Latina* 200 Desperate cuts must have desperate cures. **1659** J. RUSHWORTH *Hist. Collections* I. 120 According to the usual Proverb, A desperate disease must have a desperate remedy. **1748** RICHARDSON *Clarissa* VI. 292 I must . . have an interview with the charmer of my Soul: For desperate diseases must have desperate remedies. **1935** 'A. WYNNE' *Toll House Murder* ix. These circumstances are wholly exceptional. Desperate diseases, they say, call for desperate remedies. **1961** 'A. GILBERT' *She shall Die* xi. She'd have sold the roof over her head sooner than have you know. Desperate situations require desperate remedies. **2001** W. NORTHCUTT *Darwin Awards II* 2 Desperate times call for desperate measures, which are often sensible when you consider the bleak alternative. ■ **necessity**

destiny *see* HANGING and wiving go by destiny.

destroy *see* whom the GODS would destroy, they first make mad.

details *see* the DEVIL is in the details.

The DEVIL can quote Scripture for his own ends

The proverb alludes to the temptation of Christ by the Devil (MATTHEW iv) when the latter quotes a passage from Psalm xci.

□ **1596** SHAKESPEARE *Merchant of Venice* I. iii. 93 The devil can cite Scripture for his purpose. An evil soul producing holy witness Is like a villain with a smiling cheek. **1761** C. CHURCHILL *Apology* 15 Thus Candour's maxims flow from Rancour's throat, As devils, to serve their purpose, Scripture quote. **1843** DICKENS *Martin Chuzzlewit* xi. Is any one surprised at Mr. Jonas making such a reference to such a book for such a purpose? Does any one doubt the old saw that the Devil (being a layman) quotes Scripture for his own ends. **1937** 'C. DICKSON' *Ten Teacups* xiii. The versatile personage in our popular proverbs, who . . quotes Scripture for his own ends. **1997** *Washington Times* 25 July A4 The devil can quote Scripture, as we all know, so why not a politician? ■ **good and evil; hypocrisy**

The DEVIL finds work for idle hands to do

Idleness and mischief are linked in ST. JEROME *Letters* CXXV. xi. *fac et aliquid operis, ut semper te diabolus inveniat occupatum*, do something, so that the devil may always find you busy; cf. *c* **1386** CHAUCER *Tale of Melibee* l. 1594 Therfore seith Seint Jerome: 'Dooth somme goode dedes that the devel, which is oure enemy, ne fynde yow nat unocupied.'

□ **1715** I. WATTS *Divine Songs* 29 In Works of Labour or of Skill I would be busy too: For Satan finds some mischief still for idle Hands to do. **1721** J. KELLY *Scottish Proverbs* 221 If the Devil find a Man idle, he'll set him on Work. **1792** M. WOLLSTONECRAFT *Vindication of Rights of Woman* ix. There is a homely proverb, which speaks a shrewd truth, that whoever the devil finds idle he will employ. .. What but habitual idleness can hereditary wealth and titles produce? **1941** A. UPDEGRAFF *Hills look Down* iv. Better keep busy, and the devil won't find so much for your idle hands to do. **1997** *Spectator* 1 Nov. 25 There is potential for such a large new intake to become bored. We all know who makes work for idle hands. **2002** *Washington Times* 14 Mar. D6 (*Crock comic strip*) 'I've slaved in your salt mines for twenty years without a day off.' 'You can have thirty minutes off.' 'Why didn't you give the poor soul more time off?' 'Idle hands work for the devil, Poulet.' ■ **idleness**

Why should the DEVIL have all the best tunes?

Many hymns are sung to popular secular melodies, a practice that was especially favoured by the Methodists. This saying is commonly attributed to the English evangelist Rowland Hill (1744–1833).

□ **1859** W. CHAPPELL *Popular Music* II. 748 The Primitive Methodists.. acting upon the principle of 'Why should the devil have all the pretty tunes?' collect the airs which are sung at pot and public houses, and write their hymns to them. **1879** J. E. HOPKINS *Work amongst Working Men* vi. If Wesley could not see why the devil should have all the good tunes, still less should we be able to see why he should have all the good amusements. **1933** G. B. SHAW *Letter* 29 June in *In Great Tradition* III. 261 Why should the devil have all the fun as well as all the good tunes? **1996** *National Review* 23 Dec. 6 Not even the rule that the Devil should not have all the best tunes could save 'Happy Days Are Here Again.' **2002** *Times* 23 July 17 The Devil may have all the good tunes, but he was also, it appears, on the receiving end of one of humankind's greatest puzzles. ■ **good and evil**

The DEVIL is in the details

□ **1978** *Washington Post* 8 July C7 There is an old German saying.. that the devil is in the details. **1990** *Automotive News* 5 Mar. 1 Many issues remain unresolved. As one.. official put it, 'the devil is in the details, and we don't know what those details are yet.' **2001** *Country Life* 20/27 Dec. 39 The green paper.. gives no detail. And that is part of the trouble. In planning the devil is in the detail. We need to have much more detail before knowing what to make of the green paper. ■ **great and small**

The DEVIL is not so black as he is painted

Cf. late 15th-cent. Fr. *toutesfois n'est il pas sy deable qu'il est noir*, a man is not always as devilish as he is black.

□ **1534** MORE *Dialogue of Comfort* (1553) III. xxii. Some saye in sporte, and thinke in earnest: The devill is not so blacke as he is painted. **1642** J. HOWELL *Instructions for Foreign Travel* xiv. The Devill is not so black as he is painted, no more are these Noble Nations and Townes as they are tainted. **1834** MARRYAT *Peter Simple* II. x. Fear kills more people than the yellow fever. .. The devil's not half so black as he's painted. **1953** A. CHRISTIE *Pocket full of Rye* xxiii. Lance patted her on the arm. 'You didn't believe the devil was as black as he was painted? Well, perhaps he wasn't.' ■ **good and evil; reputation**

The DEVIL looks after his own

Cf. **1606** J. DAY *Isle of Gulls* D4v You were worse then the devil els, for they say hee helps his Servants.

□ **1721** J. KELLY *Scottish Proverbs* 310 The Dee'ls ay good to his own. .. Spoken when they whom we affect not, thrive and prosper in the World; as if they had their Prosperity from the Devil. **1837** F. CHAMIER *Arethusa* II. i. Weazel was the only midshipman saved besides myself: the devil always takes care of his own. **1940** R. A. J. WALLING *Why did Trethewy Die?* vii. 'The devil looks after his own,' said Pierce. 'Yes, doesn't he? But even he's not so clever, either.' **1985** B. KNOX *Wavecrest* vii. 140 He saw Andy Grey's worried face and winked at him. 'Cheer up. The devil looks after his own.' ■ **associates; good fortune**

The DEVIL makes his Christmas pies of lawyers' tongues and clerks' fingers

□ **1591** J. FLORIO *Second Fruits* 179 Of three things the Deuill makes his messe, Of Lawyers tongues, of Scriveners fingers, you the third may gesse [i.e. women]. **1629** T. ADAMS *Workes* 1059 Corrupt and consciencelesse lawyers you will confesse to be sharp and wounding brambles. .. The Italians haue a shrewd prouerbe against them. The Deuill makes his Christmas-pyes of lawyers tongues, and clerkes fingers. *a* **1697** J. AUBREY *Brief Lives* (1898) I. 422 Sir Robert Pye, attorney of the court of wardes, .. happened to dye on Christmas day: the newes being brought to the serjeant, said he 'The devill haz a Christmas pye.' **1952** 'E. QUEEN' *Calendar of Crime* 248 Well, well, it couldn't have happened at a more appropriate season; there's an old English proverb that says the Devil makes his Christmas pies of lawyers' tongues. **1980** *Times* 24 Dec. 8 The Devil makes his Christmas-pies of television personalities' tongues and journalists' typing fingers: old English proverb, adapted. ■ **honesty and dishonesty; law and lawyers**

The DEVIL's children have the Devil's luck

Cf. *the* DEVIL *looks after his own.*

□ **1678** J. RAY *English Proverbs* (ed. 2) 126 The Devils child the Devils luck. **1721** J. KELLY *Scottish Proverbs* 333 The Dee'ls Bairns have Dee'ls luck. Spoken enviously when ill People prosper. **1798** LD. NELSON *Letter* 20 July (1845) III. 42 It is an old saying, 'the Devil's children have the Devil's luck.' I cannot find .. where the French Fleet are gone to. **1938** R. A. J. WALLING *Corpse with Grimy Glove* vii. They must have had her hidden up somewhere .. and waited till after sundown to get away. The devil's own luck—but the devil looks after his children. **1980** G. RICHARDS *Red Kill* viii. The Devil's son has the Devil's luck. We're going to need that kind of luck. ■ **luck**

DEVIL take the hindmost

A shortened version of EVERY *man for himself, and devil take the hindmost.* A Latin version of this sentiment is HORACE *Ars Poetica* 417 *occupet extremum scabies*, may the itch take the one who is last.

□ **1620** BEAUMONT & FLETCHER *Philaster* v. i. What if .. they run all away, and cry the Devil take the hindmost. **1725** DEFOE *Everybody's Business* 29 In a few years the navigation .. will be entirely obstructed. .. Every one of these gentlemen-watermen hopes it will last his time, and so they all cry, the Devil take the hindmost. **1824** *Tales of American Landlord* I. ix. The troops .. hurried away .. with a precipitation which seemed to say 'De'il tak the hindmost.' **1953** P. GALLICO *Foolish Immortals* vii. Hannah grew up in .. a land of unlimited resources and opportunity for acquiring them and let the devil take the hindmost. **2002** *Times* 22 Feb. 24 And

Devil take the hindmost. In a better world than the infernal Circle Line, women and children first is still a noble sentiment. ■ **self-preservation**

The DEVIL was sick, the Devil a saint would be; the Devil was well, the devil a saint was he!

Promises made in adversity may not be kept in prosperity. Cf. medieval L. *aegrotavit daemon, monachus tunc esse volebat; daemon convaluit, daemon ut ante fuit*, when the Devil was ill, he wished to be a monk; when the Devil recovered, he was the Devil just as before; **1586** J. WITHALS *Dict.* (rev. ed.) K8 The diuell was sicke and crasie; Good woulde the monke bee that was lasie.

□ **1629** T. ADAMS *Works* 634 God had need to take what deuotion he can get at our hands in our misery; for when prosperity returnes, wee forget our vowes. ..The Deuill was sicke, the deuill a Monke would be, The Deuill was well, the deuill of [*sic*] Monke was he [i.e. no sort of monk at all]. **1881** D. C. MURRAY *Joseph's Coat* II. xvii. A prisoner's penitence is a thing the quality of which it is very difficult to judge until you see it.. tried outside. 'The devil was sick.' **1913** H. JAMES *Small Boy* xxviii. The old, the irrepressible adage..was to live again between them: 'When the devil was sick the devil a saint would be; when the devil was well the devil a saint was he!' **1959** E. CADELL *Alice, where art Thou?* xii. 185 Laurie..offers to do penance for his past, to make amends in the future. ..My father's comment is that the devil a monk was he. ■ **adversity**; **hypocrisy**

Devil *see also* set a BEGGAR on horseback, and he'll ride to the Devil; BETTER the devil you know than the devil you don't know; never BID the Devil good morrow until you meet him; EVERY man for himself, and devil take the hindmost; GIVE a thing, and take a thing, to wear the Devil's gold ring; GIVE the Devil his due; where GOD builds a church, the Devil will build a chapel; GOD sends meat, but the Devil sends cooks; what is GOT over the Devil's back is spent under his belly; HASTE is from the Devil; HOME is home, as the Devil said when he found himself in the Court of Session; an IDLE brain is the Devil's workshop; NEEDS must when the Devil drives; PARSLEY seed goes nine times to the Devil; it is easier to RAISE the Devil than to lay him; he who SUPS with the Devil should have a long spoon; TALK of the Devil, and he is bound to appear; TELL the truth and shame the Devil; TRUTH makes the Devil blush; YOUNG saint, old devil.

DIAMOND cuts diamond

Used of persons evenly matched in wit or cunning. Also frequently found as a descriptive phrase *diamond cut diamond*. Cf. **1593** NASHE *Christ's Tears* II. 9 An easie matter is it for anie man to cutte me (like a Diamond) with mine own dust.

□ **1604** MARSTON *Malcontent* IV. i. None cuttes a diamond but a diamond. **1629** J. FORD *Lover's Melancholy* I. 18. We're caught in our own toyles. Diamonds cut Diamonds. **1863** C. READE *Hard Cash* II. xi. You might say I robbed you. ..It is diamond cut diamond. **1958** M. STEWART *Nine Coaches Waiting* xi. I'll always have prospects. Diamond cuts diamond. **1979** *Guardian* 19 Apr. 26 *When the boat comes in*: Diamond cut diamond. James Bolam as the rough one turned smoothie. ■ **similarity and dissimilarity**

You can only DIE once

□ *c* **1435** *Torrent of Portugal* (EETS) l. 993 A man schall But onnys Dyee. **1597–8** SHAKESPEARE *Henry IV, Pt. 2* III. ii. 228 A man can die but once. *a* **1721** M. PRIOR in *Literary Works* (1971) I. 533 With great Submission I pronounce That People dye no more than once. **1818** F. HALL *Travels in Canada & United States* xxxvii. He replied .. that he was too ill to come out, and should die if she forced him; 'You can die but once,' said the beldame. **1840** MARRYAT *Olla Podrida* I. xii. 'A man cannot die more than once,' .. but .. a man can die .. once professionally or legally, and once naturally. **1980** M. GILBERT *Death of Favourite Girl* ii. 'Why not,' said Sally. 'You can only die once.' ■ **death; fate and fatalism**

die *see also* good AMERICANS when they die go to Paris; COWARDS die many times before their death; we must EAT a peck of dirt before we die; EAT, drink, and be merry, for tomorrow we die; whom the GODS love die young; the GOOD die young; call no man HAPPY till he dies; he who LIVES by the sword dies by the sword; OLD habits die hard; OLD soldiers never die; YOUNG men may die, but old men must die; *also* DYING.

diet *see* the best DOCTORS are Dr Diet, Dr Quiet, and Dr Merryman.

differ *see* TASTES differ.

DIFFERENT strokes for different folks

Of US origin: *strokes* = comforting gestures of approval or congratulation. Quickly picked up and used in a variety of parodic forms, as in a 1974 Volkswagen advertisement: Different Volks for different folks.

□ **1973** *Houston* (Texas) *Chronicle Magazine* 14 Oct. 4 The popular saying around P[almer] D[rug] A[buse] P[rogram] is 'different strokes for different folks', and that's the basis of the program. **1990** A. STODDARD *Gift of Letter* iii. Peter sends and receives letters. He dictates everything he writes. I send and receive handwritten letters. I write out everything. Different strokes for different folks. **2002** *Washington Post* 25 Feb. C2 There are many people who box for the sheer joy of it, there are even more who love to watch them do so; it's not my own cuppa—though for many years it was—but what it says here is different strokes for different folks, so let the games begin. ■ **tact; ways and means**

The DIFFICULT is done at once; the impossible takes a little longer

A version of this is well known as the slogan of the US Armed Forces: *the difficult we do immediately; the impossible takes a little longer*. The 'French Minister' to whom this saying is attributed in quot. 1873 is Charles Alexandre de Calonne (1734–1802), appointed finance minister by Louis XVI in 1783: *si c'est possible, c'est fait; impossible? cela se fera*, if a thing is possible, consider it done; the impossible? that will be done (quoted in J. Michelet *Histoire de la Révolution Française* (1847) I. ii. 8).

□ **1873** TROLLOPE *Phineas Redux* II. xxix. What was it the French Minister said. If it is simply difficult it is done. If it is impossible, it shall be done. **1967** H. HARRISON *Technicolor Time Machine* iv. The impossible may take a while, but we do it, you know the routine. **1981** P. McCUTCHAN *Shard calls Tune* iv. A well-worn precept of the British Navy was that the difficult was done at once; the impossible took a little longer. **1997** *National Review* 29 Sept. 66 That's good, utilitarian, achievement-oriented American lingo. We do the difficult immediately, the impossible takes a little longer. ■ **possibility and impossibility**

difficult *see also* it is the FIRST step that is difficult.

difficulty *see* ENGLAND's difficulty is Ireland's opportunity.

digging *see* when you are in a HOLE, stop digging.

DILIGENCE is the mother of good luck

□ **1591** W. STEPNEY *Spanish Schoolmaster* L2V Diligence is the mother of good fortune. *La diligencia es madre de la buena ventura.* **1736** B. FRANKLIN *Poor Richard's Almanack* (Feb.) Diligence is the mother of good Luck. **1875** S. SMILES *Thrift* ix. Diligence is the mother of good luck. . . A man's success in life will be proportionate to his efforts. **1972** B. EMECHETA *In Ditch* vi. Where do people get a system that allows a man to be better off when out of work?. . People. . used to say that diligence was the mother of fortune. ■ **diligence; luck**

dinner *see* AFTER dinner rest a while, after supper walk a mile; BETTER a dinner of herbs than a stalled ox where hate is.

Throw DIRT enough, and some will stick

Persistent slander will eventually pass for truth. Cf. L. *calumniare fortiter, et aliquid adhaerebit*, slander strongly and some will stick.

□ **1656** *Trepan* 34 She will say before company, Have you never had the French Pox? speak as in the sight of God: let them Reply what they will, some dirt will stick. **1678** B. R. *Letter to Popish Friends* 7 'Tis a blessed Line in Matchiavel—If durt enough be thrown, some will stick. **1705** E. WARD *Hudibras Redivivus* II. 11 Scurrility's a useful Trick, Approv'd by the most Politic; Fling Dirt enough, And some will stick. **1857** T. HUGHES *Tom Brown's Schooldays* I. viii. Whatever harm a. . venomous tongue could do them, he took care should be done. Only throw dirt enough and some of it is sure to stick. **2000** P. LOVESEY *Reaper* xvi. 201 'We both know Owen is full of wind and piss.' 'The trouble is not everyone knows that. Throw enough mud, and some will stick.' ■ **malice; slander**

dirt *see also* we must EAT a peck of dirt before we die.

DIRTY water will quench fire

Mainly used to mean that a man's lust can be satisfied by any woman, however loose or ugly.

□ **1546** J. HEYWOOD *Dialogue of Proverbs* I. v. B2 As this prouerbe saieth, for quenchyng hot desire, Foul water as soone as fayre, wyl quenche hot fire. **1796** COBBETT *Political Censor* Sept. 62 That I have made use. . of the British Corporal for a good purpose, I have little doubt—Dirty water will quench fire. **1945** O. ONIONS *Ragged Robin* vi. It's flocks and straw for us. . . Well, dirty water's good enough to quench a fire with. **1995** A. G. TAYLOR *Simeon's Bride* xxvi. 173 She had the thick ugly feet of a streetwalker. . . How could anyone go with her?' Dewi shrugged. 'They do say dirty water puts out fire just as well.' ■ **necessity; ways and means**

dirty *see also* it's an ILL bird that fouls its own nest; don't THROW out your dirty water until you get in fresh; one does not WASH one's dirty linen in public.

disappointed *see* BLESSED is he who expects nothing, for he shall never be disappointed.

DISCRETION is the better part of valour

Cf. EURIPIDES *Suppliants* l. 510 *καὶ τοῦτ᾽ ἐμοὶ τἀνδρεῖον ἡ προμηθία*, and bravery consists in foresight; *c* **1477** CAXTON *Jason* (EETS) 23 Than as wyse and discrete he withdrewe him sayng that more is worth a good retrayte than a folisshe abydinge.

□ **1597-8** SHAKESPEARE *Henry IV, Pt. 1* v. iv. 121 The better part of valour is discretion; in the which better part, I have saved my life. **1885** C. LOWE *Prince Bismarck* I. v. Napoleon.. had vowed that he would free Italy 'from the Alps to the Adriatic', but.. he acted on the maxim that discretion is the better part of valour. **2002** *Washington Times* 12 Jan. F10 (*Fox Trot comic strip*) 'Who knew you weren't supposed to club him or kick him or lob fireballs, just because he's huge and fierce and can squash you at will!' 'You've heard the saying, "Discretion is the better part of valor"? Think of this as a valuable life lesson.' ■ **discretion**; **prudence**

disease *see* DESPERATE diseases must have desperate remedies.

disgrace *see* POVERTY is no disgrace, but it is a great inconvenience.

dish *see* BETTER are small fish than an empty dish; REVENGE is a dish that can be eaten cold.

dismount *see* he who RIDES a tiger is afraid to dismount.

dispose *see* MAN proposes, God disposes.

DISTANCE lends enchantment to the view

□ **1799** T. CAMPBELL *Pleasure of Hope* I. 3 Why do those cliffs of shadowy tint appear More sweet than all the landscape smiling near?—'Tis distance lends enchantment to the view, And robes the mountain in its azure hue. **1827** T. HOOD *Poems* (1906) 78 What black Mont Blancs arose, Crested with soot and not with snows. ..I fear the distance did not 'lend enchantment to the view'. **1901** C. FITCH *Captain Jinks* II. 118 'I wish you'd taike me hout of the second row and put me in the front.'..'You forget the old adage,.. "Distance lends enchantment."' **1974** T. SHARPE *Porterhouse Blue* xviii. As ever with Lady Mary's affections, distance lent enchantment to the view, and..she was herself the intimate patroness of this idol of the media. ■ **absence**

ditch *see* when the BLIND lead the blind, both shall fall into the ditch.

DIVIDE and rule

Government is more easily maintained if factions are set against each other, and not allowed to unite against the ruler. A common maxim (in Latin *divide et impera*, in German *entzwei und gebiete*), it should not (*pace* quot. 1732) be laid at the door of the Italian political philosopher Niccolò Machiavelli (1469–1527), who in fact denounced this principle. Cf. **1588** tr. *M. Hurault's Discourse upon Present State of France* 44 It hath been alwaies her [Catherine de Medici's] custome, to set in France, one against an other, that in the meane while shee might rule in these diuisions.

□ **1605** J. HALL *Meditations* I. 109 For a Prince..is a sure axiome, Diuide and rule. **1732** SWIFT *Poems* III. 805 As Machiavel taught 'em, divide and ye govern. **1907** *Spectator* 20 Apr. 605 The cynical maxim of 'Divide and rule' has never clouded our relations with the daughter-States. **1979** D. WILLIAMS *Genesis & Exodus* ii. Matters concerning the estate were put in the hands of a secretary and a steward who were responsible not to Benson but to the Governors. But 'divide and rule' was not in his nature. ■ **power**; **rulers and ruled**

divided *see* a HOUSE divided cannot stand; UNITED we stand, divided we fall.

divine *see* to ERR is human (to forgive divine); on SAINT Thomas the Divine kill all turkeys, geese, and swine.

DO as I say, not as I do

Cf. MATTHEW xxiii. 3 (AV) Do not ye after their works: for they say, and do not.

□ *a* **1100** in N. R. Ker *Anglo-Saxons* (1959) 277 Ac theah ic wyrs do thonne ic the lære ne do thu na swa swa ic do, ac do swa ic the lære gyf ic the wel lære [Although I do worse than I teach you, do not do as I do, but do as I teach you if I teach you well]. **1546** J. HEYWOOD *Dialogue of Proverbs* II. v. H4V It is as folke dooe, and not as folke say. **1689** J. SELDON *Table-Talk* 45 Preachers say, Do as I say, not as I do. **1911** *Spectator* 24 June 957 It has always been considered allowable to say.. to children, 'Do as I say, rather than as I do.' **1979** D. CLARK *Heberden's Seat* v. I saw you spooning sugar into coffee. ..Do as I say, not as I do. **2001** *Spectator* 4 Aug. 28 Do as I say, not as I do. The government's White Paper on competition is a bad example in itself, for why should there only be one of it? ■ **hypocrisy; words and deeds**

DO as you would be done by

A pithier form of DO *unto others as you would they should do unto you*. The forms are sometimes mixed, e.g. quot. 1991.

□ *c* **1596** A. MUNDAY et al. *Sir Thomas More* 9 A [he] saies trewe: letts do as we may be doon by. **1747** CHESTERFIELD *Letter* 16 Oct. (1932) III. 1035 'Do as you would be done by,' is the surest method that I know of pleasing. **1863** C. KINGSLEY *Water Babies* v. I shall grow as handsome as my sister.. the loveliest fairy in the world;.. her name is Mrs. Doasyouwouldbedoneby. **1928** 'J. J. CONNINGTON' *Mystery at Lynden Sands* viii. 'Do unto others as you'd be done by' is my motto. **1965** M. FRAYN *Tin Men* i. 'Always treat a man as you would wish to be treated yourself. ..' 'Do as you would be done by.' 'It's good human relations. ..' Mr. Vulgurian paused and stroked his hair, doing to it as he would be done by. **1991** T. MO *Redundancy of Courage* xxix. 394 'Do unto others as you would be done by' was a more positive social prescription of societies like Toronto. ■ **reciprocity; society**

DO right and fear no man

□ *c* **1450** *Proverbs of Good Counsel* in *Book of Precedence* (EETS) 68 The beste wysdom that I Can [know], Ys to doe well, and drede no man. **1721** J. KELLY *Scottish Proverbs* 89 Do well and doubt [fear] no Man. But rest satisfied in the Testimony of a good Conscience. **1979** *Guardian* 31 Mar. 10 It used to be, 'Do right and fear no man. Don't write and fear no women.' ■ **action and consequence; conscience**

DO unto others as you would they should do unto you

See DO *as you would be done by* above. With allusion to LUKE vi. 31 (AV) As ye would that men should do to you, do ye also to them likewise.

□ *a* **901** *Laws of Alfred* in F. Liebermann *Gesetze Angelsachsen* (1903) I. 44 Thæt ge willen, thæt othre men eow ne don, ne doth ge thæt othrum monnum [What you do not wish others to do to you, do not to other men]. **1477** A. WYDEVILLE *Dicts. of Philosophers* 62 Do to other as thou woldest they should do to the, and do to noon other but as thou woldest be doon to. **1790** W. HAZLITT *Letter* 9 July (1979) 48 He wished to have him out, merely because 'he would do to others as he would be done to'. **1880** TROLLOPE *Life of Cicero* II. xii. The lesson which had governed his [Cicero's] life: 'I will do unto others as I would they should do unto me.' **1903** G. B. SHAW *Man & Superman* 227 Do not do unto others as you would that they should do unto you. Their tastes may not be the same. **2000** *Washington Post* 27 Nov. A21 Maybe all I'm doing is overcomplicating a lesson first taught two millennia ago: Do unto others as you would have others do unto you. **2002** *Times* 22 June 23 But the secret of service is the same as it was in medieval court or

Gosford Park. It is the Golden Rule: treat others as you would like to be treated yourself. ■ **reciprocity; society**

do *see also* never do EVIL that good may come of it; the KING can do no wrong; whatever MAN has done, man may do; when in ROME, do as the Romans do; if you WANT a thing done well, do it yourself; *also* DOES, DOING, DONE.

doctor *see* an APPLE a day keeps the doctor away.

The best DOCTORS are Dr Diet, Dr Quiet, and Dr Merryman

Cf. *a* **1449** LYDGATE *Minor Poems* (EETS) 704 Thre lechees [doctors] consarue a mannys myht, First *a glad hert*.. *Temperat* diet.. And best of all, for no thyng *take no thouht.* Cf. LAUGHTER *is the best medicine.*

□ **1558** W. BULLEIN *Government of Health* 50V I should not staye my selfe vpon the opinion of any one phisicion, but rather vpon three. .. The first was called doctor diet, the seconde doctor quiet, the thirde doctor mery man. **1738** SWIFT *Polite Conversation* ii. 154 The best Doctors in the World, are Doctor Dyet, Doctor Quiet, and Doctor Merryman. **1909** *Spectator* 30 Jan. 175 A proverb prescribes for sickness Dr. Diet, Dr. Quiet, and Dr. Merryman. The merry heart goes all the way in all but the worst sicknesses. ■ **doctors; health**

doer *see* EVIL doers are evil dreaders.

does *see* he who CAN, does; it's DOGGED as does it; EASY does it; HANDSOME is as handsome does; PRETTY is as pretty does.

Give a DOG a bad name and hang him

The principle is that a person's plight is hopeless once his reputation has been blackened. Similar to *he that has an* ILL *name is half hanged.*

□ **1706** J. STEVENS *Spanish & English Dict.* s.v. Perro, We say, Give a Dog an ill name and his work is done. **1721** J. KELLY *Scottish Proverbs* 124 Give a Dog an ill Name, and he'll soon be hanged. Spoken of those who raise an ill Name on a Man on purpose to prevent his Advancement. **1803** *Norfolk* (Virginia) *Herald* 14 Apr. 3 It is an old saying, 'give a dog a bad name and hang him'. **1928** G. B. SHAW *Intelligent Woman's Guide to Socialism* lvii. The Liberal impulse is almost always to give a dog a bad name and hang him: that is, to denounce the menaced proprietors as enemies of mankind, and ruin them in a transport of virtuous indignation. **2002** *Times: Weekend* 20 July 4 Give a dog a bad name seems to have become a workaday motto for the wine trade. And the sillier the name on the bottle, the less chance there is of anything drinkable inside. ■ **reputation; slander**

DOG does not eat dog

Cf. VARRO *De Lingua Latina* VII. 32 *canis caninam non est*, a dog does not eat dog's flesh.

□ **1543** W. TURNER *Hunting of Romish Fox* A2V The prouerb .. on dog will not eat of an other dogges fleshe. **1790** 'P. PINDAR' *Epistle to Bruce* 31 Dog should not prey on dog, the proverb says: Allow then brother-trav'lers crumbs of praise. **1866** C. KINGSLEY *Hereward the Wake* II. xi. Dog does not eat dog and it is hard to be robbed by an Englishman, after being robbed a dozen times by the French. **1933** F. D. GRIERSON *Empty House* viii. Dog doesn't eat dog, my dear fellow. To put it more politely, the physician attends his brother practitioner without charge. **1993** 'C. AIRD' *Going Concern* (1994) viii. 67 'Apparently Harris and Marsh've been trying for a takeover of Chernwoods' for quite a while now.' 'I always thought that dog doesn't eat dog,' objected Leeyes. 'But I suppose I'm old-fashioned.' ■ **reciprocity**

Every DOG has his day

□ **1545** R. TAVERNER tr. *Erasmus' Adages* (ed. 2) 63 A dogge hath a day. **1600–1** SHAKESPEARE *Hamlet* V. i. 286 Let Hercules himself do what he may, The cat will mew, and dog will have his day. **1611** R. COTGRAVE *Dict. French & English* s.v. Fevrier, Euerie dog hath his day. **1726** POPE *Odyssey* V. xxii. Dogs, ye have had your day; ye fear'd no more Ulysses vengeful from the Trojan shore. **1837** CARLYLE *French Revolution* III. I. i. How changed for Marat, lifted from his dark cellar!..All dogs have their day; even rabid dogs. **1863** C. KINGSLEY *Water Babies* ii. Young blood must have its course, lad, And every dog his day. **1978** 'M. CRAIG' *Were He Stranger* x. 'She could be his sister.' 'No way—not with a face like that.' 'Well, every dog deserves his day.' ■ **opportunity, taken; success**

Every DOG is allowed one bite

The proverb is based on the old common law rule (dating at least from the seventeenth century) by which the keeper of a domestic animal was not liable for harm done by it unless he knew of its vicious propensities. Quot. 1913 explains the thinking behind this.

□ **1902** V. S. LEAN *Collectanea* I. 439 Every dog is allowed his first bite i.e. is not punished. **1913** *Spectator* 15 Mar. 440 Every dog is allowed by the law one free bite. After the dog has once bitten a person it is presumed that its owner knows it to be 'savage'. **1968** P. FOOT *Politics of Harold Wilson* x. In March 1967..Wilson rounded on the Left at a Parliamentary Party meeting, warning them that 'a dog is only allowed one bite' and threatening them with a General Election unless they came to heel. **1980** 'A. BLAISDELL' *Consequence of Crime* (1981) ii. She got arrested. ..They say every dog [is] allowed one bite. ..But it was a vice thing. ..I told her to get out. ■ **reputation**

A DOG is for life, not just for Christmas

The slogan of the UK's National Canine Defence League, introduced in 1978 with the intention of dissuading people from giving puppies as Christmas presents. Widely quoted in its original form, it has also spawned any number of humorous by-forms.

□ **1998** R. RAY *Certain Age* 344 A tree is for life, not just for decorating with small shiny objects. **1999** *Jewish Chronicle* 30 July 42 And remember, a pet is for life, not just for Rosh Hashanah. **2001** *Country Life* 29 Nov. 96 (*advertisement*) A Billiard table is for life not just for Christmas. ■ **constancy and inconstancy**

The DOG returns to its vomit

The expression is frequently found in various metaphorical and allusive forms, such as *to return like a dog to his vomit*, as illustrated below. Before 1534 (see quot.), the proverb is used in more or less similar forms in earlier versions of, and commentaries upon, the Bible. The concept enjoyed wide popularity in the Middle Ages. The biblical passages involved are: PROVERBS xxvi. 11 (AV) As a dog returneth to his vomit: so a fool returneth to his folly; also 2 PETER ii. 22 (see below).

□ *c* **1390** CHAUCER *Parson's Tale* l. 137 Ye trespassen so ofte tyme as dooth the hound that retourneth to eten his spewyng. **1534** W. TYNDALE tr. *Bible* 2 Peter ii. 22 It is happened vnto them accordinge to the true proverbe: The dogge is turned to his vomet agayne. **1832** S. WARREN *Diary of Late Physician* II. vi. His infatuated wife betook herself—'like a dog to his vomit'..—to her former..extravagance and dissipation. **1981** P. McCUTCHAN *Shard calls Tune* xvi. The old saying that the dog returns to his vomit, the criminal to the scene of his crime. **1993** G. LANDRUM

Rotary Club Murder Mystery 44 'You know what the Bible says,' Harriet replied. '"The dog shall return to his vomit and the old hog to his wallowing in the mire."' ■ **habit; human nature**

A DOG that will fetch a bone will carry a bone

A gossip carries talk both ways.

□ **1830** R. FORBY *Vocabulary of East Anglia* 429 'The dog that fetches will carry.'—i.e. A talebearer will tell tales *of* you, as well as *to* you. **1941** L. I. WILDER *Little Town on Prairie* xv. So Nellie twisted what you said and told it to Miss Wilder. .. 'A dog that will fetch a bone, will carry a bone.' **1959** E. SCHIDDEL *Devil in Bucks County* II. iii. All this gossip reminded Shirley .. of the saw *The dog who brings a bone also will carry one away.* ■ **slander**

dog *see also* a BARKING dog never bites; BRAG is a good dog, but Holdfast is better; the CAT, the rat, and Lovell the dog, rule all England under the hog; he is a GOOD dog who goes to church; why KEEP a dog and bark yourself?; if you LIE down with dogs, you will get up with fleas; a LIVE dog is better than a dead lion; LOVE me, love my dog; it is a POOR dog that's not worth whistling for; let SLEEPING dogs lie; it is easy to find a STICK to beat a dog; you can't TEACH an old dog new tricks; THREE things are not to be trusted; while TWO dogs are fighting for a bone, a third runs away with it; there are more WAYS of killing a dog than choking it with butter; there are more WAYS of killing a dog than hanging it; a WOMAN, a dog, and a walnut tree, the more you beat them the better they be; *also* DOGS.

It's DOGGED as does it

Similar in form to the expression EASY *does it*.

□ **1864** M. B. CHESNUT *Diary* 6 Aug. (1949) 429 'It's dogged as does it,' says Isabella. **1867** TROLLOPE *Last Chronicle of Barset* lxi. There ain't nowt a man can't bear if he'll only be dogged. .. It's dogged as does it. It's not thinking about it. **1916** J. BUCHAN *Greenmantle* i. We've got the measure of the old Boche now, and it's dogged as does it. **1965** K. GILES *Some Beasts no More* v. It was Colonel Rodgers. 'Any progress?' .. 'Very little, it's dogged as does it, sir.' ■ **perseverance**

DOGS bark, but the caravan goes on

Quot. 1956 is a humorous inversion of the proverb. In most instances of this proverb, *caravan* is in its original sense of 'a company of people travelling together in the desert', but quot. 1956 uses the 'mobile home' sense.

□ **1891** J. L. KIPLING *Beast & Man in India* ix. 252 'The dog barks but the elephant moves on' is sometimes said to indicate the superiority of the great to popular clamour, but the best form of the phrase is, 'Though the dog may bark the caravan (*kafila*) moves on.' **1924** C. K. SCOTT MONCRIEFF tr. *Proust's Within Budding Grove* I. 45 In the words of a fine Arab proverb, 'The dogs may bark; the caravan goes on!' .. Its effect was great, the proverb being familiar to us already. It had taken the place, that year, among people who 'really counted', of 'He who sows the wind shall reap the whirlwind.' **1930** *Time* 4 July 17 I was struggling to explain the situation to an old Moor. .. After thinking it over he murmured: 'Dogs bark but the caravan goes on.' **1956** D. SMITH *Hundred & One Dalmatians* xiv. The shut-in Romany dogs heard them [the Dalmatians] and shook the caravans in their efforts to get out. .. 'The caravans bark but the dogs move on,' remarked Pongo, when he felt they were out of danger. **2002** *Spectator* 6 July 28 The dogs bark, but the caravan moves on. ICC, Kyoto, Arafat, Iraq .. early chapters in a long story. If you want to be part of it, join America. If you want to impede it, join a terrorist group. ■ **great and small; malice**

doing *see* if a THING's worth doing, it's worth doing well.

dollar *see* ANOTHER day, another dollar.

What's DONE cannot be undone

Also found in the terser, more casual form *what's done is done*. Cf. SOPHOCLES *Ajax* l. 378 *οὐ γὰρ γένοιτ᾽ ἂν ταῦθ᾽ ὅπως οὐχ ὧδ᾽ ἔχειν*, things could not now be otherwise; early 14th-cent. Fr. *mez quant ja est la chose fecte, ne puet pas bien estre desfecte*, but when a thing is already done, it cannot be undone.

□ *c* **1450** *King Ponthus* in *Publications of Modern Language Association of America* (1897) XII. 107 The thynges that be doone may not be undoone. **1546** J. HEYWOOD *Dialogue of Proverbs* I. x. C4 Things done, can not be undoone. **1605–6** SHAKESPEARE *Macbeth* III. ii. 12 Things without all remedy Should be without regard. What's done is done. *Ibid.* v. i. 65 What's done cannot be undone. **1791** G. WASHINGTON *Letter* 1 Dec. in *Writings* (1939) XXXI. 433 What has been done cannot be undone, and it would be unfortunate.. if disputes amongst the friends of the federal City should Arm the enemies of it with weapons to wound it. **1818** S. FERRIER *Marriage* III. xxi. I hope you will think twice about it. Second thoughts are best. What's done cannot be undone. **1967** H. HARRISON *Technicolor Time Machine* vii. What's done is done.. I'll see you don't suffer for it. **1998** K. NEVILLE *Magic Circle* 92 'And although I am very, very sorry I involved you in this, Ariel, what has been done cannot be undone.' ■ **past**

done *see also* DO as you would be done by; whatever MAN has done, man may do; NOTHING should be done in haste but gripping a flea; the SOONER begun, the sooner done; if you WANT something done, ask a busy person; WELL begun is half done.

A DOOR must either be shut or open

Said of two mutually exclusive alternatives. Cf. Fr. *il faut qu'une porte soit ouverte ou fermée*, it is necessary that a door be open or shut.

□ **1762** GOLDSMITH *Citizen of World* I. xlix. There are but the two ways; the door must either be shut, or it must be open. **1896** G. SAINTSBURY *Hist. Nineteenth-Century Literature* vii. Fiction.. pleads in vain for detailed treatment. For all doors must be shut or open; and this door must now be shut. **1953** S. BEDFORD *Sudden View* I. ix. We.. returned to France, the land of good sense.. where a door has got to be either open or shut. ■ **choices**

door *see also* a CREAKING door hangs longest; a GOLDEN key can open any door; when ONE door shuts, another opens; OPPORTUNITY never knocks twice at any man's door; a POSTERN door makes a thief; when POVERTY comes in at the door, love flies out of the window; it is too late to shut the STABLE-door after the horse has bolted.

doorstep *see* if every man would SWEEP his own doorstep the city would soon be clean.

When in DOUBT, do nowt

Nowt is a dialect form of 'nought' = 'nothing', here used for the rhyme.

□ **1874** G. J. WHYTE-MELVILLE *Uncle John* xx. I should wait. When in doubt what to do, he is a wise man who does nothing. **1884** G. WEATHERLY *'Little Folks' Proverb*

Painting Book 64 Err ever on the side that's safe, And when in doubt, abstain. **1917** J. C. BRIDGE *Cheshire Proverbs* 155 When in doubt, do nowt. This shows the cautious Cheshireman at his best. **1952** H. CECIL *Ways & Means* ii. I don't know. I think it's one of those occasions where it's best to follow the maxim: When in doubt, don't. **1972** E. GRIERSON *Confessions of Country Magistrate* vii. 'When in doubt say nowt' is a precept enshrined over most magistrates' courts. **1981** E. AGRY *Assault Force* i. What to do?..'When in doubt, do nowt,' had always been my grandfather's advice. ■ **action and inaction; decision and indecision**

down *see* up like a ROCKET, down like a stick; what goes UP must come down.

Whosoever DRAWS his sword against the prince must throw the scabbard away

Whoever seeks to assassinate or depose a monarch must remain constantly prepared to defend himself, and his sword will never be able to return to its scabbard.

□ **1604** R. DALLINGTON *View of France* F3^{V} His King, against whom when yee drawe the sword, ye must throw the scabberd into the riuer. **1659** J. HOWELL *Proverbs* (English) 17 Who draweth his sword against his Prince, must throw away the scabbard. **1962** S. E. FINER *Man on Horseback* viii. [The Military] must still fear the results of a fall from power. ..'Whosoever draws his sword against the prince must throw the scabbard away'..pithily express[es] the logic of the situation. ■ **hope and despair; rulers and ruled**

draws *see also* BEAUTY draws with a single hair.

dread *see* a BURNT child dreads the fire.

dreader *see* EVIL doers are evil dreaders.

DREAM of a funeral and you hear of a marriage

An illustration of the principle of DREAMS *go by contraries*, the proverb is also found in the reverse form.

□ **1639** J. CLARKE *Paræmiologia Anglo-Latina* 236 After a dreame of weddings comes a corse [corpse]. **1766** GOLDSMITH *Vicar of Wakefield* x. My wife had the most lucky dreams in the world. ..It was one night a coffin and cross-bones, the signs of an approaching wedding. **1883** C. S. BURNE *Shropshire Folklore* xx. We have the sayings..'Dream of a funeral, hear of a wedding'..and vice versa. **1909** *British Weekly* 8 July 331 'Dream of a funeral and you hear of a marriage'..has probably been verified many times in the experience of ordinary people. ■ **dreams**

dream *see also* MORNING dreams come true.

DREAMS go by contraries

□ *c* **1400** *Beryn* (EETS) l. 108 Comynly of these swevenys [dreams] the contrary man shul fynde. **1584** LYLY *Sappho & Phao* IV. iii. I dreamed last night, but I hope dreams are contrary, that..all my hair blazed on a bright flame. **1673** W. WYCHERLEY *Gentleman Dancing-Master* IV. 64 Ne're fear it, dreams go by the contraries. **1731** FIELDING *Grub-Street Opera* I. xi. Oh! the perjury of men! I find dreams do not always go by contraries. **1860** T. C. HALIBURTON *Season-Ticket* 30 The events of life, like dreams, appear in the words of the old proverb, 'to go by contraries'. **1932** J. H. WALLIS *Capital City Murder* iv. There was no sign..of Lester Armande. 'Dreams go by contraries,' said Lily. **1973** 'P. SIMPLE' *Stretchford Chronicles* (1980) 198 They say dreams go by opposites. ..Perhaps you'll dream about that AA man again. ■ **dreams**

drink *see* EAT, drink, and be merry..; you can take a HORSE to the water, but you can't make him drink.

He that DRINKS beer, thinks beer

□ **1820** W. IRVING *Sketch Book of Geoffrey Crayon* vii. 70 (*footnote*) They who drink beer will think beer. **1867** A. D. RICHARDSON *Beyond Mississippi* i. 'They who drink beer think beer,' but Catawba and Muscatel neither muddle the brain nor fire the passions. **1912** R. A. FREEMAN *Mystery of 31, New Inn* v. 'You despise the good old British John Barleycorn.' 'He that drinks beer thinks beer,' retorted Thorndyke. **1958** D. G. BROWNE *Death in Seven Volumes* xii. 'He who drinks beer, thinks beer,' was one of his favourite aphorisms. ■ **action and consequence**; **drunkenness**; **food and drink**

A DRIPPING June sets all in tune

□ **1742** *Agreeable Companion* 35 A dripping June Brings all Things in Tune. **1883** W. ROPER *Weather Sayings* 22 A dry May and a dripping June brings all things in tune. **1912** *Spectator* 28 Dec. 1094 'A dripping June sets all in tune,' and on sandy soils not only farm crops but garden flowers do best in a wet summer. ■ **weather lore**

DRIVE gently over the stones

□ **1711** SWIFT *Letter* 30 June in *Journal to Stella* (1948) I. 301 A gallop: sit fast, sirrah, and don't ride hard upon the stones. **1788** R. CUMBERLAND in *Observer* IV. cxx. We now stept into our hack, but not without a caution from Ned to the coachman to drive gently over the stones. **1844** DICKENS *Martin Chuzzlewit* xxix. Gently over the stones, Poll. Go a-tiptoe over the pimples! Poll. Go a-tiptoe over the pimples! Poll..scraped the lather off again with particular care. **1885** E. J. HARDY *How to be Happy though Married* xi. Drive gently over the stones! This piece of advice.. given to inexperienced whips, may be suggested metaphorically to the newly-married. ■ **marriage**; **tact**

You can DRIVE out Nature with a pitchfork, but she keeps on coming back

Originally HORACE *Epistles* I. x. 24 *naturam expelles furca, tamen usque recurret*, you may drive out nature with a pitchfork, but she will always return.

□ **1539** R. TAVERNER tr. *Erasmus' Adages* 44 Thurst out nature wyth a croche [staff], yet woll she styll runne backe agayne. **1831** T. L. PEACOCK *Crotchet Castle* i. Mr. Crotchet..seemed..to settle down..into an English country gentleman. ..But as, though you expel nature with a pitchfork, she will always come back. **1927** 'D. YATES' *Blind Corner* vi. There's a proverb which is rather in point. 'You can drive Nature out with a pitchfork, *but she'll always come back*.' I know you're using a bucket instead. But..the result is the same. **1980** C. GAVIN *How sleep Brave* xiv. There was feminine logic for you!..'You can drive out Nature with a pitchfork,..but she keeps on coming back.' **2002** *Times* 31 May 41 'Pitchfork nature out of doors and it will come back through a window' was a comment on many would-be papal reforms. ■ **Nature**; **persistence**

drive *see also* BAD money drives out good; HUNGER drives the wolf out of the wood; NEEDS must when the Devil drives; ONE nail drives out another.

drop *see* the LAST drop makes the cup run over.

dropping *see* CONSTANT dropping wears away a stone.

drowned *see* if you're BORN to be hanged then you'll never be drowned.

A DROWNING man will clutch at a straw

One grabs at the slightest chance when all hope is slipping away. *Clutch* is comparatively recent and is more suggestive of desperation than the earlier *catch. To clutch at a straw* (or *straws*) is frequently used as a metaphorical phrase.

□ **1534** MORE *Dialogue of Comfort* (1553) iii. Lyke a man that in peril of drowning catcheth whatsoeuer cometh next to hand .. be it neuer so simple a sticke. **1583** J. PRIME *Fruitful & Brief Discourse* I. 30 We do not as men redie to be drowned, catch at euery straw. **1623** J. HALL *Contemplations* VII. XIX. 252 The drowning man snatches at every twig. .. The messengers of Benhadad catch hastily at that stile of grace, and hold it fast. **1748** RICHARDSON *Clarissa* VII. i. A drowning man will catch at a straw, the Proverb well says. **1877** W. COLLINS *My Lady's Money* xv. His gratitude caught at those words, as the drowning man is said to catch at the proverbial straw. **1915** CONRAD *Victory* IV. viii. Wang seemed to think my insistence .. very stupid and tactless. But a drowning man clutches at straws. **1967** RIDOUT & WITTING *English Proverbs Explained* 49 A drowning man will clutch at a straw. **1967** T. STOPPARD *Rosencrantz & Guildenstern are Dead* III. 80 We drift down time, clutching at straws. But what good's a brick to a drowning man? ■ **hope and despair**

drunken *see* CHILDREN and fools tell the truth; HEAVEN protects children, sailors, and drunken men.

druv (drove, driven): *see* SUSSEX won't be druv.

dry *see* you never MISS the water till the well runs dry; sow dry and set wet; put your TRUST in God and keep your powder dry.

due *see* give CREDIT where credit is due; GIVE the Devil his due.

dumb *see* a CHERRY year a merry year.

dunghill *see* every COCK will crow upon his own dunghill.

dust *see* a PECK of March dust is worth a king's ransom.

duty *see* the FIRST duty of a soldier is obedience.

dying *see* you cannot SHIFT an old tree without it dying.

dyke *see* FEBRUARY fill dyke, be it black or be it white.

eagle *see* where the CARCASE is, there shall the eagles be gathered together.

EAGLES don't catch flies

Great or important people do not concern themselves with trifling matters or insignificant people. Cf. ERASMUS *Adages* III. ii. *aquila non captat muscas*, the eagle does not catch flies.

□ **1563** *Mirror for Magistrates* (1938) 405 The iolly Egles catche not little flees. **1581** G. PETTIE tr. *S. Guazzo's Civil Conversation* II. 48ᵛ That is the right act of a Prince, and therefore it is well saide, That the Egle catcheth not flies. **1786** H. L. PIOZZI *Anecdotes of Johnson* 185 With regard to slight insults.. 'They sting one (says he) but as a fly stings a horse; and the eagle will not catch flies.' **1942** H. C. BAILEY *Nobody's Vineyard* i. 'Eagles don't catch flies.' 'What do you mean?' 'Inspectors of Police don't trail urchins.' **1980** A. T. ELLIS *Birds of Air* (1983) 92 '*Aquila non captat muscas*,' she told him in a reassuring whisper. 'Eagles don't catch flies.' ■ **great and small**

ear *see* FIELDS have eyes, and woods have ears; LITTLE pitchers have large ears; you can't make a SILK purse out of a sow's ear; WALLS have ears.

The EARLY bird catches the worm

The corollary in quot. 2001, *it's the second mouse that gets the cheese*, is attributed to US comedian Steven Wright; it may be used independently to counsel caution.

□ **1636** W. CAMDEN *Remains concerning Britain* (ed. 5) 307 The early bird catcheth the worme. **1859** H. KINGSLEY *Geoffrey Hamlyn* II. xiv. Having worked..all the week..a man comes into your room at half-past seven..and informs you that the 'early bird gets the worm'. **1892** I. ZANGWILL *Big Bow Mystery* i. Grodman was not an early bird, now that he had no worms to catch. He could afford to despise proverbs now. **1996** R. POE *Return to House of Usher* ix. 167 'I got home at midnight last night and I'm here at seven. Where are they?.. Well, it's the early bird that catches the worm, and no mistake.' **2001** *Washington Post* 4 Sept. C13 The early bird may catch the worm, but it's the second mouse that gets the cheese. Don't be in a hurry to take a winner. ■ **diligence; efficiency and inefficiency**

The EARLY man never borrows from the late man

□ **1659** J. HOWELL *Proverbs* (English) 17 The rath [early] sower never borroweth of the late. **1732** T. FULLER *Gnomologia* no. 4492 The early Sower never borrows of the Late. **1978** R. WHITLOCK *Calendar of Country Customs* iii. Oats, too, benefit from early sowing. ..Another agricultural proverb..declares that, 'the early man never borrows from the late man'. ■ **borrowing and lending**

EARLY to bed and early to rise, makes a man healthy, wealthy, and wise

□ **1496** *Treatise of Fishing with Angle* H1 As the olde englysshe prouerbe sayth in this wyse. Who soo woll ryse erly shall be holy helthy and zely [fortunate]. **1523** J. FITZHERBERT *Husbandry* (1530) 52ᵛ At gramer scole I lerned a verse,..erly rysynge maketh a man hole in body, holer in soule, and rycher in goodes. **1639** J. CLARKE *Parœmiologia Anglo-Latina* 91 Earley to bed and early to rise, makes a man healthy, wealthy, and wise. **1853** SURTEES *Sponge's Sporting Tour* ix. Early to bed and early to rise being among Mr. Sponge's maxims, he was enjoying the view.. shortly after daylight. **2002** *New Scientist* 29 June 57 A lot of sleep doesn't make us happier. .. It's going to bed earlier that counts. There really is much to be said for 'early to bed early to rise, makes one healthy, wealthy and wise.' ■ **diligence; health; riches**

earned *see* a PENNY saved is a penny earned.

easier *see* it is easier to PULL down than to build up; it is easier to RAISE the Devil than to lay him; also EASY.

EAST is east, and west is west

□ **1892** R. KIPLING *Barrack-room Ballads* 75 Oh, East is East, and West is West, and never the twain shall meet. **1909** M. BARING *Orpheus in Mayfair* 271 Sledge said 'Goodnight' again, but when he was on the stairs he called back: 'In any case remember one thing, that East is East and West is West. Don't mix your deities.' **1994** *English Today* Oct. 19/2 East is east and west is west, and it will be a long time before fishermen from the bookends of Canada agree on delicate matters of taste over a plate of oysters. ■ **familiarity; harmony and disharmony; opposites**

EAST, west, home's best

□ **1859** W. K. KELLY *Proverbs of all Nations* 36 'East and west, at home the best' (German). .. *Ost und West, daheim das Best.* **1869** C. H. SPURGEON *John Ploughman's Talk* xiii. East and west, Home is best. **1920** E. V. LUCAS *Verena in Midst* cxiii. None the less I don't envy the traveller. 'East, west, home's best.' **1949** 'C. MACKENZIE' *Hunting Fairies* xviii. I thought what a bully time I'd had in Scotland but all the same I was glad to be going home because East West home's best. **1994** 'C. AIRD' 'Fair Cop' in *Injury Time* (1995) 27 As the police professional in Calleshire most involved with murder, Detective Inspector Sloan would have been the last man in the world to subscribe to the view that 'East or West, Home's Best' since home was where most victims of murder met their end. ■ **home**

east *see also* when the WIND is in the east, 'tis neither good for man nor beast.

EASY come, easy go

LIGHT *come, light go* and QUICKLY *come, quickly go* are less commonly found expressions of the same concept. Cf. early 15th-cent. Fr. *tost acquis tost se despens*, soon acquired, soon spent.

□ **1650** A. BRADSTREET *Tenth Muse* 126 That which easily comes, as freely goes. **1832** S. WARREN *Diary of Late Physician* II. xi. 'Easy come, easy go' is .. characteristic of rapidly acquired commercial fortunes. **1960** I. JEFFERIES *Dignity & Purity* ii. She's your only daughter, isn't she. .. Well, easy come, easy go. **2002** *National Review* 11 Mar. 28 After all, if tattoos can be removed at public expense, why bother to think very carefully about having them done in the first place? Easy come, easy go. ■ **getting and spending**

EASY does it

Also *gently does it*. Similar in form to *it's* DOGGED *as does it*.

□ **1863** T. TAYLOR *Ticket-of-Leave Man* IV. i. Easy does it, Bob. Hands off, and let's take things pleasantly. **1928** J. P. MCEVOY *Showgirl* 21 No high pressure stuff, sis. Easy does it with Dick. **1972** A. PRICE *Colonel Butler's Wolf* iii. Easy does it—the nails are big, but they are old and brittle. **1981** S. RUSHDIE *Midnight's Children* I. 103 Important to build bridges.. between the faiths. Gently does it. ■ **tact; ways and means**

easy *see* it is easy to find a STICK to beat a dog; it is easy to be WISE after the event; *also* EASIER.

You are what you EAT

Ger. *Mann ist was Mann isst*, man is what man eats; cf. the philosopher Ludwig Feuerbach (1804–72) in Jacob Moleschott *Lehre der Nahrungsmittel: Für das Volk* (1850) 'Advertisement': *Der Mensch ist, was er isst*, Man is what he eats. The saying is sometimes attributed to the French gastronome Anthelme Brillat-Savarin who wrote in his *Physiologie du Goût* (1825): *Dis-moi ce que tu manges, je te dirai ce que tu es*, Tell me what you eat, and I will tell you what you are.

□ **1930** J. GOLLOMB *Subtle Trail* ii. 55 There flashed through her mind the German saying, 'One is what one eats.' **1940** V. H. LINDLAHR (*title*) You are what you eat. **1980** FARB & ARMELAGOS *Consuming Passions* 3 Food faddists in recent decades have declared, 'You are what you eat'. **2002** *Times* 2 July 19 As obesity, chronic health problems and crime rise, we should pay far more attention to the adage 'You are what you eat'. ■ **food and drink**

We must EAT a peck of dirt before we die

A consolatory expression, frequently used in literal contexts. A *peck* is a dry measure of two gallons. Cf. **1603** H. CHETTLE et al. *Patient Grisel* A3^v I thinke I shall not eate a pecke of salt: I shall not liue long sure.

□ **1738** SWIFT *Polite Conversation* i. 48 'Why then, here's some Dirt in my Tea-cup.'.. 'Poh! you must eat a Peck of Dirt before you die.' **1819** KEATS *Letter* 19 Mar. (1952) 314 This is the second black eye I have had since leaving school.. we must eat a peck before we die. **1939** F. THOMPSON *Lark Rise* vi. The children.. were told: 'Us've all got to eat a peck o' dust before we dies, an' it'll slip down easy in this good yarb [herb] beer.' **1979** M. BABSON *Twelve Deaths of Christmas* xxix. She tried to rinse off the ice cubes. 'Never mind. .. They say, we all have to eat a peck of dirt before we die!' ■ **health; mortality**

EAT, drink, and be merry, for tomorrow we die

A conflation of two biblical sayings: ECCLESIASTES viii. 15 (AV) Then I commended mirth, because a man hath no better thing under the sun, than to eat, and to drink, and to be merry .. and ISAIAH xxii. 13 (AV) Let us eat and drink; for to morrow we shall die. There are a number of jocular variants (see for example quot. 2001).

□ **1870** D. G. ROSSETTI 'The Choice' in *House of Life*, Sonnet lxxi. Eat thou and drink; tomorrow thou shalt die. **1884** E. LYALL *We Two* xii. 240 But far from prompting him to repeat the maxim 'Let us eat and drink, for tomorrow we die!' it spurred him rather to a sort of fiery energy, never satisfied with what it had accomplished. **1960** O. MANNING *Great Fortune* (1988) 42 Inchcape.. complained: 'I've never before seen this place in such a hubbub.' 'It's the war,' said Clarence. 'Eat, drink and be merry, for tomorrow we may be starving to death.' **1975** N. GUILD *Lost and Found Man* 87 No point in getting morbid. .. What the hell. Eat, drink, and be merry, and all that crap. Lukas signaled the waiter and ordered another two croissants. **2001** *New Scientist* 22/29 Dec. 45 Eat, drink and be merry, for tomorrow we diet. ■ **life; opportunity**

He that would EAT the fruit must climb the tree

Cf. **1577** J. GRANGE *Golden Aphroditis* M1 Who will the fruyte that haruest yeeldes, must take the payne.

□ **1721** J. KELLY *Scottish Proverbs* 141 He that would eat the Fruit must climb the Tree. **1843** 'R. CARLTON' *New Purchase* I. xxiv. It is a proverb, 'He that would eat the fruit must first climb the tree and get it': but when that fruit is honey, he that wants it must first cut it down. **1970** V. CANNING *Great Affair* xiv. 'Son, are you one of those who like to eat the fruit and then walk away from the tree?' 'I want to marry her.' ■ **wanting and having**

EAT to live, not live to eat

Attributed to SOCRATES (See Diogenes Laertius *Socrates* II. xxxiv.) *ἔλεγέ τε τοὺς μὲν ἄλλους ἀνθρώπους ζῆν ἵν' ἐσθίοιεν; αὐτὸς δὲ ἐσθίειν ἵνα ζῴη*, and he said that other men live to eat, but he eats to live. Cf. CICERO *Rhetoricorum* IV. vii. *edere oportet ut vivas, non vivas ut edas*, one must eat to live, not live to eat.

□ **1387** J. TREVISA tr. *Higden's Polychronicon* (1871) III. 281 Socrates seide that meny men wil leve forto ete and drynke, and that they wolde ete and drynke.. forto lyve. *c* **1410** in *Secreta Secretorum* (1898) 67 I will ete so that y leue, and noght lyf that y ete. **1672** T. SHADWELL *Miser* 46 Eat to live, not live to eat; as the Proverb says. **1912** A. W. PINERO *Preserving Mr. Panmure* II. 85 I shall eat sufficient. .. But I eat to live; I don't live to eat. **2001** *Country Life* 20/27 Dec. 80 If I had to give a yes or a no to the old question 'Do you live to eat or eat to live?' I should say yes to the first part. ■ **food and drink**

eat *see also* the CAT would eat fish, but would not wet her feet; DOG does not eat dog; you cannot HAVE your cake and eat it; if you won't WORK you shan't eat.

eaten *see* REVENGE is a dish that can be eaten cold.

eating *see* APPETITE comes with eating; the PROOF of the pudding is in the eating.

eavesdroppers *see* LISTENERS never hear any good of themselves.

egg *see* as good be an ADDLED egg as an idle bird; you cannot make an OMELETTE without breaking eggs; there is REASON in the roasting of eggs; don't TEACH your grandmother to suck eggs.

Don't put all your EGGS in one basket

Don't chance everything on a single venture, but spread your risk. *To put all one's eggs in one basket* is commonly used as a metaphorical phrase.

□ **1662** G. TORRIANO *Italian Proverbial Phrases* 125 To put all ones Eggs in a Paniard, *viz.* to hazard all in one bottom [ship]. **1710** S. PALMER *Proverbs* 344 Don't venture all your Eggs in One Basket. **1894** 'M. TWAIN' *Pudd'nhead Wilson* in *Century Mag.* XLVII. VI. 817 Behold, the fool saith, 'Put not all thine eggs in the one basket'—which is but a manner of saying, 'Scatter your money and your attention'; but the wise man saith, 'Put all your eggs in the one basket and—*watch that basket*.' **1967** RIDOUT & WITTING *English Proverbs Explained* 46 Don't put all your eggs in one basket. **2002** *Washington Post* 23 May E3 What part of 'don't put all your eggs in one basket' isn't clear? Putting all or most of your money into one stock is gambling, not investing. ■ **prudence**

eight *see* SIX hours' sleep for a man, seven for a woman, and eight for a fool.

eleven *see* POSSESSION is nine points of the law; RAIN before seven, fine before eleven.

Every ELM has its man

Cf. **1906** R. KIPLING *Puck of Pook's Hill* 32 Ellum she hateth mankind, and waiteth Till every gust be laid To drop a limb on the head of him That any way trusts her shade.

□ **1928** *Times* 29 Nov. 10 Owing to the frequency with which this tree sheds its branches, or is uprooted in a storm, it has earned for itself a sinister reputation. 'Every elm has its man' is an old country saying. ■ **death**; **fate and fatalism**

EMPTY sacks will never stand upright

Extreme need makes survival impossible. Also used as an argument for taking food or drink (see quot. 1978)

□ **1642** G. TORRIANO *Select Italian Proverbs* 90 *Sacco vuoto non può star in piedi.* An emptie sack cannot stand upright: nota, Applied to such as either pinch themselves, or are pincht by hard fortune. **1758** B. FRANKLIN *Poor Richard's Almanack* (Introduction) Poverty often deprives a Man of all Spirit and Virtue; 'Tis hard for an empty Bag to stand up-right. **1860** G. ELIOT *Mill on Floss* I. I. viii. There's folks as things 'ull allays go awk'ard with: empty sacks 'ull never stand upright. **1958** B. BEHAN *Borstal Boy* III. 310 We've a long night before us and an empty sack won't stand. **1978** J. MCGAHERN *Getting Through* 99 'Give this man something.'.. 'A cup of tea will do fine,' he had protested. ..'Nonsense. ..Empty bags can't stand.' ■ **hunger**; **poverty**

EMPTY vessels make the most sound

Foolish or witless persons are the most talkative or noisy; also used of achievement (see quot. 1932). *Vessel* here means a receptacle, as a drinking-vessel.

□ *a* **1430** J. LYDGATE *Pilgrimage of Man* (EETS) l. 15933 A voyde vessel.. maketh outward a gret soun, Mor than.. what yt was ful. **1547** W. BALDWIN *Treatise of Moral Philosophy* IV. Q4 As emptye vesselles make the lowdest sounde: so they that haue least wyt, are the greatest babblers. **1599** SHAKESPEARE *Henry V* IV. iv. 64 I did never know so full a voice issue from so empty a heart: but the saying is true—The empty vessel makes the greatest sound. **1707** SWIFT *Essay on Faculties of Mind* I. 249 Empty Vessels sound loudest. **1967** RIDOUT & WITTING *English Proverbs Explained* 51 Empty vessels make the most sound. **1982** J. BINGHAM *Brock & Defector* xiii. 'All talk and no action. ..' 'Empty vessels make the most noise,' Brock agreed. **2002** *Times: Register* 21 Oct. 10 The adage 'empty vessels make most noise' has certainly come to mind as I have listened to other politicians. ■ **boasting**; **words and deeds**

empty *see also* BETTER are small fish than an empty dish; don't THROW the baby out with the bathwater.

enchantment *see* DISTANCE lends enchantment to the view.

The END crowns the work

Cf. L. *finis coronat opus*, the end crowns the work; 15th-cent. Fr. *la fin loe l'œuvre*, the end praises the work.

□ **1509** H. WATSON *Ship of Fools* Dd1 For the ende crowneth. **1592** G. DELAMOTHE *French Alphabet* II. 29 The end doth crowne the worke. ..La fin couronne l'œuvre. **1602** SHAKESPEARE *Troilus & Cressida* IV. v. 223 The end crowns all; And that old common arbitrator, Time, Will one day end it. **1820** SCOTT *Abbot* I. xiii. As the end crowns the work, it also forms the rule by which it must be ultimately judged.

1870 DICKENS *Edwin Drood* xviii. Proof, sir, proof, must be built up stone by stone. ..As I say, the end crowns the work. **1961** J. WEBB *One for my Dame* iii. That the end should crown the work, that I had given no more lies than I had been told made no difference. You either played it straight or you didn't. ■ **finality**

The END justifies the means

Cf. OVID *Heroides* ii. 85 *exitus acta probat*, the outcome justifies the deeds. The negative of this is also often asserted.

□ **1583** G. BABINGTON *Exposition of Commandments* 260 The ende good, doeth not by and by make the meanes good. **1718** M. PRIOR *Literary Works* (1971) I. 186 The End must justify the Means: He only Sins who Ill intends. **1941** 'H. BAILEY' *Smiling Corpse* 238 'The police don't like to have their bodies moved.'.. 'In this case the end justifies the means.' **2001** *Washington Times* 2 Aug. A16 The conservatives' war on drugs is an example of good intentions that have had unfortunate consequences. As often happens with noble causes, the end justifies the means, and the means of the drug war are inconsistent with the U.S. Constitution and our civil liberties. ■ **action and consequence**

end *see also* (noun) ALL good things must come to an end; the DEVIL can quote Scripture for his own ends; EVERYTHING has an end; he who WILLS the end, wills the means; (verb) all's WELL that ends well.

ending *see* a GOOD beginning makes a good ending

endured *see* what can't be CURED must be endured.

The ENEMY of my enemy is my friend

□ **1985** M. KORDA *Queenie* III. xiii. 347 In California, I'm an outsider. So is Wolff, so we're natural allies. "The enemy of my enemy is my friend," as I believe the Arabs say. **1992** MIEDER *Dict. American Proverbs* 181 The enemies of my enemies are my friends. **2000** *New Yorker* 25 Sept. 56/1 The enemy-of-my-enemy-is-my-friend logic.. dominates central-African politics. **2001** *Spectator* 24 Nov. 36 The hack right-wing answer.. is to quote what the quoters claim to be 'the old Arab proverb': 'The enemy of my enemy is my friend.' **2002** *National Review* 3 May (online edn) Or was she [Barbie]—as conservatives insisted, taking the view that 'the enemy of my feminist enemy is my friend'—simply good childhood fun? ■ **enemies; friends**

enemy *see also* the BEST is the enemy of the good; it is good to make a BRIDGE of gold to a flying enemy; the GOOD is the enemy of the best; there is no LITTLE enemy; SAVE us from our friends.

ENGLAND is the paradise of women, the hell of horses, and the purgatory of servants

Cf. **1558** BONAVENTURE DES PERIERS *Nouvelles Recreations* N1^v^ *Paris.. c'est le paradis des femmes, l'enfer des mules, et le purgatorie des soliciteurs*; **1583** R. D. *Mirrour of Mirth* K1^v^ *Paris* is a paradise for women, a hel for mens horses, and a Purgatorye for those that followe suits of Law.

□ **1591** J. FLORIO *Second Fruits* 205 She takes her ease, and followes her busines at home. .. England is the paradise of women, the purgatory of men, and the hell of horses. **1617** F. MORYSON *Itinerary* III. I. iii. *England*.. is said to be the Hell of Horses, the Purgatory of Seruants, and the Paradice of Weomen. **1787** F. GROSE *Provincial Glossary* s.v. England, England is the paradise of women, hell of horses, and purgatory of servants. **1962** E. S. TURNER *What Butler Saw* i. An ancient proverb said that England was 'the hell of horses, the purgatory of servants and the paradise of women'. When the eighteenth century came in, England was still the hell of horses, but there were loud complaints that it had become the paradise of servants and the purgatory of women. ■ **national characteristics**

ENGLAND's difficulty is Ireland's opportunity

□ **1856** *Tribune* 19 Jan. 188 Some few years ago, we followed O'Connell, and when he declared that 'England's difficulty is Ireland's opportunity', we threw our hats in the air. **1916** G. B. SHAW in *New York Times* (Mag.) 9 Apr. 2 The cry that 'England's Difficulty Is Ireland's Opportunity' is raised in the old senseless, spiteful way as a recommendation to stab England in the back when she is fighting some one else. **1969** T. PAKENHAM *Year of Liberty* i. Successive plantations—of Scottish Presbyterians in Ulster.. did not secure Ireland. The Catholics' watchword remained: 'England's difficulty is Ireland's opportunity.' **1997** *Times* 15 Oct. 8 Britain's difficulty became Ireland's opportunity last night when.. Sir Denis Mahon presented three Baroque paintings originally destined for Liverpool to the National Gallery of Ireland in Dublin. ■ **opportunity; politics**

England *see also* the CAT, the rat, and Lovell the dog, rule all England under the hog; what MANCHESTER says today, the rest of England says tomorrow; TURKEY, heresy, hops, and beer came into England all in one year.

The ENGLISH are a nation of shopkeepers

Attributed to Napoleon in B. E. O'Meara *Napoleon in Exile* (1822) I. 103 *L'Angleterre est une nation de boutiquiers*. The concept of the shopkeeping nation is however earlier: **1766** J. TUCKER *Letter from Merchant* 46 A Shop-keeper will never get the more Custom by beating his Customers; and what is true of a Shop-keeper, is true of a Shop-keeping Nation; **1776** A. SMITH *Wealth of Nations* II. IV. vii. To found a great empire for the sole purpose of raising up a people of customers, may at first sight appear a project fit only for a nation of shopkeepers.

□ **1831** DISRAELI *Young Duke* I. xi. Hast thou brought this, too, about that ladies' hearts should be won.. over a counter. .. We are indeed a nation of shopkeepers. **1911** *Times Weekly* 17 Feb. 132 Napoleon.. described the English as a nation of shopkeepers. Uttered in a sneering spirit, it embodied.. the profound truth that our prosperity is based upon our trade. **1981** R. RENDELL *Put on by Cunning* xiv. Americans.. are a nation of salesmen just as the English are a nation of small shopkeepers. **2002** *Times* 5 Jan. 25 England is indeed a nation of shopkeepers, but it has always preferred to draw these shopkeepers from among the newly Anglicised. ■ **national characteristics**

One ENGLISHMAN can beat three Frenchmen

Now also used of other nationalities, and in different proportions.

□ **1599** SHAKESPEARE *Henry V* III. vi. 144 When they were in health. .. I thought upon one pair of English legs Did march three Frenchmen. **1745** H. WALPOLE *Letter* 13 July (1941) IX. 17 We, who formerly.. could any one of us beat three Frenchmen, are now so degenerated that three Frenchmen can evidently beat one Englishman. **1834** MARRYAT *Peter Simple* III. viii. My men.. there are three privateers. .. It's just a fair match for you—one Englishman can always beat three Frenchmen. **1851** G. BORROW *Lavengro* I. xxvi. In the days of pugilism it was no vain boast to say, that one Englishman was a match for two of t'other race [the French]. **1913** A. LUNN *Harrovians* i. Peter knew that an Englishman can tackle three foreigners, and forgot that the inventor of this theory took care to oppose three Englishmen to one foreigner as often as possible. **1981** *London Review of Books*

16 July–5 Aug. 5 Spain's conquest of Mexico 'gave Europeans a new and potent myth', the conviction of one European as equal to twenty others. ■ **boasting; national characteristics**

An ENGLISHMAN's house is his castle

□ **1581** R. MULCASTER *Positions* xl. He is the appointer of his owne circumstance, and his house is his castle. **1642** T. FULLER *Fast Sermon* 28 It was wont to be said *A mans house is his Castle* but if this Castle of late hath proved unable to secure any, let them make their conscience their castle. **1791** BOSWELL *Life of Johnson* II. 284 In London.. a man's own house is truly his *castle*, in which he can be in perfect safety from intrusion. **1837** DICKENS *Pickwick Papers* xxiv. Some people maintains that an Englishman's house is his castle. That's gammon [nonsense]. **1998** *Garden (Royal Horticultural Society)* May 313 An Englishman's house may be his castle, but does it follow that his garden is his forest? **2002** *Washington Times* 1 Aug. A14 An Englishman's home is no longer his castle. Thanks to gun control zealots, England has become the land of choice for criminals. ■ **home; national characteristics**

An ENGLISHMAN's word is his bond

□ *c* **1500** *Lancelot of Lake* (STS) l. 1671 O kingis word shuld be o kingis bonde. *a* **1606** *Nobody & Somebody* C2^{V} Nobodies worde is as good as his bond. **1642** T. FULLER *Holy State* v. XIII. He hath this property of an honest man, that his word is as good as his band. **1754** RICHARDSON *Grandison* I. Letter ix. I am no flincher. ..The word of Sir Rowland Meredith is as good as his bond. **1841** DICKENS *Old Curiosity Shop* lviii. 'Marchioness,' said Mr. Swiveller, rising, 'the word of a gentleman is as good as his bond—sometimes better, as in the present case.' **1916** F. VANE *Letter* 14 Sept. in M. Gibbon *Inglorious Soldier* iii. [List of fictions underlying national conceit:] 3. That English justice is something much more superfine than any other sort of justice (owing to Public School training!) and that an Englishman's word is his bond. **1981** A. GRAHAM-YOOLL *Forgotten Colony* xvi. If a verbal promise is made the native, to seal the contract, usually says *palabra de inglés*,.. meaning that he will act as an Englishman, whose word is his bond. ■ **honour; national characteristics**

ENOUGH is as good as a feast

□ *c.* **1375** J. BARBOUR *Bruce* (EETS) XIV. 363 He maid thame na gud fest, perfay [truly], And nocht-for-thi [nevertheless] yneuch had thai. *c* **1470** MALORY *Morte d'Arthur* (1967) I. 246 Inowghe is as good as a feste. **1546** J. HEYWOOD *Dialogue of Proverbs* II. xi. M1 Here is enough, I am satisfied (sayde he).. For folke say, enough is as good as a feast. **1833** LAMB *Elia's Last Essays* vi. That enough is as good as a feast. Not a man, woman, or child in ten miles round Guildhall, who really believes this saying. **1928** D. H. LAWRENCE *Woman who rode Away* 165 I'll *live* with another woman but I'll never *marry* another. Enough is as good as a feast. **2000** T. & R. MAGLIOZZI *In Our Humble Opinion* 208 And now we know from our Happiness equation that the problem is high Expectations. And who comes to the rescue? Rooster Cogburn, who else? *Enough is as good as a feast.* ■ **content and discontent; food and drink**

ENOUGH is enough

From its older use as an expression of content or satisfaction (cf. ENOUGH *is as good as a feast*), this is now frequently used as a reprimand, warning someone off from persisting in an inappropriate or excessive course of action.

□ **1546** J. HEYWOOD *Dialogue of Proverbs* II. xi. M1 Sens enough is enough (sayd I) here maie we With that one word take end good. **1832** W. IRVING *Alhambra* II. 40

'I will descend for no more,' said the Moor, doggedly; 'enough is enough for a reasonable man—more is superfluous.' **1915** T. DREISER *Titan* (ed. 3) xlvii. 404 I realize all its merits just as well as you do. But enough is enough. **2002** *Times* 10 Aug. 23 We all enjoyed your encouraging letter—'Dear Sir, The bank looks forward to a return to the traditional arrangement whereby you bank with us, rather than vice-versa. Enough is enough.' ■ **content and discontent; moderation**

enough *see also* throw DIRT enough, and some will stick; give a man ROPE enough and he will hang himself; a WORD to the wise is enough.

envied *see* BETTER be envied than pitied.

To ERR is human (to forgive divine)

Although known in Latin (*humanum est errare*, it is human to err) and in earlier English versions, this saying is generally quoted in Pope's words (quot. 1711). Cf. *c* **1386** CHAUCER *Tale of Melibee* l. 1264 The proverbe seith that 'for to do synne is mannyssh, but certes for to persevere longe in synne is werk of the devel'; **1539** R. MORISON tr. *J. L. Vives' Introduction to Wisdom* D7 It is naturally gyuen to al men, to erre, but to no man to perseuer .. therein.

□ **1578** H. WOTTON tr. *J. Yver's Courtly Controversy* E3 To offend is humaine, to repent diuine, and to perseuere diuelish. **1659** J. HOWELL *Proverbs* (French) 12 To erre is humane, to repent is divine, to persevere is Diabolicall. **1711** POPE *Essay on Criticism* l. 525 Good-Nature and Good-Sense must ever join; To Err is Humane; to Forgive, Divine. **1908** *Times Literary Supplement* 27 Mar. 1 The modern moralist pardons everything, because he is not certain of anything, except that to err is human. **2000** T. DALRYMPLE *Life at Bottom* (2001) 222 To err is human, to forgive divine: and the police have now taken up the role of divinities, making allowances for wrongdoers instead of apprehending them. ■ **forgiveness; wrongdoers**

escape *see* LITTLE thieves are hanged, but great ones escape.

eternal *see* HOPE springs eternal.

Eve *see* when ADAM delved and Eve span, who was then the gentleman?

even *see* (adjective) don't get MAD, get even; never give a SUCKER an even break; (adverb) even a WORM will turn.

evensong *see* be the DAY weary or be the day long, at last it ringeth to evensong.

event *see* COMING events cast their shadows before; it is easy to be WISE after the event.

ever *see* NOTHING is for ever.

EVERY little helps

Cf. **1590** G. MEURIER *Deviz Familiers* A6 *peu ayde, disçoit le formy, pissant en mer en plein midy*, every little helps, said the ant, pissing into the sea at midday.

□ **1602** P. GAWDY *Letters* (1906) 118 The wrenn sayde all helpte when she—in the sea. **1623** W. CAMDEN *Remains concerning Britain* (ed. 3) 268 Euery thing helpes, quoth the Wren when she pist i' the sea. **1787** E. HAZARD in *Collections of Massachusetts Hist. Society* (1877) 5th Ser. II. 477 A guinea is a guinea, and every little helps. **1840** MARRYAT *Poor Jack* xiii. It's a very old saying, that every little helps. .. Almost all the men were on the larboard side. **1988** J. MORTIMER *Rumpole and Age of*

Miracles (1989) 48 'I'll get him to make a few inquiries relative to the bird in question. Every little helps.' ■ **assistance; great and small**

EVERY man for himself

See also the later expanded forms in the next two proverbs.

□ *c* **1386** CHAUCER *Knight's Tale* l. 1182 At the kynges court, my brother, Ech man for hymself, ther is noon oother. **1478** J. WHETLEY *Letter* 20 May in *Paston Letters* (1976) II. 427 Your moder..hath made her wyll, the wyche ye shall understond more when I com, for ther is every man for hym selff. **1678** J. RAY *English Proverbs* (ed. 2) (Scottish) 366 Every man for himself (quoth the Merteine). **1795** D. YANCEY *Letter* 6 June in *Virginia Magazine of Hist. & Biography* (1922) XXX. 224 The old adage might well be applied in many cases. Every man for himself. **1974** A. PRICE *Other Paths to Glory* II. vi. It was pretty much every man for himself. But I was hit quite early on. ■ **self-preservation**

EVERY man for himself, and devil take the hindmost

The two earliest examples are more closely aligned in form to the following proverb. *See also* DEVIL take the hindmost.

□ **1530** A. BARCLAY *Eclogues* (EETS) I. 1009 Eche man for him selfe, and the fiende for all. **1573** J. SANFORDE 108V Euery man for him selfe; and the Deuill for all. **1858** D. M. MULOCK *Women's Thoughts about Women* ii. The world is hard enough, for two-thirds of it are struggling for the dear life—'each for himself, and de'il tak the hindmost.' **1939** L. I. WILDER *By Shores of Silver Lake* xxv. There wasn't any standing in line. ..It was each fellow for himself and devil take the hindmost. **2001** *Spectator* 24 Nov. 29 One senses that..Tories are hostile to that extra refinement of civilisation: it's every man for himself, and devil take the hindmost. Remember what Mrs Thatcher said about not helping 'lame ducks'..? ■ **self-preservation**

EVERY man for himself, and God for us all

□ **1546** J. HEYWOOD *Dialogue of Proverbs* II. ix. L2 Praie and shifte eche one for hym selfe, as he can. Every man for hym selfe, and god for us all. **1615** T. ADAMS *White Devil* (ed. 2) 83 That by-word, Euery man for himselfe, and God for vs all, is vncharitable, vngodly. **1830** MARRYAT *King's Own* III. xiii. The captain..ordered the sailor to leave the boat. 'Every man for himself, and God for us all!' was the cool answer of the refractory sea-man. **1979** *Times* 29 Dec. 12 Each for himself, and God for us all, as the elephant said when he danced among the chickens. ■ **self-preservation**

EVERY man has his price

□ **1734** W. WYNDHAM in *Bee* VIII. 97 'It is an old Maxim, that every Man has his Price,' if you can but come up to it. **1798** W. COXE *Memoirs of Sir Robert Walpole* I. lxiv. The political axiom generally attributed to him [Walpole]..was perverted by leaving out the word *those*. ..He ascribed to the interested views of themselves..the declaration of pretended patriots, of whom he said, 'All those men have their price.' **1845** G. P. R. JAMES *Smuggler* I. x. 'You can do nothing with Mowle. He never took a penny in his life.' 'Oh, every man has his price.' **1949** N. MAILER *Naked & Dead* II. xi. It was the sort of deal his father might have pulled. 'Every man has his price.' **2000** 'C. AIRD' *Little Knell* xiv. 162 'Howard Air's accountants, sir, assure us that all their clients are men and women of unimpeachable integrity.' 'No such thing,' came back Leeyes smartly. 'Everyone's got their price.' ■ **bribery and corruption**

EVERY man is the architect of his own fortune

Although attributed to Bacon in quot. 1991, this was a saying of the Roman censor Appius Claudius Caecus (4th–3rd cent. BC): PSEUDO-SALLUST *Ad Caesarem Senem* i. *sed res docuit id verum esse, quod in carminibus Appius ait, fabrum esse suae quemque fortunae*, but experience has shown what Appius said in his verses to be true, that each man is the architect of his own fortune.

□ **1533** N. UDALL *Flowers for Latin Speaking* (1560) 24 A prouerbiall spekyng. .. Euery man.. is causer of his own fortune. **1649** MILTON *Eikonoklastes* III. 542 They in whomsoeuer these vertues dwell.. are the architects of thir own happiness. **1707** J. DUNTON *Athenian* Sport 454 We are.. architects of our own fortune. **1818** S. FERRIER *Marriage* III. vi. As every man is said to be the artificer of his own fortune, so every one.. had best be the artificer of their own friendship. **1873** *Notes & Queries* 4th Ser. XII. 514 We have not a commoner saying among us than 'Every man is the architect of his own fortune,' and we have very few much older. **1991** *Times* 5 June 18 Educationists complain of the limitations on their resources; but quantifying this in league tables proves the long-term truth of Bacon's dictum *quisque faber suae fortunae*, each the maker of his own fate. ■ **self-help**

EVERY man to his taste

Cf. STATIUS *Silvae* II. ii. 73 *sua cuique voluptas*, everyone has his own pleasures; Fr. *chacun à son goût*, each to his taste.

□ **1580** LYLY *Euphues & his England* II. 161 Betweene them it was not determined, but euery one as he lyketh. *a* **1640** MIDDLETON et al. *Old Law* II. ii. Every one to their liking. But I say An honest man's worth all. **1760** STERNE *Tristram Shandy* I. vii. I own I never could envy Didius in these kinds of fancies of his:—But every man to his own taste. **1849** BULWER-LYTTON *Caxtons* III. XVII. i. 'Sheep are dull things to look at after a bull-hunt.'.. 'Every man to his taste in the Bush.' **1929** E. LINKLATER *Poet's Pub* xxvi. 'I like fairy tales,' said the professor. .. 'Every man to his taste,' agreed the landlord. **1986** J. SMITH *Tourist Trap* xviii. Tried to get me to try one, and our son and daughter-in-law too. But we wouldn't do it. I said, '"Everybody to their own taste," said the old lady as she kissed the cow.' ■ **idiosyncrasy; taste**

EVERY man to his trade

With allusion to I CORINTHIANS vii. 20 (AV) Let every man abide in the same calling wherein he was called. Cf. **1539** R. TAVERNER tr. *Erasmus' Adages* E1 Let euerye man exercise hym selfe in the facultie that he knoweth. **1590–1** SHAKESPEARE *Henry VI, Pt. 2* IV. ii. 15 And yet it is said 'Labour in thy vocation'; which is as much to say as 'Let the magistrates be labouring men'; and therefore should we be magistrates.

□ **1597–8** SHAKESPEARE *Henry IV, Pt. 1* II. ii. 75 Every man to his business. **1605** MARSTON *Dutch Courtesan* I. i. Every man must follow his trade, and every woman her occupation. *a* **1721** M. PRIOR *Dialogues of Dead* (1907) 221 Every man to his trade, Charles, you should have challenged me at long pike or broad sword. **1930** C. BUSH *Murder at Fenwold* viii. 'I dabble in Mathematics but.. I'd rather have your Latinity.' 'Every man to his trade.' **1990** 'C. AIRD' *Body Politic* (1991) x. 110 'Too early at the crem [crematorium], of course,' said Tod, surprised. 'That's always bad.' 'Yes, I can see that,' agreed Sloan. Every man to his own trade. ■ **business; trades and skills; work**

every *see also* every CLOUD has a silver lining; every COCK will crow upon his own dunghill; every DOG has his day; every DOG is allowed one bite; every ELM has its man; there is an EXCEPTION to every rule; every HERRING must hang by its own gill; every JACK has his Jill; every LAND has its own law; every PICTURE tells a story; if every man would SWEEP his own doorstep the city would soon be clean; every TUB must stand on its own bottom; there are TWO sides to every question.

EVERYBODY loves a lord

□ **1869** F. J. FURNIVALL in *Queen Elizabeth's Academy* (EETS) p. xii. The second tract..is printed, not mainly because 'John Bull loves a Lord'..but because the question of Precedence was so important a one in old social arrangements. **1908** *Spectator* 3 July 9 It is always said that an Englishman loves a lord. It would be more exact to say that he is in love with lordliness. **1980** M. NICHOLLS *Importance of being Oscar* (1981) 58 If pressed, he would probably have admitted that he was no exception to the adage that 'Everybody Loves a Lord'. ■ **society**

What EVERYBODY says must be true

□ *a* **1400** *Legends of Saints* (STS) III. 105 For I fynd suthfastnes [truth], that al men sais, is nocht les [lies]. *c* **1475** in *Modern Philology* (1940) XXXVIII. 118 Hit ys cominly truye that all men sayth. *c* **1518** A. BARCLAY tr. *Mancinus' Mirror of Good Manners* F1[v] It nedes muste be trewe which euery man doth say. **1748** RICHARDSON *Clarissa* IV. 74 The most accomplished of women, as every one says; and what every one says must be true. **1905** A. MACLAREN *Gospel according to St. Matthew* II. 246 'What everybody says must be true' is a cowardly proverb. ..What most people say is usually false. ■ **public opinion; truth**

EVERYBODY's business is nobody's business

Cf. ARISTOTLE *Politics* II. i. *ἥκιστα γὰρ επιμελείας τυγχάνει τὸ πλείστων κοινόν*, a matter common to most men receives least attention.

□ **1611** R. COTGRAVE *Dict. French & English* s.v. Ouvrage, Euerie bodies worke is no bodies worke. **1655** I. WALTON *Compleat Angler* (ed. 2) I. ii. A wise friend of mine did usually say, That which is every bodies businesse, is no bodies businesse. **1725** DEFOE (*title*) Every-Body's Business, is No-Body's Business;..exemplified in the pride of our Woman-Servants. **1914** G. B. SHAW *Misalliance* 10 'The danger of public business is that it never ends'..'What I say is that everybody's business is nobody's business.' **1981** D. CLARK *Longest Pleasure* v. It's unfair to try to make points by misquoting. What you should have said is 'everybody's business is nobody's business', and that doesn't fit our present case at all. ■ **busybodies**

everyone *see* you can't PLEASE everyone; everyone SPEAKS well of the bridge which carries him over; everyone STRETCHES his legs according to the length of his coverlet.

EVERYTHING has an end

Cf. mid 14th-cent. Fr. *mais il n'est chose qui ne fine, ne qui ne viengne à son termine*, but there is nothing which doesn't end, which doesn't come to its conclusion.

□ *c* **1385** CHAUCER *Troilus & Criseyde* III. 615 At the laste, as every thyng hath ende, She took hire leve. **1616** N. BRETON *Crossing of Proverbs* A6 'Euery thing hath an end'..'Not so, a Ring hath none.' **1841** DICKENS *Barnaby Rudge* XX. Everything has an end. Even young ladies in love cannot read their letters for ever. **1980** D. FRANCIS *Reflex* viii. Can't go on for ever, more's the pity. Everything ends, doesn't it. ■ **finality**

everything *see also* ALL things come to those who wait; when all you have is a HAMMER, everything looks like a nail; MONEY isn't everything; a PLACE for everything, and everything in its place; there is a REMEDY for everything except death; there is a TIME and place for everything; there is a TIME for everything.

evidence *see* what the SOLDIER said isn't evidence.

EVIL communications corrupt good manners

Proper conduct is harmfully influenced by false information or knowledge; also used to assert the deleterious effect of bad example. With allusion to I CORINTHIANS xv. 33 (AV) Be not deceived: evil communications corrupt good manners.

□ *c* **1425** J. ARDERNE *Treatises of Fistula* (EETS) 5 Shrewed speche corrumpith gode maners. **1533** MORE *Debellation* [subjugation] *of Salem* xiv. (As saynt Poule speketh of such heresyes) euyl communication corrupteth good maners. **1749** FIELDING *Tom Jones* IV. XII. iii. I heartily wish you would.. not think of going among them.—Evil Communication corrupts good Manners. **1874** TROLLOPE *Phineas Redux* I. xvi. [The horse] would have taken the fence.. but Dandolo had baulked.. and evil communications will corrupt good manners. **1939** W. S. MAUGHAM *Christmas Holiday* ii. A disposition of such sweetness that no evil communication could corrupt his good manners. **1973** 'M. INNES' *Appleby's Answer* ii. One can't be too careful in choosing a well-bred cat's company. .. Evil communications corrupt good manners. ■ **conduct; example, good and bad**

EVIL doers are evil dreaders

□ *a* **1568** R. ASCHAM *Schoolmaster* (1570) I. 27 Ill doinges, breed ill thinkinges. And corrupted manners, spryng perverted iudgements. **1721** J. KELLY *Scottish Proverbs* 176 Ill doers, ill deemers. **1737** A. RAMSAY *Scots Proverbs* xix. Ill doers are ay ill dreaders. **1828** SCOTT *Fair Maid of Perth* II. v. Put me not to quote the old saw, that evil doers are evil dreaders.—It is your suspicion, not your knowledge, which speaks. **1886** R. L. STEVENSON *Kidnapped* xxvii. If you were more trustful, it would better befit your time of life. .. We have a proverb.. that evil doers are aye evil-dreaders. ■ **conscience; wrong-doers**

EVIL to him who evil thinks

Medieval Fr. *honi soit qui mal y pense* is the motto of the Order of the Garter, originated in 1348 or 1349 by King Edward III of England; the saying is well known in its French form as well as being current in a variety of English versions. Quots. 1589 and 1650 offer suggestions on the translation.

□ *c* **1460** SIR R. ROS *La Belle Dame* in Skeat (ed.) *Chaucer* VIII. 397 Who thinketh il, no good may him befal. **1546** J. HEYWOOD *Dialogue of Proverbs* I. ix. C2 And shame take him that shame thinkth. **1589** G. PUTTENHAM *Arte of English Poesie* (Arber) 116 Commonly thus Englished, Ill be to him that thinks ill, but in mine opinion better thus, Dishonoured is he that meanes dishonorably. **1650** R. COTGRAVE *Dict. French & English* (Howell's Epistle Dedicatory) We English it, Ill be to him who thinks ill; though the true sense be, let him be beray'd who thinks any ill, being a metaphor taken from a child that hath berayed [fouled] his clouts [clothes], and in France ther's not one in a hundred who understands this word nowadayes. **1668** DENHAM in Dryden *Miscellany* v. 76 Who evil thinks, may evil him confound. **1954** B. FLYNN *Doll's Done Dancing* xvii. 158 'The.. er.. *hoi polloi*.. can always be found ready to point the finger or shrug the shoulder or.. er.. nod the head. Whereas the understanding.. erudite person.. with the right instincts, makes no comment. Evil to him who evil thinks.' ■ **good and evil**

Never do EVIL that good may come of it

With allusion to ROMANS iii. 8 (AV) And not.. Let us do evil, that good may come.

□ **1583** P. STUBBES *Anatomie of Abuses* K5 We must not doo euil, that good may come of it: yet the lawes in permitting certain reasonable gain to be received for the loane of money lent..haue not doone much amisse. **1689** G. BULKELEY *Letter* in *Coll. Connecticut Hist. Society* (1860) I. 59 If I knew any thing whereby to justify the present proceeding, I should not conceal it; but we must not do evil that good may come of it. **1882** C. M. YONGE *Unknown to History* II. ix. Walsingham's agents..did evil that good might come, thinking Mary's death alone would ensure them from Pope and Spaniard. **1950** J. CANNAN *Murder Included* 127 What..were the ethics? A promise made to a silly child, was it binding? You mustn't do evil that good may come of it..but the boy was only fourteen and practically half-witted, and Lisa was an absurd little Quixote. ■ **good and evil**; **ways and means**

evil *see also* a GREAT book is a great evil; IDLENESS is the root of all evil; MONEY is the root of all evil; SEE no evil, hear no evil, speak no evil; SUFFICIENT unto the day is the evil thereof.

Of two EVILS choose the less

Cf. ARISTOTLE *Nicomachean Ethics* II. ix. 1109a κατὰ τὸν δεύτερον, φασί, πλοῦν τὰ ἐλάχιστα ληπτέον τῶν κακῶν, we must as a second-best course, it is said, take the least of the evils; CICERO *De Officiis* III. xxix. *minima de malis*, of evils choose the least.

□ *c* **1385** CHAUCER *Troilus & Criseyde* II. 470 Of harmes two, the lesse is for to chese. *c* **1440** *Gesta Romanorum* (EETS) 10 Of too Evelis the lasse Evill is to be chosyn. **1546** J. HEYWOOD *Dialogue of Proverbs* I. v. B2 Of two yls, chose the least while choyse lyth in lot. **1785** J. BOSWELL *Journal of Tour to Hebrides* 464 'O ho! Sir, (said I), you are flying to me for refuge!'..'It is of two evils choosing the least.' **1891** A. FORBES *Barracks, Bivouacs & Battles* 187 Either the Turks would make a prisoner of me..or I must..take my chance of the Russian fire. ..'Of two evils choose the less,' says the wise proverb. **1975** J. PORTER *Package Included Murder* xiv. She didn't want to wake dear Constance, who really needed all the sleep she could get, but if she didn't..Miss Jones chose the lesser of two evils. ■ **choices**

EXAMPLE is better than precept

Cf. SENECA *Letters* vi. 5 *longum iter est per precepta, breve et efficax per exempla*, long is the way by means of precepts, short and effective by examples.

□ **1400** J. MIRK *Festial* (EETS) 216 Then saythe Seynt Austeyn [Augustine] that an ensampull yn doyng ys mor commendabull then ys techyng other [or] prechyng. *a* **1568** R. ASCHAM *Schoolmaster* (1570) I. 20 One example, is more valiable..than xx. preceptes written in bookes. **1708** M. PRIOR *Literary Works* (1971) I. 535 Example draws where Precept fails, And Sermons are less read than Tales. **1828** D. M. MOIR *Mansie Wauch* xix. Example is better than precept, as James Batter observes. **1981** P. O'DONNELL *Xanadu Talisman* ii. Example is always better than precept, remember. ■ **example, good and bad**; **words and deeds**

The EXCEPTION proves the rule

'The very fact of an exception proves there must be a rule' (Brewer); now frequently misunderstood and used to justify inconsistency. Cf. L. *exceptio probat regulam in casibus non exceptis*, the exception confirms the rule in cases not excepted.

□ **1640** G. WATTS *Bacon's Advancement of Learning* VIII. iii. Exception strengthens the force of a Law in Cases not excepted. **1664** J. WILSON *Cheats* A2ᵛ I think I have sufficiently justifi'd the Brave man, even by this Reason, That the Exception proves the Rule. **1765** S. JOHNSON *Shakespeare* Preface C2ᵛ There are a few passages which may pass for imitations, but so few that the exception only confirms the rule. **1863** W. S. GILBERT in *Cornhill Mag.* Dec. VIII. 727 As for the *dictum* about Temple Bar, why, the case of Poddle and Shaddery might be one of those very exceptions whose existence is necessary to the proof of every general rule. **1907** H. W. FOWLER *Si Mihi* 80 It is one of those cryptic sayings, like 'The exception proves the rule', which always puzzle me. **1994** 'C. AIRD' 'Fair Cop' in *Injury Time* (1995) 27 [H]ome was where most victims of murder met their end. This instance, he was prepared to concede, might just be the exception that proved the rule. ■ **rules, general**

There is an EXCEPTION to every rule

See also the preceding entry and RULES *are made to be broken.*

□ **1579** T. F. *News from North* D1[v] There is no rule so generall, that it admitteth not exception, albeit i dout not.. that honors chaunge maners. **1608** T. HEYWOOD *Rape of Lucrece* V. 169 A general concourse of wise men. ..Tarquin, if the general rule have no exceptions, thou wilt have an empty consistory [council chamber]. **1773** R. GRAVES *Spiritual Quixote* III. IX. xviii. The rules of Grammar cannot, in any language, be reduced to a strict analogy; but all general rules have some exceptions. **1836** MARRYAT *Midshipman Easy* I. xii. I have little reason to speak in its favour.. but there must be exceptions in every rule. **1981** *Listener* 21 May 683 'There is still something awe-inspiring about a duke,' we are informed. Only those who share such values will want to read Heirs and Graces. Even they should remember that there is an exception to every rule. ■ **rules, general**

A fair EXCHANGE is no robbery

□ **1546** J. HEYWOOD *Dialogue of Proverbs* II. iv. G4 Chaunge be no robbry for the changed case. *c* **1590** *John of Bordeaux* (1936) l. 213 Exchaung is no roberie. *a* **1628** in M. L. Anderson *Proverbs in Scots* (1957) no. 540 Fair shifts [exchange] na robberie. **1721** J. KELLY *Scottish Proverbs* 105 Fair Exchange is no Rob'ry. Spoken when we take up one Thing, and lay down another. **1748** SMOLLETT *Roderick Random* II. xli. Casting an eye at my hat and wig.. he took them off, and clapping his own on my head, declared, that a fair exchange was no robbery. **1960** N. MITFORD *Don't tell Alfred* xx. 'So it was you who took away the Harar frescoes?' 'Took away? We exchanged them. ..A good exchange is no robbery, I believe?' **1999** J. CUTLER *Dying to Score* i. 5 'Superintendent Groom, sir, I have to report that I was just considering my spring-cleaning,' I said. 'And, since fair exchange is no robbery, what about your thoughts?' ■ **fair dealing**

excuse *see* a BAD excuse is better than none; IGNORANCE of the law is no excuse for breaking it.

He who EXCUSES, accuses himself

Cf. L. *dum excusare credis, accusas,* while you believe you excuse, you accuse; Fr. *qui s'excuse, s'accuse.*

□ **1611** R. COTGRAVE *Dict. French & English* s.v. Excuser, Some when they mean to excuse, accuse, themselues. **1884** J. PAYN *Canon's Ward* II. xxxi. It is very difficult for a person in my position to excuse without accusing himself, but I should like you to feel that Miss Gilbert's fortune has formed no part of her attraction for me. **1936** J. STAGGE *Murder gone to Earth* vi. She spoke with such venom that I remembered the good old French proverb of 'he who excuses, accuses himself.' **1968** G. WAGNER *Elegy for Corsica* xi. The tests would be underground, every precaution taken, impossible to contaminate anything. One had heard these pleas before .. Who excuses himself accuses himself. ■ **conscience; excuses**

expand *see* WORK expands so as to fill the time available.

What can you EXPECT from a pig but a grunt?

Used rhetorically with reference to coarse or boorish behaviour.

□ **1731** *Poor Robin's Almanack* C6 If we petition a Hog, what can we expect but a grunt. **1827** SCOTT *Journal* 10 Apr. (1941) 41 They refuse a draught of £20, because, in mistake, it was £8 overdrawn. But what can be expected of a *sow* but a *grumph*? **1910** P. W. JOYCE *English as We speak it in Ireland* x. Of a coarse, ill-mannered man, who uses unmannerly language: 'What could you expect from a pig but a grunt.' **1997** *Spectator* 22 Nov. 37/2 References in Mr Cole's letter to the 'bottle' were, to say the least, distasteful. But then, as they say, 'What can you expect from a pig but a grunt?' ■ **conduct; human nature**

expect *see also* BLESSED is he who expects nothing, for he shall never be disappointed.

EXPERIENCE is the best teacher

The Latin tag *experientia docet*, experience teaches, gave rise to a large number of proverbs. There is no standard form, and the sayings given below illustrate the themes that 'one learns (*also*, fools learn) by experience' and that 'experience is a hard teacher'. *See also* EXPERIENCE *keeps a dear school.*

□ *a* **1568** R. ASCHAM *Schoolmaster* (1570) I. 19 Erasmus.. saide wiselie that experience is the common scholehouse of foles. **1618** N. BRETON *Court & Country* B4 Let ignorance be an enemy to wit, and experience be the Mistris of fools. **1670** J. RAY *English Proverbs* 86 Experience is the mistress of fools. *Experientia stultorum magistra.* Wise men learn by others harms, fools by their own. **1732** T. FULLER *Gnomologia* no. 1484 Experience teacheth Fools; and he is a great one, that will not learn by it. **1856** F. M. WHITCHER *Widow Bedott Papers* xxix. I.. dident know how to do anything as well as I do now. .. Experience is the best teacher, after all. **1874** G. J. WHYTE-MELVILLE *Uncle John* I. x. Experience does *not* make fools wise. .. Most proverbs are fallacious. None greater than that which says it does. **1962** *Infantry* Nov.–Dec. 26 Experience is a hard teacher, and we cannot afford to learn on the battlefield what should be taught during normal training. **2002** *Washington Post* 11 Jan. C10 Whoever said 'experience is the best teacher' got it right—as you can certainly testify. ■ **experience**

EXPERIENCE is the father of wisdom

Cf. ALCMAN *Fragments* cxxv. (Page) *πῆρά τοι μαθήσιος ἀρχά*, experience is the beginning of knowledge.

□ **1539** R. TAVERNER *Garden of Wisdom* II. 24[v] This be commonly true, for experience is mother of prudence, yet suche prudence & wysedom cost the comon weale moch. *a* **1547** E. HALL *Chronicle* (1548) Rich. III 31 He by the longe and often alternate proof.. had gotten by greate experience the very mother and mastres of wisedome. **1581** G. PETTIE tr. *S. Guazzo's Civil Conversation* I. 11 Experience is the father of wisedom, and memorie the mother. **1788** *American Museum* III. 183 If it be true, that experience is the mother of wisdom, history must be an improving teacher. **1981** P. O'DONNELL *Xanadu Talisman* ii. Experience is the father of wisdom, remember. ■ **experience; wisdom**

EXPERIENCE keeps a dear school

□ **1743** B. FRANKLIN *Poor Richard's Almanack* (Dec.) Experience keeps a dear school, but Fools will learn in no other. **1897** C. C. KING *Story of British Army* vii. But the British leaders were to learn the fact, they might have foreseen, in the 'only school fools learn in, that of experience'. **1938** E. O. LORIMER tr. *W. Frischauer's Twilight in Vienna* vii. The various Governments had.. to learn their lesson in blood and tears, for 'experience keeps a dear school'. **2000** *Washington Post* 17 July C2 You are never going to be any of these people—for which it says here you should be eternally grateful—but that isn't going to stop you from trying, is it? In the immortal words of (talk about success gurus) Benny Franklin: 'Experience keeps a dear school, but fools will learn in no other.' ■ **experience**

EXTREMES meet

Opposite extremes have much in common. Cf. *a* **1662** PASCAL *Pensées* (new ed., 1835) I. iv. 109 *les extrèmes se touchent*, extremes meet.

□ **1762** J. WATTS in *Collections of New York Hist. Society* (1928) LXII. 48 But as extremes meet we may possibly the sooner have a peace for it. **1822** SCOTT *Nigel* III. iii. This Olifaunt is a Puritan?—not the less like to be a Papist.. for extremities meet. **1836** E. HOWARD *Rattlin the Reefer* I. xiv. Let us place at least one 'barring out' [i.e. action of schoolboys barricading themselves in a room] upon record, in order to let the radicals see, and seeing hope, when they find how nearly extremes meet, what a slight step there is from absolute despotism to absolute disorganization. **1905** J. B. CABELL *Line of Love* vi. It is a venerable saying that extremes meet. **1978** *Economist* 16 Dec. 22 Groups of the extreme left and extreme right are each other's total opposites and avowed enemies. But in some respects these extremes meet. ■ **human nature; opposites**

extremity *see* MAN's extremity is God's opportunity.

What the EYE doesn't see, the heart doesn't grieve over

Cf. ST. BERNARD *Sermon* v. *All Saints, vulgo dicitur: Quod non videt oculus cor non dolet*, it is commonly said: what the eye sees not, the heart does not grieve at; early 14th-cent. Fr. *car on dit que ce que on ne voit au cueur ne deult*, for it is said that what one does not see does not harm the heart.

□ **1545** R. TAVERNER tr. *Erasmus' Adages* (ed. 2) 13 That the eye seeth not, the hart rueth not. **1576** G. PETTIE *Petit Palace* 145 As the sence of seeinge is most sharp, so is that paine most pinching, to see the thing one seeketh, and can not possesse it. ..And as the common saying is, that which the eye seeth, the hart greeueth. **1721** J. KELLY *Scottish Proverbs* 341 What the Eye sees not, the Heart rues not. Men may have Losses, but if they be unknown to them they give them no Trouble. **1830** J. L. BURCKHARDT *Arabic Proverbs* 109 When the eye does not see, the heart does not grieve. **1883** C. S. BURNE *Shropshire Folklore* xxxvi. These.. seem to be popular legal maxims. ..What the eye doesn't see, the heart doesn't grieve. **1939** G. HEYER *No Wind of Blame* iii. Anyone knows what men are, and what the eye doesn't see the heart won't grieve over. **1986** 'J. GREENWOOD' *Mists Over Mosley* (1987) xix. 122 'But they have a saying in these parts. "What the eye don't see, the heart don't grieve," and I've always said to myself, that's not a bad motto for a man.' ■ **ignorance; trouble**

The EYE of a master does more work than both his hands

□ **1744** B. FRANKLIN *Poor Richard's Almanack* (Oct.) The eye of a Master, will do more Work than his Hand. **1876** I. BANKS *Manchester Man* I. xiv. She was wont to say, 'The eye of a master does more work than both his hands,' accordingly in house or warehouse her active supervision kept other hands from idling. ■ **employers and employees**

eye *see also* BEAUTY is in the eye of the beholder; the BUYER has need of a hundred eyes, the seller of but one; FIELDS have eyes, and woods have ears; FOUR eyes see more than two; HAWKS will not pick out hawks' eyes; PLEASE your eye and plague your heart.

The EYES are the window of the soul

Occurs in a number of variant forms: *the face is the index of the mind* is among those exemplified below. Cf. CICERO *Orator* lx. *ut imago est animi voltus sic indices oculi*, the face is a picture of the mind as the eyes are its interpreter; L. *vultus est index animi* (also *oculus animi index*), the face (also, eye) is the index of the mind.

□ **1545** T. PHAER *Regiment of Life* 14 The eyes .. are the wyndowes of the mynde, for both ioye & anger .. are seene .. through them. *a* **1575** J. PILKINGTON *Nehemiah* (1585) i. The affections of the minde declare them selues openlie in the face. **1601** JONSON *Cynthia's Revels* D3V I can refell [refute] that Paradox .. of those, which hold the face to be the Index of the minde. **1781** A. ADAMS in L. H. Butterfield et al. *Adams Family Correspondence* (1973) IV. 215 I did not study the Eye that best Index to the mind. **1864** MRS. H. WOOD *Trevlyn Hold* I. i. You have not to learn that the face is the outward index of the mind within. **1940** G. SEAVER *Scott of Antarctic* II. 48 The eye, which is the reflector of the external world, is also the mirror of the soul within. **1979** J. GERSON *Omega Factor* iii. If the old saying, the eyes are the window of the soul, were true then this young girl had misplaced her soul. **1997** *Windows Magazine* Feb. 205 If the eyes are the windows to the soul, then the monitor is the window to your system. **2000** J. W. HALL *Rough Draft* (2001) i. 23 He'd never believed in reading things into people's eyes. All that windows-of-the-soul bullshit. ■ **appearance, significant**

face *see* don't CUT off your nose to spite your face; the EYES are the window of the soul.

FACT is stranger than fiction

An alliterative version of TRUTH *is stranger than fiction.*

□ **1853** T. C. HALIBURTON *Sam Slick's Wise Saws* 5 Facts are stranger than fiction, for things happen sometimes that never entered into the mind of man to imagine or invent. **1881** A. JESSOPP *Arcady for Better or Worse* iii. I have no desire to convince the world that..in this..case fact is stranger than fiction. But the following instance of Mr. Chowne's 'cunning' may be verified. **1929** E. J. MILLWARD *Copper Bottle* 64 Facts may be stranger than fiction,..but fiction is generally truer than facts. **1980** *Christian Science Monitor* 30 May B3 Some of the research seems almost eerie to the outsider, covering some genuine fact-is-stranger-than-fiction ground. ■ **reality and illusion**

FACTS are stubborn things

□ **1732** E. BUDGELL *Liberty & Progress* ii. Plain matters of fact are terrible stubborn things. **1749** J. ELIOT *Continuation of Essay on Field Husbandry* 20 Facts are stubborn things. **1866** BLACKMORE *Cradock Nowell* III. vi. Facts, however, are stubborn things, and will not even make a bow to the sweetest of young ladies. **1942** L. THAYER *Murder is Out* xxvii. You're..too intelligent to think that suggestion would have any weight with a jury. ..Facts are stubborn things. ■ **reality and illusion**

fail *see* when all FRUIT fails welcome haws.

failure *see* SUCCESS has many fathers, while failure is an orphan.

FAINT heart never won fair lady

Cf. *c* **1390** GOWER *Confessio Amantis* v. 6573 Bot as men sein, wher herte is failed, Ther schal no castell ben assailed.

□ **1545** R. TAVERNER tr. *Erasmus' Adages* (ed. 2) 10 A coward verely neuer obteyned the loue of a faire lady. **1580** LYLY *Euphues & his England* II. 131 Faint hart Philautus neither winneth Castell nor Lady: therfore endure all thinges that shall happen with patience. **1614** W. CAMDEN *Remains concerning Britain* (ed. 2) 306 Faint heart neuer wonne faire Lady. **1754** RICHARDSON *Grandison* I. xvi. Then, madam, we will *not* take your denial. ..Have I not heard it said, that faint heart never won fair lady. **1899** G. GISSING *Crown of Life* xiii. Could he leave England, this time, without confessing himself to her? Faint heart—he mused over the proverb. **2002** *New Scientist* 11 May 37 Those who risk all might die in the attempt, but this is no worse genetically speaking than sitting around and dying childless; they might, by risking all, do very well indeed. Faint heart never won fair lady. ■ **boldness; love**

FAIR and softly goes far in a day

□ *c* **1350** *Douce MS 52* no. 50 Fayre and softe me [one] ferre gose. **1670** J. RAY *English Proverbs* 87 Fair and softly goes far in a day. ..He that spurs on too fast at first setting out, tires before he comes to his journeys end. *Festina lente*. **1818** SCOTT

Heart of Midlothian IV. viii. Reuben Butler isna the man I take him to be, if he disna learn the Captain to fuff [puff] his pipe some other gate [place] than in God's house, or [before] the quarter be ower. 'Fair and softly gangs far,' said Meiklehose. **1914** K. F. PURDON *Folk of Furry Farm* ii. Maybe I'm like the singed cat, better than I look! I'm slow, but fair and easy goes far in a day. ■ **gentleness; tact**

All's FAIR in love and war

Cf. **1578** LYLY *Euphues* I. 236 Anye impietie may lawfully be committed in loue, which is lawlesse.

□ **1620** T. SHELTON tr. *Cervantes' Don Quixote* II. xxi. Love and warre are all one. .. It is lawfull to use sleights and stratagems to .. attaine the wished end. **1845** G. P. R. JAMES *Smuggler* II. iv. In love and war, every stratagem is fair, they say. **1986** S. BRETT *Nice Class of Corpse* xl. Then Eulalie's eyes narrowed and she looked hard at her companion. 'Do you believe that all is fair in love and war?' **2002** *Spectator* 15 June 63 All is fair in love and war, and it is important that you sustain your marriage. You must therefore take the following, deceitful steps. ■ **fair dealing; love; warfare**

FAIR play's a jewel

□ **1809** W. IRVING *Hist. New York* II. VI. vii. The furious Risingh, in despight of that noble maxim .. that 'fair play is a jewel', hastened to take advantage of the hero's fall. **1823** J. F. COOPER *Pioneers* II. v. Well, fair play's a jewel. But I've got the lead of you, old fellow. **1935** E. F. BENSON *Lucia's Progress* viii. There's been a lil' mistake. .. I want my lil' rubber of Bridge. Fair play's a jewel. **1948** L. A. G. STRONG *Trevannion* iv. 'It ain't good to win crooked.' 'Good for you, Stan. I agree. Fair play's a jewel.' ■ **fair dealing**

fair *see also* none but the BRAVE deserve the fair; a fair EXCHANGE is no robbery; FAINT heart never won fair lady; GIVE and take is fair play; if SAINT Paul's day be fair and clear, it will betide a happy year; SAINT Swithun's day if thou be fair for forty days it will remain; TURN about is fair play.

FAITH will move mountains

With allusion to MATTHEW xvii. 20 (AV) If ye have faith as a grain of mustard seed, ye shall say unto this mountain; Remove hence to yonder place; and it shall remove. Cf. I CORINTHIANS xiii. 2 (AV) though I have all faith; so that I could remove mountains; and have not charity, I am nothing.

□ **1897** 'S. GRAND' *Beth Book* xvi. If mountains can be moved by faith, you can surely move your own legs! **1933** J. BETJEMAN *Ghastly Good Taste* iii. As faith can move mountains, so nothing was impossible to Holy Church. **1948** B. STEVENSON *Home Book of Proverbs* (rev. ed.) 745 Faith will move mountains. **1980** C. FREMLIN *With no Crying* xix. Faith moves mountains, they say: and Hope lights up our darkness. ■ **faith**

fall *see* (noun) hasty CLIMBERS have sudden falls; PRIDE goes before a fall; (verb) the APPLE never falls far from the tree; BETWEEN two stools one falls to the ground; the BIGGER they are, the harder they fall; when the BLIND lead the blind, both shall fall into the ditch; the BREAD never falls but on its buttered side; a REED before the wind lives on, while mighty oaks do fall; if the SKY falls we shall catch larks; when THIEVES fall out, honest men come by their own; as a TREE falls, so shall it lie; UNITED we stand, divided we fall.

fame *see* COMMON fame is seldom to blame.

FAMILIARITY breeds contempt

Cf. ST. AUGUSTINE *Scala Paradisi* 8 (Migne 40, col. 1001) *vulgare proverbium est, quod nimia familiaritas parit contemptum*, it is a common proverb, that too much familiarity breeds contempt.

□ *c* **1386** CHAUCER *Tale of Melibee* l. 1685 Men seyn that 'over-greet hoomlynesse [familiarity] engendreth dispreisynge'. **1539** R. TAVERNER *Garden of Wisdom* II. 4ᵛ Hys specyall frendes counsailled him to beware, least his ouermuche familiaritie myght breade him contempte. **1654** T. FULLER *Comment on Ruth* 176 With base and sordid natures familiarity breeds contempt. **1869** TROLLOPE *He knew He was Right* II. lvi. Perhaps, if I heard Tennyson talking every day, I shouldn't read Tennyson. Familiarity does breed contempt. **1928** D. H. LAWRENCE *Phoenix II* (1968) 598 We say.. Familiarity breeds contempt. .. That is only partly true. It has taken some races of men thousands of years to become contemptuous of the moon. **2002** *Washington Times* 12 Jan. A11 What's that saying about familiarity breeding contempt? By now, [Daniel] Snyder doesn't seem to think much of any of them. ■ **familiarity**

The FAMILY that prays together stays together

The saying was invented by Al Scalpone, a professional commercial-writer, and was used as the slogan of the Roman Catholic Family Rosary Crusade by Father Patrick Peyton (P. Peyton, *All for Her*, 1967). The crusade began in 1942 and the slogan was apparently first broadcast on 6 Mar. 1947 during the radio programme *Family Theater of the Air*. The Crusade in Britain started in 1952, and the expression now has many (often humorous) variant forms.

□ **1948** *St. Joseph Mag.* (Oregon) Apr. 3 'More things are wrought by prayer than this world dreams of', and 'The family that prays together stays together.' Such religious themes are hardly what one would expect to hear propounded over the air waves of our modern radio. **1954** *Parents' Magazine* Feb. 119 The family that plays together stays together. **1980** R. HILL *Spy's Wife* xxi. The family that spies together, sties together. Old Cockney Russian proverb. **1996** *Washington Post* 15 Mar. B3 First, Mother Teresa opined on the divorce of Princess Di and Prince Charles. .. 'The family that prays together stays together; and if you stay together, you will love one another with the same love with which God loves each one of us.' **2001** *Times* 22 Dec. 19 History has forgotten Catherine Hogarth, as her husband [Charles Dickens] eventually did. Those who cook together stay together. Maybe because they cannot decide who should get the blender. ■ **family**

family *see also* ACCIDENTS will happen (in the best-regulated families).

far *see* BLUE are the hills that are far away; FAIR and softly goes far in a day.

fare *see* GO further and fare worse.

FAR-FETCHED and dear-bought is good for ladies

Expensive or exotic articles are suitable for women.

□ *c* **1350** *Douce MS 52* no. 7 Ferre ifet and dere i-bowght is goode for ladys. **1583** B. MELBANCKE *Philotimus* 18 Pallas .. is .. hard to be found, but easy to be intreated, to be farre fetchte & deare boughte, but that we say is good for Ladies. **1616** JONSON *Epicœne* V. 163 When his cates [delicacies] are all in brought, Though there be none far fet, there will dear-bought, Be fit for ladies. **1738** SWIFT *Polite Conversation* i. 60 But you know, far-fetch'd and dear-bought is fit for Ladies. I warrant, this cost your Father Two pence half-penny. **1876** I. BANKS *Manchester Man* III. x.

'Where did these beautiful things come from?'..'India..They are "far-fetched and dear-bought", and so must be good for you, my lady.' ■ **novelty; taste**

fashion *see* BETTER be out of the world than out of the fashion; when the GORSE is out of bloom, kissing's out of fashion.

fast *see* BAD news travels fast; a MONEYLESS man goes fast through the market.

fastest *see* he TRAVELS fastest who travels alone.

fasting *see* it's ill speaking between a FULL man and a fasting.

fat *see* a GREEN Yule makes a fat churchyard; the OPERA isn't over till the fat lady sings.

Like FATHER, like son

The variant form *like father, like daughter* also occurs. *Like* MOTHER, *like daughter* evolved separately, although both it and this proverb were fixed in this form in the seventeenth century. Cf. L. *qualis pater talis filius*, as is the father, so is the son.

□ *c* **1340** R. ROLLE *Psalter* (1884) 342 Ill sunnys folous ill fadirs. **1509** A. BARCLAY *Ship of Fools* 98 An olde prouerbe hath longe agone be sayde That oft the sone in maners lyke wyll be Vnto the Father. **1616** T. DRAXE *Adages* 149 Like father like sonne. **1709** O. DYKES *English Proverbs* 30 Like Father, like Son. ..How many Sons inherit their Fathers Failings, as well as Estates? **1936** W. HOLTBY *South Riding* v. i. Perhaps Lydia might do it once too often. ..Like father, like daughter. **1983** 'M. INNES' *Appleby & Honeybath* xii. And like son, like father, if one may so vary the old expression. Neither of them reading men. ■ **children and parents; similarity and dissimilarity**

father *see also* the CHILD is father of the man; EXPERIENCE is the father of wisdom; SUCCESS has many fathers, while failure is an orphan; it is a WISE child that knows its own father; the WISH is father to the thought.

A FAULT confessed is half redressed

□ **1558** *Interlude of Wealth & Health* D2V Yf thou haue doone amisse, and be sory therfore, Then helfe a mendes is made. **1592** *Arden of Feversham* H1V A fault confessed is more than half amends, but men of such ill spirite as your selfe Worke crosses [arguments] and debates twixt man and wife. **1732** T. FULLER *Gnomologia* no. 1140 Confession of a Fault makes half amends. **1822** SCOTT *Nigel* III. v. Come, my Lord, remember your promise to confess; and indeed, to confess is, in this case, in some slight sort to redress. **1855** H. G. BOHN *Handbook of Proverbs* 285 A fault confessed is half redressed. **1981** P. O'DONNELL *Xanadu Talisman* x. A fault confessed is half redressed, so I hope he will forgive us. ■ **confession; error**

favour *see* (noun) KISSING goes by favour; (verb) FORTUNE favours fools; FORTUNE favours the brave.

FEAR the Greeks bearing gifts

The saying is often used allusively. The original Latin version is also quoted: VIRGIL *Aeneid* II. 49 *timeo Danaos, et dona ferentes*, I fear the Greeks, even when bringing gifts (said by Laocoön as a warning to the Trojans not to admit the wooden horse); thus **1777** S. JOHNSON *Letter* 3 May (1952) II. 515 Tell Mrs. Boswell that I shall taste her marmalade cautiously at first. *Timeo Danaos et dona ferentes*. Beware, says the Italian proverb, of a reconciled enemy.

□ **1873** TROLLOPE *Phineas Redux* I. xxxiii. The right honourable gentleman had prided himself on his generosity as a Greek. He would remind the right honourable gentleman that presents from Greeks had ever been considered dangerous. **1929** *Times* 26 Oct. 13 Mr. Moses .. must now be reflecting on the wisdom of the advice to 'fear the Greeks even when they bring gifts'. **1943** E. S. GARDNER *Case of Drowsy Mosquito* vi. 'It wasn't a trap, I tell you.' Nell Sims said .. 'Fear the Greeks when they bear olive branches.' **1980** J. GERSON *Assassination Run* iv. Fear the Greeks bearing gifts was the maxim to be drummed into every novice in the department. ■ **deception; giving and receiving**

fear *see also* DO right and fear no man; FOOLS rush in where angels fear to tread.

feast *see* AFTER the feast comes the reckoning; the COMPANY makes the feast; ENOUGH is as good as a feast.

feather *see* BIRDS of a feather flock together; FINE feathers make fine birds.

FEBRUARY fill dyke, be it black or be it white

February is traditionally a month of heavy rain (black) or snow (white), but see quot. 1978.

□ **1557** T. TUSSER *Husbandry* D1 Feuerell fill dyke, doth good with his snowe. **1670** J. RAY *English Proverbs* 40 February fill dike Be it black or be it white; But if it be white, It's the better to like. **1906** E. HOLDEN *Country Diary of Edwardian Lady* (1977) 13 February fill dyke Be it black or be it white. **1978** R. WHITLOCK *Calendar of Country Customs* iii. Though February is notoriously associated with floods, as in the appellation 'February fill-dyke', it is statistically one of the driest months of the year. ■ **calendar lore**

If in FEBRUARY there be no rain, 'tis neither good for hay nor grain

An earlier expression of this idea is: **1670** J. RAY *English Proverbs* 40 All the moneths in the year curse a fair Februeer.

□ **1706** J. STEVENS *Spanish & English Dict.* s.v. Febrero, When it does not rain in February, there's neither good Grass nor good Rye. **1906** E. HOLDEN *Country Diary of Edwardian Lady* (1977) 13 If February bring no rain 'Tis neither good for grass nor grain. **1978** R. WHITLOCK *Calendar of Country Customs* iii. One farming adage asserts that 'If in February there be no rain Tis neither good for hay nor grain.' ■ **weather lore**

FEED a cold and starve a fever

Probably intended as two separate admonitions, but the rationale behind the alternative interpretation is explained in quot. 2002. Early medical advice is represented by: **1574** J. WITHALS *Dict.* 66 Fasting is a great remedie in feuers.

□ **1852** E. FITZGERALD *Polonius* p. ix. 'Stuff a cold and starve a fever,' has been grievously misconstrued, so as to bring on the fever it was meant to prevent. **1867** 'M. TWAIN' *Celebrated Jumping Frog* 69 It was policy to 'feed a cold and starve a fever'. **1939** C. MORLEY *Kitty Foyle* xxxi. I said I better go downstairs and eat a square meal, 'feed a cold and starve a fever.' .. 'You misunderstand that,' he says. 'It means if you feed a cold you'll have to starve a fever later.' **1997** *Washington Times* 19 Nov. A8 'Forget about feeding a cold and starving a fever,' Dr. Edelman said, adding there is no medical reason for diet changes. **2002** *New Scientist* 9 Feb. 51 The saying should be: 'If you feed a cold you will have to starve a fever.' The theory goes that if you carry on eating when you have a cold, your body will have to use up vital energy digesting the food rather than .. fighting the cold. You are therefore more likely to allow the cold to develop and become a fever. Your body will then have no option but to shut down your desire to eat in order to direct all its energy into fighting the fever. ■ **health**

feel *see* a MAN is as old as he feels, and a woman as old as she looks; PRIDE feels no pain.

feet *see* the CAT would eat fish, but would not wet her feet; *also* FOOT.

fell *see* LITTLE strokes fell great oaks.

fellow *see* STONE-dead hath no fellow.

The FEMALE of the species is more deadly than the male.

The phrase *the female of the species* is often used with allusion to the proverb.

□ **1911** R. KIPLING in *Morning Post* 20 Oct. 7 The she-bear thus accosted rends the peasant tooth and nail, For the female of the species is more deadly than the male. **1922** WODEHOUSE *Clicking of Cuthbert* ix. The Bingley–Perkins combination, owing to some inspired work by the female of the species, managed to keep their lead. **1979** *Guardian* 28 Apr. 12 We know phrases about the female of the species being more deadly than the male, but the suffragettes.. seemed to have gone into.. abeyance. ■ **women**

fence *see* GOOD fences make good neighbours; the GRASS is always greener on the other side of the fence.

fetch *see* a DOG that will fetch a bone will carry a bone.

fever *see* FEED a cold and starve a fever.

few *see* MANY are called but few are chosen; you WIN a few, you lose a few.

fiction *see* FACT is stranger than fiction; TRUTH is stranger than fiction.

fiddle *see* there's many a GOOD tune played on an old fiddle.

fiddler *see* they that DANCE must pay the fiddler.

FIELDS have eyes, and woods have ears

The urban equivalent is WALLS *have ears*.

□ *c* **1225** in *Englische Studien* (1902) XXXI. 8 Veld haued hege [eye], and wude haued heare—*Campus habet lumen et habet nemus auris acumen*. *c* **1386** CHAUCER *Knight's Tale* l. 1522 But sooth is seyd, go sithen many yeres, That 'feeld hath eyen and the wode hath eres'. **1640** J. HOWELL *Dodona's Grove* A4^{V} Hedges have eares, the rurall Proverb sayes. **1738** SWIFT *Polite Conversation* iii. 199 'O, Miss; 'tis nothing what we say among ourselves.'.. 'Ay Madam; but they say Hedges have Eyes, and Walls have Ears.' **1905** S. J. WEYMAN *Starvecrow Farm* xxviii. Heedful of the old saying, that fields have eyes and woods have ears, she looked carefully round her before she laid her hand on the gate. ■ **eavesdroppers**

FIGHT fire with fire

An injunction to counter like with like. Cf. early 14th-cent. Fr. *lung feu doit estaindre lautre*, one fire must put out another; **1608** SHAKESPEARE *Coriolanus* IV. vii. 54 One fire drives out one fire; one nail, one nail.

□ **1846** J. F. COOPER *Redskins* III. i. If 'Fire will fight fire', 'Indian' ought to be a match for 'Injin' any day. **1869** P. T. BARNUM *Struggles & Triumphs* xl. I write to ask what your intentions are. .. Do you intend to fight fire with fire? **1980** C. SMITH

Cut-out ix. 'You think the other Palestinians have hired some heavies as well?' 'Why not? Fight fire with fire.' ■ **similarity and dissimilarity; ways and means**

fight *see also* COUNCILS of war never fight; while TWO dogs are fighting for a bone, a third runs away with it.

He who FIGHTS and runs away, may live to fight another day

The phrase *to live to fight another day* is also used allusively. Cf. MENANDER *Sent.* 56 (Jaekel) *ἀνὴρ ὁ φεύγων καὶ πάλιν μαχήσεται*, a man who flees will fight again. The present form of the saying has superseded a pithy Middle English version: *a* **1250** *Owl & Nightingale* (1960) l.176 'Wel fight that wel flight,' seth the wise.

□ **1542** N. UDALL *Erasmus' Apophthegms* II. 335ᵛ That same manne, that renneth awaye, Maye again fight, an other daye. **1678** S. BUTLER *Hudibras* III. iii. For, those that fly, may fight againe, Which he can never do that's slain. **1747** J. RAY *Complete Hist. Rebellion* 61 The Dragoons.. thought proper.. a sudden Retreat; as knowing that, He that fights and runs away, May turn and fight another Day; But he that is in Battle slain, Will never rise to fight again. **1876** J. A. AULLS *Sparks & Cinders* 5 For be it known he kept in view That ancient adage, trite but true, That 'He who fights and runs away, May live to fight another day.' **1981** *Daily Telegraph* 10 June 2 (*caption*) He who fights and runs away.. lives to fight another day! ■ **discretion; ways and means**

fill *see* FEBRUARY fill dyke, be it black or be it white; WORK expands so as to fill the time available.

find *see* the DEVIL finds work for idle hands to do; those who HIDE can find; LOVE will find a way; SAFE bind, safe find; SCRATCH a Russian and you find a Tartar; SEEK and ye shall find; SPEAK as you find; it is easy to find a STICK to beat a dog.

FINDERS keepers (losers weepers)

A colloquial variant of the succeeding proverb.

□ **1825** J. T. BROCKETT *Glossary of North Country Words* 89 No halfers—findee keepee, lossee seekee. **1856** C. READE *Never too Late* III. xiii. We have a proverb—'Losers seekers finders keepers.' **1874** E. EGGLESTON *Circuit Rider* XV. If I could find the right owner of this money, I'd give it to him; but I take it he's buried. ..'Finders, keepers,' you know. **1969** *Daily Express* 17 Mar. 9 Where I come from it's finders keepers, losers weepers. **2002** *Washington Times* 23 Jan. E4 (*Crankshaft comic strip*) 'Mr. Crankshaft.. I think I left my pencil box on your bus! Can I look in your lost and found box?' 'Forget it.. I don't have one! Haven't you ever heard of the legal concept "Finders keepers, losers weepers"?' ■ **gains and losses**

FINDINGS keepings

See also the preceding proverb. Cf. PLAUTUS *Trinummus* l. 63 *habeas ut nanctu's*, he may keep that finds. The principle was current in England before the present formulation; **1595** A. COOKE *Country Errors in Harley MS 5247* 108ᵛ That a man finds is his own, and he may keep it.

□ **1863** J. H. SPEKE *Discovery of Source of Nile* V. The scoundrels said, 'Findings are keepings, by the laws of our country; and as we found your cows, so we will keep them.' **1904** *Daily Chronicle* 27 Sept. 1 Harsh sentences of imprisonment for 'findings-keepings' offences. **1963** G. GREENE *Sense of Reality* 38 'I found them in the passage.'.. 'Finding's [i.e. the action or fact of finding, rather than the objects found, as in earlier examples] not keeping here,' he said, 'whatever it may be up there.' ■ **gains and losses**

FINE feathers make fine birds

Beautiful clothes confer beauty or status on the wearer. Cf. early 16th-cent. Fr. *les belles plumes font les beaux oiseaux*. Identified as a Basque saying by **1583** J. SPONDANUS in tr. *Odyssey* VI. 81 *apud meos Vascones.. hac parœmia..: speciosae plumae avem speciosam constituunt*, this is a proverb amongst my fellow Basques: beautiful feathers make a beautiful bird.

□ **1592** G. DELAMOTHE *French Alphabet* II. 29 The faire feathers, makes a faire foule. **1658** E. PHILLIPS *Mysteries of Love & Eloquence* 162 Fine feathers make fine birds. As you may see in Hide Park. **1858** SURTEES *Ask Mamma* x. Mrs. Joe.. essayed to pick her to pieces, intimating that she was much indebted to her dress—that fine feathers made fine birds. **1968** I. PETITE *Life on Tiger Mountain* xiv. I feel,.. if, indeed, 'fine feathers make a fine bird,' then I would just as soon *not* be that peculiar kind of fine bird. ■ **appearance, significant; dress**

FINE words butter no parsnips

Nothing is ever achieved by fine words alone. Parsnips are traditionally garnished with butter before serving.

□ **1639** J. CLARKE *Parœmiologia Anglo-Latina* 169 Faire words butter no parsnips. **1692** R. L'ESTRANGE *Fables of Aesop* cccxl. Relations, Friendships, are but Empty Names of Things, and Words Butter No Parsnips. **1763** A. MURPHY *Citizen* I. ii. What becomes of his Greek and Latin now? Fine words butter no parsnips. **1848** THACKERAY *Vanity Fair* xix. Who.. said that 'fine words butter no parsnips'? Half the parsnips of society are served and rendered palatable with no other sauce. **1997** C. M. SCHULZ *Washington Post* 27 Jan. C12 (*Peanuts comic strip*) [Charlie Brown:] 'Yes, ma'am, he's a very smart dog. Thank you for saying so.' [Snoopy:] 'Fine words butter no parsnips.' **2001** *Spectator* 1 Dec. 66 While it may be a truth universally acknowledged that fine words butter no parsnips, I have to say that in my experience parsnips are seldom cooked in butter. ■ **hypocrisy; words and deeds**

fine *see also* RAIN before seven, fine before eleven.

FINGERS were made before forks

Commonly used as a polite excuse for eating with one's hands at table.

□ **1567** *Loseley MSS* (1836) 212 As God made hands before knives, So God send a good lot to the cutler's wives. **1738** SWIFT *Polite Conversation* ii. 136 (Colonel takes them [some fritters] out with his Hand.) *Col.* Here, Miss, they say, Fingers were made before Forks, and Hands before Knives. **1857** TROLLOPE *Barchester Towers* II. iii. Miss Thorne.. was always glad to revert to anything and.. would doubtless in time have reflected that fingers were made before forks, and have reverted accordingly. **1983** J. WAINWRIGHT *Heroes no More* 37 'This is ridiculous. However, fingers were made before forks.' She lifted one of the king prawns from its resting place and began to nibble at it. ■ **excuses; manners**

fingers *see also* the DEVIL makes his Christmas pies of lawyers' tongues and clerks' fingers.

FIRE is a good servant but a bad master

□ **1615** T. ADAMS *Englands Sickness* 20 The *world*, like fire, may be a good seruant, will bee an ill Master. **1738** SWIFT *Polite Conversation* ii. 183 Why, Fire and Water are good Servants, but they are very bad Masters. **1808** J. ADAMS *Works* (1850–6) VI. 533 Like fire, they [i.e. the aristocracy] are good servants, but all-consuming masters. **1948** H. BESTON *Northern Farm* xxxvi. 'Fire is a good servant but a bad master.' So runs the proverb. **1973** J. CAIRD *Murder Remote* xx. Is not whisky the wonderful thing? But like fire, like fire—a good servant but a bad master. ■ **ways and means**

fire *see also* a BURNT child dreads the fire; DIRTY water will quench fire; FIGHT fire with fire; you should KNOW a man seven years before you stir his fire; if you PLAY with fire you get burnt; no SMOKE without fire; THREE removals are as bad as a fire.

FIRST catch your hare

Commonly thought to originate in the recipe for hare soup in Mrs Glasse's *Art of Cookery* (1747) or in Mrs Beeton's *Book of Household Management* (1851), but not found there (see quot. 1896). Similar in sentiment to CATCHING's *before hanging*. Cf. *c* **1300** BRACTON *De Legibus Angliae* IV. xxi. *vulgariter dicitur, quod primo opportet cervum capere, & postea cum captus fuerit illum excoriare*, it is commonly said that one must first catch the deer, and afterwards, when he has been caught, skin him.

□ **1801** *Spirit of Farmers' Museum* 55 How to dress a dolphin, first catch a dolphin. **1855** THACKERAY *Rose & Ring* xiv. 'To seize wherever I should light upon him—' 'First catch your hare!' .. exclaimed his Royal Highness. **1896** *Daily News* 20 July 8 The familiar words, 'First catch your hare,' were never to be found in Mrs. Glasse's famous volume. What she really said was, 'Take your hare when it is cased [skinned].' **1984** 'C. AIRD' *Harm's Way* iii. Sloan took his reply straight from the pages of an early cookery book. .. 'First, catch your hare.' ■ **ways and means**

FIRST come, first served

Cf. late 13th-cent. Fr. *qui ainçois vient au molin ainçois doit moldre*, he who comes first to the mill may grind first.

□ *c* **1390** CHAUCER *Wife of Bath's Prologue* l. 389 Whoso that first to mille comth, first grynt. **1548** H. BRINKELOW *Complaint of Roderick Mors* xvii. Ye haue a parciall lawe in making of tachmentes [attachments, i.e. judicial seizure of one's person or goods (obsolete)], first come first serued. **1608** R. ARMIN *Nest of Ninnies* D1 He found Sexton .. making nine graues .. and who so dyes next, first comes, first seru'd. **1819** SCOTT *Montrose* in *Tales of my Landlord* 3rd Ser. IV. xii. All must .. take their place as soldiers should, upon the principle of, first come, first served. **2002** *Rough Guide: Hong Kong & Macau* 170 You can't reserve seats on the ferries: it's first come, first served, so get there early at busy times. ■ **orderliness**

The FIRST duty of a soldier is obedience

The last quotation presents a variation of the proverb.

□ **1847** J. GRANT *Romance of War* IV. xv. 'What do the wiseacres at head-quarters mean, in sending a detachment there?' 'I suppose they scarcely know themselves. But obedience—We all know the adage.' **1872** G. J. WHYTE-MELVILLE *Satanella* II. xxiv. 'The first duty of a soldier is obedience,' he answered in great glee. **1915** F. M. HUEFFER *Good Soldier* III. iii. She had been taught all her life that the first duty of a woman is to obey. ■ **obedience; soldiers**

FIRST impressions are the most lasting

□ **1700** CONGREVE *Way of World* IV. i. How shall I receive him? .. There is a great deal in the first Impression. **1791** H. JACKSON in *Publications of Colonial Society of Massachusetts* (1954) XXXVI. 112 I am affraid it is too late .. and you know that first impressions are the most lasting. **1844** DICKENS *Martin Chuzzlewit* v. I didn't like to run the chance of being found drinking it .. for first impressions, you know, often go a long way, and last a long time. **1926** R. M. OGDEN *Psychology & Education* xii. Primacy is popularly expressed by the statement that 'first impressions are lasting'. **1946** J. B. PRIESTLEY *Bright Day* ii. He ought to look neat and tidy. .. It's half the battle.. making a good first impression. ■ **appearance, significant**

On the FIRST of March, the crows begin to search

□ **1846** M. A. DENHAM *Proverbs relating to Seasons, &c.* 39 On the first of March, the crows begin to search. Crows are supposed to begin pairing on this day. **1847** R. CHAMBERS *Popular Rhymes of Scotland* (ed. 2) 165 On the first of March, The craws begin to search; By the first o'April, They are sitting still. **1906** E. HOLDEN *Country Diary of Edwardian Lady* (1977) 132 By the 1.st of March the crows begin to search, By the 1.st of April they are sitting still, By the 1.st of May they are flown away, Creeping greedy back again With October wind and rain. ■ **calendar lore**

It is the FIRST step that is difficult

The proverb has various forms. The story to which the French saying alludes is referred to in quot. 1979. Cf. Fr. *ce n'est que le premier pas qui coûte*, it is only the first step that costs.

□ *c* **1596** A. MUNDAY et al. *Sir Thomas More* 11 Would I were so far on my journey. The first stretch is the worst methinks. **1616** J. WITHALS *Dict.* (rev. ed.) 576 The first step is as good as halfe ouer. **1876** A. B. MEACHAM *Wi-Ne-Ma & her People* iv. He had fortified himself against the charms of the Indian maiden, as he thought, but consented to visit her. Ah! my man, have you not learned that when the first step is taken the next follows easily. **1979** J. BARNETT *Backfire is Hostile* xi. St. Denis was executed. .. Afterwards he picked up his head and walked for six miles. .. The wise man said, 'The distance.. is not important. It was the first step that was difficult.' **1991** 'P. RUELL' *Only Game* vii. 193 What is it they said about that Frenchman who walked three miles after his head had been chopped off? It's the first step that counts. ■ **beginnings and endings**

FIRST things first

□ **1894** G. JACKSON (*title*) First things first; addresses to young men. **1920** W. RILEY *Yorkshire Suburb* 136 The dear lady was.. incapable.. of putting first things first. **1979** 'L. BLACK' *Penny Murders* iv. They dropped the talking; first things first, as Kate always felt about a pleasant meal. **2002** *Spectator* 10 Aug. 20 'I think the principle of "first things first" does apply,' says Al Gore, 'and has to be followed if we are to have any chance of success.' ■ **orderliness**

FIRST thoughts are best

□ **1922** J. JOYCE *Ulysses* 354 First kiss does the trick. The propitious moment. Something inside them goes pop. Mushy like, tell by their eye, on the sly. First thoughts are best. Remember that till their dying day. **1929** 'P. OLDFELD' *Alchemy Murder* viii. 95 'I have thought it over. First thoughts are best.' **1943** M. LOWRY *Letter* 7 Sept. in S. E. Grace *Sursum Corda!* (1995) I. 427 Don't shrink the Branches too much—first thoughts often best. ■ **decision and indecision**

There is always a FIRST time

Also, *there's a first time for everything*.

□ **1792** A. HAMILTON *Papers* (1961–) XII. 504 But there is always 'a *first time*'. **1929** W. R. BURNETT *Little Caesar* III. vii.'I ain't got nothing to spill. .. Did I ever do any spilling?' 'There's a first time for everything.' **1987** 'M. HEBDEN' *Pel among Pueblos* xvi. 'He has no record.' 'Doesn't mean a thing. There's always a first time.' **2001** R. JOHANSEN *Beyond Belief* iii. 48 'You don't think I can do it?' 'I think you can *try*.' 'I've never failed yet.' She shrugged. 'There's a first time for everything.' ■ **beginnings and endings**

first *see also* every DOG is allowed one bite; whom the GODS would destroy, they first make mad; SELF-preservation is the first law of nature; if at first you don't SUCCEED, try, try, try again; THINK first and speak afterwards; he that will THRIVE must first ask his wife; TRUTH is the first casualty of war.

The FISH always stinks from the head downwards

The freshness of a dead fish can be judged from the condition of its head. Thus, when the responsible part (as the leaders of a country, etc.) is rotten, the rest will soon follow. Gr. *ἰχθὺς ἐκ τῆς κεφαλῆς ὄζειν ἄρχεται*, a fish begins to stink from the head.

□ **1581** G. PETTIE tr. *S. Guazzo's Civil Conversation* III. 51 If the prouerbe be true, . . that a fishe beginneth first to smell at the head, . . the faultes of our seruantes will be layed vppon vs. **1611** R. COTGRAVE *Dict. French & English* s.v. Teste, Fish euer begins to taint at the head; the first thing that's deprau'd in man's his wit. **1915** W. S. CHURCHILL *Letter* 3 Dec. in M. Gilbert *Winston S. Churchill* (1972) III. Compan. II. 1309 The guilt of criminality attaches to those responsible. 'Well,' said the Aga Khan, 'fish goes rotten by the head.' **1981** *Sunday Telegraph* 3 May 16 'The fish', as the saying goes, 'always stinks from the head downwards.' Last Sunday we deplored Mr. Michael Foot's liking for the street politics of marches and 'demos'. Since then, a hundred Labour MPs . . have followed their leader's example. **2002** *Washington Post* 19 Mar. A21 Cardinal Law has to go. The Vatican has to speak up. This fish, as they say, rots from the head. ■ **rulers and ruled**

FISH and guests smell after three days

Cf. PLAUTUS *Miles Gloriosus* l. 741 *nam hospes nullus tam in amici hospitium devorti potest, quin, ubi triduom continuom fuerit, iam odiosus siet*, no host can be hospitable enough to prevent a friend who has descended on him from becoming tiresome after three days.

□ **1580** LYLY *Euphues & his England* II. 81 As we say in Athens, fishe and gestes in three dayes are stale. **1648** HERRICK *Hesperides* 169 Two dayes y'ave larded here; a third yee know, Makes guests and fish smell strong; pray go. **1736** B. FRANKLIN *Poor Richard's Almanack* (Jan.) Fish and visitors smell in three days. **1869** *Notes & Queries* 4th Ser. IV. 272 'See that you wear not out your welcome.' This is an elegant rendering of the vulgar saying that 'Fish and company stink in three days'. **1985** J. S. BORTHWICK *Down East Murders* iv. How long should she stay? She remembered the universal truth that fish and guests smell after three days. **2001** *Washington Times* 21 Nov. B1 Fish and visitors smell after three days, the old adage goes. Yet the experience of hosting a crowd for an extended time over the holidays need not leave a bad taste—or odor—for someone prepared to cope. ■ **hospitality**

There are as good FISH in the sea as ever came out of it

Now often used as a consolation to rejected lovers: 'there are plenty more fish in the sea'.

□ *c* **1573** G. HARVEY *Letter-Book* (1884) 126 In the mayne sea theres good stoare of fishe, And in delicate gardens . . Theres alwayes greate varietye of desirable flowers. **1816** T. L. PEACOCK *Headlong Hall* xiv. There never was a fish taken out of the sea, but left another as good behind. **1822** SCOTT *Nigel* III. x. Ye need not sigh sae deeply. . . There are as gude fish in the sea as ever came out of it. **1944** W. S. MAUGHAM *Razor's Edge* iii. I'm a philosopher and I know there are as good fish in the sea as ever came out. I don't blame her. You're young. I've been young too. **2000** *Washington Post* 30 Nov. C11 (*Garfield comic strip*) 'Yesiree, Garfield, there are lot of women out there. Yesiree. .. Plenty of fish in the sea. I'll just cast out the old line.' 'Your bait's dead.' ■ **love, blighted**

All is FISH that comes to the net

Everything can be used to advantage. *The* is frequently replaced by a possessive pronoun or phrase. Similar in form and sense to *all is* GRIST *that comes to the mill.*

□ *c* **1520** in *Ballads from MSS* (1868–72) I. 95 Alle ys ffysshe that commyth to the nett. **1564** W. BULLEIN *Dialogue against Fever* 70 Takyng vp commoditie [opportunity], refusyng nothyng: all is fishe that commeth to the nette. **1680** BUNYAN *Mr. Badman* 19 What was his fathers could not escape his fingers, all was fish that came to his net. **1848** DICKENS *Dombey & Son* ix. 'All's fish that comes to your net, I suppose?' 'Certainly,' said Mr. Brogley. 'But sprats an't whales, you know.' **1936** A. CHRISTIE *Murder in Mesopotamia* xix. I don't know that she cares for one more than the other. ..All's fish that comes to her net at present. ■ **gains and losses; opportunity**

fish *see also* BETTER are small fish than an empty dish; BIG fish eat little fish; the CAT would eat fish, but would not wet her feet; LITTLE fish are sweet; a WOMAN without a man is like a fish without a bicycle.

fish-guts *see* KEEP your own fish-guts for your own sea-maws.

fit *see* if the CAP fits, wear it; ONE size does not fit all; if the SHOE fits, wear it.

fix *see* if it ain't BROKE, don't fix it.

flag *see* TRADE follows the flag.

flattery *see* IMITATION is the sincerest form of flattery.

flea *see* BIG fleas have little fleas upon their backs to bite them; if you LIE down with dogs, you will get up with fleas; NOTHING should be done in haste but gripping a flea.

flesh *see* what's BRED in the bone will come out in the flesh.

flew *see* a BIRD never flew on one wing.

flight *see* BLESSINGS brighten as they take their flight.

flock *see* BIRDS of a feather flock together.

flower *see* APRIL showers bring forth May flowers.

fly *see* (noun) EAGLES don't catch flies; HONEY catches more flies than vinegar; a SHUT mouth catches no flies; (verb) TIME flies; *also* FLEW.

flying *see* it is good to make a BRIDGE of gold to a flying enemy.

folk *see* DIFFERENT strokes for different folks; there's NOWT so queer as folk; YOUNG folks think old folks to be fools, but old folks know young folks to be fools.

follow *see* TRADE follows the flag.

He that FOLLOWS freits, freits will follow him

A Scottish proverb. He that looks for portents of the future will find himself dogged by them. *Freits* are omens.

□ *c* **1700** in J. Pinkerton *Scottish Tragic Ballads* (1781) I. 47 Wha luik to freits, my master deir, Freits will ay follow them. **1721** J. KELLY *Scottish Proverbs* 128 He that follows Freets, Freets will follow him. He that notices superstitious Observations (such as spilling of Salt).. it will fall to him accordingly. **1804** M. PARK in Lockhart *Life of Scott* (1837) II. i. He answered, smiling, '*Freits* (omens) follow those who look to them.'.. Scott never saw him again. **1914** *Times Literary Supplement* 9 Apr. 178 The Kings of Scots have always been beset by omens, and.. to him who follows freits, freits follow. ■ **future**; **omens**

folly *see* where IGNORANCE is bliss, 'tis folly to be wise.

fonder *see* ABSENCE makes the heart grow fonder.

A FOOL and his money are soon parted

□ **1573** T. TUSSER *Husbandry* (rev. ed.) ix. A foole and his money be soone at debate: which after with sorow repents him too late. **1587** J. BRIDGES *Defence of Government in Church of England* xv. 1294 A foole and his money is soone parted. **1616** T. DRAXE *Adages* 166 A foole, and his money are soone parted. **1771** SMOLLETT *Humphry Clinker* I. 174 She tossed her nose in distain, saying, she supposed her brother had taken him into favour..: that a fool and his money were soon parted. **1981** C. BERMANT *Patriarch* xx. I can see now I was a fool, perhaps even a greedy fool, and a fool and his money are soon parted. **2002** *Washington Times* 1 Jan. D4 (*Herb & Jamaal comic strip*) 'Herb, you ought to know better than to get mixed up in a get-rich scheme! It's like the old saying: "A fool and his money are soon parted."' 'Yeah, you are right! So, how much did you lose?' ■ **money**; **stupidity**

A FOOL at forty is a fool indeed

Cf. **1557** R. EDGEWORTH *Sermons* 301 When he [Rehoboam] begonne hys raigne he was one and fortye yeares of age. ..And he that hath not learned some experience or practice and trade of the world by that age will neuer be wise.

□ **1725** E. YOUNG *Universal Passion* II. 16 Be wise with speed; A fool at forty is a fool indeed. **1751** N. COTTON *Visions in Verses* 13 He who at fifty is a fool, Is far too stubborn grown for school. **1908** L. MITCHELL *New York Idea* III. 112 I shall come or not [to your wedding] as I see fit. And let me add, my dear brother, that a fool at forty is a fool indeed. **1982** B. EMECHETA *Destination Biafra* i. 'What is it they say about a fool at forty?' 'I don't think you'll be a fool forever, sir.' ■ **middle age**; **stupidity**

There's no FOOL like an old fool

□ **1546** J. HEYWOOD *Dialogue of Proverbs* II. ii. F4[v] But there is no foole to the olde foole, folke saie. **1721** J. KELLY *Scottish Proverbs* 256 No fool to an old Fool. Spoken when Men of advanc'd Age behave themselves, or talk youthfully, or wantonly. **1732** T. FULLER *Gnomologia* no. 3570 No Fool like the old Fool. **1814** SCOTT *Waverley* III. xv. And troth he might hae ta'en warning, but there's nae fule like an ould fule. **1910** R. KIPLING *Rewards & Fairies* 257 'There are those who have years without knowledge.' 'Right,' said Puck. 'No fool like an old fool.' **2001** *Washington Post* 8 July B5 But these fantasies are more proper to a young person; beyond the age of, say, 50, they become the fantasy of that fool like whom we are told there is no other, the old fool. ■ **old age**; **stupidity**

A FOOL may give a wise man counsel

□ *a* **1350** *Ywain & Gawain* (EETS) l. 1477 Bot yit a fole that litel kan [knows], May wele cownsail another man. **1641** D. FERGUSSON *Scottish Proverbs* (STS) no. 84 A Fool may give a wyse man a counsell. **1721** J. KELLY *Scottish Proverbs* 25 A Fool may give a wise Man counsel by a time. An Apology of those who offer their Advice to them, who may be supposed to excel them in Parts and Sense. **1818** SCOTT *Heart of Midlothian* IV. viii. If a fule may gie a wise man a counsel, I wad hae him think twice or [before] he mells [meddles] wi' Knockdunder. **1942** E. P. OPPENHEIM *Man who changed Plea* xvii. Aren't we all fools..in one or two things?..Even a fool, though, can sometimes give good advice. ■ **advice; fools**

FOOL me once, shame on you; fool me twice, shame on me

Earlier, and still current, with the verb *deceive*.

□ **1611** *Tarlton's Jests* (1844) 11 For Who deceives me once, God forgive him; if twice, God forgive him; but if thrice, God forgive him, but not me, because I could not beware. **1650** A. WELLDON *Secret History of King James I* (1690) 88 The Italians having a Proverb, He that deceives me Once, it's his Fault; but Twice it is my fault. **1659** N. R. *Proverbs English, French, Dutch, Italian & Spanish* 54 He that deceives me once, it is his faul[t]; if twice, it is mine. **1980** *Forbes* 17 Mar. 69 The important thing in dealing with the Japanese is not to believe everything you hear. Or, as the saying goes: Fool me once, shame on you. Fool me twice, shame on me. **2001** *Washington Times* 3 Oct. A17 You know the old saying, 'Fool me once, shame on you; fool me twice, shame on me.' How does that apply in the aftermath of the Sept. 11 act of war against our country? **2002** P. LOVESEY *Diamond Dust* xxx. 297 'Did you give him any?' 'No. I wouldn't be so daft. You know that old saying? He that deceives me once, shame fall him; if he deceives me twice, shame fall me.' ■ **deception**

fool *see also* CHILDREN and fools tell the truth; FORTUNE favours fools; a man who is his own LAWYER has a fool for his client; MORE people know Tom Fool than Tom Fool knows; SIX hours' sleep for a man, seven for a woman, and eight for a fool; YOUNG folks think old folks to be fools, but old folks know young folks to be fools; *also* FOOLS.

foolish *see* PENNY wise and pound foolish.

FOOLS and bairns should never see half-done work

They may mistakenly judge the quality of the finished article from its awkwardness while it is being produced.

□ **1721** J. KELLY *Scottish Proverbs* 108 Fools should not see half done Work. Many fine Pieces of Work will look..aukward when it is a doing. **1818** SCOTT *Letter* Dec. (1933) V. 265 'Bairns and fools'..according to our old canny proverb should never see half done work. **1913** A. & J. LANG *Highways & Byways in Border* ix. To the lay eye improvement is yet barely perceptible. 'Fools and bairns', however, they tell us, 'should never see half-done work.' **1934** V. MACCLURE *Death on Set* ii. He has never really liked anybody seeing the roughs except the technical staff. Said it gave the players ideas they were better without. 'Fools and children, and unfinished work,' you know. ■ **fools; work**

FOOLS ask questions that wise men cannot answer

□ **1666** G. TORRIANO *Italian Proverbs* 249 One fool may ask more than seven wise men can answer. **1738** SWIFT *Polite Conversation* ii. 156 'Miss, can you tell which is the white Goose?'..'They say, a Fool will ask more Questions than the wisest body can answer.' **1821** SCOTT *Pirate* II. v. Bryce Snaelsfoot is a cautious man. ..He knows a fool may ask more questions than a wise man cares to answer. **1871**

J. S. JONES *Life of J. S. Batkins* liv. Bean appeared always to be fond of Amanda. . . I asked him one day. . . He looked at me, and said, 'Batkins, fools ask questions that wise men cannot answer.' ■ **fools; wisdom**

FOOLS build houses and wise men live in them

The terser form of this saying—*fools build and wise men buy*—can be applied to property other than houses (see quot. 1997).

□ **1670** J. RAY *English Proverbs* 91 Fools build houses, and wise men buy them. **1721** J. KELLY *Scottish Proverbs* 110 Fools Big [build] Houses and wise Men buy them. I knew a Gentleman buy 2000 l. worth of Land, build a House upon it, and sell both House and Land to pay the Expences of his building. **1875** A. B. CHEALES *Proverbial Folk-Lore* 43 *Fools build houses, and wise men live in them* is another proverb on this subject; it is partly true. **1911** W. F. BUTLER *Autobiography* xix. The adage says that fools build houses for other men to live in. Certainly the men who build the big house of Empire for England usually get the attic . . for their own lodgment. **1934** J. ALEXANDER *Murder at Eclipse* III. ii. 86 On his retirement, the first baron did not build himself a palace such as he could well have afforded. Perhaps he remembered the old adage that 'fools build and wise men buy.' **1997** *Country Life* 14 Aug. 28 Arthur Ransome, self-mocking, said of boating folk: 'Fools build and wise men buy.' There is a similar put-down of people who breed their own horses ■ **fools; home**

FOOLS for luck

The construction is apparent from quot. 1834. FORTUNE *favours fools* expresses the same idea. Quot. 1981 appears to be a garbled version of this saying. Cf. **1631** JONSON *Bartholomew Fair* II. ii. Bring him a sixe penny bottle of Ale; they say, a fooles handsell [gift] is lucky.

□ **1834** *Narrative of Life of David Crockett* xiii. The old saying—'A fool for luck, and a poor man for children.' **1854** J. B. JONES *Life of Country Merchant* xix. They attribute your good fortune to the old hackneyed adage, 'A fool for luck'. **1907** D. H. LAWRENCE *Phoenix II* (1968) 6 'You'll make our fortunes.' 'What!' he exclaimed, 'by making a fool of myself? They say fools for luck. What fools wise folks must be.' **1981** T. BARLING *Bikini Red North* xi. All fools are lucky; isn't that the adage? ■ **fools; luck**

FOOLS rush in where angels fear to tread

□ **1711** POPE *Essay on Criticism* l. 625 No Place so Sacred from such Fops is barr'd, Nor is Paul's Church more safe than Paul's Church-yard: Nay, fly to Altars; there they'll talk you dead; For Fools rush in where Angels fear to tread. **1858** G. J. MCREE *Iredell's Life & Correspondence* II. 277 Rash presumption illustrates the line, 'Fools rush in where angels fear to tread'. **1922** JOYCE *Ulysses* 649 Prying into his private affairs on the *fools step in where angels* principle. **1943** H. MCCLOY *Do not Disturb* ii. The folly of the officious is proverbial: don't rush in where angels fear to tread. **1975** 'C. AIRD' *Slight Mourning* xv. 'The deceased was of—er—a forceful personality. Not over-sensitive, either, from all accounts.' 'Ah, I see. Fools rush in where angels fear to tread.' ■ **fools; ignorance**

foot *see* it is not SPRING until you can plant your foot upon twelve daisies; one WHITE foot, buy him; *also* FEET.

forbear *see* BEAR and forbear.

foretold *see* LONG foretold, long last.

FOREWARNED is forearmed

Cf. L. *praemonitus, praemunitus*, forewarned, forearmed.

□ *c* **1425** J. ARDERNE *Treatises of Fistula* (EETS) 22 He that is warned afore is noght bygiled. *c* **1530** J. REDFORD *Wit & Science* l. 1093 Once warnd, half armd folk say. **1587** R. GREENE *Card of Fancy* IV. 23 I giue thee this Ring of golde, wherin is written..*Praemonitus, Premunitus*..inferring this sense, that hee which is forewarned by friendlie counsoule of imminent daungers, is fore-armed against all future mishappe. *a* **1661** T. FULLER *Worthies* (Devon) 272 Let all ships passing thereby be fore-armed because forewarned thereof. **1885** 'LE JEMLYS' *Shadowed to Europe* xxv. 'Forewarned is forearmed,' he thought, as he complimented himself upon his success in baffling the attempt to ensnare him. **2002** *Washington Times* 30 June B4 Forewarned is forearmed. Before the chemical disaster at Union Carbide's facility in Bhopal, India, the public was told an accident that has now claimed 20,000 lives could never happen. ■ **foresight and hindsight**; **prudence**

forget *see* a BELLOWING cow soon forgets her calf.

forgive *see* to ERR is human (to forgive divine); to KNOW all is to forgive all.

fork *see* FINGERS were made before forks.

FORTUNE favours fools

Cf. L. *fortuna favet fatuis*, fortune favours fools.

□ **1546** J. HEYWOOD *Dialogue of Proverbs* II. vi. I1[v] They saie as ofte, god sendeth fortune to fooles. **1563** B. GOOGE *Eclogues* E5 But Fortune fauours Fooles as old men saye And lets them lyue And take the wyse awaye. **1738** GAY *Fables* 2nd Ser. II. xii. 'Tis a gross error, held in schools, That Fortune always favours fools. **1922** E. PHILLPOTTS *Red Redmaynes* xviii. Thus he became exceedingly useful as time passed; yet fortune favours fools and his very stupidity served him well at the end. **1960** O. MANNING *Great Fortune* I. vi. Fortune favours fools. ..We were forced to tarry while he slumbered. ■ **fools**; **luck**

FORTUNE favours the brave

Cf. ENNIUS *Annals* 257 (Vahlen) *fortibus est fortuna viris data*, fortune is given to brave men; VIRGIL *Aeneid* X. 284 *audentes fortuna iuvat*, fortune aids the bold.

□ *c* **1385** CHAUCER *Troilus & Criseyde* IV. 600 Thenk ek Fortune, as wel thiselves woost, Helpeth hardy man to his enprise. *c* **1390** GOWER *Confessio Amantis* VII. 4902 And seith, 'Fortune unto the bolde Is favorable forto helpe'. *a* **1625** BEAUMONT & FLETCHER *Prophetess* IV. vi. He is the scorn of Fortune: but you'll say, That she forsook him for his want of courage, But never leaves the bold. **1724** A. RAMSAY *Works* (1953) II. 288 Fortune aye favours the active and bauld. **1752** in W. Johnson *Papers* (1939) IX. 86 Make no doubt but Fortune will favour the brave. **1885** TROLLOPE *Dr. Thorne* II. vii. Fortune, who ever favours the brave, specially favoured Frank Gresham. **2001** *Spectator* 17 Nov. 25 The luck element has aroused doubts in some quarters, but Lord Guthrie has a standard retort: 'Fortune favours the brave.' He has been proved right, so far. ■ **courage**; **luck**

fortune *see also* EVERY man is the architect of his own fortune; OPPORTUNITY never knocks twice at any man's door.

forty *see* a FOOL at forty is a fool indeed; LIFE begins at forty; SAINT Swithun's day if thou be fair for forty days it will remain.

foul *see* it's an ILL bird that fouls its own nest.

FOUR eyes see more than two

Observation by two people is better than by one alone. TWO *heads are better than one* expresses a similar idea. L. *plus vident oculi, quam oculus*, eyes see more than one eye.

□ **1591** A. COLYNET *True Hist. Civil Wars France* 37 Two eyes doo see more then one. **1592** G. DELAMOTHE *French Alphabet* II. 45 Foure eyes can see more then two. **1642** T. FULLER *Holy State* IV. v. Matters of inferiour consequence he will communicate to a fast friend, and crave his advice; for two eyes see more than one. **1898** F. M. MULLER *Auld Lang Syne* 80 But who has ever examined any translation from any language, without finding signs of.. carelessness or ignorance? Four eyes see more than two. **1962** H. REILLY *Day She Died* vii. What he wanted was a look at the cars the variegated crowd of people had arrived in. Four eyes were better than two. ■ **assistance; observation**

four *see also* there goes more to MARRIAGE than four bare legs in a bed.

There's no such thing as a FREE lunch

Originally a colloquial axiom in US economics, though now in general use. The proverb implies that you cannot get something for nothing.

□ **1967** R. A. HEINLEIN *Moon is Harsh Mistress* xi. 'Oh, "tanstaafl." Means "There ain't no such thing as a free lunch." And isn't,' I added, pointing to a FREE LUNCH sign across the room, 'or these drinks would cost half as much.' **1969** *Newsweek* 29 Dec. 52 I was taught.. the first and only law of economics: 'There is no such thing as a free lunch.' **1971** *New Yorker* 25 Sept. 76 There is no such thing as a free lunch. ..The idea has proved so illuminating for environmental problems that I am borrowing it from its original source, economics. **1979** L. ST. CLAIR *Obsessions* xi. There's no such thing as a free lunch. So, in return for your help, what do you ask? **2001** *Spectator* 29 Dec. 26 I believe that the old saying 'There is no such thing as a free lunch' applies here. Pornography and permissiveness will have a price. ■ **bribery and corruption; reciprocity**

free *see also* the BEST things in life are free; THOUGHT is free.

freit (omen): *see* he that FOLLOWS freits, freits will follow him.

Frenchman *see* one ENGLISHMAN can beat three Frenchmen.

fresh *see* don't THROW out your dirty water until you get in fresh.

Friday *see* Monday's CHILD is fair of face.

A FRIEND in need is a friend indeed

A *friend in need* is one who helps when one is in need or difficulty. Cf. EURIPIDES *Hecuba* l. 1226 ἐν τοῖς κακοῖς γὰρ ἀγαθοὶ σαφέστατοι φίλοι, for in adversity good friends are most clearly seen; ENNIUS *Scaenica* 210 (Vahlen) *amicus certus in re incerta cernitur*, a sure friend is known in unsure times.

□ *c* **1035** *Durham Proverbs* (1956) 10 Æt thearfe man sceal freonda cunnian [friend shall be known in time of need]. *a* **1400** *Titus & Vespasian* (1905) 98 I shal the save When tyme cometh thou art in nede; Than ogh men frenshep to shewe in dede. *a* **1449** LYDGATE *Minor Poems* (EETS) II. 755 Ful weele is him that fyndethe a freonde at neede. **1678** J. RAY *English Proverbs* (ed. 2) 142 A friend in need is a friend indeed. **1773** R. GRAVES *Spiritual Quixote* II. VIII. xx. (*heading*) A Friend in Need is a Friend indeed. **1866** C. READE *Griffith Gaunt* III. xv. You came to my side when I was in trouble. ..A friend in need is a friend indeed. **1985** D. WILLIAMS *Wedding Treasure*

viii. He never felt quite right about calling up scripture—at least not in private. 'Friend in need is a friend indeed,' he added. That was better. ■ **adversity; friends**

friend *see also* the BEST of friends must part; the ENEMY of my enemy is my friend; LEND your money and lose your friend; SAVE us from our friends; SHORT reckonings make long friends.

frost *see* so many MISTS in March, so many frosts in May.

When all FRUIT fails, welcome haws

Often used specifically of a person who takes of necessity an older or otherwise unsuitable lover.

□ **1721** J. KELLY *Scottish Proverbs* 350 When all Fruit fa's welcome ha's. .. Spoken when we take up with what's coarse, when the good is spent. **1914** K. F. PURDON *Folk of Furry Farm* vii. 'Lame of a leg, and grey in the head! .. That's a fancy man for a girl to take!' 'Marg was none too young herself .. and when all fruit fails, welcome haws! She wanted someone.' **1958** B. BEHAN *Borstal Boy* III. 266 So even the excommunicated will do, when it's not easy to get anyone else. When all fruit fails, welcome haws. ■ **necessity; old age**

fruit *see also* he that would EAT the fruit must climb the tree; SEPTEMBER blow soft, till the fruit's in the loft; STOLEN fruit is sweet; the TREE is known by its fruit.

FULL cup, steady hand

Used especially to caution against spoiling a comfortable or otherwise enviable situation by careless action.

□ *c* **1025** *Durham Proverbs* (1956) 15 Swa fulre fæt swa hit mann sceal fægror beran [the more full the cup, the more carefully must one carry it]. *c* **1325** *Proverbs of Hending* in *Anglia* (1881) IV. 293 When the coppe is follest, thenne ber hire feyrest. **1721** J. KELLY *Scottish Proverbs* 346 When the Cup's full carry it even. When you have arrived at Power and Wealth, take a care of Insolence, Pride, and Oppression. **1889** C. M. YONGE in *Monthly Packet* Christmas 46 Poor things! They were so happy—so open-hearted. I did long to caution them. 'Full cup, steady hand.' **1903** G. H. KNIGHT *Master's Questions* xxi I would listen .. to this question .. whenever .. I am eagerly reaching out my hands to grasp what may satisfy an unlikely ambition. All hands are not steady enough to carry a full cup. ■ **good fortune; prudence**

It's ill speaking between a FULL man and a fasting

A hungry man is never on good terms with a well-fed man; in quot. 1824, used as an incitation to eat.

□ *a* **1641** D. FERGUSSON *Scottish Proverbs* (STS) no. 1349 Thair is nothing betuix a bursten body and a hungered. **1824** SCOTT *Redgauntlet* I. xi. Ye maun eat and drink, Steenie .. for we do little else here, and it's ill speaking between a fou man and a fasting. **1934** J. BUCHAN *Free Fishers* ii. It's ill speaking between a full man and a fasting, but two fasting men are worse at a crack. ■ **hunger; quarrelsomeness**

Out of the FULLNESS of the heart the mouth speaks

With allusion to MATTHEW xii. 34 (AV) Out of the abundance of the heart the mouth speaketh.

□ *c* **1390** CHAUCER *Parson's Tale* l. 626 After the habundance of the herte speketh the mouth ful ofte. **1699** T. CHALKLEY *Fruits of Divine Meditation* in *Works* (1751) II. 26

Out of the Abundance of the Heart the Mouth speaketh. **1861** TROLLOPE *Framley Parsonage* II. x. As out of the full head the mouth speaks, so is the full heart more prone to speak at such periods of confidence as these. **1932** 'S. FOWLER' *Hand-Print Mystery* ii. The murder.. had been in the background of her mind all the time. 'Out of the fullness of the heart the mouth speaketh.' ■ **speech and silence**

One FUNERAL makes many

A similar idea to *one* WEDDING *brings another*. The thinking behind this saying is illustrated in the quots.

□ **1894** BLACKMORE *Perlycross* I. vii. It has been said, and is true too often.. that one funeral makes many. A strong east wind.. whistled through the crowd of mourners. **1935** R. C. WOODTHORPE *Shadow on Downs* V. iv. 137 The funeral went off very well. .. I am glad we had such a fine day for it. Standing about bareheaded in driving rain.. always makes such an occasion rather trying, and there is a good deal of truth in the saying that one funeral brings others. **1951** M. DURHAM *Forked Lightning* xx. 132 Poured cats and dogs for my poor father's funeral, it did. .. My poor mother took a fever and it carried her off in a fortnight. They say one funeral makes another ■ **death**

funeral *see also* DREAM of a funeral and you hear of a marriage.

further *see* GO further and fare worse.

fury *see* HELL hath no fury like a woman scorned.

When the FURZE is in bloom, my love's in tune

A corollary of *when the* GORSE *is out of bloom, kissing's out of fashion*. Cf. *c* **1225** in *Englische Studien* (1902) XXXI. 5 Whanne bloweth [flowers] the brom, thanne wogeth [woos] the grom; Whanne bloweth the furs, thanne wogeth he wurs.

□ **1752** *Poor Robin's Almanack* Aug. B3v Dog-days are in he'll say's the reason Why kissing now is out of season: but Joan says furze [gorse] in bloom still, and she'll be kiss'd if she's her will. **1908** *Spectator* 9 May 740 At almost any season of the year gorse can be found in.. flower. .. When the furze is in bloom, my love's in tune. ■ **love, prosperous**

gain *see* (noun) one man's LOSS is another man's gain; there's no great LOSS without some gain; NO pain, no gain; (verb) what you LOSE on the swings you gain on the roundabouts; NOTHING venture, nothing gain.

gallows *see* the SEA refuses no river.

game *see* LOOKERS-ON see most of the game.

gamekeeper *see* an old POACHER makes the best gamekeeper.

gander *see* what is SAUCE for the goose is sauce for the gander.

GARBAGE in, garbage out

Garbage is a colloquial term in data processing for 'incorrect input' which will, according to the proverb, inevitably produce faulty output. The acronymic form *GIGO* is also found.

□ **1964** *CIS Glossary of Automated Typesetting & Related Computer Terms* (Composition Information Services, L.A.) 15 The relationship between input and output is sometimes—when input is incorrect—tersely noted by the expression 'garbage in, garbage out'. **1966** E. J. & J. A. MCCARTHY *Integrated Data Processing Systems* v. Many data processing departments put their best operators on verifiers because they wish to avoid the effect of the GIGO principle (Garbage In—Garbage Out). **1987** *Washington Times* 10 Sept. F4 The computer rule, 'garbage in, garbage out' applies to the human mind just as much as it does to the computer. **1996** *Washington Times* 26 Feb. A19 This brings into play the old computer-industry dictum: Garbage In, Garbage Out. ■ **action and consequence**; **error**

garment *see* SILENCE is a woman's best garment.

gate *see* a CREAKING door hangs longest; one man may STEAL a horse, while another may not look over a hedge.

gather *see* a ROLLING stone gathers no moss.

gathered *see* where the CARCASE is, there shall the eagles be gathered together.

geese *see* on SAINT Thomas the Divine kill all turkeys, geese, and swine.

generation *see* from CLOGS to clogs is only three generations; from SHIRT-SLEEVES to shirtsleeves in three generations.

It takes three GENERATIONS to make a gentleman

Although apparently not expressed in this form before quot. 1823, the three-generation concept was current in the Renaissance period: e.g. **1598** J. KEPERS tr. *A. Romei's Courtier's Academy* 187 He may bee called absolutely noble, who shall have lost the memory of his ignobilitie.. during the reuolution of three generations; **1625** F. MARKHAM *Five Decades of Honour* ii. Three perfit descents, do euer so conclude a perfit Gentleman of Blood.

□ **1823** J. F. COOPER *Pioneers* I. xviii. You will find it no easy matter to make a gentleman of him. The old proverb says, that 'it takes three generations to make a gentleman'. **1915** W. S. MAUGHAM *Of Human Bondage* xxvii. He remembered his uncle's saying that it took three generations to make a gentleman: it was a companion proverb to the silk purse and the sow's ear. **1940** 'M. INNES' *Comedy of Terrors* i. It has always been possible to make a gentleman in three generations; nowadays . . the thing is done in two. ■ **family**; **gentry**

generous *see* be JUST before you're generous.

GENIUS is an infinite capacity for taking pains

Cf. **1858** CARLYLE *Frederick the Great* I. IV. iii. 'Genius' . . means transcendent capacity of taking trouble, first of all.

□ **1870** J. E. HOPKINS *Work amongst Working Men* iv. Gift, like genius, I often think, only means an infinite capacity for taking pains. **1959** M. BRADBURY *Eating People is Wrong* iv. Genius is an infinite capacity for taking pains. But we should still foster it, however much of an embarrassment it may be to us. **1974** T. SHARPE *Porterhouse Blue* xiv. The modern fashion [of research] comes, I suppose, from a literal acceptance of the ridiculous dictum that genius is an infinite capacity for taking pains. ■ **diligence**

gentleman *see* when ADAM delved and Eve span, who was then the gentleman?; an ENGLISHMAN's word is his bond; it takes three GENERATIONS to make a gentleman.

gently *see* DRIVE gently over the stones; EASY does it; if you gently touch a NETTLE it'll sting you for your pains.

get *see* you cannot get BLOOD from a stone; if you don't like the HEAT, get out of the kitchen; if you LIE down with dogs, you will get up with fleas; don't get MAD, get even; the MORE you get, the more you want; what a NEIGHBOUR gets is not lost; you cannot get a QUART into a pint pot; what you SEE is what you get; you don't get SOMETHING for nothing; *also* GOT.

Never look a GIFT horse in the mouth

A horse's age is commonly gauged by the state of its teeth. The proverb warns against questioning the quality or use of a lucky chance or gift. Cf. *a* **420** ST. JEROME *Commentary on Epistle to Ephesians* Preface *noli . . ut vulgare proverbium est, equi dentes inspicere donati*, do not, as the common proverb says, look at the teeth of a gift horse.

□ *a* **1510** J. STANBRIDGE *Vulgaria* (EETS) 27 A gyuen hors may not [be] loked in the tethe. **1546** J. HEYWOOD *Dialogue of Proverbs* I. v. B2ᵛ Where gyfts be gyuen freely, est west north or south, No man ought to loke a geuen hors in the mouth. **1659** N. R. *Proverbs* 80 No man ought to look a guift Horse in the mouth. **1710** S. PALMER *Proverbs* 40 Never look a Gift Horse in the Mouth. **1892** G. & W. GROSSMITH *Diary of a Nobody* xviii. I told him it was a present from a dear friend, and one mustn't look a gift-horse in the mouth. **2002** *Oldie* Mar. 34 Gather ye rosebuds while ye may, let not the grass grow under thy feet, and never look a gift horse in the mouth. ■ **giving and receiving**; **gratitude and ingratitude**

gift *see also* FEAR the Greeks bearing gifts.

gill *see* every HERRING must hang by its own gill.

girl *see* BOYS will be boys.

GIVE and take is fair play

□ **1778** F. BURNEY *Evelina* I. xxv. This here may be a French fashion.. but Give and Take is fair in all nations. **1832** MARRYAT *Newton Forster* III. x. Give and take is fair play. All I say is, let it be a fair stand-up fight. **1873** 'TWAIN' & WARNER *Gilded Age* xxxiii. She thought that 'give and take was fair play', and to parry an offensive thrust with a sarcasm was a neat and legitimate thing to do. ■ **fair dealing; tolerance**

GIVE a thing, and take a thing, to wear the Devil's gold ring

A rhyme used by schoolchildren when someone gives something and then asks for it back. The principle is a very old one; cf. PLATO *Philebus* 19E *καθάπερ οἱ παῖδες, ὅτι τῶν ὀρθῶς δοθέντων ἀφαίρεσις οὐκ ἔστι*, as with children, there is no taking away of what has been rightly given.

□ **1571** J. BRIDGES *Sermon at Paul's Cross* 29 Shal we make God to say the worde, and eate his worde? to giue a thing, and take a thing, little children say, This is the diuels goldring, not Gods gift. **1611** R. COTGRAVE *Dict. French & English* s.v. Retirer, To giue a thing and take a thing; to weare the diuells gold-ring. **1721** J. KELLY *Scottish Proverbs* 120 Give a Thing, and take a Thing, Is the ill Man's Goud Ring. A Cant among Children, when they demand a Thing again, which they had bestowed. **1894** *Notes & Queries* 8th Ser. VI. 155 Another saying among boys is—Give a thing and take a thing, To wear the devil's gold ring. **1959** I. & P. OPIE *Lore & Language of Schoolchildren* viii. It is a cardinal rule amongst the young that a thing which has been given must not be asked for again. .. [Somerset] Give a thing, take a thing, Dirty man's plaything. .. [Cheshire] Give a thing, take a thing, Never go to God again. ■ **giving and receiving**

GIVE the Devil his due

Also in the phrase *to give the Devil his due*.

□ **1589** LYLY *Pap with Hatchet* III. 407 Giue them their due though they were diuels.. and excuse them for taking anie money at interest. **1596** NASHE *Saffron Walden* III. 36 Giue the diuell his due. **1642** *Prince Rupert's Declaration* 2 The Cavaliers (to give the Divell his due) fought very valiantly. **1751** SMOLLETT *Peregrine Pickle* I. xvii. You always used me in an officer-like manner, that I must own, to give the devil his due. **1936** H. AUSTIN *Murder of Matriarch* xxiii. To give the devil his due.. I don't think that Irvin planned to incriminate anyone else. **1978** R. L. HILL *Evil that Men Do* vi. Giving the devil his due will always jostle the angels. ■ **fair dealing**

give *see also* it is BETTER to give than to receive; give CREDIT where credit is due; give a DOG a bad name and hang him; give a man ROPE enough and he will hang himself; never give a SUCKER an even break.

He GIVES twice who gives quickly

Cf. PUBLILIUS SYRUS *Sententia* ccxxxv. *inopi beneficium bis dat, qui dat celeriter*, he gives twice who gives quickly to the needy; mid 14th-cent. Fr. *qui tost donne, deus fois donne*. Also *c* **1385** CHAUCER *Legend of Good Women* Prologue l. 451 For whoso yeveth a yifte, or dooth a grace. Do it by tyme [in good time], his thanks ys wel the more. The Latin *bis dat qui cito dat* is perhaps better known than the Publilius Syrus version, and was quoted in this form by Francis Bacon in a speech on 17 May 1617, upon taking his seat as Keeper of the Great Seal.

□ **1553** T. WILSON *Art of Rhetoric* 65[v] He geueth twise, that geueth sone and chearefully. **1612** T. SHELTON tr. *Cervantes' Don Quixote* I. iv. It is an old proverbe, that hee that gives quickly, gives twice. **1775** J. BOSWELL *Life of Johnson* I. 443 I did really ask the favour twice; but you have been even with me by granting it so speedily. *Bis dat qui cito dat.* **1980** *Times* 17 Oct. 13 'He gives twice who gives quickly.'..We have everything to gain by generous action at once. ■ **charity; giving and receiving**

Those who live in GLASS houses shouldn't throw stones

Do not criticize or slander another if you are vulnerable to retaliation. Cf. *c* **1385** CHAUCER *Troilus & Criseyde* II. 867 Who that hath an hed of verre [glass], Fro cast of stones war hym in the werre!

□ **1640** G. HERBERT *Outlandish Proverbs* no. 196 Whose house is of glasse, must not throw stones at another. **1754** J. SHEBBEARE *Marriage Act* II. lv. Thee shouldst not throw Stones, who hast a Head of Glass thyself. ..Thee canst have no Title to Honesty who lendest the writings to deceive Neighbour Barter. **1778** T. PAINE in *Pennsylvania Packet* 22 Oct. i. He who lives in a glass house, says a Spanish proverb, should never begin throwing stones. **1861** TROLLOPE *Framley Parsonage* I. vi. Those who live in glass houses shouldn't throw stones. ..Mr. Robarts's sermon will be too near akin to your lecture to allow of his laughing. **2001** W. NORTHCUTT *Darwin Awards II* i. 16 Judea and Samaria district police jointly determined that the accidental crash was caused by the stone-throwing young men. *People who live in glass houses shouldn't throw stones.* ■ **hypocrisy; self-preservation; slander**

All that GLITTERS is not gold

'Glisters', despite its Shakespearean authority, is now less often found than 'glitters'. The variant form illustrated in quots. 1773 and 1987 is also common. L. *non omne quod nitet aurum est*, not all that shines is gold.

□ *c* **1220** *Hali Meidenhad* (EETS) ii. Nis hit nower neh gold al that ter [there] schineth. *c* **1390** CHAUCER *Canon's Yeoman's Tale* l. 962 But al thyng which that shineth as the gold Nis nat gold, as that I have herd it told. **1596** SHAKESPEARE *Merchant of Venice* II. vii. 65 All that glisters is not gold, Often have you heard that told. *c* **1628** W. DRUMMOND *Works* (1711) 222 All is not Gold which glittereth. **1773** D. GARRICK in Goldsmith *She stoops to Conquer* (Prologue) All is not gold that glitters. Pleasure seems sweet, but proves a glass of bitters [bitter-tasting medicine]. **1847** C. BRONTË *Jane Eyre* II. ix. I wished to put you on your guard. It is an old saying that 'all is not gold that glitters'. **1880** *Dict. English Proverbs* (Asprey Reference Library) 39 All that glitters is not gold. **1933** E. B. BLACK *Ravenelle Riddle* iv. All that glitters is not gold. ..Every bird who calls himself an American doesn't happen to be one. **1980** *Times* 19 Jan. 18 A young woman, perhaps grasping the unseemly spectacle of it all, suggested that all that glitters was not gold. **1987** D. FISKE *Murder Bound* (1989) ii. 11 The old saw 'all is not gold that glitters' still holds true despite its standing as a platitude. **1998** *Country Life* 22 Jan. 50 (*caption*) In the volatile world of jewellery investment, all that glisters is not gold. ■ **appearance, deceptive**

glove *see* a CAT in gloves catches no mice.

GO abroad and you'll hear news of home

□ **1678** J. RAY *English Proverbs* (ed. 2) 345 You must goe into the countrey to hear what news at London. **1887** T. HARDY *Woodlanders* I. iv. Well, what was the latest news at Shottsford. ..As the saying is, 'Go abroad and you'll hear news of home.' **1937** J. P. MARQUAND *Late George Apley* x. It seems one must leave home to learn the news of home. ■ **home; news; travel**

GO further and fare worse

□ **1546** J. HEYWOOD *Dialogue of Proverbs* II. iv. G3V You rose on your right syde here ryght. And might haue gon further, and haue faren wurs. **1738** SWIFT *Polite Conversation* ii. 58 Come, Sir *John*, you may go further, and fare worse. **1848** THACKERAY *Vanity Fair* iv. She's just as rich as most of the girls who came out of India. I might go farther and fare worse. **1938** G. GREENE in *Spectator* 12 Aug. 271 He would have said, perhaps, with his plainness and simplicity and the smirk of satisfaction you see on his portrait, that one can fare further and fare worse. ■ **content and discontent**

go *see also* EASY come, easy go; LIGHT come, light go; QUICKLY come, quickly go; he that would go to SEA for pleasure, would go to hell for a pastime; SELL in May and go away; never let the SUN go down on your anger; don't go near the WATER until you learn how to swim; the WEAKEST go to the wall; many go out for WOOL and come home shorn; *also* GOES.

You cannot serve GOD and Mammon

Quoting MATTHEW vi. 24 (AV) Ye cannot serve God and mammon. *Mammon* is the Aramaic word for 'riches', taken by medieval writers as the proper name of the devil of covetousness. Now used generally of wealth regarded as an evil influence.

□ **1531** W. BONDE *Pilgrimage of Perfection* (rev. ed.) III. vii. No person may serue god eternall and also the Mammonde of iniquite: whiche is golde and syluer and other richesse. **1860** TROLLOPE *Framley Parsonage* II. i. Lady Lufton.. would say of Miss Dunstable that it was impossible to serve both God and Mammon. **1982** P. McGINLEY *Goosefoot* v. The city and the country repel each other like oil and water. And like God and Mammon, they can't be served at the same time by the same person. ■ **money**

Where GOD builds a church, the Devil will build a chapel

Quot. 1942 cites the version of the saying found in George Herbert's *Outlandish Proverbs* (1640) no. 674.

□ **1560** T. BECON *Works* I. 516V For commonly, where so ever God buildeth a church, the Deuyll wyl builde a Chappell iuste by. **1701** DEFOE *True-born Englishman* 4 Wherever God erects a House of Prayer, The Devil always builds a Chapel there: And 'twill be found upon Examination, The latter has the largest Congregation. **1903** G. H. KNIGHT *Master's Questions* xiii. Nowhere does the devil build his little chapels more cunningly than close under the shadow of the great temple of Christian liberty. A thing in itself completely right and good, may be, in its effects on others, completely evil. **1942** M. MARLETT *Devil Builds a Chapel* (*epigraph*) No sooner is a temple built to God, but the Devil builds a chapel hard by. **2001** S. KENDRICK *Night Watch* iv. 134 'I'm beginning to think there's great truth in the old saying "Wherever God builds a church, the devil builds a chapel next door."' ■ **good and evil**

GOD helps them that help themselves

Cf. AESCHYLUS *Fragments* 395 φιλεῖ δὲ τῷ κάμνοντι συσπεύδειν θεός, God likes to assist the man who toils; early 15th-cent. Fr. *aidez uous, Dieu uos aidera*, help yourself, God will help you.

□ **1545** R. TAVERNER tr. *Erasmus' Adages* (ed. 2) 57 *Dii facientes adiuuant*. The goddes do helpe the doers. **1551** T. WILSON *Rule of Reason* S1V Shipmen cal to God for helpe, and God will helpe them, but so not withstandying, if they helpe them selfes. **1668** R. B. *Adagia Scotica* 21 Help thy self, and God will help thee. **1736** B. FRANKLIN *Poor Richard's Almanack* (June) God helps them that help themselves. **1892** H. P. LIDDON *Sermons on Some Words of Christ* iii. God does not promise us each and all that.. the ravens shall come to feed us: as the proverb most truly says, He helps them that help themselves. **1990** C. FREMLIN *Listening in Dusk* xxvii. A widow of eighty-nine.. had hit an intruder over the head with the family Bible and sent him flying. 'The Lord helps those who help themselves!' she'd declared, cackling with triumph in front of the cameras. **2002** *Spectator* 19 Jan. 33 And what does the future hold? He quotes his grandmother: 'The Lord helps those who help themselves'. ■ **providence; self-help**

GOD made the country, and man made the town

Cf. VARRO *De Re Rustica* III. i. *divina natura dedit agros, ars humana aedificavit urbes*, divine nature gave us the fields, human art built the cities.

□ **1667** A. COWLEY in J. Wells *Poems* 2 My father said.. God the first Garden made, & the first City, Cain. **1785** COWPER *Task* I. 40 God made the country, and man made the town. **1870** H. TENNYSON *Memoir* 25 Jan. (1897) II. 96 There is a saying that if God made the country, and man the town, the devil made the little country town. **1941** H. MACINNES *Above Suspicion* x. God made the country, man made the town. Pity men couldn't learn better. **1977** G. TINDALL *Field & Beneath* i. It has been said that 'God made the country and man made the town', but.. the town is simply disguised countryside. ■ **Nature**

GOD makes the back to the burden

□ **1822** COBBETT *Weekly Register* 12 Jan. 94 As 'God has made the back to the burthen,' so the clay and coppice people make the dress to the stubs and bushes. **1839** DICKENS *Nicholas Nickleby* xviii. Heaven suits the back to the burden. **1939** E. F. BENSON *Trouble for Lucia* ii. 'Spare yourself a bitty' I've said, and always she's replied 'Heaven fits the back to the burden.' **1979** E. ANTHONY *Grave of Truth* viii. So many questions and nobody to answer them; it was a true penance for her. .. God made the back for the burden. .. An Irish nun.. had taught them that saying from her native land. ■ **providence; trouble**

GOD never sends mouths but He sends meat

□ **1377** LANGLAND *Piers Plowman* B. XIV. 39 For lente neuere was lyf but lyflode [livelihood] were shapen. **1546** J. HEYWOOD *Dialogue of Proverbs* I. iv. B1 God neuer sendeth mouthe, but he sendeth meat. **1832** J. P. KENNEDY *Swallow Barn* I. xxviii. God never sends mouths.. but he sends meat, and any man who has sense enough to be honest, will never want wit to know how to live. **1905** A. MACLAREN *Gospel according to St. Matthew* I. 103 We are meant to be righteous, and shall not in vain desire to be so. God never sends mouths but He sends meat to fill them. ■ **hunger; providence**

GOD sends meat, but the Devil sends cooks

□ **1542** A. BORDE *Dietary of Health* xi. It is a common prouerbe, God may sende a man good meate, but the deuyll may sende an euyll coke to dystrue it. *c* **1607** T. DELONEY *Thomas of Reading* B3 God sends meat, and the diuel sends cookes. **1738** SWIFT *Polite Conversation* ii. 155 This Goose is quite raw: Well, God sends Meat, but the Devil sends Cooks. **1822** SCOTT *Nigel* III. iii. That homely proverb that men taunt my calling with,—'God sends good meat, but the devil sends cooks.' **1979**

Country Life 13 Sept. 807 Another old saying..that God sends good meat but the devil sends the cooks. ■ **food and drink**

GOD's in his heaven; all's right with the world

The standard form is an expression of satisfaction (see quot. 1841), which has now largely replaced the consolatory *God is where he was.*

□ **1530** J. PALSGRAVE *L'éclaircissement de la Langue Française* 213 Neuer dispayre man, god is there as he was. **1612** T. SHELTON tr. *Cervantes' Don Quixote* I. IV. iii. God is in heaven. **1678** J. RAY *English Proverbs* (ed. 2) 147 God is where he was. Spoken to encourage People in any distress. **1841** R. BROWNING *Works* (1970) 327 The snail's on the thorn: God's in his heaven—All's right with the world. **1906** R. KIPLING *Puck of Pook's Hill* 240 Cheer up, lad. ..God's where He was. **1928** E. WAUGH *Decline & Fall* I. V. When you've been in the soup as often as I have, it gives you a sort of feeling that everything's for the best, really. You know, God's in His heaven; all's right with the world. **1983** P. MORTIMER *Handyman* xv. When she heard his car draw up, on the dot of seven, it was as though she had been injected with a great feeling of calm, a reassurance that God was in his heaven and all [was] right with her world. ■ **content and discontent**

GOD tempers the wind to the shorn lamb

God mercifully ensures that misfortune does not overwhelm the weak or helpless. The phrase *to temper the wind* (*to the shorn lamb*) is also common. Cf. **1594** H. ESTIENNE *Premices 47 ces termes, Dieu mesure le froid à la brebis tondue, sont les propres termes du prouerbe*, these terms, God measures the cold to the shorn sheepe, are the correct terms of the proverb.

□ **1640** G. HERBERT *Outlandish Proverbs* no. 867 To a close shorne sheep, God gives wind by measure. **1768** STERNE *Sentimental Journey* II. 175 How she had borne it..she could not tell—but God tempers the wind, said Maria, to the shorn lamb. **1933** V. BRITTAIN *Testament of Youth* I. ii. There is an unduly optimistic proverb which declares that God tempers the wind to the shorn lamb. My subsequent history was hardly to justify such naive faith in the Deity. **1996** *American Spectator* Mar. 56 But as Laurence Sterne was wont to remind us, the Lord tempers the wind for the shorn lamb. There were bars. ■ **providence**; **trouble**

God *see also* ALL things are possible with God; EVERY man for himself, and God for us all; MAN proposes, God disposes; MAN'S extremity is God's opportunity; the MILLS of God grind slowly, yet they grind exceeding small; the NEARER the church, the farther from God; PROVIDENCE is always on the side of the big battalions; the ROBIN and the wren are God's cock and hen; TAKE the goods the gods provide; put your TRUST in God, and keep your powder dry; the VOICE of the people is the voice of God; a WHISTLING woman and a crowing hen are neither fit for God nor men; *also* GODS, HEAVEN.

godliness *see* CLEANLINESS is next to godliness.

Whom the GODS love die young

Cf. MENANDER *Dis Exapatōn* fragment 4 (Sandbach) *ὃν οἱ θεοὶ φιλοῦσιν ἀποθνήσκει νέος*, he whom the gods love dies young; PLAUTUS *Bacchides* l. 817 *quem di diligunt, Adolescens moritur*, he whom the gods favour, dies young.

□ **1546** W. HUGHE *Troubled Man's Medicine* B8^{V} Most happy be they and best belouid of god, that dye whan they be young. **1553** T. WILSON *Art of Rhetoric* 40^{V} Whom god loueth best, those he taketh sonest. **1651** G. HERBERT *Jacula Prudentum* no. 1094 Those that God loves, do not live long. **1821** BYRON *Don Juan* IV. xii. 'Whom the gods love die young,' was said of yore, And many deaths do they escape by this. **1972** A. PRICE *Colonel Butler's Wolf* xx. 'Whom the gods love die young,' the war taught us that. ■ **death; youth**

The GODS send nuts to those who have no teeth

Said of opportunities or pleasures which come too late to be enjoyed. Cf. Fr. *le pain vient à qui les dents faillent*, bread comes to those who lack teeth.

□ **1929** *American Speech* IV. 463 God gives us nuts to crack when we no longer have teeth. **1967** RIDOUT & WITTING *English Proverbs Explained* 68 The gods send nuts to those who have no teeth. In this life we either have too little of what we do want, or too much of what we don't want or can't use. **2000** 'C. AIRD' *Little Knell* (2001) xiv. 161 'It's seeing the gardens I—we—would have been going for,' insisted Sloan, 'Not the luxury.' 'Quite right,' said Leeyes, adding obscurely, 'The nuts come when the teeth have gone.' ■ **old age; opportunity, missed**

Whom the GODS would destroy, they first make mad

Cf. *Trag. Graec. Fragm. Adesp.* 296 (Nauck) *ὅταν γὰρ ὀργὴ δαιμόνων βλάπτῃ τινά, τοῦτ' αὐτὸ πρῶτον, ἐξαφαιρεῖται φρενῶν τὸν νοῦν τὸν ἐσθλόν*, when divine anger ruins a man, it first takes away his good sense; L. *quos Deus vult perdere, prius dementat.*

□ **1611** JONSON *Catiline* V. 481 A madnesse, Wherewith heauen blinds 'hem, when it would confound 'hem. **1640** G. HERBERT *Outlandish Proverbs* no. 688 When God will punish, hee will first take away the understanding. **1817** BYRON *Letter* 2 Apr. (1976) V. 204 God maddens him whom 'tis his will to lose, And gives the choice of death or phrenzy—Choose! **1875** M. THOMPSON *Hoosier Mosaics* 180 Whom the gods would destroy they first make mad. **1981** *Daily Telegraph* 24 July 4 Already Commonwealth Finance Ministers have elected not to meet on New Zealand's defiled soil. If greater penalties follow, the Commonwealth will confirm that those whom the gods would destroy they first make mad. ■ **fate and fatalism; fools**

He that GOES a-borrowing, goes a-sorrowing

□ *c* **1470** in Wright & Halliwell *Reliquiæ Antiquæ* (1841) I. 316 He that fast spendyth must nede borowe; But whan he schal paye ayen, then ys al the sorowe. **1545** R. TAVERNER tr. *Erasmus' Adages* (ed. 2) 46V He that goeth a borowynge goeth a sorowynge. **1836** MARRYAT *Midshipman Easy* I. viii. You had made your request for the loan..fully anticipating a refusal, (from the feeling that he who goes a borrowing goes a sorrowing). **1925** S. O'CASEY *Juno & Paycock* III. 84 Ah, him that goes a borrowin' goes a sorrowin'!..An' there isn't hardly a neighbour in the whole street that hasn't lent him money on the strength of what he was going to get. **1995** *American Spectator* Feb. 82 Who goes a-borrowing goes a-sorrowing. Yes, the balanced-budget amendment is sort of a dumb idea, because it can so easily be evaded by cunning congressional accounting. ■ **borrowing and lending**

What GOES around comes around

A modern proverb of US origin.

□ **1974** E. STONE *Donald writes no More* xv. No one can say why Donald Goines and Shirley Sailor were murdered. The ghetto philosophy, 'what goes around comes around', is the only answer most people can give. It is probably the answer Donald Goines himself would have provided. **1982** H. STEIN *Ethics* 108 At this juncture another, more recent, adage springs to mind: What goes around comes around. It is, all in all, a terrific statement, and I know a lot of people who would turn handsprings if only they could be assured it was true. **1989** *Washington Times* 19

Apr. F1 No sooner had the royal accusers sent Louis XVI and his queen to the guillotine, than they themselves were being hoist onto the tumbrels by men whose own heads would later drop into the basket. What goes around comes around. **2002** *Washington Post* 8 May C1 If you were given to platitudes, you would dub this an instance of What Goes Around Comes Around. Karma. Give a little, and—30 years later—watch it land a publishing deal. ■ **fate and fatalism**; **retribution**

goes *see also* there goes more to MARRIAGE than four bare legs in a bed; PRIDE goes before a fall; what goes UP must come down.

When the GOING gets tough, the tough get going

A favourite family saying of Joseph P. Kennedy (1888–1969), US politician, businessman, and father of President John F. Kennedy.

□ **1962** J. H. CUTLER *'Honey Fitz'* xx. Joe [Kennedy] made his children stay on their toes. .. He would bear down on them and tell them, 'When the going gets tough, the tough get going.' **1970** *New Yorker* 3 Oct. 33 Baron Marcel Bich, the millionaire French pen magnate probably spoke for them all last month when he said, 'When the going gets tough, the tough get going!' ('Quand le chemin devient dur, les durs se cheminent!') **1979** J. CRUMLEY *Last Good Kiss* xvi. 'When the going gets tough, the tough get going?' she asked slyly. 'Make fun if you want to, but that's what character is all about.' **2001** *Washington Post* 26 July C13 (*Hagar the Horrible comic strip*) 'I realize we're lost. .. But always remember—"When the going gets tough, the tough get going"!' 'I know. But which way do we go?' ■ **opportunity, taken**; **politics**; **stress**

GOLD may be bought too dear

□ **1546** J. HEYWOOD *Dialogue of Proverbs* II. vii. 14 Well (quoth she) a man maie bie golde to dere. **1642** T. FULLER *Holy State* II. xxi. Fearing to find the Proverb true, That Gold may be bought too dear, they returned to their ships. **1889** J. LUBBOCK *Pleasures of Life* (ed. 2) II. ii. It is well worth having.. but it does not requite too great a sacrifice. A wise proverb tells us that gold may be bought too dear. ■ **money**; **value**

gold *see also* it is good to make a BRIDGE of gold to a flying enemy; GIVE a thing, and take a thing, to wear the Devil's gold ring; all that GLITTERS is not gold.

A GOLDEN key can open any door

□ **1580** LYLY *Euphues & his England* II. 71 Who is so ignorant that knoweth not, gold be a key for euery locke, chieflye with his Ladye. **1660** W. SECKER *Nonsuch Professor* II. ix. The gates of the new Jerusalem.. are not got open by golden keys. **1842** TENNYSON *Poems* (1969) 694 Every door is barr'd with gold, and opens but to golden keys. **1945** F. THOMPSON *Lark Rise* xix. Their better-educated neighbours.. did not call on the newly rich family. That was before the days when a golden key could open any door. ■ **bribery and corruption**; **money**

golden *see also* SILENCE is golden; SPEECH is silver, but silence is golden.

If you can't be GOOD, be careful

Cf. mid 11th-cent. L. *si non caste tamen caute*; **1303** R. BRUNNE *Handlyng Synne* (EETS) l. 8316 The apostle seyth thys autoryte [dictum], 'Gyf thou be nat chaste, be thou pryue [secret].' **1528** W. TYNDALE *Obedience of Christian Man* 73 As oure lawears saye, *si non caste tamen caute*, this is, if ye live not chaste, se ye cary clene [act properly], and playe the knave secretly.

□ **1903** A. M. BINSTEAD *Pitcher in Paradise* viii. Always bear in mind what the country mother said to her daughter who was coming up to town to be apprenticed to the Bond Street millinery, 'For heaven's sake be good; but if you can't be good, be careful.' **1907** B. SCOTT *(song-title)* If you can't be good—be careful. **1982** S. GRANT DUFF *Parting of Ways* xvii. Tommy . . gave me a stern warning. . . 'Never meet a German in Prague . . Be good, and if you can't, be very careful.' ■ **caution**

A GOOD beginning makes a good ending

□ *c* **1300** *South-English Legendary* (EETS) I. 216 This was atte uerste me thingth [it seems to me] a god bygynnynge. Ther after was the betere hope to come to god endynge. *c* **1350** *Douce MS 52* no. 122 Of a gode begynnyng comyth a gode endyng. **1710** S. PALMER *Proverbs* 1 A good Beginning makes a good End. . . 'Tis a great point of Wisdom . . to begin at the right end. **1850** 'M. TENSAS' *Odd Leaves from Life of Louisiana 'Swamp Doctor'* 109 I hope my future lot will be verification of the old adage, that a 'bad beginning makes a good ending', for mine is bad enough. **1934** G. WESTON *His First Million Women* xvi. I was brought up to believe that 'Of a good beginning cometh a good ending.' . . 'You can't do a good plastering job if your laths aren't right to begin with.' ■ **beginnings and endings**

There's many a GOOD cock come out of a tattered bag

The proverb is derived from cockfighting. Similar in sentiment is: **1721** J. KELLY *Scottish Proverbs* 7 An ill Cow may have a good Calf. Bad People may have good Children.

□ **1883** C. S. BURNE *Shropshire Folklore* xxxvi. There'll come a good cock out of a ragged bag. . . A cockfighting simile, lately used by a farmer, whose buildings were out of repair, but his stock in good condition. **1953** R. SUTCLIFF *Simon* xiv. 'There's many a good cock come out of a tattered bag,' said the dark shape, slowly. There was an instant of . . silence, and then Simon said, 'And a good tune played on an old fiddle.' ■ **appearance, deceptive**

No GOOD deed goes unpunished

Sometimes attributed to Oscar Wilde, but not traced in his writings.

□ **1938** J. AGATE *Ego 3* 25 Jan. 275 Pavia was in great form to-day: 'Every good deed brings its own punishment.' **1967** J. ORTON *Diaries* (1986) 13 June 209 Very good line George came out with at dinner: 'No good deed ever goes unpunished.' **2002** *Washington Post* 11 Jan. C3 Finally, the wages of purity, naivete and an excessive love of mankind catch up with her. As they say, no good deed goes unpunished, no unloved and unimportant humans can expect not to be squashed. ■ **just deserts**

The GOOD die young

□ **1697** DEFOE *Character of Dr. Annesley* 3 The best of Men cannot suspend their Fate; The Good die early, and the Bad die late. **1814** WORDSWORTH *Excursion* I. 27 The good die first, And they whose hearts are dry as summer dust Burn to the socket. **1852** A. CARY *Clovernook* 39 Sarah . . was dead . . aged nineteen years. . . The old truth was again reasserted . . in the often repeated verse which followed, that the good die young. **1987** L. BARNES *Trouble of Fools* v. 'Live hard, die young,' I said. . . 'You got it wrong, Carlotta,' Mooney said. 'I learned it in school. It's "Only the good die young." Before they get a chance to fool around.' **2002** *Washington Post* 18 Jan. C1 It [*Black Hawk Down*] teaches stuff they don't know, only the smallest and most bitter of lessons: that ammunition is more important than water, that cover is more important than concealment, and that the good die young. ■ **death; youth**

He is a GOOD dog who goes to church

□ **1826** SCOTT *Woodstock* I. i Bevis . . fell under the proverb which avers, 'He is a good dog which goes to church'; for . . he behaved himself . . decorously. *a* **1895** F. LOCKER-LAMPSON *My Confidences* (1896) 44 Tis said, by men of deep research, He's a good dog who goes to church. ■ **conduct**

GOOD fences make good neighbours

□ **1640** E. ROGERS *Letter* in *Winthrop Papers* (1944) IV. 282 A good fence helpeth to keepe peace between neighbours; but let vs take heed that we make not a high stone wall, to keepe vs from meeting. **1815** H. H. BRACKENRIDGE *Modern Chivalry* (rev. ed.) IV. II. xiii. I was always with him [Jefferson] in his apprehensions of John Bull. . . Good fences restrain fencebreaking beasts, and . . preserve good neighbourhoods. **1914** R. FROST *North of Boston* 12 My apple trees will never get across And eat the cones under his pines, I tell him. He only says, 'Good fences make good neighbours.' **1978** T. SHARPE *Throwback* x. 'Hadn't you better go and investigate?' . . Lockhart shook his head. 'Strong fences make good neighbours.' **2001** *Washington Times* 7 Sept. A4 Mr. Fox insists that the United States overhaul immigration by the end of this year. . . He said he doesn't believe the American folk wisdom that good fences make good neighbors. ■ **harmony and disharmony; neighbours**

A GOOD horse cannot be of a bad colour

□ *a* **1628** J. CARMICHAELL *Proverbs in Scots* no. 1621 There is gude horse of all hewis. **1653** I. WALTON *Compleat Angler* iv. It is observed by some, that there is no good horse of a bad colour. **1732** T. FULLER *Gnomologia* no. 1713 Good Horses can't be of a bad Colour. **1891** J. L. KIPLING *Beast & Man* viii. 'A good horse is never of a bad colour' . . is wildly irreverent from the Oriental point of view. **1912** *Spectator* 28 Dec. 1094 Virgil . . did not hold that 'a good horse cannot be of a bad colour'; he liked bays and grays. ■ **appearance, significant; horse lore**

The only GOOD Indian is a dead Indian

Originally with reference to North American Indians; now also used derogatively of members of other nationalities or groups.

□ **1868** J. M. CAVANAUGH in *Congressional Globe* (US) 28 May 2638 I have never in my life seen a good Indian (and I have seen thousands) except when I have seen a dead Indian. **1886** A. GURNEY *Ramble through United States* 29 The Government . . is at length earnestly endeavouring to do tardy justice to the conquered race; but it was distressing to hear again and again from American lips the remark that 'A *good* Indian is a *dead* Indian.' **1895** E. S. ELLIS *People's Standard History U.S.* IV. lxxxiv. In January, 1869, . . Old Toch-a-way . . , a chief of the Comanches, . . [said]: 'Me, Tock-a-way; me good Injun.' . . General [Sheridan] . . set those standing by in a roar by saying: 'The only good Indians I ever saw were dead.' **1934** G. B. SHAW *On Rocks* (Preface) 146 'The only good nigger is a dead nigger' say the Americans of the Ku-Klux temperament. **1935** L. I. WILDER *Little House on Prairie* xvii. She did not know why the government made treaties with Indians. The only good Indian was a dead Indian. **1980** R. BUTLER *Blood-Red Sun at Noon* II. vi. The only good Jap is a dead Jap. **1994** *Washington Times* 18 Jan. A15 Unfortunately, some liberals sound as if they believe that the only good gun owner is a dead gun owner. **1998** K. NEVILLE *Magic Circle* 457 Sam had escorted me, and as we'd passed some other boys in the hallway, one had whispered just loud enough for Sam to hear: 'The only good Indian is a dead Indian.' ■ **national characteristics; reputation**

The GOOD is the enemy of the best

Also in reverse: *the* BEST *is the enemy of the good.*

□ **1912** J. KELMAN *Thoughts on Things Eternal* 108 Every respectable Pharisee proves the truth of the saying that 'the good is the enemy of the best.'.. Christ insists that we shall not be content with a second-best, though it be good. **1939** R. A. HABAS *Morals for Moderns* vii. 'The good', runs the old aphorism, 'is the enemy of the best.' Nowhere is this..better exemplified than in connection with..self-deceit. ■ **good things**

A GOOD Jack makes a good Jill

□ **1623** W. PAINTER *Palace of Pleasure* C8 A good Iacke alwaies maketh a good Gyll. **1670** J. RAY *English Proverbs* 108 A good Jack makes a good Gill. ..Inferiours imitate the manners of superiours..wives of their husbands. **1876** I. BANKS *Manchester Man* III. xv. In George Street he was refused admission, Mrs. Ashton justifying her daughter's fight with..'A good Jack makes a good Jill.' ■ **men and women**

GOOD men are scarce

□ **1609** D. TUVILL *Essays Moral & Theological* 92 Good men are scarce, no age so many brings As Thebes hath gates. **1721** J. KELLY *Scottish Proverbs* 124 Good Folks are scarce, you'll take care of one. Spoken to those who carefully provide against ill Weather, or cowardly shun Dangers. **1836** DICKENS *Sketches by Boz* I. 285 One of the women has agreed to stand a glass round, jocularly observing that 'as good people's wery scarce, what I says is, make the most on 'em.' **1979** 'J. LE CARRÉ' *Smiley's People* xii. Time you had some shut-eye, isn't it? Good men are scarce, I always say. ■ **good and evil**

There's many a GOOD tune played on an old fiddle

□ *a* **1902** S. BUTLER *Way of All Flesh* (1903) lxi. Beyond a haricot vein in one of my legs I'm as young as ever I was. Old indeed! There's many a good tune played on an old fiddle. **1979** N. FREELING *Widow* xxx. He looked at her casually. ..'Not all that bad at that. Many a good tune played on an old fiddle.' **2002** G. PHINN *Head over Heels in Dales* 9 Dun't really matter what it looks like, though, does it? It's what inside that counts, my grandad says. Same wi' people, he says. 'Many a good tune played on an owd fiddle.' ■ **appearance, deceptive; old age**

One GOOD turn deserves another

Cf. early 14th-cent. Fr. *lune bonté requiert lautre*, one good deed deserves another.

□ *c* **1400** in *Bulletin of John Rylands Library* (1930) XIV. 92 O [one] good turne asket another. **1620** J. HALL *Contemplations* V. XIV. 28 One good turne requires another. ..Justly should they haue been set at the vpper end of the table. **1638** T. RANDOLPH *Amyntas* v. vi. One good turne deserves another. **1929** S. T. WARNER *True Heart* II. 151 You've given me the best laugh I've had for months, and one good turn deserves another. **1979** T. SHARPE *Wilt Alternative* xiv. Noblesse oblige? You know, one good turn deserves another and whatnot. ■ **reciprocity**

GOOD wine needs no bush

A bunch of ivy was formerly the sign of a vintner's shop.

□ *a* **1430** J. LYDGATE *Pilgrimage of Man* (EETS) l. 20415 And at tavernys (withoute wene [doubt]) Thys tooknys [signs] nor thys bowys grene..The wyn they mende nat. **1545** R. TAVERNER tr. *Erasmus' Adages* (ed. 2) 42^{v} Wyne that is saleable and good nedeth no bushe or garland of yuye [ivy] to be hanged before. The english prouerbe is thus Good wyne neadeth no signe. **1599** SHAKESPEARE *As You like It*

(Epilogue) 3 If it be true that good wine needs no bush, 'tis true that a good play needs no epilogue. **1711** ADDISON *Spectator* 13 Nov. I was never better pleased than with a plain man's compliment, who upon his friend's telling him that he would like the *Spectator* much better if he understood the motto, replied, that good wine needs no bush. **1983** D. CLARK *Monday Theory* vi. 'Doesn't advertise much, does she, Chief?' said Reed. 'Relies on the principle that good wine needs no bush, perhaps,' replied Masters. ■ **public relations; reputation**

good *see also* as good be an ADDLED egg as an idle bird; ALL good things must come to an end; good AMERICANS when they die go to Paris; BAD money drives out good; the BEST is the enemy of the good; BETTER a good cow than a cow of a good kind; never BID the Devil good morrow until you meet him; BRAG is a good dog, but Holdfast is better; it is good to make a BRIDGE of gold to a flying enemy; a CHANGE is as good as a rest; CONFESSION is good for the soul; a clean CONSCIENCE is a good pillow; the best DEFENSE is a good offense; why should the DEVIL have all the best tunes?; DILIGENCE is the mother of good luck; ENOUGH is as good as a feast; EVIL communications corrupt good manners; never do EVIL that good may come of it; FAR-FETCHED and dear-bought is good for ladies; FIRE is a good servant but a bad master; there are as good FISH in the sea as ever came out of it; HOPE is a good breakfast but a bad supper; it's an ILL wind that blows nobody any good; JACK is as good as his master; a LIAR ought to have a good memory; LISTENERS never hear any good of themselves; a MISS is as good as a mile; MONEY, like manure, does no good till it is spread; NO news is good news; a NOD'S as good as a wink to a blind horse; there is NOTHING so good for the inside of a man as the outside of a horse; see a PIN and pick it up, all the day you'll have good luck; any PUBLICITY is good publicity; the ROAD to hell is paved with good intentions; good SEED makes a good crop; if something SOUNDS too good to be true, it probably is; one STORY is good till another is told; you can have TOO much of a good thing; when the WIND is in the east, 'tis neither good for man nor beast.

goods *see* ILL gotten goods never thrive; TAKE the goods the gods provide.

goose *see* what is SAUCE for the goose is sauce for the gander; *also* GEESE.

When the GORSE is out of bloom, kissing's out of fashion

Quots. 1846, 1860, and 2002 explain the rationale behind this proverb and also the parallel saying *when the* FURZE *is in bloom, my love's in tune*.

□ **1846** M. A. DENHAM *Proverbs relating to Seasons, &c.* 12 When whins [gorse] are out of bloom, Kissing's out of fashion. ..Whins are *never* out of bloom. **1860** G. J. WHYTE-MELVILLE *Holmby House* I. iii. 'When the gorse is out of bloom, young ladies,' quoth Sir Giles,'then is kissing out of fashion!' ..There is no day in the year when the blossom is off the gorse. **1974** A. DWYER-JOYCE *Brass Islands* 175 'What's that old jingle about the gorse?'..'When the gorse is out of bloom, kissing is out of fashion.' **2002** *Country Life* 9 May 128 Gorse can be found in flower at all seasons, hence sayings like 'When gorse is out of season, kissing's out of fashion', but in winter it yields no scent at all. ■ **love, prosperous**

What is GOT over the Devil's back is spent under his belly

What is improperly obtained is spent in reckless pleasures or debauchery.

□ **1582** S. GOSSON *Plays Confuted* G7v That which is gotten ouer the deuils backe, is spent vnder his belly. **1607** MIDDLETON *Michaelmas Term* IV. i. What's got over the devil's back (that's by knavery), must be spent under his belly (that's by lechery).

1670 J. RAY *English Proverbs* 80 What is gotten over the Devils back, is spent under his belly. . . What is got by oppression or extortion is many times spent in riot and luxury. **1821** SCOTT *Pirate* III. iv. You shall not prevail on me to go farther in the devil's road with you; for . . what is got over his back is spent—you wot how. **1952** N. TYRE *Mouse in Eternity* 93 What I say is what goes over the devil's back is sure to come under his belly. ■ **getting and spending**

got *see also* a PENNY saved is a penny earned.

grain *see* if in FEBRUARY there be no rain, 'tis neither good for hay nor grain.

grandmother *see* don't TEACH your grandmother to suck eggs.

While the GRASS grows, the steed starves

Dreams or expectations may be realized too late. Cf. medieval L. *dum gramen crescit, equus in moriendo quiescit*, while the grass grows, the horse lies dying.

□ *c* **1350** *Douce MS* 52 no. 20 While the grasse growes, the goode hors sterues. *a* **1500** in Wright & Halliwell *Reliquiæ Antiquæ* (1841) I. 208 While the grasse growes the steede starves. **1600–1** SHAKESPEARE *Hamlet* III. ii. 333 You have the voice of the King himself for your succession.—Ay, sir, but 'While the grass grows'—the proverb is something musty. **1821** J. GALT *Ayrshire Legatees* x. Until ye get a kirk there can be no marriage. But the auld horse may die waiting for the new grass. **1911** G. B. SHAW *Doctor's Dilemma* III. 56 I shall sell them next year fast enough, after my one-man-show; but while the grass grows the steed starves. **1973** 'M. INNES' *Appleby's Answer* ii. 'The working capital?' 'Well . . while the grass grows the steed mustn't starve. Say five hundred down.' ■ **expectation**

The GRASS is always greener on the other side of the fence

Cf. OVID *Ars Amatoria* I. 349 *fertilior seges est alienis semper in agris*, the harvest is always more fruitful in another man's fields.

□ **1959** H. & M. WILLIAMS in J. C. Trewin *Plays of Year* XIX. 13 (*title*) The grass is greener. **1965** *Which?* Mar. 91 'The grass always looks greener on the other side of the fence,' said another informant, explaining that while stores who do practise the system are uneasy about it . . those outside constantly wonder whether results might not justify it. **2001** *Spectator* 15/22 Dec. 26 They push their heads through fences and get stuck (the grass on the other side really is greener: sheep invented the axiom). ■ **content and discontent**

grease *see* the SQUEAKING wheel gets the grease.

A GREAT book is a great evil

Cf. CALLIMACHUS *Fragments* 465 (Pfeiffer) *τὸ μέγα βιβλίον ἴσον . . εἶναι τῷ μεγάλῳ κακῷ*, the great book is equal to a great evil.

□ **1628** BURTON *Anatomy of Melancholy* (ed. 3) 7 Oftentimes it falls out . . a great Booke is a great mischiefe. **1711** ADDISON *Spectator* 23 July We do not expect to meet with any thing in a bulky Volume. . . A great Book is a great Evil. **1933** *Oxford English Dictionary* (Preface) p. vii. If there is any truth in the old Greek maxim that a large book is a great evil, English dictionaries have been steadily growing worse ever since their inception more than three centuries ago. ■ **brevity and long-windedness**

GREAT minds think alike

Used ironically. Both verb and noun have changed in the course of this proverb's history, the earliest instance of the present form thus far discovered being quot. 1898. *Jump* used absolutely in the sense of 'agree completely' or 'coincide' is now archaic.

□ **1618** D. BELCHIER *Hans Beer-Pot* D1 Though he made that verse, Those words were made before. ..Good wits doe iumpe. **1761** STERNE *Tristram Shandy* III. ix. Great wits jump: for the moment Dr. Slop cast his eyes upon his bag..the very same thought occurred. **1889** A. JAMES *Journal* 1 Dec. (1964) 61 As great minds jump this proves..that my Mind *is Great*! **1898** C. G. ROBERTSON *Voces Academicae* 24 Curious how great minds think alike. My pupil wrote me the same explanation about his non-appearance. ..**1922** *Punch* 27 Dec. 601 Lord Riddell considers that Mr. H. G. Wells is one of the world's greatest minds. Great minds, as the saying is, think alike. **2002** *Washington Times* 28 May C9 (*Bottomliners cartoon*) 'Great minds think alike—that's why we're never in agreement.' ■ **coincidence; harmony and disharmony**

GREAT oaks from little acorns grow

□ *c* **1385** CHAUCER *Troilus & Criseyde* II. 1335 As an ook comth of a litel spir [shoot], So thorugh this letter..Encressen gan desir. **1579** S. GOSSON *School of Abuse* 20V But Tall Cedars from little graynes shoote high: great Oakes, from slender rootes spread wide. **1584** J. WITHALS *Dict.* (rev. ed.) D4 Of a nut springes an hasill, and of an Akorn an hie or tall oke. **1732** T. FULLER *Gnomologia* no. 4576 The greatest Oaks have been little Acorns. **1777** D. EVERETT in *Columbian Orator* (1797) 58 Large streams from little fountains flow, Tall oaks from little acorns grow. **1923** *Times* 13 Oct. 7 Here in England, as nowhere else in the world, 'great oaks from little acorns grow'. The oak, as the emblem of British strength, has been symbolic in many ways. **2002** *Times* 28 Mar. 27 One shouldn't sneer. From little acorns do mighty oak trees grow. ■ **beginnings and endings; great and small**

great *see also* BIG fleas have little fleas upon their backs to bite them; DEATH is the great leveller; LITTLE strokes fell great oaks; LITTLE thieves are hanged, but great ones escape; there's no great LOSS without some gain; POVERTY is no disgrace, but it is a great inconvenience; THRIFT is a great revenue; TIME is a great healer.

The GREATER the sinner, the greater the saint

□ **1773** R. GRAVES *Spiritual Quixote* II. VII. xi. It was a maxim with Mr. Whitfield, 'The greater the Sinner, the greater the Saint.' **1856** E. HINCHCLIFFE *Barthomley* vi. How well is the old proverb illustrated in this foul seducer. ..'The greater the sinner, the greater the Saint.' **1964** M. LAVIN *Stories* I. 293 Ah, well, I always heard it's the biggest divils that make the best saints, and now I can believe it! ■ **good and evil; wrong-doers**

The GREATER the truth, the greater the libel

The 'Mansfield' referred to in quots. 1787 and 1882 was William Murray, first Earl of Mansfield (1705–93), statesman and judge.

□ *c* **1787** BURNS *Poems* (1968) I. 349 Dost not know that old Mansfield, who writes like the Bible, Says the more 'tis a truth, sir, the more 'tis a libel? **1828** BULWER-LYTTON *Pelham* I. xxiv. 'You won't catch an old lawyer in such impudence.' 'The greater the truth the greater the libel,' said Warburton, with a sneer. **1882** S. A. BENT *Short Sayings of Great Men* 371 The greater the truth, the greater the libel. A maxim of the law in vogue..while Mansfield presided over the King's Bench. ..The maxim is said to have originated in the Star Chamber. **2002** *Spectator* 23 Nov. 50 On the contrary: there is an old adage, 'The greater the truth, the greater the libel', for rioting is bound to be more serious if the incitement is known to be based on fact rather than on gross exaggeration. ■ **slander; truth**

When GREEK meets Greek, then comes the tug of war

□ **1677** N. LEE *Rival Queens* IV. 48 When Greeks joyn'd Greeks, then was the tug of War. **1804** W. IRVING *Journals & Notebooks* (1969) I. 69 Two upright Postillions.. were disputing who was the greatest rogue. ..'When Greek meets Greek then comes the tug of war.' **1926** A. HUXLEY *Two or Three Graces* 175 When Greek meets Greek then comes, in this case, an exchange of anecdotes about the deposed sovereigns of eastern Europe—in a word, the tug of bores. **1979** M. A. SCREECH *Rabelais* iii. One is reminded of an adage Erasmus used.. *Magus cum mago*: 'magician meets magician'—Greek, as we say, meets Greek. ■ **enemies; similarity and dissimilarity**

Greek *see also* FEAR the Greeks bearing gifts.

A GREEN Yule makes a fat churchyard

A proverb with many variations on the theme of the unhealthiness of a mild winter.

□ **1635** J. SWAN *Speculum Mundi* V. They also say, that a hot Christmas makes a fat Church-yard. **1670** J. RAY *English Proverbs* 42 A green winter makes a fat Church-yard. This Proverb was sufficiently confuted *Anno* 1667, in which the winter was very mild; and yet no mortality.. ensued the Summer or Autumn following. **1721** J. KELLY *Scottish Proverbs* 30 A green yule makes a fat Church-yard. This, and a great many proverbial Observations, upon the Seasons of the Year, are groundless. **1858** G. ELIOT *Amos Barton* in *Scenes of Clerical Life* I. vi. I shouldn't wonder if it takes the old lady off. They say a green Yule makes a fat Churchyard; but so does a white Yule too. **1945** M. SARSFIELD (*book-title*) Green December Fills the Graveyard. **1950** B. PYM *Some Tame Gazelle* xviii. They say a green Christmas means a full churchyard. ..I dare say some old people will be taken. **1997** *Times: Weekend* 27 Dec. 16 So a green Christmas maketh a fat churchyard, as we say in SE10. ■ **death; weather lore**

greener *see* the GRASS is always greener on the other side of the fence.

The GREY mare is the better horse

The wife rules, or is more competent than, the husband. Cf. **1529** MORE *Dialogue of Images* III. v. Here were we fallen in a grete questyon of the law, whyther the gray mare be the better horse.. or whither he haue a wyse face or not that loketh as lyke a foole as an ewe loketh lyke a shepe.

□ **1546** J. HEYWOOD *Dialogue of Proverbs* II. iv. G4 The grey mare is the better hors. **1664** S. BUTLER *Hudibras* II. ii. 117 A *Riding* [charivari], us'd of Course, When the *Grey Mare's the better Horse*. When o're the Breeches greedy *Women* Fight, to extend their vast *Dominion*. **1906** J. GALSWORTHY *Man of Property* I. vi. D'you think he knows his own mind? He seems to me a poor thing. I should say the gray mare was the better horse! **1981** V. POWELL *Flora Annie Steel* vii. She did not wish it to seem, to quote an old fashioned expression, that the grey mare was the better horse. ..She strove to avoid prejudicing her husband's position. ■ **wives and husbands**

grey *see also* all CATS are grey in the dark.

grieve *see* what the EYE doesn't see, the heart doesn't grieve over.

grind *see* the MILL cannot grind with the water that is past; the MILLS of God grind slowly, yet they grind exceeding small.

gripping *see* NOTHING should be done in haste but gripping a flea.

All is GRIST that comes to the mill

Everything that is received or obtained is put to use. *Grist* is corn to be ground. *The* is freqently replaced by a possessive pronoun or phrase. Similar to the older *all is* FISH *that comes to the net*. The metaphorical expression *grist to one's mill* is also found.

□ **1655** T. FULLER *Church Hist. Britain* III. iii. Forein Casuists bring in a bundle of mortal sins, all grist for their own Mill. **1770** S. FOOTE *Lame Lover* I. 28 Well, let them go on, it brings grist to our mill: for whilst both the sexes stick firm to their honour, we shall never want business. **1896** A. WHYTE *Bible Characters* I. xii. Your stumble, your fall, your misfortune . . all is grist to the mill of the mean-minded man. **1943** A. CHRISTIE *Moving Finger* ix. You're failing to allow for the mentality of a Poison Pen—all is grist that comes to their mill. **1979** G. MITCHELL *Mudflats of Dead* iii. All was grist which came to a novelist's mill, and he was still hoping that something, somewhere, would bring him what he still thought of as inspiration. **2000** 'G. WILLIAMS' *Dr. Mortimer and Aldgate Mystery* (2001) xviii. 94 'I should very much like to know,' she said, 'what picture was there that Agar felt was so eminently worth stealing. In my pursuit of him, all is grist to my mill.' ■ **gains and losses; opportunity**

ground *see* BETWEEN two stools one falls to the ground.

grow *see* while the GRASS grows, the steed starves; GREAT oaks from little acorns grow; ONE for the mouse, one for the crow.

grunt *see* what can you EXPECT from a pig but a grunt?

guest *see* FISH and guests smell after three days.

A GUILTY conscience needs no accuser

Cf. *Disticha Catonis* I. xvii. *conscius ipse sibi de se putat omnia dici*, the man with something on his conscience thinks he is always the subject of talk.

□ *c* **1390** CHAUCER *Canon's Yeoman's Prologue* l. 688 For Catoun [Dionysius Cato] seith that he that gilty is Demeth alle thyng be spoke of him. **1597** *Politeuphuia* 10v A Guilty conscience is a worme that bites and neuer ceaseth. . . A guiltie conscience is neuer without feare. **1721** J. KELLY *Scottish Proverbs* 9 A guilty Conscience self accuses. A Man that has done ill . . shews his Guilt. **1744** *Life & Adventures Matthew Bishop* viii. It is an old saying, a guilty conscience needs no accuser. **1881** D. C. MURRAY *Joseph's Coat* I. viii. 'Where are *you* off to?' asked George with a great effort. . . A guilty conscience needs no accuser. **1952** *Ellery Queen's Mystery Mag.* Apr. 25 'Why should I think that?' I said, groping for his identity. 'Because you were thinking about me.' Then I knew he was speaking of Hinckman's murder and must be the murderer—'a guilty conscience needs no accuser.' ■ **conscience; wrong-doers**

gunner *see* the COBBLER to his last and the gunner to his linstock.

habit *see* OLD habits die hard.

What you've never HAD you never miss

□ **1912** 'J. WEBSTER' *Daddy-Long-Legs* (1913) 232 You mustn't get me used to too many luxuries. One doesn't miss what one has never had. **1939** T. BURKE *Living in Bloomsbury* ii. It has been said that what you've never had you never miss, and from all one can gather, those people were not aware of suffering from lack of holiday. **1969** R. BLYTHE *Akenfield* xiv. I castrate the male lambs..about an hour after they have been born. They say what you've never had, you never miss. **1987** S. STEWART *Lifting the Latch* 189 I ent never fled in an aeroplane. Don't want to. Too far to drop. What you've never had you never miss. ■ **content and discontent**; **gains and losses**

hair *see* BEAUTY draws with a single hair.

HALF a loaf is better than no bread

Similar in sense to SOMETHING *is better than nothing.*

□ **1546** J. HEYWOOD *Dialogue of Proverbs* I. xi. D4ᵛ Throwe no gyft agayne at the giuers head, For better is halfe a lofe then no bread. **1636** W. CAMDEN *Remains concerning Britain* (ed. 5) 297 Halfe a loafe is better than no bread at all. **1681** A. BEHN *Rover* II. II. ii. You know the Proverb of the half Loaf, Ariadne, a Husband that will deal thee some Love is better than one who can give thee none. **1841** DICKENS *Old Curiosity Shop* I. xxxiii. 'Mr. Swiveller,' said Quilp, 'being pretty well accustomed to the agricultural pursuits of sowing wild oats, Miss Sally, prudently considers that half a loaf is better than no bread.' **1979** *Guardian* 6 Aug. 10 Half a loaf is better than no bread at all. The ending of half a war is immensely better than no truce at all. **2002** A. MCNEILLIE 'Half a Loaf' in *Times Literary Supplement* 12 Apr. 4 Half a loaf's better than no bread. A crumb of wisdom finds a world, in a grain of wheat. ■ **content and discontent**

The HALF is better than the whole

A proverb advising economy or restraint. Cf. HESIOD *Works & Days* 40 *πλέον ἥμισυ παντός*, half is more than the whole.

□ **1550** H. LATIMER *Sermon before King's Majesty* G3 Ther is a proverbe..*Dimidium plus toto*: The halfe somtymes more then the hole. The meane lyfe is the best lyfe and the most quyet lyfe of al. **1828** I. DISRAELI *Curiosities of Literature* 2nd Ser. I. 419 The half is better than the whole. **1906** A. C. BENSON *From College Window* v. It is true of conversation as of many other things, that the half is better than the whole. People who are fond of talking ought to beware of being lengthy. ■ **moderation**

One HALF of the world does not know how the other half lives

Cf. **1532** RABELAIS *Pantagruel* II. xxxii. *la moytié du monde ne sçait comment l'autre vit*, one half of the world knows not how the other lives.

□ **1607** J. HALL *Holy Observations* xvii. One half of the world knowes not how the other liues: and therefore the better sort pitty not the distressed..because they knowe it not. **1640** G. HERBERT *Outlandish Proverbs* no. 907 Halfe the world knowes not how the other halfe lives. **1755** B. FRANKLIN *Poor Richard's Almanack* (Preface) It is a common saying, that One Half of the World does not know how the other Half lives. **1830** MARRYAT *King's Own* I. x. It is an old proverb that 'one half the world do not know how the other half live'. Add to it, nor *where* they live. **1945** C. S. LEWIS *That Hideous Strength* i. 'I didn't even know this was Bracton property.' 'There you are!..One half of the world doesn't know how the other half lives.' **1979** A. MORICE *Murder in Outline* vi. It just proved how true that saying is about one half knowing so little of the other, even when both halves are living under the same roof. ■ **ignorance; society**

HALF the truth is often a whole lie

□ **1758** B. FRANKLIN *Poor Richard's Almanack* (July) Half the Truth is often a great Lie. **1859** TENNYSON *Poems* (1969) 1107 That a lie which is half a truth is ever the blackest of lies, That a lie which is all a lie may be met and fought with outright, But a lie which is part a truth is a harder matter to fight. **1875** A. B. CHEALES *Proverbial Folklore* 166 Half the truth is often a whole lie..is a proverb which Tennyson has most admirably versified. **1979** H. HOWARD *Sealed Envelope* xiii. 'You've been lying.'..'Half the truth can be worse than a straight lie.' ■ **lying**

half *see also* BELIEVE nothing of what you hear, and only half of what you see; two BOYS are half a boy, and three boys are no boy at all; a FAULT confessed is half redressed; he that has an ILL name is half hanged; WELL begun is half done.

half-done *see* FOOLS and bairns should never see half-done work.

halfway *see* a LIE is halfway round the world; do not MEET troubles halfway.

hall *see* it is MERRY in hall when beards wag all.

Don't HALLOO till you are out of the wood

Do not exult until all danger or difficulty is past. *Halloo* literally means to shout in order to attract attention.

□ **1770** B. FRANKLIN *Papers* (1973) XVIII. 356 This is Hollowing before you are out of the Wood. **1800** A. ADAMS *Letter* 13 Nov. (1848) 381 It is an old and a just proverb, 'Never halloo until you are out of the woods.' **1866** C. KINGSLEY *Hereward the Wake* I. iii. Don't holla till you are out of the wood. This is a night for praying rather than boasting. **1936** 'E. C. R. LORAC' *Crime Counter Crime* i. Don't halloo till you're out of the wood. I'll bet my head to a china orange we shall have trouble before to-morrow night. **1947** M. LONG *Dull Thud* x. 99 'Don't whistle till you're out of the woods,' I advised her. 'The investigation hasn't even begun.' ■ **peril; trouble**

halved *see* a TROUBLE shared is a trouble halved.

When all you have is a HAMMER, everything looks like a nail

Principally known in North America.

□ **1981** *New York Times* 11 Nov. D13 'There is frequently a lack of understanding of what power is—I've got power, therefore I'm right,' he said. 'When you've got a hammer, everything looks like a nail.' **1989** *PC Magazine* 14 Mar. 78 That kind of crude misapplication of PCs and PC software—the computer world's equivalent of the old saw that 'when all you have is a hammer, everything starts to look like a nail'—means death for productivity. **2002** *Washington Post* 7 Apr. H7 It's a waste to use $480 worth of Office suite for such simple work. But it's not a surprise either. To paraphrase what others have said: When Microsoft Office is your only hammer, pretty much everything begins to look like a nail. Or a thumb. ■ **necessity; ways and means**

hammer *see also* the CHURCH is an anvil which has worn out many hammers.

One HAND for yourself and one for the ship

A nautical proverb, also used in variant forms in similar contexts: see the explanation in quot. 1902.

□ **1799** *Port Folio* (Philadelphia, 1812) VII. 130 Did I not tell you never to fill both hands at once. Always keep one hand for the owners, and one for yourself. **1822** J. F. COOPER *Pilot* I. vii. The maxim, which says, 'one hand for the owner, and t'other for yourself,'.. has saved many a hearty fellow from a fall that would have balanced the purser's books. **1902** B. LUBBOCK *Round Horn* 58 The old rule on a yard is, 'one hand for yourself and one for the ship,' which means, hold on with one hand and work with the other. **1968** L. MORTON *Long Wake* i. I did not know then the old adage 'one hand for oneself and one hand for the company.' **1993** B. CALLISON *Crocodile Trapp* (1994) x. 169 'Now you allus remember the seaman's golden rule from now on, Mister Despytoff,' Spew chastised gently. 'One hand f'r the ship—or in your case, f'r the *aeroplane*, eh? heh, heh.. an' one hand f'r yerself.' ■ **prudence; security**

The HAND that rocks the cradle rules the world

□ **1865** W. R. WALLACE in J. K. Hoyt *Cyclopædia of Practical Quotations* (1896) 402 A mightier power and stronger Man from his throne has hurled, For the hand that rocks the cradle Is the hand that rules the world. *a* **1916** 'SAKI' *Toys of Peace* (1919) 158 You can't prevent it; it's the nature of the sex. The hand that rocks the cradle rocks the world, in a volcanic sense. **1996** *Washington Times* 10 May A2 The habits of the home in one generation become the morals of society in the next. As the old adage says: 'The hand that rocks the cradle rules the world.' ■ **women**

One HAND washes the other

Cf. EPICHARMUS *Apophthegm* 273 (Kaibel) *ἁ δὲ χεὶρ τὰν χεῖρα νίζει*, one hand washes the other; SENECA *Apocolocyntosis* ix. *manus manum lavat*, hand washes hand.

□ **1573** J. SANFORDE *Garden of Pleasure* 110V One hand washeth an other, and both wash the face. **1611** R. COTGRAVE *Dict. French & English* s.v. Main, One hand washes the other; applyable to such as giue vpon assurance, or hope, to be giuen vnto; or vnto such as any way serue one anothers turne. **1836** P. HONE *Diary* 12 Mar. (1927) I. 203 Persons in business.. make, as the saying is, 'one hand wash the other'. **1983** H. RESNICOW *Gold Solution* ix. And three years ago, Erik was on a design jury that picked the dean's firm's entry as a winner. One hand washes the other. **2001** P. J. O'ROURKE *CEO of Sofa* xii. 250 One hand washes the other: for I the Lord thy God am a jealous God, visiting the iniquity of the fathers upon the children unto the third and fourth generation of them that hate me—unless they seek counseling, of course. ■ **reciprocity**

hand *see also* a BIRD in the hand is worth two in the bush; COLD hands, warm heart; the DEVIL finds work for idle hands to do; the EYE of a master does more work than both his hands; FULL cup, steady hand; if IFS and ands were pots and pans, there'd be no work for tinkers' hands; MANY hands make light work.

HANDSOME is as handsome does

Handsome denotes chivalrous or genteel behaviour, though it is often popularly taken to refer to good looks. At its second occurrence in the proverb the word is properly an adverb. For the common US equivalent, see PRETTY *is as pretty does.*

□ *c* **1580** A. MUNDAY *View of Sundry Examples* in J. P. Collier *John A Kent* (1851) 78 As the ancient adage is, goodly is he that goodly dooth. **1659** N. R. *Proverbs* 49 He is handsome that handsome doth. **1766** GOLDSMITH *Vicar of Wakefield* i. They are as heaven made them, handsome enough if they be good enough; for handsome is that handsome does. **1845** *Spirit of Times* 23 Aug. 297 Handsome is as handsome does. **1873** C. M. YONGE *Pillars of House* II. xvii. 'Don't you think her much better looking than Alda?' 'If handsome is that handsome does.' **1979** A. WILLIAMSON *Funeral March for Siegfried* xxiv. 'But he's such a handsome, *chivalrous*, man.' Handsome is as handsome does, thought York grimly. ■ **appearance; conduct**

HANG a thief when he's young, and he'll no' steal when he's old

□ **1832** A. HENDERSON *Scottish Proverbs* 115 Hang a thief when he's young, and he'll no [not] steal when he's auld. **1896** A. CHEVIOT *Proverbs of Scotland* 126 Hang a thief when he's young, and he'll no steal when he's auld. This was a favourite saying of Lord Justice Clerk Braxfield [Robert MacQueen, Lord Braxfield (1722–99), Scottish judge], who invariably acted upon its teaching. **1979** J. LEASOR *Love & Land Beyond* x. So much killing. . . It reminds me of the Scots proverb, 'Hang a thief when he's young, and he'll no' steal when he's old.' ■ **wrong-doers**

hang *see also* a CREAKING door hangs longest; give a DOG a bad name and hang him; every HERRING must hang by its own gill; give a man ROPE enough and he will hang himself.

One might as well be HANGED for a sheep as a lamb

The proverb alludes to the former penalty for sheep-stealing. The idea is present in: **1662** N. ROGERS *Rich Fool* 253 As some desperate Wretches, Who dispairing of life still act the more villainy, giving this desperate Reason of it, As good be hanged for a great deal, as for a little.

□ **1678** J. RAY *English Proverbs* (ed. 2) 350 As good be hang'd for an old sheep as a young lamb. *Somerset.* **1732** T. FULLER *Gnomologia* no. 683 As good be hang'd for a Sheep as a Lamb. **1836** MARRYAT *Midshipman Easy* II. ii. We may as well be hanged for a sheep as a lamb. . . I vote that we do not go on board. **1841** DICKENS *Barnaby Rudge* liii. Others . . comforted themselves with the homely proverb, that, being hung at all, they might as well be hung for a sheep as a lamb. **1915** D. H. LAWRENCE *Rainbow* vi. One might as well be hung for a sheep as for a lamb. If he had lost this day of his life, he had lost it. **1977** B. PYM *Quartet in Autumn* xv. Letty . . decided that she might as well be hung for a sheep as a lamb and make the most of her meal. ■ **conduct; risk**

hanged *see also* if you're BORN to be hanged then you'll never be drowned; CONFESS and be hanged; he that has an ILL name is half hanged; LITTLE thieves are hanged, but great ones escape; never mention ROPE in the house of a man who has been hanged.

HANGING and wiving go by destiny

□ **1546** J. HEYWOOD *Dialogue of Proverbs* I. iii. Weddyng is desteny, And hangyng lykewise. **1596** SHAKESPEARE *Merchant of Venice* II. ix. 82 The ancient saying is no heresy: Hanging and wiving goes by destiny. **1678** S. BUTLER *Hudibras* II. i. 270 If

Matrimony and *Hanging* go By *Dest'ny*, why not *Whipping* too? **1738** SWIFT *Polite Conversation* i. 78 'Twas her Fate; they say, Marriage and Hanging go by destiny. **1951** E. MARSHALL *Viking* iii. King Alfred said that wiving and hanging go by destiny. ■ **fate and fatalism; marriage**

hanging *see also* CATCHING's before hanging; there are more WAYS of killing a dog than hanging it.

ha'porth *see* do not spoil the SHIP for a ha'porth of tar.

happen *see* ACCIDENTS will happen (in the best-regulated families); the UNEXPECTED always happens.

happiness *see* MONEY can't buy happiness.

If you would be HAPPY for a week take a wife; if you would be happy for a month kill a pig; but if you would be happy all your life plant a garden

There are almost endless possibilities for variation on this theme, but marriage is generally included as one of the more ephemeral sources of content.

□ *a* **1661** T. FULLER *Worthies* Wales 6 I say the Italian-humor, who have a merry Proverb, Let him that would be happy for a Day, go to the Barber; for a Week, marry a Wife; for a Month, buy him a New-horse; for a Year, build him a New-house; for all his Life-time, be an Honest man. **1809** S. PEGGE *Anonymiana* II. xix. If you would live well for a week, kill a hog; if you would live well for a month, marry; if you would live well all your life, turn priest. .. Turning priest .. alludes to the celibacy of the Romish Clergy, and has a pungent sense, as much as to say, do not marry at all. **1973** *New Earth Catalog* 55 If you would be happy for a week take a wife; If you would be happy for a month kill a pig; But if you would be happy all your life plant a garden. **1996** *National Review* 25 Nov. 6 For those of a philosophical turn of mind, I pass on something that the distinguished economist Peter Bauer said last week: 'If you want to be happy for a day, get drunk; for a month, get married; for a lifetime, take up gardening.' ■ **happiness**

Call no man HAPPY till he dies

The story alluded to in quot. 1545 is narrated in Herodotus' *Histories* I. xxxii: when the great Athenian lawgiver Solon visited Croesus, the fabulously wealthy king of Lydia, the latter asked Solon who was the happiest man he had ever seen—expecting the answer to be himself. Cf. SOPHOCLES *Oedipus Rex* l. 1529 *μηδέν' ὀλβίζειν, πρὶν ἂν τέρμα τοῦ βίου περάσῃ μηδὲν ἀλγεινὸν παθών*, deem no man happy, until he passes the end of his life without suffering grief; OVID *Metamorphoses* iii. 135 *dicique beatus Ante obitum nemo .. debet*, nobody should be called blessed before his death.

□ **1545** R. TAVERNER tr. *Erasmus' Adages* (ed. 2) 53v Salon aunsered kynge Cresus, that no man could be named happy, tyl he had happely and prosperouslye passed the course of his lyfe. **1565** NORTON & SACKVILLE *Gorboduc* III. i. Oh no man happie, till his ende be seene. **1603** J. FLORIO tr. *Montaigne's Essays* I. xviii. We must exspect of man the latest day, Nor e'er he die, he's happie, can we say. **1891** *Times* 5 Dec. 9 Call no man happy till he dies is the motto .. suggested by the career of Dom Pedro [emperor of Brazil]. **1967** C. S. FORESTER *Hornblower & Crisis* 163 'Call no man happy until he is dead.' .. He was seventy-two, and yet there was still time for this dream .. to change to a nightmare. ■ **good fortune; happiness**

happy *see also* happy is the BRIDE that the sun shines on; happy is the COUNTRY which has no history; a DEAF husband and a blind wife are always a happy couple; happy's the WOOING that is not long a-doing.

HARD cases make bad law

Difficult cases cause the clarity of the law to be obscured by exceptions and strained interpretations.

□ **1854** G. HAYES in W. S. Holdsworth *Hist. English Law* (1926) IX. 423 A hard case. But hard cases make bad law. **1945** W. S. CHURCHILL in *Hansard* (Commons) 12 June 1478 Well, of course, hard cases do not make good laws. **1991** *Times* 17 Sept. 29 Hard cases not only make bad law. They also create bad feeling between judges. **2001** *Spectator* 21 July 18 Hard cases make bad law, no doubt, and maybe bad policy, but this case is far from unique. ■ **law and lawyers; rules, general**

HARD words break no bones

A terser statement of the sentiment in STICKS *and stones may break my bones, but words will never hurt me*. Cf. *c* **1450** *Towneley Play of Noah* (EETS) l. 380 Thise grete wordis shall not flay me.

□ **1697** G. MERITON *Yorkshire Ale* (ed. 3) 84 Foul words break neay Banes. **1806** H. H. BRACKENRIDGE *Gazette Publications* 250 Hard words, and language break nae bane. **1814** G. MORRIS *Letter* 18 Oct. (1889) II. xlix. These . . are mere words—hard words, if you please, but they break no bones. **1882** BLACKMORE *Christowell* III. xvi. 'Scoundrel, after all that I have done—.' 'Hard words break no bones, my friend.' **1980** G. NELSON *Charity's Child* i. Soft words! They butter no parsnips. . . Would you prefer hard ones? . . Hard words break no bones. ■ **malice**

hard *see also* OLD habits die hard.

harder *see* the BIGGER they are, the harder they fall.

hare *see* FIRST catch your hare; if you RUN after two hares you will catch neither; you cannot RUN with the hare and hunt with the hounds.

HASTE is from the Devil

□ **1633** J. HOWELL *Familiar Letters* 5 Sept. (1903) II. 140 As it is a principle in chemistry that *Omnis festinatio est a Diabolo*, All haste comes from Hell, so in . . any business of State, all rashness and precipitation comes from an ill spirit. **1835** SOUTHEY *Doctor* III. lxxxiii. If any of my readers should . . think that I ought to have proceeded to the marriage without delay . . I must admonish them in the words of a Turkish saying, that 'hurry comes from the Devil, and slow advancing from Allah.' **1929** *Times* 12 Sept. 14 Listening patiently to the views . . [f]or he understood the East; he knew that for an Intelligence officer 'haste is from the devil.' ■ **haste; patience and impatience**

More HASTE, less speed

The original meaning of *speed* in this proverb is 'quickness in the performance of some action or operation'.

□ *c* **1350** *Douce MS 52* no. 86 The more hast, the worse spede. **1546** J. HEYWOOD *Dialogue of Proverbs* I. ii. A3ᵛ Moste tymes he seeth, the more haste the lesse speede. **1595** *Locrine* (1908) I. ii. My penne is naught; gentlemen, lend me a knife. I thinke the more haste the worst speed. **1705** E. WARD *Hudibras Redivivus* I. i. A mod'rate pace is best indeed. The greater hurry, the worse speed. **1887** BLACKMORE *Springhaven* III. xi. Some days had been spent by the leisurely Dutchman in providing fresh supplies, and the stout bark's favourite maxim seemed to be—'the more haste the less speed.' **1919** S. J. WEYMAN *Great House* xxvii. Tell me the story from the beginning. And take time. More haste, less speed, you know. **1993** 'C. AIRD' *Going Concern* (1994) iv. 31 'Working against the clock doesn't make for considered thought.' 'More haste, less speed,' said Detective Constable Crosby helpfully. ■ **haste; patience and impatience**

HASTE makes waste

Waste properly means the squandering of time, money, etc., though it is also used with reference to material waste.

□ *c* **1386** CHAUCER *Tale of Melibee* l. 1053 The proverbe seith .. in wikked haste is no profit. **1546** J. HEYWOOD *Dialogue of Proverbs* I. ii. A3 Som thyngs .. show after weddyng, that haste maketh waste. **1663** S. BUTLER *Hudibras* I. iii. *Festina lente*, not too fast; For haste (the Proverb says) makes waste. **1853** R. C. TRENCH *On Lessons in Proverbs* i. Many Proverbs, such as Haste makes waste .. have nothing figurative about them. **1997** *Washington Post: Washington Business* 29 Dec. 15 But I've let myself be an impulsive Internet shopper, too, and I usually regret it. In '98, my motto is 'haste makes waste.' ■ **haste; patience and impatience; waste**

Make HASTE slowly

Cf. L. *festina lente*, make haste slowly; after SUETONIUS *Augustus* xxv. 4. *nihil autem minus perfecto duci quam festinationem temeritatemque convenire arbitratur. crebro itaque illa iactabat: σπεῦδε βραδέως*, he [Augustus] thought that haste and rashness were alike unsuited to a well-trained leader. So he often came out with sayings like 'make haste slowly' [etc.]; *c* **1385** CHAUCER *Troilus & Criseyde* I. 956 He hasteth wel that wisly kan [knows how to] abyde.

□ **1683** DRYDEN *Poems* (1958) I. 336 Gently make haste. .. A hundred times consider what you've said. **1744** B. FRANKLIN *Poor Richard's Almanack* (Apr.) Make haste slowly. **1989** C. G. HART *Little Class on Murder* xii. '*Festina lente*,' Miss Dora suggested slyly. 'Not bad advice,' Max said cheerfully. At Annie's glare, he added quickly, 'Make haste slowly.' ■ **haste; patience and impatience**

haste *see also* MARRY in haste and repent at leisure; NOTHING should be done in haste but gripping a flea.

hasty *see* hasty CLIMBERS have sudden falls.

hatched *see* don't COUNT your chickens before they are hatched.

hate *see* BETTER a dinner of herbs than a stalled ox where hate is.

What you HAVE, hold

□ *c* **1450** *Towneley Play of Killing of Abel* (EETS) l. 142 It is better hold that I haue then go from doore to doore and craue. **1546** J. HEYWOOD *Dialogue of Proverbs* I. x. D1 Hold fast whan ye haue it (quoth she) by my lyfe. **1876** I. BANKS *Manchester Man* I. x. Then .. rang, clear and distinct, Humphrey Chetham's motto—'Quod tuum, tene!' (What you have, hold!) **1979** *Times* 23 Nov. 5 There had been a simple 'what we have we hold' approach by the established parties. ■ **property**

You cannot HAVE your cake and eat it

You cannot consume or spend something and still keep possession of it: once the cake is eaten, it is gone. The positions of *have* and *eat* are often reversed.

□ **1546** J. HEYWOOD *Dialogue of Proverbs* II. ix. L2 I trowe ye raue, Wolde ye bothe eate your cake, and haue your cake? **1611** J. DAVIES *Scourge of Folly* no. 271 A man cannot eat his cake and haue it stil. **1812** in R. C. Knopf *Document Transcriptions of War of 1812* (1959) VI. 204 We cannot have our cake and eat it too. **1938** P. MCGUIRE *Funeral in Eden* ii. Not that the savages were especially savage. They have always been a sensitive people, and when they ate a man they probably felt genuinely sorry that they could not have their cake and eat it, so to speak. **2002** R. J. BERNSTEIN *Radical Evil* 32 Why does Kant allow himself to get entangled in such difficulties and paradoxes? It looks as if he wants to have his cake and eat it too!

have *see also* the MORE you get, the more you want; NOTHING venture, nothing have; what you SPEND, you have; you can have TOO much of a good thing.

haw *see* when all FRUIT fails, welcome haws.

HAWKS will not pick out hawks' eyes

□ **1573** J. SANFORDE *Garden of Pleasure* 104 One crowe neuer pulleth out an others eyes. **1817** SCOTT *Rob Roy* III. iii. I wadna.. rest my main dependence on the Hielandmen—hawks winna pike out hawks' een.—They quarrel amang themsells.. but they are sure to join.. against a' civilized folk. **1883** J. PAYN *Thicker than Water* III. xli. Members of his profession.. while warning others of the dangers of the table, seem to pluck from them the flower Safety. (Is it that, since hawks do not peck out hawks' een, they know they can be cured for nothing?) **1915** J. BUCHAN *Salute to Adventurers* vi. I have heard that hawks should not pick out hawks' eyes. What do you propose to gain? **1975** J. O'FAOLAIN *Women in Wall* xiv. The crow doesn't pluck out the crow's eye but poor folk bear the brunt. ■ **reciprocity**

hay *see* if in FEBRUARY there be no rain, 'tis neither good for hay nor grain; MAKE hay while the sun shines; a SWARM in May is worth a load of hay.

head *see* the FISH always stinks from the head downwards; where MACGREGOR sits is the head of the table; you cannot put an OLD head on young shoulders; a STILL tongue makes a wise head; SWEEP the house with broom in May, you sweep the head of the house away; TWO heads are better than one; YORKSHIRE born and Yorkshire bred, strong in the arm and weak in the head.

heal *see* PHYSICIAN, heal thyself.

healer *see* TIME is a great healer.

healthy *see* EARLY to bed and early to rise, makes a man healthy, wealthy, and wise.

HEAR all, see all, say nowt, tak' all, keep all, gie nowt, and if tha ever does owt for nowt do it for thysen

A proverb now traditionally associated with Yorkshire, with numerous variant forms. The precepts make up the caricature of the Yorkshireman as seen by detractors: canny, dour (*say nowt* = say nothing), grasping (*gie nowt* = give nothing), and selfish (*if tha ever does owt for nowt do it for theysen* = if you ever do anything for nothing do it for yourself).

□ *a* **1400** *Proverbs of Wisdom* in *Archiv* (1893) XC. 246 Hyre and se, and say nowght. Be ware and wyse, and lye nought.. and haue thy will. **1623** J. WODROEPHE *Spared Hours of Soldier* 276 Heare all, see all, and hold thee still If peace desirest with thy will. **1913** D. H. LAWRENCE *Letter* 1 Feb. (1962) I. 183 It seems queer, that you do it and get no profit. I should think you've forgotten the Yorkshire proverb, 'An' if tha does owt for nowt, do it for thysen.' **1925** *Notes & Queries* 412 The famous

Yorkshire motto . . is invariably recited with an air of superior bravado, and will be found upon mugs, post cards, etc. The authentic version, I believe, is, 'Hear all, see all, say now't, tak' all, keep all, gie now't, and if tha ever does ow't for now't do it for thysen.' **1984** G. SMITH *English Companion* 265 'Hear all, see all, say nowt; sup all, eat all, pay nowt', is said by detractors to be the Yorkshireman's motto. ■ **self-preservation; speech and silence**

hear *see also* ASK no questions and hear no lies; BELIEVE nothing of what you hear, and only half of what you see; there's none so DEAF as those who will not hear; DREAM of a funeral and you hear of a marriage; GO abroad and you'll hear news of home; LISTENERS never hear any good of themselves; SEE no evil, hear no evil, speak no evil.

heard *see* CHILDREN should be seen and not heard.

heart *see* ABSENCE makes the heart grow fonder; COLD hands, warm heart; what the EYE doesn't see, the heart doesn't grieve over; FAINT heart never won fair lady; out of the FULLNESS of the heart the mouth speaks; HOME is where the heart is; HOPE deferred makes the heart sick; if it were not for HOPE, the heart would break; PLEASE your eye and plague your heart; it is a POOR heart that never rejoices; put a STOUT heart to a stey brae; the WAY to a man's heart is through his stomach.

If you don't like the HEAT, get out of the kitchen

□ **1952** *Time* 28 Apr. 19 President [Truman] gave a . . down-to-earth reason for his retirement, quoting a favorite expression of his military jester, Major General Harry Vaughan: 'If you don't like the heat, get out of the kitchen.' **1970** *Financial Times* 13 Apr. 25 Property people argue that hoteliers are not facing the facts of economic life, and that if they cannot stand the heat they should get out of the kitchen. **2002** *Times* 29 Aug. 22 (*heading*) If you can't stand the Heat, then you need to get out of Hello!'s kitchen. ■ **politics; stress**

HEAVEN protects children, sailors, and drunken men

The proverb is found in various forms; latterly, American examples often add 'the United States' to the category of those favoured or in need of special protection.

□ **1861** T. HUGHES *Tom Brown at Oxford* I. xii. Heaven, they say, protects children, sailors, and drunken men; and whatever answers to Heaven in the academical system protects freshmen. **1865** G. MACDONALD *Alec Forbes* III. xi. I canna think hoo he cam' to fa' sae sair; for they say there's a special Providence watches over drunk men and bairns. **1980** S. KING *Firestarter* 57 She didn't even have a bruise—God watches over drunks and small children. **1997** *Washington Times* 18 Nov. A15 As we become once more the fool, we can only pray the old epigram is still true: 'God protects fools, drunkards and the United States.' **2001** *Washington Times* 15 Nov. A16 We've all likely heard at some time or other the stale, snide European-ism: 'The Lord looks after fools, drunks, and the United States.' Sometimes you have to wonder: Does He really? ■ **providence**

heaven *see also* CROSSES are ladders that lead to heaven; GOD's in his heaven, all's right with the world; MARRIAGES are made in heaven; *also* GOD.

hedge *see* one man may STEAL a horse, while another may not look over a hedge.

heir *see* WALNUTS and pears you plant for your heirs.

HELL hath no fury like a woman scorned

In classical mythology the Furies were avenging deities, fearful goddesses from Tartarus who avenged wrong and punished crime. *Fury* in the sense of 'frenzied rage' may also be intended, esp. in more modern quots. Cf. EURIPIDES *Medea* l. 263 *γυνὴ γὰρ τἄλλα μὲν φόβου πλέα κακή τ' ἐς ἀλκὴν καὶ σίδηρον εἰσορᾶν: ὅταν δ' ἐς εὐνὴν ἠδικημένη κυρῇ, οὐκ ἔστιν ἄλλη φρὴν μιαιφονωτέρα*, in other circumstances a woman is full of fear and shuns to confront force and iron; but when she has been wronged in a matter of sex, there is no other heart more bloodthirsty. The idea was a commonplace in the Renaissance; e.g. *a* **1625** BEAUMONT & FLETCHER *Knight of Malta* I. i. The wages of scorn'd Love is baneful hate.

□ **1696** C. CIBBER *Love's Last Shift* IV. 71 No Fiend in Hell can match the fury of a disappointed Woman!—Scorned! slighted; dismissed without a parting Pang! **1697** CONGREVE *Mourning Bride* III. 39 Heav'n has no Rage, like Love to Hatred turn'd, Nor Hell a Fury, like a Woman scorn'd. **1886** M. HOLMES *Chamber over Gate* xxvi. You know 'Hell hath no fury,' etc. If your wife should ever wake up to the true state of the case..I'm afraid she'd be an ugly customer. **2002** *Washington Post* 15 Jan. B4 'Hell hath no fury like a woman scorned,' Laura L. Martin, Calvert deputy state's attorney, told jurors yesterday at Freeman's trial on a first-degree murder charge. 'The defendant, Adele Freeman, felt like a woman scorned.' ■ **love, blighted; malice; women**

hell *see also* ENGLAND is the paradise of women; the ROAD to hell is paved with good intentions; he that would go to SEA for pleasure, would go to hell for a pastime.

help *see* EVERY little helps; GOD helps them that help themselves; a MOUSE may help a lion; help you to SALT, help you to sorrow.

hen *see* the ROBIN and the wren are God's cock and hen; a WHISTLING woman and a crowing hen are neither fit for God nor men.

herb *see* BETTER a dinner of herbs than a stalled ox where hate is.

heresy *see* TURKEY, heresy, hops, and beer came into England all in one year.

hero *see* NO man is a hero to his valet.

Every HERRING must hang by its own gill

Individuals are accountable for their own actions.

□ **1609** S. HARWARD *MS* (Trinity College, Cambridge) 85 Lett every herring hang by his owne tayle. **1639** J. CLARKE *Parœmiologia Anglo-Latina* 20 Every herring must hang by th'owne gill. **1670** J. RAY *English Proverbs* 102 Every herring must hang by its own gill. ..Every man must give an account for himself. **1865** SURTEES *Facey Romford's Hounds* xxi. One man is no more a criterion for another man than one horse is a criterion for another. ..Every herring must hang by its own head. **1890** T. H. HALL CAINE *Bondman* II. ii. Adam, thinking as little of pride, said No, that every herring should hang by its own gills. **1998** *Times* 16 June 22 You believe, like Bill Tilman who sailed leaky pilot cutters up Greenland fjords until he was 80, that 'every herring should hang by its own tail.' ■ **independence**

He who HESITATES is lost

Early uses of the proverb refer specifically to women.

□ **1713** ADDISON *Cato* IV. i. When love once pleads admission to our hearts..The woman that deliberates is lost. **1865** TROLLOPE *Can You forgive Her?* II. x. It has often been said of woman that she who doubts is lost..never thinking whether or no there be any truth in the proverb. **1878** J. H. BEADLE *Western Wilds* xxi. In Utah it is emphatically true, that he who hesitates is lost—to Mormonism. **1887** BLACKMORE *Springhaven* xlii. Dolly hesitated, and with the proverbial result. **2001** *Washington Times* 8 Nov. D6 (*Herb & Jamaal comic strip*) 'Sometimes he who hesitates is lost..and ends up several miles from the next freeway exit.' ■ **decision and indecision**

hid *see* LOVE and a cough cannot be hid.

Those who HIDE can find

Hide means 'hide something': the verb is used absolutely.

□ *c* **1400** *Seven Sages of Rome* (1845) 68 He may wel fynde that hyde him selven. **1639** J. CLARKE *Parœmiologia Anglo-Latina* 111 They that hide can find. **1842** MARRYAT *Percival Keene* I. iii. 'I could have told you where it was.' 'Yes, yes, those who hide can find.' **1922** JOYCE *Ulysses* 542 (She..unrolls the potato from the top of her stocking.) Those that hides knows where to find. **1979** 'E. PETERS' *One Corpse too Many* ix. Only those who had hidden here were likely ever to find. The full leafage covered all. ■ **concealment**

The HIGHER the monkey climbs the more he shows his tail

The further an unsuitable person is promoted, the more obvious his inadequacies become. In various more or less polite forms.

□ *c* **1395** WYCLIF *Bible* (1850) Proverbs iii. 35 (*gloss*) The filthe of her foli aperith more, as the filthe of the hynd partis of an ape aperith more, whanne he stieth [climbs] on high. *c* **1594** BACON *Promus* 102 He doth like the ape that the higher he clymbes the more he shows his ars. **1670** J. RAY *English Proverbs* 57 The higher the Ape goes, the more he shews his tail. ..The higher beggars or base bred persons are advanced, the more they discover the lowness and baseness of their spirits and tempers. **1743** POPE *Dunciad* IV. 157 (*note*) The higher you climb, the more you shew your A—. **1873** TROLLOPE *Phineas Redux* I. xxxiv. He's to be pitchforked up to the Exchequer. ..The higher a monkey climbs—; you know the proverb. **1985** *Washington Post* 3 Nov. C3 Let me tell you something Cookie and try to remember it the rest of your life, will you? The higher a monkey climbs the more he shows his ass. **2000** *Washington Post* 12 Dec. D6 The great expectations cost Norv Turner his job. And the attending soap opera quality made Dan Snyder a villainous stick figure across the nation. The lesson is obvious: The higher you attempt to climb, the more your behind shows. ■ **ambition; human nature**

hill *see* BLUE are the hills that are far away.

hindered *see* MEAT and mass never hindered man.

hindmost *see* DEVIL take the hindmost; EVERY man for himself, and devil take the hindmost.

hire *see* the LABOURER is worthy of his hire.

HISTORY repeats itself

□ **1858** G. ELIOT *Janet's Repentance* in *Scenes of Clerical Life* II. x. History, we know, is apt to repeat itself. **1865** H. SEDLEY *Marian Rooke* III. v. i. History, it is said, repeats itself. ..Few but are reminded almost every day..of something that has gone before. **1957** V. BRITTAIN *Testament of Experience* 11 History tends to defy the familiar aphorism; whether national or personal, it seldom repeats itself. **1971** A. PRICE *Alamut Ambush* xiii. Maybe history repeats itself—but I have to have facts. ■ **past**

history *see also* happy is the COUNTRY which has no history.

hog *see* the CAT, the rat, and Lovell the dog, rule all England under the hog.

hold *see* what you HAVE, hold.

Holdfast *see* BRAG is a good dog, but Holdfast is better.

When you are in a HOLE, stop digging

□ **1988** D. HEALEY *Observer* in J. Care (ed.) *Sayings of the Eighties* It is a good thing to follow the first law of holes; if you are in one, stop digging. **1989** *U.S. News & World Report* 23 Jan. CVI. iii. 46 (*headline*) When you're in a hole, stop digging. **1997** *Times* 15 Sept. 1 William Hague seems to have forgotten the first rule of politics: when you are in a hole, stop digging. **2001** *Spectator* 1 Dec. 32 Parliament would be unwise to hand to somebody in Tehran, Lambeth Palace or Salt Lake City the power, by pronouncing something hateful, to create an offence under English law. You're in a hole, Home Secretary. Stop digging. ■ **prudence**; **trouble**

HOME is home, as the Devil said when he found himself in the Court of Session

The *Court of Session* is the supreme civil tribunal of Scotland, established in 1532.

□ **1832** W. MOTHERWELL in A. Henderson *Scottish Proverbs* lxix. Nothing more bitter was ever uttered.. against our Supreme Court of Judicature, than the saying.. Hame is hamely, quo' the Deil, when he fand himself in the Court of Session. **1915** J. BUCHAN *Salute to Adventurers* iv. I saw nothing now to draw me to.. law. .. 'Hame's hame,' runs the proverb, 'as the devil said when he found himself in the Court of Session,' and I had lost any desire for that sinister company. ■ **law and lawyers**

HOME is home though it's never so homely

The archaic phrase *never so* means 'ever so'.

□ **1546** J. HEYWOOD *Dialogue of Proverbs* I. iv. B1 Home is homely, though it be poore in syght. **1569–70** *Stationers' Register* (1875) I. 192 A ballett intituled home ys homelye be yt neuer so ill. **1670** J. RAY *English Proverbs* 103 Home is home though it be never so homely. **1857** DICKENS *Little Dorrit* II. ix. 'Just as Home is Home though it's never so Homely, why you see,' said Mr. Meagles, adding a new version to the proverb, 'Rome is Rome though it's never so Romely.' **1915** J. WEBSTER *Dear Enemy* 46 Hame is hame, be't ever sae hamely. Don't you marvel at the Scotch? ■ **content and discontent**; **home**

HOME is where the heart is

□ **1870** J. J. MCCLOSKEY in Goldberg & Heffner *Davy Crockett & Other Plays* (1940) 79 'As I am to become an inmate of your home, give me a sort of a panoramic view.'.. 'Well, home, they say, is where the heart is.' **1950** H. M. GAY *Pacific Spectator* IV. 91 'Home is where the heart is,' she said, 'if you'll excuse the bromide [trite remark].' **1979** K. BONFIGLIONI *After You with Pistol* xxi. 'Where is "home", please,' I asked. .. 'Home's where the heart is,' he said. ■ **content and discontent**; **home**

home *see also* CHARITY begins at home; CURSES, like chickens, come home to roost; EAST, west, home's best; an ENGLISHMAN's house is his castle; GO abroad and you'll hear news of home; the LONGEST way round is the shortest way home; there's no PLACE like home; a WOMAN'S place is in the home; many go out for WOOL and come home shorn.

HOMER sometimes nods

Nobody, even a poet as great as the Greek epic writer Homer, can be at his best or most alert all the time. *Nods* here means 'becomes drowsy, falls asleep'; hence, 'errs due to momentary lack of attention'. The source is HORACE *Ars Poetica* 359 *indignor quandoque bonus dormitat Homerus*, I am indignant when worthy Homer nods.

□ **1387** J. Trevisa tr. *Higden's Polychronicon* (1874) V. 57 He may take hede that the grete Homerus slepeth somtyme, for in a long work it is laweful to slepe som time. **1677** DRYDEN in *State of Innocence* B1^{V} Horace acknowledges that honest Homer nods sometimes: he is not equally awake in every line. **1887** T. H. HUXLEY in *Nineteenth Century* Feb. 196 Scientific reason, like Homer, sometimes nods. **1979** D. CLARK *Heberden's Seat* vi. 'We're half asleep, not to have asked where they are before this.' 'Homer nods. .. You can't ask every question.' **2002** *National Review* 6 May 16 Thanks for the studious illumination. But isn't it easier to go the even-Homer-nods route on this, than to question the rule that plural subjects require a plural form of the verb? ■ **error**

honest *see* when THIEVES fall out, honest men come by their own.

HONESTY is the best policy

□ **1605** E. SANDYS *Europæ Speculum* K3 This over-politick..order may reach a note higher than our grosse conceipts, who think honestie the best policie. *a* **1763** J. BYROM *Poems* (1773) I. 75 I'll filch no filching;—and I'll tell no lye; Honesty's the best policy,—say I. **1854** R. WHATELY *Detached Thoughts* II. xviii. 'Honesty is the best policy'; but he who acts on that principle is not an honest man. **1928** J. GALSWORTHY *Swan Song* vi. It had been in their systems just as the proverb 'Honesty is the best policy' was in that of the private banking which then obtained. **2001** *Washington Times* 17 July A18 It is not a phrase I'm particularly fond of, for it endorses a virtue not for itself but for practical reasons, yet it bears repeating: Honesty is still the best policy. ■ **conduct**; **honesty and dishonesty**

HONEY catches more flies than vinegar

Soft or ingratiating words achieve more than sharpness.

□ **1666** G. TORRIANO *Italian Proverbs* 149 Honey gets more flyes to it, than doth viniger. **1744** B. FRANKLIN *Poor Richard's Almanack* (Mar.) Tart Words make no Friends: spoonful of honey will catch more flies than Gallon of Vinegar. **1955** W. C. MACDONALD *Destination Danger* x. I..know the old saying relative to honey catching more flies than vinegar. ..If this is an act, you might as well save your breath. **1996** *Washington Post* 25 Oct. B4 Ask his advice frequently, and thank him profusely for his wisdom and guidance. Remember that old adage 'You can catch more flies with honey than with vinegar.' ■ **tact**

honey *see also* where BEES are, there is honey.

There is HONOUR among thieves

The concept is found in *c* **1622–3** *Soddered Citizen* (1936) l. 305 Theeues haue betweene themselues, a truth, And faith, which they keepe firme, by which They doe subsist; **1703** P. A. MOTTEUX *Don Quixote* II. lx. The old proverb still holds good, Thieves are never rogues among themselves.

□ **1802** J. BENTHAM *Works* (1843) IV. 225 A sort of honour may be found (according to a proverbial saying) even among thieves. **1823** J. BEE *Dict. Turf* 98 'There is honour among thieves, but none among gamblers,' is very well antithetically spoken, but not true in fact. **1984** J. REEVES *Murder before Matins* vi. Honour among thieves was an empty phrase to all three of them: every professional criminal they'd known would sell his sidekick unhesitatingly if the price were right. **2002** R. J. BERNSTEIN *Radical Evil* 25 And a moral scoundrel may occasionally do what duty requires (honor among thieves). ■ **honour; wrong-doers**

The post of HONOUR is the post of danger

□ *a* **1533** LD. BERNERS *Huon* (EETS) xx. Where as lyeth grete parelles there lieth grete honour. **1613** T. HEYWOOD *Brazen Age* III. 211 The greater dangers threaten The greater is his honour that breaks through. *a* **1625** J. FLETCHER *Rule Wife* (1640) IV. i. I remembered your old Roman axiom, The more the danger, still the more the honour. **1711** *Spectator* 1 Dec. 1 We consider Human Life as a State of Probation, and Adversity as the Post of Honour in it. **1832** A. HENDERSON *Scottish Proverbs* 33 The post of honour is the post of danger. **1905** *British Weekly* 14 Dec. 1 The Chancellorship of the Exchequer.. is preeminently the post of danger, and therefore the post of honour in the new Government. ■ **honour; peril**

honour *see also* give CREDIT where credit is due; a PROPHET is not without honour save in his own country.

hoof *see* NO foot, no horse.

hop *see* TURKEY, heresy, hops, and beer came into England all in one year.

HOPE deferred makes the heart sick

With allusion to PROVERBS xiii., 12 (AV) Hope deferred maketh the heart sick; cf. *c* **1395** WYCLIF *Bible* (1850) Proverbs xiii. 13 Hope that is deferrid, tormenteth the soule; *c* **1527** J. RASTELL *Calisto & Melebea* A5V For long hope to the hart mych troble wyll do.

□ **1557** R. EDGEWORTH *Sermons* 130V The hope that is deferred, prolonged, and put of, vexeth the minde. **1733** J. TALCOTT in *Collections of Connecticut Hist. Society* (1892) IV. 285 As hope deferred makes the heart sick: so I am in long expectation of your answers. **1889** GISSING *Nether World* II. vii. There was a heaviness at his heart. Perhaps it came only of hope deferred. **1981** *Observer* 26 Apr. 14 If hope deferred makes the heart sick, despair is a poor counsellor also. ■ **hope and despair**

HOPE for the best and prepare for the worst

□ **1565** NORTON & SACKVILLE *Gorboduc* I. ii. Good is I graunt of all to hope the best, But not to liue still dreadles of the worst. **1581** W. AVERELL *Charles & Julia* D7 To hope the best, and feare the worst, (loe, such is Loouers gaines). **1706** E. WARD *Third Volume* 337 This Maxim ought to be carest, Provide against the worst, and hope the best. **1813** J. JAY *Correspondence* (1893) IV. 367 To hope for the best and prepare for the worst, is a trite but a good maxim. **1836** E. HOWARD *Rattlin the Reefer* II. xxix. The youngest of us cannot always escape—hoping, trusting, relying on the best, we should be prepared for the worst. **1999** 'H. CRANE' *Miss Seeton's Finest Hour* i. 7 'We must all hope for the best,' Mrs. Seeton chided him gently. 'As my nanny used to say: "Hope for the best, expect the worst—and take what comes."' ■ **foresight and hindsight**

HOPE is a good breakfast but a bad supper

□ **1661** W. RAWLEY *Resuscitatio* (ed. 2) 298 But, said the fisher men, we had hope then to make a better gain of it. Saith Mr. [Francis] Bacon well my Maisters, then Ile tell you; hope is a good Breakfast but it is a Bad supper. **1817** H. L. PIOZZI *Autobiography* (1861) II. 188 He was a wise man who said Hope is a good breakfast but a bad dinner. It shall be my supper..when all's said and done. **1986** C. M. SCHULZ *Washington Post* 27 Aug. D15 (*Peanuts comic strip*) 'I hope I get better grades this year. I hope I'll be the prettiest and smartest girl in the whole class..' '"Hope is a good breakfast, but it is a bad supper."' ■ **disappointment; hope and despair**

HOPE springs eternal

□ **1732** POPE *Essay on Man* I. 95 Hope springs eternal in the human breast. Man never Is, but always To be blest. **1865** DICKENS *Our Mutual Friend* II. III. X. Night after night his disappointment is acute, but hope springs eternal in the scholastic breast. **1935** H. SPRING *Rachel Rosing* viii. 'It was understood, wasn't it, that we could not dine together?' 'Oh yes—but you know how it is. Hope springs eternal and so forth.' **2002** *Spectator* 16 Mar. 11 But hope springs eternal in the Labour pessimist's breast. Perhaps this time Mr Blair and his American friends will get it all wrong. ■ **hope and despair**

If it were not for HOPE, the heart would break

□ *a* **1250** *Ancrene Wisse* (1962) 43 Ase me seith, yef hope nere heorte to breke [as one says, if there were not hope, the heart would break]. *c* **1440** *Gesta Romanorum* (EETS) 228 Yf hope wer not, hert schulde breke. **1616** J. WITHALS *Dict.* (rev. ed.) 582 If it were not for hope, the heart would breake. **1748** RICHARDSON *Clarissa* VI. xxix. No harm in hoping, Jack! My uncle says, Were it not for hope, the heart would break. **1911** J. LUBBOCK *Use of Life* (rev. ed.) xv. There is an old proverb that if it were not for Hope the heart would break. Everything may be retrieved except despair. ■ **hope and despair**

hope *see also* while there's LIFE, there's hope; he that LIVES in hope dances to an ill tune.

hopefully *see* it is BETTER to travel hopefully than to arrive.

You can take a HORSE to the water, but you can't make him drink

The word *the* is frequently omitted from the proverb and *lead* substituted for *take*.

□ *c* **1175** *Old English Homilies* (EETS) 1st Ser. 9 Hwa is thet mei thet hors wettrien the him self nule drinken [who can give water to the horse that will not drink of its own accord]? **1546** J. HEYWOOD *Dialogue of Proverbs* I. xi. D3 A man may well bryng a horse to the water, But he can not make hym drynke without he will. **1658** E. PHILLIPS *Mysteries of Love & Eloquence* 160 A man may lead his Horse to water, but he cannot make him drink unless he list. **1857** TROLLOPE *Barchester Towers* III. i. 'Well,' said she..'one man can take a horse to water but a thousand can't make him drink.' **1970** J. MITFORD in *Atlantic* (1979) July 50 The dropout rate [for the course] must be close to 90 percent. I guess you can take a horse to the water, but you can't make him drink. **1997** M. LAZARUS *Washington Post* 7 Dec. (*Momma comic strip*) We could send you out to a firm and convince them to hire you, but we're not sure you'd be willing to learn the job. In other words, you can lead a horse to water, but you can't make it drink. ■ **free will and compulsion**

horse *see also* don't CHANGE horses in midstream; ENGLAND is the paradise of women; never look a GIFT horse in the mouth; a GOOD horse cannot be of a bad colour; while the GRASS grows, the steed starves; the GREY mare is the better horse; because a MAN is born in a stable that does not make him a horse; NO foot, no horse; a NOD's as good as a wink to a blind horse; there is NOTHING so good for the inside of a man as the outside of a horse; don't PUT the cart before the horse; if you can't RIDE two horses at once, you shouldn't be in the circus; a SHORT horse is soon curried; it is too late to shut the STABLE-door after the horse has bolted; one man may STEAL a horse, while another may not look over a hedge; THREE things are not to be trusted; if TWO ride on a horse, one must ride behind; for WANT of a nail the shoe was lost; if WISHES were horses, beggars would ride.

horseback *see* set a BEGGAR on horseback, and he'll ride to the Devil.

HORSES for courses

Originally an expression in horse-racing: different horses are suited to different race courses. Now widely used in other contexts.

□ **1891** A. E. T. WATSON *Turf* vii. A familiar phrase on the turf is 'horses for courses'. . . The Brighton Course is very like Epsom, and horses that win at one meeting often win at the other. **1929** *Daily Express* 7 Nov. 18 Followers of the 'horses for courses' theory will be interested in the acceptance of Saracen, Norwest and Sir Joshua. **1985** 'J. GASH' *Pearlhanger* xxiii. It seemed to me I'd need a massacre, and immediately thought of Big John Sheehan. Horses for courses. **2001** *Times* 7 Nov. 16 Likewise it is horses for courses in Parliament. Mr Blair has a huge majority. There is no point in 'nursing a constituency' which offers no threat. ■ **efficiency and inefficiency**

hot *see* a LITTLE pot is soon hot; STRIKE while the iron is hot.

hound *see* you cannot RUN with the hare and hunt with the hounds.

One HOUR's sleep before midnight is worth two after

□ **1640** G. HERBERT *Outlandish Proverbs* no. 882 One houres sleepe before midnight is worth three after. **1670** J. RAY *English Proverbs* 37 One hours sleep before midnight's worth two hours after. **1829** COBBETT *Advice to Young Men* I. xxxviii. It is said by the country-people that one hour's sleep before midnight is worth more than two are worth after midnight; and this I believe to be a fact. **1937** A. THIRKELL *Summer Half* iii. Now, Mr. Winter, remember my boys when you come up! Every hour's sleep before twelve is worth two afterwards, you know. **2002** *Times* 16 Feb. 26 Some maintain that 'An hour before midnight is worth two after it', which is utter nonsense because, as everyone knows: *Early to bed, early to rise, Makes a man surly, and gives him red eyes.* ■ **health**

hour *see also* the DARKEST hour is just before the dawn; SIX hours' sleep for a man, seven for a woman, and eight for a fool.

When HOUSE and land are gone and spent, then learning is most excellent

Of similar vintage is LEARNING *is better than house and land.*

□ **1752** S. FOOTE *Taste* I. i. It has always been my Maxum . . to give my Children Learning enough; for, as the old Saying is, When house and Land are gone and spent, then Learning is most excellent. **1896** S. BARING-GOULD *Broom-Squire* xxvi.

I have..got Simon to write for me, on the fly-leaf. ..When land is gone, and money is spent, Then learning is most excellent. ■ **learning; property**

A HOUSE divided cannot stand

With allusion to MATTHEW xii. 25 (AV) Every city or house divided against itself shall not stand.

□ *a* **1050** DEFENSOR *Liber Scintillarum* (EETS) 133 Drihten segth.. ælc ceaster oththe hus todæled ongean hit sylf, hit na stynt. *c* **1704** in T. Chalkley *Journal in Works* (1751) 42 My Mother would often say, *A House divided could not stand.* **1858** A. LINCOLN *Speech* 16 June in *Works* (1953) II. 461 'A house divided against itself cannot stand.' I believe this government cannot endure, permanently half *slave* and half *free*. **2001** *Times* 12 Dec. 17 A house divided against itself cannot stand. And if Britain is to provide a secure home for all its peoples, there must be a shared sense of what values the nation holds in common. ■ **quarrelsomeness; unity and division**

house *see also* BETTER one house spoiled than two; an ENGLISHMAN'S house is his castle; FOOLS build houses and wise men live in them; those who live in GLASS houses shouldn't throw stones; LEARNING is better than house and land; never mention ROPE in the house of a man who has been hanged; SWEEP the house with broom in May, you sweep the head of the house away.

human *see* to ERR is human (to forgive divine).

hundred *see* the BUYER has need of a hundred eyes, the seller of but one.

HUNGER drives the wolf out of the wood

Cf. early 14th-cent. Fr. *la fains enchace le louf dou bois*, hunger chases the wolf from the wood.

□ **1483** CAXTON *Cato* B6V As hunger chaceth the wolfe out of the wode thus sobrete [sobriety] chaseth the deuyl fro the man. **1591** J. FLORIO *Second Fruits* 125 Hunger driues the wolfe out of the wood, if I had not great neede of monie, you should neuer haue them so dog cheape. **1748** SMOLLETT *Gil Blas* (1749) IV. XII. vii. This one..I own is the child of necessity. Hunger, thou knowest, brings the wolf out of the wood. **1872** R. BROWNING *Works* (1897) III. 323 Hunger, proverbs say, allures the wolf from the wood. **1905** J. B. CABELL *Line of Love* iv. Hunger..causes the wolf to sally from the wood. ■ **hunger; necessity**

HUNGER is the best sauce

Cf. CICERO *De Finibus* II. xxviii. *cibi condimentum esse famem*, hunger is the spice of food; early 15th-cent. Fr. *n'est sauce qui vaille fain*, there is no sauce worth so much as hunger.

□ **1530** A. BARCLAY *Eclogues* (EETS) II. 743 Make hunger thy sause be thou neuer so nice, For there shalt thou finde none other kind of spice. **1539** R. TAVERNER *Garden of Wisdom* I. B1 He [Socrates] sayd, the beste sawce is hungre. **1555** R. EDEN tr. *P. Martyr's Decades of New World* II. iii. (*margin*) Hunger is the best sauce. **1850** C. KINGSLEY *Alton Locke* I. ix. If hunger is, as they say, a better sauce than any Ude invents, you should spend..months shut out from every glimpse of Nature, if you would taste her beauties. **1929** F. M. MCNEILL *Scots Kitchen* iii. Mere hunger, which is the best sauce, will not produce cookery, which is the art of sauces. **1939** L. I. WILDER *By Shores of Silver Lake* xxi. 'The gravy is extra good too.' 'Hunger is the best sauce,' Ma replied modestly. **1996** *Washington Post* 7 Aug. A10 However, just as hunger is the best sauce for unappetizing food, political peril is the best argument for Dole to swallow his skepticism. ■ **food and drink; hunger**

A HUNGRY man is an angry man

□ *c* **1641** D. FERGUSSON *Scottish Proverbs* (STS) no. 553 Hungry men ar angry. **1659** J. HOWELL *Proverbs* (English) 13 A hungry man, an angry man. **1738** SWIFT *Polite Conversation* ii. 119 'I'm hungry.'.. 'And I'm angry, so let us both go fight.' **1909** *Spectator* 22 May 824 The Acharnians [in a play of that name by Aristophanes].. made fun of the Athenians. .. 'A hungry man is an angry man'.. and the Athenians were certainly hungry. **1922** J. JOYCE *Ulysses* 161 Hungry man is an angry man. **1981** B. MARLEY in *Times* 17 Oct. 7 A hungry mob is an angry mob, a pot a cook but the food not enough. ■ **hunger**

hunt *see* you cannot RUN with the hare and hunt with the hounds.

HURRY no man's cattle

□ **1822** SCOTT *Pirate* I. ix. 'A' in gude time,' replied the jagger [pedlar]; 'hurry no man's cattle.' **1907** W. C. HAZLITT *English Proverbs & Proverbial Phrases* 236 Hurry no man's cattle; you may come to have a donkey of your own. Sometimes said to an impatient child. **1932** J. S. FLETCHER *Murder of Ninth Baronet* xxi. I knew that in due time he would tell me the result of these mental exercises; in the meantime I stood by the old adage—hurry no man's cattle. ■ **patience and impatience**

hurt *see* don't CRY before you're hurt; what you don't KNOW can't hurt you; STICKS and stones may break my bones but words will never hurt me.

The HUSBAND is always the last to know

Said of a wife as well as a husband.

□ **1604** MARSTON *What you Will* I. i. A cuckold.. a thing that's hoodwinked with kindness. .. He must be the last must know it. **1659** N. R. *Proverbs* 95 The good man is the last that knows whats amisse at home. **1756** STERNE *Tristram Shandy* VIII. iv. 'It is with love as with cuckoldom'—the suffering party is at least the third, but generally the last who knows anything about the matter. **1893** R. KIPLING *Many Inventions* 250 The most disconnected witness knew.. the causes of offence; and the prisoner [i.e. the cuckolded husband], who naturally was the last of all to know, groaned in the dock while he listened. **1936** M. MITCHELL *Gone with Wind* liv. I thought surely the whole town knew by now. Perhaps they all do, except you. You know the old adage: 'The wife is always the last one to find out.' **1959** M. SUMMERTON *Small Wilderness* i. That over-worked truism about the wife being the last to know, wasn't in my case strictly accurate. **1979** C. MACLEOD *Family Vault* iii. 'Do you mean he hasn't heard?' Leila whooped. 'They say the husband's always the last to know,' Harry chimed in. **2002** B. MONAHAN *Sceptred Isle Club* vii. 138 John knew that, just as in affairs of the heart the wife is the last to know, with affairs of business, professional associates seldom had warnings when their seemingly secure friend went bankrupt. ■ **deception**; **wives and husbands**

husband *see also* a DEAF husband and a blind wife are always a happy couple.

I

ice *see* the RICH man has his ice in the summer and the poor man gets his in the winter.

An IDLE brain is the Devil's workshop

Recent US usage appears to conflate this proverb with *the* DEVIL *finds work for idle hands to do* (see quot. 2001).

◻ *a* **1602** W. PERKINS *Works* (1603) 906 The idle bodie and the idle braine is the shoppe [workshop] of the deuill. **1732** T. FULLER *Gnomologia* no. 3053 Idle Brains are the Devil's Workhouses. **1855** H. G. BOHN *Hand-Book of Proverbs* 311 An idle brain is the devil's workshop. **1859** S. SMILES *Self-Help* viii. Steady employment.. keeps one out of mischief, for truly an idle brain is the devil's workshop. **1930** E. D. BIGGERS *Charlie Chan Carries On* xxii. Tell him to be [a] good boy and study hard. An idle brain is the devil's workshop. **1988** C. G. HART *Design for Murder* ix. 'Idle minds are the devil's workshop.' She lifted the watch.. and stared at it accusingly. 'Five minutes after eight. Is no one else here?' **2001** *Washington Times* 3 Sept. A12 Young people need to learn to work. Their parents must not let them be idle all summer for, as they say, idle hands are the devil's workshop. ■ **idleness; wrongdoers**

IDLE people have the least leisure

The corollary of *the* BUSIEST *men have the most leisure.*

◻ **1678** J. RAY *English Proverbs* (ed. 2) 161 Idle folks have the most labour. **1853** SURTEES *Sponge's Sporting Tour* lvii. 'Got a great deal to do', retorted Jog, who, like all thoroughly idle men, was always dreadfully busy. **1855** H. G. BOHN *Hand-Book of Proverbs* 414 Idle folks have the least leisure. **1908** *Spectator* 10 Oct. 535 The difference between leisureliness and laziness runs parallel with that between quickness and haste. 'Idle people', says the proverb, 'have the least leisure.' ■ **efficiency and inefficiency; idleness**

idle *see also* as good be an ADDLED egg as an idle bird; the DEVIL finds work for idle hands to do; it is idle to SWALLOW the cow and choke on the tail.

IDLENESS is the root of all evil

The idea is attributed to St. Bernard of Clairvaux. Cf. early 14th-cent. Fr. *oiseuseté atrait viches*, idleness attracts vices; *c* **1390** CHAUCER *Second Nun's Prologue* l. 1 The ministre and the norice [nurse] unto vices, which that men clepe [call] in Englissh ydlenesse.

◻ **1422** J. YONGE in *Secreta Secretorum* (1898) 158 Idylnysse is the.. rote of vicis. **1538** T. BECON *Governance of Virtue* B8V Idleness.. is the well-spring and root of all vice. **1707** G. FARQUHAR *Beaux' Stratagem* I. i. Idleness is the Root of all Evil; the World's wide enough, let 'em bustle. **1850** DICKENS *David Copperfield* x. 'The boy will be idle there,' said Miss Murdstone, looking into a pickle-jar, 'and idleness is the root of all evil.' **1874** TROLLOPE *Phineas Redux* II. xxxvi. I much prefer downright honest figures. Two and two make four; idleness is the root of all evil.. and the rest of it. ■ **good and evil; idleness**

If IFS and ands were pots and pans, there'd be no work for tinkers' hands

Used as a humorous retort to an over-optimistic conditional expression. *ands:* the conjunction *and* 'if', of which *an* is a weakened form, is employed irregularly here as a noun to denote 'an expression of condition or doubt'.

□ **1850** C. KINGSLEY *Alton Locke* I. x. 'If a poor man's prayer can bring God's curse down.'.. 'If ifs and ans were pots and pans.' **1886** *Notes & Queries* 7th Ser. I. 71 There is also the old doggerel—If ifs and ands Were pots and pans Where would be the work for Tinkers' hands? **1981** J. ASHFORD *Loss of Culion* xvi. As my old aunt used to say, 'If ifs and ands were pots and pans, there'd be no work for tinkers' hands.' **2002** *Washington Times* 14 Aug. B5 A reader signed 'Desperate in Ohio' reported that a verse her aunt told her many years ago was rattling around in her head, but she couldn't remember the last line. It went, 'If "ifs" and "ans" were pots and pans..' My column yesterday was filled with letters from readers eager to provide the missing line, '..there'd be no work for tinkers.' ■ **wanting and having**

Where IGNORANCE is bliss, 'tis folly to be wise

Now frequently abbreviated to *ignorance is bliss.*

□ **1742** GRAY *Poems* (1966) 10 Thought would destroy their paradise. No more; where ignorance is bliss, 'Tis folly to be wise. **1865** SURTEES *Facey Romford's Hounds* lxxi. Of course Facey knew nothing about Lucy, and, upon the principle that where ignorance is bliss 'twere folly to be wise, Soapey was not extra-inquisitive about her. **1925** S. O'CASEY *Juno & Paycock* II. 49 'You ought to be ashamed o' yourself.. not to know the History o' your country.'.. 'Where ignorance's bliss 'tis folly to be wise.' **1983** 'J. GASH' *Sleepers of Erin* i. Antique dealers haven't a clue. Pathetic. God knows why, but dealers always want to prove that ignorance really is bliss. **2001** *Times* 23 Nov. 20 And the moral of our present situation is: If ignorance is bliss, why aren't more people happy? ■ **ignorance**

IGNORANCE of the law is no excuse for breaking it

There is a hoary L. legal maxim: *ignorantia iuris neminem excusat*, ignorance of the law excuses nobody.

□ *c* **1412** T. HOCCLEVE *De Regimene Principum* (EETS) 92 Excuse schal hym naght his ignorance. **1530** C. ST. GERMAN *Dialogues in English* II. xlvi. Ignorance of the law though it be inuincible doth not excuse. **1616** T. DRAXE *Adages* 100 The ignorance of the law excuseth no man. *a* **1654** J. SELDEN *Table-Talk* (1689) 30 Ignorance of the Law excuses no man; not that all Men know the Law, but because 'tis an excuse every man will plead, and no man can tell how to confute him. **1830** N. AMES *Mariner's Sketches* xxviii. Ignorance of the law excuses nobody. ..The gates of mercy are forever shut against them. **1979** *Private Eye* 17 Aug. 6 [He] was fined £5 at Marylebone Court when he learned that ignorance of the law is no excuse for breaking it. ■ **excuses; law and lawyers**

It's an ILL bird that fouls its own nest

A condemnation of a person who vilifies his own family, country, etc. Cf. medieval L. *nidos commaculans inmundus habebitur ales*, the bird is unclean that soils its nest.

□ *a* **1250** *Owl & Nightingale* (1960) l. 99 Dahet habbe [a curse on] that ilke best that fuleth his owe nest. *c* **1400** N. BOZON *Moral Tales* (1889) 205 Hyt ys a fowle brydde that fylyth hys owne neste. **1591** H. SMITH *Preparative to Marriage* 82 It becommeth not any woman to set light by her husband, nor to publish his infirmities for they say, it is an euill bird that defileth his owne nest. **1670** J. RAY *English Proverbs* 62 It's an ill bird that beraies its own nest. **1817** SCOTT *Rob Roy* II. xiii. Where's the use o' vilifying ane's country. .. It's an ill bird that files its ain nest. **1926** *Times* 7 Sept. 17 Nothing.. can excuse the bad taste of Samuel Butler's virulent attack upon his defenceless family. .. It's an ill bird that fouls its own nest. **2000** C. GOFF *Rant of Ravens* i. 2 Miriam cleared her throat. 'It's an ill bird that fouls its own nest, dear. If you ask me, it's about time you dumped him.' ■ **malice**

ILL gotten goods never thrive

Cf. CICERO *Philippica* II. xxvii. 65 *male parta, male dilabuntur*, things ill gotten slip away in evil ways. A less colourful saying on the same theme as *what is* GOT *over the Devil's back is spent under his belly.*

□ **1519** W. HORMAN *Vulgaria* 77 Euyll gotten ryches wyll neuer proue longe. *c* **1577** J. NORTHBROOKE *Treatise.. Dicing* 95 Euill gotten goods shall neuer prosper. **1609** JONSON *Case is Altered* V. xii. Ill gotten goods ne'er thriue, I plaid the thiefe, and now am robd my selfe. **1670** J. RAY *English Proverbs* 98 Ill gotten goods, seldom prosper. **1826** C. LAMB *Elia's Last Essays* (1833) ii. *That ill-gotten gain never prospers*.. is the trite consolation administered to the easy dupe, when he has been tricked out of his money or estate. **1937** D. L. SAYERS *Busman's Honeymoon* x. Ill gotten goods never thrive. .. Because he hath oppressed and forsaken the poor. ■ **action and consequence; retribution**

He that has an ILL name is half hanged

□ *a* **1400** in C. Brown *Religious Lyrics of XIVth Century* (1957) 193 Ho-so hath a wicked name Me semeth for sothe half hongid he is. **1546** J. HEYWOOD *Dialogue of Proverbs* II. vi. I2 He that hath an yll name, is halfe hangd. **1614** T. ADAMS *Devil's Banquet* IV. 156 It is a very ominous and suspitious thing to haue an ill name. The Prouerbe saith, he is halfe hanged. **1897** M. A. S. HUME *Raleigh* xii. Were.. not an ill name half hanged.. he would have been acquitted. ■ **reputation**

It's ILL waiting for dead men's shoes

The earlier form of the proverb, exemplified in quots. *c* 1549 and 1721, is no longer found. The metaphorical phrase *to wait for dead men's shoes* is also illustrated below.

□ **1530** J. PALSGRAVE *L'éclaircissement de la Langue Française* 306ᵛ Thou lokest after deed mens shoes. *c* **1549** J. HEYWOOD *Dialogue of Proverbs* I. xi. C5 Who waitth for dead men shoen, shal go long barfote. **1721** J. KELLY *Scottish Proverbs* 148 He goes long bare Foot that wears dead Mens Shoon. Spoken to them who expect to be some Man's Heir, to get his Place, or Wife, if he should dye. **1758** A. MURPHY *Upholsterer* I. ii. You have very good pretensions; but then its waiting for dead Men's Shoes. **1815** SCOTT *Guy Mannering* II. xvi. That's but sma' gear, puir thing; she had a sair time o't with the auld leddy. But it's ill waiting for dead folk's shoon. **1912** E. V. LUCAS *London Lavender* iv. I pointed out that I was executor to no fewer than three persons.. 'It's ill waiting for dead men's shoes,' Naomi quoted. **1963** C. BUSH *Case of Heavenly Twin* xvi. Perhaps I was right when I suggested he told Staffer he was waiting for a dead man's shoes. ■ **expectation**

ILL weeds grow apace

Cf. 14th-cent. Fr. *male herbe croist*, bad grass thrives.

□ *c* **1470** in *Anglia* (1918) XLII. 200 Wyl[d] weed ys sone y-growe. *Creuerat herba satis, que nil habet utilitatis.* **1546** J. HEYWOOD *Dialogue of Proverbs* I. x. C4ᵛ Ill weede growth fast Ales [Alice], wherby the corne is lorne [lost]. **1578** J. FLORIO *First Fruits* 31ᵛ An yl weede groweth apace. **1594** SHAKESPEARE *Richard III* II. iv. 13 'Ay,' quoth my uncle Gloucester, 'Small herbs have grace: great weeds do grow apace.'.. I would not grow so fast, Because sweet flow'rs are slow and weeds make haste. **1738** SWIFT *Polite Conversation* i. 23 'Don't you think Miss is grown?'..'Ay; ill Weeds grow a-pace.' **1905** A. MACLAREN *Gospel according to St. Matthew* II. 208 The roots of the old lay hid, and, in due time, showed again above ground. 'Ill weeds grow apace.' **1986** M. SLUNG *More Momilies* 67 It's always the weeds that grow the best. ■ **good and evil; wrong-doers**

It's an ILL wind that blows nobody any good

A sailing metaphor frequently invoked to explain good luck arising from the source of others' misfortune.

□ **1546** J. HEYWOOD *Dialogue of Proverbs* II. ix. L1 An yll wynde that blowth no man to good, men saie. **1591** SHAKESPEARE *Henry VI, Pt. 3* II. v. 55 Ill blows the wind that profits nobody. **1655** T. FULLER *Church Hist. Britain* II. ii. It is an ill wind which bloweth no man Profit. He is cast on the Shoar of Freezland..where the Inhabitants..were by his Preaching converted to Christianity. **1832** S. WARREN *Diary of Late Physician* I. i. My good fortune (truly it is an ill wind that blows *nobody* any good) was almost too much for me. **1979** J. SCOTT *Angels in your Beer* xxviii. It is an ill wind that blows nobody any good, but then John Quinlan..was about as close to being a nobody as anyone could get. **2002** *Washington Times* 11 Jan. A4 It's an ill wind that blows nobody any good, as the wise man said, and certain Democrats and pundits think the wind that blew Enron away was a warm breeze from Eden. ■ **misfortune**

ill *see also* BAD news travels fast; EVIL doers are evil dreaders; EVIL to him who evil thinks; it's ill speaking between a FULL man and a fasting; he that LIVES in hope dances to an ill tune; it is ill SITTING at Rome and striving with the Pope; a sow may whistle, though it has an ill mouth for it; never SPEAK ill of the dead; *also* BAD.

IMITATION is the sincerest form of flattery

□ **1820** C. C. COLTON *Lacon* I. 113 Imitation is the sincerest of flattery. **1843** SURTEES *Handley Cross* I. xv. Imitation is the sincerest of flattery. **1940** E. PAYNE *Malice Domestic* 13 Penny's [clothes] all seemed to be homemade copies of the expensive models her sister wore. ..Imitation may be the sincerest form of flattery but..I wondered whether there might not be more to it. **2001** *Washington Post* 8 Sept. C11 It has been said that 'imitation is the sincerest form of flattery,' but being stalked and copied can indeed be frightening. ■ **imitation**

impossible *see* the DIFFICULT is done at once.

impression *see* FIRST impressions are the most lasting.

IN for a penny, in for a pound

□ **1695** E. RAVENSCROFT *Canterbury Guests* v. i. It concerns you to..prove what you speak. ..In for a Penny, in for a Pound. **1815** SCOTT *Guy Mannering* III. vii. Sampson..thought to himself, in for a penny in for a pound, and he fairly drank the witch's health in a cupfull of brandy. **1841** DICKENS *Old Curiosity Shop* II. lxvi. Now, gentlemen, I am not a man who does things by halves. Being in for a penny, I am ready as the saying is to be in for a pound. **1979** P. NIESEWAND *Member of Club* viii. 'Do you want to go and have a look, sir?'..'Why not?..In for a penny, in for a pound.' **2001** *Oldie* Nov. 66 Have you ever suggested that you take the children away for a few days or even a week—in for a penny, in for a pound—after Christmas or near their birthdays? ■ **action and consequence; perseverance; risk**

inclined *see* as the TWIG is bent, so is the tree inclined.

inconvenience *see* POVERTY is no disgrace, but it is a great inconvenience.

index *see* the EYES are the window of the soul.

Indian *see* the only GOOD Indian is a dead Indian.

infinite *see* GENIUS is an infinite capacity for taking pains.

inside *see* there is NOTHING so good for the inside of a man as the outside of a horse.

intention *see* the ROAD to hell is paved with good intentions.

invention *see* NECESSITY is the mother of invention.

Ireland *see* ENGLAND's difficulty is Ireland's opportunity.

iron *see* STRIKE while the iron is hot.

Every JACK has his Jill

□ **1611** R. COTGRAVE *Dict. French & English* s.v. Demander, Like will to like; a Iacke lookes for a Gill. **1619** in C. W. Bardsley *Curiosities of Puritan Nomenclature* (1880) i. The proverb is, each Jacke shall have his Gill. **1670** J. RAY *English Proverbs* 108 Every Jack must have his Gill. . . It ought to be written *Jyll.* **1855** G. J. WHYTE-MELVILLE *General Bounce* ii. 'Every Jack has his Gill,' if he and she can only find each other out at the propitious moment. **1940** H. W. THOMPSON *Body, Boots & Britches* xix. Every Jack has his Jill; If one won't, another will. **1986** M. SLUNG *More Momilies* 47 For every Jack, there is a Jill. ■ **men and women**

JACK is as good as his master

Jack is variously used as a familiar name for a sailor, a member of the common people, a serving man, and one who does odd jobs.

□ **1706** J. STEVENS *Spanish & English Dict.* s.v. Pedro, Peter is as good as his Master. Like Master, like Man. **1868** READE & BOUCICAULT *Foul Play* II. xx. Is it the general opinion of seamen before the mast? Come, tell us. Jack's as good as his master in these matters. **1936** W. HOLTBY *South Riding* I. iv. She was far from thinking Jack as good as his master and explained failure in plebeian upstarts by saying with suave contempt: 'Well, what can you expect? Wasn't bred to power.' **1987** R. HILL *Child's Play* viii. 1945 might have seen Britain ready at last for the political assertion that Jack was as good as his master, but it was still light years away from any meaningful acknowledgement that Black Jack was as good as White Jack. ■ **employers and employees; equality**

JACK of all trades and master of none

Jack is used here in the sense of unskilled worker, as contrasted with a *master* of a trade who had completed an apprenticeship.

□ **1732** T. FULLER *Gnomologia* no. 3051 Jack of all Trades is of no Trade. **1804** M. EDGEWORTH 'The Will' in *Popular Tales* ii. 152 'How comes it that I am so unlucky?' 'Jack of all trades, and master of none!' said Goodenough, with a sneer. **1878** S. WALPOLE *History of England* I. 311 It would be unfair to say of Lord Brougham that he was 'Jack of all trades and master of none'. **1987** O. S. CARD *Seventh Son* (1988) vi. 47 To have every possible skill . . and to have it in exactly even proportions. Far from being average, the child was extraordinary . . Jack of all trades and master of none? Or master of all? **2002** *Oxford Times Weekend* 9 He is quick to point out that the reverse side of the renaissance man is jack of all trades, who, as we all know, is often considered a master of none. ■ **trades and skills**

Jack *see also* a GOOD Jack makes a good Jill; all WORK and no play makes Jack a dull boy.

JAM tomorrow and jam yesterday, but never jam today

□ **1871** 'L. CARROLL' *Through Looking-Glass* v. 'The rule is, jam to-morrow and jam yesterday—but never jam to-day.' 'It *must* come sometimes to "jam to-day",' Alice objected. 'No, it can't,' said the Queen. **1951** 'J. WYNDHAM' *Day of Triffids* xii. Just put the Americans into the jam-tomorrow-pie-in-the-sky department awhile.

1979 *Guardian* 9 June 10 The manageress of the launderette calls me darling. .. 'Jam yesterday, jam tomorrow, but never jam today.' ■ **disappointment**

jaw (rush of water): *see* JOUK and let the jaw go by.

jest *see* many a TRUE word is spoken in jest.

jewel *see* FAIR play's a jewel.

Jill *see* a GOOD Jack makes a good Jill; every JACK has his Jill.

job *see* never send a BOY to do a man's job; if a THING's worth doing, it's worth doing well.

join *see* if you can't BEAT them, join them.

JOUK and let the jaw go by

A Scottish proverb counselling prudent or evasive action when trouble threatens. The phrase *to jouk and let the jaw go by* is also found.

□ **1721** J. KELLY *Scottish Proverbs* 189 Juck [stoop], and let the jaw [rush of water] go o'er you. That is, prudently yield to a present Torrent. **1817** SCOTT *Rob Roy* II. xii. Gang your ways hame, like a gude bairn—jouk and let the jaw gae by. **1927** J. BUCHAN *Witch Wood* xv. A man must either jouk and let the jaw go bye, as the owercome [common expression] says, or he must ride the whirlwind. ■ **prudence; self-preservation**

journey *see* the LONGEST journey begins with a single step.

JOVE but laughs at lovers' perjury

Cf. HESIOD frag. 124 (M-W), ἐκ τοῦ δ' ὅρκον ἔθηκεν ἀποίνιμον ἀνθρώποισι δ'νοσφιδίων ἔργων πέρι κύπριδος, since that time he [sc. Zeus] attached no penalty for men to an oath taken in the secret works of Aphrodite; TIBULLUS *Elegies* III. vi. 49 *periuria ridet amantum Iuppiter*, Jupiter laughs at lovers' perjuries; *a* **1500** in W. W. Skeat *Chaucerian & Other Pieces* (1897) 311 Your [lovers'] othes laste No lenger than the wordes ben ago! And god, and eke his sayntes, laughe also.

□ *c* **1550** tr. *A. S. Piccolomini's Lady Lucres* E4^v Pacorus .. confesseth the faut asketh forgeuenes and .. ryghte well knewe he that Jupyter rather laughethe, then taketh angerlye the periuringe of louers. *c* **1595** SHAKESPEARE *Romeo & Juliet* II. ii. 92 At lovers' perjuries, They say Jove laughs. **1700** DRYDEN *Poems* (1958) IV. 1487 Love endures no Tie, And Jove but laughs at Lovers Perjury! **1922** *Evening Standard* 17 Oct. 5 Perjury in the Divorce Court has been openly permitted to the upper classes for many years, following the maxim .. that 'Jove but laughs at lovers' perjury.' **1973** I. MURDOCH *Black Prince* III. 299 Zeus, they say, mocks lovers' oaths. ■ **love**

No one should be JUDGE in his own cause

Cf. the Latin legal maxim: *nemo debet esse iudex in propria causa*, no one should be judge in his own cause; also **1604** SHAKESPEARE *Measure for Measure* v. i. 166 In this I'll be impartial; be you judge Of your own cause.

□ *c* **1449** R. PECOCK *Repressor of Blaming of Clergy* (1860) II. 381 Noman oughte be iuge in his owne cause which he hath anentis [against] his neighbour. **1775** WESLEY *Letter* 3 Nov. (1931) VI. 186 No man is a good judge in his own cause. I believe I am tolerably impartial. **1928** *Times* 22 Aug. 9. The principle that no judge could be a judge in his own case was generally accepted. The chairman of a meeting was in a quasi-judicial capacity. **1981** *Daily Telegraph* 16 May 18 The maxim that no one should be judge in his own cause. ■ **law and lawyers**

JUDGE not, that ye be not judged

With allusion to MATTHEW vii. 1 (AV) Judge not, that ye be not judged.

□ **1481** CAXTON *Reynard* (1880) xxix. Deme [judge] ye noman, and ye shal not be demed. **1509** H. WATSON *Ship of Fools* H1 Judge not but yf that ye wyl be judged. **1925** A. CLUTTONBROCK *Essays on Life* x. The saying, 'Judge not, that ye be not judged,' is . . a statement of fact. Nothing makes us dislike a man so much as the knowledge that he is always judging us and all men. **2001** *Washington Times* 27 Nov. A12 The purpose is neither to gloat, nor to deride nor to humiliate our enemies and adversaries. Indeed, much wisdom and prudence is captured in the biblical injunction, 'Judge not, that ye be not judged.' ■ **reciprocity; tolerance**

judge (verb) *see also* you can't tell a BOOK by its cover.

June *see* a DRIPPING June sets all in tune.

Be JUST before you're generous

□ **1745** E. HAYWOOD *Female Spectator* II. VII. 35 There is, I think, an old saying, that we 'ought to be just before we are generous'. **1780** SHERIDAN *School for Scandal* IV. i. Be just before you are generous. **1834** MARRYAT *Peter Simple* I. xi. I owe every farthing of my money. . . There's an old proverb—be just before you're generous. **1908** *Spectator* 4 Apr. 529 A likeable man is tempted to be generous before he is just. **1922** JOYCE *Ulysses* 521 Bloom—You had better hand over that cash to me to take care of. Why pay more? Stephen—Be just before you are generous. ■ **fair dealing**

JUSTICE delayed is justice denied

The idea of a link between delay and denial of justice is an old one (cf. **1215** MAGNA CARTA To no man will we sell, or deny, or delay right or justice), but this formulation appears to be modern and mainly US.

□ **1999** *Daily Nation* (Nairobi) 9 Dec. 6/1 As they say, justice delayed is justice denied, an expression that obtains especially in situations where a person may languish in remand prison for three years only to be found innocent of any charge. **2000** *Washington Times* 31 Dec. B4 Apparently, Mr. Jackson got no satisfaction from his call to Mr. Bush. A few days later, in Los Angeles, Mr. Jackson pronounced Mr. Bush's presidency 'a coup d'etat,' noting 'justice delayed is justice denied.' **2001** *Washington Times* 13 Dec. B1 The inscription on the front of the Alexandria Courthouse, next to the depiction of the tortoise and the hare, reads simply. 'Justice Delayed is Justice Denied.' That's the motto at the 'rocket docket,' the federal court known for speed, spies and a winning record for government prosecutors. ■ **justice and injustice**

justify *see* the END justifies the means.

Why KEEP a dog and bark yourself?

□ **1583** B. MELBANCKE *Philotimus* 119 It is smal reason you should kepe a dog, and barke your selfe. **1670** J. RAY *English Proverbs* 81 What? keep a dog and bark my self. That is, must I keep servants, and do my work my self. **1738** SWIFT *Polite Conversation* i. 17 'Good Miss, stir the Fire.'.. 'Indeed your Ladyship could have stirr'd it much better.'.. 'I won't keep a Dog and bark myself.' **1933** A. CHRISTIE *Thirteen at Dinner* xviii. Why keep a dog and bark yourself? **1999** S. PAWSON *Some by Fire* vii. 153 'I think you want me to start all over again at Edinburgh University and the Sorbonne, but you want me to volunteer because you daren't ask me yourself.' 'That's about it,' I admitted. '*Man with dog never has to bark.*' ■ **employers and employees; work**

KEEP a thing seven years and you'll always find a use for it

□ **1623** W. PAINTER *Palace of Pleasure* C5 Things of small value the old proverb say, Wise men seuen yeares will carefully vp lay. **1663** T. KILLIGREW *Parson's Wedding* in *Comedies & Tragedies* (1664) 100 According to the Proverb; Keep a thing seven years, and then if thou hast no use on't throw't away. **1816** SCOTT *Antiquary* II. vi. They say, keep a thing seven year, an' ye'll aye find a use for't. **1945** F. THOMPSON *Lark Rise* xx. 'I don't know that I've any use for it.' 'Use! Use! .. Keep a thing seven years and you'll always find a use for it!' ■ **thrift**

KEEP no more cats than will catch mice

□ **1673** J. DARE *Counsellor Manners* lxii. If thou hast a regard to Thrift, keep no more Cats than will kill Mice. **1678** J. RAY *English Proverbs* (ed. 2) 350 I will keep no more cats then will catch mice (*i.e.* no more in family then will earn their living). *Somerset*. **1710** S. PALMER *Proverbs* 358 Keep no more Cats than will Catch Mice. Ecquipage and Attendance.. must be agreeable to Character, Dignity and Fortune. **1910** R. KIPLING *Rewards & Fairies* 73 The King keeps no cats that don't catch mice. She must sail the seas, Master Dawe. ■ **efficiency and inefficiency; work**

KEEP your own fish-guts for your own sea-maws

□ **1721** J. KELLY *Scottish Proverbs* 118 Give your own Sea Maws [gulls] your own Fish Guts. If you have any Superfluities give them to your poor Relations, Friends, or Countrymen, rather than to others. **1816** SCOTT *Antiquary* I. xv. Ye ken my gudeman likes to ride the expresses himsel—we maun gie our ain fish-guts to our ain sea-maws. **1952** 'P. PIPER' *Death in Canongate* (1954) viii. 'Oh! it makes me a bit sick when you can be so liberal with anyone—' 'And not with you. That's what you are trying to say, isn't it?' 'I suppose so,' he said, and quoted lugubriously, '"Keep your ain fish guts for your ain sea maws."' ■ **charity; family**

KEEP your shop and your shop will keep you

Parodied by the American actress Mae West (1892–1980) in the 1937 movie *Every Day's a Holiday*: I always say, keep a diary and some day it'll keep you.

□ **1605** G. CHAPMAN et al. *Eastward Ho* A2^{V} I.. garnished my shop.. with good wholsome thriftie sentences; As, 'Touchstone, keepe thy shopp, and thy shoppe will keepe thee.' **1712** ADDISON *Spectator* 14 Oct. Sir William Turner.. would say,

Keep your Shop and your Shop will keep you. **1905** H. G. WELLS *Kipps* III. iii. A little bell jangled. 'Shop!' said Kipps. 'That's right. Keep a shop and the shop'll keep you.' **1943** S. V. BENÉT *Western Star* I. 20 I keep my shop but my shop doth not keep me. Shall I give such chances [of making a fortune] the go-by and walk the roads? **1976** H. KEMELMAN *Wednesday Rabbi got Wet* vii. 'When I was home, Dad cared a lot more about the store than he did about me,' he said bitterly. She nodded. .. 'That's because a store, if you take care of it, it takes care of you. Your father lives from that store, and your grandfather before him.' ■ **efficiency and inefficiency; money**

keep *see also* a man is known by the COMPANY he keeps; EXPERIENCE keeps a dear school; THREE may keep a secret, if two of them are dead; put your TRUST in God, and keep your powder dry.

keeper *see* FINDERS keepers (losers weepers).

keeping *see* FINDING's keepings.

key *see* a GOLDEN key can open any door.

kick *see* CORPORATIONS have neither bodies to be punished nor souls to be damned.

kill *see* it is the PACE that kills; it is not WORK that kills, but worry.

killed *see* CARE killed the cat; CURIOSITY killed the cat.

KILLING no murder

Quot. 1657 is the title of a pamphlet asserting that the assassination of Cromwell, the Protector, would be lawful and laudable.

□ **1657** SEXBY & TITUS (*title*) Killing noe murder. **1800** M. EDGEWORTH *Castle Rackrent* p. xliv. In Ireland, not only cowards, but the brave 'die many times before their death'. There killing is no murder. **1908** *Times Literary Supplement* 4 June 179 The exception is the share which he took in the conspiracy of Orsini against Napoleon III. .. It was probably a case to which Holyoake would have applied the doctrine of 'killing no murder'. **1961** C. COCKBURN *View from West* vi. The British .. made, in England, propaganda out of the phrase—attributed to the Irish—'killing no murder', they were not foolish enough to take their own propaganda seriously. ■ **violence**

killing *see also* there are more WAYS of killing a cat than choking it with cream; there are more WAYS of killing a dog than choking it with butter; there are more WAYS of killing a dog than hanging it.

kind *see* BETTER a good cow than a cow of a good kind.

The KING can do no wrong

Altered to *queen* when appropriate. Cf. the legal maxim: *rex non potest peccare*, the king can do no wrong; also *c* **1538** T. STARKEY *England in Reign of King Henry VIII* (EETS) I. iv. Wyl you make a kyng to have no more powar then one of hys lordys? Hyt ys commynly sayd .. a kyng ys aboue hys lawys.

□ *a* **1654** J. SELDEN *Table-Talk* (1689) 27 The King can do no wrong, that is no Process [action at law] can be granted against him. **1765** W. BLACKSTONE *Commentaries on Laws of England* I. vii. The King can do no wrong. .. The prerogative of the crown extends not to do any injury: it is created for the benefit of the people, and therefore cannot be exerted to their prejudice. **1888** C. M. YONGE *Beechcroft at*

Rockstone II. xxii. 'So, Aunt Jane is your Pope.' 'No; she's the King that can do no wrong,' said Gillian, laughing. **1952** 'M. COST' *Hour Awaits* 191 It was very different with Augustus. . . We had always expected that. . . In his case, was it not rather a matter of the king can do no wrong. **1981** *Times* 28 July 14 The Queen [of Holland] has no power but some influence. . . 'The Queen can do no wrong. The ministers are responsible.' ■ **rulers and ruled**

A KING'S chaff is worth more than other men's corn

The sense is explained in quot. 1738. For a similar sentiment, see **1612** T. SHELTON tr. *Cervantes' Don Quixote* I. IV. xii. A Kings crumme is more worth then a Lords loafe. The proverb in the form with *chaff* seems to be Scottish in origin.

□ *a* **1628** J. CARMICHAELL *Proverbs in Scots* (1957) 101 The kings calf [chaff] is worth other mennis corne. **1668** R. B. *Adagia Scotica* 33 Kings caff is worth other mens corn. **1738** *Gentleman's Mag.* VIII. 474 The King's chaff is worth more than other men's corn. This. . signifies that even the little perquisites, which attend the King's service, are more considerable than standing wages of private persons. **1788** BURNS *Letter* 16 Aug. (1931) I. 245 The old Scots Proverb says well—'King's caff is better than ither folks' corn.' **1817** SCOTT *Rob Roy* III. vii. They say. . kings' chaff is better than other folk's corn, but I think that canna be said o' kings' soldiers, if they let themselves be beaten wi' a wheen [few] auld carles. **1957** *Times Literary Supplement* 13 Sept. 552 A king's chaff is proverbially better than other men's corn. ■ **employers and employees; value**

king *see also* a CAT may look at a king; in the COUNTRY of the blind, the one-eyed man is king; a PECK of March dust is worth a king's ransom.

kingdom *see* in the COUNTRY of the blind, the one-eyed man is king.

KINGS have long arms

Cf. Gr. *μακραὶ τυράννων χεῖρες*, rulers' hands reach a long way; OVID *Heroides* xvii. *an nescis longas regibus esse manus?* know you not that kings have far-reaching hands?

□ **1539** R. TAVERNER tr. *Erasmus' Adages* A4[v] Kynges haue longe handes. They can brynge in men, they can pluck in thinges, though they be a great weye of. **1578** LYLY *Euphues* I. 221 Knowest thou not Euphues that kinges haue long armes, and rulers large reches? **1752** B. FRANKLIN *Poor Richard's Almanack* (Jan.) Kings haue long Arms, but misfortune longer. **1927** P. B. NOYES *Pallid Giant* iii. 'How will you insure Markham's safety if he takes refuge here?'. . 'Governments, proverbially, have long arms.' **1975** D. DUNNETT *Checkmate* V. x. 536 'I would ask you to be very careful. . in your doings when you return to Scotland. I have a long arm.' 'Monseigneur: you have no arm at all,' Lymond said, 'unless England allows you a sleeve for it.' ■ **justice and injustice; power**

kirtle *see* NEAR is my kirtle, but nearer is my smock.

kiss *see* an APPLE-PIE without some cheese is like a kiss without a squeeze.

KISSING goes by favour

□ **1616** T. DRAXE *Adages* 62 Kissing commeth by fauour. **1621** BURTON *Anatomy of Melancholy* II. iii. Offices are not alwaies given. . for worth. [*note*] Kissing goes by Favour. **1721** J. KELLY *Scottish Proverbs* 225 Kissing goes by Favour. Men shew Regard, or do Service, to People as they affect. **1880** BLACKMORE *Mary Anerley* II. iii. 'I should like. . to give you one kiss, Insie.'. . Before he could give reason in favour of a privilege which goes proverbially by favour, the young maid was gone. **1929** 'L. THAYER' *Dead Man's Shoes* i. Kissing goes by favour all along the line. **1976** K. BONFIGLIOLI *Something Nasty in Woodshed* xii. Tell you what, Jock; you forget to mention hot buttered crumpets to Mrs Mortdecai and I'll forget to mention about you pinching her caviare. Kissing goes by favour, you know. ■ **bribery and corruption**

kissing *see also* when the GORSE is out of bloom, kissing's out of fashion.

kitchen *see* if you don't like the HEAT, get out of the kitchen.

kitten *see* WANTON kittens make sober cats.

knew *see* if YOUTH knew, if age could.

knock *see* OPPORTUNITY never knocks twice at any man's door.

To KNOW all is to forgive all

Cf. **1807** MME DE STAËL *Corinne* III. XVIII. V. *tout comprendre rend très-indulgent*; also **1908** E. TERRY *Story of my Life* 116 I had taken a course for which all blamed me, perhaps because they did not know enough to pardon enough—*savoir tout c'est tout pardonner*.

□ **1864** R. H. HORNE *Prometheus the Fire-Bringer* 48 To know all, is to forgive. **1952** K. FULLER *Silken Cord* xv. After all, to know all is to forgive all, as my poor dear father used to say. **1974** 'H. CARMICHAEL' *Most Deadly Hate* xviii. 'They say to know all is to forgive all,' Piper said. 'Except the killing of Arthur Harlow.' ■ **forgiveness; tolerance**

You should KNOW a man seven years before you stir his fire

□ **1803** C. DIBDIN *Professional Life* I. p. xi. It is a well-meant saying, that you should know a man seven years before you stir his fire; or, in other words, before you venture at too much familiarity. **1904** V. S. LEAN *Collectanea* IV. 204 You may poke a man's fire after you've known him seven years, but not before. **1942** A. THIRKELL *Marling Hall* iii. 'Let me get you another drink,' said David, taking the glass. 'I know one ought to know people seven years to poke their fires, but I believe it's less for cocktails.' **1945** M. SARSFIELD *Green December Fills Graveyard* iv. 35 'I haven't known you ten years, or whatever the period is, but I'm going to poke your fire.' ■ **familiarity**

What you don't KNOW can't hurt you

□ **1576** G. PETTIE *Petit Palace* 168 Why should I seeke to take him in it? .. So long as I know it not, it hurteth mee not. **1908** E. WALTER *Easiest Way* III. 66 What a fellow doesn't know doesn't hurt him, and he'll love you just the same. **1979** 'S. WOODS' *This Fatal Writ* 54 'No, this *is* interesting. .. I didn't know—' 'What you don't know can't hurt you,' said Maitland. **1992** A. LAMBERT *Rather English Marriage* (1993) vi. 115 Everyone's entitled to their privacy and what you don't know can't hurt you. **2001** *Times* 23 Nov. 20 A little ignorance can go a long way. But what you don't know will always hurt you. Cleverness is the saving grace of our humanity. ■ **ignorance**

KNOW thyself

Cf. Gr. *γνῶθι σαυτόν* (or *σεαυτόν*), the motto inscribed on the 6th-cent. BC temple of Apollo at Delphi and quoted by several ancient writers (some attributing it to Solon): see esp. Pausanias x. 24 and Juvenal *Satires* xi; L. *nosce teipsum*.

□ **1387** J. TREVISA tr. *Higden's Polychronicon* (1865) I. 241 While the cherle smoot the victor, he schulde ofte seie to hym in this manere:.. Knowe thyself. **1545** R. ASCHAM *Toxophilus* II. 36 Knowe thy selfe: that is to saye, learne to knowe what thou arte able, fitte and apt vnto, and folowe that. **1732** POPE *Essay on Man* II. 1 Know then thyself, presume not God to scan; The proper study of Mankind is Man. **1849** BULWER-LYTTON *Caxtons* III. XVI. x. 'Know thyself,' said the old philosophy. 'Improve thyself,' saith the new. **2002** *Washington Times* 7 Feb. A21 The self-esteem movement is based on simple-minded shibboleths such as 'Love thyself,' rather than 'Know thyself.' ■ **human nature; wisdom**

You never KNOW what you can do till you try

□ **1818** COBBETT *Year's Residence in USA* II. vi. A man knows not what he can do 'till he tries. **1890** M. WILLIAMS *Leaves of Life* I. xiii. On hearing the verdict he.. shouted out: 'I told you so! You never know what you can do till you try'. **1968** D. FRANCIS *Forfeit* xiv. 'Ty, you aren't fit to drive.' 'Never know what you can do till you try.' ■ **boldness**

know *see also* BETTER the devil you know than the devil you don't know; one HALF of the world does not know how the other half lives; the HUSBAND is always the last to know; come LIVE with me and you'll know me; MORE people know Tom Fool than Tom Fool knows; NECESSITY knows no law; it TAKES one to know one; it's not WHAT you know, it's who you know; it is a WISE child that knows its own father; *see also* KNEW; KNOWN.

KNOWLEDGE is power

Similar in form to MONEY *is power* and similar in sentiment to PROVERBS xxiv. 5 (AV) A man of knowledge increaseth strength. Cf. **1597** BACON *De Haeresibus* x. *nam et ipsa scientia potestas est*, for knowledge itself is power.

□ **1598** in Bacon *Essays* 27V Knowledge it selfe is a power whereby he [God] knoweth. **1806** B. RUSH *Letter* 25 Nov. (1951) II. 935 The well-known aphorism that 'knowledge is power.' **1853** BULWER-LYTTON *My Novel* I. II. iii. He.. said half aloud,—'Well, knowledge is power!' **2002** *Washington Post* 11 Mar. A21 The assumption seems to be that if we can explain the powerful forces that control our lives, we become somehow immune to them. Knowledge, as they say, is power. ■ **power; wisdom**

knowledge *see also* a LITTLE knowledge is a dangerous thing.

known *see* a CARPENTER is known by his chips; a man is known by the COMPANY he keeps; the TREE is known by its fruit.

Who KNOWS most, speaks least

□ **1666** G. TORRIANO *Italian Proverbs* 189 Who knows most, speaks least. **1996** P. LOVESEY *Bloodhounds* xxi. 182 'Crafty old sod,' said Mr. Musgrave. .. 'What's the old saying? "Who knows most, speaks least."' ■ **speech and silence**

The LABOURER is worthy of his hire

With allusion to LUKE x. 7 (AV) The labourer is worthy of his hire.

□ *c* **1390** CHAUCER *Summoner's Tale* l. 1973 The hye God, that al this world hath wroght, Seith that the werkman worthy is his hyre. **1580** J. BARET *Alveary* D697 *Digna canis pabulo.* . . A Prouerbe declaring that the laborer is worthie of his hire: it is taken as well of the labour of the mind, as of the bodie. **1824** SCOTT *St. Ronan's Well* I. x. Your service will not be altogether gratuitous, my old friend—the labourer is worthy of his hire. **1980** *Times* 4 Mar. 7 Forget haggling. . . The labourer is worthy of his hire. **2001** R. HILL *Dialogues of Dead* ii. 11 Penn had no difficulty squaring his assertion that the labourer was worthy his hire with using Dee as his unpaid research assistant, but the librarian never complained. ■ **employers and employees; money; work**

ladder *see* CROSSES are ladders that lead to heaven.

lady *see* FAINT heart never won fair lady; FAR-FETCHED and dear-bought is good for ladies; the OPERA isn't over till the fat lady sings.

lamb *see* GOD tempers the wind to the shorn lamb; one might as well be HANGED for a sheep as a lamb; MARCH comes in like a lion, and goes out like a lamb.

Lancashire *see* what MANCHESTER says today, the rest of England says tomorrow.

Every LAND has its own law

□ *a* **1628** J. CARMICHAELL *Proverbs in Scots* no. 469 Everie land hes the laich. **1721** J. KELLY *Scottish Proverbs* 92 Every land hath its own Laugh, and every Corn its own Caff [chaff]. Every Country hath its own Laws, Customs, and Usages. **1916** *British Weekly* 2 Nov. 84 'Every land', says the old Scottish proverb, 'has its ain lauch.' And every class has its own mode of thought and expression. ■ **idiosyncrasy; national characteristics**

land *see also* you BUY land, you buy stones; when HOUSE and land are gone and spent, then learning is most excellent; LEARNING is better than house and land.

lane *see* it is a LONG lane that has no turning.

large *see* a GREAT book is a great evil; LITTLE pitchers have large ears.

lark *see* if the SKY falls we shall catch larks.

The LAST drop makes the cup run over

Similar in sense to the next proverb.

□ **1655** T. FULLER *Church Hist. Britain* XI. ii. When the Cup is brim full before, the last (though least) superadded drop is charged alone to be the cause of all the running over. **1855** H. G. BOHN *Hand-Book of Proverbs* 509 The last drop makes the cup run over. **1876** J. PAYN *Halves* I. x. An application of her brother-in-law for a five-pound note . . was the last drop that caused Mrs. Raeburn's cup of bitterness to overflow. **1888** C. M. YONGE *Beechcroft at Rockstone* I. i. Valetta burst out crying at this last drop that made the bucket overflow. ■ **excess**

It is the LAST straw that breaks the camel's back

The metaphor is also used allusively, especially in the phrase *the last straw.*

□ **1655** J. BRAMHALL *Defence of True Liberty of Human Actions* 54 It is the last feather may be said to break an Horses back. **1793** in *Publications of Colonial Society of Massachusetts* (1954) XXXVI. 298 It is certainly true that the last feather will sink the camel. **1848** DICKENS *Dombey & Son* ii. As the last straw breaks the laden camel's back, this piece of underground information crushed the sinking spirits of Mr. Dombey. **1876** I. BANKS *Manchester Man* III. xv. The last straw breaks the camel's back. **1940** 'J. J. CONNINGTON' *Four Defences* xiii. 'This final droplet turns the scale.' .. 'The last straw that breaks the camel's back?' condensed the Counsellor. **1983** R. BARNARD *Case of Missing Bronte* iii. 'This is the picture, as far as we have it,' he said, .. a sigh in his voice that suggested that the visit of the Prime Minister was the final straw that might break the camel's back of his professional equilibrium. ■ **excess**

last (noun) *see* let the COBBLER stick to his last; the COBBLER to his last and the gunner to his linstock.

last *see also* (adjective) there are no BIRDS in last year's nest; the HUSBAND is always the last to know; the THIRD time pays for all; (adverb) he LAUGHS best who laughs last; he who LAUGHS last, laughs longest.

lasting *see* FIRST impressions are the most lasting.

late *see* (adjective) the EARLY man never borrows from the late man; it is NEVER too late to learn; it is NEVER too late to mend; it is too late to shut the STABLE-door after the horse has bolted; (adverb) BETTER late than never.

LAUGH and the world laughs with you; weep and you weep alone

An alteration of the sentiment expressed by HORACE *Ars Poetica* 101 *ut ridentibus arrident, ita flentibus adsunt humani voltus*, men's faces laugh on those who laugh, and correspondingly weep on those who weep; cf. ROMANS xii. 15 (AV) Rejoice with them that do rejoice, and weep with them that weep.

□ **1883** E. W. WILCOX in *Sun* (New York) 25 Feb. 3 Laugh, and the world laughs with you; Weep, and you weep alone. For the sad old earth must borrow its mirth, But has trouble enough of its own. **1907** 'O. HENRY' *Trimmed Lamp* 211 Laugh, and the world laughs with you; weep, and they give you the laugh. **1912** 'SAKI' *Chronicle of Clovis* 127 The proverb 'Weep and you weep alone,' broke down as badly on application as most of its kind. **1997** *Oldie* Aug. 27 Laugh, said the little clown, and the world laughs with you. Cry but don't let anyone catch you at it! **2001** R. HILL *Dialogues of Dead* xviii. 153 'Right joker, this Wordman, ain't he? What's it they say? Laugh and the world laughs with you.' ■ **merriment**

Let them LAUGH that win

An older version of the next two proverbs.

□ **1546** J. HEYWOOD *Dialogue of Proverbs* I. v. B2 He laught that wynth. *a* **1596** G. PEELE *Clyomon & Clamides* F1 But I zay to you my nabor [neighbour] .. wel let them laugh that win. **1777** *Bonner & Middleton's Bristol Journal* 5 July 3 The old Proverb says, let them laugh that wins.—They glory over us, by saying that our Fund is almost exhausted—that is our look out not theirs. **1873** TROLLOPE *Phineas*

Redux I. xxxvii. 'You are laughing at me, I know.' 'Let them laugh that win.' ■ **success; winners and losers**

laugh *see also* JOVE but laughs at lovers' perjury; LOVE laughs at locksmiths.

He LAUGHS best who laughs last

See also the two adjacent proverbs. The 'French proverb' referred to in quot. 1822 is *rira bien qui rira le dernier*.

□ *c* **1607** *Christmas Prince* (1923) 109 Hee laugheth best that laugheth to the end. **1715** VANBRUGH *Country House* II. v. Does she play her jests upon me too!—but mum, he laughs best that laughs last. **1822** SCOTT *Peveril* IV. iii. Your Grace knows the French proverb, 'He laughs best who laughs last.' **1980** J. LINSSEN *Yellow Pages* lii. The mark of greatness is survival. He laughs best who laughs last. **1996** *Washington Post* 15 Jan. C2 This purchase . . was wildly out of character and the source of endless amusement to those who know me best. . . Well, in the immortal words of Sir John Vanbrugh (1664–1726): He laughs best who laughs last. ■ **revenge; winners and losers**

He who LAUGHS last, laughs longest

A modern development of the preceding proverb.

□ **1912** J. MASEFIELD *Widow in Bye Street* IV. 66 In this life he laughs longest who laughs last. **1943** J. LODWICK *Running to Paradise* xxx. He who laughs last laughs longest, and in another four days I was able to look at my mug in the mirror without wincing. **1951** M. DE LA ROCHE *Renny's Daughter* ix. 'We'll see. He who laughs last, laughs . .' So worked up was Eugene Clapperton that he could not recall the last word of the proverb. ■ **revenge; winners and losers**

LAUGHTER is the best medicine

The idea of the beneficial effects of laughter upon the health is an ancient one; e.g. PROVERBS xvii. 22 (AV) A merry heart doeth good like a medicine: but a broken spirit drieth the bones. Older English expressions of the concept include *laugh and be fat* (attested from 1596) and *laugh and be well* (1737); hence 'Laughter, the Best Medicine', the title of a long-running jokes feature in the *Reader's Digest*. Cf. *the best* DOCTORS *are Dr Diet, Dr Quiet, and Dr Merryman*.

□ **1992** MIEDER *Dict. American Proverbs* 362 Laughter is the best medicine. **2002** *Washington Post* 21 Jan. C10 Who could argue with the sage advice that an ounce of prevention is worth a pound of cure, . . or laughter is the best medicine? ■ **doctors; health; merriment**

One LAW for the rich and another for the poor

□ **1830** MARRYAT *King's Own* I. xi. Is there nothing smuggled besides gin? Now, if the husbands and fathers of these ladies,—those who have themselves enacted the laws,—wink at their *infringement*, why should not others do so? . . There cannot be one law for the rich and another for the poor. **1913** *Spectator* 8 Nov. 757 The idea prevails abroad that there is one law for the 'rich' Englishman and another for the 'poor' foreigner. **1944** A. THIRKELL *Headmistress* iv. 'You want one law for the people you think are rich and another law for the people you think are poor,' I said. 'Let me advise you to find out which are which before you make a fool of yourself.' **2001** *Spectator* 29 Dec. 48 If he gets community service and a suspended sentence the hustlers will be out in force screaming the old 'one law for the rich, another for the poor' chestnut. ■ **justice and injustice; law and lawyers**

law *see also* HARD cases make bad law; IGNORANCE of the law is no excuse for breaking it; every LAND has its own law; NECESSITY knows no law; NEW lords, new laws; POSSESSION is nine points of the law; SELF-preservation is the first law of nature.

The more LAWS, the more thieves and bandits

Attributed to Lao Tzu (*c* 604–*c* 531 BC): The more laws and orders are made prominent, The more thieves and bandits there will be (*Tao-te Ching* lvii. in Wing-Tsit Chan (ed.) *Source Book in Chinese Philosophy* (1963), 166. Cf. ARCESILAUS (3rd cent. BC): *Ὅπου νόμοι πλεῖστοι, ἐκεῖ καὶ ἀδικίαν εἶναι μεγίστην (ἔλεγε)* (in STOBAEUS *Florilegium* xliii. 91); and TACITUS *Annals* iii. 27 *Corruptissima republica plurimae leges*, the more corrupt the state the more numerous the laws.

□ **1573** J. SANFORDE *Garden of Pleasure* 4 Where there are many lawes, there be also or else haue ben many vices. *c* **1620** MIDDLETON & ROWLEY *World Tost at Tennis* (*Works* ed. Bullen VII. 176) The more laws you make The more knaves thrive by't. **1667** MILTON *Paradise Lost* xii. 283 So many Laws argue so many sins Among them. **1732** T. FULLER *Gnomologia* no. 4663 The more Laws the more offenders. **1766** O. GOLDSMITH *Vicar of Wakefield* xxvii. The multitude of laws produce new vices, and new vices call for fresh restraints. **2002** *Times* 19 Mar. 30 Citing the ancient Chinese Lao-tse's dictum, the more laws, the more thieves and bandits, Norberg insists that 'the commonest way of corupting a nation through and through is by stipulating permits and controls for production, for imports, for exports and investments'. ■ **honesty and dishonesty; law and lawyers**

A man who is his own LAWYER has a fool for his client

□ **1809** *Port Folio* (Philadelphia) Aug. 132 He who is always his own counseller will often have a fool for his client. **1850** L. HUNT *Autobiography* II. xi. The proprietor of the *Morning Chronicle* pleaded his own cause, an occasion in which a man is said to have 'a fool for his client'. **1911** *British Weekly* 21 Dec. 386 There is a popular impression, for which there is a good deal to be said, that a man who is his own lawyer has a fool for his client. **1975** D. BAGLEY *Snow Tiger* xiii. You must have heard the saying that the man who argues his own case has a fool for a lawyer. **2002** *Spectator* 30 Mar. 35 The man who is his own lawyer has a fool for a client, and that goes double for retired law lecturers from Newcastle Polytechnic. ■ **law and lawyers**

lawyer *see also* the DEVIL makes his Christmas pies of lawyers' tongues and clerks' fingers.

lay *see* it is easier to RAISE the Devil than to lay him.

LAY-OVERS for meddlers

An answer to an impertinent or inquisitive child and others. The expression is found chiefly in the north of England, and in the US. *Lay-overs*, also contracted to *layers* or *layors*, are light blows or smacks given to the meddlesome (but see also quot. 1854). Cf. **1699** B. E. *New Dict. Canting Crew* s.v. *Lare-over*, said when the true name of the thing must (in decency) be concealed.

□ **1785** F. GROSE *Classical Dict. Vulgar Tongue* s.v. *Lareovers, Lareovers for medlers*, an answer frequently given to children . . as a rebuke for their impertinent curiosity. **1854** A. E. BAKER *Glossary of Northamptonshire Words & Phrases* I. 389 *Lay-o'ers-for-meddlers*, . . a contraction of *lay-overs*, *i.e.* things *laid over*, covered up, or protected from meddlers. **1882** NODAL & MILNER *Glossary of Lancashire Dialect* 179 'What have yo' getten i' that bag?' 'Layers-for-meddlers—does ta want to know?' **1936**

M. MITCHELL *Gone with Wind* xxxii. When they asked who was going to lend the money she said: 'Layovers catch meddlers,' so archly they all laughed. **1945** B. MILLHAUSER *Whatever goes Up* xv. 'Know his address?' 'I certainly do. Ninety-seven Gramercy Park North, New York.' She closed the door firmly. 'Layovers for meddlers,' she muttered. ■ **busybodies**; **curiosity**

lazy *see* LONG and lazy, little and loud.

lead *see* when the BLIND lead the blind, both shall fall into the ditch; CROSSES are ladders that lead to heaven; all ROADS lead to Rome.

leak *see* LITTLE leaks sink the ship.

leap *see* LOOK before you leap.

learn *see* LIVE and learn; it is NEVER too late to learn; NEVER too old to learn; we must learn to WALK before we can run; don't go near the WATER until you learn how to swim.

LEARNING is better than house and land

Similar in sentiment to *when* HOUSE *and land are gone and spent, then learning is most excellent.*

□ **1773** D. GARRICK in Goldsmith *She stoops to Conquer* A3V When ign'rance enters, folly is at hand; Learning is better far than house and land. **1800** M. EDGEWORTH *Castle Rackrent* 19 I.. thanked my stars I was not born a gentleman to so much toil and trouble—but Sir Murtagh took me up short with his old proverb, 'learning is better than house or land.' **1859** J. R. PLANCHÉ *Love & Fortune* 8 'Learning is better than house and land.' A fact that I never could understand. ■ **learning**; **property**

learning *see also* when HOUSE and land are gone and spent, then learning is most excellent; a LITTLE knowledge is a dangerous thing; there is no ROYAL road to learning.

LEAST said, soonest mended

□ *c* **1460** in W. C. Hazlitt *Remains of Early Popular Poetry* (1864) III. 169 Who sayth lytell he is wyse..And fewe wordes are soone amend. **1555** J. HEYWOOD *Two Hundred Epigrams* no. 169 Lyttle sayde, soone amended. *a* **1641** D. FERGUSSON *Scottish Proverbs* (STS) no. 946 Littl said is soon mended. **1776** T. COGAN *John Buncle, Junior* I. vi. Mum's the word; least said is soonest mended. **1818** SCOTT *Heart of Midlothian* I. vi. A fine preaching has he been at the night.. but maybe least said is sunest mended. **1960** MISS READ *Fresh from Country* xii. A quiet word..should.. stop any further tale-bearing, and I really think it's a case of 'least said, soonest mended.' **1992** A. LAMBERT *Rather English Marriage* (1993) xvii. 289 He was tempted to go down and confront her,..but he knew he was in the wrong. Least said, soonest mended: no good creating a fuss now. ■ **discretion**; **speech and silence**; **tact**

least *see also* IDLE people have the least leisure; who KNOWS most, speaks least.

There is nothing like LEATHER

Also used literally.

□ **1692** R. L'ESTRANGE *Fables of Aesop* cccxlviii. There was a council of mechanics called to advise about the fortifying of a city. ..Up starts a currier [a person who dressed and coloured leather]; Gentlemen, says he, when y'ave said all that can be said, there's nothing in the world like leather. **1837** F. PALGRAVE *Merchant & Friar*

iv. King Log [the birch] was..forgotten. ..'Depend upon it, Sir, there is nothing like leather.' **1892** I. ZANGWILL *Big Bow Mystery* vi. Besides, meat might have reminded him too much of his work. There is nothing like leather, but Bow beefsteaks occasionally come very near it. **1909** *Votes for Women* 22 Oct. 63 Nothing like leather for Suffragettes' wear.—Miss M. Roberta Mills makes Ties, Bags, Belts, [etc.]. **1935** V. S. PRITCHETT (*title*) Nothing like leather. **1937** C. ST. JOHN SPRIGG *Six Queer Things* v. 115 Morgan had a leathery mind. There was no subtlety or sharpness about it, but it was tough. ..No amount of discouragement or error wore it out. There is nothing like leather. ■ **strength and weakness**

leave *see* LET well alone.

leg *see* there goes more to MARRIAGE than four bare legs in a bed; everyone STRETCHES his legs according to the length of his coverlet.

leisure *see* the BUSIEST men have the most leisure; IDLE people have the least leisure; there is LUCK in leisure; MARRY in haste and repent at leisure.

lemon *see* if LIFE hands you lemons, make lemonade.

LEND your money and lose your friend

□ **1474** CAXTON *Game of Chess* (1883) III. iv. 112 And herof speketh Domas the philosopher and sayth that my frende borrowed money of me And I haue lost my frende and my money attones [simultaneously]. **1600–1** SHAKESPEARE *Hamlet* I. iii. 75 Neither a borrower nor a lender be; For loan oft loses both itself and friend. **1721** J. KELLY *Scottish Proverbs Lend your Money, and lose your Friend.* It is not the lending of our Money that loses our Friend; but the demanding it again. **1960** H. SLESAR *Enter Murderers* xiii. You know what they say about lending money, it's a sure way to lose friends. ■ **borrowing and lending; friends.**

lend *see also* DISTANCE lends enchantment to the view.

lender *see* neither a BORROWER nor a lender be.

LENGTH begets loathing

□ **1742** C. JARVIS *Don Quixote* II. II. ix. The rest I omit, because length begets loathing. *a* **1895** F. LOCKER-LAMPSON *My Confidences* (1896) 43 'Length begets loathing.' I well remember the sultry Sunday evenings when..we simmered through Mr. Shepherd's long-winded pastorals. ■ **brevity and long-windedness**

length *see also* everyone STRETCHES his legs according to the length of his coverlet.

lengthen *see* as the DAY lengthens, so the cold strengthens.

The LEOPARD does not change his spots

With allusion to JEREMIAH xiii. 23 (AV) Can the Ethiopian change his skin, or the leopard his spots? A L. equivalent to this proverb is *lupus pilum mutat, non mentem*, the wolf changes his coat, not his nature.

□ **1546** J. BALE *First Examination of Anne Askewe* 38 Their olde condycyons wyll they change, whan the blackemoreæne change hys skynne, and the catte of the mountayne [leopard] her spottes. **1596** SHAKESPEARE *Richard II* I. i. 174 Rage must be withstood. ..Lions make leopards tame.—Yea, but not change his spots. **1869** A. HENDERSON *Latin Proverbs* 317 *Pardus maculas non deponit*, a leopard does not change his spots. **1979** J. SCOTT *Clutch of Vipers* iv. He always was a dirty old man..and the leopard doesn't change his spots. **1997** *Washington Times* 24 July

C16 Although he swears he has changed, leopards don't usually change their spots, especially those who don't cooperate in counseling. ■ **change; human nature**

LESS is more

□ **1855** R. BROWNING *Andrea del Sarto* l. 78 in *Poems* (1981) I. 645 Well, less is more, Lucrezia: I am judged. **1947** P. JOHNSON *Mies van der Rohe* 49 As in architecture, [Mies] has always been guided by his personal motto, 'less is more.' **1984** O. BANKS *Caravaggio Obsession* III. iii. Anyway, he spent years furnishing it with precious, ornamental works of art. This was in the twenties and thirties, when 'less is more' was the golden rule. **1989** *Time* 20 Feb. 108 What Chiat and his associates seem to be betting on is that there is a mass market of low-income, style-conscious people who have grasped the hip message that less is more. **2001** *Washington Times* 3 Aug. A17 It was as if the pink flamingos had been taken off a Florida lawn, the sequins off Dolly Parton's cowgirl costume, the fins off a '50s Cadillac .. There are times when less is blessedly more. ■ **moderation**

less *see also* of two EVILS choose the less; more HASTE, less speed.

LET well alone

Well is normally considered here as a noun ('what is well'), rather than an adverb. The proverb is also frequently found in the form *leave well alone*.

□ *c* **1570** *Scoggin's Jests* (1626) 76 The shomaker thought to make his house greater. ..They pulled downe foure or fiue postes of the house. ..Why said Scoggin, when it was well you could not let it alone. **1740** G. CHEYNE *Essay on Regimen* p. xxxvi. When a Person is tolerably well, and is subject to no painful or dangerous Distemper, I think it his Duty..to *let Well alone*. **1822** M. EDGEWORTH *Letter* 12 Jan. (1971) 317 Joanna quoted to me the other day an excellent proverb applied to health: 'Let well alone.' **1829** T. L. PEACOCK *Misfortunes of Elphin* ii. This immortal work..will stand for centuries. ..It is well: it works well: let well alone. **1985** R. R. IRVINE *Ratings are Murder* xx. I don't think it's ever a good idea to tamper with tradition. Leave well enough alone, I say. **2002** *Washington Post* 17 May B6 From what I can tell, most people are members of the 'Let's Leave Well Enough Alone' and 'If It Ain't Broke, Don't Fix It' clubs. ■ **busybodies; content and discontent**

let *see also* let the COBBLER stick to his last; let the DEAD bury the dead; let them LAUGH that win; LIVE and let live; let SLEEPING dogs lie; SPARE at the spigot, and let out at the bung-hole; never let the SUN go down on your anger.

leveller *see* DEATH is the great leveller.

A LIAR ought to have a good memory

Cf. QUINTILIAN *Institutio Oratoria* IV. ii. *mendacem memorem esse oportet*, a liar ought to have a good memory.

□ *a* **1542** T. WYATT in *Poetical Works* (1858) p. xxxvii. They say, 'He that will lie well must have a good remembrance, that he agree in all points with himself, lest he be spied.' *c* **1690** R. SOUTH *Twelve Sermons* (1722) IV. 167 Indeed, a very rational Saying, That a lyar ought to have a good Memory. **1721** J. KELLY *Scottish Proverbs* 50 A Lyar should have a good Memory. Lest he tell the same Lye different ways. **1945** F. THOMPSON *Lark Rise* xiii. 'A liar ought to have a good memory,' they would say. **1999** C. HITCHENS *No One Left To Lie To* (2000) i. 19 Just as the necessary qualification for a good liar is a good memory, so the essential equipment of a would-be lie detector is a good timeline, and a decent archive. ■ **lying**

libel *see* the GREATER the truth, the greater the libel.

lick *see* if you can't BEAT them, join them.

A LIE is halfway round the world before the truth has got its boots on

The speed with which falsehood travels was a classical commonplace; e.g. VIRGIL *Aeneid* iv. 174 *Fama, malum qua non aliud velocius alium*, Rumour, than whom no other evil thing is faster. This whole passage was imitated by Shakespeare in the Induction to *Henry IV, Pt. 2* (1597–8).

□ **1859** C. H. SPURGEON *Gems from Spurgeon* 74 It is well said in the old proverb, 'a lie will go round the world while truth is pulling its boots on'. **1996** *National Review* 6 May 6 'A lie is halfway round the world before the truth has got its boots on.' But, eventually, truth gets booted and spurred, and the lie gets a good licking. **2002** *Times* 21 Feb. 3 It is often said that a lie can get round the world quicker than the truth can get its shoes on. For Stephen McPherson, it was quicker than he could get his clothes on. ■ **rumour; truth**

If you LIE down with dogs, you will get up with fleas

An assertion that human failings, such as dishonesty and foolishness, are contagious. Cf. L. *qui cum canibus concumbunt cum pulicibus surgent*, they who lie with dogs will rise with fleas.

□ **1573** J. SANFORDE *Garden of Pleasure* 103V *Chi va dormir con i cani, si leua con i pulici.* He that goeth to bedde wyth Dogges, aryseth with fleas. **1640** G. HERBERT *Outlandish Proverbs* no. 343 Hee that lies with the dogs, riseth with fleas. **1721** J. KELLY *Scottish Proverbs* 129 He that sleeps with Dogs, must rise with Fleas. If you keep Company with base and unworthy Fellows, you will get some Ill by them. **1791** 'P. PINDAR' *Rights of Kings* 32 To this great truth, a Universe agrees, 'He who lies down with dogs, will rise with fleas'. **1842** C. J. LEVER *Jack Hinton* xxii. If you lie down with dogs, you'll get up with fleas, and that's the fruits of travelling with a fool. **1991** *Spectator* 9 Nov. 8 I have few genial feelings towards the *Sunday Times*, and it is possible that I was thinking of its editor when I wrote .. of the danger that those who lie with dogs will rise with fleas. **1996** *Washington Post* 26 Feb. B2 [W]e do well to bear in mind three axioms so hoary that their essential truth may no longer be adequately grasped. The first is 'He who lies down with dogs rises with fleas.' ■ **associates**

lie *see also* (noun) ASK no questions and hear no lies; HALF the truth is often a whole lie; (verb) as you MAKE your bed, so you must lie upon it; as a TREE falls, so shall it lie; TRUTH lies at the bottom of a well.

LIFE begins at forty

□ **1932** W. B. PITKIN *Life Begins at Forty* i. Life begins at forty. This is the revolutionary outcome of our New Era. .. Today it is half a truth. Tomorrow it will be an axiom. **1945** *Zionist Review* 14 Dec. 6 Among Palestine pioneers, life does not 'begin at forty'. **1952** 'M. COST' *Hour Awaits* 142 Life begins at forty. .. I know you're only in your thirties, but it leaves a nice margin. **1990** J. R. McCAHERY *Grave Undertaking* v. Life begins at forty, she reminded herself—give or take a couple of years. ■ **life; middle age**

If LIFE hands you lemons, make lemonade

□ **1996** F. POPCORN *Clicking* iii. 408 And a little stand by-the-side-of-the-road is a good spot to learn from a wise saying: If life hands you lemons, make lemonade.

But, we'd like to add, then market it, franchise it, and sell it to a major international conglomerate as a fresh fruit drink. **2000** *New York Times Mag.* 8 Oct. 57 (*advertisement*) As a family, the Upshaws have developed a unique capacity, as Martha puts it, to make 'lemonade out of lemons'—an attitude that has helped her to remain grounded. **2002** *Washington Post* 5 April C10 You are the perfect example of the adage 'When life hands you a lemon, make lemonade.' Not only have you strengthened your marriage, you have discovered new interests. ■ **adversity**

LIFE isn't all beer and skittles

Life is not unalloyed pleasure or relaxation.

□ **1855** T. C. HALIBURTON *Nature & Human Nature* I. ii. 'This life ain't all beer and skittles.' Many a time.. when I am disappointed sadly I say that saw over. **1857** T. HUGHES *Tom Brown's Schooldays* I. ii. Life isn't all beer and skittles. **1931** A. CHRISTIE *Sittaford Mystery* xxvi. 'It's an experience, isn't it?' 'Teach him life can't be all beer and skittles,' said Robert Gardner maliciously. **1985** B. J. MORISON *Beer & Skittles* iii. ' "Life," as the saying goes,' he solemnly informed Persis, ' "is not all beer and skittles." ' ■ **life**

While there's LIFE there's hope

Cf. THEOCRITUS *Idyll* iv. 42 ἐλπίδες ἐν ζωοῖσιν, there's hope among the living; CICERO *Ad Atticum* IX. x. *dum anima est, spes esse dicitur*, as the saying is, while there's life there's hope; also ECCLESIASTES ix. 4 (see *a* LIVE *dog is better than a dead lion*). A more succinct L. version *dum spiro, spero*, while I breathe I hope, is part of the motto of South Carolina.

□ **1539** R. TAVERNER tr. *Erasmus' Adages* 36^{v} The sycke person whyle he hath lyfe, hath hope. **1670** J. RAY *English Proverbs* 113 While there's life, there's hope, he cry'd; Then why such haste? so groan'd and dy'd. **1868** READE & BOUCICAULT *Foul Play* I. xi. They lost, for a few moments, all idea of escaping. But.. 'while there's life there's hope.' **1939** C. H. B. KITCHIN *Death of his Uncle* v. But so far it's only the poor gentleman's clothes that have been found, isn't it? I mean, while there's life there's hope. **1996** *Washington Times* 29 Jan. C14 I will be pleasantly surprised if corporate America acts on your 'wake-up call'—but where there's life there's hope. ■ **life; optimism**

life *see also* ART is long and life is short; the BEST things in life are free; a DOG is for life..; if you would be HAPPY for a week take a wife; my SON is my son till he gets him a wife, but my daughter's my daughter all the days of her life; VARIETY is the spice of life.

lift *see* a RISING tide lifts all boats.

LIGHT come, light go

Less often heard than EASY *come, easy go*. Cf. late 14th-cent. Fr. [*argent*] *legierement vous sont venu et legierement sont perdu*, [money] comes to you lightly and is lightly lost.

□ c **1390** CHAUCER *Pardoner's Tale* l. 781 And lightly as it comth, so wol we spende. *a* **1475** J. FORTESCUE *Works* (1869) I. 489 For thyng that lightly cometh, lightly goeth. **1546** J. HEYWOOD *Dialogue of Proverbs* II. ix. L1 Lyght come lyght go. **1712** J. ARBUTHNOT *John Bull still in his Senses* iv. A thriftless Wretch, spending the Goods and Gear that his Fore-Fathers won with the Sweet of their Brows; light come, light go. **1861** C. READE *Cloister & Hearth* II. x. Our honest customers are the thieves. ..With them and with their purses 'tis lightly come, and lightly go.

1937 G. HEYER *They found Him Dead* iv. He was a bad husband to her. Light come light go. ■ **getting and spending**

light *see also* (adjective) MANY hands make light work; (verb) BETTER to light one candle . .

LIGHTING never strikes the same place twice

□ **1857** P. H. MYERS *Prisoner of Border* xii. They did not hit me at all. . . Lightning never strikes twice in the same place, nor cannon balls either, I presume. **1942** P. WILDE *Tinsley's Bones* x. The Witness: They say that lightning never strikes twice in the same place. Mr Blodgett: It don't because the second time the place ain't there. **1979** M. YORK *Death in Account* x. His bank had been raided the moment his back had been turned. 'Well, lighting never strikes the same place twice. . . I expect we'll be safe enough now.' **2001** M. DAHL *Viking Claw* viii. 59 'You gave us our disaster for the climb,' he said. 'Most climbs have only one disaster, so now we are good for the rest of the trip.' 'Like lightning never strikes twice, eh?' said Roobick. ■ **misfortune**

LIKE breeds like

Traits in a person's character are reinforced by associating with similar people: e.g. PSALMS xviii. 25–6 (BCP) With the holy thou shalt be holy: and with a perfect man thou shalt be perfect. With the clean thou shalt be clean: and with the froward thou shalt learn frowardness.

□ **1557** R. EDGEWORTH *Sermons* 178[v] Wyth a frowarde [evilly disposed] synner, a man shall be naughtye [wicked] . . for lyke maketh like. *c* **1577** *Misogonus* 2[v] The like bredes the like (eche man sayd). **1842** TENNYSON *Poems* (1969) 703 Like men, like manners: Like breeds like, they say. **1931** 'D. FROME' *Strange Death of Martin Green* xiv. Murder is an awfully bad thing for anybody to get away with, even once. Like breeds like. **1969** A. P. HANNUM *Look back with Love* xxv. The Richard saga seemed . . summed up in her grandfather's words . . 'Like begets like in spite of the Devil.' ■ **similarity and dissimilarity**

LIKE will to like

Cf. HOMER *Odyssey* xvii. 218 *ὡς αἰεὶ τὸν ὁμοῖον ἄγει θεὸς ὡς τὸν ὁμοῖον*, the god always brings like to like; CICERO *De Senectute* III. vii. *pares autem vetere proverbio cum paribus facillime congregantur*, according to the old proverb equals most easily mix together; early 14th-cent. Fr. *lung semblable quiert lautre*, one like thing seeks another. Cf. BIRDS *of a feather flock together*.

□ *a* **1400** *Legends of Saints* (STS) I. 226 In proverbe I haf hard say That lyk to lyk drawis ay. *c* **1450** *Proverbs of Good Counsel* in *Book of Precedence* (EETS) 70 This proverbe dothe specify, 'Lyke wyll to lyke in eche company'. **1648** HERRICK *Hesperides* 378 Like will to like, each Creature loves his kinde. **1822** SCOTT *Peveril* II. ii. How could I help it? like will to like—the boy would come—the girl would see him. **1855** T. C. HALIBURTON *Nature & Human Nature* I. xi. Jessie had a repugnance to the union. . . 'Jessie . . nature, instead of forbiddin' it approves of it; for like takes to like.' **1922** S. J. WEYMAN *Ovington's Bank* xxxi. He's learned this at your d—d counter, sir! That's where it is. It's like to like. **1981** R. BARNARD *Mother's Boys* xiv. Mrs. Hodsden's connection with his house will be quite plain to you when you meet my husband. Like clings to like, they say. . . And those two certainly cling. ■ **similarity and dissimilarity**

like *see also* (adjective) like FATHER, like son; like MASTER, like man; like

MOTHER, like daughter; like PEOPLE, like priest; (verb) if you don't like the HEAT, get out of the kitchen.

linen *see* never CHOOSE your women or your linen by candlelight; one does not WASH one's dirty linen in public.

lining *see* every CLOUD has a silver lining.

link *see* a CHAIN is no stronger than its weakest link.

linstock (a forked staff to hold a lighted match): *see* the COBBLER to his last and the gunner to his linstock.

lion *see* a LIVE dog is better than a dead lion; MARCH comes in like a lion, and goes out like a lamb; a MOUSE may help a lion.

lip *see* there's MANY a slip between cup and lip.

LISTENERS never hear any good of themselves

Eavesdroppers is now very usual for *listeners*.

□ **1647** *Mercurius Elencticus* 26 Jan.–2 Feb. 76 The old Proverb is, Hearkners never heare good of them selves. **1678** J. RAY *English Proverbs* (ed. 2) 75 Listners ne'er hear good of themselves. **1839** DICKENS *Nicholas Nickleby* xlii. 'If it is fated that listeners are never to hear any good of themselves,' said Mrs. Browdie, 'I can't help it, and I am very sorry for it.' **1881** J. C. HARRIS *Uncle Remus* x. Brer Fox wuz stannin' at de back do' wid one year at de cat-hole lissenin'. Eave-drappers don't hear no good er deyse'f, en de way Brer Fox was 'bused dat day wuz a caution. **1907** E. NESBIT *Enchanted Castle* v. He..opened the door suddenly, and there..was Eliza. ..'You know what listeners never hear,' said Jimmy severely. **1977** A. NEWMAN *Evil Streak* IV. 178 They say listeners never hear any good of themselves but there is no excuse for..ingratitude. **1992** A. LAMBERT *Rather English Marriage* (1993) xvii. 289 'Eavesdroppers never hear good of themselves,' Grace would have said, and she'd have been right. ■ **eavesdroppers**

There is no LITTLE enemy

Cf. *c* **1386** CHAUCER *Tale of Melibee* l. 1322 Ne be nat necligent to kepe thy persone, nat oonly fro thy gretteste enemys, but fro thy leeste enemy. Senek seith: 'A man that is well avysed, he dredeth his leste enemy.'

□ **1659** J. HOWELL *Proverbs* 8 There's no enemy little, viz. we must not undervalue any foe. **1733** B. FRANKLIN *Poor Richard's Almanack* (Sept.) There is no little enemy. **1887** J. LUBBOCK *Pleasures of Life* I. v. To be friendly with every one is another matter; we must remember that there is no little enemy. ■ **enemies; malice**

LITTLE fish are sweet

□ **1830** R. FORBY *Vocabulary of East Anglia* 434 'Little fish are sweet.'—It means small gifts are always acceptable. **1914** K. F. PURDON *Folk of Furry Farm* vii. 'They'll sell at a loss,' he went on, with a sigh, 'but sure, little fish is sweet! and the rent has to be made up.' **1981** J. BINGHAM *Brock* 92 Wealthy proprietor of the *Melford Echo* and three or four small newspapers in the country. ('Little fish are sweet, old boy.') ■ **great and small**

A LITTLE knowledge is a dangerous thing

The *Pierian spring* in quot. 1711 refers to the classical tradition that the Muses were born in the Pieria region of northern Greece. The original *learning* is also used instead of *knowledge*.

□ **1711** POPE *Essay on Criticism* l. 215 A little Learning is a dang'rous Thing; Drink deep, or taste not the Pierian Spring. **1829** P. EGAN *Boxiana* 2nd Ser. II. 4 The sensible idea, that 'A little learning is a dangerous thing!' **1881** T. H. HUXLEY *Science & Culture* iv. If a little knowledge is dangerous, where is the man who has so much as to be out of danger? **1974** T. SHARPE *Porterhouse Blue* xviii. His had been an intellectual decision founded on his conviction that if a little knowledge was a dangerous thing, a lot was lethal. **2002** *Washington Post* 14 Jan. D9 If a little knowledge is a dangerous thing, then extensive-but-incomplete knowledge is a constant torment. ■ **ignorance; learning**

LITTLE leaks sink the ship

□ **1616** T. ADAMS *Taming of Tongue* 28 in *Sacrifice of Thankefulnesse* It is a little leake that drowneth a shippe. **1642** T. FULLER *Holy State* I. viii. If servants presume to dispose small things without their masters allowance (besides that many little leaks may sink a ship) this will widen their consciences to give away greater. **1745** B. FRANKLIN *Poor Richard's Almanack* (Jan.) Beware of little Expences; a small leak will sink a great ship. **1809** L. DOW *Chain of Lorenzo* 60 Methinks none will make that reply, but those who love and plead for a *little* sin; one leak will *sink* a ship. **1927** M. P. SHIEL *How Old Woman got Home* II. xiii. 'Don't mind spending a few pounds for me: you won't miss it.' .. 'Won't miss it. .. I don't know so much about that: it's the little leaks sink the ship.' **2002** *Washington Post* 17 March H9 I sweat the small stuff. Ben Franklin wrote: 'Beware of little expenses; a small leak will sink a great ship.' ■ **great and small**

LITTLE pitchers have large ears

Children overhear much that is not meant for them. A pitcher's *ears* are its handles.

□ **1546** J. HEYWOOD *Dialogue of Proverbs* II. v. G4^V Auoyd your children, small pitchers haue wide eares. **1594** SHAKESPEARE *Richard III* II. iv. 37 Good madam, be not angry with the child.—Pitchers have ears. **1699** B. E. *New Dict. Canting Crew* s.v. Pitcher-bawd, Little Pitchers have large ears. **1840** R. H. BARHAM *Ingoldsby Legends* 1st Ser. 226 A truth Insisted on much in my earlier years, To wit, 'Little pitchers have very long ears!' **1972** A. PRICE *Colonel Butler's Wolf* i. He watched her shoo her sisters safely away. .. He had been lamentably careless in forgetting that little pitchers had large ears. **2002** *Washington Times* 10 Feb. D2 Are you familiar with the old saying, 'Little pitchers have big ears'? Conversations .. within your son's hearing about your problems or about the problems you're having with him will affect his behavior negatively. ■ **eavesdroppers**

A LITTLE pot is soon hot

A small person is easily roused to anger or passion.

□ **1546** J. HEYWOOD *Dialogue of Proverbs* I. xi. D2 It is wood [mad] at a woorde, little pot soone whot. **1593** SHAKESPEARE *Taming of Shrew* IV. i. 6 Now were not I a little pot and soon hot, my very lips might freeze to my teeth. **1670** J. RAY *English Proverbs* 115 A little pot's soon hot. .. Little persons are commonly cholerick. **1884** C. READE *Perilous Secret* II. xv. Cheeky little beggar, But .. 'a little pot is soon hot.' **1930** R. K. WEEKES *Mignonette* xxiii. 'Oh well,' she quite obviously swallowed down her grievance, still simmering, 'I suppose you'll say little pots are soon hot.' ■ **anger; great and small**

LITTLE strokes fell great oaks

Cf. ERASMUS *Adages* I. viii. *multis ictibus deiicitur quercus*, the oak is felled by many blows.

□ *c* **1400** *Romaunt of Rose* l. 3688 For no man at the firste strok Ne may nat felle down an ok. **1539** R. TAVERNER tr. *Erasmus' Adages* 26V Wyth many strokes is an oke ouerthrowen. Nothyng is so stronge but that lyttell and lyttell maye be brought downe. **1591** SHAKESPEARE *Henry VI, Pt. 3* II. i. 54 And many strokes, though with a little axe, Hews down and fells the hardest-timber'd oak. By many hands your father was subdu'd. **1757** B. FRANKLIN *Poor Richard Improved: 1758* (Mar.) Stick to it steadily and you will see great Effects; for..Little Strokes fell great Oaks. **1869** C. H. SPURGEON *John Ploughman's Talk* xxii. 'By little strokes Men fell great oaks.' By a spadeful at a time the navvies digged..the embankment. **1981** *Family Circle* Feb. 57 From the cradle to the grave we are reminded that.. great oaks are only felled by a repetition of little strokes. ■ **great and small**

LITTLE thieves are hanged, but great ones escape

Cf. late 14th-cent. Fr. *les petits larrons sont penduez, non pas les grands*, little thieves are hanged, not big ones.

□ **1639** J. CLARKE *Parœmiologia Anglo-Latina* 172 Little theeves are hang'd, but great ones escape. **1979** *Daily Telegraph* 22 Nov. 18 In view of the Blunt affair, I am reminded of the proverb, 'Little thieves are hanged but great ones escape.' ■ **great and small; justice and injustice; wrong-doers**

LITTLE things please little minds

Cf. OVID *Ars Amatoria* I. 159 *parva leves capiunt animos*, small things enthral light minds.

□ **1576** G. PETTIE *Petit Palace* 139 A litle thyng pleaseth a foole. **1584** LYLY *Sappho & Phao* II. iv. Litle things catch light mindes. **1845** DISRAELI *Sybil* II. ii. Little things affect little minds. Lord Marney..was kept at the station which aggravated his spleen. **1880** C. H. SPURGEON *John Ploughman's Pictures* 81 Precious little is enough to make a man famous in certain companies..for..little things please little minds. **1963** D. LESSING *Man & Two Women* 74 Small things amuse small minds. **1973** *Galt Toy Catalogue* 35 As the saying goes—Little things please little minds. ■ **great and small**

little *see also* (adjective) BIG fish eat little fish; BIG fleas have little fleas upon their backs to bite them; BIRDS in their little nests agree; little BIRDS that can sing and won't sing must be made to sing; EVERY little helps; GREAT oaks from little acorns grow; LONG and lazy, little and loud; MANY a little makes a mickle; MUCH cry and little wool; (adverb) LOVE me little, love me long.

LIVE and learn

□ *c* **1620** in *Roxburghe Ballads* (1871) I. 60 A man may liue and learne. **1771** SMOLLETT *Humphry Clinker* III. 168 'Tis a true saying, live and learn—O woman, what chuckling and changing have I seen! **1894** J. LUBBOCK *Use of Life* vi. No doubt we go on learning as long as we live: 'Live and learn,' says the old proverb. **1984** J. MINAHAN *Great Diamond Robbery* xi. 'Y' want *steins*, gov, go to Germany; 'ere we only got *pints*.' Live and learn. **2002** *Washington Times* 17 May C12 Live and learn. That has become something of a mantra for mutual fund investors. ■ **experience**

LIVE and let live

□ **1622** G. DE MALYNES *Ancient Law-Merchant* I. xlv. According to the Dutche prouerbe..Leuen ende laeten leuen, To liue and to let others liue. **1641** D. FERGUSSON *Scottish Proverbs* (STS) no. 582 Live and let live. **1678** J. RAY *English Proverbs* (ed. 2) 170 Live and let live, *i.e.* Do as you would be done by. Let such pennyworths as your Tenants may live under you. **1762** SMOLLETT *Sir Launcelot*

Greaves II. xvi. He deals very little in physic stuff, . . whereby he can't expect the pothecary to be his friend. You knows, master, one must live and let live, as the saying is. **1843** SURTEES *Handley Cross* II. vii. Live and let live, as the criminal said to the hangman. **1979** C. BRAND *Rose in Darkness* iv. Not that Sari cared two hoots how other people conducted their private lives. Live and let live. **2001** *Washington Times* 30 Aug. A19 Live and let live is a pretty good philosophy. If the guy in the next lane isn't buckled up, why not leave him alone? ■ **tolerance**

If you want to LIVE and thrive, let the spider run alive

□ **1867** *Notes & Queries* 3rd Ser. XI. 32 The proverb so often used in Kent: 'He who would wish to thrive Must let spiders run alive.' **1903** V. S. LEAN *Collectanea* II. 204 He that would thrive Must let spiders live. **1957** H. P. BECK *Folklore of Maine* iv. If you want to live and thrive let the spider run alive. ■ **superstition**

A LIVE dog is better than a dead lion

With allusion to ECCLESIASTES ix. 4 (AV) To him that is joined to all the living, there is hope: for a living dog is better than a dead lion.

□ *c* **1390** in *Minor Poems of Vernon MS* (EETS) 534 Better is a quick [living] and an hol hounde Then a ded lyon . . And better is pouert with godnes Then richesse with wikkedness. **1566** J. BARTHLET *Pedigree of Heretics* 2V A lyuing Dogge, is better than a dead Lion. **1798** 'P. PINDAR' *Tales of Hoy* 41 It was a devil of a trick . . but, 'A living Dog is better than a dead Lion,' as the saying is. **1864** TROLLOPE *Can You forgive Her?* II. vii. He had so often told the widow that care killed the cat, and that a live dog was better than a dead lion. **1928** D. H. LAWRENCE *Woman who rode Away* 132 When the lion is shot, the dog gets the spoil. So he had come in for Katherine, Alan's lioness. A live dog is better than a dead lion. **1953** 'G. CULLINGFORD' *Post Mortem* iv. I take my walks without following a ball about like a dog. Which reminds me of the old proverb that a live dog is better than a dead lion. ■ **great and small; life**

They that LIVE longest, see most

Cf. early 14th-cent. Fr. *qui vit trop voit*, he who lives [long] sees much; **1605–6** SHAKESPEARE *King Lear* v. iii. 325 We that are young Shall never see so much nor live so long.

□ **1620** T. SHELTON tr. *Cervantes' Don Quixote* II. lii. My Mother was vsed to say, That 'twas needfull to liue long, to see much. **1837** T. HOOK *Jack Brag* III. ii. Them as lives longest sees the most. **1961** N. LOFTS *House at Old Vine* VI. vi. Them that live longest see most. You remember that, young man, if ever you're down on your luck. **1971** 'M. ERSKINE' *Brood of Folly* v. Mrs Parslowe gave her a glance that was both sly and knowing. 'Those that live longest will see most,' she answered cryptically. ■ **experience; old age**

Come LIVE with me and you'll know me

□ **1925** S. O'CASEY *Juno & Paycock* II. 49 I only seen him twiced; if you want to know me, come an' live with me. **1960** C. S. LEWIS *Four Loves* iii. You must really give no kind of preference to yourself; at a party it is enough to conceal the preference. Hence the old proverb 'come live with me and you'll know me'. ■ **familiarity**

live *see also* BETTER to live one day as a tiger . . ; EAT to live, not live to eat; he who FIGHTS and runs away, may live to fight another day; those who live in GLASS houses shouldn't throw stones; one HALF of the world does not know how the other half lives; MAN cannot live by bread alone; a REED before the wind lives on, while mighty oaks do fall; THREATENED men live long.

lived *see* BRAVE men lived before Agamemnon.

He who LIVES by the sword dies by the sword

Other weapons may be substituted for *the sword*, as in quot. 1997. With allusion to MATTHEW xxvi. 52 (AV) All they that take the sword shall perish with the sword; cf. **1601** A. MUNDAY et al. *Death of Robert, Earl of Huntington* L1 Alas for woe: but this is iust heauens doome On those that liue by bloode: in bloode they die.

□ **1652** R. WILLIAMS *Complete Writings* (1963) IV. 352 All that take the Sword .. shall perish by it. **1804** G. MORRIS *Diary & Letters* (1889) II. xlv. To quote the text, 'Those who live by the sword shall perish by the sword.' **1916** J. BUCHAN *Greenmantle* vi. I did not seek the war. .. It was forced on me. .. He that takes the sword will perish by the sword. **1978** 'M. CRAIG' *Were He Stranger* xiii. Mark me, Sydney, he who lives by the sword dies by the sword. **1997** *Washington Post* 12 Mar. B1 Wallace's friends, with whom he had sold dope out of a garbage can .., had pretty much summed up the situation in a sentence: 'When you live by the gun, you die by the gun.' **1998** D. HARSTAD *Eleven Days* (1999) xviii. 180 'He may be using the Satanic-related things to cover his tracks, or he might be saying to the victims, "Look, you live by the sword, you die by the sword."' ■ **retribution**

He that LIVES in hope dances to an ill tune

□ **1591** J. FLORIO *Second Fruits* 149 This argument of yours is lame and halting, but doo not you knowe that. He that dooth liue in hope, dooth dance in narrowe scope. **1640** G. HERBERT *Outlandish Proverbs* no. 1006 Hee that lives in hope danceth without musick. **1732** T. FULLER *Gnomologia* no. 2224 He that liveth in Hope, danceth without a Fiddle. **1977** J. AIKEN *Five Minute Marriage* ii. 'He that lives in hope danceth to an ill tune,' remarked Mrs. Andrews, who was full of proverbs. ■ **disappointment; hope and despair**

He LIVES long who lives well

□ **1553** T. WILSON *Art of Rhetoric* 45v They lyued long enough, that have liued well enough. **1619** W. DRUMMOND *Midnight's Trance* (1951) 29 Who liueth well, liueth long. **1642** T. FULLER *Holy State* I. vi. If he chance to die young, yet he lives long that lives well. **1861** H. BONAR in *Hymns of Faith & Hope* 2nd Ser. 129 He liveth long who liveth well! All other life is short and vain. ■ **life**

load *see* a SWARM in May is worth a load of hay.

loaf *see* HALF a loaf is better than no bread; a SLICE off a cut loaf isn't missed.

loathing *see* LENGTH begets loathing.

lock *see* it is too late to shut the STABLE-door after the horse has bolted.

locksmith *see* LOVE laughs at locksmiths.

loft *see* SEPTEMBER blow soft, till the fruit's in the loft.

London *see* what MANCHESTER says today, the rest of England says tomorrow.

LONG and lazy, little and loud; fat and fulsome, pretty and proud

□ *c* **1576** T. WHYTEHORNE *Autobiography* (1961) 23 Hy women be layzy and low be lowd, fair be sluttish, and fowll be proud. **1591** J. FLORIO *Second Fruits* 189 If long, she is lazy, if little, she is lowde. **1648** HERRICK *Hesperides* 166 *Long and lazie*. That was the Proverb. Let my mistress be Lasie to others, but be long to me— *Ibid.* 248 *Little and loud*. Little you are; for Womans sake be proud; For my sake next, (though little) *be not loud*. **1659** J. HOWELL *Proverbs* (English) 10 Long and lazy, little and loud, Fatt and fulsome, prety and proud; in point of women. **1872** BLACKMORE

Maid of Sker I. xiii. You are long enough, and lazy enough; put your hand to the bridle. ■ **women**

LONG foretold, long last; short notice, soon past

Cf. **1863** R. FITZROY *Weather Book* 15 The longer the time between the signs and the change foretold by them, the longer such altered weather will last; and, on the contrary, the less the time between a warning and a change, the shorter will be the continuance of such predicted weather.

□ **1866** A. STEINMETZ *Manual of Weathercasts* xiv. Old saws [sayings] about the barometer. Long foretold, long last; short notice, soon past. **1889** J. K. JEROME *Three Men in Boat* v. The barometer is..misleading. ..Boots..read out a poem which was printed over the top of the oracle, about 'Long foretold, long last; Short notice, soon past.' The fine weather never came that summer. ■ **future; weather lore**

It is a LONG lane that has no turning

Commonly used as an assertion that an unfavourable situation will eventually change for the better.

□ **1633** *Stationers' Register* (1877) IV. 273 (*ballad*) Long runns that neere turnes. **1670** J. RAY *English Proverbs* 117 It's a long run that never turns. **1732** T. FULLER *Gnomologia* no. 2863 It is a long Lane that never turns. **1748** RICHARDSON *Clarissa* IV. xxxii. It is a long lane that has no turning—Do not despise me for my proverbs. **1945** F. P. KEYES *River Road* VIII. xxxvii. 'You're through in politics, Gervais. You might just as well face it.'..'It's a long lane that has no turning.' **2002** *Country Life* 11 Apr. 117 'It's a long road that doesn't have to turn some time,' says Mr Plant, who intends to continue sheep farming, like his father and grandfather before him. ■ **circumstances; perseverance**

long *see also* (adjective) ART is long and life is short; be the DAY weary or be the day long, at last it ringeth to evensong; KINGS have long arms; NEVER is a long time; OLD sins cast long shadows; SHORT reckonings make long friends; a STERN chase is a long chase; he who SUPS with the Devil should have a long spoon; (adverb) he LIVES long who lives well; LOVE me little, love me long; THREATENED men live long; happy's the WOOING that is not long a-doing.

The LONGEST journey begins with a single step

Attributed to Lao-tzu (*c* 604–*c* 531 BC), founder of Taoism.

□ **1904** *Sayings of Lao Tzu* tr. L. Giles 51 A journey of a thousand miles began with a single step. **1947** L. LEE *Twisted Mirror* x. 87 Willie looked at him with all the solemnity of an old Chinese priest. 'Even a journey of a thousand miles, my honored superior,' he intoned, 'begins with but a single step.' **1983** *National Review* 29 Apr. 485 Of the 15,000 people treated there.., nearly all smoked marijuana. Which proves nothing. Except that the longest journey begins with a single step. **1997** *Spectator* 13 Dec. 27 Politicians of all sides..should remember the old adage that even that longest journey begins with a single step. Before placing another foot forward they should decide whether this actually is a journey they wish to make. **2001** *Washington Times* 28 July F9 (*Herb & Jamaal comic strip*) 'They say life is a journey. ..And there's an old saying: "A journey of a thousand miles begins with one step." My first step was into an abandoned shaft.' ■ **beginnings and endings**

The LONGEST way round is the shortest way home

The idea is found earlier: **1580** LYLY *Euphues & his England* II. 96 Thou goest about (but yet the neerest way) to hang me vp for holy-dayes. (*Go about* is used here punningly to mean both 'endeavour' and 'go around or roundabout'. The context is of a person metaphorically described as a hat which can be taken up and put down at will.)

□ **1635** F. QUARLES *Emblems* IV. ii. The road to resolution lies by doubt: The next way home's the farthest way about. **1776** G. COLMAN *Spleen* II. 24 The longest way about is the shortest way home. **1846** J. K. PAULDING *Letter* 9 May (1962) vii. The Potatoes arrived..*via* New York..in pursuance of the Old Proverb, that 'the longest way round is the shortest way home.' **1942** K. ABBEY *And let Coffin Pass* xviii. 'The longest way round is the shortest way home.'..'We'll make the best time by skirting the pines.' **1990** F. LYALL *Croaking of Raven* vi. 2. 64 '..when I was training my old boss used to say: "If in doubt take the long road round. It'll prove to be the shortest in the end."' ■ **patience and impatience; ways and means**

longest *see also* (adjective) BARNABY bright, Barnaby bright, the longest day and the shortest night; (adverb) a CREAKING door hangs longest; he who LAUGHS last, laughs longest; they that LIVE longest, see most.

LOOK before you leap

□ *c* **1350** *Douce MS 52* no. 150 First loke and aftirward lepe. **1528** W. TYNDALE *Obedience of Christian Man* 130 We say..Loke yer thou lepe, whose literall sence is, doo nothinge sodenly or without avisement. **1567** W. PAINTER *Palace of Pleasure* II. xxiv. He that looketh not before he leapeth, may chaunce to stumble before he sleapeth. **1621** BURTON *Anatomy of Melancholy* II. iii. Looke before you leape. **1836** MARRYAT *Midshipman Easy* I. vi. Look before you leap is an old proverb. ..Jack..had pitched into a small apiary, and had upset two hives of bees. **1941** C. MACKENZIE *Red Tapeworm* i. Do you remember the rousing slogan which the Prime Minister gave the voters..on the eve of the last General Election?..Look Before You Leap. **1979** D. MAY *Revenger's Comedy* ix. Changing horses, love? I should look before you leap. ■ **caution**

look *see also* a CAT may look at a king; the DEVIL looks after his own; never look a GIFT horse in the mouth; when all you have is a HAMMER, everything looks like a nail; a MAN is as old as he feels, and a woman as old as she looks; take care of the PENCE and the pounds will take care of themselves; those who PLAY at bowls must look out for rubbers; one man may STEAL a horse, while another may not look over a hedge.

LOOKERS-ON see most of the game

Recently also often with *onlooker(s)*.

□ **1529** J. PALSGRAVE in *Acolastus* (EETS) p. xxxviii. It fareth between thee and me as it doth between a player at the chess and a looker on, for he that looketh on seeth many draughts that the player considereth nothing at all. **1597** BACON *Essays* 'Of Followers' 7V To take aduise of friends is euer honorable: For lookers on many times see more then gamesters. **1666** G. TORRIANO *Italian Proverbs* III As the English say, The stander by sees more than he who plays. **1850** F. E. SMEDLEY *Frank Fairlegh* vii. Remembering the old adage, that 'lookers-on see most of the game,' I determined..to accompany him. **1983** M. GILBERT *Black Seraphim* vi. They say that the onlooker sees most of the game. It's not a very happy game that's being played here at the moment. **1998** 'C. AIRD' *Stiff News* (2000) iii. 29 So it fell out that Mrs Maisie Carruthers, still too frail to attend the funeral, but not too immobile to get to the window of her room at the Manor, became the onlooker who saw most of the game. **1999** 'H. CRANE' *Miss Seeton's Finest Hour* xix. 164 Mrs. Morris, it was clear, did not suspect that her warm regard for the works manager was no secret from her assistant—an assistant who by training was an acute observer. Was not another adage that the looker-on saw most of the game? ■ **observation**

lord *see* EVERYBODY loves a lord; NEW lords, new laws.

What you LOSE on the swings you gain on the roundabouts

A fairground metaphor used in a variety of forms.

□ **1912** P. CHALMERS *Green Days & Blue Days* 19 What's lost upon the roundabouts we pulls up on the swings. **1927** *Times* 24 Mar. 15 By screwing more money out of taxpayers he diminishes their savings, and the market for trustee securities loses on the swings what it gains on the roundabouts. **1978** G. MOORE *Farewell Recital* 129 There are compensations: what you lose on the swings you gain on the roundabouts. And let's face it, a cup of tea or a cup of coffee are all very well but they are not so much fun as polygamy. ■ **winners and losers**

You cannot LOSE what you never had

The sentiment is expressed in a number of ways: quot. 1974 represents a local equivalent. Similar to *what you've never* HAD *you never miss.*

□ *a* **1593** MARLOWE *Hero & Leander* I. 276 Of that which hath no being do not boast, Things that are not at all are never lost. **1676** I. WALTON *Compleat Angler* (ed. 5) I. v. 'He has broke all; there's half a line and a good hook lost.' 'I [Aye] and a good Trout too.' 'Nay, the Trout is not lost, for . . no man can lose what he never had.' **1788** WESLEY *Works* (1872) VII. 41 He only *seemeth* to have this. . . No man can lose what he never had. **1935** *Oxford Dict. English Proverbs* 601 You cannot lose what you never had. **1974** 'J. HERRIOT' *Vet in Harness* viii. 'Only them as has them can lose them,' she said firmly, her head tilted as always. I had heard that said many times and they were brave Yorkshire words. ■ **winners and losers**

lose *see also* a BLEATING sheep loses a bite; LEND your money and lose your friend; the SUN loses nothing by shining into a puddle; a TALE never loses in the telling; you WIN a few, you lose a few.

loser *see* FINDERS keepers (losers weepers).

One man's LOSS is another man's gain

□ *c* **1527** T. BERTHELET tr. *Erasmus' Sayings of Wise Men* D1[v] Lyghtly whan one wynneth, an other loseth. **1733** J. BARBER in *Correspondence of Swift* (1965) IV. 189 Your loss will be our gain, as the proverb says. **1821** SCOTT *Pirate* I. vi. Doubtless one man's loss is another man's gain. **1918** D. H. LAWRENCE *Letter* 21 Feb. (1962) I. 544 I am glad to have the money from your hand. But . . one man's gain is another man's loss. **1979** R. LITTELL *Debriefing* vi. Well, their loss is my gain! ■ **gains and losses**

There's no great LOSS without some gain

□ *a* **1641** D. FERGUSSON *Scottish Proverbs* (STS) no. 1408 Thair was never a grit loss without som small vantag. **1868** W. CLIFT *Tim Bunker Papers* 134 However, 'there is no great loss but what there is some small gain,' and Jake Frink claims that he has got his money's worth in experience. **1937** L. I. WILDER *On Banks of Plum Creek* XXV. The hens . . were eating grasshoppers. . . 'Well, we won't have to buy feed for the hens. . . There's no great loss without some gain.' **1957** M. P. HOOD *In Dark Night* viii. I didn't think there'd be enough business on the wharf for him to need me this afternoon. . . No loss without some small gain. ■ **gains and losses**

lost *see* BETTER to have loved and lost, than never to have loved at all; he who HESITATES is lost; what a NEIGHBOUR gets is not lost; for WANT of a nail the shoe was lost.

lottery *see* MARRIAGE is a lottery.

loud *see* LONG and lazy, little and loud.

louder *see* ACTIONS speak louder than words.

louse *see* SUE a beggar and catch a louse.

LOVE and a cough cannot be hid

Cf. L. *amor tussisque non celantur*, love and a cough cannot be concealed.

□ *a* **1325** *Cursor Mundi* (EETS) l. 4276 Luken luue at the end wil kith [concealed love will show itself in the end]. **1573** J. SANFORDE *Garden of Pleasure* 98V Foure things cannot be kept close, Loue, the cough, fyre, and sorrowe. **1611** R. COTGRAVE *Dict. French & English* s.v. Amour, We say, Loue, and the Cough cannot be hidden. **1640** G. HERBERT *Outlandish Proverbs* no. 49 Love and a Cough cannot be hid. **1863** G. ELIOT *Romola* I. vi. If there are two things not to be hidden—love and a cough—I say there is a third, and that is ignorance. **1994** R. DAVIES *Cunning Man* 458 Love and a cough cannot be hid. **2002** *Washington Times* 14 Feb. A21 Three things are hard to hide, says the Yiddish proverb: a cough, poverty and love. ■ **love**; **secrecy**

One cannot LOVE and be wise

Cf. PUBLILIUS SYRUS *Sententiae* xxii. *amare et sapere vix deo conceditur*, to love and to be wise is scarcely allowed to God.

□ *c* **1527** T. BERTHELET tr. *Erasmus' Sayings of Wise Men* B1V To have a sadde [serious] mynde and loue is nat in one person. **1539** R. TAVERNER tr. *Erasmus' Adages* II. A5 To be in loue and to be wyse is scase graunted to god. **1612** BACON *Essays* 'Of Love' xii. It is impossible to loue and bee wise. **1631** R. BRATHWAIT *English Gentlewoman* 32 The Louer is euer blinded .. with affection .. whence came that vsuall saying One cannot loue and be wise. **1872** G. ELIOT *Middlemarch* II. III. xxvii. If a man could not love and be wise, surely he could flirt and be wise at the same time? **2001** *Washington Post Book World* 29 July 1 Maybe passion is always a mistake: Yet who can love and then be wise? ■ **love**; **wisdom**

LOVE begets love

Cf. L. *amor gignit amorem*, love produces love.

□ **1648** HERRICK *Hesperides* 297 Love love begets, then never be Unsoft to him who's smooth to thee. **1812** E. NARES *I'll consider of It* iii. 'Love' says the proverb, 'produces love.' **1909** A. MACLAREN *Epistle to Ephesians* 275 Love begets love, and .. if a man loves God, then that glowing beam will glow whether it is turned to earth or turned to heaven. **1958** R. FENISONG *Death of Party* vi. The cliché that 'love breeds love' was a blatant lie. ■ **love**; **reciprocity**

LOVE is blind

Cf. THEOCRITUS Idyll x. 19 τυφλὸς .. ὁ .. Ἔρως, love is blind; PLAUTUS *Miles Gloriosus* l. 1259 *caeca amore est*, she is blinded by love.

□ *c* **1390** CHAUCER *Merchant's Tale* l. 1598 For love is blynd alday, and may nat see. **1591** SHAKESPEARE *Two Gentlemen of Verona* II. i. 61 If you love her you cannot see her.—Why?—Because Love is blind. **1978** A. MALING *Lucky Devil* xii. 'How did you ever come to marry an idiot like Irving?' .. 'Love is blind.' **2002** *Spectator* 25 May 70 And, if love is blind, how come lingerie is so popular? ■ **love**

LOVE laughs at locksmiths,

A more graphic expression of the sentiment in LOVE *will find a way*. Cf. **1592–3** SHAKESPEARE *Venus & Adonis* l. 576 Were beauty under twenty locks kept fast, Yet love breaks through and picks them all at last.

□ **1803** G. COLMAN (*title*) Love laughs at locksmiths: an operatic farce. **1901** F. R. STURGIS *Sexual Debility in Man* ix. Love is said to laugh at locksmiths, and incidentally at parental authority, and this young man was no exception. **1922** 'D. YATES' *Jonah & Co* iv. And now push off and lock the vehicle. I know Love laughs at locksmiths, but the average motor-thief's sense of humour is less susceptible. **1998** 'C. AIRD' *Stiff News* (2000) xv. 156 [A]ll the medicines at the Manor would be kept together in one place. Under lock and key, no doubt, but every policeman learned early that love wasn't the only thing that laughed at locksmiths. Murderers did, too. ■ **love**

LOVE makes the world go round

Cf. Fr. *c'est l'amour, l'amour, l'amour, Qui fait le monde A la ronde* (Dumerson & Ségur *Chansons Nationales & Populaires de France*, 1851, II. 180) it is love, love, love, that makes the world go round.

□ **1865** 'L. CARROLL' *Alice's Adventures in Wonderland* ix. ' "Oh, 'tis love, 'tis love that makes the world go round!" ' 'Somebody said,' Alice whispered, 'that it's done by everybody minding their own business.' **1902** 'O. HENRY' in *Brandur Mag.* 27 Sept. 4 It's said that love makes the world go round. The announcement lacks verification. It's the wind from the dinner horn that does it. **2002** *Washington Times* 14 Feb. A21 It is a well-known factoid that love makes the world go 'round; less well-known is love's ability to stop the planet dead flat in midspin when it ends, replacing Paris in the spring with Chicago in January. ■ **love**

LOVE me little, love me long

□ *a* **1500** in *Archiv* (1900) CVI. 274 Love me lytyll and longe. **1546** J. HEYWOOD *Dialogue of Proverbs* II. ii. G1 Olde wise folke saie, loue me lyttle loue me long. **1629** T. ADAMS *Works* 813 Men cannot brooke poore friends. This inconstant Charitie is hateful as our English phrase premonisheth; Loue me Little, and Loue me Long. **1721** J. KELLY *Scottish Proverbs* 229 Love me little, love me long. A Dissuasive from shewing too much, and too sudden Kindness. **1907** *Times Literary Supplement* 8 Mar. 77 Mrs. Bellew is a lady who cannot love either little or long. She .. tires very quickly of the men who are irresistibly drawn to her. **1991** *Washington Times* 14 Feb. G3 'Love me a little less but longer' is an old folk phrase. ■ **constancy and inconstancy; love**

LOVE me, love my dog

Cf. ST. BERNARD *Sermon: In Festo Sancti Michaelis* iii. *qui me amat, amat et canem meum*, who loves me, also loves my dog; early 14th-cent. Fr. *et ce dit le sage qui mayme il ayme mon chien*, and so says the sage, who loves me loves my dog.

□ *a* **1500** in *Archiv* (1893) XC. 81 He that lovyeth me lovyeth my hound. **1546** J. HEYWOOD *Dialogue of Proverbs* II. ix. K4^{V} Ye haue bene so veraie [veritable] a hog, To my frends. What man, loue me, loue my dog. **1692** R. L'ESTRANGE *Fables of Aesop* cvi. Love Me, Love my Dog. .. For there are certain Decencies of Respect due to the Servant for the Master's sake. **1826** LAMB *Elia's Last Essays* (1833) 262 *That you must love me, and love my dog.* .. We could never yet form a friendship .. without the intervention of some third anomaly .. the understood *dog* in the proverb. **2001**

Spectator 1 Dec. 28 Sir Michael had agreed to take his new job only on the condition that Mr Bolland remained at his right hand. 'It's a case of love me, love my dog,' a courtier told me. ■ **associates; love**

LOVE will find a way

□ *a* **1607** T. DELONEY *Gentle Craft* (1648) I. xv. Thus love you see can finde a way, To make both Men and Maids obey. **1661** 'T. B.' (*title*) Love will finde out the way. **1765** in T. Percy *Reliques* III. III. 236 Over the mountains, And over the waves;.. Love will find out the way. **1962** 'S. NASH' *Killed by Scandal* ix. But he's so fond of June that I'm sure it's going to be all right. Love will find a way. **1975** *Listener* 16 Oct. 504 The red-plush curtain fell on a reprise of 'Love will find a way'. ■ **love**

love *see also* (noun) the COURSE of true love never did run smooth; all's FAIR in love and war; when the FURZE is in bloom, my love's in tune; LUCKY at cards, unlucky in love; MONEY is the root of all evil; it is best to be OFF with the old love before you are on with the new; PITY is akin to love; when POVERTY comes in at the door, love flies out of the window; PRAISE the child, and you make love to the mother; the QUARREL of lovers is the renewal of love; (verb) EVERYBODY loves a lord; whom the GODS love die young.

loved *see* BETTER to have loved and lost, than never to have loved at all.

Lovell *see* the CAT, the rat, and Lovell the dog, rule all England under the hog.

lover *see* JOVE but laughs at lovers' perjury; the QUARREL of lovers is the renewal of love.

There is LUCK in leisure

It is often advisable to wait before acting.

□ **1683** G. MERITON *Yorkshire Dialogue* 9 There's luck in Leizur. **1859** 'SKITT' *Fisher's River* vii. Thinks I, 'There's luck in leisure,' as I've hearn folks say. .. So I jist waited a spell. **1936** J. ESTEVEN *While Murder Waits* xxii. 'You..won't decide now?'.. 'There's luck in leisure, Victoria.' ■ **patience and impatience; procrastination**

There is LUCK in odd numbers

A superstition similar to that in THIRD *time lucky.* Cf. VIRGIL *Eclogues* viii. 75 *numero deus impare gaudet*, the god delights in an uneven number.

□ **1598** SHAKESPEARE *Merry Wives of Windsor* v. i. 3 This is the third time; I hope good luck lies in odd numbers. **1837** S. LOVER *Rory O'More* I. (*title-page*) 'There's luck in odd numbers,' says Rory O'More. **1883** J. PAYN *Thicker than Water* I. i. She was..by no means averse to a third experiment in matrimony. ..'There was luck in odd numbers.' **1963** N. FITZGERALD *Day of Adder* i. You can make that five then. ..There's luck in odd numbers. ■ **luck; superstition**

luck *see also* the DEVIL's children have the Devil's luck; DILIGENCE is the mother of good luck; FOOLS for luck; see a PIN and pick it up, all the day you'll have good luck.

LUCKY at cards, unlucky in love

The idea is present in 1738 SWIFT *Polite Conversation* iii. 213 Well, Miss, you'll have a sad Husband, you have such good Luck at Cards.

□ **1866** T. W. ROBERTSON *Society* II. ii. 'I'm always lucky at cards!'.. 'Yes, I know an old proverb about that. ..Lucky at play, unlucky in—.' *a* **1871**—— *Play* (1889) III. ii. Unlucky in love, lucky at cards. **1941** P. CHEYNEY *Trap for Bellamy* iv. 'Lucky at cards, unlucky in love.'..I'm going to find out if the proverb's true. ..What are they playing tonight? **1981** *Oxford Mail* 29 Aug. 5 Arthur and Hilda Cover have defied the old proverb by being lucky at cards and lucky in love. **2003** *Times* 1 Jan. 30 You had never believed the phrase 'lucky in cards, unlucky in love' until that night when you were the victim of a drive-by shooting from a jealous ex-girlfriend shortly after being dealt a full house. ■ **love; luck**

lucky *see also* it is BETTER to be born lucky than rich; THIRD time lucky.

lunch *see* there's no such thing as a FREE lunch.

Where MACGREGOR sits is the head of the table

The proverb is sometimes attributed to Robert MacGregor of Campbell ('Rob Roy': 1671–1734), highland freebooter. Other names are used as well as MacGregor. The idea is explained in the two following quots.: **1580** LYLY *Euphues & his England* II. 39 When .. Agesilaus sonne was set at the lower end of the table, and one cast it in his teeth as a shame, he answered: this is the vpper end where I sit; **1732** T. FULLER *Gnomologia* no. 4362 That is the upper End, where the chief Person sits.

◻ **1837** EMERSON *American Scholar* 19 Wherever Macdonald [the head of the Macdonald clan] sits, there is the head of the table. Linnaeus makes botany the most alluring of studies and wins it from the farmer and the herb-woman. **1903** K. D. WIGGIN *Rebecca of Sunnybrook Farm* viii. If wherever the MacGregor sat was the head of the table, so .. wherever Rebecca stood was the centre of the stage. **1918** A. G. GARDINER *Leaves in Wind* 197 There are .. people who carry the centre of the stage with them. .. 'Where O'Flaherty sits is the head of the table.' **1940** J. W. BELLAH *Bones of Napoleon* 69 Like Macdonald—where Lord Innes sat was the head of the table. **1980** *Times* 12 May 15 (*letter from His Honour Judge MacGregor*) Sir, Where MacGregor sits is the head of the table. ■ **honour; pride**

Don't get MAD, get even

◻ **1975** J. F. KENNEDY in B. Bradlee *Conversations with Kennedy* 25 Some of the reasons have their roots in that wonderful law of the Boston Irish political jungle: 'Don't get mad; get even.' **1990** *Evening Standard* 28 Feb. 13 Nancy Reagan made more than $2 million from her 'don't get mad, get even' .. memories. **2001** *Washington Times* 25 May A22 The episode was especially moving inasmuch as forgiveness is not in the Kennedy tradition. JFK was the author of the famous dictum, 'Don't get mad, get even.' ■ **revenge**

mad *see also* whom the GODS would destroy, they first make mad.

made *see* GOD made the country, and man made the town; PROMISES, like piecrust, are made to be broken; RULES are made to be broken; *also* MAKE.

Mahomet *see* if the MOUNTAIN will not come to Mahomet, Mahomet must go to the mountain.

MAKE hay while the sun shines

◻ **1546** J. HEYWOOD *Dialogue of Proverbs* I. iii. A4 Whan the sunne shynth make hey. **1583** B. MELBANCKE *Philotimus* 24 Yt is well therefore to make hay while the sunne shines. **1835** J. CARLYLE *Letters & Memorials* (1883) I. 21 'It is good to make hay while the sun shines,' which means, in the present case .. to catch hold of a friend while she is in the humour. **1924** E. BAGNOLD *Serena Blandish* vi. The countess's enthusiasm was cooling. Martin .. said warningly, 'You must make hay, my child, while the sun shines.' **1999** 'H. CRANE' *Miss Seeton's Finest Hour* xii. 100 'Our local garage must have made a fortune out of me since this blackout nonsense began. .. Mind you,' the doctor added in a noncommittal voice, 'I imagine they think of it more along the lines of making hay while the sun shines .. ' ■ **opportunity, taken**

As you MAKE your bed, so you must lie upon it

Cf. late 15th-cent. Fr. *comme on faict son lict, on le treuve*, as one makes one's bed, so one finds it.

□ *c* **1590** G. HARVEY *Marginalia* (1913) 88 Lett them .. go to there bed, as themselues shall make it. **1640** G. HERBERT *Outlandish Proverbs* no. 340 He that makes his bed ill, lies there. **1721** J. KELLY *Scottish Proverbs* 16 As you make your bed, so you lye down. According to your Conditions you have your Bargain. **1832** S. WARREN *Diary of Late Physician* II. vi. As soon as his relatives .. heard .. they told him .. that as he had made his bed, so he must lie upon it. **1921** A. P. HERBERT *House by River* v. There's no doubt she was out with one of them .. and went further than she meant, .. but if you make your bed you must lie on it. **1997** *Spectator* 29 Nov 14 Your mother says serves you right, you've made your bed and now you lie on it, I never liked him. ■ **action and consequence**

make *see also* you cannot make BRICKS without straw; CLOTHES make the man; make HASTE slowly; if you don't make MISTAKES you don't make anything; you cannot make an OMELETTE without breaking eggs; you can't make a SILK purse out of a sow's ear.

male *see* the FEMALE of the species is more deadly than the male.

Mammon *see* you cannot serve GOD and Mammon.

MAN cannot live by bread alone

With allusion to two biblical passages (both AV): DEUTERONOMY viii. 3 Man doth not live by bread only, but by every word that proceedeth out of the mouth of the Lord doth man live; MATTHEW iv. 4 Man shall not live by bread alone.

□ **1875** EMERSON in *North American Review* May–June 418 Man does not live by bread alone, but by faith, by admiration, by sympathy. **1927** J. BUCHAN *Witch Wood* iii. Man canna live by bread alone, but he assuredly canna live without it. **1973** *Galt Toy Catalogue* 35 As the saying goes—Man cannot live by bread alone. ■ **food and drink; life**

Whatever MAN has done, man may do

There is a similar idea behind **1723** S. CRANSTON in G. S. Kimball *Correspondence of Colonial Governors of Rhode Island* (1902) I. 9 But as the Proverb is what hath been may be againe.

□ **1863** C. READE *Hard Cash* II. xiv. 'Dark Deeds are written in an unknown tongue called "Lawyerish" ..; pick it out if you can.' 'Whatever man has done man may do,' said Dr. Sampson stoutly. **1910** 'SAKI' *Reginald in Russia* 14 I fell in love .. with the local doctor's wife. .. On looking back at past events it seems to me that she must have been distinctly ordinary, but I suppose the doctor had fallen in love with her once, and what man has done man can do. ■ **possibility and impossibility**

A MAN is as old as he feels, and a woman as old as she looks

Both parts of the proverb are sometimes used on their own (see also quot. 1990).

□ **1871** V. LUSH *Thames Journal* 27 Aug. (1975) 114 She is always making me out so much older than I am and that's not fair, for a man is only as old as he *feels* and a woman is only as old as she *looks*. **1891** W. MORRIS *News from Nowhere* iii. 'How old am I, do you think?' 'Well,' quoth I, 'I have always been told that a woman is as old as she looks.' **1907** *Illustrated London News* 25 May 794 The adage that a man is as old as he feels, and a woman as old as she looks, may be said to contain much inherent truth. **1990** 'C. AIRD' *Body Politic* (1991) xi. 123 'He might still marry.' Sloan was bracing. 'A man is only as old as he feels.' ■ **men and women; old age**

MAN is the measure of all things

Cf. PROTAGORAS in Plato *Cratylus* vi. *πάντων χρημάτων μέτρον εἶναι ἄνθρωπον*, man is the measure of all things.

□ **1547** W. BALDWIN *Morall Phylosophie* III. xvi. O6[v] Man is the measure of all thynges. **1631** G. CHAPMAN *Warres of Pompey & Caesar* II. E2 As of all things, man is said the measure, So your full merits measure forth a man. **1948** 'H. BESTON' *Northern Farm* xii. 'Man the measure of all things.' A good adage. **1980** *Times Greece Supplement* 15 Dec. p. iv. The belief that man was the measure of all things . . led the Greeks into . . new disciplines. ■ **human nature**

MAN proposes, God disposes

Cf. early 14th-cent. Fr. *car se li homme mal propose, Diex . . le dispose*, for if man proposes evil, God . . disposes of it; *c* **1420** T. À KEMPIS *De Imitatione Christi* I. xix. *homo proponit, sed Deus disponit* (see quot. *c* 1450 below).

□ *c* **1440** J. LYDGATE *Fall of Princes* (EETS) I. 3291 A man off malice may a thyng purpose . . But God a-boue can graciousli dispose [determine] Ageyn such malice to make resistence. *c* **1450** tr. *T. à Kempis' De Imitatione Christi* (EETS) I. xix. For man purposith and god disposith. **1640** G. HERBERT *Outlandish Proverbs* no. 1 Man Proposeth, God disposeth. **1853** R. C. TRENCH *On Lessons in Proverbs* (ed. 2) iii. A proverb . . Man proposes, God disposes . . that every nation in Europe possesses. **1958** L. DURRELL *Mountolive* IV. 88 In diplomacy one can only propose, never dispose. That is up to God, don't you think? **1997** *Times* 9 Aug. 8 God's will is not something to be commanded; recall the saying 'Man proposes, God disposes'. ■ **fate and fatalism; providence**

MAN'S extremity is God's opportunity

□ **1629** T. ADAMS *Works* 619 Heere is now a deliuery fit for God, a cure for the Almightie hand to vndertake. Mans extremity is Gods opportunitie. **1706** LD. BELHAVEN in Defoe *Hist. Union* (1709) v. 34 Man's Extremity is God's opportunity. . . Some unforeseen Providence will fall out, that may cast the Ballance. **1916** E. A. BURROUGHS *Valley of Decision* viii. In the first winter of the war . . we were all much encouraged by tales of a new thirst for religion among the majority of the men. . . 'Man's extremity, God's opportunity.' **1949** D. SMITH *I capture Castle* xiii. 'You should look in on the church if ever you're mentally run down.' . . 'You mean "Man's extremity is God's opportunity"?' **1980** *Times* 4 Dec. 17 Those extremities which have, until now, been often God's opportunity. ■ **necessity; opportunity**

Because a MAN is born in a stable that does not make him a horse

Sometimes attributed to the Duke of Wellington (1769–1852); see quot. 1969.

□ **1833** M. SCOTT *Tom Cringle's Log* I. iv. 'I am an Englishman and no traitor, nor will I die the death of one.' . . 'Truly . . a man does sometimes become a horse by being born in a stable.' **1906** *Times Literary Supplement* 27 Apr. 147 Except on the principle that the man who is born in a stable is a horse, [he] was not an Irishman at all. **1969** E. LONGFORD *Wellington: Years of Sword* viii. If Wellington was ever chaffed for being an Irishman and replied with a notorious quip, it was probably during this period [1807]: Because a man is born in a stable that does not make him a horse. **1980** J. O'FAOLAIN *No Country for Young Men* ii. Father Casey . . has a theory that the Irish back in Ireland have less claim to Irishness than men like himself. Something to do with . . being born in a stable not necessarily making you a horse. ■ **human nature; origins**

man *see also* BETTER be an old man's darling, than a young man's slave; a BLIND man's wife needs no paint; never send a BOY to do a man's job; the CHILD is father of the man; CLOTHES make the man; in the COUNTRY of the blind, the one-eyed man is king; DO right and fear no man; a DROWNING man will clutch at a straw; the EARLY man never borrows from the late man; every ELM has its man; EVERY man for himself; EVERY man for himself, and devil take the hindmost; EVERY man for himself, and God for us all; EVERY man has his price; EVERY man is the architect of his own fortune; EVERY man to his taste; EVERY man to his trade; it's ill speaking between a FULL man and a fasting; a HUNGRY man is an angry man; you should KNOW a man seven years before you stir his fire; a man who is his own LAWYER has a fool for his client; one man's LOSS is another man's gain; MANNERS maketh man; like MASTER, like man; one man's MEAT is another man's poison; MONEY makes a man; a MONEYLESS man goes fast through the market; NEEDLES and pins, . . when a man marries, his trouble begins; NINE tailors make a man; NO man can serve two masters; NO man is a hero to his own valet; NO moon, no man; there is NOTHING so good for the inside of a man as the outside of a horse; the RICH man has his ice in the summer and the poor man gets his in the winter; give a man ROPE enough and he will hang himself; SIX hours' sleep for a man, seven for a woman, and eight for a fool; one man may STEAL a horse, while another may not look over a hedge; the STYLE is the man; TIME and tide wait for no man; for WANT of a nail the shoe was lost; the WAY to a man's heart is through his stomach; a WILFUL man must have his way; when the WIND is in the east, 'tis neither good for man nor beast; a WOMAN without a man is like a fish without a bicycle; a YOUNG man married is a young man marred; *also* MEN.

What MANCHESTER says today, the rest of England says tomorrow

The proverb occurs in a variety of forms. Quot. 1902 sets it in its historical context: the Corn Law, restricting the importation of foreign corn, was abolished in 1846, and Manchester (formerly part of Lancashire), considered the home of free trade, was in the forefront of the campaign against restrictive legislation.

□ **1898** R. KIPLING *Day's Work* 51 What the horses o' Kansas think to-day, the horses of America will think to-morrow; an' I tell *you* that when the horses of America rise in their might, the day o' the Oppressor is ended. **1902** V. S. LEAN *Collectanea* I. 116 What Lancashire thinks to-day all England will think to-morrow. This was in the days of the Anti-Corn-Law League. Since then the initiative in political movements proceeds from Birmingham. **1944** C. MILBURN *Journal* 24 Aug. in *Diaries* (1979) xiii. Manchester rang its bells yesterday—a day before St. Paul's . . thus justifying its words, so often used: 'What Manchester says today, the rest of England says tomorrow!' **1980** *Listener* 6 Mar. 300 What Manchester does today— . . is the old boast that 'What Manchester does today London thinks tomorrow.' ■ **imitation; opinions; public opinion**

Manchester *see also* YORKSHIRE born and Yorkshire bred, strong in the arm and weak in the head.

MANNERS maketh man

William of Wykeham (1324–1404), bishop of Winchester and chancellor of England, was the founder of Winchester College and New College, Oxford (see also quot. *a* **1661**).

□ *c* **1350** *Douce MS 52* no. 77 Maner makys man. *c* **1450** in *Archiv* (1931) CLIX. 88 Maners and clothying makes man. **1509** A. BARCLAY *Ship of Fools* 118 An old prouerbe.. Sayth that good lyfe and maners makyth man. *a* **1661** T. FULLER *Worthies* (Hants.) 3 Manners makes a man, Quoth William Wickham. This generally was his Motto, inscribed frequently on the places of his Founding. **1721** J. KELLY *Scottish Proverbs* 246 Meat feeds, Cloth cleeds, but Manners makes the Man. ..Good Meat, and fine Cloaths, without good Breeding, are but poor Recommendations. **1824** BYRON *Don Juan* XV. xviii. The difference is, that in days of old Men made the manners; manners now make men. **1983** R. BARNARD *Case of Missing Bronte* vi. Gracious little twit. The idea that manners makyth man clearly went out of the educational system before he went into it. ■ **manners**

manners *see also* EVIL communications corrupt good manners; OTHER times, other manners.

manure *see* MONEY, like manure, does no good till it is spread.

MANY a little makes a mickle

The proper version of the next proverb. *Pickle*, a Scottish word for 'a small quantity or amount', is also found instead of *little*. *Mickle* ('a great quantity or amount') is now only Scottish.

□ *a* **1250** *Ancrene Wisse* (1962) 32 Thys ofte as me seith, of lutel muchel waxeth. *c* **1390** CHAUCER *Parson's Tale* l. 361 The proverbe seith that 'manye smale maken a greet.' **1545** R. TAVERNER tr. *Erasmus' Adages* (ed. 2) G5 We commonly say in englyshe: Many a lyttle maketh a great. **1614** W. CAMDEN *Remains concerning Britain* (ed. 2) 310 Many a little makes a mickle. **1822** CARLYLE in J. A. Froude *Life* (1884) I. xii. 'Many a little makes a mickle.' It will be a long.. and weary job, but I must plod along. **1905** *Westminster Gazette* 29 Apr. 3 'There is the Tithe Relief. ..But that is a small item.' 'Yes, but many a pickle maks a muckle.' **1979** C. COLVIN *Maria Edgeworth in France & Switzerland* 196 Many a pickle (or little) makes a mickle. ■ **great and small**

MANY a mickle makes a muckle

A popular corruption of the preceding entry. This alternative form is in fact nonsensical, as *muckle* is merely a variant of the dialectal *mickle* 'a large quantity or amount'.

□ **1793** G. WASHINGTON *Writings* (1939) XXXII. 423 A Scotch addage, than which nothing in nature is more true..'many mickles make a muckle.' **1940** *Huntly Express* 19 Jan. 3 He said at the close of his address 'As the Scots say, and they should know, mony a mickle mak's a muckle.'..As the Scots know, he had quoted the proverb wrongly. **1993** 'C. AIRD' *Going Concern* (1994) i. 5 Amelia's mind had gone off at a complete tangent, trying to work out however many Puckles there must be in the firm. The old saw about thrift came into her mind: 'Many a mickle makes a muckle. ..' Could it be a case of many a client making a Puckle? ■ **great and small**

There's MANY a slip between cup and lip

Cf. CATO THE ELDER in Aulus Gellius *Noctes Atticae* XIII. xviii. 1 *(saepe audivi) inter os atque offam multa intervenire posse*, (I have often heard) that many things can come between mouth and morsel; PALLADAS (attrib.) in *Anthologia Palatina* x. 32 *πολλὰ μεταξὺ πέλει κύλικος καὶ χείλεος ἄκρου*, there are many things between the cup and the edge of the lip.

□ **1539** R. TAVERNER tr. *Erasmus' Adages* 15 Many thynges fall betwene the cuppe and the mouth. .. Betwene the cuppe and the lyppes maye come many casualties. **1783** in *Collections of Massachusetts Hist. Society* (1877) 5th Ser. II. 216 Have a care, and remember the old proverb of 'many a slip,' &c. **1840** R. H. BARHAM *Ingoldsby Legends* 1st Ser. 280 Doubtless the adage, 'There's many a slip 'Twixt the cup and the lip,' hath reference to medicine. **1979** E. KYLE *Summer Scandal* xiii. 'I thought you were here for life.'.. 'There's many a slip between cup and lip.' ■ **disappointment; error**

MANY are called but few are chosen

With allusion to MATTHEW xxii. 14 (AV) For many are called, but few are chosen.

□ **1871** J. S. JONES *Life J. S. Batkins* xxviii. The saying that 'many shall be called, but few chosen.' **1980** P. VAN GREENAWAY *Dissident* iii. 'Many are called.. but few are chosen.' He's right. Those of us conscious of our destinies may fairly be termed 'elitistes'. ■ **choice; fate and fatalism**

MANY hands make light work

Cf. HESIOD *Works & Days* 380 *πλείων μὲν πλεόνων μελέτη*, more hands mean more work; ERASMUS *Adages* II. iii. 95 *multae manus onus levius reddunt*, many hands make a burden lighter.

□ *c* **1330** *Sir Beves* (EETS) l. 3352 Ascopard be strong and sterk [physically powerful], Mani hondes maketh light werk! **1678** S. BUTLER *Hudibras* III. ii. Most Hands dispatch apace, And make light work, (the proverb says). **1721** J. KELLY *Scottish Proverbs* 244 Many Hands make light Work. Because it is but little to every one. **1923** *Observer* 11 Feb. 9 What is the use of saying that 'Many hands make light work' when the same copy-book tells you that 'Too many cooks spoil the broth'? **2002** B. D'AMATO *White Male Infant* i. 16 Tony immediately began to prepare the bone marrow..His assistant..simultaneously ran up smears with less usual stains..Many hands make light work. ■ **assistance; work**

many *see also* there's many a GOOD tune played on an old fiddle; many a TRUE word is spoken in jest; many go out for WOOL and come home shorn.

MARCH comes in like a lion, and goes out like a lamb

The weather is traditionally wild at the beginning of March, but fair by the end.

□ *a* **1625** J. FLETCHER *Wife for Month* (1717) II. i. 'I would chuse March, for I would come in like a Lion.'.. 'But you'd go out like a Lamb when you went to hanging.' **1670** J. RAY *English Proverbs* 41 March hack ham [hackande = annoying] comes in like a lion, goes out like a lamb. **1849** C. BRONTË *Shirley* II. iv. Charming and fascinating he resolved to be. Like March, having come in like a lion, he purposed to go out like a lamb. **1906** E. HOLDEN *Country Diary of Edwardian Lady* (1977) 25 March has come in like a lamb with a warm wind..from the South-west. **2002** *Times* 2 Mar. 26 'When March comes in like a lion, it goes out like a lamb' goes the old folklore saying..The reverse, however, is also true, and the saying continues: 'When March comes in like a lamb, it goes out like a lion,' which does not bode well for us this year. ■ **weather lore**

March *see also* APRIL showers bring forth May flowers; on the FIRST of March the crows begin to search; so many MISTS in March, so many frosts in May; a PECK of March dust is worth a king's ransom.

march *see* an ARMY marches on its stomach.

mare *see* the GREY mare is the better horse; MONEY makes the mare to go; NOTHING so bold as a blind mare.

market *see* BUY in the cheapest market and sell in the dearest; a MONEYLESS man goes fast through the market.

MARRIAGE is a lottery

□ **1642** T. FULLER *Holy State* III. xxii. Marriage shall prove no lottery to thee, when the hand of providence chuseth for thee, who, if drawing a blank, can turn into a prize by sanctifying a bad wife unto thee. **1875** S. SMILES *Thrift* xii. 'Marriage is a lottery.' It may be so, if we abjure the teachings of prudence. **1939** F. SULLIVAN *Sullivan at Bay* 14 What is marriage?.. Marriage is a lottery. ■ **luck; marriage**

There goes more to MARRIAGE than four bare legs in a bed

□ *c* **1549** J. HEYWOOD *Dialogue of Proverbs* I. viii. B1 In house to kepe household, whan folks wyll wed, Mo thyngs belong, than foure bare legs in a bed. **1623** W. CAMDEN *Remains concerning Britain* (ed. 3) 273 Longs more to marriage then foure bare legges in a bed. **1738** SWIFT *Polite Conversation* i. 84 Consider, Mr. Neverout, Four bare Legs in a Bed; and you are a younger Brother. **1958** in M. L. Wolf *Dict. Painting* p. vii. As the old proverb has it, 'there goes more to marriage than four bare legs in a bed.' ■ **marriage**

marriage *see also* DREAM of a funeral and you hear of a marriage; HANGING and wiving go by destiny.

MARRIAGES are made in heaven

□ **1567** W. PAINTER *Palace of Pleasure* xxiii. True it is, that marriages be don in Heaven and performed in earth. **1580** LYLY *Euphues & his England* II. 223 Mariages are made in heauen, though consumated in yearth. **1738** SWIFT *Polite Conversation* i. 78 They say, Marriages are made in Heaven; but I doubt, when she was married, she had no Friend there. **1932** S. GIBBONS *Cold Comfort Farm* i. I prefer the idea of arrangement to that other statement, that marriages are made in Heaven. **1980** 'S. WOODS' *Weep for Her* 187 She's a sentimental sort who believes marriages are made in heaven. ■ **marriage**

married *see* a YOUNG man married is a young man marred.

Never MARRY for money, but marry where money is

□ **1870** TENNYSON *Northern Farmer, New Style* in *The Holy Grail* 163 Doänt thou marry for munny, but goä wheer munny is! **1968** 'W. HAGGARD' *Cool Day for Killing* ii. He'd have heard the ancient saw. Never marry for money, but marry where money is. **1991** *Bookseller* 16 Aug. 403 'Never marry money but go where money is.' For the book as an entity to make news consistently, it must go where news is consistently made—as with the royal family. ■ **marriage; money**

MARRY in haste and repent at leisure

This formula can be applied to rash steps other than marriage: e.g. **1998** *Spectator* 10 Jan. 6 All modern governments legislate in haste and repent at leisure. A frequent recent variant is *act in haste, repent at leisure*: e.g. **1998** *Times* 26 Jan. 21 'Act in haste, repent at leisure' would be a poor epitaph for the UK's presidency [of the EU].

□ **1568** E. TILNEY *Duties in Marriage* B4 Some haue loued in post hast, that afterwards haue repented them at leysure. **1615** J. DAY *Festivals* x. Marrying in hast, and

Repenting by leasure. **1734** B. FRANKLIN *Poor Richard's Almanack* (May) Grief often treads upon the heels of pleasure, Marry'd in haste, we oft repent at leisure. **1872** W. STIRLING-MAXWELL *Works* (1891) VI. xvii. 'Marry in haste and repent at leisure' is a proverb that may be borne in mind with advantage in the choice of a party as well as of a wife. **2002** *National Review* 11 Mar. 28 One might with justice adapt the old proverb about marriage to the adorning of the skin in this savage fashion: Tattoo in haste, repent at leisure. ■ **haste; marriage; regrets**

MARRY in May, rue for aye

Some earlier related proverbs are also illustrated below. There are a number of old beliefs about the malign influence of this month, e.g. MAY *chickens come cheeping*. Cf. OVID *Fasti* v. 489 *si te proverbia tangunt, mense malum Maio nubere volgus ait*, if proverbs influence you, the common people say it is bad luck to marry in May.

□ **1675** *Poor Robin's Almanack* May, The Proverb saies..Of all the Moneths 'tis worst to Wed in May. **1821** J. GALT *Annals of Parish* vi. We were married on the 29th day of April..on account of the dread that we had of being married in May, for it is said, 'Of the marriages in May, The bairns die of a decay.' **1879** W. HENDERSON *Notes on Folk-Lore of Northern Counties* (rev. ed.) i. The ancient proverb still lives on the lips of the people of Scotland and the Borders—Marry in May, Rue for aye. **1913** E. M. WRIGHT *Rustic Speech* xiii. May..is an evil month for marriage. .. Marry in May, you'll rue it for aye, is a Devonshire saying. **1981** *Observer Magazine* 28 June 27 On weddings and engagements we are told that May is an unlucky month for getting married, 'Marry in May, rue for aye.' ■ **calendar lore; marriage; regrets**

marry *see also* BETTER to marry than to burn.

martin *see* the ROBIN and the wren are God's cock and hen.

martyr *see* the BLOOD of the martyrs is the seed of the Church.

mass *see* MEAT and mass never hindered man.

Like MASTER, like man

Man here is in the sense of 'servant'. The female equivalent is *like mistress like maid*. Cf. PETRONIUS *Satyricon* lviii. *qualis dominus, talis et servus*, as is the master, so is the servant; early 14th-cent. Fr. *lon dit a tel seigneur tel varlet*, it is said, for such a lord such a manservant.

□ **1530** J. PALSGRAVE *L'éclaircissement de la Langue Française* 120v Suche maystre suche man. **1538** T. ELYOT *Dict.* s.v. Similes, A lewde [foolish] servaunt with an yll master. ..Lyke master lyke man. **1620** T. SHELTON tr. *Cervantes' Don Quixote* II. x. The Prouerbe be true that sayes, 'like master, like man', and I may add, 'like lady, like maid'. Lady Hercules was fine, but her maid was still finer. **1979** M. G. EBERHART *Bayou Road* iv. 'Like master, like man,' Marcy's father had said bitterly ..of the disappearance of an entire set of Dresden plates. **1990** 'C. AIRD' *Body Politic* (1991) xii. 131 'I'm sorry,' said Miss Finch, 'but she just doesn't like men.' Like mistress, like maid, was what Sloan's grandmother would have said to that, but Sloan himself, wise in his own generation, kept silent. ■ **employers and employees**

master *see also* the EYE of a master does more work than both his hands; FIRE is a good servant but a bad master; JACK is as good as his master; JACK of all trades and master of none; NO man can serve two masters.

What MATTERS is what works

□ **1998** Department of Transport, Environment, and the Regions *Modernising Local Government: Improving Local Services through Best Value* ii. 9 There is no reason why services should be delivered directly if other more efficient means are available. What matters is what works. **2001** *Spectator* 3 Nov. 22 Given that the unions had all bought into 'what matters is what works', it struck me as confrontational. ■ **efficiency and inefficiency**

MAY chickens come cheeping

The proverb literally means that the weakness of chickens born in May is apparent from their continual feeble cries.

□ **1868** A. HISLOP *Proverbs of Scotland* 223 May birds are aye cheeping. This refers to the popular superstition against marrying in.. May, the children of which marriages are said to 'die of decay'. **1895** S. O. ADDY *Household Tales* II. viii. Children born in the month of May require great care in bringing up, for 'May chickens come cheeping.' ■ **calendar lore; misfortune**

May *see also* APRIL showers bring forth May flowers; ne'er CAST a clout till May be out; MARRY in May, rue for aye; so many MISTS in March, so many frosts in May; SELL in May and go away; a SWARM in May is worth a load of hay; SWEEP the house with broom in May, you sweep the head of the house away.

may *see* he that WILL not when he may, when he will he shall have nay.

means *see* the END justifies the means; he who WILLS the end, wills the means.

There is MEASURE in all things

Similar to MODERATION *in all things.* HORACE *Satires* I. i. 106 *est modus in rebus*, there is measure in things.

□ *c* **1385** CHAUCER *Troilus & Criseyde* II. 715 In every thyng, I woot, there lith mesure [moderation]. **1598–9** SHAKESPEARE *Much Ado about Nothing* II. i. 59 If the prince be too important, tell him there is measure in every thing. **1616** T. DRAXE *Adages* 131 There is a measure in all things. **1910** R. KIPLING *Rewards & Fairies* 84 There's no clean hands in the trade. But steal in measure. .. There is measure in all things made. **1942** A. THIRKELL *Marling Hall* iii. 'Good God, mamma dear,' said Oliver. 'You cannot throw old governesses together like that. There is measure in everything.' **1958** M. RENAULT *King must Die* II. i. One expects some fooling when they bring the bridegroom, but there is measure in everything. ■ **moderation**

measure *see also* MAN is the measure of all things.

MEAT and mass never hindered man

□ *a* **1628** J. CARMICHAELL *Proverbs in Scots* no. 134 A mease [mess = serving] of meat hinderit never man. **1639** J. CLARKE *Parœmiologia Anglo-Latina* 273 Meat and mattens hinder no mans journey. **1641** D. FERGUSSON *Scottish Proverbs* (STS) no. 644 Meat and masse never hindred no man. **1817** SCOTT *Rob Roy* III. ii. 'What the devil are ye in sic a hurry for?' said Garschattachin; 'meat and mass never hindered wark.' **1893** R. L. STEVENSON *Catriona* I. xix. Meat and mass never hindered man. The mass I cannot afford you, for we are all good Protestants. But the meat I press on your attention. ■ **Christianity; food and drink**

One man's MEAT is another man's poison

Cf. LUCRETIUS *De Rerum Natura* IV. 637 *quod ali cibus est aliis fuat acre venenum*, what is food to one person may be bitter poison to others.

□ *c* **1576** T. WHYTHORNE *Autobiography* (1961) 203 On bodies meat iz an otherz poizon. **1604** *Plato's Cap* B4 That ould moth-eaten Prouerbe.. One mans meate, is another mans poyson. *a* **1721** M. PRIOR *Dialogues of Dead* (1907) 246 May I not nauseate the food which you Covet; and is it not even a Proverb, that what is meat to one Man is Poyson to another. **1883** TROLLOPE *Autobiography* x. It is more true of novels than perhaps of anything else, that one man's food is another man's poison. **1986** J. S. SCOTT *Knife between Ribs* xvi. 'I don't see what he sees in her.' 'One man's meat is another man's poison.' **2000** *Washington Post* 9 Mar. C2 If one man's meat is another man's poison, then by the same token one man's joke is another man's snooze. ■ **idiosyncrasy; taste**

meat *see also* you BUY land you buy stones; GOD never sends mouths but He sends meat; GOD sends meat, but the Devil sends cooks; the NEARER the bone, the sweeter the meat.

medicine *see* LAUGHTER is the best medicine.

meddler *see* LAY-OVERS for meddlers.

Do not MEET troubles halfway

There are a number of sayings along similar lines, e.g. *never* TROUBLE *trouble till trouble troubles you.* Cf. SENECA *Epistle* XIII. x. *quid iuvat dolori suo occurrere?* what help is it to run out to meet your troubles?; **1598–9** SHAKESPEARE *Much Ado about Nothing* I. i. 82 Are you come to meet your trouble? The fashion of the world is to avoid cost, and you encounter it.

□ **1896** J. C. HUTCHESON *Crown & Anchor* xvi. I can't see the use of anticipating the worst and trying to meet troubles halfway. **1940** M. SADLEIR *Fanny by Gaslight* III. ii. What happens when she goes?.. Do not meet troubles half way. ..When need arises we will see what can be done. **1980** G. THOMPSON *Murder Mystery* xx. Don't go meeting trouble half-way. There might just be something we can do. ■ **misfortune**

meet *see also* never BID the Devil good morrow until you meet him; EXTREMES meet; when GREEK meets Greek then comes the tug of war.

memory *see* a LIAR ought to have a good memory.

So many MEN, so many opinions

Cf. TERENCE *Phormio* II. iv. *quot homines tot sententiae*, so many men, so many opinions; mid 14th-cent. Fr. *que tant de testes, tant de sens*, so many heads, so many opinions.

□ *c* **1390** CHAUCER *Squire's Tale* l. 203 As many heddes, as manye wittes ther been. **1483** *Vulgaria abs Terencio* Q3ᵛ Many men many opinyons. Euery man has his guyse. **1692** R. L'ESTRANGE *Fables of Aesop* ccclviii. So many Men, so many Minds; and this Diversity of Thought must necessarily be attended with Folly, Vanity, and Error. **1754** RICHARDSON *Grandison* VI. xx. Doctors differ. So many persons, so many minds. **1924** 'A. CARP' *Augustus Carp, Esq.* xii. They were all those things, and they would remember the old saying, so many men, so many opinions. ■ **idiosyncrasy; opinions**

men *see also* the BEST-laid schemes of mice and men gang aft agley; the BEST of men are but men at best; BRAVE men lived before Agamemnon; the BUSIEST men have the most leisure; DEAD men don't bite; DEAD men tell no tales; GOOD men are scarce; when THIEVES fall out, honest men come by their own; THREATENED men live long; one VOLUNTEER is worth two pressed men; YOUNG men may die, but old men must die.

mend *see* it is NEVER too late to mend; when THINGS are at the worst they begin to mend.

mended *see* LEAST said, soonest mended.

mending *see* a WOMAN and a ship ever want mending.

mention *see* never mention ROPE in the house of a man who has been hanged.

merrier *see* the MORE the merrier.

It is MERRY in hall when beards wag all

□ *c* **1300** *King Alisaunder* (EETS) l. 1164 Swithe [so] mury hit is in halle, When the burdes wawen alle! **1546** J. HEYWOOD *Dialogue of Proverbs* II. vii. 13V It is mery in halle, When berds wag all. **1598** SHAKESPEARE *Henry IV, Pt. 2* V. iii. 35 Be merry, be merry, my wife has all. .. 'Tis merry in hall when beards wag all. **1738** SWIFT *Polite Conversation* ii. 170 Come; they say, 'Tis merry in Hall, when Beards wag all. **1857** TROLLOPE *Barchester Towers* III. iv. ''Twas merry in the hall when the beards wagged all;' and the clerical beards wagged merrily.. that day. **1976** 'J. DAVEY' *Treasury Alarm* i. Presumably this is how the Treasury greybeards get their fun. Are they in fact grey-bearded. One rather assumes a great wagging of beards: *'tis merry in hall when beards wag all.* ■ **hospitality**; **merriment**

merry *see also* a CHERRY year, a merry year; EAT, drink, and be merry…

Merryman *see* the best DOCTORS are Dr Diet, Dr Quiet, and Dr Merryman.

mice *see* the BEST-laid schemes of mice and men gang aft agley; a CAT in gloves catches no mice; when the CAT's away, the mice will play; KEEP no more cats than will catch mice.

mickle *see* MANY a little makes a mickle; MANY a mickle makes a muckle.

midge *see* the MOTHER of mischief is no bigger than a midge's wing.

midnight *see* one HOUR's sleep before midnight is worth two after.

mid-stream *see* don't CHANGE horses in mid-stream.

MIGHT is right

Cf. PLATO *Republic* I. 338C *φημὶ γὰρ ἐγὼ εἶναι τὸ δίκαιον οὐκ ἄλλο τι ἢ τὸ τοῦ κρείττονος ξυμφέρον*, for I [Thrasymachus] say that justice is nothing else than the interest of the stronger; LUCAN *Pharsalia* I. 175 *mensuraque iuris vis erat*, might was the measure of right.

□ *a* **1327** in T. Wright *Political Songs* (1839) 254 For miht is right, the lond is laweless. **1546** J. HEYWOOD *Dialogue of Proverbs* II. v. H2V We se many tymes myght ouercomth ryght. **1790** J. TRUSLER *Proverbs Exemplified* 78 The law is so expensive. ..Might too often overcomes right. **1892** J. NICHOL *Carlyle* iv. [In] *Chartism*.. he clearly enunciates 'Might is right'—one of the few strings on which.. he played through life. **1979** *Guardian* 17 May 24 By adult examples, pupils are being taught such evil doctrines as 'Might is right'. **2001** *Times* 7 Nov. 16 All this means is that in politics, as in war, might is right. ■ **justice and injustice**; **power**

mightier *see* the PEN is mightier than the sword.

mighty *see* a REED before the wind lives on, while mighty oaks do fall.

mile *see* a MISS is as good as a mile.

milk *see* why buy a cow when milk is so cheap?; it is no use CRYING over spilt milk.

The MILL cannot grind with the water that is past

□ **1616** T. DRAXE *Adages* 151 The water that is past, cannot make the mill goe. **1640** G. HERBERT *Outlandish Proverbs* no. 153 The mill cannot grind with the water that's past. **1856** R. C. TRENCH *Poems* 197 Oh seize the instant [present] time; you never will With waters once passed by impel the mill. **1980** G. RICHARDS *Red Kill* xiv. It did no good to think back. The mill cannot grind with the water that is past, as the old people in the mountains used to say. ■ **opportunity, missed; past**

mill *see also* all is GRIST that comes to the mill.

The MILLS of God grind slowly, yet they grind exceeding small

Quoted in SEXTUS EMPIRICUS *Against Professors* I. 287 *ὀψὲ θεῶν ἀλέουσι μύλοι, ἀλέουσι δὲ λεπτά*, the mills of the gods are late to grind, but they grind small.

□ **1640** G. HERBERT *Outlandish Proverbs* no. 747 Gods Mill grinds slow, but sure. **1870** LONGFELLOW *Poems* (1960) 331 Though the mills of God grind slowly, yet they grind exceeding small; Though with patience he stands waiting, with exactness grinds he all. **1942** 'F. BEEDING' *Twelve Disguises* i. That's my business. . . The mills of God grind slowly, but they grind exceeding small. **1989** R. HART *Remains to be Seen* vii. Military record keepers were like the mills of God. They ground slow, and exceeding small, but only at their own pace. ■ **justice and injustice; retribution**

mind *see* the EYES are the window of the soul; GREAT minds think alike; LITTLE things please little minds; OUT of sight, out of mind; TRAVEL broadens the mind.

The age of MIRACLES is past

□ **1599** SHAKESPEARE *Henry V* I. i. 67 It must be so; for miracles are ceas'd; And therefore we must needs admit the means How things are perfected. **1602**—— *All's Well that Ends Well* II. iii. 1 They say miracles are past; and we have our philosophical persons to make modern and familiar things supernatural and causeless. **1840** CARLYLE *On Heroes & Hero Worship* iv. The Age of Miracles past? The Age of Miracles is for ever here! **1988** J. MORTIMER *Rumpole and Age of Miracles* (1989) 108 'A total victory,' I agreed. 'The Age of Miracles is not past.' ■ **marvels**

mischief *see* the MOTHER of mischief is no bigger than a midge's wing.

MISERY loves company

Now predominantly current in the United States. Cf. mid 14th-cent. L. *gaudium est miseris socios habuisse penarum*, it is a comfort to the wretched to have companions in woes; *a* **1349** R. ROLLE *Meditations on Passion* in C. Horstmann *Yorkshire Writers* (1895) I. 101 It is solace to haue companie in peyne.

□ **1578** LYLY *Euphues* I. 238 In miserie Euphues it is a great comfort to haue a companion. **1620** T. SHELTON tr. *Cervantes' Don Quixote* II. xiii. If that which is commonly spoken be true, that to haue companions in misery is a lightner of it, you may comfort me. **1775** T. GILBERT *Letter* 4 May in W. B. Clark et al. *Naval Documents of American Revolution* (1964) I. 279 All my Letters are inter septed by those Rebels who want Every one to be kept in Dark like themselves. (Misery

Loves Company). **1851** H. D. THOREAU *Journal* 1 Sept. (1949) II. 440 If misery loves company, misery has company enough. **2002** *Washington Post* 21 Aug. F1 The question is how to salvage a difficult season. Refusing to open our depressing 401(k) statements may work for a little while, but most of us need something more emotionally nourishing. (And besides, misery loves company.) ■ **malice; misfortune**

MISFORTUNES never come singly

Cf. early 14th-cent. Fr. *ung meschief ne vient point seul*, a misfortune does not come alone.

□ *c* **1300** *King Alisaunder* (EETS) l. 1276 Men telleth in olde mone [lament] The qued [harm] comuth nowher alone. **1509** A. BARCLAY *Ship of Fools* 236 Wyse men sayth, and oft it fallyth so..That one myshap fortuneth neuer alone. **1622** J. MABBE tr. *Aleman's Guzman d'Alfarache* I. iii. Misfortunes seldome come alone. **1711** J. ADDISON *Spectator* 8 Mar. The Lady..said to her Husband with a Sigh, My Dear, Misfortunes never come single. **1791** T. BURR *Letter* 27 July in M. L. Davis *Memoirs of Aaron Burr* (1836) I. 301 We certainly see the old proverb very often verified. 'That misfortunes never come singly,' that poor little woman is a proof. **1894** BLACKMORE *Perlycross* II. vii. As misfortunes never come single, the sacred day robbed him of another fine resource. **1931** 'L. CHARTERIS' *Wanted for Murder* v. Blessings, like misfortunes, never come singly. There was even a packet of Havana cigarettes..behind the bath salts. **1981** G. MITCHELL *Death-Cap Dancers* v. 'The car..skidded and hit a tree.' 'Misfortunes never come singly.' ■ **misfortune**

A MISS is as good as a mile

The syntax of the proverb has been distorted by abridgement: the original structure is apparent from quot. 1614.

□ **1614** W. CAMDEN *Remains concerning Britain* (ed. 2) 303 An ynche in a misse is as good as an ell [a former measure of length equal to about 1.1 m]. **1655** T. FULLER *Hist. Cambridge* 37 An hairs breadth fixed by a divine-finger, shall prove as effectuall a separation from danger as a miles distance. **1788** *American Museum* Apr. 382 A miss is as good as a mile. **1825** SCOTT *Journal* 3 Dec. (1939) 28 He was very near being a poet—but a miss is as good as a mile, and he always fell short of the mark. **1978** T. SHARPE *Throwback* vii. If you aimed at a grouse it was hit or miss and a miss was as good as a mile. ■ **error**

You never MISS the water till the well runs dry

□ *a* **1628** J. CARMICHAELL *Proverbs in Scots* no. 1140 Manie wats [know] not quhairof [whereof] the wel sauris [tastes] quhill [until] it fall drie. **1659** J. HOWELL *Proverbs* (British) 24 Of the Well we see no want, till either dry, or Water skant. **1721** J. KELLY *Scottish Proverbs* 351 We'll never know the worth of Water 'till the well go dry. **1874** H. LINN *You never miss Water* 5 Do not let your chances, like sunbeams pass you by; For you never miss the water till the well runs dry. **1996** *Washington Times* 18 July A6 'There is an old adage,' Sen. Robert Byrd..recalled this week, 'that "you never miss the water until the well runs dry."' ■ **blessings; gratitude and ingratitude**

miss *see also* what you've never HAD you never miss; a SLICE off a cut loaf isn't missed.

If you don't make MISTAKES you don't make anything

□ **1896** CONRAD *Outcast of Islands* III. ii. It's only those who do nothing that make no mistakes, I suppose. **1925** *Times* 9 Nov. 17 The comforting assurance that 'a man who never makes mistakes never makes anything.' **1980** M. DRABBLE *Middle Ground* 86 If you don't make mistakes you don't make anything, she said, a motto which Hugo seemed to remember having seen pinned over the desk. ■ **error; risk**

mistress *see* like MASTER, like man.

So many MISTS in March, so many frosts in May

□ **1612** A. HOPTON *Concordancy of Years* xxx. Some say, so many mistes in March, so many hoare frosts after Easter. **1678** J. RAY *English Proverbs* (ed. 2) 344 So many frosts in March so many in May. **1978** R. WHITLOCK *Calendar of Country Customs* iii. Many old country beliefs are not content with generalities but strive to be more precise. A well-known proverb is: So many mists in March, So many frosts in May. ■ **weather lore**

mixen *see* BETTER wed over the mixen than over the moor.

MODERATION in all things

A more recent formulation of the idea contained in *there is* MEASURE *in all things*. The Latin word *modus* can be translated as either 'moderation' or 'measure', but the former seems to be gaining currency at the expense of the latter, possibly because 'measure' has several meanings and so could be misunderstood. HESIOD *Works & Days* l. 694 *μέτρα φυλάσσεσθαι· καιρὸς δ' ἐπὶ πᾶσιν ἄριστος*, observe due measure; moderation is best in all things; PLAUTUS *Poenulus* l. 238 *modus omnibus rebus.. optimus est habitu*, moderation in all things is the best policy.

□ **1849** H. MELVILLE *Mardi* II. lxxvii. I am for being temperate in these things. ..All things in moderation are good; whence, wine in moderation is good. **1879** W. H. G. KINGSTON tr. *Swiss Family Robinson* ii. 'Oh, father, sugar canes. ..Do let us take a lot home to mother.'..'Gently there. ..Moderation in all things.' **1980** S. T. HAYMON *Death & Pregnant Virgin* ii. Norfolk..[is] on the same scale I am. No Niagaras, no hills higher than hills..ought to be. Moderation in all things. **2002** *Times Crème* 3 July 5 It can hardly be described as good for you..but all things in moderation, as they say. ■ **moderation**

Monday *see* Monday's CHILD is fair of face.

MONEY can't buy happiness

A recurrent theme in invectives against materialism down the ages, but this formulation of it appears to be comparatively recent.

□ **1856** G. C. BALDWIN *Representative Women* 215 Gold cannot buy happiness, and parents who compel their daughters to marry for money, or station, commit a grievous sin against humanity and God. **1873** E. KELLOGG *Arthur Brown* vii. 118 'I had rather have friends who love me for my own sake..than all the money in the world.' 'Money won't buy happiness, Walter.' **1984** ANON. in R. Byrne *Other 637 Best Things Anybody Ever Said* (1985) I. no. 220 Whoever said money can't buy happiness didn't know where to shop. **2002** *Washington Post* 19 June C15 (*Blondie comic strip*) 'Bumstead, your problem is that you worry too much about money. Money can't buy happiness, you know.' 'Has it bought you happiness, boss?' 'Yeah, but that's just me!' ■ **happiness; money**

MONEY has no smell

L. *non olet*, it [money] does not smell. Titus, son of the Roman emperor Vespasian, had criticized a tax on public lavatories. Vespasian held a coin from the first payment to his son's nose and asked him whether the smell was offensive. Titus said no. Vespasian replied 'And yet it comes from urine' (Suetonius *Vespasian* xxiii).

□ **1914** 'E. BRAMAH' *Max Carrados* 45 The Romans, Parkinson, had a saying to the effect that gold carries no smell. That is a pity sometimes. What jewellery did Miss Hutchins wear? **1922** A. BENNETT *Mr. Prohack* iii. The associations of the wealth scarcely affected him. He understood in the flesh the deep wisdom of that old proverb.. that money has no smell. **1940** R. CHANDLER *Farewell, my Lovely* xxxiv. He punched the cash-register and dropped the bill into the drawer. They say money don't stink. I sometimes wonder. **2002** *Times* 20 Feb. 3 Mr Justice Jacob.. asked rhetorically: 'Should procurers, pimps, panders.. pay VAT? That is the question on this appeal.. In this case, as the Latin poet [*sic*] said, *pecunia non olet*—money doesn't smell. I allow the appeal.' ■ **money**

MONEY isn't everything

□ **1927** E. O'NEILL *Marco Millions* iii. Money isn't everything, not always. *a* **1947** F. THOMPSON *Still glides Stream* (1948) ii. He said quite angrily that money was not everything, there was the satisfaction of knowing you'd turned out a good job. **1975** J. I. M. STEWART *Young Pattullo* xv. If one owns property one can always have a little money follow one around. But we all know that money isn't everything. ■ **money**

MONEY is power

A more worldly alternative to KNOWLEDGE *is power*.

□ **1741** N. AMES *Almanack* 4 Laws bear Name, but Money has the Power. **1789** F. AMES *Letter* 16 May in *Works* (1854) I. 39 Money is power, a permanent revenue is permanent power, and the credit which it would give was a safeguard to the government. **1818** M. EDGEWORTH *Letter* 13 Oct. (1971) 115 Now he had money 'and money is power'. **1930** MEANS & THACKER *Strange Death of President Harding* iv. One can do nothing—be nothing, without money, not even in the White House. Money is power. **1980** J. O'FAOLAIN *No Country for Young Men* i. The lads would have to have.. money if they were to get guns. .. Money was power. ■ **money**; **power**

MONEY is the root of all evil

Cf. I TIMOTHY vi. 10 (AV) The love of money is the root of all evil. Both the biblical original and the shorter version are current.

□ *c* **1000** AELFRIC *Homilies* (1843) I. 256 Seo gytsung is ealra yfelra thinga wyrtruma [covetousness is the root of all evil things]. *c* **1449** R. PECOCK *Repressor of Blaming of Clergy* (1860) II. 555 Loue to money.. is worthi to be forborn.. as Poul seith, it is 'the roote of al yuel'. **1616** J. WITHALS *Dict.* (rev. ed.) 546 Riches are the root of all euill. **1777** in L. H. Butterfield et al. *Adams Family Correspondence* (1963) II. 345 Many have been loth to believe.. That Money is the Root of all Evil. **1858** TROLLOPE *Dr. Thorne* I. xii. 'But, doctor, you'll take the money.'.. 'Quite impossible..' said the doctor,.. valiantly rejecting the root of all evil. **1978** W. L. DEANDREA *Killed in Ratings* ii. Magazines have got these funny little sayings. .. Here's one. 'Money is the root of all evil.. but that's one evil I'm rooting for.' **2001** R. HILL *Dialogues of Dead* xliii. 355 'Anyway there we have it, a dollar sign and a Roman coin. I suppose it could be some kind of statement about money being the root of all evil?' ■ **good and evil**; **money**

MONEY, like manure, does no good till it is spread

□ **1625** F. BACON 'Of Seditions and Troubles' in *Essays* 85 Money is like muck; not good except it be spread. **1816** W. MAVOR *English Spelling-Book* (ed. 198)

103 Money, like manure, does no good till it is spread. **2001** *Las Vegas Review-Journal* 7 Oct. (electronic ed.) 'Jack always says,' Wagner recalled, 'money's like manure. You've got to spread it around in your company to make things grow.' ■ **money**

MONEY makes a man

Cf. L. *divitiae virum faciunt*, wealth makes the man.

□ *a* **1500** in R. L. Greene *Early English Carols* (1935) 263 Yt ys allwayes sene now-adayes That money makythe the man. *a* **1661** T. FULLER *Worthies* (Hants.) 3 We commonly say.. In the Change [Exchange], Money makes a man, which puts him in a solvable condition. **1828** BULWER-LYTTON *Pelham* I. xxxiv. The continent only does for us English people to see. ..Here, you know, 'money makes the man.' **1920** D. H. LAWRENCE *Letter* 7 May (1962) I. 629 Money maketh a man; even if he was a monkey to start with. **1950** C. E. VULLIAMY *Henry Plumdew* 203 I doubt whether he understands the place of money in vulgar estimation. ..Money maketh man. ■ **money**

MONEY makes money

□ **1572** T. WILSON *Discourse upon Usury* 54ᵛ Mony getteth money. *a* **1654** J. SELDEN *Table-Talk* (1689) 57 'Tis a vain thing to say, Money begets not Money; for that no doubt it does. **1776** A. SMITH *Wealth of Nations* I. I. ix. Money, says the proverb, makes money. When you have got a little, it is often easy to get more. **1865** DICKENS *Our Mutual Friend* III. v. We have got to recollect that money makes money, as well as makes everything else. **1935** A. CHRISTIE *Miss Marple's Final Cases* (1979) 60 Everything she did turned out well. Money made money. **1988** C. H. SAWYER *J. Alfred Prufrock Murders* v. Well.. maybe she made some clever investments? But no, she would have had to have money to begin with—it takes money to make money, my husband always said. ■ **money**

MONEY makes the mare to go

□ *a* **1500** in R. L. Greene *Early English Carols* (1935) 262 In the heyweyes [highways] ther joly [spirited] palfreys Yt [money] makyght to.. praunce. **1573** J. SANFORDE *Garden of Pleasure* 105ᵛ Money makes the horsse to goe. **1670** J. RAY *English Proverbs* 122 It's money makes the mare to go. **1748** RICHARDSON *Clarissa* IV. 187 A leading man in the House of Commons, is a very important character; because that house has the giving of money: And *Money makes the mare to go.* **1930** L. MEYNELL *Mystery at Newton Ferry* xiii. 'Tis money makes the mare go. ..They're all after it, every one of them. **1978** *Countryman* Spring 193 Weardale farmer's advice to daughter about to reject a proposal of marriage from a wealthy tradesman: 'Never cock your snoop at money, my lass, 'cos it's money that makes the mare to go'. ■ **money**

MONEY talks

Meaning that money has influence.

□ **1666** G. TORRIANO *Italian Proverbs* 179 Man prates, but gold speaks. **1681** A. BEHN *Rover* II. III. i. Money speaks in a Language all Nations understand. **1903** *Saturday Evening Post* 5 Sept. 12 When money talks it often merely remarks 'Good-by'. **1915** WODEHOUSE *Something Fresh* iii. The whole story took on a different complexion for Joan. Money talks. **1984** A. BROOKNER *Hotel du Lac* (1985) xi. 'At least I assume they are millionaires?' 'That is what they would like you to assume, certainly. And if money talks,.. they are certainly making the right amount of noise.' **2002** *Washington Post* 15 Jan. E3 Why did all these people look the other way for so long? Money talks. Or, with Enron, shouts. ■ **money**; **power**

money *see also* BAD money drives out good; a FOOL and his money are soon parted; LEND your money and lose your friend; never MARRY for money, but marry where money is; where there's MUCK there's brass; you PAYS your money and you takes your choice; TIME is money.

A MONEYLESS man goes fast through the market

The proverb is explained in quot. 1721. The last example represents a variation of the original proverb, asserting that a person rushes to wherever what he lacks may be found. Cf. late 14th-cent. Fr. *cilz qui n'a point d'argent n'a que faire au marchié*, he who has no money can only go to (i.e. cannot buy anything at) the market.

□ **1721** J. KELLY *Scottish Proverbs* 10 A silverless Man goes fast through the Market. Because he does not stay to cheapen [bargain] or buy. **1732** T. FULLER *Gnomologia* no. 330 A Moneyless Man goes fast thro' the Market. **1977** J. AIKEN *Five-Minute Marriage* iv. Found your way here at last, then, miss, have you? A moneyless mare trots fast to the market. ■ **buying and selling; poverty**

monk *see* the COWL does not make the monk.

monkey *see* the HIGHER the monkey climbs, the more he shows his tail; if you PAY peanuts, you get monkeys; SOFTLY, softly, catchee monkey.

moon *see* NO moon, no man.

moor *see* BETTER wed over the mixen than over the moor.

MORE people know Tom Fool than Tom Fool knows

Tom Fool is a name traditionally given to a simpleton, or to one who acts the part of a fool, as in a drama or morris dance.

□ **1656** S. HOLLAND *Wit & Fancy* II. i. In all Comedies more know the Clown, then the Clown knows. **1723** DEFOE *Colonel Jack* (ed. 2) 347 It was no satisfaction to me that I knew not their faces, for they might know mine..according to the old English proverb, 'that more knows Tom Fool, than Tom Fool knows'. **1865** SURTEES *Facey Romford's Hounds* xxxii. 'Good mornin', Mr. Swig,' said the man; for the aphorism that 'more people know Tom Fool than Tom Fool knows,' holds particularly good as regards huntsmen and field servants. **1980** L. MEYNELL *Hooky & Prancing Horse* iv. Hooky asked..'How's the great pulsating world of journalism?' Mac was..surprised; but he consoled himself with the thought that more people know Tom Fool than Tom Fool knows. **2000** 'C. AIRD' *Little Knell* (2001) xv. 170 'I reckon that just at this minute, sir, there's more that we don't know about this girl's murder than what we do..' 'More people always know Tom Fool, Crosby.' ■ **associates; fame and obscurity**

The MORE the merrier

□ *c* **1380** *Pearl* (1953) l. 850 The mo [more] the myryer, so God me blesse. **1546** J. HEYWOOD *Dialogue of Proverbs* II. vii. I3 The mo the merier, we all daie here [hear] and se. Ye but the fewer the better fare (saied he). **1614** T. ADAMS *Devil's Banquet* IV. 196 The company is..all the Patriarchs, Prophets, Saints. ..The more the mirrier, yea, and the better cheare to. **1855** C. KINGSLEY *Westward Ho!* III. iv. The old proverb comes true—'the more the merrier: but the fewer the better fare.' **1976** L. ALTHER *Kinflicks* xiii. 'Take my word for it. Have another baby.'..'The more, the merrier!' **2001** M. DAHL *Viking Claw* vii. 56 A third rope was tossed through the hole. 'Clip that on, too!' yelled out Uncle Stoppard. Why not? The more the merrier. ■ **hospitality; merriment**

The MORE you get, the more you want

An observation more succinctly stated as MUCH *would have more*. Cf. HORACE *Epistles* II. ii. 147 *quanto plura parasti, tanto plura cupis*, you want as much again as you have already got.

□ *c* **1340** R. ROLLE *Psalter* (1884) 97 The mare that a man has the brennandere [more ardently] he askis. *a* **1450** *Castle of Perseverance* l. 3268 *in Macro Plays* (EETS) The more he hadde, the more he cravyd, Whyl the lyf lefte hym with-Inne. **1578** J. FLORIO *First Fruits* 32 The more a man hath, the more he desireth. **1798** W. MANNING *Key of Liberty* (1922) 9 In short he is never easy, but the more he has the more he wants. **1940** G. H. COXE *Glass Triangle* x. I was averaging eighty to a hundred [dollars] a week. Well, you know how it is. The more you get the more you want. ■ **greed**; **riches**

more *see also* more HASTE, less speed; the more LAWS, the more thieves and bandits; LESS is more; MUCH would have more; the more you STIR it the worse it stinks; there are more WAYS of killing a cat than choking it with cream; there are more WAYS of killing a dog than choking it with butter; there are more WAYS of killing a dog than hanging it.

MORNING dreams come true

Cf. MOSCHUS *Europa* 2 *νυκτὸς ὅτε τρίτατον λάχος ἵσταται, ἐγγύθι δ'ἠώς,.. εὖτε καὶ ἀτρεκέων ποιμαίνεται ἔθνος ὀνείρων*, at the third watch of the night, when dawn is near,.. and when the flock of true dreams is out grazing; HORACE *Satires* I. X. 33 *post mediam noctem visus, cum somnia vera*, he appeared to me after midnight, when dreams are true.

□ **1540** J. PALSGRAVE *Acolastus* II. i. After mydnyght men saye, that dreames be true. **1616** JONSON *Love Restored* VIII. 385 All the morning dreames are true. **1813** W. B. RHODES *Bombastes Furioso* III. 7 This morn.. I dreamt (and morning dreams come true, they say). **1909** A. MACLAREN *Romans* 87 Our highest anticipations and desires are not unsubstantial visions, but morning dreams, which are proverbially sure to be fulfilled. ■ **dreams**

morning *see also* never BID the Devil good morrow until you meet him; RED sky at night shepherd's delight.

moss *see* a ROLLING stone gathers no moss.

most *see* who KNOWS most, speaks least.

Like MOTHER, like daughter

The female equivalent of *like* FATHER, *like son*. EZEKIEL xvi. 44 (AV) Every one.. shall use this proverb against thee, saying, As is the mother, so is her daughter.

□ *a* **1325** *Cursor Mundi* (EETS) l. 18857 O suilk [such] a moder, wel slik [such] a child. **1474** CAXTON *Game of Chess* II. ii. For suche moder suche doughter comunely. **1644** R. WILLIAMS *Bloody Tenent of Persecution* xcix. Is not this as the Prophet speaks, Like mother, like daughter? **1861** C. READE *Cloister & Hearth* II. xvii. 'Mother, you were so hot against her.'.. 'Ay. .. Like mother like daughter: cowardice it is our bane.' **1992** A. LAMBERT *Rather English Marriage* (1993) xi. 188 'Darling, you are hopeless! Why are you always so broke?' (Like mother, like daughter, she thought to herself.) ■ **children and parents**; **similarity and dissimilarity**

The MOTHER of mischief is no bigger than a midge's wing

□ *a* **1628** J. CARMICHAELL *Proverbs in Scots* no. 1468 The mother of mischief, is na mair nor [than] a midgewing. **1796** M. EDGEWORTH *Parent's Assistant* (ed. 2) 149 'The mother of mischief', says an old proverb, 'is no bigger than a midge's wing.' **1858** D. M. MULOCK *Woman's Thoughts about Women* viii. Fatal and vile as her [Gossip's] progeny may be, 'the mother of mischief', says the proverb, 'is no bigger than a midge's wing.' ■ **beginnings and endings; great and small; trouble**

mother *see also* DILIGENCE is the mother of good luck; NECESSITY is the mother of invention; PRAISE the child, and you make love to the mother.

If the MOUNTAIN will not come to Mahomet, Mahomet must go to the mountain

Quot. 1625 gives the anecdote behind this saying.

□ **1625** BACON *Essays* 'Of Boldness' xii. Mahomet cald the Hill to come to him.. And when the Hill stood still, he was neuer a whit abashed, but said; If the Hill will not come to Mahomet, Mahomet wil go to the hil. **1732** T. FULLER *Gnomologia* no. 2707 If the Mountain will not come to Mahomet, Mahomet must go to the Mountain. **1975** D. BAGLEY *Snow Tiger* xvii. You couldn't go to see him, so the mountain had to go to Mahomet. It was.. important to him. **2001** *Washington Times* 27 Jan. F23 (*Herb & Jamaal comic strip*) 'I've waited too long for Jamaal to ask me out. It's time for me to take action! As they say, "If the mountain won't come to Mohammed, then Mohammed will go to the mountain".' ■ **necessity; obstinacy**

mountain *see also* FAITH will move mountains.

A MOUSE may help a lion

The proverb alludes to Aesop's fable of the lion and the rat, which is told by Caxton in *Fables* (1484) 40.

□ **1563** *Mirror for Magistrates* (1938) 274 The mouse may sometyme help the Lyon in nede. .. O prynces seke no foes. **1732** T. FULLER *Gnomologia* no. 264 A Lyon may come to be beholding to a Mouse. **1842** MARRYAT *Percival Keene* I. xvii. A mouse may help a lion, as the fable says. **1935** J. BUCHAN *House of Four Winds* xi. I only offer to show my gratitude by doing what I can. .. A mouse may help a lion. ■ **assistance; great and small**

mouse *see also* ONE for the mouse, one for the crow; *also* MICE.

mouth *see* out of the FULLNESS of the heart the mouth speaks; never look a GIFT horse in the mouth; GOD never sends mouths but He sends meat; a SHUT mouth catches no flies; a SOW may whistle, though it has an ill mouth for it.

Out of the MOUTHS of babes—

Young children may speak disconcertingly wisely or aptly at times. The proverb is used in a variety of abbreviated and allusive forms, often without a knowledge of the complete biblical quotations (both AV): PSALMS viii. 2 Out of the mouth of babes and sucklings hath thou ordained strength; MATTHEW xxi. 16 Jesus saith unto them [the Pharisees], Yea; have ye never read, Out of the mouth of babes and sucklings thou hast perfected praise.

□ **1899** R. KIPLING *Stalky & Co.* II In the present state of education I shouldn't have thought any three boys would be well enough grounded. ..But out of the mouths—. **1906** —— *Puck of Pook's Hill* 285 Out of the mouths of babes do we learn.

1979 'C. AIRD' *Some die Eloquent* xviii. It was something Crosby said. ..'About the source of the money.' 'Out of the mouths,' conceded Leeyes. ■ **children; wisdom**

move *see* FAITH will move mountains.

MUCH cry and little wool

□ *a* **1475** J. FORTESCUE *On Governance of England* (1885) x. His hyghnes shall haue theroff, but as hadd the man that sherid is [sheared his] hogge, much crye and litil woll. **1659** J. HOWELL *Proverbs* (English) 13 A Great cry and little wooll, quoth the Devil when he sheard the hogg. **1711** J. ADDISON *Spectator* 18 Dec. Those..make the most noise, who have least to sell..to whom I cannot but apply that old Proverb of *Much cry, but little wool.* **1922** *Punch* 29 Nov. 520 Ministers have taken good care that the adage, 'Much cry and little wool,' shall not apply to them. **1958** M. RENAULT *King must Die* I. v. They keep it [the codpiece] on under their kilts ..; much cry and little wool as the saying goes. ■ **boasting; words and deeds**

MUCH would have more

Cf. *the* MORE *you get, the more you want.*

□ *c* **1350** *Douce MS 52* no. 65 Mykull [much] wulle more. *a* **1400** *Wars of Alexander* (EETS) l. 4397 Mekill wald have mare as many man spellis [tells]. **1597** T. MORLEY *Plain Introduction to Music* II. 70 The Common Prouerb is in me verified, that much would have more. **1732** T. FULLER *Gnomologia* no. 3487 Much would have more; but often meets with less. **1897** J. McCARTHY *Hist. Own Times* V. 131 Expedition after expedition has been sent out to extend the Egyptian frontier. ..'Much will have more,' the old proverb says; but in this case..much is compelled for the sake of..security to try to have more. **1928** J. S. FLETCHER *Ransom for London* V. iv. Why should ten millions satisfy these people?..There is an old adage to the effect that much wants more. ■ **greed; riches**

much *see also* you can have TOO much of a good thing.

Where there's MUCK there's brass

Brass is a slang and dialectal word for 'money' here.

□ **1678** J. RAY *English Proverbs* (ed. 2) 179 Muck and money go together. **1855** H. G. BOHN *Hand-Book of Proverbs* 564 Where there is muck there is money. **1943** J. W. DAY *Farming Adventure* xii. 'Where there's muck there's money' is as true now as then. But farms today lack the mud. **1967** *Punch* 13 Sept. 396 'Where there's muck there's brass' synopsised for many a North-country businessman the value of dirt in the profit-making process. **2001** *Spectator* 15/22 Dec. 28 Where there's muck, there's brass, and it was the job of the *stercorarius* to empty the cesspits and sell on the contents to farmers on city outskirts. ■ **money**

muckle *see* MANY a mickle makes a muckle.

mud *see* throw DIRT enough, and some will stick.

multitude *see* CHARITY covers a multitude of sins.

MURDER will out

Similar in form to TRUTH *will out.*

□ *c* **1325** *Cursor Mundi* (EETS) l. 1084 For-thi [therefore] men sais into this tyde [time], Is no man that murthir may hide. *c* **1390** CHAUCER *Nun's Priest's Tale* l. 4242 Mordre wol out that se we day by day. **1596** SHAKESPEARE *Merchant of Venice* II. ii. 73 Truth will come to light; murder cannot be hid long. **1860** W. COLLINS *Woman in White* II. 64 Crimes cause their own detection, do they? And murder will out (another moral epigram), will it? **1978** F. NEUMANN *Seclusion Room* ix. 'Murder will out,' Berman announced, smiling fatuously. ■ **concealment; violence**

murder *see also* KILLING no murder.

What MUST be, must be

Cf. Ital. *che sarà sarà,* what will be, will be (this English form is also used).

□ *c* **1386** CHAUCER *Knight's Tale* l. 1466 Whan a thyng is shapen, it shal be. **1519** W. HORMAN *Vulgaria* 20^{V} That the whiche muste be wyll be. **1546** J. HEYWOOD *Dialogue of Proverbs* II. i. F3 That shalbe, shalbe. **1616** BEAUMONT & FLETCHER *Scornful Lady* III. i. I must kiss you. ..What must be, must be. **1841** S. WARREN *Ten Thousand a Year* I. i. It's really very inconvenient..for any of my young men to be absent..but—I suppose—what must be must be. **1850** DICKENS *David Copperfield* lvii. 'My love,' observed Mr. Micawber, '..I am always willing to defer to your good sense. What will be—will be.' **1981** J. BINGHAM *Brock* 70 Oh well, what must be, must be. ■ **fate and fatalism**

nail *see* when all you have is a HAMMER, everything looks like a nail; ONE nail drives out another; for WANT of a nail the shoe was lost.

name *see* give a DOG a bad name and hang him; he that has an ILL name is half hanged; NO names, no pack-drill.

nation *see* happy is the COUNTRY which has no history; the ENGLISH are a nation of shopkeepers.

NATURE abhors a vacuum

Cf. L. *natura abhorret vacuum*, Nature abhors a vacuum.

□ **1551** CRANMER *Answer to Gardiner* 299 Naturall reason abhorreth vacuum. **1642** T. FULLER *Holy State* v. ii. Queen Joan .. (hating widowhood as much as Nature doth vacuum) maried James King of Majorca. **1686** R. BOYLE *Free Inquiry* VII. 292 The Axiom of the Schools, that Nature abhors a Vacuum. **1771** S. JOHNSON *Letter* 20 June (1952) I. 249 Whatever philosophy may determine of material nature, it is certainly true of intellectual nature, that it abhors a vacuum: our minds cannot be empty. **2001** *Washington Times* 30 Oct. A4 The White House should have expected this, of course, since the media, like nature, abhors a vacuum. ■ **Nature; opportunity, taken**

nature *see also* you can DRIVE out Nature with a pitchfork, but she keeps on coming back; SELF-preservation is the first law of nature.

nay *see* he that WILL not when he may, when he will he shall have nay.

NEAR is my kirtle, but nearer is my smock

A justification for looking after one's own closest interests; see also the next proverb. A *kirtle* is a woman's skirt or gown; a *smock* is an undergarment. Cf. PLAUTUS *Trinummus* l. 1154 *tunica propior palliost*, my tunic is closer than my cloak.

□ **1461** *Paston Letters* (1976) II. 228 Nere is my kyrtyl but nerre is my smok. **1545** R. TAVERNER tr. *Erasmus' Adages* (ed. 2) B7ᵛ The Englysshe prouerbe sayethe thus: nere is my cote, but nerer is my shyrt. **1622** J. HOWELL *Familiar Letters* 1 May (1903) I. 126 That king .. having too many irons in the fire at his own home .. answered them that his shirt was nearer to him than his doublet. **1861** C. READE *Cloister & Hearth* IV. xxix. You must not think all of him and none of yourself. Near is your kirtle, but nearer is your smock. ■ **self-preservation**

NEAR is my shirt, but nearer is my skin

See also the preceding proverb. Cf. early 14th-cent. Fr. *plus pres m'est char que n'est chemise*, my skin is nearer to me than my shirt.

□ *c* **1570** in J. P. Collier *Old Ballads* (1840) 99 Neerer is my skin then shirte. **1631** J. HENSHAW *Spare Hours of Meditations* 63 His charitie beginnes at home, and there it ends; neere is his coat, but neerer is his skinne. **1712** J. ARBUTHNOT *Lewis Baboon* v. My Shirt (quoth he) is near me, but my Skin is nearer: Whilst I take care of the Welfare of other Folks, no body can blame me, to apply a little Balsam to my own

Sores. **1890** T. H. HALL CAINE *Bondman* II. x. 'We can't trust you.'.. 'Not your own brother?' said Jacob. '"Near is my shirt, but nearer is my skin," as the saying is.' ■ **self-preservation**

The NEARER the bone, the sweeter the meat

□ *a* **1398** J. TREVISA tr. *Bartholomew's On Properties of Things* (1975) xix. 1 The nerer the boon the swetter is the flesshe. *a* **1661** T. FULLER *Worthies* (Wales) 2 As the sweetest flesh is said to be nearest the bones, so most delicious vallies are interposed betwixt these Mountains. **1778** in B. Franklin *Writings* (1906) VIII. 258 We all agree the nearer the bone the sweeter the meat. **1945** F. THOMPSON *Lark Rise* i. 'The nearer the bone the sweeter the meat,' they used to say, and they were getting very near the bone. .. Their children.. would have to depend wholly upon whatever was carved for them from the communal joint. **1979** 'TREVANIAN' *Shiborni* I. 38 A little skinny.. for my taste, but, like my ol' daddy used to say: the closer the bone, the sweeter the meat. **1996** *Washington Post* 27 Nov. B7 He inserts the rib in his mouth. 'The closer to the bone, the sweeter the meat,' he notes. ■ **value**

The NEARER the church, the farther from God

□ **1303** R. BRUNNE *Handlyng Synne* (EETS) l. 9242 Tharfor men seys, an weyl ys trowed [believed], 'the nere the cherche, the fyrther fro God.' **1620** T. SHELTON tr. *Cervantes' Don Quixote* II. xlvii. Eat nothing of all this meat.. for this dinner was presented by Nunnes, and it is an olde saying, The neerer the Church, the farther from God. **1879** J. E. HOPKINS *Work amongst Working Men* i. I fear it was a practical comment on the truth of the uncomfortable proverb, 'The nearer the church, the farther from God,' that so bad a district should adjoin one of the great head-quarters of the church. **1957** R. GRAVES *They hanged my Saintly Billy* ii. 'The nearer the church, the farther from God,' is a proverb of doubtful truth. But true it is that William Palmer, as a child, had two churches frowning down on him. ■ **Christianity**

NECESSITY is the mother of invention

Cf. PERSIUS *Satires* Prologue 10 *magister artis ingeniique largitor venter*, the belly is the teacher of art and the giver of wit. The idea is stated more succinctly in **1519** W. HORMAN *Vulgaria* 52 Nede taught hym wytte. *Necessitas ingenium dedit.*

□ **1545** R. ASCHAM *Toxophilus* II. 18^{V} Necessitie, the inuentor of all goodnesse (as all authours in a maner, doo saye).. inuented a shaft heed. **1608** G. CHAPMAN *Tragedy of Byron* IV. i. The great Mother, Of all productions (graue Necessity). **1658** R. FRANCK *Northern Memoirs* (1694) 44 Art imitates Nature, and Necessity is the Mother of Invention. **1726** J. SWIFT *Gulliver's Travels* IV. x. I soaled my Shoes with wood, which I cut from a Tree. .. No man could more verify the Truth.. That, Necessity is the Mother of Invention. **1861** C. READE *Cloister & Hearth* II. vi. 'But, dame, I found language too poor to paint him. I was fain to invent. You know Necessity is the mother of—.' 'Ay! ay, that is old enough, o' conscience'. **2001** *Washington Post* 18 Nov. B7 If necessity is the mother of invention, calamity is not uncommonly the source of legislation. ■ **necessity**

NECESSITY knows no law

Cf. L. *necessitas non habet legem*, necessity has no law.

□ **1377** LANGLAND *Piers Plowman* B. xx. 10 Nede ne hath no lawe, ne neure shal falle in dette. *c* **1530** W. TYNDALE *Answer to More* B1 Two things are without law, God and necessity. *a* **1555** N. RIDLEY *Lamentation of Miserable Estate of Church* (1556) D4 The latter reason.. includeth a necessitie which after the common sayinge hathe no law. **1680** DRYDEN *Kind Keeper* III. ii. Necessity has no Law; I must be patient. **1776** F. RHINELANDER *Letter* 23 Feb. in H. C. Van Schaack *Life of Peter Van Schaack* (1842) 54 Troops..quarter themselves in any houses they find shut up. Necessity knows no law. **1864** MRS H. WOOD *Trevlyn Hold* II. xiv. Necessity has no law, and he was obliged to rise. **1939** 'D. YATES' *Gale Warning* vi. '"Don't speak to the man at the wheel" is a very good rule.' 'So', said I, 'is "Necessity knows no law."' **1977** S. T. WARNER *Kingdoms of Elfin* 107 Necessity knows no law. I must admit it. From time to time, I flew. ■ **necessity**

need *see* (noun) a FRIEND in need is a friend indeed; (verb) GOOD wine needs no bush; a GUILTY conscience needs no accuser.

NEEDLES and pins, needles and pins, when a man marries, his trouble begins

□ **1843** J. O. HALLIWELL *Nursery Rhymes of England* 122 Needles and pins, needles and pins, When a man marries his trouble begins. **1876** R. D. BLACKMORE *Cripps* III. 214 Cripps was come to a turn of the track—for it scarcely could be called a road—and was sadly singing to Dobbin and himself that exquisite elegiac—'Needles and pins, needles and pins, When a man marries, his trouble begins!' **1952** 'J. CANNAN' (1983) *Body in Beck* vii. 165 Thank God I steered clear of females. *Needles and pins, needles and pins, when a man marries his trouble begins.* Good God, where did I get that from? **2000** *Washington Times* 15 Nov. E12 (*Herb & Jamaal comic strip*) They say, 'Needles and pins, needles and pins, when a man marries, his troubles begin,'.. But I'll tell ya, among the things they say, what I'm most curious about is..who are '*they*'? ■ **marriage**

NEEDS must when the Devil drives

Needs must is used elliptically for 'one needs must (i.e. must of necessity) go'.

□ *c* **1450** J. LYDGATE *Assembly of Gods* (EETS) l. 21 Hit ys oft seyde by hem that yet lyues He must nedys go that the deuell dryues. **1602** SHAKESPEARE *All's Well that ends Well* I. iii. 29 He must needs go that the devil drives. **1835** SOUTHEY *Doctor* III. lxxxiii. Needs must go when the Devil drives. **1843** SURTEES *Handley Cross* III. xi. Needs must when the devil drives!..But I'd rather do any thing than injure that poor blue-eyed beauty. **1978** T. SHARPE *Throwback* iii. I don't want to marry the damned woman either, but needs must when the devil drives. **2002** *Times* 22 Feb. 24 Applied conscientiously in the rush hour it [the rule 'women and children first'] would ensure that no male adult would ever reach his office on time, if at all. Needs must when the Devil drives is a more realistic motto for the Underground. ■ **necessity**

What a NEIGHBOUR gets is not lost

Often with *friend* instead of *neighbour*.

□ **1567** L. WAGER *Mary Magdalene* D4[v] There is nothyng lost that is done for such a friende. **1721** J. KELLY *Scottish Proverbs* 198 It is no tint [not lost], a Friend gets. **1891** J. L. KIPLING *Beast & Man* viii. The public at large have reaped much of the crop sown by Government for its own army, but, as the Scottish saying has it, 'What a neighbour gets is not lost.' **1933** N. GORDON *Shakespeare Murders* xv. 237 'Every one is naturally interested in the whereabouts of a million pounds, even if it does not belong to oneself. It isn't lost, what a friend gets.' 'You mean that you can always borrow from him?' 'I meant rather that one delights in his good fortune.' ■ **neighbours; winners and losers**

neighbour *see also* GOOD fences make good neighbours.

nest *see* there are no BIRDS in last year's nest; BIRDS in their little nests agree; it's an ILL bird that fouls its own nest.

In vain the NET is spread in the sight of the bird

With allusion to PROVERBS i. 17 (AV) Surely in vain the net is spread in the sight of any bird; cf. *c* **1395** WYCLIF *Bible* (1850) Proverbs i. 17 A net is leid in veyn before the ighen [eyes] of briddis.

□ **1581** G. PETTIE tr. *S. Guazzo's Civil Conversation* I. 20^{V} In vaine (as the Prouerb sayth) The net is pitcht in the sight of the birdes. **1888** J. E. T. ROGERS *Economic Interpretation of Hist.* xxi. The landowners in Pitt's time foresaw this. ..They would certainly be caught, and the net was spread in vain in sight of the bird. **1941** 'M. COLES' *They tell No Tales* x. 'Keep a good look out.'.. 'In vain is the net spread in the sight of the bird, anyway.' **1961** L. S. DE CAMP *Dragon of Ishtar Gate* viii. 'If they come, we shall be ready,' said Bessas. 'In vain the net is spread in the sight of the bird.' ■ **deception; futility**

net *see also* all is FISH that comes to the net.

If you gently touch a NETTLE it'll sting you for your pains; grasp it like a lad of mettle, an' as soft as silk remains

The metaphorical phrase *to grasp the nettle*, to tackle a difficulty boldly, is often found.

□ **1578** LYLY *Euphues* I. 212 True it is Philautus that he which toucheth ye nettle tenderly, is soonest stoung. **1660** W. SECKER *Nonsuch Professor* I. 156 Sin is like the nettle, that stings when it is gently touched, but doth hurt not when it is ruggedly handled. **1753** A. HILL *Works* IV. 120 Tender-handed stroke a nettle, And it stings you, for your pains: Grasp it like a man of mettle, And it soft as silk remains. **1830** R. FORBY *Vocabulary of East Anglia* 430 'Nip a nettle hard, and it will not sting you'— i.e. Strong and decided measures prevail best with troublesome people. **1925** S. O'CASEY *Juno & Paycock* I. 35 Be firm, Captain. ..If you gently touch a nettle it'll sting you for your pains; grasp it like a lad of mettle, an' as soft as silk remains. ■ **boldness**

NEVER is a long time

□ *c* **1390** CHAUCER *Canon's Yeoman's Tale* l. 1411 Nevere to thryve were to long a date. **1721** J. KELLY *Scottish Proverbs* 260 Never is a long Term. ..Spoken to them that say they will never get such a Thing effected. **1887** BLACKMORE *Springhaven* I. xvii. She never could pay her rent. But 'never is a long time'.. and.. she stood clear of all debt now. **1979** H. HOWARD *Sealed Envelope* iii. 'I never reveal my sources.'.. 'Never is a long time.' ■ **future**

NEVER say never

Probably a pithy modern reformulation of the preceding proverb.

□ **1977** *Economist* 9 Apr. 6 Mr Colley.. is politician enough never to say never. **1978** *Washington Post* 2 Mar. A1 Marshall did not rule out a resumption of talks, saying 'you can never say "never" in this business.' **1984** *Washington Post* 27 Apr. A23 A president should 'never say never.' **2002** *Washington Times* 18 Apr. B5 That proves you should never say 'Never.' ■ **future**

It is NEVER too late to learn

A later variation of the next two proverbs.

□ **1678** R. L'ESTRANGE *Seneca's Morals* II. xx. It is never too late to learn what it is always necessary to know. **1721** J. KELLY *Scottish Proverbs* 266 Never too late to learn. **1856** W. COLLINS *Lady of Glenwith Grange* in *After Dark* II. 3 'It is never too late to learn,' cried he. 'I will make a fisherman of you in no time, if you will only attend to my directions.' **1927** E. F. BENSON *Lucia in London* ii. We want to know what the cosmopolitan mind is thinking about. Of course we're old, but it is never too late to learn. **2002** *Washington Times* 17 Feb. B3 To his credit, Norman Mailer later said that he felt 'a very large responsibility' for Mr. Adan's murder, and admitted that he 'never thought Abbott was close to killing... I was not sensitive to the fact.' It's never too late to learn. ■ **lateness; learning**

It is NEVER too late to mend

See also the two adjacent proverbs.

□ **1590** R. GREENE (*title*) Never too late. **1594** LODGE & GREENE *Looking-Glass for London* I3^{V} Amends may neuer come too late. *c* **1645** J. HOWELL *Familiar Letters* 9 Nov. (1903) III. 139 We have both of us our failings that way.. but it is never over late to mend. **1856** C. READE (*title*) It is never too late to mend. **1934** H. SPRING *Shabby Tiger* iv. Adolf shrugged a shoulder which suggested that it's never too late to mend. **1961** I. JEFFERIES *It wasn't Me!* i. How kind. ..Never too late to mend. ■ **improvement; lateness**

NEVER too old to learn

See also the two preceding proverbs. Cf. SENECA *Epistle* LXXVI. iii. *tamdiu discendum est, quamdiu nescias: si proverbio credimus, quamdiu vivas*, we must go on learning as long as we are ignorant; or, if we believe the proverb, as long as we live.

□ **1530** A. BARCLAY *Eclogues* (EETS) II. 538 Coridon thou art not to olde for to lere. **1555** *Institution of Gentleman* B7^{V} No man can be to olde to learne. **1670** J. RAY *English Proverbs* 112 Never too old to learn. **1712** J. ARBUTHNOT *Law is Bottomles Pit* I. vii. A Lawyer I was born, and a Lawyer I will be; one is never too Old to learn. **1858** TROLLOPE *Dr. Thorne* I. x. One should never be too old to learn—there's always something new worth picking up. **1990** 'C. AIRD' 'Lord Peter's Touch' in *Injury Time* (1995) 45 'All right then, tell me. I suppose I'm never too old to learn.' ■ **learning; old age**

never *see also* BETTER late than never; never send a BOY to do a man's job; never do EVIL that good may come of it; what you've never HAD you never miss; PAY beforehand was never well served; never let the SUN go down on your anger.

NEW brooms sweep clean

The phrase *new broom* (one newly appointed to a position who makes changes in personnel or procedures) derives from this proverb.

□ **1546** J. HEYWOOD *Dialogue of Proverbs* II. i. F3^{V} Som therto said, the grene new brome swepith cleene. **1578** LYLY *Euphues* I. 232 Ah well I wotte [know] that a newe broome sweepeth cleene. **1616** J. WITHALS *Dict.* (rev. ed.) 569 New bromes sweepe cleane, yet old friendship still retaine. **1776** G. COLMAN *New Brooms!* 15 I am glad he is gone—Glad!—To be sure. *New Brooms*, you know. **1877** J. A. FROUDE *Short Studies* 3rd Ser. 55 New brooms sweep clean. Abbot Thomas, like most of his predecessors, began with attempts at reformation. **1979** F. OLBRICH *Sweet & Deadly* iv. He was all right at first. It was a case of a new broom sweeping clean. ■ **improvement; innovation**

What is NEW cannot be true

□ **1639** J. CLARKE *Parœmiologia Anglo-Latina* 228 The newest things, not always truest. **1791** J. BOSWELL *Life of Johnson* II. 283 I found that generally what was new was false. **1880** J. NICHOL *Byron* ix. We are told..that he knew little of art or music. ..It is true but not new. But when Hunt proceeds to say that Byron had no sentiment..it is new enough, but is manifestly not true. **1928** *Times* 4 Feb. 8 Sir Arthur Evans has fallen a victim..to the old slogan 'What is new cannot be true.' ■ **innovation**

NEW lords, new laws

Cf. *a* **1450** *St. Editha* (1883) 96 Willyham Conquerour was made here kyng, And made newe lordus and eke new lawe.

□ *a* **1547** E. HALL *Chronicle* (1548) Hen. VI 169 Tholde spoken prouerbe, here toke place: New Lordes, new lawes. **1824** SCOTT *St. Ronan's Well* II. i. But new lords new laws—naething but fine and imprisonment, and the game no a feather the plentier. **1874** T. HARDY *Far from Madding Crowd* I. viii. 'I was lately married to a woman, and she's my vocation now.'..'New lords new laws, as the saying is.' ■ **change; circumstances**

You can't put NEW wine in old bottles

With allusion to MATTHEW ix. 17 (AV) Neither do men put new wine into old bottles: else the bottles break, and the wine runneth out, and the bottles perish. The idea is also expressed allusively as a metaphorical phrase.

□ **1912** L. STRACHEY *Landmarks in French Literature* vi. The new spirits had animated the prose of Chateaubriand and the poetry of Lamartine; but..the *form* of both these writers retained most of the important characteristics of the old tradition. It was new wine in old bottles. **1948** A. J. TOYNBEE *Civilization on Trial* vi. The new wines of industrialism and democracy have been poured into old bottles and they have burst the old bottles beyond repair. **1960** I. JEFFERIES *Dignity & Purity* viii. 'I don't think you can put new wine in old bottles.' I looked doubtful. ..'A lot of this could be rationalized.' **1974** T. SHARPE *Porterhouse Blue* x. 'Motives?..Good old-fashioned lust.' 'That hardly explains the explosive nature of his end.'..'You can't put new wine in old bottles.' ■ **innovation**

There is always something NEW out of Africa

L. *ex Africa semper aliquid novi*, a variant of a passage in the *Naturalis Historia* (viii. 16) of Pliny the Elder referring to hybridization of African animals: *unde etiam vulgare Graeciae dictum semper aliquid novi African afferre*, hence that common saying of the Greek that Africa is always bringing forth something new; the allusion is to a passage in Aristotle's *De Animalibus Historia* viii. 28, 7 *Ἀεὶ Λιβύη φέρει τι καινόν*, Libya is always showing something new. Versions of the Latin saying have been current in England since Erasmus' *Adagia* (1500).

□ **1559** W. BAVARDE tr. *A Woorke of Ioannes Ferrarius* 81 It is saied that Affricque bringeth foorthe alwaies some newe thing. **1642** J. HOWELL *Instructions for Forreine Travel* (Arber ed.) iii. 22 *France*, which as Africk produceth always something New, for I never knew week passe in *Paris* but it brought forth some new kinds of Authors. **1976** D. ARDEN (*title*) Out of Africa something new? **1983** R. KELLY 'Stone Wall in Providence' in *Under Words* 112 Always something new / out of Africa. Rubadubdub of the new desires squeezing / into the convenient old places of the sleepstonewall. **2000** CBS NEWS (web site) 11 June It is a thing of rare beauty nonetheless: Humans and dangerous animals at peace and in harmony with each other—proving once again that there is always something new out of Africa. ■ **novelty**

new *see also* there is NOTHING new under the sun; it is best to be OFF with the old love before you are on with the new; you can't TEACH an old dog new tricks.

news *see* BAD news travels fast; GO abroad and you'll hear news of home; NO news is good news.

nibble *see* a BLEATING sheep loses a bite.

NIGHT brings counsel

Cf. MENANDER *Sententiae* no. 222 *Ἐν νυκτὶ βουλὴ τοῖς σοφοῖσι γίγνεται*, at night comes counsel to the wise; L. *in nocte consilium*, in night is counsel.

□ **1590** SPENSER *Faerie Queene* I. i. 291 Vntroubled night.. giues counsell best. **1640** G. HERBERT *Outlandish Proverbs* no. 746 Night is the mother of Councels. **1660** DRYDEN *Astræa Redux* l. 93 Well might the Ancient Poets then confer On Night the honour'd name of *Counseller*. **1928** L. THAYER *Darkest Spot* xviii. The saying that night brings counsel is often true. .. Peter.. woke next morning with a plan of campaign fully developed. **1967** N. FREELING *Strike out where not Applicable* 184 'Home you go, boy. Night brings counsel.' Night did bring counsel. Or rather Verbiest, the young inspector, brought it. ■ **advice**

night *see also* BARNABY bright, Barnaby bright, the longest day and the shortest night; all CATS are grey in the dark; RED sky at night shepherd's delight; SING before breakfast, cry before night.

NINE tailors make a man

The literal meaning is that a gentleman must select his attire from various sources. It is now sometimes specifically associated with bell-ringing (see quots. 1908 and 1934).

□ **1613** *Tarlton's Jests* C1 Two Taylors goes to a man. **1647** N. WARD *Simple Cobbler* 26 It is a more common then convenient saying, that nine Taylers make a man; it were well if nineteene could make a woman to her minde. **1776** *Poor Robin's Almanack* II. C6^{V} Do ye know how many Taylors make a Man? Why Nine—Nine Taylors make a Man. **1819** SCOTT *Letter* 26 July (1933) V. 427 They say it take *nine* tailors to make a man—apparently, *one* is sufficient to ruin him. **1908** H. B. WALTERS *Church Bells* v. When the Knell is rung, it is a frequent practice to indicate the.. sex of the deceased. .. The old saying 'nine tailors make a man' is really 'nine tellers' [strokes], or three times three. **1912** A. BRAZIL *New Girl at St. Chad's* i. There's a saying that it takes nine tailors to make a man, so if your name is Taylor you can only be the ninth part of a lady! **1934** D. L. SAYERS *Nine Tailors* IV. iii. The voice of the bells of Fenchurch St. Paul. .. Nine Tailors Make a Man. ■ **dress**

nine *see also* PARSLEY seed goes nine times to the Devil; POSSESSION is nine points of the law; it is not SPRING until you can plant your foot upon twelve daisies; a STITCH in time saves nine.

NO cross, no crown

Cross is used here punningly as in CROSSES *are ladders that lead to heaven.*

□ **1609** T. BRETNOR *Almanac* March Good days A crosse before a Crowne. **1621** F. QUARLES *History of Queene Ester: Meditations* ix. The way to Blisse lyes not on beds of Downe, And he that had no Crosse, deserues no Crowne. **1669** W. PENN (*title*) No Cross no Crown. **1944** 'A. GILBERT' *Death at Door* (1945) xiii. 135 They were always at loggerheads, those two. No Cross, No Crown, that's their motto. **1996** L. ANDREWS *Sinister Side* vii. 123 He sighed piteously. 'I suppose I'll have to hang on for it.' 'No cross, no crown, Julian.' He realised he had overplayed the martyr. ■ **misfortune**

NO cure, no pay

The expression is known principally from its use on Lloyd's of London's Standard Form of Salvage Agreement; cf. the earlier *no purchase, no pay* and similar proverbs.

□ *c* **1877** G. W. H. GRIFFIN (*title*) No Cure, No Pay. **1888** R. R. DOUGLAS *Alphabetical Reference Index to Recent & Important Maritime Law Decisions* 194 Agreement—'no cure no pay'. **1907** A. R. KENNEDY *Treatise.. Law of Civil Salvage* (ed. 2) 270 (*heading*) Salvage agreement on basis of Lloyd's standard form of 'no cure—no pay' agreement. **1933** *Reports of Tax Cases (Inland Revenue)* XVII. 352 The charges of those accountants.. were made on the 'No cure, no pay' principle. **1965** *Lloyd's List Law Reports* I. 429 The master.. made a bargain with.. Mr. Bezikis.. who.. agreed to make good the steering engine.. at a cost of what was described as £420 'no cure no pay'. **1982** *Listener* 6 May 10 The divers.. will earn their money. .. If they find nothing, they will receive nothing. .. No cure, no pay. ■ **just deserts**

NO foot, no horse

In North America as *no hoof, no horse*.

□ **1751** J. BRIDGES (*title*) No Foot, No Horse. An essay on the anatomy of the foot of.. a horse. **1893** A. T. FISHER *The Farrier or 'No Foot, No Horse'* 2 'No foot, no horse' exactly expresses that which I desire to impress on the reader in the following pages. Without the full and perfect use of its feet, the horse is useless. **1999** G. WILLIAMS & M. DEACON *No Foot, No Horse* 139 Shoeing will no longer be regarded as a necessary evil but vital for performance and soundness—and the expression 'no foot, no horse' will be a thing of the past. **2001** R. FREEMAN *www.horseshoes.com* (web site) It was while hanging around the barns with a friend who trained horses that I quickly gained an appreciation for the old adage, 'no hoof, no horse'. ■ **horse lore**

NO man can serve two masters

With allusion to MATTHEW vi. 24 (AV) No man can serve two masters (the verse which concludes *you cannot serve* GOD *and Mammon*).

□ *c* **1330** in T. Wright *Political Songs* (1839) 325 No man may wel serve tweie lordes to queme [please] *c* **1477** CAXTON *Jason* (EETS) 57 No man may wel serve two maistres, for that one corumpeth that other. **1642** D. ROGERS *Naaman* vi. You cannot have your will.. and Christ too; no man can serve two masters. **1853** R. C. TRENCH *On Lessons in Proverbs* v. Our lord.. has said: 'No man can serve two masters.'.. So the Spanish proverb: He who has to serve two masters, has to lie to one. **1979** 'C. AIRD' *Some die Eloquent* v. The Coroner's Officer existed in a sort of leaderless no-man's-land. Hostilities had broken out over this more than once. .. No man can serve two masters. ■ **employers and employees**

NO man is a hero to his valet

Attributed to Mme Cornuel (1605–94): *il n'y a pas de héros pour son valet-de-chambre*, no man is a hero to his valet. Cf. **1603** J. FLORIO tr. *Montaigne's Essays* III. ii. Few men haue beene admired of their familiers. .. In my climate of Gascoigne they deeme it as iest to see mee in print.

□ **1764** S. FOOTE *Patron* II. 31 It has been said.. that no man is a hero to his valet de chambre; now I am afraid when you and I grow a little more intimate.. you will be horribly disappointed in your high expectations. **1910** *Times* 20 Jan. (Literary

Supplement) 17 Many men have been heroes to their valets, and most (except Pope and Poe) to their biographers. **1940** A. CHRISTIE *One, Two, buckle my Shoe* i. It has been said that no man is a hero to his valet. To that may be added that few men are heroes to themselves at the moment of visiting their dentist. **2002** *Washington Times* 9 May C2 All of which is a mere footnote to the longest presidency in American history, and one of the greatest. But it is a useful reminder that just as no man is a hero to his valet so, it seems, not even a president is immune to the ministrations of a Chef From Hell. ■ **employers and employees; familiarity**

NO moon, no man

□ **1878** T. HARDY *Return of Native* I. I. iii. 'No moon, no man.' 'Tis one of the truest sayings ever spit out. The boy never comes to anything that's born at new moon. **1878** T. F. THISTELTON-DYER *English Folk-Lore* ii. In Cornwall, when a child is born in the interval between an old moon and the first appearance of a new one, it is said that it will never live to reach the age of puberty. Hence the saying 'No moon, no man.' ■ **calendar lore; children**

NO names, no pack-drill

If nobody is named as being responsible for something, then nobody can be blamed and punished. Also used more generally in favour of reticence on a subject. *Pack-drill* is a military punishment in which the offender is compelled to march up and down in full marching order.

□ **1923** O. ONIONS *Peace in our Time* I. ii. Men had a way of omitting the names of those of whom they spoke; no names no pack-drill. **1925** S. O'CASEY *Juno & Paycock* II. 61 I know some as are as sweet as the blossoms that bloom in the May—oh, no names, no pack drill. **2000** P. LOVESEY *Reaper* iv. 47 'Do you know, I've heard of churches—no names, no pack-drill—who wait until the end of the year before stomping up.' ■ **speech and silence**

NO news is good news

□ **1616** JAMES I in *Loseley MSS* (1836) 403 No newis is bettir then evill newis. **1640** J. HOWELL *Familiar Letters* 3 June (1903) II. 144 I am of the Italians mind that said, 'Nulla nuova, buona nuova', (no news, good news). **1850** F. E. SMEDLEY *Frank Fairlegh* x. Arguing..(on the 'no news being good news' system) that I should have heard again if anything had gone wrong, I dismissed the subject from my mind. **1974** T. SHARPE *Porterhouse Blue* xxi. 'He can't reply,' the Senior Tutor pointed out. 'I find that most consoling. After all no news is good news.' **2002** *Washington Post* 12 Feb. C13 (*Mother Goose & Grimm comic strip*) 'Sigh..No news is good news.' 'I'll say..It means no rolled-up newspaper.' ■ **news**

NO pain, no gain

□ **1577** N. BRETON *Works of Young Wit* 33v They must take pain that look for any gayn. **1648** HERRICK *Hesperides* 298 *No Paines, no Gaines*. If little labour, little are our gaines: Mans fortunes are according to his paines. **1853** R. C. TRENCH *On Lessons in Proverbs* iv. For the most part they courageously accept the law of labour, *No pains, no gains,—No sweat, no sweet*, as the appointed law and condition of man's life. **1985** *Washington Post* 22 May (Health Supplement) 14 Forget the coach's rule of 'no pain, no gain'. Today, exercise researchers are replacing it with the 'talk rule'. **2000** M. BERMAN *Twilight of American Culture* i. 58 As Peter Sacks shows.., there is very little tolerance on the part of students for any real work; 'no pain, no gain' is not part of their emotional vocabulary. ■ **wanting and having**

NO penny, no paternoster

□ **1528** W. TYNDALE *Obedience of Christian Man* fo. lxxxii^v After the commune sayenge, no peny no Pater noster. **1648** HERRICK *Hesperides* 302 Who..Can't send for a gift A Pig to the Priest for a Roster [roast], Shall heare his Clarke say, .. *No pennie, no Pater Noster.* **1721** J. KELLY *Scottish Proverbs* 259 No Penny, no Pater Noster. **1925** J. I. C. CLARKE *My Life* ix. If the churchly motto 'No penny, no Paternoster' was true, how could a church..stay downtown when its congregation was moving north. **1940** D. TEILHET *Broken Face Murders* ii. No penny, no paternoster. I neither pay the piper nor do I dance. ■ **just deserts**

no *see also* HALF a loaf is better than no bread; there's no great LOSS without some gain; there's no PLACE like home; if there were no RECEIVERS, there would be no thieves; there is no ROYAL road to learning; SEE no evil, hear no evil, speak no evil; SHROUDS have no pockets; no SMOKE without fire; TIME and tide wait for no man; no TIME like the present.

nobody *see* EVERYBODY'S business is nobody's business; it's an ILL wind that blows nobody any good.

A NOD's as good as a wink to a blind horse

A fanciful assertion, often abbreviated as in quot. 1822, that the slightest hint is enough to convey one's meaning in the case.

□ **1794** W. GODWIN *Caleb Williams* I. viii. Say the word; a nod is as good as a wink to a blind horse. **1822** B. MALKIN *Gil Blas* (rev. ed.) I. II. ix. I shall say no more at present; a nod is as good as a wink. **1925** S. O'CASEY *Shadow of Gunman* in *Two Plays* I. 142 You needn't say no more—a nod's as good as a wink to a blind horse. **1979** L. MEYNELL *Hooky & Villainous Chauffeur* vi. The way he behaves..Other men's wives. Still, I expect you know as much about that as I do. ..They say a nod's as good as a wink to a blind horse. **1992** W. DONALDSON *Root into Europe* ii. 34 Got a good PR machine working for you, I expect. Say no more. ..Nod's as good as a wink. ■ **hints; tact**

nod *see also* (verb) HOMER sometimes nods.

noise *see* EMPTY vessels make the most sound.

none *see* a BAD excuse is better than none; there's none so BLIND as those who will not see; none but the BRAVE deserve the fair; there's none so DEAF as those who will not hear; JACK of all trades and master of none; TWO is company, but three is none..

no one *see* no one should be JUDGE in his own cause.

NORTH wind doth blow, we shall have snow

□ **1805** *Songs for Nursery* 3 The north wind doth blow, And we shall have snow, And what will poor Robin do then? Poor thing! **1980** A. T. ELLIS *Birds of Air* (1983) 113 Mary was thinking, 'The north wind doth blow and we shall have snow and what will the robin do then..' ■ **weather lore**

nose *see* don't CUT off your nose to spite your face.

NOTHING comes of nothing

Cf. ALCAEUS *Fragment* cccxx. (Lobel-Page) *οὐδὲν ἐκ δενὸς γένοιτο*, nothing comes of nothing; L. *ex nihilo nihil fit.*

□ *c* **1380** CHAUCER *Boethius* v. pr. i. For this sentence is verray and soth, that 'no thing hath his beynge of naught'. **1551** CRANMER *Answer to Gardiner* 369 *Sicut ex nihilo nihil fit, Ita nihil in nihilum redigitur*, As nothyng can be made of nought, so nothynge can be tourned into nought. **1605-6** SHAKESPEARE *King Lear* I. i. 89 Nothing will come of nothing. Speak again. **1818** SCOTT *Heart of Midlothian* I. i. You are to give me all your business. .. If you have none, the learned gentleman here knows nothing can come of nothing. **1946** E. R. CURTIS *Lady Sarah Lennox* iv. 'What did you think of it?' 'Nothing, Sir.' 'Nothing comes of nothing!' the King exclaimed impatiently. **1998** T. DALRYMPLE *Life at Bottom* (2001) 233 Well, as King Lear said, nothing comes of nothing: and the journalist's hatred of the police was unlikely to have sprung completely at random and fully informed from his consciousness. ■ **reciprocity**

NOTHING for nothing

□ *a* **1704** T. BROWN *Works* (1707) I. 131 Thou know'st the proverb, nothing due for nought. **1800** M. EDGEWORTH *Castle Rackrent* 167 Nothing for nothing, or I'm under a mistake with you, Jason. **1858** G. J. WHYTE-MELVILLE *Interpreter* xxv. Sir Harry.. recollected the old-established principle of himself and his clique, 'Nothing for nothing, and very little for a halfpenny.' **1908** A. MACLAREN *Ezekiel* 172 The last touch in the picture is meanness, which turned everything into money. .. Is not 'nothing for nothing' an approved maxim to-day? **1981** N. FREELING *One Damn Thing after Another* iv. Their heart's not in it. Nothing for nothing and not much for sixpence. ■ **reciprocity**

NOTHING is certain but death and taxes

□ **1726** DEFOE *Hist. Devil* II. vi. Not the Man in the Moon, .. not the Inspiration of Mother Shipton, or the Miracles of Dr. Faustus, Things as certain as Death and Taxes, can be more firmly believ'd. **1789** B. FRANKLIN *Letter* 13 Nov. in *Writings* (1907) X. 69 In this world nothing can be said to be certain, except death and taxes. **1939** L. I. WILDER *By Shores of Silver Lake* xxv. Everything's more or less a gamble. .. Nothing is certain but death and taxes. **2001** *Washington Times* 20 Dec. C10 In 1789, Benjamin Franklin said, 'In this world, nothing is certain but death and taxes.' Well, there is one way to avoid capital-gains taxes on investments—hold them until you die. ■ **certainty and uncertainty**

NOTHING is certain but the unforeseen

Similar to *the* UNEXPECTED *always happens*.

□ **1886** J. A. FROUDE *Oceana* vii. There is a proverb that 'nothing is certain but the unforeseen,' and in fact few things turn out as we expect them. **1905** A. MACLAREN *Gospel according to St. Matthew* I. 322 There is nothing certain to happen, says the proverb, but the unforeseen. Tomorrow *will have* its cares. ■ **certainty and uncertainty; foresight and hindsight**

NOTHING is for ever

□ **1984** *Defense Electronics* 144/2 Nothing is forever, and political-military alliances are less forever than most. **1992** MIEDER *Dict. American Proverbs* 433 Nothing can last for ever. **2001** *Times* 7 Nov. 16 Mr Blair may treat Parliament's support as unconditional, but nothing is for ever. ■ **change**

There is NOTHING new under the sun

With allusion to ECCLESIASTES i. 9 (AV) There is no new thing under the sun.

□ **1592** G. DELAMOTHE *French Alphabet* II. 7 Under the large Cope of heauen, we see not a new thing. **1664** A. BRADSTREET *Works* (1867) 53 There is no new thing under the sun. **1801** T. JEFFERSON *Writings* (1904) X. 229 We can no longer say there is nothing new under the sun. **1850** C. KINGSLEY *Alton Locke* I. xviii. There is nothing new under the sun; all that, is stale and trite to a septuagenarian, who has seen where it all ends. **2002** *Times* 4 Jan. 16 Cliché is the element in which political hacks live and move and have our being. Not just situation cliché. There is nothing new under the sun in politics. ■ **familiarity; novelty**

NOTHING should be done in haste but gripping a flea

□ *a* **1655** N. L'ESTRANGE in *Anecdotes & Traditions* (1839) I. 55 A grave gentleman in this Kingdome us'd this phrase often: 'Do nothing rashly, but catching of fleas.' **1678** J. RAY *English Proverbs* (ed. 2) 151 Nothing most be done hastily but killing of fleas. **1721** J. KELLY *Scottish Proverbs* 261 Nothing to be done in haste, but gripping of Fleas. ..Spoken when we are unreasonably urged to make haste. **1927** J. BUCHAN *Witch Wood* xii. What's the need o' hurry when the body's leg is still to set. As my auld mither used to say, naething suld be done in haste but grippin' a flea. **1969** B. LEHANE *Compleat Flea* i. 'Do nothing hastily but catching of fleas,' warns a wary proverb.

NOTHING so bad but it might have been worse

A more positive version is **1817** SCOTT *Rob Roy* II. xiii. There's naething sae gude on this side o' time but it might hae been better.

□ **1876** I. BANKS *Manchester Man* III. xiii. However, there is nothing so bad but it might be worse. **1885** E. J. HARDY *How to be Happy though Married* xxi. Let us resolve to look at the bright side of things. ..'Nothing so bad but it might have been worse.' **1908** *Times* 5 Oct. 3 Farmers.. will regard the.. meteorological changes as illustrating the ancient axiom to the effect that circumstances are never so bad that they cannot be worse. ■ **good and evil; optimism**

NOTHING so bold as a blind mare

□ *a* **1628** J. CARMICHAELL *Proverbs in Scots* no. 1435 The blind horse is hardiest. **1721** J. KELLY *Scottish Proverbs* 266 Nothing so bold as a blind Mare. **1922** J. BUCHAN *Huntingtower* x. He spoke of the still unconquered enemy with.. disrespect, so that Mrs Morran was moved to observe that there was 'naething sae bauld as a blind mear'. ■ **boldness; ignorance**

There is NOTHING so good for the inside of a man as the outside of a horse

A proverb asserting the benefit of horse-riding to health.

□ **1906** G. W. E. RUSSELL *Social Silhouettes* xxxii. The Squire will wind up.. with an apocryphal saying which he attributes to Lord Palmerston—'There's nothing so good for the inside of a man as the outside of a horse.' **1946** M. C. SELF *Horseman's Encyclopædia* 338 'There is something about the outside of a horse which is good for the inside of a man.' This adage is wiser than might first appear. But one should not consider just the hours spent in the saddle as beneficial. **1987** *Time* 28 Dec. 52 There is nothing better for the inside of a man than the outside of a horse. *Ronald Reagan* President. ■ **health**

NOTHING succeeds like success

Cf. Fr. *rien ne réussit comme le succès*, nothing succeeds like success.

□ **1867** A. D. RICHARDSON *Beyond Mississippi* xxxiv. 'Nothing succeeds like success.' There *was* much Southern sympathy on the island; now all are our dear friends. **1872** W. BESANT *Ready-Money Mortiboy* I. ix. In Mr. Mortiboy's judgment no proverb could be better than.. 'Nothing succeeds like success.' Success dazzled him. **1980** H. TREVOR-ROPER *History & Imagination* 9 Nothing succeeds like success, and if Hitler had founded his empire..we can well imagine how later historians would have treated him. ■ **success**

NOTHING venture, nothing gain

A variant of the next proverb. Cf. late 14th-cent. Fr. *qui onques rien n'enprist riens n'achieva*, he who never undertook anything never achieved anything; **1481** CAXTON *Reynard* (1880) xii. He that will wynne he muste laboure and auenture.

□ **1624** T. HEYWOOD *Captives* IV. i. I see hee that nought venters, nothinge gaynes. **1668** C. SEDLEY *Mulberry Garden* III. ii. Who ever caught any thing With a naked hook? nothing venture, nothing Win. **1876** BLACKMORE *Cripps* III. iv. We must all have been in France.. if—well, never mind. Nothing venture, nothing win. **1967** D. MORRIS *Naked Ape* iv. For him [the withdrawn individual] the old saying: 'Nothing ventured, nothing gained' has been rewritten: 'Nothing ventured, nothing lost'. **1979** A. PRICE *Tomorrow's Ghost* vii. That was decidedly interesting—'And Pearson Cole?' Nothing venture, nothing gain. **1990** R. D. EDWARDS *English School of Murder* vi. 'I'd need a little training before I could take on a proper class.' 'Nonsense, old man,' cried Rich. 'Nothing ventured, nothing gained.' **2001** *Washington Times* 15 Dec. B2 Though there are no guarantees, it does seem sad that a chance at true love was stillborn because one of the parties had low self-esteem. Nothing ventured, nothing gained. ■ **boldness; wanting and having; risk**

NOTHING venture, nothing have

□ *c* **1385** CHAUCER *Troilus & Criseyde* II. 807 He which that nothing undertaketh, Nothing n'acheveth, be hym looth or deere [be it hateful or pleasing to him]. **1546** J. HEYWOOD *Dialogue of Proverbs* I. xi. E1 Noght venter noght haue. **1559** T. COOPER *Bibliotheca* (ed. 3) s.v. Fortis, Fortune foretherethe [furthers] bolde aduenturers, nothyng venture, nothyng haue. **1791** J. BOSWELL *Life of Johnson* II. 166 I am, however, generally for trying 'Nothing venture, nothing have'. **1841** DICKENS *Old Curiosity Shop* I. xxix. I'm sorry the gentleman's daunted—nothing venture, nothing have—but the gentleman knows best. **1957** R. DOWNING *All Change Here* v. 36 'Jonah, aren't you taking a hell of a risk?' 'Of course. We all are. But then "nothing venture nothing have."' ■ **boldness; wanting and having; risk**

nothing *see also* BELIEVE nothing of what you hear, and only half of what you see; BLESSED is he who expects nothing, for he shall never be disappointed; CIVILITY costs nothing; there is nothing like LEATHER; you don't get SOMETHING for nothing; SOMETHING is better than nothing; the SUN loses nothing by shining into a puddle.

notice *see* LONG foretold, long last.

There's NOWT so queer as folk

Nowt is a dialect variant of 'nought' i.e. 'nothing'.

□ **1905** *English Dialect Dict.* IV. 304 There's nowt sae queer as folk, *Old saying*. **1939** J. WOOD *Letter* 30 May in J. Chambers *Letters* (1979) 186 I trust you.. find plenty of interest in people & their doings. Really 'there is nowt so funny as folk'. **1955** R. E. MEGARRY *Miscellany-at-Law* I. 72 There is the infinite charm and variety of human nature itself: 'there's nowt so queer as folk.' **1993** B. D'AMATO *Hard Women* xxi. 243 'You never really *know* anything about people. As LJ sometimes says, "There's nowt so strange as folk." It's not like you can work people out on a chessboard.'

2002 *Oldie* Apr. 57..and his creed that everyone is good copy. Or, as they would put it up North, that there's nowt so queer as folk. ■ **idiosyncrasy**

nowt *see also* when in DOUBT, do nowt; HEAR all, see all, say nowt.

number *see* there is LUCK in odd numbers; there is SAFETY in numbers.

nut *see* the GODS send nuts to those who have no teeth.

When the OAK is before the ash, then you will only get a splash; when the ash is before the oak, then you may expect a soak

A traditional way of predicting whether the summer will be wet or dry on the basis of whether the oak or the ash is first to come into leaf in the spring.

□ **1852** *Notes & Queries* 1st Ser. V. 581 When the oak comes out before the ash, there will be fine weather in harvest. I..find it generally correct. **1911** *Times Literary Supplement* 4 Aug. 285 One of the commonest weather rhymes in most parts of England deals with the budding of the oak and the ash:—When the oak's before the ash Then you'll only get a splash, When the ash is before the oak Then you may expect a soak. But in North Germany the signs are exactly inverted, and also in Cornwall. **1987** *Daily Telegraph* 22 June 12 My farmer neighbour and myself have always been great believers in the saying: 'Ash before oak, we'll get a soak Oak before ash, we'll only have a splash.' ■ **weather lore**

Beware of an OAK, it draws the stroke; avoid an ash, it counts the flash; creep under the thorn, it can save you from harm

Advice on where to shelter from lightning during a thunderstorm.

□ **1878** *Folk-Lore Record* I. 43 Mothers teach their children to say—Beware of an oak, It draws the stroke; Avoid an ash; It counts the flash; Creep under the thorn, It can save you from harm. **1945** F. THOMPSON *Lark Rise* xvii. Some one would.. warn him to keep away from trees during a thunderstorm. ..Others would quote: Under oak there comes a stroke, Under elm there comes a calm, And under ash there comes a crash. ■ **necessity; security**

oak *see also* GREAT oaks from little acorns grow; LITTLE strokes fell great oaks; a REED before the wind lives on, while mighty oaks do fall.

obedience *see* the FIRST duty of a soldier is obedience.

He that cannot OBEY cannot command

Cf. SENECA *De Ira* II. xiv. *nemo regere potest nisi qui et regi*, no one can rule unless he can also be ruled.

□ *a* **1500** tr. *T. à Kempis' De Imitatione Christi* (1893) xxiv. No man surely comaundith but he that hath lerned to obeye. **1581** G. PETTIE tr. *S. Guazzo's Civil Conversation* III. 48ᵛ Those onely knowe well how to commaund, which know well howe to obaye. **1734** B. FRANKLIN *Poor Richard's Almanack* (Aug.) He that cannot obey, cannot command. **1850** H. MELVILLE *White Jacket* vi. As the only way to learn to command, is to learn to obey, the usage of a ship of war is such that midshipmen are constantly being ordered about by the Lieutenants. **1972** S. CLOETE *Victorian Son* ix. I did not mind the army because I knew I must learn to obey before I could command. ■ **obedience; rulers and ruled**

OBEY orders, if you break owners

A nautical proverb; for the meaning see quot. 1924.

□ **1782** W. GORDON *Letter* 30 Nov. in *Proceedings of Massachusetts Hist. Society* (1930) LXIII. 476 You will be safe, though you break orders that would break your owners. **1823** J. F. COOPER *Pilot* vii. The old rule runs, 'Obey orders, if you break owners.' **1924** R. CLEMENTS *Gipsy of Horn* iii. What could be sounder than 'Obey orders, if you break owners'—meaning, do as you're told, even if you know it's wrong. **1976** J. R. L. ANDERSON *Death on North Sea* iv. I was brought up on the old sea maxim, 'Obey orders if you break owners.' ■ **obedience**

odd *see* there is LUCK in odd numbers.

odious *see* COMPARISONS are odious.

It is best to be OFF with the old love before you are on with the new

□ **1801** M. EDGEWORTH *Belinda* I. x. I can give you my advice gratis, in the formula of an old Scotch song. ..''Tis good to be off with the old love, Before you be on with the new.' **1819** SCOTT *Bride of Lammermoor* III. ii. It is best to be off wi' the old love Before you be on wi' the new. **1891** A. LANG *Essays in Little* 6 Dumas..met the great man at Marseilles, where..Alexandre chanced to be 'on with the new love' before being completely 'off with the old'. **1923** E. V. LUCAS *Advisory Ben* xxxix. That proverb about being off with the old love is a very sound one. **1980** I. ST. JAMES *Money Stones* III. vi. Off with the old and on with the new. Why not just come out with it? Tell her it's all finished. ■ **constancy and inconstancy; love**

OFFENDERS never pardon

□ **1640** G. HERBERT *Outlandish Proverbs* no. 561 The offender never pardons. **1672** DRYDEN *Conquest of Granada* II. I. ii. Forgiveness to the Injur'd does belong; But they ne'r pardon who have done the wrong. **1876** I. BANKS *Manchester Man* III. xiii. He was of Mrs. Ashton's mind, that, 'as offenders never pardon', Augusta needed a friend. ■ **forgiveness; wrong-doers**

offense *see* ATTACK is the best form of defence; the best DEFENSE is a good offense.

OLD habits die hard

□ **1758** B. FRANKLIN in *London Chronicle* 26–28 Dec. 632 I hear the reader say, Habits are hard to break, and those..accustomed to idleness or extravagance do not easily change their manners. **1792** J. BELKNAP *Foresters* ix. Old habits are not easily broken, and..they endeavoured..to transfer the blame from him to his wife. **1944** 'H. TALBOT' *Rim of Pit* xv. 'Miss Daventry..started to run. Naturally I ran after her.' Rogan smiled. 'Old habits die hard.' **2002** *Washington Times* 6 Mar. A2 Lately, we've heard high French officials denounce our nation's anti-terrorism policies as 'simplistic' and seen a French Olympic skating judge given the heave for apparently conspiring to aid the Russians (old habits die hard). ■ **habit**

You cannot put an OLD head on young shoulders

□ **1591** H. SMITH *Preparative to Marriage* 14 It is not good grafting of an olde head vppon young shoulders, for they will neuer beare it willingly but grudgingly. **1794** E. DRINKER *Journal* 31 Dec. (1889) 256 Tis not the way I could wish my children to conclude the year—in parties—but we can't put old heads on young shoulders. **1951** *Sport* 30 Mar.–5 Apr. 11 I no longer believe in the old proverb that you cannot put an old head on young shoulders. **1975** J. PORTER *Package included Murder* xvi. The Hon. Con generously forgave her. Well, you can't expect old heads on young shoulders, can you? ■ **wisdom; youth**

OLD sins cast long shadows

Cf. **1638** SUCKLING *Aglaura* v. in *Plays* (1971) 110 Our sins, like to our shadowes, When our day is in its glorie scarce appear: Towards our evening how great and monstrous they are!

□ **1924** D. VANE *Scar* xxiii. 'You don't look well. . . No fresh worry, I hope.' 'No,' wearily. 'Only old sins have long shadows.' **1957** V. BRITTAIN *Testament of Experience* I. iii. If he hadn't been killed, they would probably never have become what they were. . . Bygone battles, like old sins, cast long shadows. **1987** C. GRAHAM *Killings at Badger's Drift* viii. 'The father was no good. Drove his poor wife into her grave.' 'So I understood.' 'Old sins cast long shadows.' ■ **past**; **wrong-doers**

OLD soldiers never die

□ *a* **1920** J. FOLEY (*song-title*) Old soldiers never die. **1930** BROPHY & PARTRIDGE *Songs & Slang of British Soldier 1914–18* II. 67 Old soldiers never die—They simply fade away. **1933** F. RICHARDS *Old Soldiers never Die* xxviii. We generally wound up our evenings with the old song, set to the tune of a well-known hymn, 'Old soldiers never die, they simply fade away'. **1940** *Times* 6 Apr. 4 There is an old saying that 'Old soldiers never die'—but they may starve. . when other State pensioners are receiving increased benefits. **2000** *Washington Times* 7 Apr. A18 Meanwhile, regardless of the case's outcome, Gen. Kennedy plans to retire this summer, proving, once again, that old soldiers never die. These days, they just file harassment charges. ■ **old age**; **soldiers**

old *see also* BETTER be an old man's darling, than a young man's slave; you cannot CATCH old birds with chaff; there's no FOOL like an old fool; there's many a GOOD tune played on an old fiddle; HANG a thief when he's young and he'll no' steal when he's old; a MAN is as old as he feels, and a woman as old as she looks; NEVER too old to learn; you can't put NEW wine in old bottles; it is best to be OFF with the old love before you are on with the new; an old POACHER makes the best gamekeeper; you cannot SHIFT an old tree without it dying; you can't TEACH an old dog new tricks; YOUNG folks think old folks to be fools but old folks know young folks to be fools; YOUNG men may die but old men must die; YOUNG saint, old devil.

You cannot make an OMELETTE without breaking eggs

Cf. Fr. *on ne fait pas d'omelette sans casser des œufs*, one does not make an omelette without breaking eggs.

□ **1859** T. P. THOMPSON *Audi Alteram Partem* II. xc. We are walking upon eggs and. . the omelet will not be made without the breaking of some. **1897** R. L. STEVENSON *St. Ives* viii. You cannot make an omelette without breaking eggs, . . and it is no bagatelle to escape from Edinburgh Castle. One of us, I think, was even killed. **1974** J. MANN *Sticking Place* iv. 'In your philosophy, it seems that some men have no right to live at all.' . . 'You can't make an omelette without breaking eggs, Mother.' **2000** *National Review* 20 Mar. 22 Nor should anyone be satisfied with the argument that eggs must be broken to make an omelet—the idea, in other words, that effective law enforcement requires the occasional slaying of an innocent citizen. ■ **necessity**; **ways and means**

ONCE a—, always a—

This formula produces a limitless variety of proverbs, many of them depreciatory. Some are of long standing, while others appear to be one-offs. A small selection of sayings in this form is illustrated below and in the next two entries.

□ **1622** J. MABBE tr. *Aleman's Guzman* I. I. i. Once a knaue, and euer a knaue:..For he that hath once beene naught, is presumed to bee so still..not considering.. whether..hee had reformed his manners or no. **1655** T. FULLER *Church Hist. Britain* VII. xxviii. Latimer by the courtesie of England (once a bishop, and ever a bishop) was in civility saluted Lord. **1706** J. STEVENS *Spanish & English Dict.* s.v. Hurtar, Once a Thief, always a Thief. **1820** M. EDGEWORTH *Letter* 15 Nov. in *Maria Edgeworth in France & Switzerland* (1979) 277 She loses her rank..by marrying one of inferior rank. ..French and Russians are with reason surprised with the superior gallantry of our customs which say once a Lady and always a lady. **1953** R. CHANDLER *Long Good-bye* xliv. I went out of the door and got out of the building fast. Once a patsy [dupe], always a patsy. **2002** *Times 2* 21 May 6 Yet although lapsed Catholics may rebel on the surface, they cannot escape the Once a Catholic, Always a Catholic dictum. ■ **constancy and inconstancy**; **human nature**

ONCE a priest, always a priest

An act enabling the clergy of the Church of England to unfrock themselves (the Clerical Disabilities Act) was passed on 9 Aug. 1870.

□ **1859** G. A. SALA *Twice round Clock* 290 The great case of Horne Tooke *versus* the House of Commons—'Once a priest forever a priest'. **1865** L. STEPHEN *Life & Letters* (1906) ix. As in this..country we stick to the maxim, 'once a parson, always a parson,' I could not..go in for law. **1916** JOYCE *Portrait of Artist* (1967) iv. You must be quite sure, Stephen, that you have a vocation because it would be terrible if you found afterwards that you had none. Once a priest always a priest, remember. **2002** *Washington Times* 14 June A1 'Once a priest, always a priest' is a fundamental belief among Catholics. But that tenet may be tested as bishops consider firing hundreds of priests. ■ **constancy and inconstancy**

ONCE a whore, always a whore

□ **1613** H. PARROT *Laquei Ridiculosi* II. cxxi. Well you may change your name, But once a Whore, you shall be still the same. **1659** N. R. *Proverbs* 82 Once a whore and alwaies a whore. **1754** *World* 31 Jan. 344 Supposing him to have acquired so much wealth, the proverb of 'Once a whore, and always a whore', is less significant. **1824** H. MARSHALL *Hist. Kentucky* II. v. 'Once a prostitute, and always a prostitute,' is a fair mode of argument—at least, among politicians. **1981** N. LOFTS *Old Priory* V. iii. There is a saying, 'Once a whore, always a whore.' ■ **constancy and incontancy**; **wrong-doers**

ONCE bitten, twice shy

The variant *once burned, twice shy* is particularly common in the US, perhaps influenced by *a* BURNT *child dreads the fire*.

□ **1853** SURTEES *Sponge's Sporting Tour* xxxvii. Jawleyford had been bit once, and he was not going to give Mr. Sponge a second chance. **1894** G. F. NORTHALL *Folk-Phrases* 20 Once bitten, twice shy. **1920** CONRAD *Rescue* III. ix. Once bit twice shy. He had no mind to be kidnapped. **1949** 'S. STERLING' *Dead Sure* xv. She was especially on her guard..because she'd been victimized in a stupid swindle herself, recently. Once burned, twice shy, you know. **1981** H. ENGEL *Ransom Game* xvi. I can't imagine why this man would be harassing my wife again, Mr. Cooperman. You'd think 'Once burned, twice shy', wouldn't you. **1998** *Times* 7 Jan. 27/6 Once bitten, twice shy when thinking of certain shops. ■ **experience**

once *see also* you can only DIE once; FOOL me once, shame on you.

When ONE door shuts, another opens

□ **1586** D. ROWLAND tr. *Lazarillo* D3v This proverbe was fulfild, when one doore is shut the other openeth. **1620** T. SHELTON tr. *Cervantes' Don Quixote* III. vii. Where one door is shut another is opened. **1710** S. PALMER *Proverbs* 49 When one Door Shuts another Opens. ..How often does the Divine Bounty surprize us with unthought of Felicity! **1821** J. GALT *Annals of Parish* xxvi. Here was an example..of the truth of the old proverb that as one door shuts another opens;..A full equivalent for her [the light-headed Lady Macadam] was given in this hot and fiery Mr. Cayenne. **1925** S. O'CASEY *Juno & Paycock* I. 16 'The job couldn't come at a betther time.'..'Ah, God never shut wan door but he opened another.' **1987** S. STEWART *Lifting the Latch* 105 They say one door in life doesn't close without another opening. **2002** *Washington Post* 30 Jan. C15 (*Rhymes with Orange comic strip*) 'I always say, "When one door closes, another will open." In this case, when my office door closes behind you, Security will escort you to the exit and open that door for you.' ■ **opportunity**

ONE for sorrow, two for mirth; three for a wedding, four for a birth

A traditional country proverb found in a variety of forms, which refers to the number of magpies seen on a particular occasion.

□ *a* **1846** B. HAYDON *Autobiography* (1853) I. v. During the journey four magpies rose..and flew away. ..I repeated..the old saw, 'one for sorrow, two for mirth, three for a wedding, and four for death.' **1846** M. A. DENHAM *Proverbs relating to Seasons, &c.* 35 One for sorrow: two for mirth: three for a wedding: four for a birth: five for silver: six for gold: seven for a secret, not to be told: eight for heaven: nine for hell: and ten for the devil's own sel [self]. **1913** A. C. BENSON *Along Road* 162 I never see magpies myself without relating the old rhyme: 'One for sorrow, Two for mirth, Three for a death, Four for a birth; Five, you will shortly be In a great company.' **1981** J. GARDNER *Licence Renewed* ii. Bond thought of the old adage, 'One for sorrow, two for joy.' There were a lot of single magpies swooping near the car. ■ **bird lore; omens**

ONE for the mouse, one for the crow, one to rot, one to grow

Other forms of this traditional country saying relating to sowing are also illustrated here.

□ **1850** *Notes & Queries* 1st Ser. II. 515 How to sow Beans. 'One for the mouse, One for the crow, One to rot, One to grow.' **1941** L. I. WILDER *Little Town on Prairie* ii. 'Kernels,' said Pa. 'Four kernels. ..One for the blackbird, One for the crow, And that will leave Just two to grow.' **1961** N. LOFTS *House at Old Vine* I. 34 Careful farmers..sow their seed broadcast, saying: One for wind and one for crow One to die and one to grow. ■ **garden lore**

ONE nail drives out another

Cf. ARISTOTLE *Politics* 1314a ἥλῳ γὰρ ὁ ἧλος, ὥσπερ ἡ παροιμία, one nail knocks out another, according to the proverb.

□ *a* **1250** *Ancrene Wisse* (1962) 206 An neil driueth ut then other. **1555** J. HEYWOOD *Two Hundred Epigrams* no. 112 One nayle dryueth out an other. **1591** SHAKESPEARE *Two Gentlemen of Verona* II. iv. 189 As one nail by strength drives out another, So the remembrance of my former love Is by a newer object quite forgotten. *c* **1645** J. HOWELL *Familiar Letters* 17 Sept. (1903) III. 87 Languages and words..may be said to stick in the memory like nails or pegs in a wainscot door, which used to thrust out one another oftentimes. **1852** E. FITZGERALD *Polonius* cxvii. One nail drives out another. **1979** V. CANNING *Satan Sampler* ix. He needed a home with a woman in it. One nail drove out another. ■ **change**

ONE size does not fit all

Earlier versions of this saying are based on the metaphor of different size shoes for different feet; cf. **1587** J. BRIDGES *Defence of Government of Church of England* 86 Diverse feete have diverse lastes. The shooe that will serve one, may wring another.

□ **1616** B. RICH *My Ladie's Looking Glasse* 21 As every shooe is not fit for every foote, nor every medicine to be applyed to every maladie, so every fashion, doth not befit every person, not every colour agree with every complexion. **1712** J. KELLY *Scottish Proverbs* 96 Every shoe fits not every foot. Every condition of life, every behaviour, every speech and gesture becomes not every body; that will be decent in one, which will be ridiculous in another. **1874** Ascott House, Buckinghamshire, UK (*painted on cornice*) Every shoe fits not every foot. **2002** *Times* 20 Mar. 26 Yesterday Sir Howard Davies . . gave warning that there was a danger that Europe's approach to financial markets was in danger of trying to strap the different European markets into rigid rules that risked damaging their international competitiveness. One size does not fit all, he said. ■ **ways and means**

ONE year's seeding makes seven years' weeding

On the danger of allowing weeds to grow and seed themselves: also used figuratively.

□ **1866** *Rural American* 1 Dec. 354 It has been truly remarked that 'one year's seeding may cost ten years' weeding'. **1873** HARLAND & WILKINSON *Lancashire Legends* 190 One year's seeding makes seven years' weeding. **1889** T. F. THISTELTON-DYER *Folklore of Plants* xi. A weed that runs to seed Is a seven years' weed . . implies that disagreeable actions . . only too frequently cling to man in after years. **1980** *Daily Telegraph* 19 Jan. 20 My advice to weed-persons is: do not let your weeds grow to maturity and seed—'one year's seeding means seven years' weeding'. ■ **action and consequence; garden lore**

one *see also* BETTER one house spoiled than two; BETTER to live one day as a tiger . . ; a BIRD never flew on one wing; two BOYS are half a boy, and three boys are no boy at all; the BUYER has need of hundred eyes, the seller of but one; every DOG is allowed one bite; don't put all your EGGS in one basket; one ENGLISHMAN can beat three Frenchmen; one FUNERAL makes many; one GOOD turn deserves another; one HALF of the world does not know how the other half lives; one HAND for yourself and one for the ship; one HAND washes the other; one HOUR's sleep before midnight is worth two after; one man's LOSS is another man's gain; one man's MEAT is another man's poison; one PICTURE is worth ten thousand words; one man may STEAL a horse, while another may not look over a hedge; one STEP at a time; from the SUBLIME to the ridiculous is only a step; one SWALLOW does not make a summer; it TAKES one to know one; TWO heads are better than one; if TWO ride on a horse, one must ride behind; one VOLUNTEER is worth two pressed men; one WEDDING brings another.

one-eyed *see* in the COUNTRY of the blind, the one-eyed man is king.

open *see* (adjective) A DOOR must either be shut or open; (verb) a GOLDEN key can open any door; when ONE door shuts, another opens.

The OPERA isn't over till the fat lady sings

Attempts to determine the identity of the diva concerned have been inconclusive.

□ **1978** *Washington Post* 13 June B1 The opera isn't over till the fat lady sings. . . One day three years ago, Ralph Carpenter, who was then Texas Tech's sports information director, declared to the press box contingent in Austin, 'The rodeo ain't over till the bull riders ride.' Stirred to top that deep insight, San Antonio sports editor Dan Cook countered with, 'The opera ain't over till the fat lady sings.' **1988** D. L. GILBERT *Black Star Murders* viii. As soon as the big blond Brünnhilde finished, it was over. All I could think about was the classic line about the opera never being over until the fat lady sings. **1992** *Independent* 11 Aug. 7 'You know, they say that the show's never over until the fat lady sings,' Mr Bolger said. 'Well, I think it was her we heard warming up in the wings this week.' **2002** *Times* 2 July 19 [T]he Royal Opera House's leading lady whose dress was set on fire by an on-stage candle is a classic case of it ain't over till the fat lady singes. ■ **finality**

opinion *see* he that COMPLIES against his will is of his own opinion still; so many MEN, so many opinions.

OPPORTUNITY makes a thief

□ *c* **1220** *Hali Meidenhad* (EETS) 23 Man seith that eise maketh theof. **1387** J. TREVISA tr. *Higden's Polychronicon* (1879) VII. 379 At the laste the bischop seide to hym, 'Me thenke that opportunitie makethe a thefe'. **1623** W. CAMDEN *Remains concerning Britain* (ed. 3) 275 Opportunity makes the thief. **1670** J. RAY *English Proverbs* 129 Opportunity makes the thief. . . Therefore, masters . . ought to secure their moneys and goods under lock and key, that they do not give . . a temptation to steal. **1835** SOUTHEY *Doctor* III. cv. Opportunity, which makes thieves, makes lovers also. **1979** *Daedalus* Summer 107 A child steals from the sleeping woman's pocket, acting out the proverb 'Opportunity makes a thief.' ■ **honesty and dishonesty; opportunity, taken**

OPPORTUNITY never knocks twice at any man's door

Fortune occurs instead of *opportunity* in earlier forms of the saying. Several quotations below represent slightly different ideas based on the original proverb. In quots. 1809 and 1981, Opportunity is said to knock once or more, but in other quotations, once only. Cf. early 15th-cent Fr. *il n'est chance qui ne retourne*, there is no opportunity which comes back again.

□ **1567** G. FENTON *Bandello* 216 Fortune once in the course of our life, dothe put into our handes the offer of a good torne. **1809** *Port Folio* (Philadelphia) Nov. 431 Fortune knocks once, at least, at every man's door. **1889** W. F. BUTLER *C. G. Gordon* iii. Fate, it is said, knocks once at every man's door. . . Gordon had just passed his thirtieth year when Fortune . . knocked at . . the door which was to lead him to fame. **1891** J. J. INGALLS *Opportunity* in *Truth* (NY) 19 Feb. 17 I [Opportunity] knock unbidden once at every gate! If sleeping, wake: if feasting rise before I turn away . . [for] I return no more! **1941** 'P. WENTWORTH' *Unlawful Occasions* xxiv. It was an opportunity with a capital O, and if she threw it away it would never come back again. Opportunity never knocks twice at any man's door. **2001** *Washington Post* 18 Nov. F2 Experts are uniquely vulnerable to one weakness: Opportunity may knock only once, but the temptation to try to make a contract the hard way—and make the newspapers—is always pounding at the expert's door. ■ **opportunity**

opportunity *see also* ENGLAND'S difficulty is Ireland's opportunity; MAN'S extremity is God's opportunity.

opposite *see* DREAMS go by contraries.

orders *see* OBEY orders, if you break owners.

orphan *see* SUCCESS has many fathers, while failure is an orphan.

OTHER times, other manners

The proverb occurs in various forms and languages: cf. PINDAR *Fragment* CCXXV. (Bowra), *ἄλλοτ᾽ ἀλλοῖα φρόνει*, think different thoughts at different times; Fr. *autres temps, autres mœurs*, other times, other customs.

□ **1576** G. PETTIE *Petit Palace* 34 Other times, other wayes. **1902** A. DOBSON *Samuel Richardson* iv. Notwithstanding the favourite explanation of 'other times, other manners', contemporary critics of Clarissa found very much the same fault with her history as people do to-day. **1945** F. THOMPSON *Lark Rise* viii. Other days, other ways. ..The old country midwives did at least succeed in bringing into the world many generations of our forefathers. **1978** G. GREENE *Human Factor* IV. ii. 'We used to have better funerals in Africa.'..'Oh well—other countries, other manners.' ■ **change; circumstances; past**

other *see also* DO unto others as you would they should do unto you; the GRASS is always greener on the other side of the fence; one HALF of the world does not know how the other half lives; one HAND washes the other.

An OUNCE of practice is worth a pound of precept

A number of proverbs similar in form are illustrated below. *An ounce* used figuratively for 'a small quantity' is found in **1567** W. CECIL *Letter* in C. Read *Mr. Secretary Cecil* (1955) xxi. Marry [to be sure], an ounce of advice is more worth to be executed aforehand than in the sight of perils. Quot. 2002 suggests some convergence between this saying and PREVENTION *is better than cure.*

□ *c* **1576** T. WHYTHORNE *Autobiography* (1961) 142 I ment not to be on of thoz who waith [esteems] A chip of chauns [luck] mor then A pownds wurth of witt. **1592** G. DELAMOTHE *French Alphabet* II. 55 An ounce of discretion, is better worth, then a pound of hardinesse [audacity]. **1616** T. ADAMS *Sacrifice of Thankfulness* 19 The prouerbe is true; an Ounce of Discretion, is worth a pound of Learning. **1748** J. ELIOT *Essays upon Field Husbandry* 12 It used to be the Saying of an old Man, That an Ounce of Experience is better than a Pound of Science. **1866** BLACKMORE *Cradock Nowell* II. ix. Remember that rigid probity, and the strictest punctuality..are the very soul of business, and that an ounce of practice is worth a pound of precept. **1925** J. GALSWORTHY *Caravan* 667 'Define it [Beauty], Mr. Vaness.' 'An ounce of fact is worth a ton of theory.—It stands before me.' **1981** P. O'DONNELL *Xanadu Talisman* ix. She said rather primly, 'An ounce of wisdom is worth a pound of wit.' **2002** *Washington Times* 5 Apr. A20 Yet, if the IRS is attempting to reduce the incidence of obesity,..shouldn't it permit deduction for activities and products that prevent one from becoming obese in the first place? After all, an ounce of prevention could be worth a literal pound of cure. ■ **example, good and bad; words and deeds**

OUT of debt, out of danger

□ **1639** J. CLARKE *Parœmiologia Anglo-Latina* 82 Out of debt and deadly danger. **1667** H. PEACHAM *Worth of Penny* (ed. 2) 8 How bold, confident, merry, lively, and ever in humour are moneyed men (for being out of debt, they are out of danger). **1710** S. PALMER *Proverbs* 132 Out of Debt out of Danger. ..A Man in Debt is a Slave, and can't act with Liberty. **1908** E. M. SNEYD-KYNNERSLEY *H.M.I.* xxi. Call it 'distributing capital expenditure over a term of years', and even a rural dean succumbs. 'Out of debt, out of danger,' but 'out of debt, out of progress.' **1977** 'C. AIRD' *Parting Breath*

vii. 'Well, they're important, aren't they?' said Leeyes largely. 'Out of debt, out of danger.' ■ **security; thrift**

OUT of sight, out of mind

Cf. L. *absens haeres non erit*, an absent person will not be an heir.

□ *c* **1250** *Proverbs of Alfred* (1907) 46 He that is ute bi-loken [shut out] He is inne sone foryeten [forgotten]. *c* **1450** tr. *T. à Kempis' De Imitatione Christi* (EETS) I. xxxiii. Whan Man is oute of sight, son be he passith oute of mynde. **1545** R. TAVERNER tr. *Erasmus' Adages* (ed. 2) D6V Whereunto also agreethe oure Englyshe proverbe which sayethe: Oute of syght, oute of mynde. **1797** A. RADCLIFFE *Italian* III. ix. Old women now-a-days are not much thought of; out of sight out of mind with them. **1863** C. KINGSLEY *Water Babies* i. Sir John and the rest saw no more of her; and out of sight was out of mind. **1979** 'S. WOODS' *This Fatal Writ* 45 The brief.. was promptly concealed. ..He was working on the principle 'out of sight, out of mind'. **2002** *Spectator* 13 Apr. 38 'Once word gets out, people will come,' they say. 'Out of sight, out of mind.' ■ **absence; forgetfulness**

out *see also* BETTER be out of the world than out of the fashion; there are as good FISH in the sea as ever came out of it; when the GORSE is out of bloom, kissing's out of fashion; don't HALLOO till you are out of the wood; out of the MOUTHS of babes—; MURDER will out; never tell TALES out of school; TRUTH will out.

outside *see* there is NOTHING so good for the inside of a man as the outside of a horse.

over *see* the OPERA isn't over till the fat lady sings; the SHARPER the storm, the sooner it's over.

own *see* the DEVIL looks after his own; when THIEVES fall out, honest men come by their own.

owner *see* OBEY orders, if you break owners.

owt *see* HEAR all, see all, say nowt; you don't get SOMETHING for nothing.

ox *see* BETTER a dinner of herbs than a stalled ox where hate is.

It is the PACE that kills

□ **1855** S. A. HAMMETT *Wonderful Adventures of Captain Priest* XV. The well-known sporting maxim, that 'It is the pace that kills'. **1901** S. LANE-POOLE *Sir H. Parkes in China* XX. There is an old proverb about the pace that kills, and.. Sir Harry was killing himself by work at high pressure. **1936** N. MARSH *Death in Ecstasy* II. xvii. Don't overdo it. .. This is the pace that kills. ■ **haste; stress**

package *see* the BEST things come in small packages.

pack-drill *see* NO names, no pack-drill.

padlock *see* WEDLOCK is a padlock.

pain *see* GENIUS is an infinite capacity for taking pains; NO pain, no gain; PRIDE feels no pain.

paint *see* a BLIND man's wife needs no paint.

painted *see* the DEVIL is not so black as he is painted.

pan *see* if IFS and ands were pots and pans, there'd be no work for tinkers' hands.

paradise *see* ENGLAND is the paradise of women.

parcel *see* the BEST things come in small packages.

pardon *see* OFFENDERS never pardon.

Paris *see* good AMERICANS when they die go to Paris.

PARSLEY seed goes nine times to the Devil

□ **1658** in Mennis & Smith *Wit Restored* 35 There is a saying in the North Riding of Yorkshire that The weed [parsley] before it's borne Nine times the devill sees. **1885** *Notes & Queries* 6th Ser. XI. 467 Parsley seed (when it has been sown) goes nine times to the devil. **1908** D. H. LAWRENCE *Letter* 4 May (1962) I. 7 People say parsley seed goes seven times (some are moderate, discarding the holy number as unfit, and say five) to the Old Lad, it is so long a-germinating. **1981** in A. Hewins *Dillen* xiv. It's a queer plant, parsley: 'sow on Good Friday, seven times down to Hell afore it chits [sprouts (dialect)].' ■ **garden lore; superstition**

parsnip *see* FINE words butter no parsnips.

part *see* (noun) DISCRETION is the better part of valour; if you're not part of the SOLUTION, you're part of the problem; (verb) the BEST of friends must part.

parted *see* a FOOL and his money are soon parted.

Things PAST cannot be recalled

Cf. late 14th-cent. Fr. *ce qui est passé ne poet on recouver*, that which is past one cannot recall.

□ *a* **1500** H. MEDWALL *Nature* H3v A thyng don can not be called agayn. *a* **1535** MORE *Edward V* in J. Hardyng *Chronicle* (1543) II. 36 Sith [since] thynges passed cannot be gaine called, muche more ought wee to bee ware. **1616** T. DRAXE *Adages* 151 That that is past, cannot be recalled or helped. **1804** M. EDGEWORTH *Popular Tales* II. 130 Since a thing past can't be recalled.. we may be content. **1979** *Country Life* 24 May 1683 Visually, another period's realities are palpably inaccessible. Things past cannot be—perfectly—recalled. ■ **past; regrets**

pastime *see* he that would go to SEA for pleasure, would go to hell for a pastime.

paternoster *see* NO penny, no paternoster.

PATIENCE is a virtue

Cf. *Disticha Catonis* I. xxxviii. *maxima enim.. patientia virtus*, patience is the greatest virtue; mid 14th-cent. Fr. *patience est une grant vertu*, patience is a great virtue.

□ **1377** LANGLAND *Piers Plowman* B. XI. 370 Suffraunce [forbearance] is a souereygne vertue. *c* **1386** CHAUCER *Tale of Melibee* l. 1517 Pacience is a greet vertu of perfeccioun. **1594** LYLY *Mother Bombie* V. iii. Patience is a vertue, but pinching is worse than any vice! **1754** RICHARDSON *Grandison* II. xvii. Aunt Prue in Yorkshire.. will be able to instruct you, that patience is a virtue; and that you ought not to be in haste to take a first offer, for fear you should not have a second. **1858** TROLLOPE *Dr. Thorne* I. xiv. That was only three days ago. Why don't you.. ferret her out?.. Patience is and always was a virtue. **1979** A. FOX *Threat Warning Red* iv. 'I.. can't *wait* for you.'.. 'Patience is and said to be a virtue?' ■ **patience and impatience**

Paul *see* if SAINT Paul's day be fair and clear, it will betide a happy year.

paved *see* the ROAD to hell is paved with good intentions.

PAY beforehand was never well served

□ **1591** J. FLORIO *Second Fruits* 39 He that paieth afore hand, hath neuer his worke well done. **1721** J. KELLY *Scottish Proverbs* 278 *Pay beforehand was never well serv'd*. It is common to see.. Labourers, to go about a piece of Work with great Uneasiness, which is to pay a just Debt. **1786** G. WASHINGTON *Letter* 7 Jan. in *Writings* (1938) XXVIII. 370 I have had some reason to remember an old adage, that one of the bad paymasters is him that pays before hand. **1819** SCOTT *Bride of Lammermoor* iii. 'Your honour is the bad pay-master,' he said, 'who pays before it is done.' **1928** A. C. BROWN *Dr. Glazebrook's Revenge* xi. The old Scots adage that 'fore-hand payments mak' hint-hand wark'. ■ **employers and employees; work**

He that cannot PAY, let him pray

□ **1611** R. COTGRAVE *Dict. French & English* s.v. Argent, He that cannot pay let him pray. **1732** T. FULLER *Gnomologia* no. 6362 He that cannot pay, Let him pray. **1954** R. STOUT *Three Men Out* v. They're quotations from things. One of them says, 'He that cannot pay, let him pray.' ■ **money; poverty**

If you PAY peanuts, you get monkeys

Peanuts in the sense of 'a small sum of money' (esp. when considered as inadequate payment) originated as mid 20th-cent. US slang.

□ **1966** L. COULTHARD in *Director* Aug. 228 Shareholders want the best available businessmen to lead the companies and recognise that you get what you pay for. If you pay in peanuts, you must expect to get monkeys. **1979** P. ALEXANDER *Show me Hero* iii. 'That's forty thousand we're giving away. Seems an awful lot.' 'If you pay peanuts,' said Ashman, 'you get monkeys.' **1979** *Guardian* 11 Sept. 30 The companies' chief negotiator.. was greeted with shouts of 'if you pay peanuts, you get monkeys'. **1994** S. REUBEN *Origin and Cause* xvii. 107 'How much is.. this photo-enhancement going to cost my client?' 'A bundle. .. But in my experience, if you pay peanuts, you get monkeys.' ■ **employers and employees; money**

pay *see also* (noun) NO cure, no pay; (verb) CRIME doesn't pay; they that DANCE must pay the fiddler; DEATH pays all debts; SPEAK not of my debts unless you mean to pay them; the THIRD time pays for all.

He who PAYS the piper calls the tune

Reversing the emphasis of *they that* DANCE *must pay the fiddler*.

□ **1895** *Daily News* 18 Dec. 9 Londoners had paid the piper, and should choose the tune. **1910** *Spectator* 22 Oct. 643 Until British electors know that the dollars have been returned they will be wise in placing little trust in Nationalist 'loyalty'. He who pays the piper calls the tune. **2002** *Times* 2 Jan. 14 In no profession is the saying 'He who pays the piper, calls the tune' more apt than government. ■ **action and consequence; money**

You PAYS your money and you takes your choice

Both *pays* and *takes* are non-standard, colloquial forms.

□ **1846** *Punch* X. 16 'Which *is* the Prime Minister?'.. 'Which ever you please, my little dear. You pays your money, and you takes your choice.' **1904** V. S. LEAN *Collectanea* IV. 205 You pays your money and you takes your choice. You pays your money and what you sees is A cow or a donkey just as you pleases. **2001** *Washington Post Book World* 23 Dec. 11 Which is the right answer? You pays your money, as another saying goes, and you takes your choice. ■ **choices; money**

If you want PEACE, you must prepare for war

Translating the 4th-cent. AD Roman military writer FLAVIUS VEGETIUS *Epitoma Rei Militaris* III. (Introd.) *qui desiderat pacem, praeparet bellum*, he who desires peace must prepare for war.

□ *a* **1547** E. HALL *Chronicle* (1548) Edw. IV 209 He forgat the olde adage, saynge in tyme of peace prouyde for warre. **1593** M. SUTCLIFFE *Practice of Arms* A2V He that desireth peace, he must prepare for warres. **1624** BURTON *Anatomy of Melancholy* (ed. 2) II. iii. The Commonwealth of Venice in their Armory haue this inscription, Happy is that Citty which in time of peace thinkes of warre, a fit Motto for euery mans priuate house. **1885** C. LOWE *Prince Bismarck* II. x. Lord Beaconsfield had acted on the maxim that 'if you want peace, you must prepare for war'. **1929** *Listener* 28 Aug. 278 'If you want peace, prepare for peace.' This is the reverse of the old motto, 'If you want peace, prepare for war'. **2001** *Washington Times* 13 July A17 Peace is pro-family, pro-economy and—hear this environmentalists—pro-turtle. Do you want peace? Scipio Africanus, the Roman who defeated Hannibal, put it this way: 'If you want peace, prepare for war.' ■ **peace; prudence**

peanut *see* if you PAY peanuts, you get monkeys.

pear *see* WALNUTS and pears you plant for your heirs.

Do not throw PEARLS to swine

With allusion to MATTHEW vii. 6 (AV) Give not that which is holy unto the dogs, neither cast ye your pearls before swine. Often in the phrase *to cast pearls before swine*.

□ **1340** *Ayenbite of Inwit* (EETS) 152 Thet we ne thrauwe naght oure preciouse stones touore the zuyn. **1362** LANGLAND *Piers Plowman* A. XI. *Noli mittere Margeri*, perles Among hogges. **1526** *Pilgrimage of Perfection* II. iii. The holy fathers thought it nat expedient to disclose the secrete misteryes to euery worldly person. .. Cast not your perles before hogges. **1550** R. CROWLEY *Epigrams* A3^{v} Before suche swyne no pearles maye be caste. **1816** S. SMITH *Letter* in S. Holland *Memoir* (1855) II. 134 Elgin has done a very useful thing in taking them [the Elgin Marbles] away from the Turks. Do not throw pearls to swine. **1925** WODEHOUSE *Sam the Sudden* xi. 'Young women do not interest me.' The proverb about casting pearls before swine occurred to Sam. **2001** *Spectator* 3 Nov. 8 I am always inclined to toss such people a copy of *The Way of All Flesh* to show them what great late-Victorian fiction-writing was really about, but that would be pearls before swine. ■ **gratitude and ingratitude; waste**

A PECK of March dust is worth a king's ransom

The month of March is traditionally wet and blustery. A *peck* in former times was a dry measure of two gallons. Thomas Fuller, discussing this saying in his *Worthies of England* (1662, p. 87), links the 'king's ransom' to the £100,000 raised in 1193–4 to pay for the release of King Richard I, who, on his way home from crusading in the Holy Land, was being held captive in Germany.

□ **1533** J. HEYWOOD *Play of Weather* D1 And now to mynde there is one olde prouerbe come: 'One bushell of march dust is worth a kynges raunsome.' **1685** R. BOYLE *Discourse of Causes of Insalubrity of Air* 55 It is proverbially said in England, that a Peck of March Dust is worth a King's Ransom: So infrequent is dry Weather, during that Month. **1836** E. HOWARD *Rattlin the Reefer* III. viii. A spoonful of the soup to-day will be worth a king's ransom—a peck of March dust! pooh! **1936** H. C. BAILEY *Clue for Mr. Fortune* 36 The flower borders .. were planted with bush roses .. stunted by the rigours of that grim March. .. 'Bushel of March dust worth a king's ransom,' Reggie murmured. **1978** R. WHITLOCK *Calendar of Country Customs* iii. [The farmer] values dry, cold weather, such as often occurs in late February and March. 'A peck of dust in March is worth a king's ransom,' is still an oft-quoted proverb. ■ **weather lore**

peck *see also* we must EAT a peck of dirt before we die.

The PEN is mightier than the sword

Cf. CICERO *De Officiis* I. xxii. *cedant arma togae*, arms give way to persuasion.

□ **1582** G. WHETSTONE *Heptameron of Civil Discourses* iii. The dashe of a Pen, is more greeuous then the counter use of a Launce. *a* **1712** W. KING *Eagle & Robin* in *Poetical Works* (1781) III. 49 Poor Bob .. A goosequill on for weapon ty'd, Knowing by use that now and then A sword less hurt does than a pen. **1839** BULWER-LYTTON *Richelieu* II. ii. Beneath the rule of men entirely great, The pen is mightier than the sword. **1976** T. SHARPE *Wilt* iii. The man who said the pen was mightier than the sword ought to have tried reading *The Mill on the Floss* to Motor Mechanics. **2002** *Washington Post* 6 Mar. C1 In the long run, casualties and causality may be equally important—or maybe Laura Bush and her conference on education had the edge, yesterday, the pen being mightier than the sword and all. ■ **tact**

Take care of the PENCE and the pounds will take care of themselves

The 'Mr. Lowndes' to whom quot. 1750 attributes this saying was William Lowndes (1652–1724).

□ **1750** CHESTERFIELD *Letter* 5 Feb. (1932) IV. 1500 Old Mr. Lowndes, the famous Secretary of the Treasury, .. used to say .. Take care of the pence, and the pounds will take care of themselves. **1912** G. B. SHAW *Pygmalion* II. 132 Take care of the pence and the pounds will take care of themselves is as true of personal habits as of money. **1979** R. CASSILIS *Arrow of God* IV. xvii. Little things, Master Mally. Look after the pennies, Master Mally, and the pounds will look after themselves. **1999** 'H. CRANE' *Miss Seeton's Finest Hour* xi. 92 'Yes, it sounds on the melodramatic side,' he said cheerfully, 'but in wartime you can't be too careful about the smallest detail. Think of it as along the lines of taking care of the pennies, and the pounds will take care of themselves.' ■ **money; thrift**

A PENNY saved is a penny earned

□ **1640** G. HERBERT *Outlandish Proverbs* no. 506 A penny spar'd is twice got. *a* **1661** T. FULLER *Worthies* (Hunts.) 51 By the same proportion that a penny saved is a penny gained, the preserver of books is a Mate for the Compiler of them. **1695** E. RAVENSCROFT *Canterbury Guests* II. iv. This I did to prevent expences, for..a penny sav'd, is a penny got. **1853** DICKENS *Bleak House* ix. I saved five pounds out of the brickmaker's affair. ..It's a very good thing to save one, let me tell you: a penny saved, is a penny got! **1923** WODEHOUSE *Inimitable Jeeves* xi. I can save money this way; and believe me, laddie, nowadays..a penny saved is a penny earned. **2001** *Washington Post* 6 Dec. C11 (*Family Circus comic strip*) 'A penny saved is a penny earned, but what can I buy with it?' ■ **thrift**

PENNY wise and pound foolish

□ **1607** E. TOPSELL *Four-footed Beasts* 609 If by couetousnesse or negligence, one withdraw from them their ordinary foode, he shall be penny wise, and pound foolish. **1712** J. ADDISON *Spectator* 7 Feb. I think a Woman who will give up herself to a Man in Marriage, where there is the least room for such an Apprehension.. may very properly be accused..of being Penny wise and Pound foolish. **1864** MRS H. WOOD *Trevlyn Hold* II. xxi. He never would insure his ricks. ..Miss Diana has often told him he deserved to have his ricks take fire for being penny wise and pound foolish. **2001** *Washington Post* 17 June H1 I didn't stop because I was too focused on saving that 2 cents a gallon. I was, without a doubt, being penny-wise and pound-foolish. ■ **meanness; stupidity**

penny *see also* a BAD penny always turns up; IN for a penny, in for pound; NO penny, no paternoster.

Like PEOPLE, like priest

With allusion to HOSEA iv. 9 (AV) Like people, like priest.

□ **1589** *Pasquil's Return* C3 Like people, like Priest begins now to be verified. **1670** J. RAY *English Proverbs* 114 Like priest, like people. ..Always taken in the worse sense. **1893** R. HEATH *English Peasant* IV. iii. He had so deep a reverence for the clergy, that it never entered into his mind that perhaps, after all, it was 'like people, like priest'. ■ **similarity and dissimilarity**

people *see also* IDLE people have the least leisure; MORE people know Tom Fool than Tom Fool knows; the VOICE of the people is the voice of God.

perfect *see* PRACTICE makes perfect.

perish *see* he who LIVES by the sword dies by the sword.

perjury *see* JOVE but laughs at lovers' perjury.

PHYSICIAN, heal thyself

With allusion to LUKE iv. 23 (AV) Ye will surely say unto me this proverb, Physician, heal thyself. (VULGATE *medice cura teipsum.*)

□ *c* **1400** tr. *Honorius of Autun's Elucidarium* (1909) 29 Blynde leches [doctors], heeleth first youre silf! **1519** J. COLET *Sermon to Convocation* B5v If you wyll ponder and loke vpon oure mottis [motes] fyrst take awaye the blockes out of your eies. Hit is an olde Prouerbe: Phisition heale thy selfe. **1780** T. FRANCKLIN tr. *Lucian's Works* I. 320 According to the old adage, 'physician, cure thyself'. **1875** S. SMILES *Thrift* ii. How can a man.. teach sobriety or cleanliness, if he be himself drunken or foul? 'Physician, heal thyself,' is the answer of his neighbours. **1979** G. SWARTHOUT *Skeletons* 150 Tell me the truth. Don't dig yourself in any deeper. Physician, heal thyself. **2002** *National Review* 11 Feb. 26 As for those who get bent out of shape when they're 'Dr.'-less, all we can say is, 'Ph.D., heal thyself.' ■ **doctors**

pick *see* HAWKS will not pick out hawks' eyes; see a PIN and pick it up, all the day you'll have good luck.

pickle (small quantity): *see* MANY a little makes a mickle.

One PICTURE is worth ten thousand words

There is no foundation to the ascription of Chinese origin in quot. 1927.

□ **1921** *Printers' Ink* 8 Dec. 96 One look is worth a thousand words. **1927** *Ibid.* 10 Mar. 114 *Chinese proverb*, One picture is worth ten thousand words. **1954** R. HAYDN *Journal of Edwin Carp* 90 'One picture speaks louder than ten thousand words.' Mr. Bovey repeated the adage this morning when.. he handed me my finished portrait. **1979** *Scientific American* Oct. 118 A picture is worth a thousand words. **2001** *New Scientist* 17 Nov. 59 [In a photograph] the mask is being worn with the bottom strap cut off or dangling. A picture is worth a thousand words, but here are eight to redress the balance: 'If there's only one strap, it's probably crap.' ■ **example, good and bad; illustration**

Every PICTURE tells a story

Quot. 1847 antedates the use of this saying as an advertiser's catch-phrase.

□ **1847** C. BRONTË *Jane Eyre* I. i. The letter-press.. I cared little for. .. Each picture told a story. **1904** *Daily Mail* 26 Feb. 8 A London woman and Doan's Backache Kidney Pills. .. 'Every picture tells a story.' **1967** E. WILLIAMS *Beyond Belief* IV. xxiii. Every Picture Tells a Story. .. Sergeant Carr stood with his.. back to the fireplace, the lady next to the budgie, the dog next to her. **2001** *Times Literary Supplement* 2 Nov. 8 'We extend that which is limited by a frame to before and after, and through the craft of telling stories.. we lend the immutable picture an infinite and inexhaustible life.' This is not merely a gloss on 'every picture tells a story', but an unfashionably specific and an unfashionably true observation. ■ **example, good and bad; illustration**

pie *see* the DEVIL makes his Christmas pies of lawyers' tongues and clerks' fingers.

pie-crust *see* PROMISES, like pie-crust, are made to be broken.

pig *see* what can you EXPECT from a pig but a grunt?

pillow *see* a clean CONSCIENCE is a good pillow.

See a PIN and pick it up, all the day you'll have good luck; see a pin and let it lie, bad luck you'll have all the day

Similarly extolling the virtues of thrift in small matters is **1668** S. PEPYS *Diary* 2 Jan. (1976) IX. 7 The King answered to it with great indifferency. Sir W. Coventry answered: 'I see your Majesty doth not remember the old English proverb, 'He that will not stoop for a pin will never be worth a pound'.

□ **1843** J. O. HALLIWELL *Nursery Rhymes* 120 See a pin and let it lay, Bad luck you'll have all the day! **1883** C. S. BURNE *Shropshire Folklore* xxi. Pins are held.. unlucky.. in the North of England.. but side by side with this we have the thrifty maxim—See a pin and let it lie, You'll want a pin another day; See a pin and pick it up, All the day you'll have good luck. **1935** A. CHRISTIE *Tape-Measure Murder* in *Miss Marple's Final Cases* (1979) 'There's a pin in your tunic.'.. He said, 'They do say, "See a pin and pick it up, all the day you'll have good luck."' **1966** D. FRANCIS *Flying Finish* ix. In the little hall hung more time-worn poker work. 'See a pin and pick it up, all the day you'll have good luck. See a pin and let it lie, you will want before you die.' ■ **luck; thrift**

pin *see also* NEEDLES and pins,.. when a man marries, his trouble begins; it's a SIN to steal a pin.

pint *see* you cannot get a QUART into a pint pot.

piper *see* he who PAYS the piper calls the tune.

pitch *see* he that TOUCHES pitch shall be defiled.

The PITCHER will go to the well once too often

A warning against pushing one's luck too far. Cf. early 14th-cent. Fr. *tant va pot a eve qu'il brise*, the pot goes so often to the water that it breaks.

□ **1340** *Ayenbite of Inwit* (EETS) 206 Zuo longe geth thet pot to the wetere: thet hit comth to-broke hom. **1584** J. WITHALS *Dict.* (rev. ed.) Bl So oft goeth the pitcher to the well, that at last it commeth broken home. **1777** N. SHAW *Collections of New London County Hist. Society* (1933) I. 223 I shall send down what I have, but dont you think the Pitcher will go to the well once too often? **1880** *Church Times* 30 Apr. 275 Some of Mr. Gladstone's feats in the way of sweeping obstacles out of his path have been wonderful; but the proverb tells us that the pitcher which goes oft to the well will be broken at last. **1996** 'C. AIRD' *After Effects* xvi. 187 Superintendent Leeyes would have to be disturbed on a Saturday all over again. And it was odds on that he wouldn't like it. That quotation about the pitcher going to the well once too often had more than a ring of truth to it as far as the superintendent was concerned. ■ **misfortune; persistence**

pitcher *see also* LITTLE pitchers have large ears.

pitchfork *see* you can DRIVE out Nature with a pitchfork, but she keeps on coming back.

pitied *see* BETTER be envied than pitied.

PITY is akin to love

□ **1601** SHAKESPEARE *Twelfth Night* III. i. 119 I pity you.—That's a degree to love. **1696** T. SOUTHERNE *Oroonoko* II. i. Do, pity me: Pity's a-kin to Love. *a* **1895** F. LOCKER-LAMPSON *My Confidences* (1896) 95 They say that Pity is akin to Love, though only a Poor Relation; but Amy did not even pity me. **1942** 'C. KINGSTON' *Murder Tunes In* (1943) iii. 44 'It may not be love—it may be only pity.' 'You're wrong,' said Mrs. Armitage with the cheerfulness of one discussing something exceedingly pleasurable. 'It's not the pity that is akin to love—it's love itself.' ■ **love; pity**

A PLACE for everything, and everything in its place

□ **1640** G. HERBERT *Outlandish Proverbs* no. 379 All things have their place, knew wee how to place them. **1842** MARRYAT *Masterman Ready* II. i. In a well-conducted man-of-war.. every thing in its place, and there is a place for every thing. **1855** T. C. HALIBURTON *Nature & Human Nature* I. vi. There was a place for everything, and everything was in its place. **1928** D. L. SAYERS *Lord Peter views Body* x. 'I thought you were rather partial to anatomical specimens.' 'So I am, but not on the breakfast-table. "A place for everything and everything in its place," as my grandmother used to say.' **2002** A. VANNEMAN *Sherlock Holmes and Giant Rat of Sumatra* ix. 80 The sailor's apothegm—'a place for everything, and everything in its place'—guided us, until at length everything was stowed away.. ■ **orderliness**

There's no PLACE like home

Cf. HESIOD *Works & Days* l. 365 *οἴκοι βέλτερον εἶναι*, there's no place like home.

□ **1571** T. TUSSER *Husbandry* (rev. ed.) H1v Though home be but homely, yet huswife is taught, That home hath no fellow to such as haue aught. **1823** J. H. PAYNE *Clari* I. i. 'Mid pleasures and palaces though we may roam, Be it ever so humble, there's no place like home.' **1939** E. F. BENSON *Trouble for Lucia* xi. 'What a joy to have it back at Mallards again!'.. 'No place like home is there, dear?' **2002** *Spectator* 16 Mar. 26 And then there is the tortoise who refused to come to Zeus' party, arguing that there was no place like home. So Zeus angrily condemned him to carry his house with him wherever he went. ■ **content and discontent; home**

place *see also* LIGHTNING never strikes the same place twice; there is a TIME and place for everything; a WOMAN's place is in the home.

plague *see* PLEASE your eye and plague your heart.

plant *see* it is not SPRING until you can plant your foot upon twelve daisies; WALNUTS and pears you plant for your heirs.

Those who PLAY at bowls must look out for rubbers

Rubber is apparently an alteration of *rub*, an obstacle or impediment to the course of a bowl. Cf. **1595** SHAKESPEARE *Richard II* III. iv. 4 Madam, we'll play at bowls.—'Twill make me think the world is full of rubs.

□ **1762** SMOLLETT *Sir Launcelot Greaves* I. x. (*heading*) Which sheweth that he who plays at bowls, will sometimes meet with rubbers. **1824** SCOTT *Redgauntlet* III. vi. 'And how if it fails?' said Darsie. 'Thereafter as it may be—' said Nixon; 'they who play at bowls must meet with rubbers.' **1874** L. STEPHEN *Hours in Library* I. 384 De Quincey.. admits.. that the fanaticism of the rub was 'much more reasonable' than the fanaticism of Priestly; and that those who play at bowls must look out for rubbers. **1907** F. W. HACKWOOD *Old English Sports* xi. Another term used in common speech and derived from this game [bowls] is 'rub'; as when we say.. 'he who plays at bowls must look out for rubs'—that is, he must consider the inequalities of the ground, and.. make due allowance for them. ■ **caution; foresight and hindsight; trouble**

If you PLAY with fire you get burnt

The metaphorical phrase *to play with fire*, to tinker with something potentially dangerous, is also commonly found. Cf. **1655** H. VAUGHAN *Silex Scintillans* II. 15

I played with fire, did counsell spurn,.. But never thought that fire would burn, Or that a soul could ake.

□ **1884** R. H. THORPE *Fenton Family* xiv. If people will play with fire, they must expect to be burned by it some time. If I had not learned the game, and thought myself a good player, I'd never have lost Mother's money. **1980** P. KINSLEY *Vatchman Switch* xxiv. If you play with fire you get burnt. Shouldn't mess around in Crown Colonies. ■ **action and consequence; peril**

play *see also* (noun) FAIR play's a jewel; GIVE and take is fair play; TURN about is fair play; all WORK and no play makes Jack a dull boy; (verb) when the CAT's away, the mice will play.

You can't PLEASE everyone

□ **1472** E. PASTON *Letter* 16 May in *Paston Letters* (1971) I. 635 I am in serteyn the contrary is true—yt is nomore but that he can not plese all partys. **1616** T. DRAXE *Adages* 45 One can hardly please all men. **1844** RUSKIN *Journal* 30 Apr. in *Diaries 1835–47* (1956) 274 At Ward's about window—nothing done. Gastineau came up and don't like mine: can't please everybody. **1981** *Daily Telegraph* 16 May 18 The old adage, 'you can't please everyone', holds good. ■ **conduct; public relations**

PLEASE your eye and plague your heart

□ *c* **1617** A. BREWER *Lovesick King* (1655) III. E3[v] She may please your eye a little.. but vex your heart. **1748** SMOLLETT *Roderick Random* II. xl. Many a substantial farmer.. would be glad to marry her; but she was resolved to please her eye, if she should plague her heart. **1829** COBBETT *Advice to Young Men* III. cxxic. 'Please your eye and plague your heart' is an adage that want of beauty invented, I dare say, more than a thousand years ago. **1876** I. BANKS *Manchester Man* III. vi. But I *will* marry him, mamma—I'll please my eye, if I plague my heart. ■ **appearance; beauty; love**

please *see also* LITTLE things please little minds.

pleasure *see* BUSINESS before pleasure; he that would go to SEA for pleasure, would go to hell for a pastime.

plum *see* a CHERRY year a merry year.

An old POACHER makes the best gamekeeper

□ *c* **1390** CHAUCER *Physician's Tale* l. 83 A theef of venysoun, that hath forlaft His likerousnesse [depravity] and al his olde craft, Kan kepe a forest best of any man. **1695** T. FULLER *Church Hist. Britain* IX. iii. Alwayes set a—to catch a—; and the greatest dear-stealers, make the best Parke-keepers. **1878** R. JEFFERIES *Gamekeeper at Home* ix. There is a saying that an old poacher makes the best gamekeeper, on the principle of setting a thief to catch a thief. **1970** V. CANNING *Great Affair* iii. What the Church needed, possibly, was a good leavening of sinners in its ministry, on the principle that poachers make the best gamekeepers. **1978** T. SHARPE *Throwback* i. 5 'You'll have heard the saying that a poacher makes the best gamekeeper?.. Well, Dodd's the reverse. He's a gamekeeper who would have made the best poacher.' ■ **guile; wrong-doers**

pocket *see* SHROUDS have no pockets.

point *see* POSSESSION is nine points of the law.

poison *see* one man's MEAT is another man's poison.

poke *see* you should KNOW a man seven years before you stir his fire.

policy *see* HONESTY is the best policy.

politeness *see* CIVILITY costs nothing; PUNCTUALITY is the politeness of princes.

POLITICS makes strange bedfellows

Politics has long been considered a plural noun; its use with a singular verb is comparatively recent. A well-established variant of ADVERSITY *makes strange bedfellows*.

□ **1839** P. HONE *Diary* 9 July (1927) I. 404 Party politics, like poverty, bring men 'acquainted with strange bedfellows'. **1870** C. D. WARNER *My Summer in Garden* (1871) 187 The Doolittle raspberries have sprawled all over the strawberry-beds: so true is it that politics makes strange bed-fellows. **1936** M. MITCHELL *Gone with Wind* lviii. Ashley Wilkes and I are mainly responsible. Platitudinously but truly, politics make strange bedfellows. **1980** P. VAN GREENAWAY *Dissident* vii. Even enemies have something in common. Statecraft produces strange bedfellows. **1995** *Washington Times* 31 Mar. A4 Politics makes strange bedfellows, if Mr. Hyde will forgive the unforgivable but irresistible metaphor. ■ **associates; politics**

It is a POOR dog that's not worth whistling for

□ **1546** J. HEYWOOD *Dialogue of Proverbs* I. xi. It is, as I haue learned in lystnyng, A poore dogge, that is not worth the whistlyng. **1614** W. CAMDEN *Remains concerning Britain* (ed. 2) 303 A poore dog that is not worth the whystling. **1738** SWIFT *Polite Conversation* i. 41 Because, Miss, you never ask'd me; and 'tis an ill Dog that's not worth whistling for. **1952** W. S. HOOLE *Alias Simon Suggs* i. It was a poor dog indeed that wasn't worth whistling for. ■ **value**

It is a POOR heart that never rejoices

□ **1834** MARRYAT *Peter Simple* I. v. 'Well,' continued he, 'it's a poor heart that never rejoiceth.' He then poured out half a tumbler of rum. **1841** DICKENS *Barnaby Rudge* iv. What happened when I reached home you may guess. ..Ah! Well, it's a poor heart that never rejoices. **1935** E. F. BENSON *Lucia's Progress* viii. They were all men together, he said, and it was a sad heart that never rejoiced. **1979** J. SCOTT *Clutch of Vipers* iv. 'It's a poor heart', Frankie told him, 'that never rejoices.' ■ **happiness**

poor *see also* one LAW for the rich and another for the poor; the RICH man has his ice in the summer and the poor man gets his in the winter.

Pope *see* it is ill SITTING at Rome and striving with the Pope.

port *see* ANY port in a storm.

POSSESSION is nine points of the law

There is no specific legal ruling which supports this proverb—though the concept is widely acknowledged—but in early use the satisfaction of ten (sometimes twelve) points was commonly asserted to attest full entitlement or ownership. Possession, represented by nine (or eleven) points, is therefore the closest substitute for this. Cf. **1595** *Edward III* E3 Tis you are in possession of the Crowne, And thats the surest poynt of all the Law.

□ **1616** T. DRAXE *Adages* 163 Possession is nine points in the Law. **1659** J. IRETON *Oration* 5 This Rascally-devill.. denys to pay a farthing of rent. Tis true, possession is nine points of the Law, Yet give Gentlemen, right's right. **1709** O. DYKES *English Proverbs* 213 Possession is a mighty Matter indeed; and we commonly say, 'tis eleven Points of the Law. It goes a great Way to the giving of Security, but not any

Right. **1822** T. L. PEACOCK *Maid Marian* v. In those days possession was considerably more than eleven points of the Law. The baron was therefore convinced that the earl's outlawry was infallible. **1920** J. GALSWORTHY *In Chancery* II. xiv. We're the backbone of the country. They [Leftists] won't upset us easily. Possession's nine points of the Law. **2002** *Washington Times* 17 Feb. B2 Mrs. Clinton told the New York Post, 'You know, we followed every single law.' And they did. So what if it was the law of the jungle (possession is nine-tenths of the law)..? ■ **property**

possible *see* ALL things are possible with God; all's for the BEST in the best of all possible worlds.

post *see* the post of HONOUR is the post of danger.

A POSTERN door makes a thief

Similar to OPPORTUNITY *makes a thief.* A postern door is a back door or small entrance distinct from the main access.

□ *c* **1450** *Proverbs of Good Counsel* in *Book of Precedence* (EETS) 69 A nyse wyfe, and a back dore, Makyth often tymus A ryche man pore. **1573** J. SANFORDE *Garden of Pleasure* 107 The posterne dore destroyeth the house. **1611** J. DAVIES *Scourge of Folly* 146 The Posterne doore makes theefe and whore. But, were that dam'd with Stone, or Clay, Whoores and Theeues would find a way. **1732** T. FULLER *Gnomologia* no. 6176 The Postern Door Makes Thief and Whore. **1977** J. AIKEN *Five-Minute Marriage* xi. 'I shall never be able to sleep securely in this room, if thieves are to be always breaking in and waking me up!' 'A postern door do always make a thief.' ■ **honesty and dishonesty; opportunity, taken**

pot *see* if IFS and ands were pots and pans, there'd be no work for tinkers' hands; a LITTLE pot is soon hot; you cannot get a QUART into a pint pot; a WATCHED pot never boils.

pound *see* IN for a penny, in for a pound; an OUNCE of practice is worth a pound of precept; take care of the PENCE and the pounds will take care of themselves; PENNY wise and pound foolish.

pour *see* it never RAINS but it pours.

When POVERTY comes in at the door, love flies out of the window

Similar in sentiment to **1474** CAXTON *Game of Chess* III. iii. Herof men saye a comyn prouerbe in englond that loue lastest as longe as the money endurith.

□ **1631** R. BRATHWAIT *English Gentlewoman* vi. It hath been an old Maxime; that as pouerty goes in at one doore, loue goes out at the other. **1639** J. CLARKE *Parœmiologia Anglo-Latina* 25 When povertie comes in at doores, love leapes out at windowes. **1790** *Universal Asylum* Aug. 84 I hope, ladies, none of you may ever experience, that 'when poverty comes in at the door, love flies out at the windows'. **1894** J. LUBBOCK *Use of Life* iii. It is a mean proverb that, 'When poverty comes in at the door, love flies out of the window'. **1968** J. N. LOCH *Fringe of Blue* 6 Edith's family all believed that love flew out of the window when poverty came in at the door. ■ **love, blighted; poverty**

POVERTY is no disgrace, but it is a great inconvenience

□ **1591** J. FLORIO *Second Fruits* 105 Neuer be ashamed of thy calling, for Pouertie is no vice, though it be an inconvenience. **1721** J. KELLY *Scottish Proverbs* 278 Poortha [poverty] is a Pain, but no Disgrace. Unless it be the Effects of Laziness, and Luxury. **1945** F. THOMPSON *Lark Rise* i. 'Poverty's no disgrace, but 'tis a great inconvenience' was a common saying among the Lark Rise people; but.. their poverty was no less than a hampering drag upon them. ■ **poverty**

POVERTY is not a crime

□ **1591** J. FLORIO *Second Fruits* 105 Pouertie is no vice. **1640** G. HERBERT *Outlandish Proverbs* no. 844 Poverty is no sinne. **1785** C. MACKLIN *Man of World* IV. 56 Her Poverty is not her crime, Sir, but her misfortune. **1839** DICKENS *Nicholas Nickleby* lv. 'Remember how poor we are.' Mrs. Nickleby.. said through her tears that poverty was not a crime. **1945** F. THOMPSON *Lark Rise* ii. There's nothing the matter with Lark Rise folks but poverty, and that's no crime. If it was, we should likely be hung ourselves. **1973** G. MIKES *Spy who died of Boredom* 50 The English say: poverty is not a sin but something much worse. ■ **poverty**

poverty *see also* ADVERSITY makes strange bedfellows.

powder *see* put your TRUST in God, and keep your powder dry.

POWER corrupts

The proverb is now commonly used in allusion to quot. 1887.

□ **1876** TROLLOPE *Prime Minister* IV. viii. We know that power does corrupt, and that we cannot trust kings to have loving hearts. **1887** LD. ACTON *Letter* in *Life & Letters of Mandel Creighton* (1904) I. xiii. Power tends to corrupt, and absolute power corrupts absolutely. Great men are almost always bad men, even when they exercise influence and not authority. **1957** V. BRITTAIN *Testament of Experience* II. ix. The processes by which 'power corrupts' are perhaps inevitable. **1979** McCARRY *Better Angels* IV. xii. He doesn't *know* that power corrupts; there's nothing dark in him. **2001** *Washington Times* 1 Sept. A10 To paraphrase Lord Acton: Power corrupts. Extended service in Congress corrupts absolutely. ■ **power**

power *see also* KNOWLEDGE is power; MONEY is power.

PRACTICE makes perfect

□ **1553** T. WILSON *Art of Rhetoric* 3 Eloquence was vsed, and through practise made parfect. **1599** H. PORTER *Two Angry Women of Abington* l. 913 Forsooth as vse makes perfectnes, so seldome seene is soone forgotten. **1761** J. ADAMS *Diary* (1961) I. 192 Practice makes perfect. **1863** C. READE *Hard Cash* III. iv. He lighted seven fires, skillfully on the whole, for practice makes perfect. **1979** D. LESSING *Shikasta* 185 It is like playing the piano or riding a bicycle. Practice makes perfect. **2002** *Country Life* 14 Feb. 49 The quality of the [blackbird's] song improves as the season progresses. .. This, presumably, is a matter of practice makes perfect. ■ **diligence**

practice *see also* an OUNCE of practice is worth a pound of precept.

PRACTISE what you preach

□ **1377** LANGLAND *Piers Plowman* B. XIII. 79 This goddes gloton.. Hath no pyte on vs pore. He perforneth yuel [does evil], That he precheth he preueth [demonstrates] nought. **1639** T. FULLER *Holy War* I. xxiii. The Levites.. had 48 cities.. being better provided for then many English ministers, who may preach of hospitalitie to their people, but cannot go to the cost to practice their own doctrine. **1678** R. L'ESTRANGE *Seneca's Morals* II. ii. We must practise what we preach. **1725** E. YOUNG *Universal Passion* III. 48 Ye doctors sage, who thro' *Parnassus* teach, Or quit the tub, or practise what you preach. **1854** THACKERAY *Newcomes* I. xiv. Take counsel by an old soldier, who fully practises what he preaches, and beseeches you to beware of the bottle. **1945** F. THOMPSON *Lark Rise* iv. Songs of a high moral tone, such as:.. practise what you preach. **1970** D. CLARK *Deadly Pattern* iv. He was more than scornful of drink know-alls who practised what they preached even against their own palates. ■ **words and deeds**

PRAISE the child, and you make love to the mother

□ **1829** COBBETT *Advice to Young Men* IV. clxxxi. It is an old saying, 'Praise the child, and you make love to the mother'; and it is surprising how far this will go. **1885** E. J. HARDY *How to be Happy though Married* xix. 'Praise the child, and you make love to the mother,' and it is a thing that no husband ought to overlook. ■ **children and parents**

praise *see also* (noun) SELF-praise is no recommendation.

pray *see* the FAMILY that prays together stays together; he that cannot PAY, let him pray.

precept *see* EXAMPLE is better than precept; an OUNCE of practice is worth a pound of precept.

prepare *see* HOPE for the best and prepare for the worst; if you want PEACE, you must prepare for war.

present *see* no TIME like the present.

preservation *see* SELF-preservation is the first law of nature.

pressed *see* one VOLUNTEER is worth two pressed men.

PRETTY is as pretty does

US equivalent to HANDSOME *is as handsome does.*

□ **1853** T. C. HALIBURTON *Sam Slick's Wise Saws* i. 136 A very smart little boy; and Old Hundreth.. tells me you are a very good boy, and that's better, for pretty is as pretty does. *a* **1871** A. CARY 'Pretty is that Pretty Does' in M. C. Ames *Memorial of Alice and Phoebe Cary* (1874) 238 My child, who reads this simple lay With eyes down-dropt and tender, Remember the old proverb says That pretty is, which pretty does And that worth does not go nor stay For poverty nor splendor. **1991** H. P. MCADOO in *Journal of Negro Education* lx. 362 On special occasions a big (and I do mean big) bow was placed on top of my head. As my mother wrestled with my hair she often tossed out little proverbs such as 'Pretty is as pretty does.' **2002** *Washington Times* 23 July B5 There is an old saying, 'Pretty is as pretty does.' It's a wise woman who learns that lesson early. ■ **appearance; conduct**

PREVENTION is better than cure

Cf. *c* **1240** BRACTON *De Legibus* V. x. *melius & utilius [est] in tempore occurrere, quam post causam vulneratam quaerere remedium*, it is better and more useful to meet a problem in time than to seek a remedy after the damage is done.

□ **1618** T. ADAMS *Happiness of Church* 146 Preuention is so much better then healing, because it saues the labour of being sicke. **1732** T. FULLER *Gnomologia* no. 3962 Prevention is much preferable to Cure. **1826** J. PINTARD *Letter* 19 Apr. (1940) II. 257 Prevention is better than cure. ..With perseverance we shall save numbers of little Devils from becoming big ones. **1954** R. HAYDN *Journal of Edwin Carp* 148 'Why do you wear those old galoshes when the sun's shining?' .. 'Prevention's better than Cure.' **1996** 'C. AIRD' *After Effects* iii. 28 'Glad to hear it, sir,' said Sloan, adding prosaically, 'You could say that prevention's better than cure in the police world as well as the medical one.' ■ **foresight and hindsight; prudence**

price *see* EVERY man has his price.

PRIDE feels no pain

□ **1614** T. ADAMS *Devil's Banquet* II. 73 Pride is neuer without her own paine, though shee will not feele it: be her garments what they will, yet she will neuer be too hot, nor too colde. **1631** JONSON *New Inn* II. i. Thou must make shift with it. Pride feeles no pain. Girt thee hard, Pru. **1721** J. KELLY *Scottish Proverbs* 277 Pride finds no cold. Spoken . . to Beaus [fops] with their open Breasts, and Ladies with their extravagant Hoops [hooped skirts]. **1865** SURTEES *Facey Romford's Hounds* xxxii. It was hard upon the old boy, who . . was not at all adapted for the sport; but pride feels no pain, and he went at it like a man. **1981** *Radio Times* 28 Feb.–6 Mar. 43 (*advertisement*) Pride feels no pain, the saying goes. Thankfully, with Clarks [shoes] it doesn't have to. ■ **pride**

PRIDE goes before a fall

Pride precedes disaster. An elliptical version of PROVERBS xvi. 18 (AV) Pride goeth before destruction, and an haughty spirit before a fall.

□ *c* **1390** GOWER *Confessio Amantis* I. 3062 Pride . . schal doun falle. **1509** A. BARCLAY *Ship of Fools* 195V First or last foule pryde wyll haue a fall. **1784** S. JOHNSON *Letter* 2 Aug. (1952) III. 191 I am now reduced to think . . of the weather. Pride must have a fall. **1856** H. MELVILLE *Piazza Tales* 431 The bell's main weakness was where man's blood had flawed it. And so pride went before the fall. **1930** W. S. MAUGHAM *Cakes & Ale* V. I suppose he thinks he'd be mayor himself. . . Pride goeth before a fall. **1980** M. L. WEST in K. J. Dover *Ancient Greek Literature* iii. The spectacle of Xerxes' defeat tremendously reinforced the traditional conviction that pride goes before a fall. **2001** K. HALL PAGE *Body in Moonlight* epilogue 233 Millicent had disagreed. Vanity, pure and simple. Pride goeth before a fall. It was one of the maxims by which Millicent lived. ■ **pride; retribution**

priest *see* ONCE a priest, always a priest; like PEOPLE, like priest.

prince *see* whosoever DRAWS his sword against the prince must throw the scabbard away; PUNCTUALITY is the politeness of princes.

problem *see* if you're not part of the SOLUTION you're part of the problem; a TROUBLE shared is a trouble halved.

PROCRASTINATION is the thief of time

□ **1742** E. YOUNG *Night Thoughts* I. 18 Procrastination is the Thief of Time; Year after year it steals, till all are fled. **1850** DICKENS *David Copperfield* xii. Never do to-morrow what you can do to-day. Procrastination is the thief of time. **1935** O. NASH *Primrose Path* 100 Far from being the thief of Time, procrastination is the king of it. **2000** D. LINDSAY *Cutting Edge of Barney Thomson* xxi. 219 'Ach, well, ye know how it is, . . an' so I procrastinated, I must admit. I know what ye must be thinking, laddie . . Procrastination is the thief of time, aye, isn't that the truth.' ■ **procrastination**

PROMISES, like pie-crust, are made to be broken

□ **1681** *Heraclitus Ridens* 16 Aug. He makes no more of breaking Acts of Parliaments, than if they were like Promises and Pie-crust made to be broken. **1871** TROLLOPE *Ralph the Heir* II. iv. 'Promises like that are mere pie-crust,' said Ralph. **1981** *Family Circle* Feb. 66 Promises, like pie-crusts, they say, are made to be broken. Not at Sainsbury's. Every single pie they sell lives up to the promise of its famous name. **2002** *Oldie* Aug. 26 Unhappily for most of those zillionaire twenty-somethings—and for those who invested in the New Economy they thought they had invented—their promises turned out to be piecrust. ■ **deception**

The PROOF of the pudding is in the eating

Proof means 'test' rather than the more normal 'verification, proving to be true'.

□ *c* **1300** *King Alisaunder* (EETS) l. 4038 Jt is ywrite that euery thing Hymself sheweth in the tastyng. **1623** W. CAMDEN *Remains concerning Britain* (ed. 3) 266 All the proofe of a pudding, is in the eating. **1666** G. TORRIANO *Italian Proverbs* 100 (*note*) As they say at the winding up, or the proof of the pudding is in the eating. **1738** SWIFT *Polite Conversation* ii. 132 The Proof of the Pudden is in the Eating. **1842** R. H. BARHAM *Ingoldsby Legends* 2nd Ser. 25 With respect to the scheme.. I've known soldiers adopt a worse stratagem. ..There's a proverb however, I've always thought clever..The proof of the Pudding is found in the eating. **1924** J. GALSWORTHY *White Monkey* III. xii. Let us..look at the thing more widely. The proof of the pudding is in the eating. **1997** *New Scientist* 19 July 41 Lindzen for one argues that if the models get the detail wrong, they will get the big picture wrong, too. But modellers say the proof of the pudding is in the eating. ■ **appearance; reality and illusion**

A PROPHET is not without honour save in his own country

With allusion to MATTHEW xiii. 57 (AV) A prophet is not without honour, save in his own country, and in his own house.

□ *a* **1485** CAXTON in Malory *Works* (1967) I. p. cxlv. The word of God.. sayth that no man is accept for a prophete in his owne contreye. **1603** J. FLORIO tr. *Montaigne's Essays* III. ii. No man hath beene a Prophet..in his owne country, saith the experience of histories. **1771** SMOLLETT *Humphry Clinker* III. 92 The captain, like the prophets of old, is but little honoured in his own country. **1946** W. S. MAUGHAM *Then & Now* xxx. In Florence..they had no great confidence in his judgment and never followed his advice. 'A prophet is not without honour save in his own country.' **2002** *Spectator* 2 Feb. 48 'I hope you don't mind, but my wife is in love with your Prime Minister.' 'Mind? Not I,' I coughed. 'A prophet is not without honour save in his own country,' another quoted. ■ **familiarity; honour**

propose *see* MAN proposes, God disposes.

prosper *see* CHEATS never prosper.

protect *see* HEAVEN protects children, sailors, and drunken men.

prove *see* the EXCEPTION proves the rule.

provide *see* TAKE the goods the gods provide.

PROVIDENCE is always on the side of the big battalions

Cf. **1673** MME DE SÉVIGNÉ *Letter* 22 Dec. *la fortune est toujours, comme disait le pauvre M. de Turenne, pour les gros bataillons*, fortune is always, as poor Mr. de Turenne used to say, for the big battalions.

□ **1822** A. GRAYDON *Memoirs* v. Heaven was ever found favourable to strong battalions. **1842** A. ALLISON *Hist. Europe* X. lxxviii. Providence was always on the side of dense battalions. **1904** 'SAKI' *Reginald* 63 Someone has observed that Providence is always on the side of the big dividends. **1943** R. A. J. WALLING *Corpse by any Other Name* iii. Our statesmen..ought to have learned years ago that Providence is always on the side of the big battalions. **1979** *Guardian* 9 July 9 Many thousands more voices now are raised in the name of sanity. But I dare say God is still on the side of the big battalions. ■ **great and small; providence**

public *see* one does not WASH one's dirty linen in public.

Any PUBLICITY is good publicity

□ **1933** R. CHANDLER in *Black Mask* Dec. 26 Rhonda Farr said: 'Publicity, darling. Just publicity. Any kind is better than none at all.' **1974** P. CAVE *Dirtiest Picture Postcard* xiv. Haven't you ever heard the old adman's adage.. 'any publicity is good publicity'? **1986** 'C. AIRD' *Dead Liberty* xii. Bill wasn't too worried. Like the old trouper he is, he insisted that all publicity is good publicity. **2002** *Washington Times* 9 May C8 Mike Tyson may have disproved the adage that any publicity is good publicity. ■ **public relations**

pudding *see* the PROOF of the pudding is in the eating.

puddle *see* the SUN loses nothing by shining into a puddle.

It is easier to PULL down than to build up

□ **1577** R. STANYHURST *Hist. Ireland* in Holinshed *Chronicles* 89 It is easie to raze, but hard to buylde. **1587** J. BRIDGES *Defence of Government in Church of England* VI. 518 We may quicklier pull downe with one hande, than wee can easilie builde againe with both. **1644** J. HOWELL *Dodona's Grove* 134 In politicall affaires, as well as mechanicall, it is farre easier to pull downe, then build up. **1909** *Times* 29 Apr. 9 Turkey and her new rulers.. have astonished those who thought they knew the Turks best by.. the vigour.. with which the great change has been conducted. .. But it is easier always and everywhere to pull down than to build up. ■ **destruction**

PUNCTUALITY is the politeness of princes

Fr. *l'exactitude est la politesse des rois*, punctuality is the politeness of kings (attributed to Louis XVIII, 1755–1824).

□ **1834** M. EDGEWORTH *Helen* II. ix. 'Punctuality is the virtue of princes.'.. Mr. Harley.. would have ridiculed so antiquated a notion. **1854** SURTEES *Handley Cross* (ed. 2) xli. Punctuality is the purlitness o' princes, and I doesn't like keepin' people waitin'. **1930** G. MITCHELL *Mystery of Butcher Shop* (1990) iii. 31 'Now do try to be down in time for breakfast to-morrow morning. Remember—"Punctuality is the politeness of princes." So charming of them, I always think.' **1981** P. MCCUTCHAN *Shard calls Tune* xv. One should never keep people waiting; punctuality was the politeness of princes. ■ **politeness; punctuality**

PUNCTUALITY is the soul of business

□ **1853** T. C. HALIBURTON *Wise Saws* I. iii. 'Punctuality,' sais I, 'my lord, is the soul of business.' **1911** W. CROSSING *Folk Rhymes of Devon* 16 Punctuality is the soul of business, and in these days of cheap watches there can be no excuse for anybody failing to cultivate the habit. **1940** C. DICKSON *And so to Murder* 181 Punctuality.. has been called the politeness of kings. It's more than that: it's plain good business. ■ **business; punctuality**

punished *see* CORPORATIONS have neither bodies to be punished nor souls to be damned.

To the PURE all things are pure

With allusion to TITUS i. 15 (AV) Unto the pure all things are pure: but unto them that are defiled and unbelieving is nothing pure.

□ **1854** S. M. HAYDEN *Early Engagements* ii. Would that our earth were more frequently brightened and purified by such spirits. .. 'To the pure all things are pure.' **1895** G. ALLEN *Woman who Did* vii. Herminia, for her part, never discovered she was talked about. To the pure all things are pure. **1996** 'C. AIRD' *After Effects* xiv. 161 Sloan's mother, a great churchwoman in her day, always insisted that to the pure all things were pure. ■ **virtue**

purgatory *see* ENGLAND is the paradise of women.

purpose *see* the DEVIL can quote Scripture for his own ends.

purse *see* you can't make a SILK purse out of a sow's ear.

Don't PUT the cart before the horse

Most commonly as the phrase (*putting*) *the cart before the horse*.

□ *c* **1520** R. WHITTINGTON *Vulgaria* (1527) 2 That techer setteth the carte before the horse that preferreth imitacyon before preceptes. **1589** G. PUTTENHAM *Arte of English Poesie* (Arber) 181 We call it in English prouerbe, the cart before the horse, the Greeks call it Histeron proteron. **1801** M. EDGEWORTH *Belinda* iii. Esteem ever followed affection, instead of affection following esteem. Woe be to all who in morals preposterously put the cart before the horse! **2002** CAI TRANSCRIPTION (web site) 17 May We at CAI say not to put the cart before the horse. Don't invest heavily in reference materials that you most probably will not even use in the future during your career as a Medical Transcriptionist. ■ **patience and impatience; ways and means**

Never PUT off till tomorrow what you can do today

The proverb is often humorously reversed (see quots. 1869 and 1980). Cf. mid 14th-cent. Fr. *le bien que tu peus faire au matin, n'attens pas le soir ne l'endemain*, do not wait for the evening or the next day (to do) the good which you can do in the morning.

□ *c* **1386** CHAUCER *Tale of Melibee* l. 1793 An olde proverbe..seith that 'the goodnesse that thou mayst do this day, do it, and abide nat ne delaye it nat til tomorwe'. **1616** T. DRAXE *Adages* 42 Deferre not vntill to morrow, if thou canst do it to day. **1633** J. HOWELL *Familiar Letters* 5 Sept. (1903) II. 140 Secretary Cecil..would ofttimes speak of himself, 'It shall never be said of me that I will defer till tomorrow what I can do to-day.' **1749** CHESTERFIELD *Letter* 26 Dec. (1932) IV. 1478 No procrastination; never put off til to-morrow what you can do to-day. **1869** C. H. SPURGEON *John Ploughman's Talk* vii. These slow coaches think that to-morrow is better than to-day, and take for their rule an old proverb turned topsy-turvy—'Never do to-day what you can put off till tomorrow.' **1980** J. LEES-MILNE *Harold Nicolson* xv. Lord Sackville was..a lovable, easy-going but indolent peer whose philosophy is best summarized in one of his pet sayings: 'Never do today what you can possibly put off until tomorrow.' **2002** *Washington Post* 16 Feb. C13 (*Born Loser comic strip*) 'Brutus, weren't you going to take down the Christmas lights this weekend?' 'No..Next weekend, Gladys! Never put off till tomorrow what you can put off till next weekend!' ■ **efficiency and inefficiency; procrastination**

put *see also* don't put all your EGGS in one basket; you can't put NEW wine in old bottles; you cannot put an OLD head on young shoulders; put a STOUT heart to a stey brae; put your TRUST in God, and keep your power dry.

The QUARREL of lovers is the renewal of love

Cf. TERENCE *Andria* l. 555 *amantium irae amoris integratiost*, lovers' quarrels are a strengthening of love.

□ *c* **1520** *Terence in English* C1 The angers of louers renew love agayn. **1576** R. EDWARDES *Paradise of Dainty Devises* 42 Now haue I founde, the prouerbe true to proue, The fallyng out of faithfull frends, is the renuyng of love. **1624** BURTON *Anatomy of Melancholy* (ed. 2) III. ii. She would . . picke quarrells vpon no occasion, because she would be reconciled to him againe. . . The falling out of lovers is the renuing of loue. **1754** RICHARDSON *Grandison* III. xviii. The falling out of Lovers . . is the renewal of Love. Are we not now better friends than if we had never differed? **1874** TROLLOPE *Phineas Redux* II. xxix. She knew that 'the quarrel of lovers is the renewal of love'. At any rate, the woman always desires that it may be so, and endeavours to reconcile the parted ones. **1905** *Graphic* (Christmas) 14 (*caption*) The quarrel of lovers is the renewal of love. **1980** M. GILBERT *Death of Favourite Girl* ii. Bear in mind, ladies, that a lovers' quarrel sometimes signifies the rebirth of love. ■ **love**

quarrel *see also* (noun) it takes TWO to make a quarrel; (verb) a BAD workman blames his tools.

You cannot get a QUART into a pint pot

A *quart* is an imperial measure of two pints. The metaphorical phrase *to get* (or *put*) *a quart into a pint pot* is also used.

□ **1896** *Daily News* 23 July 4 They had been too ambitious. They had attempted what he might describe in homely phrase as putting a quart into a pint pot. **1934** C. F. GREGG *Execution of Diamond Deutsch* xi. He whistled thoughtfully. 'You can't get a quart into a pint pot—is that it?' asked the South African officer, quick to see the reason. **1948** P. M. WARNER *Embroidery Mary* xi. When they . . got down to . . packing it was found to be a case of 'quarts into pint pots will not go.' **1974** W. FOLEY *Child in Forest* I. 101 A quart may not go into a pint pot, but my feet had to go into those boots. ■ **great and small; possibility and impossibility**

queer *see* there's NOWT so queer as folk.

quench *see* DIRTY water will quench fire.

question *see* ASK a silly question and you get a silly answer; ASK no questions and hear no lies; a CIVIL question deserves a civil answer; FOOLS ask questions that wise men cannot answer; there are TWO sides to every question.

QUICKLY come, quickly go

Similar to EASY *come, easy go*.

□ **1583** B. MELBANCKE *Philotimus* 151 Quickly spent, thats easely gotten. **1631** J. MABBE tr. *F. de Rojas' Celestina* I. 8 Quickly be wonne, and quickly be lost. **1869** W. C. HAZLITT *English Proverbs* 322 Quickly come, quickly go. **1947** C. MACKENZIE *Whisky Galore* iii. Quick come, quick go. The wind got up in a moment and it will drop just as suddenly. **1979** N. GOLLER *Tomorrow's Silence* iv. 'Was he alright when you came home?'..'Yes, what comes quickly must go quickly, that's what I say.' ■ **getting and spending**

quickly *see also* he GIVES twice who gives quickly.

quiet *see* the best DOCTORS are Dr Diet, Dr Quiet, and Dr Merryman.

quote *see* the DEVIL can quote Scripture for his own ends.

The RACE is not to the swift, nor the battle to the strong

With allusion to ECCLESIASTES ix. 11 (AV) The race is not to the swift, nor the battle to the strong.

▫ **1632** BURTON *Anatomy of Melancholy* (ed. 4) II. iii. It is not honesty, learning, worth, wisdome, that preferres men, The race is not to the swift, nor the battell to the stronger [1638 strong]. **1873** C. M. YONGE *Pillars of House* III. xxxii. Poor child! she lay.. trying to work out.. why the race is not to the swift, nor the battle to the strong. **1901** G. B. SHAW *Caesar & Cleopatra* in *Three Plays for Puritans* 96 The descendants of the gods did not stay to be butchered, cousin. The battle was not to the strong; but the race was to the swift. **2002** *Washington Times* 7 Mar. A16 The race is not to the swift, nor the battle to the strong—but how come? One good reason: Ours is an imperfect world, full to the brim with imperfect people. ■ **success**

race *see also* SLOW and steady wins the race.

ragged *see* there's many a GOOD cock come out of a tattered bag.

RAIN before seven, fine before eleven

▫ **1853** *Notes & Queries* 1st Ser. VIII. 218 Weather Proverbs. ..Rain before seven, fine before eleven. **1909** *Spectator* 20 Mar. 452 'Rain before seven, shine before eleven,' is one of the most trustworthy of all country saws. **1940** B. DE VOTO (*title*) Rain before seven. **1961** THIRKELL & LEJUNE *Three Score & Ten* vii. The morning of the Agricultural dawned fair and bright. Naturally there were wisebeards who shook their heads over this and said Ar, that were a bad sign for certain sure, rain before seven, fine before eleven, and stands to reason the contrairy [*sic*] holds. ■ **weather lore**

rain *see also* blessed are the DEAD that the rain rains on; if in FEBRUARY there be no rain, 'tis neither good for hay nor grain; SAINT Swithun's day if thou be fair for forty days it will remain.

It never RAINS but it pours

An archaic use of *but* to introduce an inevitable accompanying circumstance.

▫ **1726** J. ARBUTHNOT (*title*) It cannot rain but it pours. **1770** C. BURNEY *Music, Men and Manners in France and Italy* (1974) 22 July 54 The singers were the same as I had heard at the Burletta. ..'It never rains, but it pours!' **1857** TROLLOPE *Barchester Towers* III. xii. A wife with a large fortune too. It never rains but it pours, does it, Mr. Thorne? **1979** L. BARNEA *Reported Missing* vii. I listened to the radio. Ben Gurion had suffered a stroke. ..It never rains but it pours. **2002** *Washington Post* 1 Mar. C5 When it rains, it pours, and Matt Sullivan is being flooded out by women who want to have sex with him. ■ **misfortune**

It is easier to RAISE the Devil than to lay him

▫ **1655** T. FULLER *Church Hist. Britain* x. iv. The Boy having gotten a habit of counterfeiting.. would not be undeviled by all their Exorcisms, so that the Priests raised up a Spirit which they could not allay. **1725** N. BAILEY tr. *Erasmus' Colloquies*

202 'Tis an old Saying and a true, 'Tis an easier Matter to raise the Devil, than 'tis to lay him. **1845** MACAULAY *Works* (1898) XII. 136 Did you think, when, to serve your turn, you called the Devil up, that it was as easy to lay him as to raise him? **1890** 'R. BOLDREWOOD' *Miner's Right* II. viii. Exorcists of all lands.. have ever found the fiend more easy to invoke than to lay. ■ **good and evil; prudence**

ransom *see* a PECK of March dust is worth a king's ransom.

rat *see* the CAT, the rat, and Lovell the dog, rule all England under the hog.

reach *see* STRETCH your arm no further than your sleeve will reach.

reap *see* as you sow, so you reap; they that sow the wind shall reap the whirlwind.

There is REASON in the roasting of eggs

There is reason behind every action, however odd it may seem.

□ **1659** J. HOWELL *Proverbs* (English) 12 Ther's reason in rosting of Eggs. **1785** J. BOSWELL *Journal of Tour of Hebrides* 24 (*note*) Every man whatever is more or less a cook, in seasoning what he himself eats.—Your definition is good, said Mr. Burke, and I now see the full force of the common proverb, 'There is *reason* in roasting of eggs'. **1867** TROLLOPE *Last Chronicle of Barset* II. lxxv. But there's reason in the roasting of eggs, and.. money is not so plentiful.. that your uncle can afford to throw it into the Barchester gutters. **1915** SOMERVILLE & ROSS *In Mr. Knox's Country* ix. I seemed to myself merely an imbecile, sitting in heavy rain, staring at a stone wall. Half an hour, or more, passed. 'I'm going out of this,' I said to myself defiantly; 'there's reason in the roasting of eggs.' ■ **idiosyncrasy**

recalled *see* things PAST cannot be recalled.

receive *see* it is BETTER to give than to receive.

If there were no RECEIVERS, there would be no thieves

□ *c* **1390** CHAUCER *Cook's Tale* l. 4415 There is no theef with-oute a lowke [accomplice], That helpeth hym to wasten and to sowke [cheat]. **1546** J. HEYWOOD *Dialogue of Proverbs* I. xii. F1 This prouerbe preeues, Where be no receyuers, there be no theeues. **1614** T. ADAMS *Devil's Banquet* II. 67 The Calumniator is a wretched Thiefe, and robs man of the best thing he hath. .. But if there were no receiuer, there would be no Thiefe. **1884** R. JEFFERIES *Red Deer* v. No one would buy a stolen deer, knowing the inevitable consequences, and as there are no receivers.. there are no thieves. **1926** *Times* 22 Nov. 11 It had often been said in those Courts that if there were no receivers there would be no thieves. ■ **associates; wrong-doers**

reckoning *see* AFTER the feast comes the reckoning; SHORT reckonings make long friends.

recommendation *see* SELF-praise is no recommendation.

RED sky at night, shepherd's delight; red sky in the morning, shepherd's warning

One of the most persistent of the weather sayings, used by sailors as well as shepherds (see quots. 1893 and 1996). With allusion to MATTHEW xvi. 2–3 (AV) When it is evening, ye say, It will be fair weather: for the sky is red. And in the morning, It will be foul weather to day: for the sky is red and louring. *c* **1395**

WYCLIF *Bible* Matthew xvi. 2 The eeuenynge maad, ye seien, It shal be cleer, for the heuene is lijk to reed; and the morwe, To day tempest, for heuen shyneth heuy, or sorwful.

□ *c* **1454** R. PECOCK *Follower to Donet* (EETS) 54 We trowen [believe] that this day schal be a reyny day for that his morowynyg was reed, or that to morow schal be a fayre day for that his euentide is reed. **1592–3** SHAKESPEARE *Venus & Adonis* l. 453 Like a red morn, that ever yet betoken'd Wreck to the seaman..Sorrow to shepherds. **1893** R. INWARDS *Weather Lore* 53 Sky red in the morning Is a sailor's sure warning; Sky red at night Is the sailor's delight. **1920** *Punch* 14 July 36 Red sky at night shepherd's delight. ..Red sky in the morning shepherd's warning. **1979** P. ALEXANDER *Show me Hero* xxv. 'Going to be a fine day,' he said at last. 'Red sky in the morning, shepherd's warning,' Ashman said. **1995** R. ORMEROD *And Hope to Die* ii. 15 The next morning it was raining steadily, this in spite of the flush of sunset the evening before. ..Red sky at night, shepherds' delight. Well all right, perhaps so, if they'd been praying for rain. **2002** M. DAHL *Coral Coffin* ii. 16 Pink clouds sailed high over the island. What was that saying I had heard from Uncle Stoppard? *Red skies at night: a sailor's delight Red skies at morning: a sailor takes warning.* ■ **weather lore**

redressed *see* a FAULT confessed is half redressed.

A REED before the wind lives on, while mighty oaks do fall

□ *c* **1385** CHAUCER *Troilus & Criseyde* II. 1387 And reed that boweth down for every blast, Ful lightly, cesse wynd, it wol aryse. **1621** BURTON *Anatomy of Melancholy* II. iii. Though I liue obscure, yet I liue cleane and honest, and when as the lofty oake is blowne downe, the silly [frail] reed may stand. **1732** T. FULLER *Gnomologia* no. 3692 Oaks may fall, when Reeds stand the Storm. **1954** R. HAYDN *Journal of Edwin Carp* 20 Remembering that 'a reed before the wind lives on—while mighty oaks do fall,' I attempted to remove the pencil marks with my pocket eraser. ■ **great and small; strength and weakness**

refuse *see* the SEA refuses no river.

regulated *see* ACCIDENTS will happen (in the best-regulated families).

rejoice *see* it is a POOR heart that never rejoices.

There is a REMEDY for everything except death

Cf. medieval L. *contra malum mortis, non est medicamen in hortis*, against the evil of death there is no remedy in the garden.

□ *c* **1430** J. LYDGATE *Dance of Machabree* (EETS) l. 432 Agens deeth is worth [useful] no medicine. **1573** J. SANFORDE *Garden of Pleasure* 52 There is a remedie for all things, sauing for death. **1620** T. SHELTON tr. *Cervantes' Don Quixote* II. lxiv. There is a remedy for everything but death, said Don Quixote; for tis but hauing a Barke ready at the Sea side, and in spite of all the world we may embarke our selues. *a* **1895** F. LOCKER-LAMPSON *My Confidences* (1896) 95 There is a remedy for everything except Death..so the bitterness of this disappointment has long passed away. ■ **death; finality**

remedy *see also* DESPERATE diseases must have desperate remedies.

removal *see* THREE removals are as bad as a fire.

renewal *see* the QUARREL of lovers is the renewal of love.

repair *see* a WOMAN and a ship ever want mending.

repeat *see* HISTORY repeats itself.

repent *see* MARRY in haste and repent at leisure.

rest *see* (noun) a CHANGE is as good as a rest; (verb) AFTER dinner rest a while, after supper walk a mile.

return *see* a BAD penny always turns up; the DOG returns to his vomit; the TONGUE always returns to the sore tooth.

REVENGE is a dish that can be eaten cold

Vengeance need not be exacted immediately; but cf. **1620** T. SHELTON tr. *Cervantes' Don Quixote* II. lxiii. Reuenge is not good in cold bloud.

□ **1885** C. LOWE *Prince Bismarck* I. iv. He had defended Olmütz, it is true, but..with a secret resolution to 'eat the dish of his revenge cold instead of hot'. **1895** J. PAYN *In Market Overt* xvii. Invective can be used at any time; like vengeance, it is a dish that can be eaten cold. **1975** J. O'FAOLAIN *Women in Wall* iii. Revenge..is a meal that's as tasty cold as hot. Tastier cold sometimes. **1997** *Washington Post* 6 Nov. E6 Revenge is a dish best served cold. Let's see what happens one of these cold Octobers. **2002** *Times* 20 Aug. 6 Revenge is a dish best eaten cold. Or in Margaret Cook's case, three years later. Cook, who mercilessly exposed the character defects of her former husband, Robin, in her memoirs..has now completed *Lords of Creation—The Demented World of Men in Power.* ■ **patience and impatience; revenge**

REVENGE is sweet

Cf. HOMER *Iliad* XVIII. 109 *χόλος .. ὅς τε πολὺ γλυκίων μέλιτος καταλειβομένοιο ἀνδρῶν ἐν στήθεσσιν ἀέξεται ἠΰτε καπνός*, anger..that far sweeter than trickling honey wells up like smoke in the breasts of men.

□ **1566** W. PAINTER *Palace of Pleasure* 300 Vengeance is sweete vnto him, which in place of killing his enemy, giueth life to a perfect frende. **1609** JONSON *Silent Woman* IV. v. O reuenge, how sweet art thou! **1658** *Whole Duty of Man* XVI. 346 'Tis a devilish phrase in the mouth of men, that revenge is sweet. ..Is it possible there can be any such sweetnesse in it? **1775** SHERIDAN *St. Patrick's Day* II. 22 'Revenge is sweet'..and though disappointed of my designs upon your daughter,..I'm revenged on her unnatural father. **1861** H. KINGSLEY *Ravenshoe* II. x. Revenge is sweet—to some. Not to him. **1980** J. PORTER *Dover beats Band* xv. He came to the conclusion that though revenge may be sweet, knowledge..is better than money in the bank. ■ **revenge**

revenue *see* THRIFT is a great revenue.

REVOLUTIONS are not made with rose-water

With reference to **1789** CHAMFORT in Marmontel *Works* (1818) II. 294 *voulez-vous qu'on vous fasse des révolutions à l'eau rose*, do you require that revolutions be made with rose-water?

□ **1819** BYRON *Letter* 3 Oct. (1976) VI. 226 On either side harm must be done before good can accrue—revolutions are not to be made with rose water. **1894** J. LUBBOCK *Use of Life* xi. It is sometimes said that Revolutions are not made with rose-water. Greater changes, however, have been made in the constitution of the world by argument than by arms. *a* **1931** T. M. HEALY letter in F. Callanan *T. M. Healy* (1996) The Sinns won in three years what we did not win in forty. You cannot make revolutions with rosewater, or omelettes without breaking eggs. ■ **politics; rulers and ruled; ways and means**

reward *see* VIRTUE is its own reward.

The RICH man has his ice in the summer and the poor man gets his in the winter

□ **1921** W. B. MASTERSON in *Morning Telegraph* (NY) 27 Oct. 7 There are those who argue that everything breaks even in this old dump of a world of ours. .. These ginks who argue that way hold that because the rich man gets ice in the Summer and the poor man gets it in the winter things are breaking even for both. *a* **1957** L. I. WILDER *First Four Years* (1971) ii. Everything evens up in the end. .. The rich man has his ice in the summer and the poor man gets his in the winter. **1986** J. W. RIDER *Jersey Tomatoes* xi. The rich get ice in the summer and the poor get it in the winter, so some people figure everyone gets an even break. ■ **equality; poverty; riches**

rich *see also* it is BETTER to be born lucky than rich; one LAW for the rich and another for the poor.

If you can't RIDE two horses at once, you shouldn't be in the circus

James Maxton, to whom this saying is attributed (quot. 1935), was a British Independent Labour Party MP (1932–46). Denis Healey (see quot. 2002), another British Labour politician, was probably consciously quoting Maxton.

□ **1935** G. McALLISTER *James Maxton* xiv. Maxton made a brief intervention in the debate to say.. that he did not believe it was necessary to pass a resolution for disaffiliation [of the ILP from the Labour Party]. He had been told that he could not ride two horses. 'My reply to that is', he said.. 'that if my friend cannot ride two horses—what's he doing in the bloody circus?' **1979** *Daily Telegraph* 15 Mar. 15 A producer who 'can't ride two horses at the same time shouldn't be in the circus.'.. Current affairs television should be both serious and entertaining. **2002** *National Review* 3 June 18 But politics is a practical activity, not an intellectual one. As Denis Healey once said, if you can't ride two horses at once, you shouldn't be in the bloody circus. ■ **efficiency and inefficiency; stress**

ride *see also* set a BEGGAR on horseback, and he'll ride to the Devil; if TWO ride on a horse one must ride behind; if WISHES were horses beggars would ride.

He who RIDES a tiger is afraid to dismount

Once a dangerous or troublesome venture is begun, the safest course is to carry it through to the end.

□ **1875** W. SCARBOROUGH *Collection of Chinese Proverbs* no. 2082 He who rides a tiger is afraid to dismount. .. *Ch'i 'hu nan hsia pei.* **1902** A. R. COLQUHOUN *Mastery of Pacific* xvi. These colonies are .. for her [France] the tiger which she has mounted (to use the Chinese phrase) and which she can neither manage nor get rid of. **1983** W. HARRISS *Bay Psalm Book Murder* x. 'But no doubt about it, I've got a tiger by the tail now.' 'And there's an Oriental saying that the man who rides the tiger is afraid to get off. Watch your step.' ■ **peril**

ridiculous *see* from the SUBLIME to the ridiculous is only a step.

right *see* the CUSTOMER is always right; DO right and fear no man; GOD's in his heaven, all's right with the world; MIGHT is right; TWO wrongs don't make a right.

ring *see* GIVE a thing, and take a thing, to wear the Devil's gold ring.

ripe *see* SOON ripe, soon rotten.

rise *see* EARLY to bed and early to rise, makes a man healthy, wealthy, and wise; a STREAM cannot rise above its source.

A RISING tide lifts all boats

Principally known in the United States, this is one of several proverbs popularized by the Kennedy family. It is generally used in economic contexts, the *tide* being that of prosperity.

□ **1963** J. F. KENNEDY *Address* 25 June in *Public Papers of Presidents of U.S.* (1964) 519 As they say on my own Cape Cod, a rising tide lifts all the boats. And a partnership, by definition, serves both partners, without domination or unfair advantage. **1988** *Washington Post* 7 Mar. A12 The theory used to be that all Americans had a stake in prosperity. The comforting notion was that the rising tide would lift all boats. Now, however, both the theory and some of the boats have holes in them. **1990** *Washington Times* 6 Mar. C2 The country was in a sharp economic expansion coming out of '82. This made everybody look smart—you know, the rising tide lifts all boats. **2001** *Washington Post* 16 Aug. E1 'In the high-growth environment of the past, a rising tide lifted all boats,' said Magid Abraham, chief executive of ComScore Networks, a Reston firm that measures online activity. ■ **good fortune**

river *see* the SEA refuses no river.

The ROAD to hell is paved with good intentions

Earlier forms of the proverb omit the first three words. Cf. ST. FRANCIS DE SALES, *Letter* lxxiv. *le proverbe tiré de notre saint Bernard, 'L'enfer est plein de bonnes volontés ou désirs'*, the proverb taken from our St. Bernard, 'Hell is full of good intentions or desires.'

□ **1574** E. HELLOWES tr. *Guevara's Epistles* 205 Hell is full of good desires. **1654** R. WHITLOCK *Observations on Manners of English* 203 It is a saying among Divines, that Hell is full of good Intentions, and Meanings. **1736** WESLEY *Journal* 10 July (1910) I. I. 246 It is a true saying,'Hell is paved with good intentions'. **1847** J. A. FROUDE *Shadows of Clouds* ix. I shall have nothing to hand in, except intentions,—what they say the road to the wrong place is paved with. **1855** H. G. BOHN *Hand-Book of Proverbs* 514 The road to hell is paved with good intentions. **2001** *Washington Times* 5 Dec. D8 (*Herb & Jamaal comic strip*) 'I'm sorry if I made things a mess with you and Yolanda. But I'll have you know that I had nothing but good intentions.' 'They say, "The road to ruin is paved with good intentions."..and you keep making potholes.' ■ **action and inaction; intentions**

road *see also* there is no ROYAL road to learning.

All ROADS lead to Rome

Cf. medieval L. *mille vie ducunt hominem per secula Romam*, a thousand roads lead man for ever towards Rome. *c* **1391** CHAUCER *Astrolabe* Prologue l. 40 Right as diverse pathes leden diverse folk the righte way to Rome.

□ **1806** R. THOMSON tr. *La Fontaine's Fables* IV. XII. xxiv. All roads alike conduct to Rome. **1872** W. BLACK *Strange Adventures of Phaeton* vi. You know all roads lead to Rome, and they say that Oxford is half-way to Rome. **1912** J. S. HUXLEY *Individual in Animal Kingdom* vi. All roads lead to Rome: and even animal individuality throws a ray on human problems. **2002** *Spectator* 16 Feb. 21 All roads, of course, led to Rome: an expression of Rome's control over the empire's landscape and populace. ■ **beginnings and endings; ways and means**

roasting *see* there is REASON in the roasting of eggs.

robbery *see* a fair EXCHANGE is no robbery.

The ROBIN and the wren are God's cock and hen; the martin and the swallow are God's mate and marrow

Marrow is an obsolete word (except in dialect), meaning 'something that makes a pair with another'. The rhyme is found in a variety of forms, as in *a* **1508** J. SKELTON *Poems* (1969) 45 The prety wren . . is our Ladyes hen.

□ **1787** F. GROSE *Provincial Glossary* (Popular Superstitions) 64 There is a particular distich in favour of the robin and wren: A robin and wren Are God Almighty's cock and hen. Persons killing [them] . . or destroying their nests, will infallibly, within the course of a year, break a bone, or meet with some other dreadful misfortune. On the contrary, it is deemed lucky to have martins and swallows build their nests in the eaves of a house. **1826** R. WILBRAHAM *Cheshire Glossary* (ed. 2) 105 The following metrical adage is common in Cheshire: The Robin and the Wren Are God's cock and hen, The Martin and the Swallow are God's mate and marrow. **1945** F. THOMPSON *Lark Rise* ix. No boy would rob a robin's or a wren's nest . . for they believe that: The robin and the wrens Be God Almighty's friends. And the martin and the swallow Be God Almighty's birds to follow. ■ **bird lore**

ROBIN Hood could brave all weathers but a thaw wind

A *thaw wind* is 'a cold piercing wind from the S. or SE. which often accompanies the breaking up of a long frost' (J. Bridge, *Cheshire Proverbs*).

□ **1855** W. NEVILLE *Life & Exploits of Robin Hood* ii. Every one, at least every Yorkshireman, is familiar with the observation that Robin Hood could brave all weathers but a thaw wind. **1931** J. BUCHAN *Blanket of Dark* xii. I dread the melting wind which makes seas of rivers and lakes of valleys. Robin Hood feared little above ground, but he feared the thaw-wind. ■ **weather lore**

rock *see* (noun) who won't be RULED by the rudder must be ruled by the rock; (verb) the HAND that rocks the cradle rules the world.

Up like a ROCKET, down like a stick

The origin of this is Thomas Paine's gibe about Edmund Burke's oratory in a House of Commons debate on the subject of the French Revolution (see quot. 1792).

□ **1792** T. PAINE *Letter to Addressers on Late Proclamation* 4 As he rose like a rocket, he fell like the stick. **1922** JOYCE *Ulysses* 364 Up like a rocket, down like a stick. **1974** A. MENEN *Fonthill* (1975) 53 I believe he died loaded with debts. Well, up like a rocket and down like the stick, I always say. **2002** *Oldie* Aug. 26 The value of the shares they had so vaingloriously promoted performed like the proverbial rocket and its equally proverbial stick. ■ **ambition**; **pride**

rod *see* SPARE the rod and spoil the child.

A ROLLING stone gathers no moss

Cf. ERASMUS *Adages* III. iv. *λίθος κυλινδόμενος τὸ φῦκος οὐ ποιεῖ*, a rolling stone does not gather sea-weed; *musco lapis volutus haud obducitur*, a rolling stone is not covered with moss.

□ **1362** LANGLAND *Piers Plowman* A. x. 101 Selden Moseth [becomes mossy] the Marbelston that men ofte treden. **1546** J. HEYWOOD *Dialogue of Proverbs* I. xi. D2 The rollyng stone neuer gatherth mosse. **1579** S. GOSSON *Ephemerides* of Phialo 5^v

A rowling stone gathers no mosse, and a running hed wil neuer thriue. **1710** A. PHILIPS *Pastorals* II. 8 A Rolling Stone is ever bare of Moss. **1841** DICKENS *Old Curiosity Shop* II. xlviii. Your popular rumour, unlike the rolling stone of the proverb, is one which gathers a deal of moss in its wanderings up and down. **1979** *Listener* 5 July 16 A roadside notice.. said in one long line: *Loose stones travel slowly*. Well, I dare say they do: rolling stones, we know, gather no moss. ■ **constancy and inconstancy; human nature**

When in ROME, do as the Romans do

Cf. ST. AMBROSE, quoted in ST. AUGUSTINE *Letters* xxxvi. 32 (Migne), *quando hic sum, non ieiuno sabbato; quando Romae sum, ieiuno sabbato*, when I am here [i.e. Milan], I do not fast on Saturday; when I am in Rome, I fast on Saturday; **1660** quoted in verse form in JEREMY TAYLOR, *Ductor Dubitantium* (1851) I. i. 5. 5 *cum fueris Romae, Romano vivito more, cum fueris alibi, vivito sicut ibi*, when you're in Rome, then live in Roman fashion; when you're elsewhere, then live as there they live.

□ *c* **1475** in *Modern Philology* (1940) XXXVIII. 122 Whan tho herd hat Rome Do so of ther the dome [when you are at Rome do as they do there]. **1552** R. TAVERNER tr. *Erasmus' Adages* (ed. 3) 51ᵛ That which is commonly in euery mans mouth in England Whan you art at Rome, do as they do at Rome. **1766** in L. H. Butterfield et al. *Adams Family Correspondence* (1963) I. 55 My advice to you is among the Romans, do as the romans do. **1836** E. HOWARD *Rattlin the Reefer* I. xxii. 'Do at Rome as the Romans do,' is the essence of all politeness. **1960** N. MITFORD *Don't tell Alfred* viii. 'I thought the English never bothered about protocol?' 'When in Rome, however, we do as the Romans do.' **2001** *Washington Post* 8 Dec. A25 One woman stationed there [Saudi Arabia] who purports to be comfortable with the rules said, 'When in Rome, do as the Romans do.' But how far does that go? To feeding the lions? ■ **circumstances; conduct**

ROME was not built in a day

Cf. medieval Fr. *Rome ne fut pas faite toute en un jour*, Rome was not made in one day.

□ **1545** R. TAVERNER tr. *Erasmus' Adages* (ed. 2) D1ᵛ Rome was not buylt in one daye. **1546** J. HEYWOOD *Dialogue of Proverbs* I. xi. D4 Rome was not bylt on a daie (quoth he) and yet stood Tyll it was fynysht. **1646** in *Publications of Prince Society* (1865) I. 236 Rome was not built in a day. .. Let them produce any colonie.. where more hath been done in 16 yeares. **1849** C. BRONTË *Shirley* I. vi. As Rome.. had not been built in a day, so neither had Mademoiselle Gerard Moore's education been completed in a week. **2001** *Times 2* 6 Nov. 15 Even then, £14 million must still be found from private sources. Not easy.. . Still, Rome wasn't built in a day. ■ **haste; patience and impatience**

Rome *see also* all ROADS lead to Rome; it is ill SITTING at Rome and striving with the Pope.

There is always ROOM at the top

The remark is popularly attributed to the American politician Daniel Webster (1782–1852), and is said to have been his riposte after he had been advised against joining the legal profession on the grounds that it was already overcrowded.

□ **1888** *Clothier and Furnisher* Jan. 38 The sage who so confidently remarked that 'there is always room at the top' might have added 'because too many are pushed off.' **1900** W. JAMES *Letter* 2 Apr. (1920) II. 121 Verily there is room at the top. S—seems to be the only Britisher worth thinking of. **1914** A. BENNETT *Price of Love* vii. The Imperial had set out to be the most gorgeous cinema in the Five Towns; and it simply was. Its advertisements read: 'There is always room at the top.' **1957** J. BRAINE *Room at Top* xxviii. You're the sort of young man we want. There's always room at the top. **1980** M. DRABBLE *Middle Ground* 140 There's room at the top, maybe, but only for the clever ones. ■ **ambition**

roost *see* CURSES, like chickens, come home to roost.

root *see* IDLENESS is the root of all evil; MONEY is the root of all evil.

Give a man ROPE enough and he will hang himself

Rope is used both literally, and figuratively—'licence, freedom'.

□ **1639** T. FULLER *Holy War* v. vii. they were suffered to have rope enough, till they had haltered themselves. **1670** J. RAY *English Proverbs* 148 Give a thief rope enough, and he'll hang himself. **1698** in *William & Mary College Quarterly* (1950) VII. 106 The Kings prerogative..will be hard for his Successor to retrieve, though there's a saying give Men Rope enough, they will hang themselves. **1876** TROLLOPE *Prime Minister* II. xvii. Give Sir Orlando rope enough and he'll hang himself. **1941** G. BAGBY *Red is for Killing* x. 'I like to build a pretty complete case before making an arrest.'..'If you give a man enough rope he hangs himself.' **1968** H. CECIL *No Fear or Favour* xvi. 'Judges always give a lot of rope to prisoners when they're defending themselves, don't they, sir?' 'That's true,' said Stokes. 'Let's hope he hangs himself with it,' said the superintendent. ■ **ways and means; wrong-doers**

Never mention ROPE in the house of a man who has been hanged

□ **1599** J. MINSHEU *Spanish Dialogues* i. A man ought not to make mention of a halter in the house of a man that was hanged. **1620** T. SHELTON tr. *Don Quixote* III. xi. why doe I name an Asse with my mouth, seeing one should not make mention of a rope in ones house that was hanged? **1890** J. PAYN *Burnt Million* xxxii. Miss Grace, whom he pictured..as sensitive upon the matter as though if her parent had been hung she would have been to an allusion to a rope. **1958** 'J. S. STRANGE' *Night of Reckoning* viii. Never mention rope in the house of a man who has been hanged. **1995** *Washington Times* 14 July A4 Whenever he hears the very word 'Vietnam' shame could compel Mr. Clinton to excuse himself. ..He should remember FDR's famous admonition to avoid speaking of rope in the house of a man recently hanged. ■ **tact**

No ROSE without a thorn

Cf. CLAUDIAN *In Nuptias Honorii..Fescennina* iv. 10 *Armat spina rosas, mella tegunt apes*, a thorn arms roses, bees conceal their honey.

□ **1430–40** LYDGATE *Bochas* Prol. ix There is no rose..in garden, but there be sum thorne. **1579** LYLY *Euphues* i. 184 The sweetest Rose hath his prickel. **1603** J. FLORIO tr. *Montaigne's Essays* III. iii. 68 But no good without paines; no Roses without prickles. **1670** J. RAY *English Proverbs* 138 No rose without a thorn. **1922** JOYCE *Ulysses* Queer the number of pins they always have. No roses without thorns. **1965** H. ACTON *Old Lamps* 218 'But everything depends on the baby. What a bore.' 'No rose without a thorn, eh?' ■ **good and evil**

rose-water *see* REVOLUTIONS are not made with rose-water.

rot *see* ONE for the mouse, one for the crow; WINTER never rots in the sky.

The ROTTEN apple injures its neighbour

The proverb is also found in a number of variant forms, some of which are illustrated below. Cf. L. *pomum compunctum cito corrumpit sibi junctum*, a rotten apple quickly infects its neighbour.

□ **1340** *Ayenbite of Inwit* (EETS) 205 A roted eppel amang the holen [whole ones], maketh rotie the yzounde [sound]. **1577** J. NORTHBROOKE *Treatise against Dicing* 95 A peny naughtily [dishonestly] gotten, sayth Chrysostome, is like a rotten apple layd among sounde apples, which will rot all the rest. **1736** B. FRANKLIN *Poor Richard's Almanack* (July) The rotten apple spoils his companion. **1855** H. G. BOHN *Hand-Book of Proverbs* 514 The rotten apple injures its neighbour. **1979** D. MACKENZIE *Raven feathers his Nest* 19 The police.. have a deserved reputation for uprightness. ..But one bad apple can spoil the whole barrel. ■ **associates; example, good and bad**

rotten *see also* SMALL choice in rotten apples; SOON ripe, soon rotten.

roundabout *see* what you LOSE on the swings you gain on the roundabouts.

There is no ROYAL road to learning

Cf. PROCLUS *Commentary on Euclid* (Friedlein) 68, *μὴ εἶναι βασιλικὴν ἀτραπὸν ἐπὶ γεωμετρίαν*, there is no royal short cut to geometry (quoting Euclid). **1745** E. STONE tr. *Euclid's Elements* (ed. 2) II. A2v There is no other Royal Way or Path to Geometry.

□ **1824** EMERSON *Journal* (1961) II. 268 There is no royal road to Learning. **1857** TROLLOPE *Barchester Towers* II. i. There is no royal road to learning; no short cut to the acquirement of any valuable art. **1941** H. G. WELLS *You can't be too Careful* II. vi. 'There's no Royal Road to Learning,' said Mr. Myame. 'No. "Thorough" has always been my motto.' **1995** *Nature* 26 Jan. 297/3 There are well-established criteria by which to distinguish homology from homoplasy but there is still no royal road to truth. ■ **diligence; learning; ways and means**

rubber *see* those who PLAY at bowls must look out for rubbers.

rudder *see* who won't be RULED by the rudder must be ruled by the rock.

rue *see* MARRY in May, rue for aye.

rule *see* (noun) the EXCEPTION proves the rule; there is an EXCEPTION to every rule; (verb) DIVIDE and rule; the HAND that rocks the cradle rules the world.

Who won't be RULED by the rudder must be ruled by the rock

□ **1666** G. TORRIANO *Italian Proverbs* 286 That ship which will have no *rudder*, must have a rock. **1823** I. DISRAELI *Curiosities of Literature* 2nd Ser. I. 459 There is a Cornish proverb, 'Those who will not be ruled by the rudder must be ruled by the rock'—the strands of Cornwall, so often covered with wrecks, could not fail to impress on the imaginations of its inhabitants the two objects from whence they drew this salutary proverb. **1911** B. WILBERFORCE *Secret of Quiet Mind* 79 Jesus.. is weeping because the spiritual blindness of the people made.. the destruction of Jerusalem.. inevitable. 'He who will not be ruled by the rudder must be ruled by the rock,' but ruled he must be. **1984** R. HENDERSON *Salty Words* 165 The nautical saying *Who won't be ruled by the rudder must be ruled by the rock*.. means 'those who won't listen to reason must bear the consequences'. ■ **action and consequence; discipline**

RULES are made to be broken

□ **1938** F. VIVIAN *Black Alibi* xxiii. 212 'An old rule says Tell your lawyer everything, Mr. Moy.'..'An old saying asserts that rules were made to be broken. You must remember that also!' **1954** A. C. CLARKE *Expedition to Earth* 58 It is a fundamental rule of space-flight that..the minimum crew on a long journey shall consist of not less than three men. But rules are made to be broken. **1978** D. CLARK *Libertines* i. 20 '..it's an unwritten law that the Libertines don't use the house.' 'Rules are made to be broken.' **2001** *Washington Post Book World* 28 Jan. 13 It's a rule of crime fiction that recurring main characters rarely get knocked off; but during Flavia's final confrontation with a sadistic murderer, Pears gives his uneasy readers cause to remember that rules are made to be broken. ■ **rules, general**

If you RUN after two hares you will catch neither

Cf. ERASMUS *Adages* III. ccxxxvii. *duos insequens lepores, neutrum capit*, he who chases two hares catches neither.

□ **1509** A. BARCLAY *Ship of Fools* H5 A fole is he..Whiche with one haunde tendyth [intends] to take two harys in one instant. **1580** LYLY *Euphues & his England* II. 157 I am redie to take potions..yet one thing maketh to feare, that in running after two Hares, I catch neither. **1732** T. FULLER *Gnomologia* no. 2782 If you run after two Hares, you will catch neither. **1880** C. H. SPURGEON *John Ploughman's Pictures* 24 If we please one we are sure to get another grumbling. We shall be like the man who hunted many hares at once and caught none. **1981** P. O'DONNELL *Xanadu Talisman* v. Let's take things a step at a time. You know what they say. If you run after two hares you will catch neither. ■ **decision and indecision**; **wanting and having**

You cannot RUN with the hare and hunt with the hounds

Also used in the metaphorical phrase *to run with the hare and hunt with the hounds*. In quot. 1546 *tytifils* comes from Titivil, formerly a common name for a demon.

□ *a* **1449** J. LYDGATE *Minor Poems* (EETS) 821 He..holdeth bothe with hounde and hare. **1546** J. HEYWOOD *Dialogue of Proverbs* I. x. C3 There is no mo [more] suche tytifils [scoundrels] in Englands grounde, To holde with the hare, and run with the hounde. **1694** *Trimmer's Confession of Faith* I I can hold with the Hare, and run with the Hound: Which no Body can deny. **1896** M. A. S. HUME *Courtships of Queen Elizabeth* xii. Leicester, as usual, tried to run with the hare and hunt with the hounds, to retain French bribes and yet to stand in the way of French objects. **1975** J. O'FAOLAIN *Women in Wall* v. Clotair's henchmen say: 'You cannot *run* with the hare and hunt with the hounds.' The peasants have an even clearer way of putting this: 'You cannot', they say, 'side with the cow and the clover'. ■ **choices**

run *see also* he who FIGHTS and runs away, may live to fight another day; the LAST drop makes the cup run over; STILL waters run deep; while TWO dogs are fighting for a bone, a third runs away with it; we must learn to WALK before we can run.

rush *see* FOOLS rush in where angels fear to tread.

Russian *see* SCRATCH a Russian and you find a Tartar.

rust *see* BETTER to wear out than to rust out.

Sabbath *see* Monday's CHILD is fair of face.

sack *see* EMPTY sacks will never stand upright.

SAFE bind, safe find

□ **1546** J. HEYWOOD *Dialogue of Proverbs* I. iii. A4 Than catche and hold while I may, fast bind, fast fynde. **1573** T. TUSSER *Husbandry* (rev. ed.) II. 8 Drie sunne, drie winde, safe bind, safe find. **1655** T. FULLER *Church Hist. Britain* IV. iv Because sure binde, sure finde, he [Richard III] is said, and his Queen, to be Crowned again in York with great solemnity. **1890** D. C. MURRAY *John Vale's Guard* I. vi. 'Safe bind, safe find,' said Uncle Robert, locking the door and pocketing the key. **1937** D. L. SAYERS *Busman's Honeymoon* xx. As I says to Frank Crutchley, safe bind, safe find, I says. **1947** M. GILBERT *Close Quarters* viii. 'A careful man, the late head verger,' remarked Hazlerigg. 'Careful of his own and his master's property. Fast bind, fast find.' ■ **gains and losses; security**

safe *see also* it is BEST to be on the safe side; BETTER be safe than sorry.

There is SAFETY in numbers

Now much more general in its application than its possible biblical source: PROVERBS xi.14 (AV) In the multitude of counsellors there is safety.

□ **1680** BUNYAN *Mr. Badman* 133 I verily think, (since in the multitude of Counsellors there is safety) that if she had acquainted the Congregation with it, .. she had had more peace. **1816** J. AUSTEN *Emma* II. i. She determined to call upon them and seek safety in numbers. **1914** T. DREISER *Titan* xvii. He was beginning to run around with other women. There was safety in numbers. **2001** *Washington Post* 12 Sept. C15 (*Jeff MacNelly's Shoe comic strip*) 'Whoever said there's safety in numbers.. never took a math test.' ■ **associates; security**

said *see* LEAST said, soonest mended; what the SOLDIER said isn't evidence.

sailor *see* HEAVEN protects children, sailors, and drunken men.

If SAINT Paul's day be fair and clear, it will betide a happy year

The Conversion of St. Paul is traditionally celebrated on 25 January. Cf. *c* **1340** ROBERT OF AVESBURY *Hist.* (1720) 266 *clara dies Pauli bona tempora denotat anni*, a clear St. Paul's day denotes good times for the year.

□ **1584** R. SCOT *Discovery of Witchcraft* XI. xv. If Paule th'apostles daie be cleare, it dooth foreshew a luckie yeare. **1687** J. AUBREY *Gentilism & Judaism* (1881) 94 The old verse so much observed by Countrey-people: 'If Paul's day be faire and cleare It will betyde a happy yeare.' **1846** M. A. DENHAM *Proverbs relating to Seasons, &c.* 24 If St. Paul's day be fine and clear, It doth betide a happy year; But if by chance it then should rain, It will make dear all kinds of grain. **1975** M. KILLIP *Folklore of Isle of Man* xiii. In January the testing day was.. the 25th: St. Paul's Day stormy and windy, Famine in the world and great death of mankind, Paul's day fair and clear, Plenty of corn and meal in the world. ■ **weather lore**

SAINT Swithun's day, if thou be fair, for forty days it will remain; Saint Swithun's day, if thou bring rain, for forty days it will remain

St. Swithun (or Swithin) was a bishop of Winchester. He died in 862 and his feast-day is 15 July. The association of St. Swithun with persistent rain is at least as old as the early 14th-century MS 27 in Emmanuel College, Cambridge (fo. 163; quoted in I. Opie and M. Tatem *Dictionary of Superstitions*): In the daye of seynte Svithone rane ginneth rinigge Forti dawes mid ywone [on St. Swithun's day it usually starts to rain for forty days]. The rhyme has many variants.

□ **1600** JONSON *Every Man out of Humour* I. iii. O, here, S. Swithin's the xv day, variable weather, for the most part raine. .. Why, it should raine fortie daies after, now, more or lesse, it was a rule held afore I was able to hold a plough. **1697** *Poor Robin's Almanack* July B2V In this month is St. Swithin's day; On which, if that it rain, they say, Full forty days after it will, Or more or less some rain distill. **1846** M. A. DENHAM *Proverbs relating to Seasons, &c.* 52 St. Swithin's day, if thou dost rain, For forty days it will remain: St. Swithin's day, if thou be fair, For forty days 'twill rain na mair. **1892** C. M. YONGE *Old Woman's Outlook* 169 St. Swithin's promise is by no means infallible, whether for wet or fair weather. In.. Gloucestershire, they prefer a shower on his day, and call it christening the apples; but Hampshire.. hold[s] that—If Swithun's day be fair and clear, It betides a happy year; If Swithun's day be dark with rain, Then will be dear all sorts of grain. **1978** R. WHITLOCK *Calender of Country Customs* viii. Even today innumerable people take note of the weather on St. Swithun's Day, 15 July. .. St. Swithun's Day, if thou be fair, For forty days it will remain. St. Swithun's Day, if thou bring rain, For forty days it will remain. ■ **weather lore**

On SAINT Thomas the Divine kill all turkeys, geese, and swine

The feast-day of St. Thomas the Apostle has been traditionally celebrated on 21 December in the West.

□ **1742** *Agreeable Companion* 59 Thomas Divine, Brewing and Baking, and Killing of Swine. **1846** M. A. DENHAM *Proverbs relating to Seasons, &c.* 64 The day of St. Thomas, the blessed divine, Is good for brewing, baking, and killing fat swine. **1979** C. MORSLEY *News from English Countryside* 164 This couplet reminded farmers of the day on which they should make their last slaughters for the Christmas table. On St. Thomas the Divine Kill all turkeys, geese and swine. ■ **calendar lore**

saint *see also* the DEVIL was sick, the Devil a saint would be; the GREATER the sinner, the greater the saint; YOUNG saint, old devil.

Help you to SALT, help you to sorrow

□ **1666** G. TORRIANO *Italian Proverbs* 245 At table, one ought not to present any one, either salt, or the head of any creature. **1872** J. GLYDE *Norfolk Garland* i. The spilling of salt is very ominous, and the proverb is well known: Help me to salt, Help me to sorrow. **1945** F. THOMPSON *Lark Rise* xxxvi. No one would at table spoon salt on to another person's plate, for 'Help you to salt, help you to sorrow'. **1969** 'S. MAYS' *Reuben's Corner* xiv. There was no end to the prohibitions we learned as youngsters. .. Never help anyone to salt: Help you to salt, help you to sorrow. ■ **misfortune; superstition**

Saturday *see* Monday's CHILD is fair of face.

What's SAUCE for the goose is sauce for the gander

What is suitable for a woman is suitable for a man. The proverb is also occasionally used in non-sexist contexts.

□ **1670** J. RAY *English Proverbs* 98 That that's good sawce for a goose, is good for a gander. ..This is a woman's Proverb. **1692** R. L'ESTRANGE *Fables of Aesop* cccii. Sauce for a Goose is Sauce for a Gander.. **1894** BLACKMORE *Perly-cross* III. v. A proverb of large equity..declares..that 'sauce for the goose is sauce for the gander'. This maxim is pleasant enough to the goose. **2002** *National Review* 28 Jan. 39 To buttress his case, the Russian leader pointed out that NATO itself had recently insisted that Macedonia implement this same principle in behalf of its Albanian ethnic minority. What was sauce for the Albanian goose was sauce for the Baltic gander. ■ **men and women**

sauce *see also* HUNGER is the best sauce.

SAVE us from our friends

The idea that friends may be more dangerous than professed enemies because precautions are taken against the latter, whereas a friend is trusted, is an old one; cf. OVID *Ars Amatoria* I. 751 *Non est hostis metuendus amanti. Quos credis fidos effuge: tutus eris*, an enemy is not to be feared by the lover. Shun those whom you believe friends; then you will be safe. Both this short form and the expanded form represented by quot. 1604 are found.

□ **1477** A. WYDEVILLE *Dicts. of Philosophers* 127 Ther was one that praied god to kepe him from the daunger of his frendis. **1585** Q. ELIZABETH in J. E. Neale *Elizabeth I & her Parliament* (1957) iv. There is an Italian proverb which saith, From my enemy let me defend myself; but from a pretensed friend, good Lord deliver me. **1604** J. MARSTON *Malcontent* IV. ii. Now, God deliver me from my friends..for from mine enemies I'll deliver myself. **1884** *Railway Engineer* V. 265 The old proverb, 'Save us from our friends', may be well applied to the diligent gentlemen who..toiled through labyrinths of reports since 1877, to dress up a few exaggerated cases against the..brake. **1979** 'S. WOODS' *Proceed to Judgement* 140 Heaven save us from our friends! **2002** *Washington Times* 26 Mar. B5 'Defend me from my friends; I can defend myself from my enemies.' So cried a famous French general to Louis XIV long before bridge was invented. ■ **friends**

save *see also* a STITCH in time saves nine.

saved *see* a PENNY saved is a penny earned.

say *see* DO as I say, not as I do; when in DOUBT, do nowt; what EVERYBODY says must be true; HEAR all, see all, say nowt; what MANCHESTER says today, the rest of England says tomorrow; NEVER say never; *also* SAID.

Who SAYS A must say B

Only recorded in English from North American sources. Cf. Du. *wie a zegt, moet ook b zeggen*, who says a must also say b.

□ **1838** J. C. NEAL *Charcoal Sketches* 190 Not so easy as you think. ..If you say A, they'll make you say B. **1988** *Washington Times* 16 Sept. F3 But who says 'A' must say 'B', Mr. McCarthy. You can't talk about victims and caring and knowing cows individually while, at the same time, you treat carrots as nobodies! **2001** *National Review* 11 June 8 Either the state has the right to take life in cold blood,.. or it does not. If it does not, then McVeigh must be carefully supported, at public expense, even to the point of guarding him from other prisoners who might do him harm, for the rest of his natural days. Who says A, must say B. ■ **action and consequence; necessity**

scabbard *see* whosoever DRAWS his sword against the prince must throw the scabbard away.

scarce *see* GOOD men are scarce.

scarlet *see* an APE's an ape, a varlet's a varlet, though they be clad in silk or scarlet.

scheme *see* the BEST-laid schemes of mice and men gang aft agley.

school *see* EXPERIENCE keeps a dear school; never tell TALES out of school.

scorned *see* HELL hath no fury like a woman scorned.

You SCRATCH my back, I'll scratch yours

Similar in sentiment to *one* HAND *washes the other* (see quot. 1961).

□ **1704** E. WARD *All Men Mad* 18 Scratch me, says one, and I'll scratch thee. **1858** 'A. WARD' *Letter* 27 Jan. in *Maine: Guide 'Down East'* (1937) III. 363 You scratch my back and i will scratch your back. **1928** *Manchester Guardian Weekly* 10 Aug. 104/1 He goes on to spoil the effect by accusing Liberals of hypocrisy and being false to the principle of justice embodied in the phrase 'Scratch me and I'll scratch you'. **1961** J. HELLER *Catch-22* (1962) iv. 33 A little grease is what makes this world go round. One hand washes the other. Know what I mean? You scratch my back, I'll scratch yours. **2002** *Washington Times* 3 Mar. D1 Psychologist Lawrence Kohlberg outlined the stages of moral development in children:..2. Doing right for self-serving reasons: 'You scratch my back, and I'll scratch yours.' ■ **reciprocity**

SCRATCH a Russian and you find a Tartar

The proverb is also used allusively, especially of other nationalities. Cf. Fr. *grattez le Russe et vous trouverez le Tartare*, scratch the Russian and you will find the Tartar (attributed to Napoleon).

□ **1823** J. GALLATIN *Diary* 2 Jan. (1914) 229 Very true the saying is, 'Scratch the Russian and find the Tartar.' *c* **1863** J. R. GREEN in *Notes & Queries* (1965) CCX. 348 They say, if you scratch a Russian you always find the Tartar beneath. **1899** F. A. OBER *Puerto Rico* xii. Scratch a Puerto Rican and you find a Spaniard underneath, so the language and home customs of Spain prevail here. **1911** *Spectator* 2 Dec. 964 Until a short time ago the aphorism, 'Scratch a Russian and you find a Tartar,' was the sum of British comprehension of the Russian character. **1947** J. FLANNER in *New Yorker* 31 May 6 Scratch a Pole and you find a Pole, even if he is a Communist. **1967** D. BLOODWORTH *Chinese Looking Glass* xxxiv. Mao.. discovered many years ago that you only had to scratch a Russian Communist to find a Tatar. ■ **human nature; national characteristics**

Scripture *see* the DEVIL can quote Scripture for his own ends.

He that would go to SEA for pleasure, would go to hell for a pastime

A sailors' proverb.

□ **1899** A. J. BOYD *Shellback* viii. Shentlemens vot goes to sea for pleasure vould go to hell for pastime. **1910** D. W. BONE *Brassbounder* xxvi. He gave a half-laugh and muttered the old formula about 'the man who would go to sea for pleasure, going to hell for a pastime!' **1924** R. CLEMENTS *Gipsy of Horn* iii. 'He who would go to sea for pleasure, would go to hell for a pastime' is an attempt at heavy satire. **1933** M. LOWRY *Ultramarine* i. 'What made you come to sea anyway?' 'Search me. ..To amuse myself, I suppose.' 'Well, a man who'd go to sea for fun'd go to hell for a pastime. ..It's an old sailor expression.' **1986** *Newsweek* 27 Jan. 62 Just before

Steven Callahan set out to sail alone from Penzance to Martinique, a Cornish seaman warned him that 'a fella who'd go to sea for pleasure'd sure go to hell for pastime.' ■ **idiosyncrasy**

The SEA refuses no river

□ **1614** T. GENTLEMAN *England's Way to win Wealth* 45 (*marginal note*) The Sailors Prouerbe: The Sea and the Gallowes refuse none. **1699** E. WARD *Trip to New England* 4 It often puts me in mind of the old Proverb, *The Sea and the Gallows refuses none.* **1850** H. MELVILLE *White Jacket* II. xliii. 'The gallows and the sea refuse nothing,' is a very old sea saying. **1969** R. NYE *Tales I told my Mother* 124 The sea refuses no river. ■ **greed**

sea *see also* there are as good FISH in the sea as ever came out of it.

sea-maws *see* KEEP your own fish-guts for your own sea-maws.

search *see* on the FIRST of March, the crows begin to search.

SECOND thoughts are best

Cf. EURIPIDES *Hippolytus* l. 436 *αἱ δεύτεραί πως φροντίδες σοφώτεραι*, the second thoughts are invariably wiser.

□ **1577** HOLINSHED *Chronicles* 438 Oftentymes it chaunceth, that latter thoughts are better aduised than the first. **1581** G. PETTIE tr. *S. Guazzo's Civil Conversation* i. 23v I finde verified that Prouerbe, That the second thoughts are euer the best. **1681** DRYDEN *Spanish Friar* II. 22 Second thoughts, they say, are best: I'll consider of it once again. **1813** BYRON *Letter* 11 Dec. (1974) III. 196 In composition I do not think *second* thoughts are best, though *second* expressions may improve the first ideas. **1908** C. FITCH *Beau Brummel* I. i. Second thoughts seem to be always the best. **1981** P. O'DONNELL *Xanadu Talisman* v. That was my first thought. ..But second thoughts are always best. ■ **prudence**

secret *see* THREE may keep a secret, if two of them are dead.

What you SEE is what you get

Of American origin: often shortened to the acronym *wysiwyg* (especially in computing) of a system capable of reproducing the screen format of text on a printout.

□ **1971** *New York Times* 14 Nov. 17 'What you see, is what you get' .. is one of those recurring gag lines from the Flip Wilson Show that has quickly drifted into the language, all but become a household expression. **1983** G. PETIEVICH *To die in Beverly Hills* vii. The teleprinter raced as it printed the names of arrestees nicknamed Bones. 'What you see is what you get,' she said, squirming to point her breasts. 'I mean the printout of course.' **1990** *Washington Post* 10 Sept. (Business Section) 59 The lenders who would lend to anyone who said 'real estate' aren't lending now. So we aren't going to build any more product. What you see is what you get. **2001** *Spectator* 17 Nov. 12 With this prime minister, what you see is closer to what you get than has been the case with most of his predecessors. ■ **appearance, significant**

SEE no evil, hear no evil, speak no evil

The proverb is conventionally represented by figurines or pictures of three monkeys covering respectively their eyes, ears, or mouth with their hands.

□ **1926** *Army & Navy Stores Catalogue* 197 The three wise monkeys. 'Speak no evil, see no evil, hear no evil.' **1939** I. OELLRICHS *Man who didn't Answer* viii. 'Hear no evil, see no evil and speak no evil' was all right in its place, but Matt knew.. they gossiped as much there as in any other smallish town. **1978** T. L. SMITH *Money War* III. 233 It's the sort of thing they want done but do not want to know about. See no evil, hear no evil, speak no evil. **2001** *Washington Times* 18 July A14 Now, the International Olympic Committee—a bastion of 'hear no evil, see no evil, speak no evil'..—will send the sports equivalent of missionaries to the 2008 Summer Games. ■ **good and evil**

see *see also* BELIEVE nothing of what you hear, and only half of what you see; there's none so BLIND as those who will not see; what the EYE doesn't see, the heart doesn't grieve over; HEAR all, see all, say nowt; they that LIVE longest, see most; LOOKERS-on see most of the game; see a PIN and pick it up, all the day you'll have good luck; *also* SEEING, SEEN.

Good SEED makes a good crop

The obverse is found earlier in 1492 *Dialogue of Salomon & Marcolphus* (1892) 5 He that sowyth chaf shall porely mowe.

□ **1569** W. WAGER *Longer Thou Livest* A2 To be a good man it is also expedient Of good Parents to be begotten and borne. ..Commonly of good Seed procedeth good Corne. **1700** T. TRYON *Letters* i. If the Seed he Sowes be good..his Crop is according;..If he Sows Tares..will he expect Wheat? **1940** L. I. WILDER *Long Winter* xvii. Seed-time's pretty sure to come around. ..And good seed makes a good crop. ■ **beginnings and endings**

seed *see also* the BLOOD of the martyrs is the seed of the Church; PARSLEY seed goes nine times to the Devil.

seeding *see* ONE year's seeding makes seven years' weeding.

SEEING is believing

□ **1609** S. HARWARD *MS* (Trinity College, Cambridge) 85 Seeing is leeving. **1639** J. CLARKE *Parœmiologia Anglo-Latina* 90 Seeing is beleeving. **1712** J. ARBUTHNOT *Lewis Baboon* iv. There's nothing like Matter of Fact; Seeing is Believing. **1848** J. C. & A. W. HARE *Guesses at Truth* (ed. 2) 2nd Ser. 497 Seeing is believing, says the proverb. ..Though, of all our senses, the eyes are the most easily deceived, we believe them in preference to any other evidence. **2001** *Washington Times* 14 Dec. A4 Seeing, as the old saw goes, is believing, and in the post-literate age the visual is more persuasive than it used to be. ■ **trust and scepticism**

SEEK and ye shall find

Cf. SOPHOCLES *Oedipus Tyrannus* l. 110–11 *τὸ δὲ ζητούμενον ἁλωτόν, ἐκφεύγειν δὲ τἀμελούμενον*, what is sought is found; what is neglected evades us. A more direct source is MATTHEW vii. 7 (AV) Ask, and it shall be given you: seek, and ye shall find.

□ **1530** in J. Palsgrave *L'éclaircissement de la Langue Française* A5 He that wyll seke may fynde And in a brefe tyme attayne to his utterest desire. *c* **1538** J. BALE *King Johan* (1931) l. 192 Serche and ye shall fynd, in every congregacyn that long [belongs] to the pope. **1783** J. JAY *Letter* 14 Nov. (1891) III. 95 'Seek and you shall find' does not, it seems, always extend to that [health] of the body. **1980** R. COLLINS *Case of Philosopher's Ring* xiii. There is danger in the saying, 'Seek and ye shall find'. ■ **diligence; wanting and having**

seem *see* BE what you would seem to be.

seen *see* CHILDREN should be seen and not heard.

SELF-praise is no recommendation

Cf. L. *laus in proprio ore sordescit*, praise in one's own mouth is offensive.

□ **1826** COBBETT *Weekly Register* 17 June 743 In general it is a good rule.. that self-praise is no commendation. **1853** DICKENS *Bleak House* lv. Self-praise is no recommendation, but I may say for myself that I am not so bad a man of business. **1967** RIDOUT & WITTING *English Proverbs Explained* 137 'I admit I didn't score any of the goals, but it was largely due to me that we won the game.' 'Self-praise is no recommendation.' ■ **boasting**

SELF-preservation is the first law of nature

Cf. CICERO *De Finibus* IV. x. 25 *primamque ex natura hanc habere appetitionem, ut conservemus nosmet ipsos*, by nature our first impulse is to preserve ourselves.

□ *a* 1631 DONNE *Biathanatos* (1646) I. ii. It is onely upon this reason, that selfe-preservation is of Naturall Law. **1675** [MARVELL] *Complete Poems* (1872) I. 439 Self-preservation, Nature's first great Law. **1681** DRYDEN *Spanish Friar* IV. ii. Self-preservation is the first of Laws:.. When Subjects are oppress'd by Kings, They justifie Rebellion by that Law. **1821** SCOTT *Pirate* I. v. Triptolemus.. had a reasonable share of that wisdom which looks towards self-preservation as the first law of nature. **1952** 'A. A. FAIR' *Top of Heap* xvii. Loyalty is a fine thing.. but self-preservation is the first law of nature. **1975** P. D. JAMES *Black Tower* vii. What it amounted to was that he'd do a great deal for dear Maggie but that self-preservation was the first law of nature. ■ **self-preservation**

SELL in May and go away

A saying relating originally to the cycle of activity on the London Stock Exchange. May, shortly after the start of the financial year, was a busy time, but during the following months a bear market prevailed as trading was slack and Londoners (stockbrokers included) enjoyed their summer breaks away from the capital. Also current in the expanded version represented by quot. 2002, referring to the classic St. Leger horse race run at Doncaster in early September, the traditional end of the English summer social calendar.

□ **1979** *Daily Telegraph* 27 July 19 That hoary old adage sell in May and go away, has yet again been vindicated with the Financial Times 30 share index falling 97 points, from 559 on the May 4 post-election day to last night's 462 and with little immediate relief in sight. **1992** *Economist* 11 July 87/1 'Sell in May and go away,' says the old adage. This year it has been right on the button: a bad June for world stockmarkets is being followed by a worse July. **2001** *New York Times* The pattern [of stock market fluctuation] is the factual basis for the saying 'Sell in May and go away.' **2002** *Times* 15 May 34 In the City, you are about as likely to hear someone utter the old adage 'sell in May, go away, come back on St Leger's Day' as you are to spot gentlemen wearing bowler hats and carrying rolled umbrellas. ■ **business**

Don't SELL the skin till you have caught the bear

The origin of this saying is to be found in a fable added by Lorenzo Astemio (Laurentius Abstemius) to a collection of Aesop's fables compiled in the 1490s.

□ **1578** H. WOTTON tr. J. Yver *Courtly Controversie of Cupids Cantles* N4ᵛ His eyes, greedily fixed vpon his faire Mistresse, solde vnto him (as men say) the skin before the beast is taken. **1580** LYLY *Euphues & his England* ii. 53 I trusted so much, that I solde the skinne before the Beaste was taken. **1641** CHARLES I *Comment* (on

Remonstrance) 1 Dec. in *Rushworth Historical Collections* (1692) III. v. 1, 436 We must not dispose of the Bears skin till the Bear be dead. **1692** R. L'ESTRANGE *Aesop* (ed. 3) 270 He bade me have a care for the future, to make sure of the bear before I sell his skin. **1721** KELLY *Scottish Proverbs* 376 You sell the Bear Skin on his Back. **1999** R. CARPENTER *Scarlet Pimpernel* (*BBC TV, episode 1*) [CHAUVELIN:] The trap is set, and he's about to walk into it. [MARGUERITE:] Don't sell the skin till you've caught the bear. ■ **optimism**

sell *see also* BUY in the cheapest market and sell in the dearest.

seller *see* the BUYER has need of a hundred eyes, the seller of but one.

send *see* never send a BOY to do a man's job; GOD never sends mouths but He sends meat; GOD sends meat, but the Devil sends cooks.

SEPTEMBER blow soft, till the fruit's in the loft

□ **1571** T. TUSSER *Husbandry* (rev. ed.) F2 September blowe soft, Till fruite be in loft. **1732** T. FULLER *Gnomologia* no. 6214 September, blow soft, Till the Fruit's in the Loft. **1906** E. HOLDEN *Country Diary of Edwardian Lady* (1977) 121 September blow soft,—Till the fruit's in the loft. **1928** *Daily Mail* 3 Sept. 10 'September blow soft till the apple's in the loft' is what we desire of this traditionally beautiful month. ■ **weather lore**

servant *see* ENGLAND is the paradise of women; FIRE is a good servant but a bad master.

serve *see* you cannot serve GOD and Mammon; NO man can serve two masters.

If you would be well SERVED, serve yourself

Very similar to *if you* WANT *a thing done well, do it yourself*.

□ **1659** G. TORRIANO *English & Italian Dict.* 39 Who hath a mind to any thing let him go himself. **1706** J. STEVENS *Spanish & English Dict.* s.v. Querer, If you would be well serv'd, serve your self. **1871** J. E. AUSTEN-LEIGH *Memoir of Jane Austen* (ed. 2) ii. 'If you would be well served, serve yourself.' Some gentlemen took pleasure in being their own gardeners. **1981** *Times* 28 Apr. 15 Absurd that the important things in one's life should be made by another person—'One is never so well served as by oneself.' ■ **efficiency and inefficiency**; **self-help**

served *see also* FIRST come, first served; PAY beforehand was never well served; YOUTH must be served.

session *see* HOME is home, as the Devil said when he found himself in the Court of Session.

set *see* set a BEGGAR on horseback, and he'll ride to the Devil; sow dry and set wet; set a THIEF to catch a thief.

seven *see* KEEP a thing seven years and you'll always find a use for it; you should KNOW a man seven years before you stir his fire; ONE year's seeding makes seven years' weeding; PARSLEY seed goes nine times to the Devil; RAIN before seven, fine before eleven; SIX hours' sleep for a man, seven for a woman, and eight for a fool.

shadow *see* COMING events cast their shadows before; OLD sins cast long shadows.

shame *see* (noun) FOOL me once, shame on you; (verb) TELL the truth and shame the Devil.

shared *see* a TROUBLE shared is a trouble halved.

The SHARPER the storm, the sooner it's over

Cf. SENECA *Natural Questions* VII. ix. *procellae, quanto plus habent virium, tanto minus temporis*, the harder storms are, the shorter they last.

□ **1872** F. KILVERT *Diary* 9 June (1977) II. 207 Mrs. Vaughan will have a good family soon. Her children come fast. But the harder the storm the sooner 'tis over. **1913** *Folk-Lore* XXIV. 76 The sharper the storm, the sooner it's over. **2002** *Washington Post* 11 Feb. C13 (*One Big Happy comic strip*) '.. She'll be very, very angry!' 'I know, but the sharper the storm, the sooner it's over.' 'I'm about to be killed, and you're giving me weather reports?!' ■ **weather lore**

sheep *see* BETTER to live one day as a tiger than a thousand years as a sheep; a BLEATING sheep loses a bite; one might as well be HANGED for a sheep as a lamb.

shepherd *see* RED sky at night shepherd's delight.

You cannot SHIFT an old tree without it dying

□ *c* **1518** A. BARCLAY tr. *Mancinus' Mirror of Good Manners* G4^v An old tre transposed shall fynde smal auauntage. **1670** J. RAY *English Proverbs* 22 Remove an old tree, and it will wither to death. **1721** J. KELLY *Scottish Proverbs* 284 Remove an old Tree, and it will wither. Spoken by a Man who is loth to leave a Place in his advanc'd years, in which he has long lived. **1831** W. M. PRAED *Political & Occasional Poems* (1888) 166 I'm near three-score; you ought to know You can't transplant so old a tree. **1906** R. KIPLING *Puck of Pook's Hill* 259 'You've cleaved to your own parts pretty middlin' close, Ralph.' 'Can't shift an old tree 'thout it dyin'.' ■ **habit; old age**

shine *see* happy is the BRIDE that the sun shines on; MAKE hay while the sun shines.

shining *see* the SUN loses nothing by shining into a puddle.

Do not spoil the SHIP for a ha'porth of tar

Ship is a dialectal pronunciation of *sheep*, and the original literal sense of the proverb was 'do not allow sheep to die for the lack of a trifling amount of tar', tar being used to protect sores and wounds on sheep from flies. *Hog* (quots. 1623 and 1670) seems to have been understood by Ray (quot. 1670 note) as a swine, but it was also a widely used dialect term for a young sheep older than a lamb but before its first shearing. The current form of this proverb was standard by the mid nineteenth century. The metaphorical phrase *to spoil the ship for a ha'porth of tar* is also found.

□ **1623** W. CAMDEN *Remains concerning Britain* (ed. 3) 265 A man will not lose a hog, for a halfeperth [halfpennyworth] of tarre. **1631** J. SMITH *Advertisements for Planters* XIII. 30 Rather.. lose ten sheepe, than be at the charge of halfe penny worth of Tarre. **1670** J. RAY *English Proverbs* 103 Ne're lose a hog for a half-penny-worth of tarre [(ed. 2) 154 Some have it, lose not a sheep, &c. Indeed tarr is more used about sheep than swine]. **1861** C. READE *Cloister & Hearth* I. i. Never tyne [lose] the ship for want of a bit of tar. **1869** W. C. HAZLITT *English Proverbs* 432 To spoil the ship for a halfpennyworth of tar. In Cornwall, I heard a different version, which appeared to me to be more consistent with probability: 'Don't spoil the sheep for a ha'porth of tar.' **1910** *Spectator* 19 Feb. 289 The ratepayers.. are accused of.. cheeseparing, of spoiling the ship for a ha'p'orth of tar. **1992** 'C. AIRD' 'Man Who Rowed for Shore' in *Injury Time* (1995) 22 As Millicent, his late wife, would have said, it was just like Norman to spoil the ship for a ha'p'orth of tar. ■ **meanness**

ship *see also* one HAND for yourself and one for the ship; LITTLE leaks sink the ship; a WOMAN and a ship ever want mending.

shirt *see* NEAR is my shirt, but nearer is my skin.

From SHIRTSLEEVES to shirtsleeves in three generations

Shirtsleeves denote the need to work hard for one's living. This saying has been attributed to A. Carnegie (1835–1919), manufacturer and philanthropist, but is not found in his published writings. *From* CLOGS *to clogs is only three generations* expresses the same idea.

□ **1907** N. M. BUTLER *True & False Democracy* ii. No artificial class distinctions can long prevail in a society like ours [in the US] of which it is truly said to be often but three generations 'from shirt-sleeves to shirt-sleeves'. **1957** J. S. BRUNER in *Psychological Review* LXIV. 125 From shirtsleeves to shirtsleeves in three generations: we are back with the founding and founded content of the pre-Gestalt Gestalters. **1980** J. KRANTZ *Princess Daisy* xvii. What's this? Shirtsleeves to shirtsleeves in three generations. ■ **family; poverty**

If the SHOE fits, wear it

A predominantly US variant of *if the* CAP *fits, wear it.*

□ **1773** *New-York Gazette & Weekly Mercury* 17 May Why should Mr. Vanderbeek apply a general comparison to himself? Let those whom the shoe fits wear it. **1876** W. G. NASH *Century of Gossip* 125 If the shoe fits you, you can wear it a little wile [*sic*], Jack; but we won't quarrel about that. **1934** J. GREGORY *Emerald Murder Trap* 260 Some one, devilishly inspired, had made a noose in the end and the knot was what is so widely known as a Hangman's knot. .. 'There's an old saying, you know; if the shoe fits, wear it. The words might be made to apply to knots, I suppose!' **2001** *Washington Post* 13 Dec. C11 (*Baby Blues comic strip*) 'Zee, you're a know-it-all-crybaby-tattletale brat!' 'I'm telling Mommy that you said that!' .. 'What did Mommy say?' 'She said, "If the shoe fits, wear it!"' ■ **conduct; reputation**

shoe *see also* it's ILL waiting for dead men's shoes; for WANT of a nail the shoe was lost.

The SHOEMAKER's son always goes barefoot

A skilled or knowledgeable person commonly neglects to give his own family the benefit of his expertise. Found in a number of variants.

□ **1546** J. HEYWOOD *Dialogue of Proverbs* I. xi. E1v But who is wurs shod, than the shoemakers wyfe, With shops full of newe shapen shoes all hir lyfe? **1773** R. GRAVES *Spiritual Quixote* I. III. ii. The Shoe-maker's wife often goes in ragged shoes. .. Although there had been a [Methodist] Society begun here by Mr. Whitfield, yet .. the people of Gloucester are not much the better for having had so great a Prophet born amongst them. **1876** S. SMILES *Life of Scotch Naturalist* xvii. His large family .. were all .. well shod, notwithstanding the Scottish proverb to the contrary. 'The Smith's meer [mare] and the shoemaker's bairns are aye the worst shod.' **1981** 'E. PETERS' *Saint Peter's Fair* 30 Spruce in his dress, but down at heel, Cadfael noticed—proof of the old saying that the shoemaker's son is always the one who goes barefoot! **1987** S. STEWART *Lifting the Latch* 58 They say the cobbler's children go the worst shod. Dad made sure we children went dry-shod by giving us a penny-a-week for the Boot-fund. **2001** *Spectator* 4 Aug. 28 The cobbler's children go barefoot, and Pearson, which publishes the *Financial Times*, has lost £233 million in six months. ■ **family**

shoemaker *see also* let the COBBLER stick to his last.

shop *see* KEEP your shop and your shop will keep you.

shopkeeper *see* the ENGLISH are a nation of shopkeepers.

shorn *see* GOD tempers the wind to the shorn lamb; many go out for WOOL and come home shorn.

A SHORT horse is soon curried

A slight task is soon completed. *Curried* here means 'groomed with a curry-comb'.

□ *c* **1350** *Douce MS 52* no. 17 Short hors is son j-curryed. *a* **1530** R. HILL *Commonplace Book* (EETS) 128 A shorte hors is son curried. **1732** T. FULLER *Gnomologia* no. 395 A short Horse is soon curried. **1820** SCOTT *Abbot* I. xi. A short tale is soon told—and a short horse soon curried. **1939** L. I. WILDER *By Shores of Silver Lake* xxx. A short horse is soon curried. This is our tightest squeeze yet, .. but it's only a beginning. **1948** F. P. KEYES *Dinner at Antoine's* xx. That's a short horse and soon curried. Let's go see this Captain Murphy and put an end to it. ■ **efficiency and inefficiency**; **work**

SHORT reckonings make long friends

A *short reckoning* is the speedy settlement of an account.

□ **1530** R. WHITFORDE *Work for Householders* A4 The commune prouerbe is that ofte rekenynge holdest longe felawship. **1641** D. FERGUSSON *Scottish Proverbs* (STS) no. 668 Oft compting makes good friends. **1673** J. DARE *Counsellor Manners* xciii. Short reckonings (we say) make long friends. **1842** S. LOVER *Handy Andy* viii. There must be no nonsense about the wedding. .. Just marry her off, and take her home. Short reckonings make long friends. **1918** BARONESS ORCZY *Man in Grey* 15 Short reckonings make long friends. I'll have a couple of hundred francs now. ■ **business**; **punctuality**

short *see also* ART is long and life is short; LONG foretold, long last.

shortest *see* BARNABY bright, Barnaby bright, the longest day and the shortest night; the LONGEST way round is the shortest way home.

shoulder *see* you cannot put an OLD head on young shoulders.

show *see* TIME will tell.

shower *see* APRIL showers bring forth May flowers.

SHROUDS have no pockets

□ **1854** R. C. TRENCH *On Lessons in Proverbs* (ed. 2) v. With an image Dantesque in its vigour, that 'a man shall carry nothing away with him when he dieth', take this Italian, *Our last robe*, that is our winding sheet, is made *without pockets*. **1909** A. MACLAREN *Epistle to Ephesians* 41 There is nothing that is truly our wealth which remains outside of us, and can be separated from us. 'Shrouds have no pockets.' **1961** M. KELLY *Spoilt Kill* II. 20 'He had a win on the pools and it's burning him.' 'Shrouds don't need pockets, love,' he said with a grin. **2002** *Spectator* 13 Apr. 57 So we take into the afterlife only what we have given away. Shrouds have no pockets. ■ **death**; **money**

A SHUT mouth catches no flies

□ **1599** J. MINSHEU *Spanish Grammar* 83 In a closed vp mouth a flie cannot get in. **1640** G. HERBERT *Outlandish Proverbs* no. 219 Into a mouth shut flies flie not. **1659** T. FULLER *Appeal of Injured Innocence* I. 12 The *Spanish* Proverb..is necessary in dangerous..Times, *Where the mouth is shut no Fly doth enter.* **1742** B. FRANKLIN *Poor Richard's Almanack* (Feb.) Speak and speed: the close mouth catches no flies. **1897** 'H. S. MERRIMAN' *In Kedar's Tents* xxiii. Concha, remembering..that no flies enter a shut mouth, was silent. **1926** T. A. WILLARD *City of Sacred Well* xv. Tell each of them that a shut mouth catches no flies. We may find..nothing..and..we do not want the other men laughing at us behind our backs. **1984** 'M. HEBDEN' *Pel and Pirates* (1987) v. 43 'People keep a tight lip. *In bocca chiusa non entra mai mosca*.. . It's an old Italian saying. The people on the island use it.' 'What's it mean?' 'A fly never enters a closed mouth. They don't talk much.' ■ **discretion; speech and silence**

shut *see also* a DOOR must either be shut or open; when ONE door shuts, another opens; it is too late to shut the STABLE-door after the horse has bolted.

shy *see* ONCE bitten, twice shy.

sick *see* the DEVIL was sick, the Devil a saint would be; HOPE deferred makes the heart sick.

side *see* it is BEST to be on the safe side; the BREAD never falls but on its buttered side; the GRASS is always greener on the other side of the fence; PROVIDENCE is always on the side of the big battalions; there are TWO sides to every question.

sight *see* in vain the NET is spread in the sight of the bird; OUT of sight, out of mind.

SILENCE is a woman's best garment

Cf. SOPHOCLES *Ajax* l. 293 γυναιξὶ κόσμον ἡ σιγὴ φέρει, silence is a woman's ornament. The passage of St. Paul alluded to in quot. 1539 is I CORINTHIANS xiv. 34 (AV) Let your women keep silence in the churches, for it is not permitted unto them to speak.

□ **1539** R. TAVERNER tr. *Erasmus' Adages* 50 *Mulierem ornat silentium*. Silence garnysheth a woman..whych thynge also the Apostle Paule requyreth. **1659** J. HOWELL *Proverbs* (English) 11 Silence the best ornament of a woman. **1732** T. FULLER *Gnomologia* no. 4166 Silence is a fine Jewel for a Woman; but it's little worn. **1977** J. AIKEN *Five-Minute Marriage* iv. Quiet, miss! Silence is a woman's best garment. ■ **speech and silence; women**

SILENCE is golden

Sometimes in the fuller version SPEECH *is silver, but silence is golden.*

□ **1865** W. WHITE *Eastern England* II. ix. Silence is golden, says the proverb. We apprehend the full significance..in some lone hamlet situate amid a 'thousand fields'. **1923** A. HUXLEY *Antic Hay* xx. Silence is golden, as her father used to say when she used to fly into tempers and wanted to say nasty things to everybody within range. **2002** *Washington Post* 4 Apr. C13 (*Mother Goose & Grimm comic strip*) 'What I don't understand is..how can campaign money be free speech..but silence is golden?' ■ **speech and silence**

SILENCE means consent

This is not a principle accepted in modern English law. However, Sir Thomas More (1478–1535) is said to have riposted with the Latin maxim when asked at his trial why he kept silent when asked to acknowledge the King's supremacy over the Church. Cf. L. *qui tacet consentire videtur*, he who is silent seems to consent.

□ *c* **1380** WYCLIF *Select English Works* (1871) III. 349 Oo [one] maner of consent is, whanne a man is stille and tellith not. **1591** LYLY *Endymion* v. iii. Silence, Madame, consents. *c* **1616–30** *Partial Law* (1908) v. iv. 'I will nothing say.' .. 'Then silence gives consent.' **1847** A. HELPS *Friends in Council* ix. I have known a man..bear patiently..a serious charge which a few lines would have entirely answered.'.. 'Silence does not give consent in these cases.' **1914** L. WOOLF *Wise Virgins* v. He..did not speak. 'I assume that silence means consent,' said Arthur. **1986** 'C. AIRD' *Dead Liberty* ii. 'Silence is consent,' said the superintendent. His knowledge of law had a magpie quality about it and he had picked up the phrase from somewhere. ■ **speech and silence**

silence *see also* SPEECH is silver, but silence is golden.

You can't make a SILK purse out of a sow's ear

□ **1518** A. BARCLAY *Eclogues* (EETS) v. 360 None can..make goodly silke of a gotes flece. **1579** S. GOSSON *Ephemerides of Phialo* 62v Seekinge..too make a silke purse of a Sowes eare, that when it shoulde close, will not come togeather. **1672** W. WALKER *English & Latin Proverbs* 44 You cannot make a..silk purse of a sows ear; a scholar of a blockhead. **1834** MARRYAT *Peter Simple* I. xii. The master..having been brought up in a collier, he could not be expected to be very refined. .. 'It was impossible to make a silk purse out of a sow's ear.' **1915** D. H. LAWRENCE *Rainbow* i. You can't make a silk purse out of a sow's ear, as he told his mother very early, with regard to himself. **1985** M. SLUNG *Momilies* 83 You can't make a silk purse out of a sow's ear. ■ **possibility and impossibility**

silk *see also* an APE's an ape, a varlet's a varlet, though they be clad in silk or scarlet.

silly *see* ASK a silly question and you get a silly answer.

silver *see* every CLOUD has a silver lining; SPEECH is silver, but silence is golden.

It's a SIN to steal a pin

□ **1875** A. B. CHEALES *Proverbial Folk-Lore* 129 It is a sin To steal a pin, as we, all of us, used to be informed in the nursery. **1945** F. THOMPSON *Lark Rise* xiii. Children were taught to 'know it's a sin to steal a pin'..when they brought home some doubtful finding. **1956** D. M. DISNEY *Unappointed Rounds* xvii. I brought that boy up..and I taught him to be honest. ..I used to say to him. ''Tis a sin to steal a penny or a pin,' and he'd say it after me. ■ **honesty and dishonesty; theft**

sin *see also* CHARITY covers a multitude of sins; OLD sins cast long shadows.

sincerest *see* IMITATION is the sincerest form of flattery.

SING before breakfast, cry before night

Also occurs in reverse form; see quot. 1954.

□ **1530** J. PALSGRAVE *L'éclaircissement de la Langue Française* 404 You waxe mery this morning god gyue grace you wepe nat or [before] nyght. **1611** R. COTGRAVE *Dict. French & English* s.v. Soir, Some laugh amornings who ere night shed teares. **1721** J. KELLY *Scottish Proverbs* 332 They that laugh in the Morning may greet [weep] e'er Night. **1940** 'T. CHANSLOR' *Our First Murder* xii. 'You remember the saying. "Sing before breakfast—"' 'Oh dear—"cry before night."' **1954** A. SETON *Katherine* xxxi. Cry before breakfast, sing before supper. ■ **merriment**

sing *see also* little BIRDS that can sing and won't sing must be made to sing; the OPERA isn't over till the fat lady sings.

single *see* BEAUTY draws with a single hair; the LONGEST journey begins with a single step.

singly *see* MISFORTUNES never come singly.

sink *see* LITTLE leaks sink the ship.

sinner *see* the GREATER the sinner, the greater the saint.

sit *see* where MACGREGOR sits is the head of the table.

It is ill SITTING at Rome and striving with the Pope

□ *a* **1628** J. CARMICHAELL *Proverbs in Scots* no. 1847 Ye may not sit in Rome and strive with the Pape. **1721** J. KELLY *Scottish Proverbs* 194 It is hard to sit in Rome, and strive against the Pope. It is foolish to strive with our Governours, Landlords, or those under whose Distress we are. **1908** A. MACLAREN *Ezekiel* 58 'It is ill sitting at Rome and striving with the Pope.' Nebuchadnezzar's palace was not precisely the place to dispute with Nebuchadnezzar. ■ **conduct; prudence**

sitting *see also* it is as CHEAP sitting as standing.

situation *see* DESPERATE diseases must have desperate remedies.

SIX hours' sleep for a man, seven for a woman, and eight for a fool

□ **1623** J. WODROEPHE *Spared Hours of Soldier* 310 The Student sleepes six Howres, the Traueller seuen; the Workeman eight, and all Laizie Bodies sleepe nine houres and more. **1864** J. H. FRISWELL *Gentle Life* 259 John Wesley.. considered that five hours' sleep was enough for him or any man. ..The old English proverb, so often in the mouth of George III, was 'six hours for a man, seven for a woman, and eight for a fool'. **1908** *Spectator* 19 Dec. 1047 Is there not a proverb that a man requires six hours' sleep, a woman seven, a child eight and only a fool more? If this be true, thousands of great men were, and are, fools. ■ **health**

size *see* ONE size does not fit all.

skin *see* (noun) NEAR is my shirt, but nearer is my skin; don't SELL the skin till you have caught the bear; (verb) there is more than one WAY to skin a cat.

skin-deep *see* BEAUTY is only skin-deep.

skittle *see* LIFE isn't all beer and skittles.

If the SKY falls we shall catch larks

'In ridicule of those who talk of doing many things, if certain other things, not likely, were to happen': Fielding, *Proverbs of all Nations* (1824) 22.

□ *c* **1445** *Peter Idley's Instructions to his Son* (1935) I. 178 We shall kacche many larkis whan heuene doith falle. **1546** J. HEYWOOD *Dialogue of Proverbs* I. iv. B1^{v} When the sky falth we shal haue larks. **1670** J. RAY *English Proverbs* 143 If the sky falls we shall catch larks. **1721** J. KELLY *Scottish Proverbs* 343 What if the Lift [sky] fall, you may gather Laverocks [larks]. **1914** G. B. SHAW *Misalliance* p. xxx. I cannot be put off by the news that our system would be perfect if it were worked by angels.. just as I do not admit that if the sky fell we should all catch larks. **1950** C. S. LEWIS in *Month*

Oct. 234 If.. the total content of time were spread out before me.. I could do what the Historicist says he is doing. .. Yes; and if the sky fell we should all catch larks. ■ **possibility and impossibility**

sky *see also* RED sky at night, shepherd's delight; WINTER never rots in the sky.

slave *see* BETTER be an old man's darling, than a young man's slave.

sleep *see* one HOUR's sleep before midnight is worth two after; SIX hours' sleep for a man, seven for a woman, and eight for a fool.

Let SLEEPING dogs lie

Cf. early 14th-cent. Fr. *n'esveillez pas lou chien qui dort*, wake not the sleeping dog.

□ *c* **1385** CHAUCER *Troilus & Criseyde* III. 764 It is nought good a slepyng hound to wake. **1546** J. HEYWOOD *Dialogue of Proverbs* I. x. D1^V It is euill wakyng of a slepyng dog. **1681** S. COLVIL *Whigs' Supplication* II. 27 It's best To let a sleeping mastiff rest. **1824** SCOTT *Redgauntlet* I. xi. Take my advice, and speer [ask] as little about him as he does about you. Best to let sleeping dogs lie. **1976** T. SHARPE *Wilt* xx. He would be better off sticking to indifference and undisclosed affection. 'Let sleeping dogs lie,' he muttered. **1996** M. MACDONALD *Death's Autograph* ix. 98 'They don't have to prove it! He's dead. It can't do him any harm now.' She said distinctly, 'Let sleeping dogs lie, then.' ■ **action and inaction; busybodies**

sleeve *see* STRETCH your arm no further than your sleeve will reach.

A SLICE off a cut loaf isn't missed

□ **1592** SHAKESPEARE *Titus Andronicus* II. i. 87 More water glideth by the mill Than wots [knows] the miller of; and easy it is Of a cut loaf to steal a shive [slice]. **1639** J. CLARKE *Parœmiologia Anglo-Latina* 118 'Tis safe taking a shive of a cut loafe. **1732** T. FULLER *Gnomologia* no. 3012 It is safe taking a slice off a Cut Loaf. **1901** F. E. TAYLOR *Wit & Wisdom of South Lancashire Dialect* 11 A shoive off a cut loaf's never miss't. (A satirical remark.) **1981** N. LOFTS *Old Priory* v. iii. I went into this with my eyes open and a slice off a cut loaf ain't missed. ■ **gains and losses**

slip *see* there's MANY a slip between cup and lip.

SLOW and steady wins the race

Sometimes merged with SLOW *but sure*.

□ **1762** R. LLOYD *Poems* 38 You may deride my awkward pace, But slow and steady wins the race. **1894** G. F. NORTHALL *Folk-Phrases* 22 Slow and steady wins the race. **2002** *Washington Post Book World* 14 Apr. 4 In Gould's theory, slow and steady sometimes wins the race, but more often than not life is punctuated by catastrophic contingencies that fall in the realm of unique historical narratives rather than predictable natural laws. ■ **patience and impatience; ways and means**

SLOW but sure

Sure means properly 'sure-footed, deliberate' and is frequently contrasted with *slow* as in **1562** G. LEGH *Accidence of Armoury* 97 Although the Asse be slowe, yet is he sure. Closely related to the previous proverb.

□ **1692** R. L'ESTRANGE *Fables of Aesop* ccclxix. Slow and sure in these cases, is good counsel. **1859** S. SMILES *Self-Help* xi. Provided the dunce has persistency and application, he will inevitably head the cleverer fellow without these qualities. Slow but sure, wins the race. **1947** M. PENN *Manchester Fourteen Miles* xvii. No dressmaker.. ever learnt her trade in a hurry. 'Slow but sure' was the beginner's motto. **1985** D. & S. ROSEN *Death & Blintzes* xxi. But you know how we work, slow but sure. Getting the facts first and then narrowing things down. ■ **patience and impatience; ways and means**

slowly *see* make HASTE slowly; the MILLS of God grind slowly, yet they grind exceeding small.

SMALL choice in rotten apples

□ **1593** SHAKESPEARE *Taming of Shrew* I. i. 129 Faith, as you say, there's small choice in rotten apples. **1931** C. WELLS *Umbrella Murder* iv. 'I'm going upstairs, and you can come with me, or stay behind, as you choose.' 'Small choice in rotten apples.' **1958** 'S. DEAN' *Dishonor among Thieves* xxiii. It's a choice of rotten apples. ■ **choices; necessity**

SMALL is beautiful

□ **1973** E. F. SCHUMACHER (*title*) Small is beautiful. **1977** D. JAMES *Spy at Evening* xxiv. Small Is Beautiful—but big pays more. **1991** *Washington Post* 13 Jan. G8 In the 19th century, some classical composers forgot (if they had ever known) the principle that 'small is beautiful.' **2002** *Times* 2 May 23 Small isn't always beautiful and really small, like *Nanoarchaeum equitans*, which measures a whole 100 millionth of a millimetre less than the tiniest bacterium, may be a long way from even being visible to the naked eye. ■ **great and small**

small *see also* the BEST things come in small packages; BETTER are small fish than an empty dish; LITTLE things please little minds; there's no great LOSS without some gain; the MILLS of God grind slowly, yet they grind exceeding small.

smell *see* (noun) MONEY has no smell; (verb) FISH and guests smell after three days.

smock *see* NEAR is my kirtle, but nearer is my smock.

No SMOKE without fire

Cf. PLAUTUS *Curculio* 53 *flamma fumo est proxima*, the flame is right next to the smoke; late 13th-cent. Fr. *nul feu est sens fumee ne fumee sens feu*, no fire is without smoke, nor smoke without fire; *c* **1375** J. BARBOUR *Bruce* (EETS) IV. 81 And thair may no man fire sa covir, [Bot] low or reyk [flame or smoke] sall it discovir.

□ *c* **1422** T. HOCCLEVE *Works* (EETS) I. 134 Wher no fyr maad is may no smoke aryse. **1592** G. DELAMOTHE *French Alphabet* II. 39 No smoke without fire. **1655** T. FULLER *Church Hist. Britain* II. x. There was no Smoak but some Fire: either he was dishonest, or indiscreet. **1869** TROLLOPE *He knew He was Right* II. lii. He considered that..Emily Trevelyan had behaved badly. He constantly repeated..the old adage, that there was no smoke without fire. **1948** 'M. INNES' *Night of Errors* iv. 'Chimneys!..Who the deuce cares whether there's smoke from every chimney in the house.' 'I do. No smoke without fire.' **2002** *Times* 8 July 8 'I've been found not guilty, but mud sticks. Some people will say: "There's no smoke without fire."' ■ **public opinion; rumour**

smooth *see* the COURSE of true love never did run smooth.

snow *see* NORTH wind doth blow, we shall have snow.

so *see* so many MEN, so many opinions.

sober *see* WANTON kittens make sober cats.

A SOFT answer turneth away wrath

With allusion to PROVERBS xv. 1 (AV) A soft answer turneth away wrath. Cf. *c* **1395** WYCLIF *Bible* (1850) Proverbs xv. 1 A soft answere brekith ire.

□ *c* **1445** *Peter Idley's Instructions to his Son* (1935) I. 84 A softe worde swageth [assuages] Ire. **1693** C. MATHER *Wonders of Invisible World* 60 We would use to one another none but the Soft Answers, which Turn away Wrath. **1826** SOUTHEY *Letter* 19 July (1912) 414 A soft answer turneth away wrath. There is no shield against wrongs so effectual as an unresisting temper. **1922** JOYCE *Ulysses* 597 A soft answer turns away wrath. **1979** J. SCOTT *Clutch of Vipers* vi. 'Yes, sir!'.. Soft answer, no wrath. ■ **anger; tact**

soft *see also* SEPTEMBER blow soft, till the fruit's in the loft.

SOFTLY, softly, catchee monkey

□ **1907** G. BENHAM *Cassell's Book of Quotations* 849 (Proverbs) 'Softly, softly,' caught the monkey—(Negro). **1939** H. C. BAILEY *Veron Mystery* xx. 'Softly talkee, catchee monkey,' Hopley summed up the method thus prescribed to him. **1941** F. VIVIAN *Death of Mr. Lomas* iv. 80 'Managed to dig out a suitable motive for Steadfall?' the Chief Constable asked slyly. 'I haven't done with him yet,' came the slow reply. 'Softly, softly, catchee monkee. ..' **1978** E. ST. JOHNSTON *One Policeman's Story* vii. They took with them the unique motto of the Lancashire Constabulary Training School, 'Softly, Softly, Catchee Monkey' which inspired the new programme's title, 'Softly, Softly'. ■ **guile; patience and impatience; ways and means**

softly *see also* FAIR and softly goes far in a day.

What the SOLDIER said isn't evidence

□ **1837** DICKENS *Pickwick Papers* III. xxxiii. 'You must not tell us what the soldier.. said, sir,' interposed the judge; 'it's not evidence.' **1931** 'V. LODER' *Red Stain* xii. 'It was true!'.. 'True to you,.. but you have no means of proving it to us. What the soldier said is not evidence.' **1971** P. MOYES *Season of Snows & Sins* ix. 'There is an English *mot* about a *poilu*—no?.. What *le poilu* say cannot be in Court—is that it?' Henry grinned. 'What the soldier said isn't evidence.' ■ **rumour; soldiers; truth**

soldier *see also* the FIRST duty of a soldier is obedience; OLD soldiers never die.

If you're not part of the SOLUTION, you're part of the problem

□ **1968** E. CLEAVER *Speech* (in R. Scheer, *Eldridge Cleaver* (1969) 32) What we're saying today is that you're either part of the solution or you're part of the problem. **1975** M. BRADBURY *History Man* v. 'If you're not the solution,' says Peter Madden, 'you're part of the problem.' 'It would be terribly arrogant of me to believe I was the solution to anything.' **1977** C. MCFADDEN *Serial* xxvi. Listen, don't you realize if you're not part of the solution you're part of the problem. **2001** *New Scientist* 24 Nov. 112 MTV used to broadcast environmental messages featuring the punchline 'if you're not part of the solution, you're part of the problem'. Indeed. ■ **assistance; trouble**

some *see* you WIN a few, you lose a few.

You don't get SOMETHING for nothing

A variant of this, originally from the north country, runs *you don't get owt* [anything] *for nowt* [nothing]. Cf. **1845** DISRAELI *Sybil* I. I. v. To do nothing and get something formed a boy's ideal of a manly career.

□ **1870** P. T. BARNUM *Struggles & Triumphs* viii. When people expect to get 'something for nothing' they are sure to be cheated. **1947** M. PENN *Manchester Fourteen Miles* xiii. No stranger, she declared emphatically, ever sent to another stranger 'summat for nowt'. It would .. be against nature. **1952** F. PRATT *Double Jeopardy* i. You don't get something for nothing, even in medicine. Perizone has a peculiar secondary effect. It releases all inhibitions. **1979** *Guardian* 18 June 10 Stravinsky and Auden .. [are] saying 'You don't get something for nothing.' If you want the lovely things .. you can't have them unless you're prepared to pay for them. **1979** *Church Times* 29 June 13 You don't get owt for nowt. ■ **reciprocity**

SOMETHING is better than nothing

Similar in sentiment to HALF *a loaf is better than no bread*. Cf. early 15th-cent. Fr. *mieulx vault aucun bien que neant*, something is better than nothing.

□ **1546** J. HEYWOOD *Dialogue of Proverbs* I. ix. D1 And by this prouerbe appereth this o [one] thyng, That alwaie somwhat is better than nothyng. **1612** T. SHELTON tr. *Cervantes' Don Quixote* III. vii. I will weare it as I may: for something is better then nothing. **1842** J. T. IRVING *Attorney* xvii. Something is better than nothing—nothing is better than starving. **1980** *Country Life* 24 Apr. 1283 Mrs Smith worked out her own charitable rules: give what can be given in kind (for something is better than nothing) but never give money. ■ **content and discontent**

something *see also* if ANYTHING can go wrong, it will.

My SON is my son till he gets him a wife, but my daughter's my daughter all the days of her life

□ **1670** J. RAY *English Proverbs* 53 My son's my son, till he hath got him a wife, But my daughter's my daughter all days of her life. **1863** C. READE *Hard Cash* I. v. 'Oh, mamma,' said Julia warmly, 'and do you think all the marriage in the world .. can make me lukewarm to my .. mother? .. It's a son who is a son only till he gets him a wife: but your daughter's your daughter, all-the-days-of her life. **1943** A. THIRKELL *Growing Up* iii. She doesn't hear from him for months at a time now of course and then it's only a wire as often as not, but your son's your son till he gets him a wife, as the saying is. **1981** *Listener* 27 Aug. 206 There's a very old-fashioned sort of saying we have in the North which goes, 'My son is my son till he finds him a wife, but my daughter is my daughter the rest of her life.' ■ **children and parents**

son *see also* CLERGYMEN's sons always turn out badly; the DEVIL's children have the Devil's luck; like FATHER, like son; the SHOEMAKER's son always goes barefoot.

SOON ripe, soon rotten

Cf. L. *cito maturum cito putridum*, quickly ripe, quickly rotten.

□ **1393** LANGLAND *Piers Plowman* C. XIII. 233 And that that rathest [earliest] rypeth, roteth most saunest. **1546** J. HEYWOOD *Dialogue of Proverbs* I. x. C4v In youth she was towarde [promising] and without euill. But soone rype sone rotten. **1642** D. ROGERS *Naaman* x. Some indeed .. are moved to .. disdaine by their inferiours forwardnesse, called them hastings, soone ripe, soone rotten. **1887** S. SMILES *Life & Labour* vi. Very few prize boys and girls stand the test of wear. Prodigies are almost always uncertain; they illustrate the proverb of 'soon ripe, soon rotten'. **1976** L. ROSTEN *O KAPLAN! My KAPLAN!* II. iii. 'Parkhill,' Mr. Robinson steelily murmured, 'we may all profit from the ancient adage: "*Presto maturo, presto marcio?!*" Yes: "The sooner ripe, the sooner rotten!" That applies to pupils no less than fruit!' ■ **youth**

The SOONER begun, the sooner done

□ **1578** T. GARTER *Most Virtuous Susanna* (1937) l. 948 The sooner that we do begin, the sooner is it done. **1872** TROLLOPE *Golden Lion* xx. 'I suppose I might as well go to him alone,' said Michel, groaning. 'Well, yes. ..Soonest begun, soonest over.' **1955** M. BOROWSKY *Queen's Knight* 46 Sooner task's begun, sooner task is done—so it's said. **1987** B. J. MORISON *Voyage of Chianti* vii. 'Would you like Viola and me to begin on her book tomorrow?' Amy asked him. 'The sooner begun, the sooner done.' ■ **beginnings and endings; efficiency and inefficiency**

sore *see* the TONGUE always returns to the sore tooth.

sorrow *see* ONE for sorrow, two for mirth; help you to SALT, help you to sorrow.

sorrowing *see* he that GOES a-borrowing goes a-sorrowing.

sorry *see* BETTER be safe than sorry.

sort *see* it takes ALL sorts to make a world.

soul *see* BREVITY is the soul of wit; CONFESSION is good for the soul; CORPORATIONS have neither bodies to be punished nor souls to be damned; the EYES are the window of the soul; PUNCTUALITY is the soul of business.

sound *see* EMPTY vessels make the most sound.

If something SOUNDS too good to be true, it probably is

□ **1997** *Washington Times* 3 June B7 I'm sure you've heard the expression, 'If something sounds too good to be true, it probably is.' Well, in the investment world, I say, 'If something sounds too good to be true, it definitely is.' **2001** *Washington Times* 24 Aug. E18 Apparently the old adage still applies: If a deal seems too good to be true, it probably is. Pass it up, or at least check it out with a call to your Department of Motor Vehicles. **2002** *Times: Weekend* 5 Jan. 4 And beware gambling on big bins of wine with lengthy, glowing descriptions; if the wine sounds too good to be true, it is. ■ **reality and illusion**

source *see* a STREAM cannot rise above its source.

SOW dry and set wet

Seed put into wet soil will rot before it germinates: **1580** T. TUSSER *Husbandry* (rev. ed.) xxxv. 38V By sowing in wet, Is little to get.

□ **1660** S. RIDERS *Riders: 1660 British Merlin* [observation on Apr.] In gardning never this rule forget To sowe dry, and set wet. **1846** M. A. DENHAM *Proverbs relating to Seasons, &c.* 11 This rule in gardening never forget—Sow dry and plant wet. **1985** *Observer* 3 Mar. 51 There is an adage for March which says 'This rule in gardening ne'er forget: Sow dry and set wet.' March is the month when most people's gardening year starts. ■ **garden lore**

A SOW may whistle, though it has an ill mouth for it

The 'Lord Granard' mentioned in quot. 1802 was George Forbes (1760–1837), sixth Earl and first Baron Granard.

□ **1802** M. EDGEWORTH *Letter* 19 Oct in *Maria Edgeworth in France & Switzerland* (1979) 10 He waddles on dragging his boots along in a way that would make a pig laugh. As Lord Granard says, a pig may whistle though he has a bad mouth for it. **1846** J. GRANT *Romance of War* I. xii. 'I dare say the Spanish sounds very singular to your ear.' 'Ay, sir; it puts me in mind o' an auld saying o' my faither the piper.

"A soo may whussle, but its mouth is no made for't."' **1927** J. BUCHAN *Witch Wood* xvii. Ye say he has the speech o' a guid Christian? Weel-a-weel, a soo may whistle, though it has an ill mouth for it. ■ **possibility and impossibility**

As you SOW, so you reap

With allusion to GALATIANS vi. 7 (AV) Whatsoever a man soweth, that shall he also reap.

□ *a* **900** CYNEWULF *Christ* in *Anglo-Saxon Poetic Records* (1936) III. 5 Swa eal manna bearn sorgum sawath, swa eft ripath [just as each son of man sows in grief, so he also reaps]. *c* **1470** *Mankind* in *Macro Plays* (1962) l. 180 Such as thei haue sowyn, such xall thei repe. **1664** S. BUTLER *Hudibras* II. ii. And look before you ere you leap; For as you sow, you are like to reap. **1871** J. A. FROUDE *Short Studies* 2nd Ser. 10 As men have sown they must still reap. The profligate.. may recover.. peace of mind.. but no miracle takes away his paralysis. **1978** F. WELDON *Praxis* xxiv. 'You should never have left them,' said Irma. 'As you sow, Praxis, so you reap.' **2000** 'C. AIRD' *Little Knell* (2001) iii. 29 'But like it says in the Bible,' said Jennifer, 'as you sow, so shall you reap.' ■ **action and consequence**

They that SOW the wind shall reap the whirlwind

The proverb is also used as a metaphorical phrase *to sow the wind (and reap the whirlwind)*. With allusion to HOSEA viii. 7 (AV) They have sown the wind, and they shall reap the whirlwind.

□ **1583** J. PRIME *Fruitful & Brief Discourse* II. 203 They who sowed a winde, shall reap a whirlewind, but they that sowed in iustice shall reape mercie. **1853** G. W. CURTIS in *Putnam's Magazine* Apr. 386 Ask the Rev. Cream Cheese to.. preach from this text: 'They that sow the wind shall reap the whirlwind.' **1923** O. DAVIS *Icebound* III. 98 Well—what's passed is passed. Folks that plant the wind reap the whirlwind! **1981** J. STUBBS *Ironmaster* xvii. I know that he who sows the wind shall reap the whirlwind. I dislodge a clod of earth, and start a landslide. ■ **action and consequence**

sow *see also* (noun) you can't make a SILK purse out of a sow's ear.

span *see* when ADAM delved and Eve span, who was then the gentleman?

SPARE at the spigot, and let out at the bung-hole

The meaning is explained in quot. 1721. The *spigot* is the peg or pin used to regulate the flow of liquid through the tap on a cask, while the *bung-hole* is the (much larger) opening through which a cask is filled or emptied and which is closed by a plug (the bung).

□ **1642** G. TORRIANO *Select Italian Proverbs* 50 He holdeth in at the spicket, but letteth out at the bunghole. **1670** J. RAY *English Proverbs* 193 Spare at the spigget, and let it out at the bung-hole. **1721** J. KELLY *Scottish Proverbs* 299 Spare at the Spiggot, and let out at the Bung Hole. Spoken to them who are careful and penurious in some trifling Things, but neglective in the main Chance. **1885** E. J. HARDY *How to be Happy though Married* xiii. People are often saving at the wrong place. .. They spare at the spigot, and let all run away at the bunghole. **1935** H. ZINSSER *Rats, Lice & History* xvi. It is all a part of the strange contradictions between idealism and savagery that characterize the most curious of all mammals. It leads to the extraordinary practice of what is spoken of as 'saving at the spigot and wasting at the bung'. **1966** L. BEERS *Wild Apples & North Wind* xxvii. That might fix it now, but next summer you'd be in as bad a squeeze. .. If you save at the spigot you lose at the bung. ■ **getting and spending; waste**

SPARE the rod and spoil the child

And introduces a consequence. With allusion to PROVERBS xiii. 24 (AV) He that spareth his rod, hateth his son.

□ *c* **1000** AELFRIC *Homilies* (1843) II. 324 Se the sparath his gyrde [stick], he hatath his cild. **1377** LANGLAND *Piers Plowman* B. v. 41 Salamon seide.. *Qui parcit virge, odit filium.* The Englich of this latyn is.. Who-so spareth the sprynge [switch], spilleth [ruins] his children. **1560** *Nice Wanton* A1[v] He that spareth the rod, the chyld doth hate. **1639** J. CLARKE *Parœmiologia Anglo-Latina* 161 Spare the rod and spoyle the child. **1876** I. BANKS *Manchester Man* II. vii. 'Spare the rod and spoil the child' had not been abolished from the educational code fifty-five years back. **1907** E. GOSSE *Father & Son* ii. This action [caning] was justified, as everything he did was justified, by reference to Scripture—'Spare the rod and spoil the child'. **2002** *Oldie* Aug. 64 It was good to hear.. how the Lord Chamberlain, the wonderfully named Sir Norman Bodkin, changed 'Spare the rod and spoil the child' to 'Spare the cane and spoil the child.' ■ **children; discipline**

SPARE well and have to spend

□ **1541** M. COVERDALE tr. *H. Bullinger's Christian State of Matrimony* xix. Spare as though thou neuer shuldest dye and yet as mortall spend mesurably. To spare that thou mayest haue to spend in honestye for goodes sake. **1635** J. GORE *Way to Well-doing* 25 A good sparer makes a good spender. **1721** J. KELLY *Scottish Proverbs* 297 Spare when you're young, and spend when you're old. .. He that saveth his Dinner will have the more for his Supper. **1832** A. HENDERSON *Scottish Proverbs* 16 Spare weel and hae weel. **1977** J. AIKEN *Five-Minute Marriage* x. I've given them a polish and they've come up real tip-top! Spare well and have to spend, I allus say. ■ **thrift**

SPEAK as you find

□ **1594–8** SHAKESPEARE *Taming of Shrew* II. i. 66 Mistake me not; I speak but as I find. **1666** TORRIANO *Italian Proverbs* 294 no. 115 The English say, Let every one speak as he finds. **1937** A. QUILLER-COUCH 'Captain Knot' in *Q's Mystery Stories* 150 'There's a silly proverb tells ye to speak of a man as you find him. I found Kennedy well enough.' **1988** H. MANTEL *Eight Months on Ghazzah Street* 175 Look, I don't have any theories. I just go issue by issue. I just speak as I find. ■ **reputation**

Never SPEAK ill of the dead

Cf. Gr. *τὸν τεθνηκότα μὴ κακολογεῖν*, speak no evil of the dead (attributed to the Spartan ephor [civil magistrate] Chilon, 6th cent. BC); L. *de mortuis nil nisi bonum*, say nothing of the dead but what is good.

□ **1540** R. TAVERNER tr. *Erasmus' Flores Sententiarum* A6 Rayle not vpon him that is deade. **1609** S. HARWARD *MS* (Trinity College, Cambridge) 81[v] Speake not evill of the dead. **1682** W. PENN *No Cross, No Crown* (ed. 2) xix. Speake well of the dead. **1783** S. JOHNSON *Lives of Poets* (rev. ed.) IV. 381 He that has too much feeling to speak ill of the dead.. will not hesitate.. to destroy.. the reputation.. of the living. **1945** F. THOMPSON *Lark Rise* xiv. 'Never speak ill of the dead' was one of their maxims. **2002** K. HALL PAGE *Body in Bonfire* viii. 201 Faith remembered the conversation she'd overhead. No need to speak ill of the dead. But devastating as it might be, his wife's death had solved a major problem for the headmaster. ■ **reputation; slander**

SPEAK not of my debts unless you mean to pay them

□ **1640** G. HERBERT *Outlandish Proverbs* no. 998 Speake not of my debts, unlesse you meane to pay them. **1875** A. B. CHEALES *Proverbial Folk-Lore* 88 Special proverbs supply us with some excellent admonitions. ..Dont talk of my debts unless you mean to pay them. **1981** *Times* 2 Jan. 10 An old proverb recommends you not to speak of my debts unless you mean to pay them. ■ **money; tact**

speak *see also* ACTIONS speak louder than words; out of the FULLNESS of the heart the mouth speaks; who KNOWS most, speaks least; SEE no evil, hear no evil, speak no evil; TALK of the Devil, and he is bound to appear; THINK first and speak afterwards; *also* SPOKEN.

speaking *see* it's ill speaking between a FULL man and a fasting.

Everyone SPEAKS well of the bridge which carries him over

□ **1678** J. RAY *English Proverbs* (ed. 2) 106 Let every man praise the bridge he goes over. *i.e.* Speak not ill of him who hath done you a courtesie, or whom you have made use of to your benefit; or do commonly make use of. **1797** F. BAILY *Journal* 11 May (1856) 279 Let every one speak well of the bridge which carries him safe over. **1850** C. KINGSLEY *Alton Locke* I. x. Every one speaks well of the bridge which carries him over. Every one fancies the laws which fill his pockets to be God's laws. **1886** G. DAWSON *Biographical Lectures* i. Our love of compromise.. has also been our great strength. ..We speak well of the bridge that carries us over. ■ **assistance; public opinion**

species *see* the FEMALE of the species is more deadly than the male.

If you don't SPECULATE, you can't accumulate

□ **1925** WODEHOUSE 'Bit of Luck for Mabel' in *Eggs, Beans and Crumpets* (1963) 127 You can't accumulate if you don't speculate. So, though funds were running a bit low by this time, I invested a couple of bob in a cab. **1941** D. DODGE *Death & Taxes* xxiii. Krebs took out his billfold. 'Can you give me any assurance that you have useful information?' 'Nope.'..'You never accumulate if you don't speculate.' **1957** WODEHOUSE *Something Fishy* iv. Don't spoil the ship for a ha'porth of tar, or, putting it another way, if you don't speculate, you can't accumulate. **1984** J. S. SCOTT *All Pretty People* ix. 'Bloody liquor's becoming an expense.' 'Won't be for long. You have to speculate to accumulate, if we kept her sober we couldn't do it our way.' ■ **gains and losses; riches; risk**

SPEECH is silver, but silence is golden

See also the abbreviated form SILENCE *is golden.*

□ **1834** CARLYLE in *Fraser's Magazine* June 668 As the Swiss Inscription says: *Sprechen ist silbern, Schweigen ist golden* (Speech is silvern, Silence is golden). **1865** A. RICHARDSON *Secret Service* ii. A taciturn but edified listener, I pondered upon.. 'speech is silver, while silence is golden'. **1936** W. HOLTBY *South Riding* I. iv. She will give a pound note to the collection if I would cut my eloquence short, so in this case, though speech is silver, silence is certainly golden. **1961** M. SPARK *Prime of Miss Jean Brodie* i. Speech is silver but silence is golden. Mary, are you listening? ■ **speech and silence**

speed *see* more HASTE, less speed.

What you SPEND, you have

The original of quot. 1579, which is quoted inexactly by Spenser, was the epitaph on the tomb of Edward Courtenay Earl of Devon (d. 1509) and his wife in St. Peter's church, Tiverton, Devon.

□ *c* **1300** in M. R. James *Catalogue of Library Pembroke College* (1905) 35 That ich et [I ate] that ich hadde. That ich gaf that ich habbe. That ich ay held that i nabbe [do not have]. **1579** SPENSER *Shepherd's Calendar* (May) 56 (Glossary) Ho, ho, who lies here? I the good Earle of Deuonshere, And Maulde my wife, that was ful deare. .. That we spent, we had: That we gaue, we haue: That we lefte we lost. **1773** S. JOHNSON *Letter* 12 Aug. (1952) I. 338 The monument of Robert of Doncaster.. says.. something like this. What I gave, that I have; what I spent, that I had; what I left that I lost. **1862** *Times* 15 Dec. 8 The most common maxim of the rank and file of British industry is that what you spend you have for it alone cannot be taken away from you. ■ **getting and spending**

spend *see also* SPARE well and have to spend.

spent *see* what is GOT over the Devil's back is spent under his belly.

sphere *see* a WOMAN's place is in the home.

spice *see* VARIETY is the spice of life.

spider *see* if you want to LIVE and thrive, let the spider run alive.

spigot *see* SPARE at the spigot, and let out at the bung-hole.

spilt *see* it is no use CRYING over spilt milk.

spite *see* don't CUT off your nose to spite your face.

splash *see* when the OAK is before the ash, then you will only get a splash.

spoil *see* do not spoil the SHIP for a ha'porth of tar; SPARE the rod and spoil the child; TOO many cooks spoil the broth.

spoiled *see* BETTER one house spoiled than two.

spoken *see* many a TRUE word is spoken in jest.

spoon *see* he who SUPS with the Devil should have a long spoon.

spot *see* the LEOPARD does not change his spots.

spread *see* MONEY, like manure, does no good till it is spread; in vain the NET is spread in the sight of the bird.

It is not SPRING until you can plant your foot upon twelve daisies

□ **1863** R. CHAMBERS *Book of Days* I. 312 We can now plant our 'foot upon nine daisies' and not until that can be done do the old-fashioned country people believe that spring is really come. **1878** T. F. THISELTON-DYER *English Folk-Lore* i. 'It ain't spring until you can plant your foot upon twelve daisies,' is a proverb still very prevalent. **1910** *Spectator* 26 Mar. 499 Spring is here when you can tread on nine daisies at once on the village green; so goes one of the country proverbs. **1972** CASSON & GRENFELL *Nanny Says* 52 When you can step on six daisies at once, summer has come. ■ **calendar lore**

spring (verb) *see* HOPE springs eternal.

The SQUEAKING wheel gets the grease

Attention is only given to a troublesome person or thing.

□ *a* **1937** in J. Bartlett *Familiar Quotations* 518 The wheel that squeaks the loudest Is the one that gets the grease. **1948** in B. Stevenson *Home Book of Proverbs* 2483 I hate to be a kicker, I always long for peace, But the wheel that does the squeaking is the one that gets the grease. **1974** *Hansard* (Commons) 17 Oct. 502 It is the old story: the squeaky wheel gets the grease. **2001** *Washington Times* 29 June A20 We are all acquainted with the adage 'the squeaky wheel gets the grease.' For the past decade or so, liberals have been squeaking loudly and getting more than their fair share of the grease, many times even from Republicans. ■ **trouble**

squeeze *see* an APPLE-PIE without some cheese is like a kiss without a squeeze.

stable *see* because a MAN is born in a stable that does not make him a horse.

It is too late to shut the STABLE-door after the horse has bolted

In early use the proverb referred to horse-stealing; *has bolted* is a modern substitution for the traditional *is stolen*. Cf. medieval Fr. *a tart ferme on l'estable, quant li chevaux est perduz*, the stable is shut too late, when the horse is lost.

□ *c* **1350** *Douce MS* 52 no. 22 When the hors is stole, steke [lock] the stabull-dore. *c* **1490** in *Anglia* (1918) XLII. 204 Whan the stede ys stole, than shytte the stable-dore. **1578** LYLY *Euphues* I. 188 It is to late to shutte the stable doore when the steede is stolen: The Trojans repented to late when their towne was spoiled. **1719** DEFOE *Robinson Crusoe* II. 92 A dead Bush was cram'd in [the hedge] to stop them [the Spaniards] out for the present, but it was only shutting the Stable-door after the Stead was stolen. **1886** R. L. STEVENSON *Kidnapped* xiv. A guinea-piece .. fell .. into the sea. .. I now saw there must be a hole, and clapped my hand to the place. .. But this was to lock the stable door after the steed was stolen. **1940** N. MARSH *Death of Peer* x. The horse having apparently bolted, I shall be glad to assist at the ceremony of closing the stable-door. **1979–80** *Verbatim* Winter 2 It is too late .. to shut the stable door after the horse has bolted. **1998** D. HARSTAD *Eleven Days* (1999) viii. 71 'Mike, maybe we should talk to Rothberg ..' 'Doesn't do much good to close the barn door after the horse is out.' ■ **foresight and hindsight; futility; lateness**

stalled *see* BETTER a dinner of herbs than a stalled ox where hate is.

stand *see* EMPTY sacks will never stand upright; if you don't like the HEAT, get out of the kitchen; a HOUSE divided cannot stand; every TUB must stand on its own bottom; UNITED we stand, divided we fall.

standing *see* it is as CHEAP sitting as standing.

starve *see* FEED a cold and starve a fever; while the GRASS grows, the steed starves.

stay *see* the FAMILY that prays together stays together.

steady *see* FULL cup, steady hand; SLOW and steady wins the race.

One man may STEAL a horse, while another may not look over a hedge

People may take different degrees of liberty depending on our opinion of them.

□ **1546** J. HEYWOOD *Dialogue of Proverbs* II. ix. K4 This prouerbe .. saith, that some man maie steale a hors better, Than some other maie stande and loke vpone. **1591** LYLY *Endymion* III. iii. Some man may better steale a horse, then another looke ouer the hedge. **1670** J. RAY *English Proverbs* 128 One man may better steal a horse, then another look over the hedge. If we once conceive a good opinion of a man, we will not be perswaded he doth any thing amiss; but him whom we have a prejudice against, we are ready to suspect on the sleightest occasion. **1894** J. LUBBOCK *Use of Life* ii. 'One man may steal a horse, while another may not look over a hedge'.. because the one does things pleasantly, the other disagreeably. **1921** A. BENNETT *Things that have interested Me* 315 Strange how one artist may steal a horse while another may not look over a hedge. **1957** R. WEST *Fountain Overflows* xi. Fancy him caring for her after all these years. Particularly when she treated him the way she did. But there, some people can steal a horse, and others aren't allowed to look over the gate. ■ **reputation**

steal *see also* HANG a thief when he's young, and he'll no' steal when he's old; it's a SIN to steal a pin.

steed *see* while the GRASS grows, the steed starves.

One STEP at a time

□ **1853** C. M. YONGE *Heir of Redclyffe* II. i. One step at a time is all one wants. **1901** R. KIPLING *Kim* vi. It's beyond me. We can only walk one step at a time in this world. **1919** J. BUCHAN *Mr. Standfast* xvi. I did not allow myself to think of ultimate escape. ..One step at a time was enough. **1986** M. SLUNG *More Momilies* 69 One step at a time is all it takes to get there. ■ **caution; patience and impatience**

step *see also* it is the FIRST step that is difficult; the LONGEST journey begins with a single step; from the SUBLIME to the ridiculous is only a step.

A STERN chase is a long chase

A *stern chase* is one in which the pursuing ship follows directly in the wake of the pursued.

□ **1823** J. F. COOPER *Pilot* xv. 'If we can once get him in our wake I have no fears of dropping them all.' 'A stern chace is a long chase.' **1919** J. A. BRIDGES *Victorian Recollections* xiv. English poetry has had a start of some centuries, and a stern chase is proverbially a long one. **1929** G. B. VALE *Mystery of Papyrus* vii. 52 Followed again to-day by shabby native, but threw him off with complete success by getting rapidly into a taxi and driving round about. A stern chase is a long chase. ■ **futility; persistence**

stey (*steep*): *see* put a STOUT heart to a stey brae.

It is easy to find a STICK to beat a dog

An excuse to justify a harsh action or opinion is easy to find.

□ **1564** T. BECON *Works* I. C5V Howe easye a thyng it is to fynde a staffe if a man be mynded to beate a dogge. **1581** G. PETTIE tr. *S. Guazzo's Civil Conversation* III. 50 It is an easie matter to finde a staffe to beate a dog. **1782** F. HOPKINSON *Miscellaneous Essays* I. 266 A proverb.. naturally occurs on this occasion: It is easy to find a stick to beat a dog. **1875** S. SMILES *Thrift* xiv. Excuses were abundant. ..It is easy to find a stick to beat a sick dog. **1908** *Times Literary Supplement* 6 Nov. 391 The reviewer seems.. predisposed to the view that any stick is good enough to beat a dog with. **1987** *Washington Times* 30 Apr. 11A When you want to beat a dog, any stick will do. ■ **excuses**

stick *see* (noun) up like a ROCKET, down like a stick; (verb) let the COBBLER stick to his last; throw DIRT enough, and some will stick.

STICKS and stones may break my bones, but words will never hurt me

Similar to HARD *words break no bones.*

□ **1894** G. F. NORTHALL *Folk-Phrases* 23 Sticks and stones will break my bones, but names will never hurt me! Said by one youngster to another calling names. **1980** *Cosmopolitan* Dec. 137 'Sticks and stones may break my bones,' goes the children's rhyme, 'but words will never hurt me.' One wonders whether the people on the receiving end..would agree. **2001** *Times* 28 Dec. 20 Sticks and stones may break some bones, but, as every journalist knows, words truly hurt. They rouse the fiends of fury, litigation and letters to the press. ■ **malice; words and deeds**

A STILL tongue makes a wise head

□ **1562** J. HEYWOOD *Works* Dd3[v] Hauyng a styll toung he had a besy head. **1776** T. COGAN *John Buncle, Junior* I. 238 Mum's the word. ..A quiet tongue makes a wise head, says I. **1869** W. C. HAZLITT *English Proverbs* 35 A still tongue makes a wise head. **1892** A. QUILLER-COUCH *I saw Three Ships* vii. A still tongue makes a wise head. **1937** J. WORBY *Other Half* iv. 'I believe in the old saying "A still tongue keeps a wise head".' 'I guess you're right. ..It's no business of mine.' ■ **speech and silence; wisdom**

STILL waters run deep

Now commonly used to assert that a placid exterior hides a passionate or subtle nature. Cf. Q. CURTIUS *De Rebus Gestis Alexandri Magni* VII. iv. 13 *altissima quaeque flumina minimo sono labi*, the deepest rivers flow with least sound [said there to be a Bactrian saying].

□ *c* **1400** *Cato's Morals* in *Cursor Mundi* (EETS) 1672 There the flode is deppist the water standis stillist. *c* **1410** J. LYDGATE *Minor Poems* (EETS) 476 Smothe waters ben ofte sithes [oftentimes] depe. **1616** T. DRAXE *Adages* 178 Where riuers runne most stilly, they are the deepest. **1721** J. KELLY *Scottish Proverbs* 287 Smooth Waters run deep. **1858** D. M. MULOCK *Woman's Thoughts about Women* xii. In maturer age..the fullest, tenderest tide of which the loving heart is capable may be described by those 'still waters' which 'run deep'. **1979** M. UNDERWOOD *Victim of Circumstances* II. 86 As for her, still waters run deep, it seems. She always looked so solemn. ..Fancy her shooting him! **2001** *National Review* 30 Apr. 60 Still waters run deep, so they say. The stillest and deepest belonged to Greta Garbo, who abruptly ended a dispute with Hollywood's moguls by saying, 'I tink I go home now.' She meant Sweden. ■ **appearance, deceptive; speech and silence**

sting *see* if you gently touch a NETTLE it'll sting you for your pains.

stink *see* the FISH always stinks from the head downwards; FISH and guests smell after three days; the more you STIR it the worse it stinks.

The more you STIR it the worse it stinks

□ **1546** J. HEYWOOD *Dialogue of Proverbs* II. vi. The more we stur a tourde, the wours it will stynke. **1639** J. CLARKE *Parœmiologia Anglo-Latina* 200 The more you stirre it the worse it stinkes. **1706** P. A. MOTTEUX tr. *Cervantes' Don Quixote* II. xii. The more ye stir, the more 'twill stink. **1929** T. COBB *Crime without Clue* xx. The more we stir the worse it stinks, inspector. One would never imagine there were so many shady histories in this harmless-looking village. **1971** H. VAN DYKE *Dead Piano* iv. I could tell you. ..But like my mama always used to say, 'The more you stir shit, the more it stinks.' ■ **action and consequence; busybodies**

stir *see also* you should KNOW a man seven years before you stir his fire.

A STITCH in time saves nine

The proverb was originally a couplet. The number *nine* was apparently introduced fancifully for the sake of assonance.

□ **1732** T. FULLER *Gnomologia* no. 6291 A Stitch in Time May save nine. **1797** F. BAILY *Journal* 30 Apr. (1856) 268 After a little while we acquired a method of keeping her [a boat] in the middle of the stream, by watching the moment she began to vary, and thereby verifying the vulgar proverb, 'A stitch in time saves nine.' **1868** READE & BOUCICAULT *Foul Play* I. ix. Repairing the ship. Found a crack or two in her inner skin. . . A stitch in time saves nine. **1979** *Homes & Gardens* June 105 Looking after oneself is like looking after a house: a stitch in time . .

STOLEN fruit is sweet

The proverb is used in a variety of forms, principally in allusion to the temptation of Eve (Genesis iii. 6): e.g. *c* **1390** CHAUCER *Parson's Tale* l. 332 The fleesh hadde delit in the beautee of the fruyt defended [forbidden]. See also the next entry.

□ **1614** T. ADAMS *Devil's Banquet* III. 98 But as the Proverbe hath it . . Apples are sweet, when they are plucked in the Gardiners absence. Eve liked no Apple in the Garden so well as the forbidden. **1668** F. KIRKMAN *English Rogue* II. B1[v] So eager are these sort of people to buy any thing that is unlicensed, following the Proverb, that stollen meat is sweetest. **1855** GASKELL *North & South* II. vi. I can remember . . your being in some disgrace . . for stealing apples. . . Some one had told you that stolen fruit tasted sweetest. **1935** H. SPRING *Rachel Rosing* xxiv. He knew that he did not love her. . . What else, then? . . He was not going to pretend that this stolen fruit was not sweet. **1961** N. LOFTS *House at Old Vine* II. 137 Old men are like children, of whom they say 'Stolen apples are sweetest'. **1971** E. H. COHEN *Mademoiselle Libertine* iii. The truth was that at the Minimes the show was better than in the Place Royale, perhaps because stolen fruits are sweeter. ■ **theft**

STOLEN waters are sweet

With allusion to PROVERBS ix. 17 (AV) Stolen waters are sweet. Cf. *c* **1395** WYCLIF *Bible* Proverbs ix. 17 Stoln watris ben swettere. Less frequent than the preceding entry.

□ *c* **1548** *Will of Devil* (1863) 9 This saiyng of the retcheles [reckless] woman in Salomon (Stollen waters ar sweete). **1614** T. ADAMS *Devil's Banquet* I. 3 Sinne shewes you a faire Picture—Stollen waters are sweet. **1721** J. KELLY *Scottish Proverbs* 298 Stoln Waters are sweet. People take great Delight in that which they can get privately. **1976** A. J. RUSSELL *Pour Hemlock* ii. Lucarelli, fond of quoting scripture, ended the memo with 'Stolen waters are sweet'. ■ **theft**

stomach *see* an ARMY marches on its stomach; the WAY to a man's heart is through his stomach.

stone *see* you cannot get BLOOD from a stone; you BUY land, you buy stones; CONSTANT dropping wears away a stone; DRIVE gently over the stones; those who live in GLASS houses shouldn't throw stones; a ROLLING stone gathers no moss; STICKS and stones may break my bones, but words will never hurt me.

STONE-dead hath no fellow

Predominantly used by advocates of the death penalty. *Fellow* here means 'equal' or 'counterpart'.

□ *c* **1633** *Soddered Citizen* (1936) l. 2618 'Is your ffather dead?'..'Laid with both Leggs Sir, in one lynnen bootehose That has noe fellowe, stone dead. *c* **1641** CLARENDON *Hist. Rebellion* (1702) I. III. 191 The Earl of Essex..answer'd, 'Stone Dead hath no Fellow.' **1828** MACAULAY *Essays* (1843) I. 144 Stonedead hath no fellow. **1926** *Times* 27 Aug. 11 The execution of the death sentence had been postponed for a week, an unusual period in a country where the adage 'stone-dead hath no fellow' wins general support. **1980** G. BLAKISTON *Woburn & Russells* v. Bedford, who was against the death penalty for Stratford, sought to moderate the violent opinions of some of his fellow peers, the Earl of Essex being heard to declare vehemently: 'stone dead hath no fellow'. ■ **death**; **finality**

stool *see* BETWEEN two stools one falls to the ground.

stop *see* when you are in a HOLE, stop digging.

storm *see* AFTER a storm comes a calm; ANY port in a storm; the SHARPER the storm, the sooner it's over.

One STORY is good till another is told

□ **1593** R. GREENE *Mamillia* II. 222 One tale is alwayes good vntil another is heard. *a* **1661** T. FULLER *Worthies* (Kent) 65 One story is good till another is heard. **1769** *Boston Gazette* 24 Apr. 2 The proverb, however homely it may be, will be allow'd by impartial men to be just, that 'one story is good, till another is told.' **1831** MACAULAY in *Edinburgh Review* Jan. 515 A theory is not proved..because the evidence in its favour looks well at first sight. ..'One story is good till another is told!' **1922** JOYCE *Ulysses* 121 One story good till you hear the next. ■ **good things**; **novelty**

story *see also* every PICTURE tells a story.

Put a STOUT heart to a stey brae

A Scottish proverb also used as a metaphorical phrase. A *stey brae* is a 'steep slope'.

□ *a* **1585** A. MONTGOMERIE *Cherry & Sloe* (1821) xxxvi. So gets ay, that sets ay, Stout stomackis to the brae. **1721** J. KELLY *Scottish Proverbs* 287 Set a stout Heart to a stay Brea. Set about a difficult Business with Courage and Constancy. **1821** J. GALT *Annals of Parish* i. I began a round of visitations; but oh, it was a steep brae that I had to climb, and it needed a stout heart. For I found the doors..barred against me. **1916** J. BUCHAN *Greenmantle* xii. He..shouted to me..to 'pit a stoot hert tae a stey brae'. **1937** S. SCOTT *Crazy Murder Show* v. Like the walls of Jericho, their resistance will eventually crumble if you peg away long enough. A stout heart to a stey brae, as my Inverness grandmother used to say. ■ **boldness**; **perservance**

strange *see* ADVERSITY makes strange bedfellows; POLITICS makes strange bed-fellows.

stranger *see* FACT is stranger than fiction; TRUTH is stranger than fiction.

straw *see* you cannot make BRICKS without straw; a DROWNING man will clutch at a straw; it is the LAST straw that breaks the camel's back.

STRAWS tell which way the wind blows

The phrase 'a straw in the wind', a sign of the prevailing opinion, action, etc., is also found.

□ *a* **1654** J. SELDEN *Table-Talk* (1689) 31 Take a straw and throw it up into the Air, you shall see by that which way the Wind is. . . More solid things do not shew the Complexion of the times so well, as Ballads and Libels. **1799** COBBETT *Porcupine's Works* (1801) X. 161 'Straws' (to make use of Callender's old hackneyed proverb) . . 'served to show which way the wind blows.' **1927** A. ADAMS *Ranch on Beaver* vii. As straws tell which way the wind blows . . this day's work gives us a clean line on these company cattle. **1968** R. H. R. SMITHIES *Shoplifter* vii. You must remember that I was present at the contretemps which occurred at your house two days ago. Straws show which way the wind blows, Mrs. Pride! ■ **hints; omens**

A STREAM cannot rise above its source

□ **1663** S. TUKE *Adventures of Five Hours* (Prologue) He would be ever w'you, but wants force; The Stream will rise no higher than the Source. **1732** T. FULLER *Gnomologia* no. 4771 The Stream can never rise above the Spring-head. **1905** H. A. VACHELL *Hill* 84 Clever chap. . . But one is reminded that a stream can't rise higher than its source. **1921** T. R. GLOVER *Pilgrim* 125 It is held that a stream cannot rise above its source; but . . [a] river may have many tributaries, and one of them may change the character of what we call the main stream. **1952** R. A. KNOX *Hidden Stream* iv. Because after all the stream doesn't rise higher than its source, and God, however we conceive him, must be higher in the scale of being than anything he has created. ■ **beginnings and endings**

stream *see also* don't CHANGE horses in mid-stream.

strength *see* UNION is strength.

strengthen *see* as the DAY lengthens, so the cold strengthens.

STRETCH your arm no further than your sleeve will reach

Do not spend more than you can afford. Similar to CUT *your coat according to your cloth.*

□ **1541** M. COVERDALE tr. *H. Bullinger's Christian State of Matrimony* xix. Strech out thine arme no farther then thy sleve wyll retche. **1639** J. CLARKE *Parœmiologia Anglo-Latina* 211 Stretch your arme no further than your sleeve will reach. **1721** J. KELLY *Scottish Proverbs* 277 Put your Hand no farther than your Sleeve will reach. That is, spend no more than your Estate will bear. **1881** W. WESTALL *Old Factory* II. ii. It would leave me short of working capital, and . . I mustn't stretch my arm further than th'coat-sleeve will reach. ■ **circumstances; poverty; prudence**

Everyone STRETCHES his legs according to the length of his coverlet

□ *a* **1300** WALTER OF HENLEY *Husbandry* (1890) 4 Wo that stretchet fortherre than his wytel [blanket] wyle reche, in the straue [straw] his fet he mot streche. **1550** W. HARRYS *Market* D5^v Then must many a man . . stretche out his legges accordynge to the length of his coverlet. **1640** G. HERBERT *Outlandish Proverbs* no. 147 Everyone stretcheth his legges according to his coverlet. **1897** 'H. S. MERRIMAN' *In Kedar's Tents* iv. 'The English . . travel for pleasure.' . . 'Every one stretches his legs according to the length of his coverlet,' he said. ■ **circumstances; prudence**

STRIKE while the iron is hot

A proverb originally alluding to the blacksmith's art. Cf. late 13th-cent. Fr. *len doit batre le fer tandis cum il est chauz*, one must strike the iron while it is hot.

□ *c* **1386** CHAUCER *Tale of Melibee* l. 1035 Whil that iren is hoot, men sholden smyte. **1546** J. HEYWOOD *Dialogue of Proverbs* I. iii. A4 And one good lesson to this purpose I pyke [pick] From the smiths forge, whan thyron is hote stryke. **1576** G. PETTIE *Petit*

Palace 181 I think it wisdome to strike while the iron is hot. **1682** BUNYAN *Holy War* 18 Finding..the affections of the people warmly inclining to him, he, as thinking 'twas best striking while the iron is hot, made this..speech. **1771** SMOLLETT *Humphry Clinker* III. 242 If so be as how his regard be the same, why stand shilly shally? Why not strike while the iron is hot, and speak to the 'squire without loss of time? **1848** THACKERAY *Vanity Fair* xxi. Let George cut in directly and win her. ..Strike while the iron's hot. **1974** T. SHARPE *Porterhouse Blue* xx. 'It seems an inopportune moment,' said the Senior Tutor doubtfully. ..'We must strike while the iron is hot,' said the Dean. **2000** 'G. WILLIAMS' *Dr. Mortimer and Aldgate Mystery* (2001) xxxii. 158 'Excellent!' I replied. 'Let us take up the invitation this very weekend: strike while the iron is hot.' ■ **opportunity**

strike *see also* LIGHTNING never strikes the same place twice.

striving *see* it is ill SITTING at Rome and striving with the Pope.

stroke *see* DIFFERENT strokes for different folks; LITTLE strokes fell great oaks; beware of an OAK, it draws the stroke.

strong *see* GOOD fences make good neighbours; the RACE is not to the swift, nor the battle to the strong; YORKSHIRE born and Yorkshire bred, strong in the arm and weak in the head.

stronger *see* a CHAIN is no stronger than its weakest link.

stubborn *see* FACTS are stubborn things.

The STYLE is the man

Cf. L. *stylus virum arguit*, the style shows the man; G. L. LE CLERC, CONTE DE BUFFON in *Histoire Naturelle* (1753) VII. p. xvii. *Le style est l'homme même*, the style is the man himself.

□ **1901** A. WHYTE *Bible Characters* V. civ. If the style is the man in Holy Scripture also..we feel a very great liking for Luke. **1942** H. F. HEARD *Reply Paid* ix. Usually I don't like to have my style modified. 'The style is the man.' ■ **human nature; idiosyncrasy**

From the SUBLIME to the ridiculous is only a step

In this form, from a remark made by Napoleon to the Polish ambassador De Pradt (D. G. De Pradt *Histoire de l'Ambassade*..(1815) 215), following the retreat from Moscow in 1812: *Du sublime au ridicule il n'y a qu'un pas*, there is only one step from the sublime to the ridiculous. The idea, however, was not original to Napoleon: **1795** T. PAINE *Age of Reason* II. 20 The sublime and the ridiculous are often so nearly related, that it is difficult to class them separately. One step above the sublime, makes the ridiculous; and one step above the ridiculous, makes the sublime again.

□ **1879** M. PATTISON *Milton* 116 The Hague tittle-tattle..is set forth in the pomp of Milton's loftiest Latin. ..The sublime and the ridiculous are here blended without the step between. **1909** *Times Literary Supplement* 17 Dec. 492 In the case of Louis XVIII, indeed, the ridiculous was, as it is commonly said to be, only a step removed from the sublime. **1940** W. & E. MUIR tr. *L. Feuchtwanger's Paris Gazette* II. xxxviii. From the sublime to the ridiculous is only a step, but there's no road that leads back from the ridiculous to the sublime. **1983** 'M. INNES' *Appleby & Honeybath* iii. 'At least,' he said, 'we can now go next door. Architecturally speaking, it's to move from the sublime to the ridiculous.' ■ **great and small**

If at first you don't SUCCEED, try, try, try again

The short poem *Try (try) again* was often quoted in nineteenth-century children's literature, especially in the United States (see quot. 1840). It is popularly attributed to W. E. Hickson, who quoted it (with three *try*'s) in his *Moral Songs* (1857) p. 8, but Palmer's use is earlier. The saying was soon used independently as a proverb.

□ **1840** T. H. PALMER *Teacher's Manual* 223 'Tis a lesson you should heed, Try, try again. If at first you do n't succeed, Try, try again. **1915** E. B. HOLT *Freudian Wish* iii. The child is frustrated, but not instructed; and it is in the situation where, later on in life, we say to ourselves, 'If at first you don't succeed, Try, try, try again!' *a* **1979** A. CHRISTIE *Miss Marple's Final Cases* 39 You mustn't give up, Mr. Rossiter, 'If at first you don't succeed, try, try, try again.' **2001** *Washington Times* 3 Aug. A17 John F. Harris reports, 'Bill Clinton this week will begin a second attempt at beginning his ex-presidency.' (If at first you don't succeed, try and try again.) ■ **perseverance; success**

succeed *see also* NOTHING succeeds like success.

SUCCESS has many fathers, while failure is an orphan

Cf. **1942** G. CIANO *Diary* 9 Sept. (1946) II. 196 *La vittoria trova cento padri, e nessuno vuole riconoscere l'insuccesso.* Victory has a hundred fathers, and no one acknowledges a failure.

□ **1961** J. F. KENNEDY *News Conference* 21 Apr. in *Public Papers of Presidents of U.S.* (1962) 312 There's an old saying that victory has 100 fathers and defeat is an orphan. **1991** *Washington Times* 29 Jan. G1 In the aftermath of the impeccably executed aerial attack that initiated the war with Iraq, the old saw that success has many fathers while failure is an orphan comes to mind. **2002** *Times* 11 June 19 In war, it has often been noted, victory has a hundred fathers, but defeat is an orphan. ■ **success**

suck *see* don't TEACH your grandmother to suck eggs.

Never give a SUCKER an even break

This saying has been attributed to various people, including E. F. Albee and W. C. Fields. It was popularized by Fields, who is said to have used it in the musical comedy *Poppy* (1923), though it does not occur in the libretto. *Poppy* was made into a silent film in 1925 and called *Sally of the Sawdust*. This was in turn remade as a 'talkie' in 1936 (see quot. 1936). The proverb means that one should not allow a fair chance to a fool, or one who may be easily deceived.

□ **1925** *Collier's* 28 Nov. 26 'That line of mine that brings down the house always was true, wasn't it?' 'Which line?' I asked. 'Never give a sucker an even break' he [W. C. Fields] answered. **1936** *N. Y. Herald Tribune* 15 Mar. v. 1 Wasn't it 'Poppy' that provided him with his immortal motto, 'Never give a sucker an even break'? **1940** WODEHOUSE *Eggs, Beans & Crumpets* 158 Never give a sucker an even break. . . But your sermon has made me see that there is something higher and nobler than a code of business ethics. **1979** *Daily Telegraph* 3 Nov. 24 The basic American business philosophy of 'never give a sucker an even break' runs rampant in those [money] markets. ■ **fair dealing; fools**

suckling *see* out of the MOUTHS of babes—.

sudden *see* hasty CLIMBERS have sudden falls.

SUE a beggar and catch a louse

□ **1639** J. CLARKE *Parœmiologia Anglo-Latina* 72 Sue a begger and get a louse. **1659** J. HOWELL *Proverbs* (English) 2 Goe to Law with a beggar, thou shalt gett a lowse. **1732** T. FULLER *Gnomologia* no. 4285 Sue a Beggar, and catch a Louse. **1819** SCOTT *Bride of Lammermoor* iii. I guess it is some law phrase—but sue a beggar, and—your honour knows what follows. **1937** R. WINSTON *It's a Far Cry* xi. Such suit would have been useless as he was insolvent. The case indeed would have been the old one of suing a beggar and catching a louse! ■ **futility; law and lawyers**

SUFFICIENT unto the day is the evil thereof

With allusion to MATTHEW vi. 34 (AV) Sufficient unto the day is the evil thereof.

□ **1766** in L. H. Butterfield et al. *Adams Family Correspondence* (1963) I. 56 Sufficient to the Day is the Evil thereof. **1836** J. CARLYLE *Letter* 1 Apr. in *Letters & Memorials* (1893) I. 57 In the meanwhile there were no sense in worrying over schemes for a future, which we may not live to see. 'Sufficient for the day is the evil thereof.' **1979** M. BABSON *So soon done For* vii. 'I'll deal with these [bills] later.' .. 'Sufficient unto the day,' Kay agreed. ■ **good and evil**

sufficient *see also* a WORD to the wise is enough.

summer *see* the RICH man has his ice in the summer and the poor man gets his in the winter; one SWALLOW does not make a summer.

Never let the SUN go down on your anger

With allusion to EPHESIANS iv. 26 (AV) Let not the sun go down upon your wrath.

□ **1642** T. FULLER *Holy State* III. viii. S. Paul saith, *Let not the Sunne go down on your wrath*; to carry news of the Antipodes in another world of thy revengefull nature. **1709** O. DYKES *English Proverbs* 189 We ought not to let the Sun go down upon our Wrath, or our Impenitence; neither ought we to let it conclude our Sluggishness. **1972** CASSON & GRENFELL *Nanny Says* 37 Never let the sun go down on your anger. **1981** M. MCMULLEN *Other Shoe* ii. Never let the sun go down on your anger, Clare's grandmother Herne used to say. ■ **anger; forgiveness; malice**

The SUN loses nothing by shining into a puddle

Cf. DIOGENES LAERTIUS VI. lxiii. *ὁ ἥλιος εἰς τοὺς ἀποπάτους, ἀλλ' οὐ μιαίνεται*, the sun shines into dung but is not tainted (attributed to Diogenes); TERTULLIAN *De Spectaculis* xx. *sol et in cloacam radios suos defert nec inquinatur*, the sun spreads his rays even into the sewer, and is not stained.

□ **1303** R. BRUNNE *Handlyng Synne* (EETS) l. 2299 The sunne, hys feyrnes neuer he tynes [loses], Thogh hyt on the muk hepe shynes. *c* **1390** CHAUCER *Parson's Tale* l. 911 Though that hooly writ speke of horrible synne, certes hooly writ may nat been defouled, namoore than the sonne that shyneth on the mixne [midden]. **1578** LYLY *Euphues* I. 193 The Sun shineth vppon the dungehill and is not corrupted. **1732** T. FULLER *Gnomologia* no. 4776 The Sun is never the worse for shining on a Dunghill. **1943** E. M. ALMEDINGEN *Frossia* iv. Dreadful words did fly about then, but the sun loses nothing by shining into a puddle. ■ **associates; great and small**

sun *see also* happy is the BRIDE that the sun shines on; MAKE hay while the sun shines; there is NOTHING new under the sun.

sunny *see* if CANDLEMAS day be sunny and bright, winter will have another flight.

supper *see* AFTER dinner rest a while, after supper walk a mile; HOPE is a good breakfast but a bad supper.

He who SUPS with the Devil should have a long spoon

A proverb advocating caution when dealing with dangerous or malevolent persons.

□ *c* **1390** CHAUCER *Squire's Tale* l. 602 Therfore bihoueth hire a ful long spoon That shal ete with a feend. **1545** R. TAVERNER tr. *Erasmus' Adages* (ed. 2) 9^V He had nede to haue a longe spone that shuld eate with the deuyl. **1590** SHAKESPEARE *Comedy of Errors* IV. iii. 59 He must have a long spoon that must eat with the devil.—What tell'st thou me of supping? **1641** D. FERGUSSON *Scottish Proverbs* (STS) no. 350 He should have a long shafted spoon that sups kail [vegetable broth] with the devil. **1721** J. KELLY *Scottish Proverbs* 147 He had need of a long Spoon that sups Kail with the Dee'l. He that has to do with wicked.. Men, had need to be cautious. **1840** R. H. BARHAM *Ingoldsby Legends* 1st Ser. 270 Who suppes with the Deville sholde have a longe spoone! **1979** 'E. ANTHONY' *Grave of Truth* viii. Hindenburg and the army thought they could use [Hitler]. .. Who sups with the devil needs a long spoon. ■ **associates; caution; peril**

sure *see* SLOW but sure.

suspicion *see* CAESAR's wife must be above suspicion.

SUSSEX won't be druv

A local proverb which asserts that Sussex people have minds of their own, and cannot be forced against their will. *Druv* is a dialect variant of *drove* (standard English *driven*).

□ **1910** in T. Wales *Sussex Garland* (1979) i. (*postcard*) Have got as fat as a Sussex [pig]—and 'wunt be druv' from Brighton. **1924** H. DE SELINCOURT *Cricket Match* vi. 'Well, we'd better be going, I suppose,' Gauvinier announced.. well aware that 'Sussex won't be druv'. **1939** 'D. FROME' *Pinkerton at Old Angel* vi. The sudden weariness in her frail face testified to years of patient leading. Mr. Pinkerton thought of the boast of the men of Sussex. They too couldn't be druv, they said. **1979** T. WALES *Sussex Garland* i. There ant no place like Sussex, Until ye goos above, For Sussex will be Sussex, And Sussex won't be druv! ■ **obstinacy**

One SWALLOW does not make a summer

Cf. Gr. *μία χελιδὼν ἔαρ οὐ ποιεῖ*, one swallow does not make a spring; ERASMUS *Adages* I. vii. *una hirundo non facit ver*.

□ **1539** R. TAVERNER tr. *Erasmus' Adages* 25 It is not one swalowe that bryngeth in somer. It is not one good qualitie that maketh a man good. **1546** J. HEYWOOD *Dialogue of Proverbs* II. v. H3 One swalow maketh not sommer. **1659** J. HOWELL *Proverbs* (English) 11 One Swallow doth not make a Summer. **1844** DICKENS *Martin Chuzzlewit* xlii. One foul wind no more makes a winter, than one swallow makes a summer. **2000** 'G. WILLIAMS' *Dr. Mortimer and Aldgate Mystery* (2001) xiv. 78 One or two alfresco afternoons in the garden under the supervision of Ord and Demmy did not spell liberation any more than one swallow made a summer.. ■ **omens**

It is idle to SWALLOW the cow and choke on the tail

Quot. 1721 explains the meaning.

□ **1659** J. HOWELL *Proverbs* (English) 13 To swallow an Ox, and be choaked with the tail. **1721** J. KELLY *Scottish Proverbs* 190 It is a Shame to eat the Cow, and worry [choke] on the Tail. It is a Shame to perform a great Task all but a little, and then give over. **1915** J. BUCHAN *Salute to Adventurers* xviii. We had gone too far to turn back, and as our proverb says, 'It is idle to swallow the cow and choke on the tail.' **1935** C. M. RUSSELL *Murder at Old Stone House* xvi. I'm not one to swallow a cow and choke on the tail. ■ **perseverance**

swallow (noun) *see also* the ROBIN and the wren are God's cock and hen.

swap *see* don't CHANGE horses in mid-stream.

A SWARM in May is worth a load of hay; a swarm in June is worth a silver spoon; but a swarm in July is not worth a fly

□ **1655** S. HARTLIB *Reformed Commonwealth of Bees* 26 It being a Proverb, that a Swarm of Bees in May is worth a Cow and a Bottle [bundle] of Hay, whereas a Swarm in July is not worth a Fly. **1710** *Tusser Redivivus* May 11 The Proverb says, 'A Swarm in May is worth a Load of Hay'. **1879** R. JEFFERIES *Wild Life in Southern County* vii. 'A swarm in May is worth a load of hay; a swarm in June is worth a silver spoon; but a swarm in July is not worth a fly'—for it is then too late . . to store up . . honey before the flowers begin to fade. **1945** F. THOMPSON *Lark Rise* v. As she reminded the children: A swarm in May's worth a rick of hay; And a swarm in June's worth a silver spoon; while A swarm in July isn't worth a fly. **1985** D. FOSTER *Dog Rock* ii. *A swarm of bees in May is worth a load of hay, A swarm of bees in June is worth a silver spoon, A swarm of bees in July is worth not a fly.* On that basis, a swarm of bees now would be worth a milking cow, but I won't be joining it to one of my colonies. ■ **calendar lore**

If every man would SWEEP his own doorstep the city would soon be clean

□ **1624** T. ADAMS *Temple* 65 When we would haue the street cleansed, let euery man sweep his owne doore, and it is quickly done. **1666** G. TORRIANO *Italian Proverbs* 41 If every one will sweep his own house, the City will be clean. **1930** *Times* 25 Mar. 10 It appears to be hard to draw a clear distinction between deciding a question of right and wrong for one's self and deciding it for others. . . 'If every man would sweep his own doorstep the city would soon be clean.' **2002** *Washington Times* 14 Aug. B5 You're right—and if everyone swept his own doorstep, this world would be a cleaner place. ■ **cleanliness**; **society**

SWEEP the house with broom in May, you sweep the head of the house away

There was a widespread folk belief associating broom with witches and magic; hence, flowering broom was considered unlucky and a harbinger of death in any house into which it was brought.

□ **1873** *Folk-Lore Record* I. 52 The old gentleman . . strictly forbade green brooms being used in his house during the month of May, and, as a reason for the prohibition, used to quote the adage—'If you sweep the house with broom in May, You'll sweep the head of that house away'. **1943** H. C. BAILEY *Mr. Fortune Finds Pig* (1948) xvi. 64 'What hadn't you thought of?' Rosen demanded sharply. ' "Sweep the house with broom in May",' Reggie murmured, ' "You sweep the head of the house away." ' ■ **calendar lore**; **superstition**

sweep *see also* NEW brooms sweep clean.

sweet *see* LITTLE fish are sweet; REVENGE is sweet; STOLEN fruit is sweet; STOLEN waters are sweet.

sweeter *see* the NEARER the bone, the sweeter the meat.

From the SWEETEST wine, the tartest vinegar

□ **1578** LYLY *Euphues* I. 197 As the best wine doth make the sharpest vinaigar, so the deepest loue tourneth to the deadliest hate. **1637** J. HOWELL *Familiar Letters* 3 Feb. (1903) II. 140 He swears he had rather see a basilisk than her [his former love]. The sweetest wines may turn to the tartest vinegar. **1852** E. FITZGERALD *Polonius* 9 'It is . . the sweetest wine that makes the sharpest vinegar,' says an old proverb. **1979** *Daedalus* Summer 121 The juxtaposition silently signals the cautionary maxim 'From the sweetest wine, the tartest vinegar'. ■ **opposites**

swift *see* the RACE is not to the swift, nor the battle to the strong.

swim *see* don't go near the WATER until you learn how to swim.

swine *see* do not throw PEARLS to swine; on SAINT Thomas the Divine kill all turkeys, geese, and swine.

swing *see* what you LOSE on the swings you gain on the roundabouts.

Swithun *see* SAINT Swithun's day if thou be fair for forty days it will remain.

sword *see* whosoever DRAWS his sword against the prince must throw the scabbard away; he who LIVES by the sword dies by the sword; the PEN is mightier than the sword.

table *see* where MACGREGOR sits is the head of the table.

tail *see* every HERRING must hang by its own gill; the HIGHER the monkey climbs the more he shows his tail; it is idle to SWALLOW the cow and choke on the tail.

tailor *see* NINE tailors make a man.

TAKE the goods the gods provide

Cf. PLAUTUS *Rudens* l. 1229 *habeas quod di dant boni*, you may keep what good the gods give.

□ **1697** DRYDEN *Alexander's Feast* 5 Lovely Thais sits beside thee, Take the good the gods provide thee. **1880** TROLLOPE *Duke's Children* III. xiv. 'It is only because I am the governor's son,' Silverbridge pleaded. ..'What of that? Take the goods the gods provide you.' **1980** M. MCMULLEN *Something of Night* viii. Take the goods the gods provide, and don't..sulk when they are snatched away. ■ **good fortune; opportunity**

take *see also* it takes ALL sorts to make a world; you can take the BOY out of the country but you can't take the country out of the boy; GIVE a thing, and take a thing, to wear the Devil's gold ring; GIVE and take is fair play; you can take a HORSE to the water, but you can't make him drink; you PAYS your money and you takes your choice; take care of the PENCE and the pounds will take care of themselves; it takes TWO to make a bargain; it takes TWO to make a quarrel; it takes TWO to tango.

It TAKES one to know one

□ **1977** *National Journal* 9 July 1090 In the it-takes-one-to-know-one category. Lester L. Kinsolving, among other jobs, is serving as national editor for the Panax Corp. newspapers. **1997** *Buffalo News* 27 Aug. 9D We hear that a local dude discourages his wife from buying antiques by saying, 'It takes one to know one.' **2001** R. HILL *Dialogues of Dead* xxiii. 200 'Sam just wasn't the suicidal type.' 'Takes a one to know a one, does it?' said Dalziel. ■ **similarity and dissimilarity**

A TALE never loses in the telling

Also used in the phrase *to lose* (or *grow*) *in the telling*, often implying exaggeration. **1541** *Schoolhouse of Women* A4ᵛ What soeuer commeth to memorye Shall not be loste, for the tellinge. **1581** *Stationers' Register* (1875) II. 388 A good tale Cannot to[o] often be Tolde.

□ **1609** S. HARWARD *MS* (Trinity College, Cambridge) 121 Tales lose nothing by the cariadge. **1721** J. KELLY *Scottish Proverbs* 44 A Tale never loses in the telling. Fame or Report..commonly receives an Addition as it goes from hand to Hand. **1907** *Spectator* 16 Nov. 773 A story never loses in the telling in the mouth of an Egyptian. **1954** L. P. HARTLEY *White Wand* 15 No doubt Antonio was telling the story to his fellow-gondoliers and it would lose nothing in the telling. **1979** M. STEWART *Last Enchantment* 19 Like all strange tales, it will grow with the telling. ■ **rumour**

tale *see also* DEAD men tell no tales.

Never tell TALES out of school

The phrase *to tell tales out of school* is also used.

□ **1530** W. TYNDALE *Practice of Prelates* B1V So that what cometh once in may never out for feare of tellinge tales out of scole. **1616** J. WITHALS *Dict.* (rev. ed.) 573 You must not tel tales out of the Tauerne. **1721** J. KELLY *Scottish Proverbs* 303 Tell no School Tales. Do not blab abroad what is said in drink, or among Companions. **1876** I. BANKS *Manchester Man* I. xv. All attempts to make known school troubles and grievances were met with 'Never tell tales out of school'. **1963** A. CHRISTIE *Clocks* xxiv. 'Well—.'..'I understand. Mustn't tell tales out of school.' ■ **malice**

TALK is cheap

Cf. *c* **1600** A. MUNDAY et al. *Sir T. More* (1911) 23 Woords are but wordes, and payes not what men owe; **1639** CHAPMAN & SHIRLEY *Ball* v. i. You may heare talke; but give me the man That has measur'd 'em: talkes but talke.

□ **1668** R. B. *Adagia Scotica* 47 Seying goes good cheap. **1843** T. C. HALIBURTON *Attaché* I. ii. Talk is cheap, it don't cost nothin' but breath. **1929** K. C. STRAHAN *Footprints* i. Talk's cheap. You could never make me believe that. **2002** *Washington Times* 16 Mar. F15 (*Herb & Jamaal comic strip*) 'Talk is cheap..because the supply always exceeds the demand.' ■ **boasting; words and deeds**

TALK of the Devil, and he is bound to appear

Also abbreviated to *talk of the Devil!*, used when a person just spoken of is suddenly seen.

□ **1666** G. TORRIANO *Italian Proverbs* 134 The English say, Talk of the Devil, and he's presently at your elbow. **1721** J. KELLY *Scottish Proverbs* 299 Speak of the Dee'l, and he'll appear. Spoken when they, of whom we are speaking, come in by Chance. **1773** R. GRAVES *Spiritual Quixote* II. VIII. v. 'How free he had made with the Devil's name.'..'Talk of the Devil, and he will appear.' **1830** MARRYAT *King's Own* II. v. The unexpected appearance of Mrs. Rainscourt made him involuntarily exclaim, 'Talk of the devil—' 'And she appears, Sir,' replied the lady. **1979** *Radio Times* 27 Oct.–2 Nov. 66 Talk of the Devil..and he's bound to appear, they say. **2001** R. HILL *Dialogues of Dead* xiii. 107 'Talk of the devil, there he is. How do, Your Lordship! Who's looking after the maggots?' ■ **coincidence**

talk *see also* MONEY talks.

tango *see* it takes TWO to tango.

tar *see* do not spoil the SHIP for a ha'porth of tar.

Tartar *see* SCRATCH a Russian and you find a Tartar.

tartest *see* from the SWEETEST wine, the tartest vinegar.

taste *see* there is no ACCOUNTING for tastes; EVERY man to his taste.

TASTES differ

□ **1803** J. DAVIS *Travels in USA* ii. Tastes sometimes differ. **1868** W. COLLINS *Moonstone* I. xv. Tastes differ. ..I never saw a marine landscape that I admired less. **1924** H. DE SELINCOURT *Cricket Match* iii. It's no use arguing about that. ..Tastes differ. **1940** 'J. J. CONNINGTON' *Four Defences* xii. Tastes differ. One has to admit it. **1974**

'M. INNES' *Appleby's Other Story* xi. She seemed as alive as an electric eel, and no more comfortable for the purpose of making passes at. But tastes of course differ. ■ **idiosyncrasy; taste**

tattered *see* there's many a GOOD cock come out of a tattered bag.

tax *see* NOTHING is certain but death and taxes.

You can't TEACH an old dog new tricks

□ **1530** J. FITZHERBERT *Husbandry* (ed. 2) G1^v The dogge must lerne it when he is a whelpe, or els it wyl not be; for it is harde to make an olde dogge to stoupe. **1636** W. CAMDEN *Remains concerning Britain* (ed. 5) 300 It is hard to teach an old dog trickes. **1672** W. WALKER *English & Latin Proverbs* 46 An old dog will learn no new tricks. **1806** J. RANDOLPH *Letter* 15 Feb. (1834)14 There is an old proverb, 'You cannot teach an old dog new tricks.' **1987** J. HIGGINS *Little Death Music* v. He's listening to records with Vance. Downright rude, if you ask me, but you can't teach an old dog new tricks. **2002** *Times* 18 May 5 If ever there was a teacher who gave the lie to the proverb about old dogs and new tricks it is 89-year-old Donald Turner, whose classes on subjects as wide-ranging as line dancing and geography have left pupils asking for more. ■ **habit; innovation; old age**

Don't TEACH your grandmother to suck eggs

A caution against offering advice to someone wiser and more experienced than oneself. The metaphorical phrase *to teach one's grandmother* (*to suck eggs*) is also found.

□ **1707** J. STEVENS tr. *Quevedo's Comical Works* IV. 403 You would have me teach my Grandame to suck Eggs. **1738** SWIFT *Polite Conversation* i. 57 'I'll mend it, Miss.' .. 'You mend it! go, Teach your Grannam to suck Eggs.' **1882** BLACKMORE *Christowell* II. iii. A .. twinkle, which might have been interpreted—'instruct your grandfather in the suction of gallinaceous products'. **1967** RIDOUT & WITTING *English Proverbs Explained* 48 Don't teach your grandmother to suck eggs. **2000** S. BOOTH *Black Dog* xxvii. 433 Hitchens was really warming up now. 'Teaching your grandmother to suck eggs' was an expression that sprang to the DCI's mind. ■ **advice**

teach *see also* he who CAN, does.

teacher *see* EXPERIENCE is the best teacher.

teeth *see* the GODS send nuts to those who have no teeth.

TELL the truth and shame the Devil

□ **1548** W. PATTEN *Expedition into Scotland* A5 An Epigram .. the whiche I had, or rather (to saie truth and shame the deuel, for out it wool) I stale .. from a frende of myne. **1576** G. GASCOIGNE *Grief of Joy* II. 555 I will tell trewth, the devyll hymselfe to shame. **1597–8** SHAKESPEARE *Henry IV, Pt 1* III. i. 58 And I can teach thee, coz [cousin], to shame the devil By telling truth: tell truth, and shame the devil. **1639** J. CLARKE *Parœmiologia Anglo-Latina* 316 Tell the truth, and shame the Devill. **1738** SWIFT *Polite Conversation* i. 93 Well; but who was your Author? Come, tell Truth and shame the Devil. **1945** F. THOMPSON *Lark Rise* xiv. A few homely precepts, such as .. 'Tell the truth and shame the devil.' **2000** V. McDERMID *Place of Execution* III. iii. 255 'Questions are no trouble to me,' she snapped. 'Tell truth and shame the devil. I've nothing to fear from your questions, so ask away.' ■ **truth**

tell *see also* BLOOD will tell; you can't tell a BOOK by its cover; CHILDREN and fools tell the truth; DEAD men tell no tales; every PICTURE tells a story; STRAWS tell which way the wind blows; never tell TALES out of school; TIME will tell.

telling *see* a TALE never loses in the telling.

temper *see* GOD tempers the wind to the shorn lamb.

ten *see* one PICTURE is worth ten thousand words.

thaw *see* ROBIN Hood could brave all weathers but a thaw wind.

themselves *see* GOD helps them that help themselves; LISTENERS never hear any good of themselves.

thick *see* YORKSHIRE born and Yorkshire bred, strong in the arm and weak in the head.

thicker *see* BLOOD is thicker than water.

Set a THIEF to catch a thief

Cf. CALLIMACHUS *Epigram* xliii. *φωρὸς δ' ἴχνια φὼρ ἔμαθον*, being a thief myself I recognized the tracks of a thief.

□ **1654** E. GAYTON *Pleasant Notes upon Don Quixote* IV. ii. As they say, set a fool to catch a fool; a Proverb not of that gravity (as the Spaniards are), but very usefull and proper. **1665** R. HOWARD *Four New Plays* 74 According to the old saying, Set a Thief to catch a Thief. **1812** M. EDGEWORTH *Tales of Fashionable Life* VI. 446 'You have all your life been evading the laws. ..Do you think this has qualified you peculiarly for being a guardian of the laws?' Sir Terence replied, 'Yes, sure, set a thief to catch a thief is no bad maxim.' **2002** *Washington Times* 13 Jan. A9 A pickpocket specialist with the Washington Metro Transit Police Department says it may take a thief to catch a thief, but cops who are trained to think like crooks can do just as well. ■ **guile; wrong-doers**

thief *see also* HANG a thief when he's young, and he'll no' steal when he's old; there is HONOUR among thieves; the more LAWS, the more thieves and bandits; LITTLE thieves are hanged, but great ones escape; OPPORTUNITY makes a thief; a POSTERN door makes a thief; PROCRASTINATION is the thief of time; if there were no RECEIVERS, there would be no thieves.

When THIEVES fall out, honest men come by their own

□ **1546** J. HEYWOOD *Dialogue of Proverbs* II. ix. L1 And olde folke vnderstood, Whan theues fall out, true men come to their good, Which is not alwaie true. *a* **1640** DAY & CHETTLE *Blind Beggar* (1659) IV. G2ᵛ Here's the old Proverb right, When false Theeves fall out, true men come to their own. **1681** S. COLVIL *Whigs' Supplication* II. 53 When thieves reckon, it's oft-times known That honest people get their own. **1838** A. JACKSON *Letter* 26 Mar. in *Correspondence* (1931) V. 545 You must recollect the old adage, 'When rogues fall out, truth is revealed, and honest men get justice.' **1866** C. KINGSLEY *Hereward the Wake* XV. The rogues have fallen out, and honest men may come by their own. **1980** M. BABSON *Queue here for Murder* xiii. 'She's pretty tied up with that Arab fellow, isn't she? They seem thick as thieves.' 'But thieves fall out.'.. 'You're a disgraceful old matchmaker!' ■ **honesty and dishonesty; wrong-doers**

If a THING'S worth doing, it's worth doing well

Job is sometimes used instead of *thing*.

□ **1746** CHESTERFIELD *Letter* 9 Oct. (1932) III. 783 Care and application are necessary. ..In truth, whatever is worth doing at all is worth doing well. **1910** G. K. CHESTERTON *What's Wrong with World* IV. xiv. The elegant female, drooping her ringlets over her water-colours,.. was maintaining the prime truth of woman, the universal mother: that if a thing is worth doing, it is worth doing badly. **1915** H. G. WELLS *Bealby* V. 'If a thing's worth doing at all,' said the professor.. 'it's worth doing well.' **1980** *Church Times* 22 Feb. 12 'Things worth doing are worth doing well,' was the motto at my first school. **1992** A. LAMBERT *Rather English Marriage* (1993) iii. 62 She'd never cared for dripdry, ..she'd rather see everything starched and crisply ironed. 'If a job's worth doing, it's worth doing well' was Gracie's motto. **2002** *Washington Times* 11 Mar. B5 Children should learn the value of completing tasks properly. The old saying, 'A job worth doing is worth doing well,' holds true. ■ **work**

thing *see also* ALL good things must come to an end; ALL things are possible with God; ALL things come to those who wait; BAD things come in threes; the BEST things come in small packages; the BEST things in life are free; FACTS are stubborn things; FIRST things first; there's no such thing as a FREE lunch; GIVE a thing, and take a thing, to wear the Devil's gold ring; KEEP a thing seven years and you'll always find a use for it; LITTLE things please little minds; there is MEASURE in all things; MODERATION in all things; things PAST cannot be recalled; to the PURE all things are pure; THREE things are not to be trusted; you can have TOO much of a good thing; if you WANT a thing done well, do it yourself; the WORTH of a thing is what it will bring.

When THINGS are at the worst they begin to mend

□ **1582** G. WHETSTONE *Heptameron of Civil Discourses* vi. Thinges when they are at the worst, begin again to amend. The Feauer giueth place to health, when he hath brought the pacyent to deathes door. **1600** *Sir John Oldcastle* H1ᵛ Patience good madame, things at worst will mend. **1623** J. WEBSTER *Duchess of Malfi* IV. i. Things being at the worst, begin to mend. **1748** RICHARDSON *Clarissa* III. liv. When things are at the worst they must mend. **1889** GISSING *Nether World* I. ii. When things are at the worst they begin to mend. ..It can't be much longer before he gets work. **1928** M. SUMMERS *Vampire* V. If there be any truth in the old adage, that 'When things are at the worst they must amend,' the bettering of Spectral Melodrama is not distant. ■ **optimism**

THINK first and speak afterwards

□ **1557** R. EDGEWORTH *Sermons* B6 Thinke well and thou shalt speak wel. **1623** W. PAINTER *Chaucer New Painted* B1ᵛ Thinke twise, then speak, the old Prouerbe doth say. Yet Fooles their bolts will quickely shoot away. **1639** J. CLARKE *Parœmiologia Anglo-Latina* 133 First thinke and then speak. **1640** R. BRATHWAIT *Art asleep Husband?* vii. You thinke twice before you speake, and may be demanded twice before you answer. **1855** H. G. BOHN *Hand-Book of Proverbs* 528 Think to-day and speak to-morrow. **1902** E. HUBBARD in *Philistine* May 192 Think twice before you speak and then talk to yourself. **1943** L. I. WILDER *Happy Golden Years* i. You must do your thinking first and speak afterward. If you will.. do that, you will not have any trouble. **1981** P. O'DONNELL *Xanadu Talisman* iv. Please think before you speak. ■ **discretion; tact**

think *see also* EVIL to him who evil thinks; GREAT minds think alike; what MANCHESTER says today, the rest of England says tomorrow.

THIRD time lucky

□ *c* **1840** R. BROWNING *Letter* (1933) 5 'The luck of the third adventure' is proverbial. **1862** A. HISLOP *Proverbs of Scotland* 194 The third time's lucky. **1882** R. L. STEVENSON *New Arabian Nights* II. 59 'The next time we come to blows—' 'Will make the third,' I interrupted. .. 'Ay, true. .. Well, the third time's lucky.' **1942** N. MARSH *Death & Dancing Footman* vii. It was a glancing blow. .. It might have been my head. .. One of them's saying to himself: 'Third time lucky.' **1993** 'C. AIRD' 'Slight of Hand' in *Injury Time* (1995) 62 'And after the second time,' murmured the Commander into his drink, 'he said he hoped it would be a case of third time lucky.' ■ **luck; superstition**

The THIRD time pays for all

□ **1574** J. HIGGINS *Mirror for Magistrates* (1946) 93 The third payes home, this prouerbe is to true. **1599** *Warning for Fair Women* E3 The third time payes for all. **1855** GASKELL *North & South* I. xvii. 'This is th' third strike I've seen,' said she.. 'Well, third time pays for all.' **1922** *Punch* 20 Dec. 594 Mrs. Ellison has already been twice married. The third time pays for all, so they say. **1978** S. KING *Stand* III. liv. If I could have brought myself to jump once.. I might not be here. Well, last time pays for all. ■ **perseverance; superstition**

third *see also* while TWO dogs are fighting for a bone, a third runs away with it.

Thomas *see* on SAINT Thomas the Divine kill all turkeys, geese, and swine.

thorn *see* beware of an OAK, it draws the stroke; no ROSE without a thorn.

THOUGHT is free

□ *c* **1390** GOWER *Confessio Amantis* V. 4485 I have herd seid that thoght is fre. **1601** SHAKESPEARE *Twelfth Night* I. iii. 64 Fair lady, do you think you have fools in hand?—Now, sir, thought is free. **1874** G. MACDONALD *Malcolm* II. xvii. 'How do you come to think of such things?' 'Thought's free, my lord.' ■ **opinions**

thought *see also* FIRST thoughts are best; SECOND thoughts are best; the WISH is father to the thought.

thousand *see* one PICTURE is worth ten thousand words.

THREATENED men live long

Cf. early 14th-cent. Fr. *le[s] menaciez encore vivent*, threatened men live long.

□ **1534** LADY E. WHEATHELL in M. St. C. Byrne *Lisle Letters* II. ii. Ther es a nolde sayeng thretend men lyue long. *c* **1555** in H. L. Collman *Ballads of Elizabethan Period* (1912) 69 It is a true prouerbe: the threatned man lyues long. **1607** T. HEYWOOD *Fair Maid of Exchange* II. 68 Threatened men live long. **1655** T. FULLER *Church Hist. Britain* VIII. iii. Gardiner.. vowed.. to stop the sending of all supplies unto them. .. But threatned folke live long. **1865** G. W. THORNBURY *Haunted London* ii. Temple Bar was doomed to destruction by the City as early as 1790. .. 'Threatened men live long.' .. Temple Bar still stands. **1930** A. CHRISTIE *Murder at Vicarage* iv. Archer.. is vowing vengeance against me, I hear. Impudent scoundrel. Threatened men live long, as the saying goes. **1980** L. EGAN *Hunters & Hunted* i. The threat was an old one; and, the proverb ran, threatened men live long. ■ **mortality; peril**

THREE may keep a secret, if two of them are dead

□ **1546** J. HEYWOOD *Dialogue of Proverbs* II. v. G4[v] We twayne are one to many (quoth I) for men saie, Three maie keepe a counsell, if two be awaie. *c* **1595**

SHAKESPEARE *Romeo & Juliet* II. iv. 190 Is your man secret? Did you ne'er hear say Two may keep counsel, putting one away? **1735** B. FRANKLIN *Poor Richard's Almanack* (July) Three may keep a secret, if two of them are dead. **1979** D. CLARK *Heberden's Seat* ii. Two of everything..two bodies, two causes of death. ..What was it? 'Three may keep a secret, if two of them are dead.' ■ **concealment; discretion**

THREE removals are as bad as a fire

□ **1758** B. FRANKLIN *Poor Richard's Almanack* (Preface) I never saw an oft removed Tree, Nor yet an oft removed Family, That throve so well, as those that settled be. And again, Three Removes are as bad as a Fire. **1839** DICKENS *Letter* 14 Nov. (1965) I. 602 Did you ever 'move'?..There is an old proverb that three removes are as bad as a fire. **1931** E. PEARSON in *Liberty* 5 Sept. 28 Mr. Small's historians have traced at least six removals from place to place after he left his native Portland, and by reckoning 'three moves as bad as a fire'..you may estimate the extent of his misfortune. **1999** *Washington Post* 17 Sept. E12 In terms of general disruption, it's been said that two moves equal one fire. But unlike fires, moves can be planned and budgeted. ■ **change**

THREE things are not to be trusted: a cow's horn, a dog's tooth, and a horse's hoof

Cf. 13th-cent. Fr. *dent de chael, pé de cheval, cul d'enfant ne sunt pas a crere*, a dog's tooth, a horse's hoof, and a baby's bottom are not to be trusted.

□ *c* **1383** JOHN OF FORDUN *Scotichronicon* (1759) II. XIV. xxxii. Till horsis fote thou never traist, Till hondis tooth, no womans faith. **1585** S. ROBSON *Choice of Change* K2 Trust not 3 things. Dogs teeth. Horses feete. Womens Protestations. **1910** P. W. JOYCE *English as We speak it in Ireland* 110 Three things are not to be trusted—a cow's horn, a dog's tooth and a horse's hoof. **1948** T. H. WHITE *Elephant & Kangaroo* xiii. He was..beginning to worry about being employed by a venomous Englishman. 'Four things not to trust,' said the Cashelmor proverb: 'a dog's tooth, a horse's hoof, a cow's horn, and an Englishman's laugh.' ■ **caution; trust and scepticism**

three *see also* BAD things come in threes; two BOYS are half a boy, and three boys are no boy at all; from CLOGS to clogs is only three generations; one ENGLISHMAN can beat three Frenchmen; FISH and guests smell after three days; it takes three GENERATIONS to make a gentleman; from SHIRTSLEEVES to shirtsleeves in three generations; TWO is company, but three is none

THRIFT is a great revenue

Cf. CICERO *Paradox* 49 *non intellegunt homines quam magnum vectigal sit parsimonia*, men do not realize how great a revenue thrift is.

□ **1659** J. HOWELL *Proverbs* (French) 15 Parsimony is the best revenue. **1855** H. G. BOHN *Hand-Book of Proverbs* 530 Thrift is a good revenue. **1930** *Times* 10 Oct. 13 Thrift..is not only a great virtue but also 'a great revenue'. ■ **thrift**

He that will THRIVE must first ask his wife

□ *a* **1500** in R. L. Greene *Early English Carols* (1935 276 Hym that cast hym for to thryve, he must ask leve of his wyff. *c* **1549** J. HEYWOOD *Dialogue of Proverbs* I. xi. B8v He that will thryue, must aske leaue of his wyfe. *a* **1790** B. FRANKLIN *Autobiography* (1905) I. 324 He that would thrive, must ask his wife. It was lucky for me that I had one as much dispos'd to industry and frugality as myself. **1875** S. SMILES

Thrift viii. There is an old English proverb which says, 'He that would thrive must first ask his wife.' ■ **wives and husbands**

thrive *see also* ILL gotten goods never thrive; if you want to LIVE and thrive, let the spider run alive.

Don't THROW out your dirty water until you get in fresh

□ *c* **1475** in *Modern Philology* (1940) XXXVIII. 121 He ys a fole that castith a-way his olde water or he have new. **1623** W. PAINTER *Palace of Pleasure* C4ᵛ The wise prouerbe wish all men to saue Their foule water vntill they fayrer haue. **1710** S. PALMER *Proverbs* 89 Don't throw away Dirty Water till you have got Clean. . . The Man being possess'd with Avarice, throws away a Certain Benefit upon uncertain . . Expectations. **1842** S. LOVER *Handy Andy* xxix. 'I'll change my clothes.' . . 'You had better wait. . . You know the old saying, "Don't throw out your dirty wather until you get in fresh."' **1911** G. B. SHAW *Fanny's First Play* III. 208 Dont you throw out dirty water til you get in fresh. Dont get too big for your boots. **1986** M. SLUNG *More Momilies* 67 Don't throw out dirty water until you have clean. ■ **innovation**

Don't THROW the baby out with the bathwater

The proverb is often used allusively, especially in the metaphorical phrase *to throw* (or *empty*) *out the baby with the bathwater*. Known in German from at least as early as the start of the sixteenth century; cf. **1610** J. KEPLER *Tertius Interveniens* (sub-heading) *Das ist Warnung . . das sie . . nicht das Kindt mit dem Badt ausschütten*, this is a caution . . lest you throw out the baby with the bath.

□ **1853** CARLYLE *Nigger Question* (ed. 2) 29 The Germans say, 'You must empty out the bathing-tub, but not the baby along with it.' . . How to abolish the abuses of slavery, and save the precious thing in it: also, I do not pretend that this is easy. **1911** G. B. SHAW *Getting Married* (Preface) 186 We shall in a very literal sense empty the baby out with the bath by abolishing an institution [marriage] which needs nothing more than a little . . rationalizing to make it . . useful. **1979** J. P. YOUNG *Art of Learning to Manage* 91 Do be careful that you don't throw the baby out with the bath water, and find yourself with too many people who lack experience. **2002** *Times* 9 Apr. 22 So let reform and trimming continue; but don't throw the baby out with the bathwater. ■ **prudence**

throw *see also* throw DIRT enough, and some will stick; those who live in GLASS houses shouldn't throw stones; do not throw PEARLS to swine.

Thursday *see* Monday's CHILD is fair of face.

thyself *see* KNOW thyself; PHYSICIAN, heal thyself.

thysen (yourself): *see* HEAR all, see all, say nowt.

tide *see* a RISING tide lifts all boats; TIME and tide wait for no man.

tiger *see* BETTER to live one day as a tiger . .; he who RIDES a tiger is afraid to dismount.

There is a TIME and place for everything

An expanded version of *there is a* TIME *for everything*.

□ **1509** A. BARCLAY *Ship of Fools* 94 Remember: there is tyme and place for euery thynge. **1862** G. BORROW *Wild Wales* II. x. There is a time and place for everything, and sometimes the warmest admirer of ale would prefer the lymph of the hill-side fountain to the choicest ale. **1986** 'C. AIRD' *Dead Liberty* iv. A memory from

A Midsummer Night's Dream to do with Snout serving the office of a wall welled up in Sloan's mind, but he suppressed it instantly. There was a time and a place for everything. ■ **opportunity; orderliness; time**

TIME and tide wait for no man

□ *c* **1390** CHAUCER *Clerk's Tale* l. 118 For thogh we slepe or wake, or rome, or ryde, Ay fleeth the tyme; it nil no [will no] man abyde. *a* **1520** *Everyman* (1961) l. 143 The Tyde abydeth no man. **1592** R. GREENE *Disputation between He Cony-catcher & She Cony-catcher* X. 241 Tyde nor time tarrieth no man. **1639** J. CLARKE *Parœmiologia Anglo-Latina* 233 Time and tide tary on no man. **1767** 'A. BARTON' *Disappointment* II. i. Let's step into the state-room, and turn in: Time and tide waits for no one. **1822** SCOTT *Nigel* III. ii. Come, come, master, let us get afloat. . . Time and tide wait for no man. **2002** *Washington Post* 10 Mar. SC11 (*Family Circus comic strip*) Time and tide wait for no man. 'And a school bus waits for no boy.' ■ **opportunity; time**

TIME flies

Cf. L. *tempus fugit*, time flies.

□ *c* **1390** CHAUCER *Clerk's Tale* l. 118 For though we slepe or wake, or rome, or ryde, Ay fleeth the tyme. **1639** J. CLARKE *Parœmiologia Anglo-Latina* 308 Time flyeth away without delay. **1776** J. W. FLETCHER *Letter* 21 Mar. in *Works* (1803) IX. 197 Time flies! Years of plenty. . disappear before the eternity to which we are all hastening. **2002** *Washington Post* 29 Mar. C9 (*Classic Peanuts comic strip*) 'Quick, Marcie, I need the answer to the third question!' 'There is no third question, sir. . we did that test last week. . .' 'Time flies when you're having fun.' ■ **time**

There is a TIME for everything

With allusion to ECCLESIASTES iii. 1 (AV) To every thing there is a season.

□ *c* **1390** CHAUCER *Clerk's Prologue* l. 6 But Salomon seith 'every thyng hath tyme'. **1540** CRANMER *Bible* (Prologue) +3 Ther is tyme for euery thynge. **1590** SHAKESPEARE *Comedy of Errors* II. ii. 63 Well, sir, learn to jest in good time; there's time for all things. **1818** J. AUSTEN *Northanger Abbey* xxx. Your head runs too much upon Bath; but there is a time for every thing—a time for balls. . and a time for work. **1980** 'M. INNES' *Going It Alone* I. x. There is a time for everything, and he hoped that, in the present exigency, Tim wasn't going to be. . frivolous. ■ **opportunity; time**

TIME is a great healer

There are numerous expressions derived from the ancient concept that time heals, several of which are illustrated here. Predominantly used in the context of feelings and emotions rather than physical suffering. Cf. MENANDER *Fragments* dclxxvii. (Kock) *πάντων ἰατρὸς τῶν ἀναγκαίων κακῶν χρόνος ἐστίν*, time is the healer of all necessary evils.

□ *c* **1385** CHAUCER *Troilus & Criseyde* v. 350 As tyme hem [them] hurt, a tyme doth hem cure. **1591** J. HARINGTON tr. *Ariosto's Orlando Furioso* VI. ii. He hurt the wound which time perhaps had healed, weening [thinking] with greater sinne the lesse to mend. **1622** H. PEACHAM *Complete Gentleman* iv. Time, the Phisition of all. **1837** DISRAELI *Henrietta Temple* III. VI. ix. Time is the great physician. **1926** G. B. SHAW *Translations & Tomfooleries* 60 Time is the great healer. **1942** A. CHRISTIE *Body in Library* viii. He had a terrible shock and loss. . . But Time, as my dear mother used to say, is a great healer. **2001** *Washington Times* 23 Sept. C17 Time is the greatest of healers, and during the next few weeks, sports again will provide us with a much-needed respite from our everyday worries. ■ **time**

TIME is money

Gr. *τὸ πολυτελέστατον .. ἀνάλωμα, τὸν χρόνον*, the most costly outlay is time (attributed to Antiphon).

□ **1572** T. WILSON *Discourse upon Usury* 33 They saye tyme is precious. **1748** B. FRANKLIN *Papers* (1961) III. 306 Remember that Time is Money. He that can earn Ten Shillings a Day.. and.. sits idle one half of that Day.. has really.. thrown away Five Shillings. **1840** BULWER-LYTTON *Money* III. vi. 'You don't come often to the club, Stout?'.. 'No, time is money.' **1980** H. R. F. KEATING *Murder of Maharajah* xv. I can't wait here day after day. .. Time's money, you know. **2002** *Washington Times* 2 Feb. A11 When a quarterback is chosen as the Most Valuable Player in the National Football League for the second time in three years, time is money. He can rake in big bucks for appearing in ads, and he can also do his bit for charity by appearing in a United Way commercial. ■ **efficiency and inefficiency; time**

No TIME like the present

□ **1562** G. LEGH *Accidence of Armoury* 225^V Mary [to be sure] sir no time better then euen now. **1696** M. MANLEY *Lost Lover* IV. i. No time like the present. **1888** M. OLIPHANT *Second Son* I. iv. 'If you were a-passing this way, sir, some time in the morning—.' 'There's no time like the present,' answered Roger. **2000** 'G. WILLIAMS' *Dr. Mortimer and Aldgate Mystery* (2001) i. 7 '..I was thinking in terms of an immediate start..' 'Oh, capital!' the doctor exclaimed. ..'No time like the present, hey?' ■ **opportunity; time**

TIME will tell

Cf. MENANDER *Monosticha* 11 *ἄγει δὲ πρὸς φῶς τὴν ἀλήθειαν χρόνος*, time brings the truth to light.

□ **1539** R. TAVERNER tr. *Erasmus' Adages* 37 *Tempus omnia reuelat*. Tyme discloseth all thynges. **1616** T. DRAXE *Adages* 205 Time reuealeth all things. **1771** C. STUART *Letter* 15 Apr. in *Publications of Mississippi Hist. Society* (1925) V. 50 Time only will shew how far those Informations have been well founded. **1863** C. READE *Hard Cash* I. vi. I will answer.. that she will speak as distinctly to music as you do in conversation—Time will show, madam. **1913** E. H. PORTER *Pollyanna* xxiii. The doctor had looked very grave.. and had said that time alone could tell. **1929** 'J. J. CONNINGTON' *Eye in Museum* xiv. 'I'm not.. bringing any charge.'.. 'Oh.. a bright idea, perhaps. Or perhaps not so bright.' 'Time will tell,' the Superintendent retorted. **2002** *New Scientist* 30 Mar. 7 'But if you look at the general principles, it's a wonderful system,' says Richard Mulligan.. 'Time will tell.' ■ **future; time**

TIME works wonders

□ **1588** A. MARTEN *Exhortation to defend Country* F2 You.. thinke that time will worke wonders, though you your selves follow your owne pleasures. **1815** BYRON *Letter* 7 Jan. (1975) IV. 252 Time does wonders. **1845** D. W. JERROLD (*title*) Time works wonders. **1872** G. J. WHYTE-MELVILLE *Satanella* II. xxiv. 'I want you to like me.'.. 'They say time works wonders.. and I feel I shall.' **1982** R. DAVIES *Rebel Angels* 4 But there was time, and I was to be in his outer room, constantly under his eye. Time works wonders. ■ **time**

time *see also* there is always a FIRST time; NEVER is a long time; OTHER times, other manners; PARSLEY seed goes nine times to the Devil; PROCRASTINATION is the thief of time; one STEP at a time; a STITCH in time saves nine; THIRD time lucky; the THIRD time pays for all; WORK expands so as to fill the time available.

TIMES change and we with time

Cf. L. *omnia* (also *tempora*) *mutantur nos et mutamur in illis*, all things (*also* times) are changing and we with them (attributed to Lothar I, Holy Roman Emperor 840–55).

□ **1578** LYLY *Euphues* I. 276 The tymes are chaunged as Ouid sayeth, and wee are chaunged in the times. **1666** G. TORRIANO *Italian Proverbs* 281 Times change, and we with them. ..The Latin says the same, *Tempora mutantur, et nos mutamur in illis*. **1943** C. MILBURN *Diary* 21 Feb. (1979) 168 In English cities the Red Flag has been flown. ..Times change indeed, and we with time. **1981** J. BINGHAM *Brock* 31 Times were changing and Melford with them. ■ **circumstances; innovation**

tinker *see* if IFS and ands were pots and pans, there'd be no work for tinkers' hands.

TODAY you; tomorrow me

Cf. L. *hodie mihi, cras tibi*, today it is my turn, tomorrow yours.

□ *a* **1250** *Ancrene Wisse* (1962) 143 *Ille hodie, ego cras.* He to dei, and ich to marhen [he today, and I tomorrow]. **1620** T. SHELTON tr. *Cervantes' Don Quixote* II. lxv. To day for thee, and to-morrow for me. **1855** C. KINGSLEY *Westward Ho!* II. i. To-day to thee, to-morrow to me. **1906** A. CONAN DOYLE *Sir Nigel* xv. 'It is the custom of the Narrow Seas,' said they: 'To-day for them; to-morrow for us.' **1929** A. W. WHEEN tr. *E. M. Remarque's All Quiet on Western Front* ix. 'Comrade,' I say to the dead man, but I say it calmly, 'To-day you, to-morrow me.' ■ **future**

today *see also* JAM tomorrow and jam yesterday, but never jam today; what MANCHESTER says today, the rest of England says tomorrow; never PUT off till tomorrow what you can do today.

told *see* one STORY is good till another is told.

Tom *see* MORE people know Tom Fool than Tom Fool knows.

TOMORROW is another day

□ *c* **1527** J. RASTELL *Calisto & Melebea* C1^V Well mother to morrow is a new day. **1603** J. FLORIO tr. *Montaigne's Essays* II. iv. A letter..beeing delivered him..at supper, he deferred the opening of it, pronouncing this by-word. To morrow is a new day. **1824** SCOTT *St. Ronan's Well* III. vii. We will say no more of it at present. ..To-morrow is a new day. **1927** P. GREEN *Field God* I. 148 Go to it, you Mag and Lonie! To-morrow's another day, and you'll need all you can hold. **2001** K. HALL PAGE *Body in Moonlight* vii. 127 'Maybe tomorrow,' Faith said, trying to turn the corners of her mouth up. 'Tomorrow's another day.' ■ **future**

TOMORROW never comes

□ **1523** LD. BERNERS *Froissart* (1901) II. 309 It was sayde every day among them, we shall fight tomorowe, the whiche day came never. **1602** J. CHAMBERLAIN *Letter* 8 May (1939) I. 142 Tomorrow comes not yet. **1678** J. RAY *English Proverbs* (ed. 2) 343 Tomorrow come never. **1756** B. FRANKLIN *Poor Richard's Almanack* (July) To-morrow, every Fault is to be amended; but that To-morrow never comes. **1889** GISSING *Nether World* III. ix. 'It's probably as well for you that *to-morrow* never comes.' 'Now just see how things turn out!' went on the other. **2001** *Washington Post* 27 Mar. C11 (*Jeff MacNelly's Shoe comic strip*) 'They say tomorrow never comes.' 'I sure hope so. That's when I have a math test.' ■ **future; procrastination**

tomorrow *see also* EAT, drink, and be merry, for tomorrow we die; JAM tomorrow and jam yesterday, but never jam today; what MANCHESTER says today, the rest of England says tomorrow; never PUT off till tomorrow what you can do today; TODAY you, tomorrow me.

The TONGUE always returns to the sore tooth

□ **1586** G. PETTIE tr. *S. Guazzo's Civil Conversation* (1925) II. 201 The tongue rolles there where the tooth aketh. **1659** J. HOWELL *Proverbs* (Spanish) 27 There the tongue goes where the tooth akes. **1746** B. FRANKLIN *Poor Richard's Almanack* (July) The Tongue is ever turning to the aching tooth. **1817** J. K. PAULDING *Letters from South* II. 167 The tongue touches where the tooth aches, as the saying goes; the English of which is that people are apt to talk of what annoys them most at the moment. **1949** W. KRASNER *Walk Dark Streets* ii. He would stop.. to find the flaws in his case were standing over him, implacable, like the certainty of guilt. The tongue always returned to the sore tooth. **1985** K. S. ROBINSON in G. Dozois *Isaac Asimov's Mars* (1991) 155 In the same way that a tongue will go to a sore tooth over and over, Roger finds himself following Hans and Arthus to hear the areologist's explanation. ■ **persistence**

tongue *see also* the DEVIL makes his Christmas pies of lawyers' tongues and clerks' fingers; a STILL tongue makes a wise head.

TOO many cooks spoil the broth

□ **1575** ?J. HOOKER *Life of Carew* (1857) 33 There is the proverb, the more cooks the worse potage. **1662** B. GERBIER *Principles of Building* 24 When.. an undertaking hath been committed to many, it caused but confusion, and therefore it is a saying.. Too many Cooks spoils the Broth. *c* **1805** J. AUSTEN *Watsons* (1972) VI. 318 She professes to keep her own counsel. .. 'Too many Cooks spoil the Broth.' **1855** C. KINGSLEY *Westward Ho!* II. vii. As Amyas sagely remarked, 'Too many cooks spoil the broth, and half-a-dozen gentlemen aboard one ship are as bad as two kings of Brentford.' **1979** *Guardian* 7 Nov. 6 It was a great mistake to think that administration was improved by taking on more administrators. .. 'Too many cooks spoil the broth.' **1997** *Times* 8 Aug. 25 Too many cooks spoil the broth and at Apple there is now the equivalent of Marco Pierre White, Anton Mosimann and Nico Ladenis. ■ **assistance; busybodies; work**

You can have TOO much of good thing

□ **1483** B. BURGH *Cato* in *Archiv* (1905) CXV. 313 To much is nouht of any maner thyng [too much of anything is nothing]. **1546** J. HEYWOOD *Dialogue of Proverbs* II. iv. G4[v] Well (quoth I) to muche of one thyng is not good, Leaue of this. **1611** R. COTGRAVE *Dict. French & English* s.v. Manger, A man may take too much of a good thing. **1738** SWIFT *Polite Conversation* i. 77 Fie, Miss! you said that once before; and, you know, Too much of one Thing is good for nothing. **1906** CHESTERTON *Charles Dickens* iv. We believe that you can have too much of a good thing—a blasphemous belief, which at one blow wrecks all the heavens that men have hoped for. **1985** *Washington Post* 2 Mar. A18 A more modestly sized delegation.. might have spared Congress a certain ridicule. Mae West once said it was possible to have too much of a good thing and it was wonderful. **1995** *Washington Times* 25 Apr. A17 Modern liberals feel that a more tolerant society is good thing, and they are right. Yet, it is possible to have too much of a good thing. ■ **excess; good things**

tool *see* a BAD workman blames his tools.

tooth *see* the TONGUE always returns to the sore tooth.

top *see* there is always ROOM at the top.

touch *see* if you gently touch a NETTLE it'll sting you for your pains.

He that TOUCHES pitch shall be defiled

Cf. APOCRYPHA *Ecclesiasticus* xiii. 1 (AV) He that toucheth pitch, shall be defiled therewith.

□ **1303** R. BRUNNE *Handlyng Synne* (EETS) l. 6578 Who-so handlyth pycche wellyng hote, He shal haue fylthe therof sumdeyl [in some degree]. **1578** LYLY *Euphues* I. 250 He that toucheth pitche shall be defiled. **1710** S. PALMER *Proverbs* 249 Touch Pitch and you'll be Defil'd. ..There is Danger every Way in Ill Company. **1886** H. CONWAY *Living or Dead* II. ix. The next two months of my life..made me take a lower and more debased view of the world. ..I was touching pitch, yet striving to keep myself from being defiled. **1979** *Listener* 13 Sept. 345 The makers of the series believe that those who meddle with pitch may be defiled. ■ **associates; example, good and bad**

tough *see* when the GOING gets tough, the tough get going.

town *see* GOD made the country, and man made the town.

TRADE follows the flag

□ **1870** J. A. FROUDE in *Fraser's Magazine* Jan. 4 The removal of a million poor creatures to Canada and the establishment of them there..would probably have turned out..a profitable investment. Trade follows the flag. **1945** R. HARGREAVES *Enemy at Gate* 152 There is a glib saying..that 'trade follows the flag'; an apophthegm that succeeds in putting the cart before the horse with greater aplomb than almost any other cant phrase in common use. **1979** in C. Allen *Tales from Dark Continent* i. There is a famous old quotation that 'Trade follows the Flag' but..in West Africa..the reverse was true. ■ **business**

trade *see also* EVERY man to his trade; JACK of all trades and master of none; there are TRICKS in every trade; TWO of a trade never agree.

transplant *see* you cannot SHIFT an old tree without it dying.

TRAVEL broadens the mind

□ **1911** 'SAKI' 'Way to Dairy' in *Chronicles of Clovis* (*Short Stories of Saki*, 1958) 195 'Travel enlarges the mind, my dear Christine,' said her aunt. 'Yes, dear aunt, travel undertaken in the right spirit,' agreed Christine; 'but travel pursued merely as a means towards gambling and extravagant living is more likely to contract the purse than to enlarge the mind.' **1929** G. K. CHESTERTON *Poet & Lunatics* iii. He may be a trifle cracked,..but that's only because his travels have been too much for his intellect. They say travel broadens the mind; but you must have the mind. **1949** N. STREATFEILD *Painted Garden* iii. Foreign travel broadens the mind..and a broadened mind helps all art. **1969** 'E. LATHEN' *When in Greece* xvii. 'The Americans we have met compare very favorably with most other nationals.' Travel, after all, can broaden only so many minds. **1981** C. KING *Commonplace Book* 22 It has so truly been said that travel—anywhere—broadens the mind. **1997** *Times* 24 Dec. 14 The past may be a foreign country through which we travel as strangers. But travel still broadens the mind. ■ **experience; travel**

travel (verb) *see* BAD news travels fast; it is BETTER to travel hopefully than to arrive.

He TRAVELS fastest who travels alone

Cf. **1854** H. D. THOREAU *Walden* 78 The man who goes alone can start today; but he who travels with another must wait till that other is ready.

□ **1888** R. KIPLING *Story of Gadsby* (1889) 94 Down to Gehenna, or up to the Throne, He travels fastest who travels alone. **1921** E. WAUGH *Journal* 19 June in *Diaries* (1979) 129 Hale's gone already. I suppose he will have to. 'He travels fastest who travels alone' anyway. **1989** F. KING *Reflections in Jaundiced Eye* iv. The reason I can 'do what I do' is because I've never married. He travels fastest who travels alone, and that goes double for she. ■ **efficiency and ineffiency**; **independence**; **travel**

tread *see* FOOLS rush in where angels fear to tread.

As a TREE falls, so shall it lie

One must not change long-established beliefs, etc., in the face of death. With allusion to ECCLESIASTES xi. 3 (AV) If the tree fall toward the South, or toward the North, in the place where the tree falleth, there it shall be.

□ **1549** H. LATIMER *Seven Sermons* IV. M3[v] Wheresoeuer the tre falleth..there it shall reste. **1578** LYLY *Euphues* I. 308 Where the tree falleth there it lyeth..and every ones deathes daye is his domes day. **1678** J. RAY *English Proverbs* (ed. 2) 296 As a man lives so shall he die, As a tree falls so shall it lie. **1836** M. SCOTT *Cruise of Midge* II. ii. It is of no use. ..As the tree falls, so must it lie—it is a part of my creed. **1937** 'F. HEDLEY' *Cavalier of Crime* x. 130 'No use trying to account for the vagaries of fate, is it, Inspector? Where the tree falleth, there shall it lie.' ■ **death**; **fate and fatalism**

The TREE is known by its fruit

With allusion to MATTHEW xii. 33 (AV) The tree is known by his fruit.

□ **1528** W. TYNDALE *Obedience of Christian Man* 88[v] Judge the tre by his frute, and not by his leves. **1597–8** SHAKESPEARE *Henry IV, Pt. 1* II. iv. 414 If then the tree may be known by the fruit..there is virtue in that Falstaff. **1670** J. RAY *English Proverbs* 11 A tree is known by the fruit, and not by the leaves. **1896** J. A. FROUDE *Council of Trent* iv. Lutherans said the tree is known by its fruit. Teach a pure faith, and abuses will disappear. **1928** D. H. LAWRENCE *Lady Chatterley's Lover* iv. The mental life..[is] rooted in spite and envy. ..Ye shall know the tree by its fruit. **1955** S. N. GHOSE *Flame of Forest* I. 15 'I never judge a man by his mask.' 'A tree should be judged by its fruits,' Myna responded. ■ **appearance**; **human nature**

tree *see also* the APPLE never falls far from the tree; he that would EAT the fruit must climb the tree; you cannot SHIFT an old tree without it dying; as the TWIG is bent, so is the tree inclined; WALNUTS and pears you plant for your heirs; a WOMAN, a dog, and a walnut tree, the more you beat them the better they be.

trick *see* you can't TEACH an old dog new tricks.

There are TRICKS in every trade

□ **1632** M. PARKER (*title*) Knavery in all Trades. **1654** *Mercurius Fumigosus* 12–19 July 49 If there be not Knavery in All Trades, I shrewdly am mistaken. **1692** R. L'ESTRANGE *Fables of Aesop* clxxxiii. Jupiter appointed Mercury to make him a Composition of Fraud and Hypocrisie, and to give Every Artificer his Dose on't. ..Mercury..gave the Taylors the Whole Quantity that was Left; and from hence comes the Old Saying, There's Knavery in All Trades, but Most in Taylors. **1857** E. BENNETT *Border Rover* vi. 'I would be willing to swear you had bewitched this rifle.'..'Thar's tricks to all trades 'cept ourn.' **1978** L. BLOCK *Burglar in Closet* xvii.

You age them [bills, paper money]..by cooking them with a little coffee—well, there are tricks in every trade—and I don't..know some of the ones the counterfeiters have come up with. **1987** S. STEWART *Lifting the Latch* 87 'Theer's a trick in every trade,' he was fond of saying, 'bar besom[broom]-making, and the biggest stick goes in the middle theer.' ■ **business; trades and skills**

A TROUBLE shared is a trouble halved

□ **1931** D. L. SAYERS *Five Red Herrings* ix. 'Unbosom yourself,' said Wimsey. 'Trouble shared is trouble halved.' **1966** A. CARTER *Shadow Dance* viii. He found he wanted to share the experience of the previous night with Edna (a trouble shared is a trouble halved). **1987** C. GRAHAM *Killings at Badger's Drift* 7 She had never felt more keenly the truth of the saying 'a trouble shared is a trouble halved'. But she had lived in a small village long enough to know that what she had discovered could safely be discussed with no one. **2002** *Times* 18 Mar. 12 Thorpe's estranged wife,..acting under the principle of a problem shared is a problem halved, wanted 'the truth to come out'. ■ **trouble**

Never TROUBLE trouble till trouble troubles you

□ **1884** *Folk-Lore Journal* II. 280 Never trouble trouble, till trouble troubles you. **1945** 'D. B. OLSEN' *Cats don't Smile* i. Never trouble trouble until trouble troubles you. I always wondered: what then? **1983** *Good Housekeeping* Oct. 75 Talking of proverbs, there is an old Yorkshire saying: never trouble trouble, till trouble troubles thee. To which I would add the rider: and when it does trouble thee, keep it to thyself. **2002** *Spectator* 20 July 31 He was a master of procrastination or of misunderstanding what he had been told to do. 'Never trouble trouble until trouble troubles you': that was Junor's maxim where Beaverbrook was concerned. ■ **trouble**

trouble (noun) *see also* do not MEET troubles halfway; NEEDLES and pins,..when a man marries, his trouble begins.

Many a TRUE word is spoken in jest

□ *c* **1390** CHAUCER *Monk's Prologue* l. 1964 Be nat wrooth, my lord, though that I pleye. Ful ofte in game a sooth [truth] I have herd seye! *a* **1628** J. CARMICHAELL *Proverbs in Scots* no. 1099 Manie suith word said in bourding [jesting]. *c* **1665** in *Roxburghe Ballads* (1890) VII. 366 Many a true word hath been spoke in jest. **1738** SWIFT *Polite Conversation* I. iii. 'I did a very foolish thing yesterday.'.. 'They say, many a true Word's spoken in Jest.' **1898** G. B. SHAW *Widower's Houses* I. in *Plays Pleasant & Unpleasant* I. 10 There actually are Johannis churches here..as well as Apollinaris ones. ..There is many a true word spoken in jest. **1979** D. LESSING *Shikasta* 356 By the time we have finished I expect we shall have a dozen or more [children]. ..Many a true word is spoken in jest. ■ **truth**

true *see also* the COURSE of true love never did run smooth; what EVERYBODY says must be true; MORNING dreams come true; what is NEW cannot be true; if something SOUNDS too good to be true, it probably is.

Put your TRUST in God, and keep your powder dry

Advice attributed to Oliver Cromwell (see quot. 1834), combining spiritual exhortation with the practical measure of making sure that one's gunpowder is kept serviceable. The second half of the saying is often used allusively in the phrase *to keep one's powder dry*.

□ **1834** COLONEL BLACKER *Oliver's Advice* in E. Hayes *Ballads of Ireland* (1856) I. 192 Put your trust in God, my boys, and keep your powder dry. **1856** E. HAYES *Ballads of*

Ireland (ed. 2) I. 191 Cromwell . . when his troops were about crossing a river . . concluded an address . . with these words—'put your trust in God; but mind to keep your powder dry.' **1908** *Times Literary Supplement* 6 Nov. 383 In thus keeping his powder dry the bishop acted most wisely, though he himself ascribes the happy result entirely to the observance of the other half of Cromwell's maxim. **1979** V. CANNING *Satan Sampler* iv. God . . created us for a better end. . . We must put our trust in Him and keep our powder dry. ■ **prudence; self-help**

There is TRUTH in wine

Cf. Gr. *ἐν οἴνῳ ἀλήθεια*, there is truth in wine (attributed to the 6th-cent. BC lyric poet Alcaeus); L. *in vino veritas*. The Latin version, used in Erasmus' *Adages*, is widely known and perhaps more frequently used than the English proverb.

□ **1545** R. TAVERNER tr. *Erasmus' Adages* (ed. 2) H5[v] In wyne is trouthe. **1659** T. PECKE *Parnassi Puerperium* 5 Grant but the Adage true, that Truth's in wine. **1869** TROLLOPE *He knew He was Right* II. li. There is no saying truer than that . . there is truth in wine. Wine . . has the merit of forcing a man to show his true colours. **1934** R. GRAVES *Claudius the God* ix. The man who made the proverb 'There's truth in wine' must have been pretty well soaked when he made it. **2002** P. LOVESEY *Diamond Dust* xi. 87 He was trying to decide if the man was capable of coherent answers. *In vino veritas* is a maxim reliable only up to a certain intake of the vino. ■ **drunkenness; truth**

TRUTH is the first casualty of war

The originator of this saying is sometimes said to be Hiram Johnson, addressing the US Senate in 1918, but it does not occur in the record of the relevant speech.

□ **1928** A. PONSONBY *Falsehood in Wartime* (*epigraph*) When war is declared, Truth is the first casualty. **1975** P. KNIGHTLEY (title) The First Casualty: the war correspondent as hero, propagandist, and myth maker from the Crimea to Vietnam **1992** *English Today* Jan. 48/1 In war, the first casualty is language. . . It was the 'pacification' of Gaul by Julius Caesar, not the brutal and bloody subjugation of Gaul. **1998** *Independent* 12 June I. 29/1 If truth is the first casualty of war then words are the first to be crocked in the World Cup. **2002** *Consumer Reports* Feb. 62 We've all heard that truth is the first casualty of war. Still, it was surprising how fast the victim expired after the terrorist attacks of Sept. 11. By the 12th, Internet watchdogs were already warning against online frauds. ■ **truth; warfare**

TRUTH is stranger than fiction

Similar to FACT *is stranger than fiction*.

□ **1823** BYRON *Don Juan* XIV. ci. Truth is always strange, Stranger than Fiction. **1863** C. READE *Hard Cash* II. xv. Sampson was greatly struck with the revelation: he . . said truth was stranger than fiction. **1905** G. K. CHESTERTON *Club of Queer Trades* 133 'Do you believe that truth is stranger than fiction?' 'Truth must of necessity be stranger than fiction,' said Basil placidly. 'For fiction is the creation of the human mind, and therefore congenial to it.' **2001** *Washington Post* 25 June C2 There are times when truth is indeed stranger than fiction, when the teller of true tales can report things that we would dismiss as preposterous inventions should a novelist try to put them over on us. ■ **reality and illusion**

TRUTH lies at the bottom of a well

Cf. Gr. *ἐτεῇ δὲ οὐδὲν ἴσμεν, ἐν βυθῷ γάρ ἡ ἀλήθεια*, we know nothing certainly, for truth lies in the deep (attributed to Democritus); LACTANTIUS *Institutiones Divinae* III. xxviii. *in puteo . . veritatem iacere demersam*, truth lies sunk in a well.

□ **1562** J. WIGAND *De Neutralibus* G6^V The truth lyeth yet still drowned in the depe. **1578** H. WOTTON tr. *J. Iver's Courtly Controversy* 90 I shall conduct you..vnto the Mansion where the truth so long hidden dothe inhabite, the which sage Democritus searched in the bottom of a well. *a* **1721** M. PRIOR *Dialogues of Dead* (1907) 225 You know the Antient Philosophers said Truth lay at the bottom of a Well. **1887** J. R. LOWELL *Democracy* 30 Truth..is said to lie at the bottom of a well. *c* **1943** J. CORBETT *Murder minus Motive* xii. Truth..is reputed to reside at the bottom of a well. I've often conned that old saw over to myself, and..its originators must have meant that truth is often damned hard to discern. **2001** *Times 2* 31 Oct. 12 Truth may be found at the bottom of the well, but there was no well in London deep enough for that commodity. ■ **concealment; truth**

TRUTH makes the Devil blush

Perhaps a variant of TELL *the truth and shame the Devil.*

□ **1944** 'A. GILBERT' *Death at Door* (1945) viii. 81 Crook caught back a quick exclamation. Truth may make the devil blush but that doesn't mean the devil doesn't frequently get the best of it. **1955** H. KEMP *Death of Dwarf* ix. 82 'So I shall not break my rule: never to say a thing about anybody until I'm sure it's true, and not always then. *Truth makes the devil blush.* That's true enough; but if it turns out not to be the truth after all, it only sets him giggling.' ■ **truth**

TRUTH will out

Similar in form to MURDER *will out.*

□ **1439** LYDGATE *Life of St. Alban* (1974) 203 Trouthe wil out. ..Ryghtwysnesse may nat ben hid. **1596** SHAKESPEARE *Merchant of Venice* II. ii. 73 Truth will come to light; murder cannot be hid long; a man's son may, but in the end truth will out. **1822** M. EDGEWORTH *Letter* 17 Jan. (1971) 324 Whether about a novel or a murder the truth will out. **2001** *Spectator* 17 Nov. 35 It has just been announced that the EU is to hold its own public inquiry into the [foot-and-mouth] epidemic, in Strasbourg next year. At last, perhaps, truth will out. ■ **concealment; truth**

truth *see also* CHILDREN and fools tell the truth; the GREATER the truth, the greater the libel; HALF the truth is often a whole lie; a LIE is halfway round the world; TELL the truth and shame the Devil.

try *see* you never KNOW what you can do till you try; if at first you don't SUCCEED, try, try, try, again.

Every TUB must stand on its own bottom

A proverb advocating independence and initiative.

□ **1564** W. BULLEIN *Dialogue against Fever* 48^V Let euery Fatte [vat] stande vpon his owne bottome. **1639** J. CLARKE *Parœmiologia Anglo-Latina* 66 Every tub must stand on his owne bottome. **1721** C. CIBBER *Refusal* v. 721 I have nothing to do with that. ..Let every Tub stand on its own Bottom. **1948** F. THOMPSON *Still glides Stream* iv. 'Every tub must stand on its own bottom,' was one of his homely ways of expressing the individual independence desirable in children. **1994** H. N. THOMAS *Spirits in Dark* xviii. 214 I know the Old Testament tell us that the sins o' the fathers get visited on the children, but yo' mustn' have a hand in that. Let 'every tub must sit 'pon its own bottom.' ■ **independence**

Tuesday *see* Monday's CHILD is fair of face.

tug *see* when GREEK meets Greek, then comes the tug of war.

tune *see* why should the DEVIL have all the best tunes?; a DRIPPING June sets all in tune; when the FURZE is in bloom, my love's in tune; there's many a GOOD tune played on an old fiddle; he that LIVES in hope dances to an ill tune; he who PAYS the piper calls the tune.

TURKEY, heresy, hops, and beer came into England all in one year

□ **1599** H. BUTTES *Diet's Dry Dinner* G4 I know not how it happened (as he merrily saith) that herisie and beere came hopping into England both in a yeere. **1643** R. BAKER *Chronicle* Henry VIII 66 About [1524] .. it happened that divers things were newly brought into England, whereupon this Rime was made: 'Turke[y]s, Carps, Hoppes, Piccarell [young pike], and Beere, Came into England all in one yeere.' **1906** R. KIPLING *Puck of Pook's Hill* 235 We say—'Turkey, Heresy, Hops, and Beer Came into England all in one year.' **1979** *Observer* 16 Dec. 56 'Turkeys, heresies, hops and beer All came to England in the one year' says the rhyme, but the Romans gave us hops. ■ **innovation**

turkey *see also* on SAINT Thomas the Divine kill all turkeys, geese, and swine.

TURN about is fair play

□ **1755** *Life of Captain Dudley Bradstreet* 338 Hitherto honest Men were kept from shuffling the Cards, because they would cast knaves out from the Company of Kings, but we would make them know, Turn about was fair Play. **1854** SURTEES *Handley Cross* xviii. 'Turn about is fair play,' as the devil said to the smoke-jack [an apparatus for turning a roasting spit]. **1986** J. SMITH *Tourist Trap* xi. 'And if you hear anything about Les, you'll let me know, won't you?' 'I'll be glad to. But turn-about's fair play—if *you* hear something, will you let me know?' **2002** *Washington Times* 10 Apr. A16 And let's not forget: Turnabout is fair play. If we let the IRS impose U.S. tax laws on foreign banks, what's to stop foreign tax collectors from seeking to impose their laws on U.S. banks? ■ **fair dealing**

turn *see also* (noun) one GOOD turn deserves another; (verb) a BAD penny always turns up; CLERGYMEN's sons always turn out badly; even a WORM will turn.

turneth *see* a SOFT answer turneth away wrath.

turning *see* it is a LONG lane that has no turning.

twelve *see* it is not SPRING until you can plant your foot upon twelve daisies.

twice *see* FOOL me once, shame on you; fool me twice, shame on me; he GIVES twice who gives quickly; LIGHTNING never strikes the same place twice; ONCE bitten, twice shy; OPPORTUNITY never knocks twice at any man's door.

As the TWIG is bent, so is the tree inclined

Cf. **1530** J. PALSGRAVE *L'éclaircissement de la Langue Française* 161 A man may bende a wande [shoot] while it is grene [pliant] and make it strayght though it be neuer so croked.

□ **1732** POPE *Epistles to Several Persons* I. 102 'Tis Education forms the common mind, Just as the Twig is bent, the Tree's inclined. **1818** T. G. FESSENDEN *Ladies Monitor* 75 ' 'Tis education forms the tender mind, Just as the twig is bent the tree's inclined.' This hacknied adage, not more trite than true. **1940** P. MCGINLEY *Primary Education* in *Pocketful of Wry* 16 As bends the twig, thus grows the el-em .. So, twice a month, we're bound to sell 'em The doctrine of Impartial Minds. **1979** 'C. AIRD' *Some die Eloquent* viii. 'Nature, not nurture?' murmured the biologist. .. 'As the twig is bent,' Sloan came back. **1996** *National Review* 9 Dec. 63 Older, bigger children defend their privileges, while younger kids try to subvert the status quo. As the twig is bent, so grows the tree. ■ **children; human nature; nature and nurture**

TWO blacks don't make a white

Similar to TWO *wrongs don't make a right.*

□ **1721** J. KELLY *Scottish Proverbs* 321 Two Blacks make no White. An Answer to them who, being blam'd, say others have done as ill or worse. **1822** SCOTT *Letter* 14 Mar (1934) VII. 96 To try whether I cannot contradict the old proverb of 'Two blackies [Lockhart *Life*: blacks] not making a white'. **1882** A. AINGER *Charles Lamb* vii. As two blacks do not make a white, it was beside the mark to make laborious fun over Southey's youthful ballads. **1932** G. B. SHAW *Adventures of Black Girl* 28 Never forget that two blacks do not make a white. **1966** A. E. LINDOP *I start Counting* viii. 'What's the modern murderer got to fear?.. They'll only go to prison.'.. 'Two blacks don't make a white.' ■ **good and evil**

While TWO dogs are fighting for a bone, a third runs away with it

□ *c* **1386** CHAUCER *Knight's Tale* l. 1177 We stryve as dide the houndes for the boon. .. Ther cam a kyte, whil that they were so wrothe, And baar awey the boon betwixe hem bothe. **1534** MORE *Dialogue of Comfort* (1553) I Aiii^v Now strive there twain for vs, our lord send the grace, that the thyrde dog cary not awaie the bone from them both. **1639** J. CLARKE *Parœmiologia Anglo-Latina* 94 Two dogs strive for a bone, and the third runs away with it. **1784** *Gazette of State of S. Carolina* 17 July 2 Verifying the coarse proverb, while two dogs are fighting for a bone, a third comes and runs away with it. **1983** *Practical Computing* June 5 While the major companies continue to argue among themselves they are in a poor position to police the rest of the industry. When two alsatians are fighting over a large bone, a passing poodle can easily walk off with it. ■ **opportunity, taken**

TWO heads are better than one

Similar to FOUR *eyes see more than two*. Quot. 2001 relies on a slang use of *head* to mean 'lavatory'.

□ *c* **1390** GOWER *Confessio Amantis* I. 1021 Tuo han more wit then on. **1530** J. PALSGRAVE *L'éclaircissement de la Langue Française* 269 Two wyttes be farre better than one. **1546** J. HEYWOOD *Dialogue of Proverbs* I. ix. C2^v But of these two thynges he wolde determyne none Without ayde. For two hedds are better than one. **1778** S. FOOTE *Nabob* I. 5 Here comes brother Thomas; two heads are better than one; let us take his opinion. **1979** J. RATHBONE *Eurokillers* xviii. Two heads are better than one. .. I'd value your advice. **2001** *Washington Post* 14 July C12 (*Jeff MacNelly's Shoe comic strip*) 'Roz is having another restroom installed here.' 'Then it's true. Two heads are better than one.' ■ **assistance**

TWO is company, but three is none

The alternative ending is *three's a crowd.*

□ **1706** J. STEVENS *Spanish & English Dict.* s.v. Compañia, A Company consisting of three is worth nothing. It is the Spanish Opinion, who say that to keep a Secret three are too many, and to be Merry they are too few. **1860** T. C. HALIBURTON *Season Ticket* viii. Three is a very inconvenient limitation, constituting, according to an old adage, 'no company'. **1869** W. C. HAZLITT *English Proverbs* 442 Two is company, but three is none. **1944** *Modern Language Notes* LIX. 517 Two's company, three's a crowd. **1979** J. LEASOR *Love & Land Beyond* viii. Two's company and three's none, so one of the three has been taken out of the game. **2002** *Washington Post* 10

Mar. SC11 (*Family Circus comic strip*) Two's company, three's a crowd. ''Specially on a tandem bike.' ■ **friends**

TWO of a trade never agree

□ **1630** DEKKER *Second Part of Honest Whore* II. 154 It is a common rule, and 'tis most true, Two of one trade never loue. **1673** E. RAVENSCROFT *Careless Lovers* A2v Two of a Trade can seldome agree. **1727** GAY *Fables* I. xxi. In every age and clime we see, Two of a trade can ne'er agree. **1887** G. MEREDITH *Poems* (1978) I. 148 Two of a trade, lass, never agree! Parson and Doctor!—don't they love rarely, Fighting the devil in other men's fields! **1914** 'SAKI' *Beasts & Super-Beasts* 96 The snorts and snarls.. went far to support the truth of the old saying that two of a trade never agree. **1981** E. LONGFORD *Queen Mother* vii. There is an old adage, 'Two of a kind never agree.' ■ **quarrelsomeness; similarity and dissimilarity; trades and skills**

If TWO ride on a horse, one must ride behind

□ **1598–9** SHAKESPEARE *Much Ado about Nothing* III. v. 34 An two men ride of a horse, one must ride behind. *c* **1628** J. SMYTH *Berkeley MSS* (1885) III. 32 If two ride upon an horse one must sit behinde; meaninge, That in each contention one must take the [defeat]. **1874** G. J. WHYTE-MELVILLE *Uncle John* I. x. There is an old adage.. 'When two ride on a horse, one must ride behind.' **1942** V. RATH *Posted for Murder* VI. iii. There comes a point when you are very exasperating. ..'When two ride on one horse, one must ride behind.' But I'm getting off for a while. **1986** A. CLARKE *Mystery Lady* (1988) iv. Collaboration on a book is an awkward business. If two people ride one horse, one of them must ride behind. ■ **co-operation**

There are TWO sides to every question

Cf. PROTAGORAS *Aphorism* (in Diogenes Laertius *Protagoras* IX. li.) *καὶ πρῶτος ἔφη* [Protagoras] *δύο λόγους εἶναι περὶ παντὸς πράγματος ἀντικειμένους ἀλλήλοις*, Protagoras was the first to say that there are two sides to every question, one opposed to the other.

□ **1802** J. ADAMS *Autobiography* (1966) III. 269 There were two Sides to a question. **1817** T. JEFFERSON *Letter* 5 May in L. J. Cappon *Adams–Jefferson Letters* (1959) II. 513 Men of energy of character must have enemies: because there are two sides to every question, and.. those who take the other will of course be hostile. **1863** C. KINGSLEY *Water Babies* vi. Let them recollect this, that there are two sides to every question, and a downhill as well as an uphill road. **1957** E. SITWELL *Letter* in V. Glendinning *Edith Sitwell* (1981) xxviii. It's more than platitudinous to say that there are two sides to every question but there is something to be said on both sides. **1971** C. FITZGIBBON *Red Hand* iii. From the English point of view which inevitably they have applied to.. Ireland, the art of politics consists in realizing that there are two sides to every question. ■ **fair dealing**

It takes TWO to make a bargain

□ **1597** BACON *Colours of Good & Euill* x. 68 The seconde worde makes the bargaine. **1598** *Mucedorus* B2 Nay, soft, sir, tow words to a bargaine, *a* **1637** MIDDLETON et al. *Widow* v. i. There's two words to a bargain ever.. and if love be one, I'm sure money's the other. **1766** GOLDSMITH *Vicar of Wakefield* II. xii. 'Hold, hold, Sir,' cried Jenkinson, 'there are two words to that bargain.' **1943** M. FLAVIN *Journey in Dark* iv. Takes two to make a bargain, and you both done mighty wrong. **1973** E. McGIRR *Bardel's Murder* iv. My father was in skins and he had to carry a life-preserver, they got so nasty. *Caveat emptor*, he used to say, it taking two to make a bargain. ■ **buying and selling**

It takes TWO to make a quarrel

□ **1706** J. STEVENS *Spanish & English Dict.* s.v. Barajar, When one will not, two do not Quarrel. **1732** T. FULLER *Gnomologia* no. 4942 There must be two at least to a Quarrel. **1859** H. KINGSLEY *Geoffrey Hamlyn* II. xiii. It takes two to make a quarrel, Cecil, and I will not be one. **1979** *Times* 3 Dec. 13 If it were not for the truism that it takes at least two to make a quarrel, the French and the Germans.. could fairly claim that the fault lay wholly with the United Kingdom. ■ **anger, quarrelsomeness**

It takes TWO to tango

Probably based on earlier sayings of the *it takes two to*.. form (see above). Sung by Pearl Bailey, the Hoffman and Manning song (quot. 1952) was a worldwide hit, giving this saying instant international currency.

□ **1952** HOFFMAN & MANNING *Takes Two to Tango (song-title)* 2 There are lots of things you can do alone! But, takes two to tango. **1965** *Listener* 24 June 923 As for negotiation.. the President has a firm, and melancholy, conviction: it takes two to tango. **1991** *Times* 22 May 14 Remember. It only takes two to tango, and neither of them has to be you. **1999** *Bella* 25 May 16/2 Deep down, I know it takes two to tango and the blame should lie with them equally. ■ **co-operation**

TWO wrongs don't make a right

Similar to TWO *blacks don't make a white*.

□ **1783** B. RUSH *Letter* 2 Aug. (1951) I. 308 Three wrongs will not make one right. **1814** J. KERR *Several Trials of David Barclay* 249 Two wrongs don't make one right. **1905** S. WEYMAN *Starvecrow Farm* xxiv. He ought to see this!.. After all, two wrongs don't make a right. **1991** *Washington Post* 26 Apr. Even in law school, two wrongs don't make a right. **2002** *Washington Times* 30 Jan. A16 Moreover, in the Austrian view, two wrongs don't make a right. The central bank cannot undo its mistakes by reversing course. ■ **good and evil**

two *see also* BETTER one house spoiled than two; BETWEEN two stools one falls to the ground; a BIRD in the hand is worth two in the bush; two BOYS are half a boy, and three boys are no boy at all; of two EVILS choose the less; FOUR eyes see more than two; one HOUR's sleep before midnight is worth two after; NO man can serve two masters; ONE for sorrow, two for mirth; if you can't RIDE two horses at once, you shouldn't be in the circus; if you RUN after two hares you will catch neither; THREE may keep a secret, if two of them are dead; one VOLUNTEER is worth two pressed men.

undone *see* what's DONE cannot be undone.

The UNEXPECTED always happens

Similar to NOTHING *is certain but the unforeseen.* Cf. PLAUTUS *Mostellaria* I. iii. 197 *insperata accidunt magi' saepe quam quae speres*, unexpected things happen more often than those you hope for.

□ **1885** E. J. HARDY *How to be Happy though Married* xxv. A woman may have much theoretical knowledge, but this will not prevent unlooked-for obstacles from arising. . . It is the unexpected that constantly happens. **1909** *Times Weekly* 12 Nov. 732 No place in the world is more familiar than the House of Commons with 'the unforeseen that always happens'. **1938** E. WAUGH *Scoop* I. iii. Have nothing which in a case of emergency you cannot carry in your own hands. But remember that the unexpected always happens. **1977** L. J. PETER *Peter's Quotations* 296 Peter's Law—The unexpected always happens. ■ **certainty and uncertainty**; **foresight and hindsight**

unforeseen *see* NOTHING is certain but the unforeseen.

UNION is strength

Unity is a popular alternative for *union*, especially when used as a trade-union slogan. Cf. HOMER *Iliad* XIII. 237 *συμφερτὴ δ᾽ἀρετὴ πέλει ἀνδρῶν καὶ μάλα λυγρῶν*, even weak men have strength in unity; L. *vis unita fortior*, force united is stronger; *c* **1527** T. BERTHELET tr. *Erasmus' Sayings of Wise Men* A4v Concorde maketh those thynges that are weake, mighty and stronge.

□ **1654** R. WILLIAMS *Complete Writings* (1963) VI. 280 Union strengthens. **1837** in D. Porter *Early Negro Writing* (1971) 228 In Union is strength. **1848** S. ROBINSON *Letter* 29 Dec. in *Indiana Hist. Collections* (1936) XXII. 178 'Union is strength,' and that is the only kind that can control the floods of such a 'great father of rivers [the Mississippi]'. **1877** E. WALFORD *Tales of Great Families* I. 264 The prosperity of the House of Rothschild [is due to] the unity which has attended the co-partnership of its members, . . a fresh example of the saying that 'union is strength'. **1933** H. ADAMS *Strange Murder of Hatton* xxix. Union is strength. We, by pooling our resources, . . are able . . to secure a steady income. **1981** E. AGRY *Assault Force* ix. This unfortunate misunderstanding; we must clear it up. . . After all, unity is strength. ■ **strength and weakness**; **unity and division**

UNITED we stand, divided we fall

□ **1768** J. DICKINSON *Liberty Song* in *Boston Gazette* 18 July Then join Hand in Hand brave Americans all, By uniting we stand, by dividing we fall. **1849** G. P. MORRIS *Flag of our Union* in *Poems* (1853) 41 'United we stand—divided we fall!'—It made and preserves a nation! **1894** J. JACOBS *Fables of Aesop* 122 Then Lion attacked them one by one and soon made an end of all four [oxen]. United we stand, divided we fall. **2002** *Times 2* 13 June 7 Threatened . . , mocked . . , hounded . . , the churches—or at least, their more enlightened leaders—are belatedly moving towards the view that 'united we might just stand, but divided we most certainly fall'. ■ **unity and division**

unity *see* UNION is strength.

unlucky *see* LUCKY at cards, unlucky in love.

unpunished *see* no GOOD deed goes unpunished.

What goes UP must come down

Originally associated with wartime bombing and anti-aircraft shrapnel.

□ **1929** F. A. POTTLE *Stretchers* vii. The antiaircraft guns always took a shot for luck. What goes up must come down, and one can be killed quite as neatly by a fragment of his own shrapnel as by the enemy's. **1949** N. MAILER *Naked & Dead* III. vi. Gravity would occupy the place of mortality (what goes up must come down). **1967** F. J. SINGER *Epigrams at Large* 57 'What goes up, must come down' is really a time-worn statement which wore out after the Venus and Mars probes. **2001** *Washington Post* 7 Sept. B1 What goes up must come down, even 26 years later. And the aged Russian rocket that came down just before dawn yesterday did so with a glowing, protracted brilliance that startled the early birds who saw it from New York to North Carolina. ■ **fate and fatalism**

up *see also* up like a ROCKET, down like a stick.

upright *see* EMPTY sacks will never stand upright.

use *see* KEEP a thing seven years and you'll always find a use for it.

vacuum *see* NATURE abhors a vacuum.

vain *see* in vain the NET is spread in the sight of the bird.

valet *see* NO man is a hero to his valet.

valour *see* DISCRETION is the better part of valour.

VARIETY is the spice of life

Cf. EURIPIDES *Orestes* 234 *μεταβολὴ πάντων γλυκύ*, a change is always nice.

□ **1785** COWPER *Task* II. 76 Variety's the very spice of life, That gives it all its flavour. **1854** 'M. LANGDON' *Ida May* vi. Take all de wives you can get,—bariety am de spite of life. **1954** 'M. COST' *Invitation from Minerva* 174 'Your signal is different from ours?' .. 'Variety is the spice of life,' he retorted. **2002** *Washington Post* 7 Aug. C15 (*Broom Hilda comic strip*) 'I have prepared our annual financial statement.' .. 'Last year you chewed it up and swallowed it.' 'Variety, lads. Spice of life and all that!' ■ **novelty; variety**

varlet *see* an APE's an ape, a varlet's a varlet, though they be clad in silk or scarlet.

vengeance *see* REVENGE is a dish that can be eaten cold.

venture *see* NOTHING venture, nothing gain; NOTHING venture, nothing have.

vessel *see* EMPTY vessels make the most sound.

view *see* DISTANCE lends enchantment to the view.

vinegar *see* HONEY catches more flies than vinegar; from the SWEETEST wine, the tartest vinegar.

VIRTUE is its own reward

Cf. OVID *Ex Ponto* II. iii. *virtutem pretium .. esse sui*, virtue is its own reward.

□ **1509** A. BARCLAY *Ship of Fools* 10[v] Vertue hath no rewarde. **1596** SPENSER *Faerie Queene* III. xii. Your vertue selfe her owne reward shall breed, Euen immortall praise, and glory wyde. **1642** BROWNE *Religio Medici* I. 87 That vertue is her owne reward, is but a cold principle. **1673** DRYDEN *Assignation* III. i. Virtue .. is its own reward: I expect none from you. **1844** DICKENS *Martin Chuzzlewit* xv. It *is* creditable to keep up one's spirits here. Virtue's its own reward. **1988** H. MANTEL *Eight Months on Ghazzah Street* (1989) 19 His patience was not like other people's, a rather feeble virtue, which had, by its nature, to be its own reward. **2002** *Spectator* 12 Jan. 18 Humble people lack self-esteem, and chastity is just another sexual dysfunction. Virtue is not so much its own reward as a condition requiring therapeutic intervention. ■ **just deserts; virtue**

virtue *see also* PATIENCE is a virtue.

visitor *see* FISH and guests smell after three days.

The VOICE of the people is the voice of God

Cf. *a* **804** ALCUIN *Letter* clxiv. in *Works* (1863) I. 438 *solent dicere: vox populi, vox Dei,* they often say: the voice of the people is the voice of God.

□ *c* **1412** T. HOCCLEVE *Regimen of Princes* (EETS) 104 Peples vois is goddes voys, men seyne. **1450** in T. Wright *Political Poems* (1861) II. 227 The voice of the people is the voice of God. **1646** BROWNE *Pseudodoxia Epidemica* I. iii. Though sometimes they are flattered with that Aphorisme, [they] will hardly beleeve the voyce of the people to bee the voyce of God. **1822** C. C. COLTON *Lacon* II. 266 The voice of the People is the voice of God; this axiom has manifold exceptions. **1914** G. B. SHAW *Misalliance* p. lxxii. An experienced demagogue comes along and says, 'Sir: *you* are the dictator: the voice of the people is the voice of God.' **1989** *Washington Post* 24 Mar. C2 I imagine they are fine citizens. After all, we elected them and the voice of the people is the voice of God, remember that. ■ **politics; power; rulers and ruled**

One VOLUNTEER is worth two pressed men

Pressed men were those who were forced into military service.

□ **1705** T. HEARNE *Journal* 31 Oct. in *Remarks & Collections* (1885) I. 62 'Tis s^{d} my Ld Seymour presently after M^{r}. Smith was pronounc'd Speaker, rose up, and told them, Gentlemen; you have got a Low Church man; but pray remember that 100 Voluntiers are better than 200 press'd men. **1834** MARRYAT *Jacob Faithful* I. xiii. 'Shall I give you a song?' 'That's right, Tom; a volunteer's worth two pressed men.' **1837** F. CHAMIER *Arethusa* I. iii. Don't fancy you will be detained against your will; one volunteer is worth two pressed men. **1897** R. KIPLING *Captains Courageous* x. He presumed Harvey might need a body-servant some day or other, and.. was sure that one volunteer was worth five hirelings. **1979** M. M. KAYE *Shadow of Moon* (rev. ed.) iv. The Earl could not be persuaded to send her away. .. In any case, said the Earl, Winter would need a personal maid, and in his opinion one volunteer was worth three pressed men. ■ **co-operation; free will and compulsion**

vomit *see* the DOG returns to his vomit.

wag *see* it is MERRY in hall when beards wag all.

wait *see* ALL things come to those who wait; TIME and tide wait for no man.

waiting *see* it's ILL waiting for dead men's shoes.

We must learn to WALK before we can run

The metaphorical phrase *to run before one can walk* is also common.

□ *c* **1350** *Douce MS 52* no. 116 Fyrst the chylde crepyth and after gooth [walks]. *c* **1450** *Towneley Play of First Shepherds* (EETS) l. 100 Ffyrst must vs crepe and sythen [afterwards] go. **1670** J. RAY *English Proverbs* 75 You must learn to creep before you go. **1794** G. WASHINGTON *Letter* 20 July in *Writings* (1940) XXXIII. 438 We must walk as other countries have done before we can run. **1851** G. BORROW *Lavengro* II. ii. Ambition is a very pretty thing; but sir, we must walk before we run. **1876** J. PLATT *Business* 124 More fail from doing too much than too little. We must learn and be strong enough to walk before we can run. **1947** M. PENN *Manchester Fourteen Miles* xv. Mrs. Winstanley reproved her for being impatient. She pointed out.. that everybody must learn to walk before they could run. **1980** K. AMIS *Russian Hide & Seek* iv. At the moment we can't leave it to the English to do anything. We must learn to walk before we can run. ■ **patience and impatience**

walk *see also* AFTER dinner rest a while, after supper walk a mile.

wall *see* the WEAKEST go to the wall.

WALLS have ears

Similar to FIELDS *have eyes, and woods have ears.*

□ **1575** G. GASCOIGNE *Supposes* I. i. The table.., the portals, yes and the cupbords them selves have eares. **1592** G. DELAMOTHE *French Alphabet* II. 29 The walles may have some eares. ..*Les murailles ont des aureilles.* **1620** T. SHELTON tr. *Cervantes' Don Quixote* II. xlviii. They say Walls haue eares. **1766** D. GARRICK *Neck or Nothing* II. i. Not so fast and so loud, good master of mine—walls have ears. **1822** SCOTT *Nigel* I. vi. It is not good to speak of such things. ..Stone walls have ears. **1958** L. DURRELL *Mountolive* XII. 232 She lay in the silence of a room which had housed (if walls have ears) their most secret deliberations. **2000** J. ALTMAN *Gathering of Spies* v. 91 He realized that Himmler was waiting to gain distance from the house before speaking. Walls had ears, and Nazi walls had more ears than most. ■ **eavesdroppers**

walnut *see* a WOMAN, a dog, and a walnut tree, the more you beat them the better they be.

WALNUTS and pears you plant for your heirs

The idea of 'planting trees for posterity' is much older than the specific references to walnuts and pears. Cf. CICERO *Cato Major* vii. 24 *'serit arbores, quae alteri saeclo prosint,' ut ait Statius noster in Synephebis*, 'he plants trees, which will be of use to another age,' as [Caecilius] Statius says in his *Synephebi.*

□ **1640** G. HERBERT *Outlandish Proverbs* no. 198 The tree that growes slowly, keepes it selfe for another. **1732** T. FULLER *Gnomologia* no. 2401 He who plants a

Walnut-Tree, expects not to eat of the Fruit. **1863** A. SMITH *Dreamthorp* xi. My oaks are but saplings; but what undreamed-of English kings will they not outlive?.. A man does not plant a tree for himself; he plants it for posterity. **1907** W. C. HAZLITT *English Proverbs* 361 Plant pears for your heirs. A proverb which no longer holds true, since pears are now made to yield well after a few years. **1941** C. MACKENZIE *Red Tapeworm* xv. 'Better to plant them promptly,' said Miss Quekett. 'It's only walnuts and pears you plant for your heirs.' ■ **children and parents**

If you WANT a thing done well, do it yourself

Very similar to *if you would be well* SERVED, *serve yourself.*

□ **1541** M. COVERDALE tr. *H. Bullinger's Christian State of Matrimony* xix. If thou wilt prospere, then loke to euery thynge thyne owne self. **1616** T. DRAXE *Adages* 163 If a man will haue his business well done, he must doe it himselfe. **1858** LONGFELLOW *Poems* (1960) 160 That's what I always say; if you want a thing to be well done, You must do it yourself. **1927** *Times* 14 Nov. 15 Lastly there is the illustration of the great principle: if you want a thing done, do it yourself. **1975** 'E. LATHEN' *By Hook or by Crook* xxi. Do you know how I got it done in the end? I went down to Annapolis myself. I always say, if you want a thing done well, do it yourself! **1998** *Times* 20 Jan. 7 After everything that's happened, pregnancy was the last thing on my mind. .. there's a lot to be said for the old adage that if you want a job doing properly, do it yourself. ■ **efficiency and inefficiency; self-help**

For WANT of a nail the shoe was lost; for want of a shoe the horse was lost; and for want of a horse the man was lost

The proverb is found in a number of forms. Cf. late 15th-cent. Fr. *par ung seul clou perd on ung bon cheval*, by just one nail one loses a good horse; *c* **1390** GOWER *Confessio Amantis* v. 4785 For sparinge of a litel cost Fulofte time a man hath lost The large cote for the hod [hood].

□ **1629** T. ADAMS *Works* 714 The French-men haue a military prouerbe, The losse of a nayle, the losse of an army. The want of a nayle looseth the shooe, the losse of shooe troubles the horse, the horse indangereth the rider, the rider breaking his ranke molests the company, so farre as to hazard the whole Army. **1640** G. HERBERT *Outlandish Proverbs* no. 499 For want of a naile the shoe is lost, for want of a shoe the horse is lost, for want of a horse the rider is lost. **1880** S. SMILES *Duty* x. 'Don't care' was the man who was to blame for the well-known catastrophe:—'For want of a nail the shoe was lost, for want of a shoe the horse was lost, and for want of a horse the man was lost.' **1925** S. O'CASEY *Juno & Paycock* I. 16 You bring your long-tailed shovel, an' I'll bring me navvy [device for excavating earth]. We mighten' want them, an', then agen, we might: for want of a nail the shoe was lost, for want of a shoe the horse was lost, an' for want of a horse the man was lost—aw, that's a darlin' proverb, a daarlin'. **1979** M. MCCARTHY *Missionaries & Cannibals* viii. No detail.. was too small to be passed over. .. 'For want of a nail,' as the proverb said. **1995** *National Review* 12 June 10 For want of nail the battle was lost. Well, Republicans may have found just the right nail to win the entitlement battle. ■ **action and consequence; great and small**

If you WANT something done, ask a busy person

The rationale behind this apparent paradox is indicated in quot. 1997.

□ **1984** *Christian Science Monitor* 26 Oct. 38 It means. specifically, that you must banish all idleness; and it also means, in a general way, that if you want something done, you should ask a busy person—like me—to do it. **1997** *Life Association News* Aug. 60 It's the old story: If you want something done, ask a busy person. They know how to manage their time. **1998** *Times* 9 Jan. 33 They do say that if you want something done you should ask a busy person, but there must be limits. ■ **efficiency and inefficiency**

want *see also* (noun) WILFUL waste makes woeful want; (verb) the MORE you get, the more you want; if you want PEACE, you must prepare for war; WASTE not, want not.

WANTON kittens make sober cats

□ **1732** T. FULLER *Gnomologia* no. 5415 Wanton [frolicsome] Kitlins may make sober old Cats. **1832** A. HENDERSON *Scottish Proverbs* 97 Wanton kittens make douce [sedate] cats. **1855** H. G. BOHN *Hand-Book of Proverbs* 551 Wanton kittens may make sober cats. **1975** J. O'FAOLAIN *Women in Wall* I. I was fleshy.. in my youth. Carnal. But wanton kittens make sober cats. ■ **youth**

war *see* COUNCILS of war never fight; all's FAIR in love and war; when GREEK meets Greek, then comes the tug of war; if you want PEACE, you must prepare for war; TRUTH is the first casualty of war.

warling (one who is despised or disliked): *see* BETTER be an old man's darling, than a young man's slave.

warm *see* COLD hands, warm heart.

One does not WASH one's dirty linen in public

It is unwise to publicize private disputes or scandals. The saying is very often used in the metaphorical phrase *to wash one's dirty linen in public*. Cf. Fr. *c'est en famille, ce n'est pas en publique, qu'on lave son linge sale*, one washes one's dirty linen amongst the family, not in public.

□ **1809** T. G. FESSENDEN *Pills* 45 The man has always had a great itch for scribbling, and has mostly been so fortunate as to procure somebody who pitied his ignorance, to 'wash his dirty linen'. **1867** TROLLOPE *Last Chronicle of Barset* II. xliv. I do not like to trouble you with my private affairs;—there is nothing.. so bad as washing one's dirty linen in public. **1886** E. J. HARDY *How to be Happy though Married* i. Married people.. should remember the proverb about the home-washing of soiled linen. **1942** 'P. WENTWORTH' *Danger Point* xlviii. The case.. will be dropped. .. There's nothing to be gained by washing a lot of dirty linen in public. **1980** T. HOLME *Neapolitan Steak* 199 Her look raked him from head to toe. 'One does not wash one's Dirty Linen in Public, commissario.' ■ **discretion**

wash *see also* one HAND washes the other.

WASTE not, want not

Want is variously used in the senses 'lack' and 'desire'. Another proverb making the connection between *waste* and *want* is WILFUL *waste makes woeful want*.

□ **1772** WESLEY *Letter* 10 Aug. (1931) V. 334 he will waste nothing; but he must want nothing. **1872** T. HARDY *Under Greenwood Tree* I. I. viii. Helping her to vegetable she didn't want, and when it had nearly alighted on her plate, taking it across for his own use, on the plea of waste not, want not. **1941** C. MACKENZIE *Red Tapeworm* xxii. 'The lorry's full of children as well as rubbish.'.. 'And what is printed on the banner?'.. 'Waste Not Want Not.' **2002** *Washington Times* 8 Apr. B5 Your cousin was a practical woman. 'Waste not, want not.' ■ **thrift; waste**

waste (noun) *see* HASTE makes waste; WILFUL waste makes woeful want.

A WATCHED pot never boils

□ **1848** GASKELL *Mary Barton* II. xiv. What's the use of watching? A watched pot never boils. **1880** M. E. BRADDON *Cloven Foot* III. viii. Don't you know that vulgar old proverb that says that 'a watched pot never boils'? **1940** C. BOOTHE *Europe in Spring* x. 'He [Mussolini] is waiting to see how the next battle turns out,' they said. . . 'A watched pot never boils,' they said—only this one finally did. **2002** *Washington Post* 26 Apr. C10 (*Born Loser comic strip*) 'Whoever said, "A watched pot never boils" obviously didn't own a microwave.' ■ **patience and impatience**

Don't go near the WATER until you learn how to swim

□ **1855** H. G. BOHN *Hand-Book of Proverbs* 459 Never venture out of your depth till you can swim. **1975** D. BAGLEY *Snow Tiger* xv. 'There I was. . . Over-protected and regarded as a teacher's pet into the bargain.' '"Don't go near the water until you learn how to swim,"' quoted McGill. ■ **prudence**

water *see also* BLOOD is thicker than water; DIRTY water will quench fire; you can take a HORSE to the water, but you can't make him drink; the MILL cannot grind with the water that is past; you never MISS the water till the well runs dry; STILL waters run deep; STOLEN waters are sweet; don't THROW out your dirty water until you get in fresh.

The WAY to a man's heart is through his stomach

□ **1814** J. ADAMS *Letter* 15 Apr. in *Works* (1851) VI. 505 The shortest road to men's hearts is down their throats. **1845** R. FORD *Hand-Book for Travellers in Spain* I. i. The way to many an honest heart lies through the belly. **1857** D. M. MULOCK *John Halifax, Gentleman* xxx. 'Christmas dinners will be much in request.' 'There's a saying that the way to an Englishman's heart is through his stomach.' **1975** A. PRICE *Our Man in Camelot* v. The way to a man's heart wasn't through his stomach, it was through an appreciation of what interested him. **1986** J. W. RIDER *Jersey Tomatoes* xv. What she meant was in a home she could bake things and make meals for him. . . The way to man's heart is through his stomach. **2001** *Washington Post* 6 Jan. C11 (*Piranha Club comic strip*) 'And remember ladies—the way to a man's heart is through his stomach.' 'Unfortunately, you have to get it past his gag reflex first.' ■ **food and drink**

There is more than one WAY to skin a cat

□ **1854** S. SMITH *'Way down East* viii. 166 This is a money digging world of ours and, as it is said, 'there are more ways than one to skin a cat,' so there are more ways than one of digging for money. **1918** W. FAULKNER *Letter* 17 Oct. in J. G. Watson *Thinking of Home* (1992) So you see, there is more than one way to skin a cat. **2001** K. TOPPING *Slayer* (rev. ed.) 232 The Mayor [in a 1999 episode of *Buffy the Vampire Slayer*] knows that the statement 'There's more than one way to skin a cat' is factually accurate. ■ **ways and means**

way *see also* the LONGEST way round is the shortest way home; LOVE will find a way; OTHER times, other manners; STRAWS tell which way the wind blows; a WILFUL man must have his way; where there's a WILL there's a way.

There are more WAYS of killing a cat than choking it with cream

See also the following two entries and *there is more than one* WAY *to skin a cat.*

□ **1839** S. SMITH *John Smith's Letters* 91 There's more ways to kill a cat than one. **1855** C. KINGSLEY *Westward Ho!* II. xii. Hold on yet awhile. More ways of killing a cat than choking her with cream. **1941** 'R. WEST' *Black Lamb* I. 506 Now I see the truth of the old saying that there are more ways of killing a cat than choking it with cream. In Bosnia the Slavs did choke the Turk with cream, they glutted him with their wholesale conversions. . . But here cream just did not come into the question. **1974** T. SHARPE *Porterhouse Blue* ii. I have yet to meet a liberal who can withstand the attrition of prolonged discussion of the inessentials. . . There are more ways of killing a cat than stuffing it with . . ■ **ways and means**

There are more WAYS of killing a dog than choking it with butter

See also the adjacent entries.

□ **1845** W. T. THOMPSON *Chronicles of Pineville* 35 There's more ways to kill a dog besides choking him with butter. **1945** F. THOMPSON *Lark Rise* xvi. A proverb always had to be capped. No one could say, 'There's more ways of killing a dog than hanging it' without being reminded, 'nor of choking it with a pound of fresh butter.' **1955** W. C. MACDONALD *Destination, Danger* x. It [liquor] was a life-saver and I'm much obliged. But you can kill a dog without choking him with butter. ■ **ways and means**

There are more WAYS of killing a dog than hanging it

See also the two preceding entries.

□ **1678** J. RAY *English Proverbs* (ed. 2) 127 There are more ways to kill a dog then hanging. **1721** J. KELLY *Scottish Proverbs* 253 Many ways to kill a Dog, and not to hang him. There be many ways to bring about one and the same Thing, or Business. **1725** SWIFT *Drapier's Letters* X. 165 I know that very homely Proverb, more ways of killing a Dog than hanging him. **1945** F. THOMPSON *Lark Rise* xvi. A proverb always had to be capped. No one could say, 'There's more ways of killing a dog than hanging it' without being reminded, 'nor of choking it with a pound of fresh butter.' ■ **ways and means**

weak *see* YORKSHIRE born and Yorkshire bred, strong in the arm and weak in the head.

The WEAKEST go to the wall

Usually said to derive from the installation of seating (around the walls) in the churches of the late Middle Ages. *To go to the wall* means figuratively 'to succumb in a conflict or struggle'.

□ *a* **1500** *Coventry Plays* (EETS) 47 The weykist gothe eyuer to the walle. *c* **1595** SHAKESPEARE *Romeo & Juliet* I. i. 14 That shows thee a weak slave; for the weakest goes to the wall. **1714** DEFOE (*title*) The weakest go to the wall, or the Dissenters sacrific'd by all parties. **1834** MARRYAT *Peter Simple* I. v. You will be thrashed all day long. . . The weakest always goes to the wall there. **1888** C. M. DOUGHTY *Travels in Arabia Deserta* I. x. There perished many among them; . . it is the weak which go to the wall. **1916** 'J. OXENHAM' *My Lady of Moor* i. He saw to it that I had a good education, . . knowing the necessity and value of it in these strenuous days of the 'weak to the wall'. **1955** T. WARRINER *Doors of Sleep* i. 'As in the early church, the weakest go to the wall,' the Archdeacon said, seating himself on the low parapet. ■ **strength and weakness; winners and losers**

weakest *see also* a CHAIN is no stronger than its weakest link.

wealthy *see* EARLY to bed and early to rise, makes a man healthy, wealthy, and wise.

wear *see* BETTER to wear out than to rust out; if the CAP fits, wear it; CONSTANT dropping wears away a stone; GIVE a thing, and take a thing, to wear the Devil's gold ring; if the SHOE fits, wear it.

weary *see* be the DAY weary or be the day long, at last it ringeth to evensong.

weather *see* there is no such thing as BAD weather, only the wrong clothes; ROBIN Hood could brave all weathers but a thaw wind.

wed *see* BETTER wed over the mixen than over the moor.

One WEDDING brings another

Similar to *one* FUNERAL *makes many*, the idea in this case being that the social gathering of the bride's and groom's families and friends is likely to result in other romantic attachments.

□ **1634** M. PARKER in *Roxburghe Ballads* (1880) III. 54 'Tis said that one wedding produceth another. **1713** GAY *Wife of Bath* I. i. One Wedding, the Proverb says, begets another. **1885** C. H. SPURGEON *Salt-Cellars* I. 88 Bridesmaids may soon be made brides. One wedding.. brings on another. **1929** S. T. WARNER *True Heart* I. 54 Cheer up, Suke! I dare say you'll get a boy in time—they do say one wedding brings another. **1957** A. THIRKELL *Double Affair* i. But when he said 'One marriage always brings on another, Mrs. Hubback,' I slapped his face with a nice bit of cod's tail. ■ **weddings**

WEDLOCK is a padlock

□ **1678** J. RAY *English Proverbs* (ed. 2) 56 Wedlock is a padlock. **1821** BYRON *Don Juan* (1857) V. clviii. Thus in the East they are extremely strict, And wedlock and a padlock mean the same. **1950** C. E. VULLIAMY *Henry Plumdew* 211 Wedlock is a padlock, says our proverb. ■ **marriage**

Wednesday *see* Monday's CHILD is fair of face.

weed *see* ILL weeds grow apace.

weeding *see* ONE year's seeding makes seven years' weeding.

week *see* if you would be HAPPY for a week take a wife.

weep *see* LAUGH and the world laughs with you.

weeper *see* FINDERS keepers (losers weepers).

welcome *see* when all FRUIT fails, welcome haws.

WELL begun is half done

Cf. PLATO *Laws* 753e ἀρχὴ γὰρ λέγεται μὲν ἥμιον παντὸς ἐν ταῖς παροιμίαις ἔργου, proverbially it is said that the beginning is the half of every task; HORACE *Epistles* I. ii. 40 *dimidium facti qui coepit habet*, he who has made a beginning, has half done.

□ *c* **1415** *Middle English Sermons* (EETS) 148 The wise man seth that halfe he hath don that wel begynneth is werke. **1542** N. UDALL *Erasmus' Apophthegms* I. 16 Laertius ascrybeth to hym [Socrates] this saiyng also: to haue well begoone is a thyng halfe dooen. **1616** J. WITHALS *Dict.* (rev. ed.) 555 Well begun, is halfe done. **1703** P. A. MOTTEUX *Don Quixote* IV. xli. Let me.. get.. ready for our Journey. ..'Twill be soon done, and A Business once begun, you know, is half ended. **1883** C. S. BURNE *Shropshire Folklore* 273 They also account it very unlucky to give trust [credit] for the first article sold. 'Well begun is half done,' is evidently their principle. **1907** A. MACLAREN *Acts* I. 176 Satan spoils many a well-begun work. ..Well begun is half—but only half—ended. **1981** P. O'DONNELL *Xanadu Talisman* iv. The nannie-like proverbs..Well begun is half done, The early bird catches the worm. ■ **beginnings and endings**

All's WELL that ends well

Cf. *c* **1250** *Proverbs of Hending in Anglia* (1881) IV. 182 Wel is him that wel ende mai.

□ **1381** in J. R. Lumby *Chronicon Henrici Knighton* (1895) II. 139 If the ende be wele, than is alle wele. *c* **1530** R. HILL *Commonplace Book* (EETS) 110 'All ys well that endyth well,' said the gud wyff. **1602** SHAKESPEARE *All's Well that ends Well* IV. iv. 35 All's Well That Ends Well. Still the fine's [end's] the crown. **1836** MARRYAT *Midshipman Easy* I. vi. I had got rid of the farmer,..bull, and the bees—all's well that ends well. **1979** G. HAMMOND *Dead Game* xviii. My rank's been confirmed. So all's well that ends well. **2002** *Washington Post* 25 June C12 Thanks for telling us the rest of the story. All's well that ends well. ■ **beginnings and endings; good fortune**

well *see also* (noun) you never MISS the water till the well runs dry; the PITCHER will go to the well once too often; TRUTH lies at the bottom of a well.

well *see also* (noun) LET well alone; (adjective) the DEVIL was sick, the Devil a saint would be; (adverb) he LIVES long who lives well; PAY beforehand was never well served; if you would be well SERVED, serve yourself; SPARE well and have to spend; everyone SPEAKS well of the bridge which carries him over; if a THING's worth doing, it's worth doing well; if you WANT a thing done well, do it yourself.

west *see* EAST is east, and west is west; EAST, west, home's best.

wet *see* (adverb) sow dry and set wet; (verb) the CAT would eat fish, but would not wet her feet.

It's not WHAT you know, it's who you know

□ **1992** *Economist* 26 Dec. 20/1 'It's not what you know, it's who you know,' is the cry of the disappointed and excluded around the world. How true: intelligence and application help in life, but contacts are what count. **1998** *Housing Agenda* Apr. 12/1 Take getting a job. The old adage that 'it's not what you know but who you know' has more than a kernel of truth in it. ■ **bribery and corruption**

what *see also* what you don't KNOW can't hurt you; what MATTERS is what works; what MUST be must be; what you SEE is what you get; what goes UP must come down.

wheel *see* the SQUEAKING wheel gets the grease.

while *see* while there's LIFE there's hope.

whirlwind *see* they that sow the wind shall reap the whirlwind.

whistle *see* don't HALLOO till you are out of the wood; a sow may whistle, though it has an ill mouth for it.

A WHISTLING woman and a crowing hen are neither fit for God nor men

The rhyme has at least three common variants.

□ **1721** J. KELLY *Scottish Proverbs* 33 A crooning cow, a crowing Hen and a whistling Maid boded never luck to a House. The two first are reckoned ominous, but the Reflection is on the third. **1850** *Notes & Queries* 1st Ser. II. 164 A whistling woman and a crowing hen, Is neither fit for God nor men. **1891** J. L. KIPLING *Beast & Man* ii. 'A whistling woman and a crowing hen are neither fit for God nor men,' is a mild English saying. **1917** J. C. BRIDGE *Cheshire Proverbs* 28 A whistling woman and a crowing hen will fear the old lad [the Devil] out of his den. **1933** L. I. WILDER *Farmer Boy* xi. Royal teased her, Whistling girls and crowing hens Always come to some bad ends. **1979** G. DUFF *Country Wisdom* (1983) 55 A whistling woman and a crowing hen, Will bring Old Harry out of his den. **1995** B. HOLLAND *Endangered Pleasures* 116 I was the wrong sex. Boys whistled. . . As grandmothers used to say, *A whistling girl and a crowing hen Both will come to a bad end.* ■ **women**

whistling *see also* it is a POOR dog that's not worth whistling for.

One WHITE foot, buy him; two white feet, try him; three white feet, look well about him; four white feet, go without him

A horse-dealing proverb.

□ **1882** *Notes & Queries* 6th Ser. V. 427 One white foot—buy him. Two white feet—try him. Three white feet—look well about him. Four white feet—go without him. **1957** H. P. BECK *Folklore of Maine* iv. One white foot, buy him. Two white feet, try him. Three white feet, deny him. Four white feet and a slip in his nose, take him out and feed him to the crows. ■ **buying and selling; horse lore**

white *see also* FEBRUARY fill dyke, be it black or be it white; TWO blacks don't make a white.

whole *see* the HALF is better than the whole; HALF the truth is often a whole lie.

whore *see* ONCE a whore, always a whore.

wife *see* a BLIND man's wife needs no paint; CAESAR's wife must be above suspicion; a DEAF husband and a blind wife are always a happy couple; if you would be HAPPY for a week take a wife; the HUSBAND is always the last to know; my SON is my son till he gets him a wife, but my daughter's my daughter all the days of her life; he that will THRIVE must first ask his wife.

A WILFUL man must have his way

□ **1816** SCOTT *Antiquary* I. vi. A wilful man must have his way. **1907** W. DE MORGAN *Alice-for-Short* xxxvii. 'A wilful man will have his way,' says Peggy, laughing. . . Alice replies: 'Never mind!' **1931** J. BUCHAN *Blanket of Dark* xii. 'Take one of my men with you.' . . He shook his head. . . 'A wilful man must have his way,' she said. ■ **obstinacy**

WILFUL waste makes woeful want

The connection between *waste* and *want* predates the present form of this proverb, e.g. **1576** R. EDWARDS *Paradise of Dainty Devices* 88 For want is nexte to waste, and shame doeth synne ensue.

□ **1721** J. KELLY *Scottish Proverbs* 353 Wilful waste makes woeful want. **1866** GASKELL *Wives & Daughters* II. xxix. Now young folks go off to Paris, and think nothing of the cost: and it's well if wilful waste don't make woeful want before they die. **1946** 'R. FINNEGAN' *Lying Ladies* vi. 'Well, do you want the drink or not?' . . Regan . . emptied his glass and shoved forward. 'Willful waste makes woeful want,' he declared. ■ **action and consequence; waste**

He that WILL not when he may, when he will he shall have nay

□ *a* **1000** in *Anglia* (1889) XI. 388 Nu sceal ælc man efsten, thæt he to gode gecerre tha hwile the he muge, thelæste, gyf he nu nelle tha hwile the he muge, eft thone he wyle, he ne mæig [Now shall each man hasten to turn to God while he may, lest if he will not now while he may, later when he will, he may not]. **1303** R. BRUNNE *Handlyng Synne* (EETS) l. 4795 He that wyl nat when he may, He shal nat, when he wyl. *c* **1450** in Brown & Robbins *Index of Middle English Verse* (1943) 186 He that will not when he may, When he will he shall have nay [denial]. **1624** BURTON *Anatomy of Melancholy* (ed. 2) III. ii. They omit oportunities. . . *He that will not when he may, When he will he shall haue nay.* **1893** R. L. STEVENSON *Catriona* xix. That young lady, with whom I so much desired to be alone again, sang . . 'He that will not when he may, When he will he shall have nay.' **1935** N. MITCHISON *We have been Warned* III. 297 'She that will not when she may, When she will she shall have nay.' Aren't you feeling a bit like that? **1958** B. PYM *Glass of Blessings* xi. 'It was a rather pretty little box, just the kind of thing you like. . . ' 'I know,' I said. ' "If you will not when you may, when you will you shall have nay." ' ■ **opportunity, missed**

Where there's a WILL, there's a way

□ **1640** G. HERBERT *Outlandish Proverbs* no. 730 To him that will, wais are not wanting. **1822** W. HAZLITT in *New Monthly Mag.* Feb. 102 Where there's a will, there's a way.—I said so to myself, as I walked down Chancery-lane . . to inquire . . where the fight the next day was to be. **1979** E. KOCH *Good Night Little Spy* xi. I've no idea how it can be done. But where there's a will, there's a way. **2002** *Washington Times* 26 Mar. A17 Where there's a will, there's a way. And the one thing campaign-finance reform does not do, because it cannot, is diminish the will to influence elections and politicians. ■ **persistence; ways and means**

will *see also* (noun) he that COMPLIES against his will is of his own opinion still; (verb) if ANYTHING can go wrong, it will; there's none so BLIND as those who will not see; there's none so DEAF as those who will not hear; what MUST be must be.

He who WILLS the end, wills the means

□ **1692** R. SOUTH *Twelve Sermons* 497 That most true aphorism, that he who wills the end, wills also the means. **1910** *Spectator* 29 Oct. 677 We won a Trafalgar . . because we not only meant to win, but knew how to win—because we understood . . the maxim, 'He who wills the end wills the means.' **1980** *Listener* 13 Mar. 332 I could offer a text . . from Aneurin Bevan: 'It's no good willing the end unless you're also ready to will the means.' ■ **action and consequences; ways and means**

You WIN a few, you lose a few

An expression of consolation or resignation of American origin, also frequently found in the form *you win some, you lose some*. See also the next entry. Cf. **1897** R. KIPLING *Captains Courageous* x. 'Thirty million dollars' worth of mistake, wasn't it? I'd risk it for that.' 'I lost some; and I gained some.'

□ **1966** P. O. DONNELL *Sabre-Tooth* XIV. You win a few, you lose a few, and it's no good getting sore. **1976** *Times* 23 Nov. 14 You look like being saddled with the uninspiring Willy. . . On the other hand, you seem to have got your way over Mrs. Thatcher's nominee. . . You win some, you lose some. **1998** *Oldie* Jan. 32/3 Ah well, as they say in the Silver Ring, win a few, lose a few. **2001** *National Review* 19 Nov. 6 At a big Madison Square Garden event, Hillary was booed, Bill was cheered. Win some, lose some. ■ **winners and losers**

You can't WIN them all

Similar in sentiment to the preceding entry.

□ **1953** R. CHANDLER *Long Good-bye* xxiv. Wade took him by the shoulder and spun him round. 'Take it easy, Doc. You can't win them all.' **1984** 'C. AIRD' *Harm's Way* xviii. 'The finger being found on the footpath was just bad luck on the murderer's part.' 'You can't win them all,' said Crosby ambiguously. **2002** *Washington Post* 18 Mar. C11 (*Born Loser comic strip*) 'They say you can't win them all.. however, as evidenced by Brutus Thornapple, evidently you can lose them all!' ■ **winners and losers**

win *see also* let them LAUGH that win; *also* WINS, WON.

When the WIND is in the east, 'tis neither good for man nor beast

□ **1600** R. CAWDREY *Treasury of Similies* 750 The East wind is accounted neither good for man or beast. **1659** J. HOWELL *Proverbs* (English) 19 When the wind is in the east it is good for neither man nor beast. **1670** J. RAY *English Proverbs* 41 When the wind's in the East, It's neither good for man nor beast. .. The East-wind with us is commonly very sharp, because it comes off the Continent. **1929** A. WYNNE *Room with Iron Shutters* xx. 'When the wind is in the East.. 'Tis neither good for man nor beast.' Has it ever occurred to you.. to relate the incidence of crime to meteorological conditions? **2002** *Times* 13 Mar. 24 'When the wind is from the east, 'tis neither good for man nor beast,' the old saying goes, meaning that a cold, raw, easterly wind blowing off the Continent will make life miserable. ■ **weather lore**

wind *see also* APRIL showers bring forth May flowers; GOD tempers the wind to the shorn lamb; it's an ILL wind that blows nobody any good; NORTH wind doth blow, we shall have snow; ONE for the mouse, one for the crow; a REED before the wind lives on, while mighty oaks do fall; ROBIN Hood could brave all weathers but a thaw wind; they that sow the wind shall reap the whirlwind; STRAWS tell which way the wind blows.

window *see* the EYES are the window of the soul; when POVERTY comes in at the door, love flies out of the window.

When the WINE is in, the wit is out

Wit is used in the sense of 'intelligence', rather than 'clever or amusing talk'.

□ *c* **1390** GOWER *Confessio Amantis* VI. 555 For wher that wyn doth wit aweie [does away with wit], Wisdom hath lost the rihte weie [path]. **1529** MORE *Dialogue of Images* III. xvi. Whan the wyne were in and the wyt out, wolde they take vppon them.. to handle holy scrypture. **1560** T. BECON *Works* I. 536V When the wine is in, the wit is out. **1710** S. PALMER *Proverbs* 18 When the Wine's In, the Wit's Out. **1854** J. W. WARTER *Last of Old Squires* vi. None is a Fool always, every one sometimes. When the Drink goes in, then the Wit goes out. **1937** V. WILKINS *And so—Victoria* iii. Remember what I told you last night—that with wine in, wits go out. ■ **drunkenness**

wine *see also* GOOD wine needs no bush; you can't put NEW wine in old bottles; from the SWEETEST wine, the tartest vinegar; there is TRUTH in wine.

wing *see* a BIRD never flew on one wing; the MOTHER of mischief is no bigger than a midge's wing.

wink *see* a NOD's as good as a wink to a blind horse.

wins *see* SLOW and steady wins the race.

WINTER never rots in the sky

□ **1621** J. HALL *Contemplations* XIII in *Recollections* 32 God.. chooses out a fit season for the execution; As we vse to say of winter, the iudgements of God doe neuer rot in the skie, but shall fall (if late, yet) surely. **1670** J. RAY *English Proverbs* 42 Winter never rots in the sky. **1817** W. BENTLEY *Diary* 24 Jan. (1914) IV. 434 'Winter does not rot in the sky.' We have a deep snow and for the first time this season the Earth is completely covered. **1959** *Boston Herald* 13 Mar. 42 Winter never rots in the sky, says the old proverb. ■ **retribution**

winter *see also* if CANDLEMAS day be sunny and bright, winter will have another flight; a GREEN Yule makes a fat churchyard; the RICH man has his ice in the summer and the poor man gets his in the winter.

wisdom *see* EXPERIENCE is the father of wisdom.

It is easy to be WISE after the event

Cf. *c* **1490** P. DE COMMYNES *Mémoires* (1924) I. I. xvi. *Les deux ducz.. estoient saiges après le coup (comme l'on dit des Bretons)*; **1596** T. DANNETT tr. *Commynes' Mémoires* I. xvi. These two Dukes were wise after the hurt received (as the common prouerbe saith) of the Brittons.

□ **1616** JONSON *Epicœne* II. iv. Away, thou strange iustifier of thy selfe, to bee wiser then thou wert, by the euent. **1717** R. WODROW *Letter* 28 Sept. (1843) II. 319 Had we not verified the proverb of being wise behind the time, we might for ever [have] been rid of them. **1900** A. CONAN DOYLE *Great Boer War* xix. It is easy to be wise after the event, but it does certainly appear that.. the action at Paardeberg was as unnecessary as it was expensive. **1977** J. PORTER *Who the Heck is Sylvia?* ii. 'It's easy enough to be wise after the event,' Babette pointed out sullenly. ■ **foresight and hindsight**

It is a WISE child that knows its own father

□ **1584** J. WITHALS *Dict.* (rev. ed.) L4 Wise sonnes they be in very deede, That knowe their Parents who did them breede. **1589** R. GREENE *Menaphon* VI. 92 Wise are the Children in these dayes that know their owne fathers, especially if they be begotten in Dogge daies [the heat of summer], when their mothers are frantick with love. **1596** SHAKESPEARE *Merchant of Venice* II. ii. 69 It is a wise father that knows his own child. **1613** G. WITHER *Abuses* I. ii. Is't not hence this common Prouerbe growes, 'Tis a wise child that his owne father knowes? **1762** GOLDSMITH *Mystery Revealed* 21 She called her father John instead of Thomas.. but perhaps she was willing to verify the old proverb, that It is a wise child that knows its own father. **1823** SCOTT *Peveril* III. x. I only laughed because you said you were Sir Geoffrey's son. But no matter—'tis a wise child that knows his own father. **1983** R. DAVIES *High Spirits* 119 It's a wise child that knows its own father. How wise does a child have to be to know its own great-great-grandfather? ■ **children and parents**

wise *see also* EARLY to bed and early to rise, makes a man healthy, wealthy, and wise; a FOOL may give a wise man counsel; FOOLS ask questions that wise men cannot answer; FOOLS build houses and wise men live in them; where IGNORANCE is bliss, 'tis folly to be wise; one cannot LOVE and be wise; PENNY wise and pound foolish; a STILL tongue makes a wise head; a WORD to the wise is enough.

The WISH is father to the thought

□ **1597–8** SHAKESPEARE *Henry IV, Pt. 2* IV. v. 93 I never thought to hear you speak again.—Thy wish was father, Harry, to that thought. **1783** P. VAN SCHAACK *Letter* 5 Jan. in H. C. Van Schaack *Life* (1842) 321 My 'wish is father to the thought'. **1860** TROLLOPE *Framley Parsonage* III. xiv. The wish might be father to the thought.. but the thought was truly there. **1940** E. F. BENSON *Final Edition* iii. She spied a smallish man.. walking away from us. The wish was father to the thought. 'Ah, there is Lord Ripon,' she said. ..He turned round. It wasn't Lord Ripon at all. **1980** A. T. ELLIS *Birds of Air* (1983) 40 Somewhere in that area of the human mind where the wish is father to the thought activity was taking place. **1988** *Washington Times* 13 Jan. A 13 The wish is father to the thought, and that timeless truism fits federal judges like a glove. ■ **wanting and having**

If WISHES were horses, beggars would ride

□ *a* **1628** J. CARMICHAELL *Proverbs in Scots* no. 140 And [if] wishes were horses pure [poor] men wald ryde. **1721** J. KELLY *Scottish Proverbs* 178 If Wishes were Horses, Beggars would ride. **1844** J. O. HALLIWELL *Nursery Rhymes of England* (ed. 4) 501 If wishes were horses, Beggars would ride; If turnips were watches, I would wear one by my side. **1912** *British Weekly* 18 Jan. 480 If wishes were horses Unionists would ride rapidly into office. **1992** A. LAMBERT *Rather English Marriage* (1993) ix. 153 'If wishes were horses then beggars should ride,' he told her. 'Don't be too sure.' **2002** *Washington Times* 14 Aug. B5 Not only do I remember my mother quoting the same phrase to me, she had another one: 'If wishes were horses, beggars would ride.' Both are from a bygone generation that held no truck with the 'if only' and 'I wish' mentality. ■ **wanting and having**

wit *see* BREVITY is the soul of wit; when the WINE is in, the wit is out.

wiving *see* HANGING and wiving go by destiny.

woeful *see* WILFUL waste makes woeful want.

wolf *see* HUNGER drives the wolf out of the wood.

A WOMAN, a dog, and a walnut tree, the more you beat them the better they be

'The old custom of beating a walnut-tree was carried out firstly to fetch down the fruit and secondly to break the long shoots and so encourage the production of short fruiting spurs': M. Hadfield *British Trees* (1957) Cf. L. *nux, asinus, mulier verbere opus habent*, a nut tree, an ass, and a woman need a beating.

□ **1581** G. PETTIE tr. *S. Guazzo's Civil Conversation* III. 20 I have redde, I know not where, these verses. A woman, an asse, and a walnut tree, Bring the more fruit the more beaten they bee. **1670** J. RAY *English Proverbs* 50 A spaniel, a woman and a walnut tree, The more they're beaten the better still they be. **1836** T. C. HALIBURTON *Clockmaker* 1st Ser. xxv. There was an old sayin there [Kent], which.. is not far off the mark: A woman, a dog, and a walnut tree, The more you lick 'em, the better they be. **1929** E. LINKLATER *Poet's Pub* xii. A woman, a dog, and a walnut tree, The more you beat 'em, the better they be. **1945** F. THOMPSON *Lark Rise* v. A handsome pie was placed before him.. such as seemed to.. illustrate the old saying, 'A woman, a dog and a walnut tree, the more you beat 'em the better they be'. **1981** *Daily Telegraph* 5 Feb. 17 It's not right to batter your wife. It is like the old saying, 'A wife, a dog and a walnut tree, the more you beat them the better they be.' It's just not true. ■ **women**

A WOMAN and a ship ever want mending

Cf. PLAUTUS *Poenulus* ll. 210–15 *negoti sibi qui volet vim parare, navem et mulierem, haec duo comparato. .. Neque umquam satis hae duae res ornantur, neque is ulla ornandi satis satietas est*, whoever wants to acquire a lot of trouble should get himself a ship and a woman. For neither of them is ever sufficiently equipped, and there is never enough means of equipping them.

□ **1578** J. FLORIO *First Fruits* 30 Who wil trouble hym selfe all dayes of his life, Let hym mary a woman, or buy hym a shyp. **1598** *Mirror of Policy* (1599) X2 Is it not an old Prouebe. That Women and Shippes are neuer so perfect, but still there is somewhat to bee amended. **1640** G. HERBERT *Outlandish Proverbs* no. 780 A shippe and a woman are ever repairing. **1840** R. H. DANA *Two Years before Mast* iii. As has often been said, a ship is like a lady's watch, always out of repair. **1928** A. T. SHEPPARD *Here comes Old Sailor* II. vi. There are special proverbs for us shipmen: .. 'A woman and a ship ever want mending.' ■ **women**

A WOMAN without a man is like a fish without a bicycle

This remark is now widely attributed to the American feminist Gloria Steinem (born 1934), but seems to have originated as an anonymous graffito (see quot. 1979).

□ **1979** N. REES *Graffiti Lives OK* 80 'A woman without a man is like a fish without a bicycle.' Penned as a Woman's Lib slogan, this was met by the male response: 'Yes, but who needs a stationary haddock?' **2001** *Times Literary Supplement* 28 Dec. 8 Women may have decided they need men like a fish needs a bicycle, but the pram in the hall is with us still, ruthlessly demanding attention. ■ **women**

A WOMAN'S place is in the home

□ **1844** 'J. SLICK' *High Life* II. 121 A woman's place is her own house, a taking care of the children. **1897** 'S. GRAND' *Beth Book* (1898) xix. If we had .. done as we were told, the woman's-sphere-is-home would have been as ugly and comfortless a place for us today as it used to be. **1936** R. A. J. WALLING *Corpse with Dirty Face* iv. Mrs. Franks, being a dutiful wife, was always on the premises. 'Ah, yes—woman's place is in the home,' said Pierce. **1943** A. CHRISTIE *Moving Finger* vi. I go up in arms against the silly old-fashioned prejudice that women's place is always the home. **1979** G. WAGNER *Barnardo* v. Barnardo .. firmly believed that a woman's place was in the home. ■ **women**

A WOMAN'S work is never done

□ **1570** T. TUSSER *Husbandry* (rev. ed.) 26 Some respite to husbands the weather doth send, but huswiues affaires haue never none ende. **1629** in *Roxburghe Ballads* (1880) III. 302 (*title*) A woman's work is never done. **1722** B. FRANKLIN *Papers* (1960) I. 19 If you go among the Women, you will learn .. that a Woman's work is never done. **1920** *Times Weekly* 12 Mar. 209 'Women's work is never done.' .. We shall never hear the whole of woman's work during the war. **1981** 'G. GAUNT' *Incomer* xiv. My grannie used to say, A woman's work is never done when it never gets started! ■ **women; work**

woman *see also* HELL hath no fury like a woman scorned; a MAN is as old as he feels, and a woman as old as she looks; SILENCE is a woman's best garment; SIX hours' sleep for a man, seven for a woman, and eight for a fool; a WHISTLING woman and a crowing hen are neither fit for God nor men.

women *see* never CHOOSE your women or your linen by candlelight; ENGLAND is the paradise of women.

won *see* FAINT heart never won fair lady.

wonder *see* TIME works wonders.

WONDERS will never cease

□ **1776** H. BATES in T. Boaden *Private Correspondence of D. Garrick* (1823) II. 174 You have heard, no doubt, of his giving me the reversion of a good living in Worcestershire. . . Wonders will never cease. **1843** C. J. LEVER *Jack Hinton* I. xx. The bystanders . . looked from one to the other, with expressions of mingled surprise and dread. . . 'Blessed hour. . . Wonders will never cease.' **1974** A. PRICE *Other Paths to Glory* I. vii. Wonders will never cease. . . Early Tudor—practically untouched. ■ **marvels**

wood *see* FIELDS have eyes, and woods have ears; don't HALLOO till you are out of the wood; HUNGER drives the wolf out of the wood.

Happy's the WOOING that is not long a-doing

□ **1576** R. EDWARDS *Paradise of Dainty Devices* 71 Thrise happie is that woying That is not long a doyng. **1624** BURTON *Anatomy of Melancholy* (ed. 2) III. ii. Blessed is the wooing, That is not long a doing. **1754** RICHARDSON *Grandison* I. ix. What signifies shilly-shally? What says the old proverb? 'Happy's the wooing, That is not long a doing.' **1842** R. H. BARHAM *Ingoldsby Legends* 2nd Ser. ii. 40 'Thrice happy's the wooing that's not long a-doing!' So much time is saved in the billing and cooing. **1930** A. CHRISTIE *Mysterious Mr. Quin* iii. The old saying . . 'Happy the wooing that's not long doing.' ■ **weddings**

Many go out for WOOL and come home shorn

Many seek to better themselves or make themselves rich, but end by losing what they already have.

□ **1599** J. MINSHEU *Dialogues in Spanish* 61 You will goe for wooll, and returne home shorne. **1612** T. SHELTON tr. *Cervantes' Don Quixote* I. vii. To wander through the world . . without once considering how many there goe to seeke for wooll, that returne againe shorne themselues. **1678** J. RAY *English Proverbs* (ed. 2) 220 Many go out for wooll and come home shorn. **1858** S. A. HAMMETT *Piney Woods Tavern* xxiii. There's a proverb about going out after wool, and coming home shorn. **1910** G. W. E. RUSSELL *Sketches & Snapshots* 315 Some go [to Ascot] intent on repairing the ravages of Epsom or Newmarket; and in this speculative section not a few . . who go for wool come away shorn. **1981** N. FREELING *One Damn Thing after Another* iii. One always comes back tired from holidays. 'Go for wool and come back—?' 'Shaved—no, cropped.' 'Sheared. Yes.' ■ **ambition**; **misfortune**; **poverty**

wool *see also* MUCH cry and little wool.

A WORD to the wise is enough

Now often abbreviated to *a word to the wise*. Cf. L. *verbum sat sapienti*, a word is sufficient to a wise man; also *verb. sap.*

□ *a* **1513** DUNBAR *Poems* (1979) 206 Few wordis may serve the wyis. **1546** J. HEYWOOD *Dialogue of Proverbs* II. vii. 14ᵛ Fewe woords to the wise suffice to be spoken. *a* **1605** W. HAUGHTON *Englishmen for my Money* (1616) D3 They say, a word to the Wise is enough: so by this little French that he speakes, I see he is the very man I seeke for. **1768** STERNE *Sentimental Journey* III. 164 A word, Mons. Yorick, to the wise . . is enough. **1841** DICKENS *Old Curiosity Shop* ii. 'Fred!' cried Mr. Swiveller, tapping his nose, 'a word to the wise is sufficient for them—we may be good and happy without riches, Fred.' **2002** *Washington Times* 25 Apr. C10 (*heading*) The Man With the Proverbial Word to the Wise. ■ **hints**

word *see also* ACTIONS speak louder than words; an ENGLISHMAN'S word is his bond; FINE words butter no parsnips; HARD words break no bones; one PICTURE is worth ten thousand words; STICKS and stones may break my bones, but words will never hurt me; many a TRUE word is spoken in jest.

All WORK and no play makes Jack a dull boy

□ **1659** J. HOWELL *Proverbs* (English) 12 All work and no play, makes Jack a dull boy. **1825** M. EDGEWORTH *Harry & Lucy Concluded* II. 155 All work and no play makes Jack a dull boy. All play and no work makes Jack a mere toy. **1859** S. SMILES *Self-Help* xi. 'All work and no play makes Jack a dull boy'; but all play and no work makes him something greatly worse. **1898** C. G. ROBERTSON *Voces Academicae* I. i. 'Is that why you give garden parties yourself, eh?.. all work and no play makes Jill a very—' .. 'Plain girl. She is that already.' **1979** R. MUTCH *Gemstone* xi. 'All work and no play makes Jack a dull boy,' he observed, pouring the champagne into a glass. **2001** *Washington Post* 4 Oct. C13 (*Jeff MacNelly's Shoe comic strip*) 'What about your homework?' 'Later. All work and no Playstation makes Jack a dull boy.' ■ **recreation; work**

WORK expands so as to fill the time available

Commonly known as 'Parkinson's Law', after Professor C. Northcote Parkinson, who first propounded it.

□ **1955** C. N. PARKINSON in *Economist* 19 Nov. 635 It is a commonplace observation that work expands so as to fill the time available for its completion. **1972** M. ARGYLE *Social Psychology of Work* viii. 'Parkinson's Law' is that 'work expands so as to fill the time available'. **1976** *Scotsman* 25 Nov. 14 Though there are fewer Bills than usual, MPs, being well known as exemplars of Parkinson's law, can be relied on to stretch their work to fill all the time available and more. ■ **efficiency and inefficiency; work**

It is not WORK that kills, but worry

□ **1879** D. M. MULOCK *Young Mrs. Jardine* III. ix. Working.. all day, writing.. at night.. Roderick had yet.. never spent a happier three months.. for it is not work that kills, but 'worry'. **1909** *British Weekly* 8 July 333 It is worry that kills, they say, and not work. .. The canker of care seems to eat the life away. **1930**[?] S. K. HOCKING *Mystery Man* vi. 42 'Please don't talk about bother,' she said gently and sincerely. 'Naturally we've been worried and anxious.' 'Oh, but you shouldn't worry,' and he grinned again. 'It's worry that kills, so I've been told.' ■ **stress; work**

If you won't WORK you shan't eat

With allusion to 2 THESSALONIANS iii. 10 (AV) If any would not work, neither should he eat.

□ *c* **1535** D. LINDSAY *Satire of Three Estates* (EETS) 475 *Qui non laborat, non manducet.* .. Quha labouris nocht he sall not eit. **1624** CAPT. J. SMITH *General Hist. Virginia* III. x. He that will not worke shall not eate. **1891** R. KIPLING *Life's Handicap* 362 If you won't work you shan't eat. .. You're a wild elephant, and no educated animal at all. Go back to your jungle. **1938** N. STREATFEILD *Circus is Coming* v. Proper termagent she was, bless her. 'Them as can't work can't eat,' she always said. **1981** J. STUBBS *Ironmaster* xx. I say them as don't work shan't eat. ■ **idleness; work**

work *see also* (noun) the DEVIL finds work for idle hands to do; the END crowns the work; the EYE of a master does more work than both his hands; FOOLS and bairns should never see half-done work; if IFS and ands were pots and pans, there'd be no work for tinkers' hands; MANY hands make light work; a WOMAN's work is never done; (verb) what MATTERS is what works; TIME works wonders.

workman *see* a BAD workman blames his tools.

workshop *see* an IDLE brain is the Devil's workshop.

world *see* it takes ALL sorts to make a world; all's for the BEST in the best of all possible worlds; BETTER be out of the world than out of the fashion; GOD's in his heaven, all's right with the world; one HALF of the world does not know how the other half lives; the HAND that rocks the cradle rules the world; LAUGH and the world laughs with you; a LIE is halfway round the world; LOVE makes the world go round.

Even a WORM will turn

Even the humblest will strike back if harassed or imposed upon too far.

□ **1546** J. HEYWOOD *Dialogue of Proverbs* II. iv. G4[v] Treade a worme on the tayle, and it must turne agayne. **1592** R. GREENE *Groatsworth of Wit* XII. 143 Stop shallow water still running, it will rage. Tread on a worme and it will turne. **1854** 'M. LANGDON' *Ida May* xi. Even the worm turns when he is trodden upon. **1889** W. JAMES in *Mind* XIV. 107 Since even the worm will 'turn', the space-theorist can hardly be expected to remain motionless when his Editor stirs him up. **1962** A. CHRISTIE *Mirror Crack'd* xii. He's a very meek type. Still, the worm will turn, or so they say. **1975** 'M. INNES' *Appleby File* 98 Signs were not wanting that she was putting stuffing into Charles Vandervell, of late so inclined to unwholesome meditation of headlong dying. It was almost as if a worm were going to turn. ■ **retribution**

worm *see also* the EARLY bird catches the worm.

worry *see* it is not WORK that kills, but worry.

worse *see* GO further and fare worse; NOTHING so bad but it might have been worse; the more you STIR it the worse it stinks.

worst *see* HOPE for the best and prepare for the worst; when THINGS are at the worst they begin to mend.

The WORTH of a thing is what it will bring

Cf. L. *valet quantum vendi potest*, it is worth as much as it can be sold for; 15th-cent. Fr. *tant vault la chose comme elle peut estre vendue*, a thing is worth just so much as it can be sold for.

□ **1569** J. SANFORDE tr. *H. C. Agrippa's Vanity of Arts & Sciences* xci. The thinge is so muche worthy as it maye be solde for. **1664** S. BUTLER *Hudibras* II. i. For what is Worth in any thing, But so much Money as 'twill bring? **1813** SOUTHEY *Life of Nelson* I. ii. Vouchers, he found in that country were no check whatever; the principle was, that 'a thing was always worth what it would bring'. **1847** J. O. HALLIWELL *Dict.* II. 864 The worth of a thing is what it will bring. **1908** *Spectator* 4 Apr. 535 'The real worth of anything Is just as much as it will bring'. You cannot get beyond that piece of ancient wisdom as to the determination of value. ■ **buying and selling; value**

worth *see also* a BIRD in the hand is worth two in the bush; a KING's chaff is worth more than other men's corn; an OUNCE of practice is worth a pound of precept; a PECK of March dust is worth a king's ransom; one PICTURE is worth ten thousand words; it is a POOR dog that's not worth whistling for; a SWARM in May is worth a load of hay; if a THING's worth doing, it's worth doing well; one VOLUNTEER is worth two pressed men.

worthy *see* the LABOURER is worthy of his hire.

wrath *see* a SOFT answer turneth away wrath.

wren *see* the ROBIN and the wren are God's cock and hen.

wrong *see* (noun) he who is ABSENT is always in the wrong; the KING can do no wrong; TWO wrongs don't make a right; (adverb) if ANYTHING can go wrong, it will; (adjective) there is no such thing as BAD weather, only the wrong clothes.

year *see* there are no BIRDS in last year's nest; a CHERRY year a merry year; KEEP a thing seven years and you'll always find a use for it; you should KNOW a man seven years before you stir his fire; ONE year's seeding makes seven years' weeding; TURKEY, heresy, hops, and beer came into England all in one year.

yesterday *see* JAM tomorrow and jam yesterday, but never jam today.

YORKSHIRE born and Yorkshire bred, strong in the arm and weak in the head

The names of other (chiefly, northern) English counties and towns are also used instead of *Yorkshire*.

□ **1852** *Notes & Queries* 1st Ser. V. 573 Derbyshire born and Derbyshire bred, Strong i' th' arm, and weak i' th' head. **1869** W. C. HAZLITT *English Proverbs* 273 Manchester bred: Long in the arms, and short in the head. **1920** C. H. DOUGLAS *Credit-Power & Democracy* vi. Organised labour at this time shows considerable susceptibility to the Border gibe of being 'strong i' th' arm and weak i' th' head'. **1966** J. BINGHAM *Double Agent* ii. He thought, Yorkshire born and Yorkshire bred, strong in th' arm and weak in't head; but it wasn't true, most of them were as quick as weasels and sharp as Sheffield steel. ■ **human nature**

YOUNG folks think old folks to be fools, but old folks know young folks to be fools

□ **1577** J. GRANGE *Golden Aphroditis* O2ᵛ Young men thinks old men fooles, but old men knoweth well, Yong men are fooles. **1605** W. CAMDEN *Remains concerning Britain* 221 Wise was that saying of Doctor Medcalfe: You Yong men do thinke vs olde men to be fooles, but we olde men do know that you yong men are fooles. **1790** R. TYLER *Contrast* V. ii. Young folks think old folks to be fools; but old folks know young folks to be fools. **1850** F. E. SMEDLEY *Frank Fairlegh* xxx. 'Young folks always think old ones fools, they say.' 'Finish the adage, Sir, that old folks know young ones to be so, and then agree with me that it is a saying founded on prejudice.' **1930** A. CHRISTIE *Murder at Vicarage* xxxi. I remember a saying of my Great Aunt Fanny's. I was sixteen at the time and thought it particularly foolish. .. She used to say, 'The young people think the old people are fools—but the old people *know* the young people are fools!' ■ **fools; old age; youth**

A YOUNG man married is a young man marred

□ **1589** G. PUTTENHAM *Art of English Poesy* III. xix. 173 The maide that soone married is, soone marred is. **1602** SHAKESPEARE *All's Well that ends Well* II. iii. 291 A young man married is a man that's marr'd. **1961** R. KIRK *Old House of Fear* i. Don't forget this, though, Duncan—'You can grave it on his tombstone, you can cut it on his card: A young man married is a young man marred.' ■ **marriage; youth**

YOUNG men may die, but old men must die

Cf. the words of a Roman noblewoman rejecting an elderly suitor after the death of her young husband: *juvenis quidem potest cito mori; sed senex diu vivere non potest*, a young man may indeed die early, but an old man cannot live long (quoted by ST. JEROME, *Letter* cxxvii. 2).

□ **1534** MORE *Dialogue of Comfort* (1553) II. ii. As the younge man maye happe some time to die soone, so the olde man can never liue long. **1623** W. CAMDEN *Remains concerning Britain* (ed. 3) 276 Young men may die, but old men must die. **1758** LADY M. W. MONTAGU *Letter* 5 Sept. (1967) III. 174 According to the good English Proverb, young people may die, but old must. **1863** B. I. WILEY *Life of Billy Yank* (1952) xii. That is the Way of the World. The old must die and the young may die. **1970** 'D. CRAIG' (*title*) Young men may die. **1993** 'C. AIRD' *Going Concern* (1994) i. 9 Mary-Louise was the holiday party's language specialist and immediately said: '"The young die sometimes, but the old always die." That's an old Breton proverb.' ■ **death; necessity; old age**

YOUNG saint, old devil

□ *c* **1400** *Middle English Sermons* from MS Royal 18 B xxiii (EETS) 159 Itt is a comond prouerbe bothe of clerkes and of laye men, 'younge seynt, old dewell'. **1552** H. LATIMER *Seventh Sermon, Lord's Prayer* in *Sermons* (1844–5) 431 The old proverb, 'Young saints, old devils'.. is.. the devil's own invention; which would have parents negligent in bringing up their children in goodness. **1636** S. WARD *Collection of Sermons & Treatises* 269 Young Saints, will prove but old Devils.. But.. such as proove falling starres, never were ought but meteors. **1936** V. MCHUGH *Caleb Catlum's America* xxvii. Young saint, old devil.. looks to me like you been leadin' too virtyus a life. ■ **good and evil; human nature; youth**

young *see also* BETTER be an old man's darling than a young man's slave; whom the GODS love die young; the GOOD die young; HANG a thief when he's young, and he'll no' steal when he's old; you cannot put an OLD head on young shoulders.

YOUTH must be served

□ **1829** P. EGAN *Boxiana* 2nd Ser. II. 60 Tom Cannon made his appearance in the Prize Ring rather too late in life, under the idea that 'Youth must be served'. **1900** A. CONAN DOYLE *Green Flag* 125 There were.. points in his favour. ..There was age—twenty-three against forty. There was an old ring proverb that 'Youth will be served'. **1941** G. HEYER *Envious Casca* iv. You're just an old curmudgeon, and you're upset because you didn't like young Roydon's play. ..But, my dear chap, youth must be served! **2001** *Washington Times* 19 Aug. B1 And why wouldn't your clone, poor thing, have just as much claim to your constituent organs, if not more? (Youth will be served.) ■ **opportunity; youth**

If YOUTH knew, if age could

Cf. H. ESTIENNE *Les Premices* (1594) 173 *O si la ievnesse scavoit, O si la vieillesse povvoit*; often quoted in its modern French form *si jeunesse savait; si vieillesse pouvait*.

□ **1611** R. COTGRAVE *Dict. French & English* s.v. jeunesse If youth knew what to doe, and age could doe what it knowes, no man would ever be poore. **1922** J. JOYCE *Ulysses* 30 I know, I know. If youth but knew. But what does Shakespeare say? **2002** *Times* 9 July 19 The old adage, 'If youth knew, if age but could', has been replaced by a scenario in which youth doesn't know, but age still can. ■ **old age; youth**

Yule *see* a GREEN Yule makes a fat churchyard.

Bibliography

of Major Proverb Collections and Works cited from Modern Editions

Quotations are taken from the first edition of the work in question unless otherwise stated. Standard modern editions of several major authors, particularly from the medieval and Renaissance periods, have been used for ease of reference.

Major Proverb Collections

Apperson, G. L., *English Proverbs and Proverbial Phrases* (London, 1929).

Bohn, H. G., *Hand-Book of Proverbs* (London, 1855).

Carmichaell, J., *James Carmichaell Collection of Proverbs in Scots*, ed. M. L. Anderson (Edinburgh, 1957).

[Clarke, J.,] *Parœmiologia Anglo-Latina.. or Proverbs English, and Latine, methodically disposed according to the Common-place heads, in Erasmus his Adages* (London, 1639).

Denham, M. A., *Collection of Proverbs and Popular Sayings relating to the seasons, the weather, and agricultural pursuits* (London, 1846).

Draxe, T., *Bibliotheca Scholastica Instructissima, or, a Treasurie of ancient Adagies, and sententious Prouerbes, selected out of the English, Greeke, Latine, French, Italian, and Spanish* (London, 1616).

Dykes, O., *English Proverbs, with Moral Reflexions* (London, 1709).

Fergusson, D., *Fergusson's Scottish Proverbs from the Original Print of 1641 together with a larger Manuscript Collection of about the same period hitherto unpublished*, ed. E. Beveridge (Edinburgh, 1924).

Franklin, B., *Poor Richard's Almanack: Sayings of Poor Richard*, ed. P. L. Ford (Brooklyn, 1890).

Fuller, T., *Gnomologia: Adagies and Proverbs; Wise Sentences and Witty Sayings, Ancient and Modern, Foreign and British* (London, 1732).

Hassell, J. W., Jun., *Middle French Proverbs, Sentences, and Proverbial Phrases* (Toronto, 1982).

Hazlitt, W. C., *English Proverbs and Proverbial Phrases* (London, 1869). Later editions are also cited.

Henderson, A., *Scottish Proverbs* (Edinburgh, 1832).

H[erbert]., G., *Outlandish Proverbs* (1640), and *Jacula Prudentum* (1651), in *Works*, ed. F. E. Hutchinson (Oxford, 1941).

Heywood, J., *Dialogue conteinyng the nomber in effect of all the prouerbes in the englishe tongue* (London, 1546). Later editions are also cited.

Hislop, A., *Proverbs of Scotland* (Glasgow, 1862).

H[owell]., J., *Paroimiographia. Proverbs, or Old sayed sawes & adages in English,.. Italian, French, and Spanish, whereunto the British.. are added* (London, 1659).

Kelly, J., *Complete Collection of Scottish Proverbs Explained and made Intelligible to the English Reader* (London, 1721).

Lean, V. S., *Collectanea* (5 vols., Bristol, 1902–4).

[Mapletoft, J.,] *Select Proverbs, Italian, Spanish, French, English, Scotish, British, &c. Chiefly Moral* (London, 1707).

Mieder, W., Kingsbury, S. A., and Harder, K. B., *A Dictionary of American Proverbs* (New York and Oxford, 1992).

Oxford Dictionary of English Proverbs, ed. F. P. Wilson (ed. 3, Oxford, 1970).

Palmer, S., *Moral Essays on some of the most Curious and Significant English, Scotch, and Foreign Proverbs* (London, 1710).

R[ay]., J., *Collection of English Proverbs* (Cambridge, 1670). Later editions are also cited.

Stevenson, B., *Home Book of Proverbs, Maxims, and Familiar Phrases* (rev. ed., New York, 1961).

Taverner, R., *Proverbs or adagies with newe addicions gathered out of the Chiliades of Erasmus* (London, 1539).

Taylor, A., and Whiting, B. J., *Dictionary of American Proverbs and Proverbial Phrases 1820–1880* (Cambridge, Massachusetts, 1958).

Tilley, M. P., *Dictionary of the Proverbs in England in the Sixteenth and Seventeenth Centuries* (Ann Arbor, 1950).

Torriano, G., *Dictionary English & Italian, with severall Proverbs*, first published with J. Florio's *Vocabolario Italiano & Inglese, a Dictionary Italian & English* (rev. ed., London, 1659).

—— *Piazza universale di proverbi Italiani; or, a common place of Italian proverbs and proverbial phrases* (London, 1666).

—— *Second alphabet consisting of proverbial phrases* (London, 1662).

—— *Select Italian Proverbs* (Cambridge, 1642).

Tusser, T., *Husbandry: Hundreth good pointes of husbandrie* (London, 1557), *Five hundreth points of good husbandry united to as many of good huswiferie* (1573, various revised and augmented editions).

Whiting, B. J., *Early American Proverbs and Proverbial Phrases* (Cambridge, Massachusetts, 1977).

—— *Modern Proverbs and Proverbial Sayings* (Cambridge, Massachusetts, 1989).

—— *Proverbs, Sentences, and Proverbial Phrases from English Writings mainly before 1500* (Cambridge, Massachusetts, 1968).

Works Cited from Modern Editions

Beaumont, F., and Fletcher, J., *Works*, ed. A. Glover and A. R. Waller (10 vols., Cambridge, 1905–12).

Bible: Authorised Version of the English Bible 1611 ed. W. A. Wright (5 vols., Cambridge, 1909).

Chaucer, G., *Works*, ed. F. N. Robinson (ed. 2, London, 1966).

Dekker, T., *Dramatic Works*, ed. F. T. Bowers (4 vols., Cambridge, 1953–61). Non-dramatic works are cited from the first edition.

Douce MS 52: Förster, M., 'Die Mittelenglische Sprichwörtersammlung in Douce 52', *Festschrift zum XII. Allgemeinen Deutschen Neuphilologentage in München, Pfingsten 1906* (Erlangen, 1906), 40–60.

Ford, J., *Dramatic Works*, ed. W. Bang and H. de Vocht (2 vols., Louvain, 1908, 1927).

Gascoigne, G., *Complete Works*, ed. J. W. Cunliffe (2 vols., Cambridge, 1907–10).

Gower, J., *English Works*, ed. G. C. Macaulay (2 vols., London, 1900–1).

Greene, R., *Life and Complete Works in prose and verse*, ed. A. B. Grosart (15 vols., London, 1881–6).

Heywood, T., *Dramatic Works*, ed. R. H. Shepherd (6 vols., London, 1874). *Captives* is cited from the first publication of 1885.

Jonson, B., *Works*, ed. C. H. Herford, P. and E. M. Simpson (11 vols., Oxford, 1925–52). *Cynthia's Revels* is cited from the first edition.

Langland, W., *Vision of William concerning Piers Plowman*, ed. W. W. Skeat (5 vols., London, 1867–85).

Lyly, J., *Complete Works*, ed. R. W. Bond (3 vols., Oxford, 1902). Principal works cited are *Euphues: the anatomy of wit* (1578) and *Euphues and his England* (1580).

Marlowe, C., *Works and Life*, ed. R. H. Case et al. (6 vols., London, 1930–3).

Marston, J., *Works*, ed. A. H. Bullen (3 vols., London, 1887).

Massinger, P., *Plays and Poems*, ed. P. Edwards and C. Gibson (Oxford, 1976).

Middleton, T., *Works*, ed. A. H. Bullen (8 vols., London, 1885–6).

Milton, J., *Complete Prose Works*, ed. D. M. Wolfe et al. (8 vols., New Haven, 1953–).

—— *Works*, ed. F. A. Patterson (18 vols., New York, 1931–8). Cited for poetical works.

Nashe, T., *Works*, ed. R. B. McKerrow (5 vols., London, 1904–10; corrected reprint 1958, 1966).

Pope, A., *Twickenham edition of the poems*, ed. J. Butt et al. (10 vols., London, 1939–67). The *Dunciad* and the translation of the *Odyssey* are cited from the first edition; *Letters* are cited as marked in the text.

Porter, H., *Pleasant Historie of the two angrie women of Abington*, ed. W. W. Greg (Oxford, for the Malone Society, 1912).

Romaunt of the Rose: in Chaucer, G., *Works*, supra.

Shakespeare, W., *Complete Works*, ed. P. Alexander (London, 1951).

Skelton, J., *Poems*, ed. R. S. Kinsman (Oxford, 1969). Items not found here are cited from *Poetical Works*, ed. A. Dyce (2 vols., London, 1843).

Spenser, E., *Works: a variorum edition*, ed. E. Greenlaw et al. (10 vols., Baltimore, 1932–57).

Swift, J., *Poems*, ed. H. Williams (3 vols., ed. 2, Oxford, 1958).

—— *Prose Works*, ed. H. Davis (14 vols., Oxford, 1939–68). The *Polite Conversation* ('S. W[agstaff].', *Complete collection of genteel and ingenious conversation, according to the most polite mode and method now used at court, and in the best companies of England* (London, 1738)) is cited from the first edition.

Thompson, F., *Lark Rise to Candleford:* cited from the first collected edition of 1945.

Webster, J., *Complete Works*, ed. F. L. Lucas (4 vols., London, 1927).

Thematic Index

Oxford Paperback Reference

The Concise Oxford Dictionary of Art & Artists
Ian Chilvers

Based on the highly praised *Oxford Dictionary of Art*, over 2,500 up-to-date entries on painting, sculpture, and the graphic arts.

'the best and most inclusive single volume available, immensely useful and very well written'

Marina Vaizey, *Sunday Times*

The Concise Oxford Dictionary of Art Terms
Michael Clarke

Written by the Director of the National Gallery of Scotland, over 1,800 entries cover periods, styles, materials, techniques, and foreign terms.

A Dictionary of Architecture
James Stevens Curl

Over 5,000 entries and 250 illustrations cover all periods of Western architectural history.

'splendid ... you can't have a more concise, entertaining, and informative guide to the words of architecture'

Architectural Review

'excellent, and amazing value for money ... by far the best thing of its kind'

Professor David Walker

Oxford Paperback Reference

The Kings of Queens of Britain
John Cannon and Anne Hargreaves

A detailed, fully-illustrated history ranging from mythical and pre-conquest rulers to the present House of Windsor, featuring regional maps and genealogies.

A Dictionary of Dates
Cyril Leslie Beeching

Births and deaths of the famous, significant and unusual dates in history – this is an entertaining guide to each day of the year.

'a dipper's blissful paradise ... Every single day of the year, plus an index of birthdays and chronologies of scientific developments and world events.'

Observer

A Dictionary of British History
Edited by John Cannon

An invaluable source of information covering the history of Britain over the past two millennia. Over 3,600 entries written by more than 100 specialist contributors.

Review of the parent volume
'the range is impressive ... truly (almost) all of human life is here'

Kenneth Morgan, *Observer*

Oxford Paperback Reference

Oxford Paperback Reference

The Concise Oxford Companion to English Literature
Margaret Drabble and Jenny Stringer

Based on the best-selling *Oxford Companion to English Literature*, this is an indispensable guide to all aspects of English literature.

Review of the parent volume
'a magisterial and monumental achievement'

Literary Review

The Concise Oxford Companion to Irish Literature
Robert Welch

From the ogam alphabet developed in the 4th century to Roddy Doyle, this is a comprehensive guide to writers, works, topics, folklore, and historical and cultural events.

Review of the parent volume
'Heroic volume ... It surpasses previous exercises of similar nature in the richness of its detail and the ecumenism of its approach.'

Times Literary Supplement

A Dictionary of Shakespeare
Stanley Wells

Compiled by one of the best-known international authorities on the playwright's works, this dictionary offers up-to-date information on all aspects of Shakespeare, both in his own time and in later ages.

Oxford Paperback Reference

The Concise Oxford Dictionary of Quotations
Edited by Elizabeth Knowles

Based on the highly acclaimed *Oxford Dictionary of Quotations*, this paperback edition maintains its extensive coverage of literary and historical quotations, and contains completely up-to-date material. A fascinating read and an essential reference tool.

The Oxford Dictionary of Humorous Quotations
Edited by Ned Sherrin

From the sharply witty to the downright hilarious, this sparkling collection will appeal to all senses of humour.

Quotations by Subject
Edited by Susan Ratcliffe

A collection of over 7,000 quotations, arranged thematically for easy look-up. Covers an enormous range of nearly 600 themes from 'The Internet' to 'Parliament'.

The Concise Oxford Dictionary of Phrase and Fable
Edited by Elizabeth Knowles

Provides a wealth of fascinating and informative detail for over 10,000 phrases and allusions used in English today. Find out about anything from the 'Trojan horse' to 'ground zero'.

Oxford Paperback Reference

The Oxford Dictionary of Dance
Debra Craine and Judith Mackrell

Over 2,500 entries on everything from hip-hop to classical ballet, covering dancers, dance styles, choreographers and composers, techniques, companies, and productions.

'A must-have volume ... impressively thorough'
Margaret Reynolds, *The Times*

Who's Who in Opera
Joyce Bourne

Covering operas, operettas, roles, perfomances, and well-known personalities.

'a generally scrupulous and scholarly book'
Opera

The Concise Oxford Dictionary of Music
Michael Kennedy

The most comprehensive, authoritative, and up-to-date dictionary of music available in paperback.

'clearly the best around ... the dictionary that everyone should have'
Literary Review